# Alan S. Milward and a
# of European Change

## Routledge Studies in Modern European History

1 **Facing Fascism**
The Conservative Party and the European dictators 1935–1940
*Nick Crowson*

2 **French Foreign and Defence Policy, 1918-1940**
The Decline and Fall of a Great Power
*Edited by Robert Boyce*

3 **Britain and the Problem of International Disarmament**
1919-1934
*Carolyn Kitching*

4 **British Foreign Policy 1874–1914**
The Role of India
*Sneh Mahajan*

5 **Racial Theories in Fascist Italy**
*Aaron Gilette*

6 **Stormtroopers and Crisis in the Nazi Movement**
Activism, Ideology and Dissolution
*Thomas D. Grant*

7 **Trials of Irish History**
Genesis and Evolution of a Reappraisal 1938–2000
*Evi Gkotzaridis*

8 **From Slave Trade to Empire**
European Colonisation of Black Africa 1780s–1880s
*Edited by Olivier Pétré-Grenouilleau*

9 **The Russian Revolution of 1905**
Centenary Perspectives
*Edited by Anthony Heywood and Jonathan D. Smele*

10 **Weimar Cities**
The Challenge of Urban Modernity in Germany
*John Bingham*

11 **The Nazi Party and the German Foreign Office**
*Hans-Adolf Jacobsen and Arthur L. Smith, Jr.*

12 **The Politics of Culture in Liberal Italy**
From Unification to Fascism
*Axel Körner*

13 **German Colonialism, Visual Culture and Modern Memory**
*Edited by Volker M. Langbehn*

14 **German Colonialism and National Identity**
*Edited by Michael Perraudin and Jürgen Zimmerer*

15 **The Great War on the Western Front**
Strange Hells
*Ross J. Wilson*

16 **West Germans and the Nazi Legacy**
*Caroline Sharples*

# Alan S. Milward and a Century of European Change

Edited by Fernando Guirao, Frances M. B. Lynch, and Sigfrido M. Ramírez Pérez

LONDON AND NEW YORK

First published 2012 by Routledge

2 Park Square, Milton Park, Abingdon, Oxon OX14 4RN
711 Third Avenue, New York, NY 10017, USA

*Routledge is an imprint of the Taylor & Francis Group, an informa business*

First issued in paperback 2017



*Library of Congress Cataloging-in-Publication Data*

Alan S. Milward and a century of European change / edited by Fernando Guirao, Frances M. B. Lynch, and Sigfrido M. Ramírez Pérez.
p. cm. — (Routledge studies in modern European history ; 17)
Includes bibliographical references and index.
1. Milward, Alan S. 2. Economists—Europe—Biography. 3. Europe—Economic conditions—1945– 4. Europe—Economic integration. I. Guirao, Fernando, 1962– II. Lynch, Frances M. B., 1955– III. Ramírez Pérez, Sigfrido M.
HC240.A598 2011
330.092—dc23
[B]
2011033899

ISBN13: 978-0-415-87853-1 (hbk)
ISBN13: 978-1-138-10753-3 (pbk)

Typeset in Sabon
by IBT Global.

# Contents

# Abbreviations and Acronyms

| | |
|---|---|
| AB | Aluminiumwerk GmbH in Bitterfeld |
| AIAG | Aluminium-Industrie-Aktiengesellschaft |
| Alcoa | Aluminum Company of America |
| ARBED | Aciéries réunies de Burbach-Eich-Dudelange |
| ASP | American Selling Price |
| ASSIDER | Associazione industrie siderurgiche italiane |
| Benelux | Belgium, Netherlands and Luxembourg |
| BLEU | Belgium and Luxembourg Economic Union |
| CAP | Common Agricultural Policy |
| CEA | Confédération européenne de l'agriculture |
| CECA | Communauté européenne du charbon et de l'acier |
| CEE | Communauté économique européenne |
| CEEC | Committee of European Economic Cooperation |
| CET | Common External Tariff |
| CGIL | Confederazione generale italiana del lavoro |
| Cominform | Communist Information Bureau |
| COPA | Comité des organisations professionnelles agricoles |

| | |
|---|---|
| CSSF | Chambre syndicale de la sidérurgie française |
| DAI | Dansk Aluminium Industri |
| DC | Democrazia cristiana |
| DM | Dürener Metallwerke |
| EC | European Community; also, European Commission |
| ECA | Economic Cooperation Administration |
| ECE | Economic Commission for Europe |
| ECSC | European Coal and Steel Community |
| EDC | European Defense Community |
| EEC | European Economic Community |
| EFTA | European Free Trade Association |
| EMS | European Monetary System |
| EMU | European Monetary Union |
| EPA | European Productivity Agency |
| EPC | European Political Community |
| EPU | European Payments Union |
| ERP | European Recovery Program |
| EU | European Union |
| EUI | European University Institute |
| Euratom | European Atomic Energy Community |
| EWG | Europäische Wirtschaftsgemeinschaft |
| FAO | Food and Agriculture Organization |
| GATT | General Agreement on Tariffs and Trade |

| | |
|---|---|
| GHFAB | Groupement des hauts-fourneaux et aciéries belges |
| GISL | Groupement des industries sidérurgiques luxembourgeoises |
| HL | Hansa Leichtmetall |
| IAR | International Authority for the Ruhr |
| IGF | Interessen-Gemeinschaft Farbenindustrie |
| IMF | International Monetary Fund |
| IR | International Relations |
| IRMA | International Rail Makers Association |
| ISA | Industrie siderurgiche associate |
| ITO | International Trade Organization |
| JEIH | Journal of European Integration History |
| JFM | Junkers Flugzeug und Motorenwerke |
| LSE | London School of Economics and Political Science |
| LTA | Long-Term Arrangement on Cotton Textiles |
| MEP | Member of the European Parliament |
| NA | Nordische Aluminium |
| NACO | Norsk Aluminium Company |
| NAI | Nordisk Aluminiumindustri |
| NATO | North Atlantic Treaty Organization |
| NLA | Nordisk Lettmetall |
| OECD | Organization for Economic Cooperation and Development |
| OEEC | Organization for European Economic Cooperation |
| PCE | Partido Comunista de España |

| | |
|---|---|
| PCF | Parti communiste français |
| PCI | Partito comunista italiano |
| PSI | Partito socialista italiano |
| RLM | Reichsluftfahrtministerium |
| RWM | Reichswirtschaftsministerium |
| SABAP | Société anonyme de bauxite et alumines de Provence |
| SAKO | A/B Svenska Aluminiumkompaniet |
| SEB | Skandinaviska Enskilda Banken |
| SITC | Standard International Trade Classification |
| SPD | Sozialdemokratische Partei Deutschlands |
| TA | Technical Assistance program under the ERP |
| UEA | University of East Anglia |
| UMIST | University of Manchester Institute of Science and Technology |
| UNECE | United Nations Economic Commission for Europe |
| UPF | Pompeu Fabra University, Barcelona |
| USSBS | United States Strategic Bombing Survey |
| USSR | Union of Soviet Socialist Republics |
| VAW | Vereinigte Aluminium Werke |
| VIAG | Vereinigte Industrieunternehmungen AG |
| WVESI | Wirtschaftsvereinigung Eisen- und Stahlindustrie |

# Archives

Archiv für Christlich-Soziale Politik der Hanns-Seidel-Stiftung, Munich

| | |
|---|---|
| AECB | Archives of the European Commission in Brussels |
| ANLux | Archives nationales de Luxembourg |
| ARBED-P | Archives of Aciéries réunies de Burbach-Eich-Dudelange—Presidency |
| Archivio PCI | Fondazione Istituto Gramsci, Archives of the Italian Communist Party |
| BA/K | Bundesarchiv, Koblenz |
| Ba-Ma | Bundesarchiv-Militärarchiv, Freiburg |
| CAC | Centre des Archives Contemporaines, Fontainebleau |
| CEAB | Commission européenne, Archives Bruxelles |
| CEC | Cabinet Economic Committee (Denmark) |
| CM2 | Archives, Council of Ministers of the European Union, Brussels |
| EB PA | Erik Brofoss' private archive, Norwegian Labor Archive, Oslo |
| HADIR-CP | Archives of the Hauts-fourneaux et aciéries de Differdange-St.Ingbert-Rumelange, Committee of Presidents |
| HADIR-DC | Archives of the Hauts-fourneaux et aciéries de Differdange-St.Ingbert-Rumelange, Dossier confidentiel |

| | |
|---|---|
| HAEU | Historical Archives of the European Union |
| LBJL | Lyndon B. Johnson Library |
| MAEF | Ministère des Affaires Etrangères (Quai d'Orsay), Paris DE/CE Direction économique / Coopération européenne (files on European cooperation from the General Directorate of Economic and Financial Affairs) |
| NARA | United States National Archives, College Park, Maryland |
| PA/AA | Politisches Archiv des Auswärtigen Amtes, Berlin |
| RA | Riksarkivet (the Norwegian National Archives) |
| UD | Archive of the Norwegian Foreign Office |
| UM | Archive of the Danish Ministry of Foreign Affairs, National Archive, Copenhagen |

# Figures and Tables

FIGURES



TABLES

*Alan Steele Milward was born on 19 January 1935 in Stoke-on-Trent, United Kingdom, and died on 28 September 2010 in London. Photograph by Dr. Andreas Frijdal.*

# Preface

*Alan S. Milward and a Century of European Change* was initially conceived as a token of belated gratitude prompted by the shocking news that Alan Milward had been diagnosed with vascular dementia toward the end of 2007.[1] Although his general health had been deteriorating slowly for some time the diagnosis of vascular dementia was not expected by his medical consultants or by him. Indeed, long after his retirement in January 2003 from the chair in the History of European Integration at the European University Institute (EUI), a chair which he himself had helped to establish in 1983, he had continued to work as an official historian in the United Kingdom (commissioned to write the official history of the United Kingdom's relations with the European Communities), going to conferences, attending seminars and meetings, and participating in other research projects.

Yet after that time travel to give academic papers or examine doctoral theses in Italy, Norway, France, Sweden, Portugal, and Poland was increasingly fraught with difficulty. His last two pieces of work were written in 2005.[2] The last thesis which he examined was in December 2006.[3] His last lecture was at a conference held in Warsaw in March 2007, and his last recorded conference attendance was at the fourth workshop of the Balzan project held at Birkbeck College, University of London, in June

---

1. Unlike the most common form of dementia, Alzheimer's, which on account of its organic nature usually takes the form of a gradual deterioration of the brain, vascular dementia is caused by a restriction of the blood supply to the brain, its onset is often sudden, and its course is always unpredictable.
2. Milward, 'History, Political Science and European Integration', in Jørgensen, Pollack, and Rosamond, *Handbook of European Union Politics*, 99–103 (the original manuscript was submitted in February 2005) and Milward, 'Was the Middle East the Birthplace of a Common European Foreign Policy?' in Petersen, *Controlling the Uncontrollable? The Great Powers in the Middle East*, 23–36 (manuscript submitted in September 2005).
3. Lucia Coppolaro, 'Trade and Politics across the Atlantic: The European Economic Community and the United States of America in the GATT Negotiations of the Kennedy Round (1962–1967)', European University Institute, Florence, December 2006.

2007.[4] His last book review appeared in September 2007. It was of a book on the troubled relationship of Germany and European unification, which best symbolized one of the important themes in his scholarly career.[5] His effort to attend a meeting of the European Union Liaison Committee of Historians in Paris in September 2007 was to be the last time that he traveled outside Britain.[6] His final experience on the Continent was to be held by the Belgian police after he was found wandering and confused near the Franco-Belgian border in the early morning.

As the news of his illness spread many of his colleagues and former students began to discuss how they could show their respect and sadness but also celebrate and analyze what the work of Alan Milward had meant in academic terms. What else could be done apart from writing a book commemorating his scholarship? This is, mainly, what scholars do, particularly when elder colleagues retire or are no longer able to command their own research agenda.

There were many initiatives, but the specific one that ended up as *Alan S. Milward and a Century of European Change* was due to Dr. Sigfrido Ramírez, one of Alan Milward's former doctoral students who had just defended his thesis at the EUI in December 2007 without the presence of his first academic mentor among the members of the examining board. Informed of the reason for the absence, he proposed organizing a *Festschrift*. The idea as such was not very original since there were many scholars already thinking about editing books to honor Alan Milward. It was generally seen as a good thing that so many scholars were interested in such celebratory publications because it meant that Alan Milward's work would become more accessible to future generations. What made Dr. Ramírez's proposal successful were two circumstances. First of all, he addressed himself not to his peers but directly to Professor Milward's wife, and second, that the moment was quite propitious as her husband's health deteriorated so seriously that he had to be taken into hospital for constant medical supervision before being moved into a care home. This was precisely the

4. In 2003 Eric Hobsbawm was awarded the prestigious Balzan Prize for his contribution to European history since 1900. The prize money was used to fund a project entitled 'Reconstruction in the Immediate Aftermath of War: A Comparative Study of Europe, 1945–1950', directed by Professor Mark Mazower (Columbia University) and Professor David Feldman (Birkbeck College, University of London).
5. Milward's review of *Die Bundesrepublik Deutschland und die Europäische Einigung, 1949–2000*, edited by Mareike Konig and Matthias Schulz, *The English Historical Review* 122: 498 (September 2007): 1112–1113.
6. It is no surprise that, despite his condition at that time, Alan Milward tried to attend this meeting, as he had been 'one of the most reliable members of the EU Liaison Committee of Historians' since the creation of this group, which he had helped to establish in January 1982 as the *Groupe de liaison des professeurs d'histoire contemporaine auprès de la Commission européenne*; Loth, 'In memoriam Alan S. Milward (1935–2010)'.

moment when Alan Milward's prodigious scholarly ability came to an end. After much hesitation, the prospects of the book lifted her spirits, and thus she finally agreed to move on in defining the project.

Dr. Frances M. B. Lynch was Alan Milward's spouse. Having the wife of the honoree as an editor has not been a standard academic procedure, partly because it has not been common in the past for academic historians to share both their academic and personal lives. Since this is now changing we do not apologize for setting a precedent in inviting the spouse, who is a historian in her own right, to be a joint editor. Particular care has been taken to avoid any unintentional lack of objectivity on her part. The positive aspects of having Dr. Lynch's active support were seen as more than outnumbering any potentially negative ones. That her husband was to die on 28 September 2010, in the middle of the most intense period of editorial work on the volume, could not have been predicted.[7]

Frances Lynch recruited Professor Fernando Guirao, a historian from the Universitat Pompeu Fabra of Barcelona (UPF), to become the third editorial partner. Guirao, a long-standing colleague of Alan Milward on the Liaison Committee of Historians, was aware of the different proposals to honor Alan Milward's scholarship and, crucially, was prepared to devote sufficient energy and commitment to steering this particular project through to its conclusion.

The three editors barely knew each other before committing themselves to carry out the process that was to lead to *Alan S. Milward and a Century of European Change*. Since they had never previously worked together, they soon found themselves holding very different approaches to the project. There is no doubt that this project was complicated, and the fact that it materialized into the volume that the reader is now holding, to these signing editors' delighted relief, is an achievement in itself. It is up to future readers and reviewers to express judgment upon the final outcome of this project and the validity of many decisions made along the way, the most important of which we would like to explain in the following paragraphs.

The nature of the book was not obvious from the outset. It was clear that the intention was to honor Alan Milward by celebrating his lifelong research, but how could this be best accomplished? Two possibilities

7. Obituaries were published in *The Times* on 14 October 2010, *The Guardian* on 28 October (by Charles S. Maier), *The Guardian* on 3 November 2010 (by Christopher Smout), *The Daily Telegraph* on 9 November 2010, *The Independent* on 6 December 2010 (by David McKittrick), in the University Association for Contemporary European Studies' newsletter (*UACES News*), Winter 2010: 6 and 7 (by Wolfram Kaiser and Morten Rasmussen respectively), in the European University Institute's newsletter (*EUI news*), Winter 2010: 28 (by Federico Romero), in the *JEIH* 16: 2 (December 2010) (by Wilfried Loth), in LSE alumni magazine, *Connect* 23: 1 (Summer 2011): 45 (by Leslie Hannah), and in The Economic History Association's on-line publication http://eh.net/content/alan-s-milward-1935-2010 (by John Komlos) (posted on 20 June 2011 - last accessed on 13 December 2011).

emerged, one after the other. A first one was the classic *Festschrift*, that is, a compilation of essays in honor of Alan Milward, a book where a selective group of scholars would write pieces on a topic of their specialization but at a level of excellence on a par with that of Alan Milward himself. The editors believed that this could perhaps be accomplished within six months. This option, which was in fact conceived as a gift for Alan Milward, as a placebo to help the patient's speedy recovery, was abandoned when the editors realized that, no matter how quickly they could produce the book, Alan Milward would not be able to read any of the contributions nor recognize any of the contributors.

The second option was to produce a collection of essays which aimed to provide a better understanding of Alan Milward's extensive intellectual work for future scholars and facilitate the knowledge and transmission of his published work and of the full magnitude of his scientific accomplishments to present and future generations of students, scholars in the various disciplines concerned, and the general public. The project was thus transformed into the gathering of a series of original contributions which were, in some way, to relate to or reflect upon Alan Milward's own contributions to the various academic fields. The intention was to honor him through a better understanding of his many pioneering contributions in the fields of contemporary European history in general and the history of European integration in particular.

The problem of deciding who should be invited to contribute was no easy task. There were many possible approaches to this question, and the three editors did not necessarily hold identical views. Alan Milward's work covered many different fields and his network of scholars was vast. The list of prospective contributors had to include those with the clearest understanding of his research so that they could judge and explain to others the relative importance of his scholarly contribution, possible shortcomings in his views and research outcomes, as well as their relevance for today. The list of authors also had to include those who had been close to Alan Milward as well as those holding well-constructed critical views on his work, since the editors were persuaded that the best way to honor his scholarly work was through a rigorous evaluation of his contributions and of the novel research supervised by him. It was to be as multinational as Alan Milward's own research was. The list had also to include senior and junior scholars, Alan Milward's colleagues, as well as a representation of his former students.

The latter constituted a numerous and dispersed set, as the reader may infer from the list of Ph.D. theses supervised by Alan Milward (Appendix 3 of this volume). Alan Milward had supervised doctoral students first as Professor of European Studies at the University of Manchester Institute of Science and Technology (UMIST) (1971–83), then as Professor of the History of European Integration at the EUI (first in 1983–86 and then in 1996–2003), and in between as Professor of

Economic History at the University of London School of Economics and Political Science (LSE) (1986–96). The editors wanted to invite representatives of the different generations, those with the most successful academic careers, as well as the most recent Ph.D. students—the very ones who used to refer to him, behind his back, as 'Milwy': *un modo carino per chiamare un vecchio leone*!*

This was certainly not an initiative limited to historians but was to be multidisciplinary in nature, as was Alan Milward's own work. Given the variety of topics and subjects falling within his scholarly interests, the original list was to include scholars from all the disciplines that, one way or other, were influenced by his work. Economists, political scientists, sociologists, European Union experts of all sorts, in addition to historians from all possible areas of academic specialization were invited to take part in this initiative. Striking the right balance on all these counts was not easy. The range of subjects covered and the number of contributors considered were, simply, enormous.

Another important aspect of this project was finding the publisher. Selecting the ideal publisher was easy: Routledge, the editors believed, was obviously the most appropriate publishing house for the project. It had published most of Alan Milward's books: *The European Rescue of the Nation-State* (1992, reprinted 2000); *The Frontier of National Sovereignty: History and Theory 1945–1992* (1993); *Britain's Place in the World. A historical enquiry into import controls 1945–60* (1996); a reprint in 2003 of *The Reconstruction of Western Europe 1945–51* (originally published by Methuen in 1984); and finally, *Politics and Economics in the History of the European Union* (2005). It had also, as George Allen and Unwin, published the two-volume textbook which Alan Milward had written with S. Berrick Saul, *The Economic Development of Continental Europe 1780–1870* (1973, 1979, 2011, to be reprinted in 2012) and *The Development of the Economies of Continental Europe 1850–1914* (1977, 2011, to be reprinted in 2012). The kind of general assessment of Alan Milward's main scientific achievements which this project was intended to carry out would keep most of these works in the public eye. Thus Routledge was informed in March 2008, even before the project was well defined, of our interest in proposing the volume to them. Both the publisher and the reviewers were overwhelmingly positive once the editors had managed to put forward a formal proposal. In August 2009 the editors were finally able to sign a contract for the volume.[8]

---

* 'Milwy': an affectionate term for an old lion!

8. Perry Anderson, overcommitted to many writing projects, was to publish a book, which he dedicated to Alan, long before the present volume went to the publisher: 'Unable, by reason of circumstance, to contribute to a volume in honour of Alan Milward, I have dedicated this book to him, though it is so unlike his work. It was his writing, of which I express my admiration in these pages, that first made me want to say something about Europe' (*The New Old World*, ix).

The themes of the essays gathered in this volume reflect the main areas of interest in Alan Milward's lifelong program of historical research, namely the social, economic, and political development of Europe since the nineteenth century and the role played by the state in that development; the overall social and economic impact of the two world wars; the reconstruction of western Europe after 1945; the rationale behind the United States' official intervention in European affairs, particularly the program of assistance popularly known as the Marshall Plan and its short-, medium-, and long-term consequences; and the multidisciplinary study of the processes of the political and economic integration and interdependence within the western part of Europe in a long-term perspective. Certainly not all these subjects are reflected in this volume with the same intensity, partly due to the absence of original research in some areas, partly due to the constraints of space, and partly due to the changes in individual circumstances, during the project's three and a half years of life, of a number of the scholars who had initially been involved. Our basic intention has not been to be exhaustive but qualitative. Not all of Alan Milward's work can possibly be explained to future students in this volume, nor does this volume aim to be a substitute for the work itself. The editors hope that the volume will serve to make his publications attractive and valuable for future generations of students and scholars. It is our firm conviction that the best way of preserving and presenting Alan Milward's rich and varied intellectual contribution is to read his complete oeuvre itself. This is the purpose of including a commentary by way of introduction and a full list of his publications as an appendix, in addition to the twenty-three chapters in total.

The introduction to this volume has several objectives. First, it aims to summarize and explain Alan Milward's scholarship, quite often in his own words and in those of the main reviewers of his books. This in itself proved to be a voyage of discovery for the editors. Second, it tries to place his writing within the framework of prevailing scholarship. Third, it aims to show how his work was received on publication and how it has stood the test of time. The purpose of the introduction, combined with the analysis carried out in many of the contributions, is to stand on Alan Milward's own shoulders for a better understanding of historical and present realities. Since we are already breaking one sacred Milwardian tradition of keeping the preface short, we might well break a second one, that of avoiding Latin, by referring to the allegory attributed to Bernard of Chartres by his disciple John of Salisbury in The Metalogicon (book three), completed in 1159: gigantium humeris insidentes, ut possimus plura eis et remotiora videre ('standing on the shoulders of giants, we can see more and further'), which represents a good metaphor of the significance of Alan Milward's research for future generations:

> Bernard of Chartres used to compare us with [puny] dwarfs perched on the shoulders of giants. He pointed out that we see more and further than

our predecessors, not because we have keener vision or greater height, but because we are lifted up and borne aloft on their gigantic stature.[9]

*

* *

*Alan S. Milward and a Century of European Change* has entailed a long and fascinating journey during which many debts have been accumulated. The editors are, first of all, indebted to Routledge: to Laura Stearns, the Research Editor on the History list, based in New York for showing immediate interest in the project, to Stacy Noto for providing such efficient assistance to Laura Stearns; to Alan Jarvis, the editorial director of social sciences books based in Oxford, and his assistant Adam Micklethwaite, for leading the project toward a successful outcome; and finally, to Michael R. Watters, of Integrated Book Technology Global, based in Troy, New York, who handled the copyediting and composition of this book magnificently. Second, we would like to acknowledge the positive assessment that three scholars carried out for Routledge. Their comments and criticisms undoubtedly helped the editors to refine the definition of their project.

Third, we would like to acknowledge our sources of financial assistance and to thank EUI President Professor Yves Mény, in office until 31 December 2009, who warmly welcomed the initiative from its earliest stages and gave us significant financial help toward meeting the editorial costs. We would like to acknowledge and thank Professor Helen Wallace, former director of the Schuman Center at the EUI, for assisting us in securing this funding and Ms. Sandra Brière, from the Office of the EUI President, for her practical help. The Historical Archives of the European Union in Florence, directed by Dr. Jean-Marie Palayret, also provided generous financial support to defray part of the administrative costs involved and for which we are very grateful.

Fourth, we are in debt to Peter Kennealy and Silvia Losa Vidal for their altruistic assistance. The former, a librarian at the EUI, helped mainly in the tricky task of compiling the list of EUI Ph.D. theses of which Alan Milward was officially the main supervisor. He also offered his expertise whenever the editors found themselves in trouble. Silvia Losa, a librarian at the law section of UPF central library, assisted the editorial team in three apparently trivial tasks which proved to be cumbersome in the extreme and quite time consuming. Her first task was that of establishing Alan Milward's bibliography in all its many details, which included first editions, reeditions, reimpressions, and translations. Professor Milward himself would not have

9. *The Metalogicon of John of Salisbury: A Twelfth-Century Defense of the Verbal and Logical Arts of the Trivium*, translated with an Introduction and Notes by Daniel D. McGarry (Berkeley and Los Angeles, University of California Press, 1962), 167.

done it better! Secondly, Ms. Losa compiled the list of book reviews that Alan Milward had written in numerous journals since 1965. As a result of her work the editors discovered an important although relatively neglected aspect of Alan Milward's rich intellectual activity. He was an avid reader and reviewer of books, to which the long list in Appendix Two testifies, ever-ready to update his own views in the light of serious research done by others. Ms. Losa's third task has been the compilation of reviews of Professor Milward's publications, which is as exhaustive as possible. The footnotes in the introduction section of this volume will reveal the richness of such a compilation. The intense use made of this material serves as a token of our high esteem for the assistance that she has provided.

Fifth, the editors are indebted to Helena Scott, a research assistant at the University of Westminster with experience in translating, editing, and preparing books for publication. Since her incorporation into the project, in September 2008, she has taken care of what turned out to be an extremely delicate matter, that of handling correspondence with contributors during the last two years of the project. She also performed final English editing as well as formatting and unifying styles to that of Routledge—altogether preparing the final manuscript for submission to the publisher. Without Ms. Scott's assistance this extremely complex project would have neither reached a safe haven nor met the contractual deadline. Although at some points, her work schedule was stakhanovite, no mistakes should be attributed to her. The editors assume the full responsibility for all the editorial tasks performed and for any remaining mistakes in the volume.

The fact that these editors are not gifted with the same range of linguistic skills as Alan Milward has made it necessary to seek some specialist assistance. Therefore, the editors would like to express their gratitude to Karl Oskar Tein for solving specific linguistic problems with the Norwegian language, to Dolores Lojo Casal and Mayumi Sano for the transliteration of a Japanese title, and to Abel Losa Vidal, a tireless, enthusiastic linguist, for general multilinguistic assistance. The latter's collaboration was rendered possible thanks to Aitor Canal Cases' expertise in optical character recognition software.

The good offices provided by the personnel of the interlibrary loan service of UPF central library, directed by Marta Comadran Junyent, particularly Fanny Ferran Cuadrat, Maria del Mar Magem Vila, and Ramon Vendrell Olivé, made it possible for an anxious scholar to collect in Barcelona what might perhaps be the most complete collection of Milward publications outside Islington and the British Library. We would like to underline the importance of such public assistance for academic work particularly at a time when basic public services in academic and cultural activities are subject to strong criticism and financial strain.

The editors would also like to express their gratitude to Maria Rosa Laorden Delàs for general administrative support; to Dr. Andreas Frijdal for providing the photograph of his friend and colleague Alan Milward which is included in this volume; to Dr. Andreas Beierwaltes from the publisher Nomos and Dr. Charles Barthel from the *JEIH* Secretariat for granting and taking care of a necessary copyright authorization respectively; to Professor Christopher Smout, Professor Albert Carreras de Odriozola, Dr. Xavier Tafunell Sambola, and many contributors to this volume for their scholarly advice on countless matters as well as their constant support. A special mention is reserved for Professor S. Berrick Saul for his kindness and enthusiasm in attending to our request for factual information. Last but not least, we would like to express our gratitude to all the contributors to this volume for generously giving their time and expertise to writing original contributions and for their patience during the long editorial process involved. Without each and every one of them, this volume would have been a poorer one.

All of those mentioned so far helped to alleviate the burden on the editors which a project on such a scale necessarily involves. Most unfortunately, the editors in their turn could not spare their families the great burden of what has proved to be an all-consuming process. They remain indebted to their respective families for their unconditional love and support during three and a half long and demanding years of work.

It is to Alan Milward's youngest daughter, Laura, that this book is offered.

The Editors,<br>
Barcelona, London, Brussels<br>
31 December 2010<br>
(updated on 31 May 2011)

# A Lifetime's Search for a Theory of Historical Change

## An Introduction to the Work of Alan S. Milward

*Frances M. B. Lynch and Fernando Guirao*

Alan Steele Milward (1935–2010) was first and foremost a historian, a contemporary historian. Although he was not a Marxist he shared with Karl Marx a belief that the material basis of existence was the starting point for an understanding of the world and, since he believed that 'all history is change', he sought to explain contemporary history through an understanding of the forces responsible for economic change.[1] Unlike most neoclassical economic historians, he considered that one of the most powerful of these forces in contemporary Europe was the state. Therefore in his research, which focused mainly on twentieth-century Europe with some excursions into earlier times, he sought to uncover the interaction of the political and the economic. Accordingly, it spanned several academic disciplines, with his professorships ranging from economics at Stanford University to European studies at the University of Manchester Institute of Science and Technology (UMIST), to contemporary history and later the history of European integration at the European University Institute (EUI), Florence, and to economic history first as a lecturer at the University of Edinburgh and later as a professor at the London School of Economics and Political Science (LSE). From all these fields and several others Alan Milward drew inspiration for his historical research.

'When through some obstinate and now unredeemable error of judgement', as he himself wrote, 'I first decided I would be an historian "Contemporary History" was a phrase spoken in Britain only with an accompanying sneer.' That was in 1956 when, with a first class degree in Medieval and Modern History from University College London, he could find in Britain 'only one Professor of History [ . . . ] who would accept as a research student someone who wanted to work on the history of the Nazi period. "That is not history", they said, or, more cunningly, "there are no sources".'[2] His supervisor at the LSE was the renowned diplomatic historian and author

1. Milward, *The European Rescue of the Nation-State* (1992), 437 (quotation).
2. Milward, 'Now as available as pornography . . . ' (1975), 92 (both quotations).

of two volumes in the British Official History series of the Second World War, Professor William Norton Medlicott.[3] After three years of research, Alan Milward submitted a Ph.D. thesis entitled 'The Armaments Industry in the German Economy in the Second World War', which granted him, at 25 years of age, a doctorate in Economic History.

When he was working on his thesis in the second half of the 1950s the two dominant views of the Nazi regime were, on the one hand, the orthodox Marxist-Leninist view as defined by the Communist International (known as *Comintern*) in 1935, namely that it was a form of Fascism and was the direct agent of monopoly capitalism; and on the other, the liberal-bourgeois view which saw it as a form of totalitarianism and thus a state-controlled command economy similar to Communism in the Soviet Union.[4] As a first demonstration of one of the most enduring features of his work, Alan Milward preferred to develop his own understanding by ferreting in all the available sources of information which he, as a young British student with a reading knowledge of German and French, was able to find.[5] On the strength of an unusual linguistic ability, he adopted a method which was to characterize his research activity throughout the next fifty years: to be among the first to uncover and read in a systematic way hitherto secret government archives from many countries and to combine his documentary findings with a wide range of statistical material often ignored by historians.

For his thesis, from which his first scholarly publications were to be derived, he based his research on the largely unexplored captured records of the German Ministry for Armaments and Ammunition and the Economic and Armaments Office of the High Command of the Armed Forces, as well as other documents then kept in the Air Historical Branch of the Air Ministry in London. He also consulted the records of the United States' Strategic Bombing Survey (USSBS), the purpose of which had been to examine the relative success of the various Allied bombing policies during the war.[6] This survey provided him with valuable material for his thesis in so far as it presented a detailed study of the German war economy which the strategic bombing was meant to cripple. One of the authors of the survey, the economist Burton H. Klein, was at that time writing his own book based largely

3. Medlicott, *The Economic Blockade* (vol. 1, 1952; vol. 2, 1959).
4. Kershaw, *The Nazi Dictatorship* (2000), 12–13.
5. Milward's linguistic skills were learned entirely at high school in Stoke-on Trent. His first visit outside the British Isles was in 1955 when he won a university competition for his project to cycle around Finland and Northern Norway. At a later stage of his academic career, he would also be able to read Danish, Dutch, Italian, Norwegian, Portuguese, Romanian, Spanish, and Swedish, and speak many fluently.
6. USSBS, *The Effects of Strategic Bombing on the German War Economy* (1945).

on the results of that survey.[7] But the young Alan Milward, who defended his thesis in 1960, shortly after the publication of Klein's book, and shortly before becoming assistant lecturer, then Lecturer, in Economic History at the University of Edinburgh (1960–1965), reached very different conclusions than those of Klein.

## THE GERMAN ECONOMY AT WAR (1965)

The most succinct and accessible account of Alan Milward's argument about Nazi Germany's war economy can be found in his first article, published in *The Economic History Review* in 1964.[8] The following year his first book, *The German Economy at War*, now considered a classic, was published.[9] In spite of its title, Alan Milward did not consider his book to be a history of the German war economy as a whole. He himself pointed to the fact that, by 1965, there were still 'too many serious gaps' in the documentary and statistical knowledge of the German economy from 1939 to 1945 for his own study to be taken as 'a comprehensive history of German war production to serve as a counterpart of the United Kingdom Official History of the Second World War, Civil Series', which his own doctoral supervisor and mentor had completed shortly beforehand.[10] His research focused on determining the turning points in Germany's wartime economic strategy.

Milward's main thesis was that until 1942 Nazi Germany was being prepared to wage a war of a special kind which was most suited to the German economy and to the political nature of the Nazi party and its ideology. That war was briefly referred to as 'the *Blitzkrieg*', a term commonly translated into English as 'lightning wars'. It rested on a military strategy which implied a succession of rapid knock-out blows delivered against the enemy's forces from a position of strength without requiring the full-scale and permanent mobilization of the country's economy and society. Temporary efforts to boost the production of particular sectors were to precede each military campaign. The degree of wartime resource mobilization was to be flexible, varying in accordance with the military needs of each successive aggressive campaign between September 1939 and the summer of 1941. These campaigns were based on German military forces being superior in number and capacity to the opposing forces at the time of each surprise attack.

In Milward's interpretation, the Blitzkrieg was an economic and political as much as a military strategy. In this sense, the Blitzkrieg strategy was

7. Klein, *Germany's Economic Preparations for War* (1959).
8. Milward, 'The End of the Blitzkrieg' (1964).
9. Milward, *The German Economy at War* (1965).
10. Ibid., v.

based on operating a war economy within the general framework of the heavily mobilized economy which Nazi Germany had sustained since 1936. It thus required balancing the preparation of the country for war, which was an intrinsic goal of Nazi ideology, with the maintenance of consumption at levels necessary to retain sufficient domestic support for the Nazi regime. The Third Reich would impose on German civilians the rigors of a full-scale war economy only if and when it was forced to do so. Thus, for Alan Milward, the Blitzkrieg was 'a method of waging war which would avoid misery which war seemed destined to bring to the [German] civilian population.'[11] It was based on achieving the Nazi party's ultimate political objectives with less disruption to the national economy and society than would otherwise have been possible. In Alan Milward's own words, the Blitzkrieg economy

> was pre-eminently suited to the structure of the National Socialist state. It was the system of warfare best suited to the character and institutions of Hitler's Germany. For a democratic country such a method of waging war would have presented immense difficulties, for Germany, it was politically and economically convenient.[12]

As a political strategy, it was to prepare the country to wage successfully the sort of war which would lay the basis for the future German dominance of continental Europe under the leadership of the National Socialist party. The subsequent simplified depiction of his argument as that of 'a peacetime economy at war' is at best a distortion.[13] Indeed, Alan Milward stressed that '[n]o nation had ever previously spent so vast a sum in peace time on preparations for war', as Charles S. Maier reminds us in Chapter 1 of this volume.[14]

What Alan Milward set out to do was explain, first, how Nazi Germany was able to conquer most of continental Europe within a short space of time while maintaining living standards, and thus support for the regime at home; and second, when and why the initial strategy was changed. It was at the beginning of 1942 that, as he claimed, due to the immense cost generated by the invasion of the Soviet Union, Germany was forced to abandon the economic and military strategy of the Blitzkrieg and develop an alternative one aimed at sustaining a prolonged war effort. Given the Allied superiority in the quantity of strategic resources at their disposal, the emphasis in Germany was placed on achieving qualitative superiority. Adolf Hitler and the Ministry of Armaments and Munitions assumed that it was impossible for Germany to out-produce its enemies in armaments

---

11. Ibid., 7.
12. Ibid., 31.
13. For further elaboration on this question see below, 59.
14. Quotation taken from Milward, *The German Economy*, 27.

but that it 'could still win a war of mass production by harnessing her technology and science to the task of keeping a qualitative superiority in many individual armaments.'[15] This illusion was abandoned in turn, Alan Milward argued, in the summer of 1944, when Germany geared itself toward a total-war effort which required the full mobilization of all available resources at the expense of both the quality of armaments and domestic living standards. Hitler's 'Concentration Order' (*Konzentrationserlass*) of 19 June 1944 marked, he said, a desperate effort to postpone disaster by abandoning Germany's qualitative superiority and focusing all efforts on the mass production of the existing weapon types, as did the appointment in July 1944 of Josef Goebbels as Reich Plenipotentiary for the Mobilization of Total War. This question of when Nazi Germany was organized or aimed to be organized for 'total war' dominated scholarly debates for many years after the 1960s.[16]

If the Blitzkrieg strategy had been successful in the first twenty months of the war in defeating the armed forces of Poland, Denmark, Norway, Belgium, the Netherlands, Luxembourg, France, Yugoslavia, and Greece, the total-war effort which the Third Reich initiated in 1942 was insufficient, however impressive its actual results, against the combined resources and capabilities of powers which were not only economically stronger but, through an efficient system of cooperation, proved themselves to be better suited for the kind of command over all the resources which was necessary to win the war. Thus, in his first book, Milward was making a persuasive case for the importance of economic and political as well as military strategy in explaining the outcome of the war and for the importance of the Soviet Union, along with Britain, to Allied victory by defeating the Blitzkrieg before the United States joined the Allies.

The first (recorded) reviewer of *The German Economy at War* aptly described the social and academic atmosphere in which Alan Milward carried out his first academic research:

> It is not unfair to use the British war economy as a standard of comparison for the German economy. For, at the time, the British were spurred on to sacrifice partly by their belief that the Germans had won their victories because they had learned long ago the lessons of giving up butter in order to have guns. It came as a shock to read the [USSBS] after the war and to discover how wrong we were. The Germans had, it seemed, maintained high civilian standards throughout the war: even the number of domestic servants had increased. Unfortunately, apart from articles by one or two notable economists who worked in

15. Ibid., 101.
16. Detailed information about the changing interpretation of the concept of total war can be found in Beckett, 'Total War' (1988).

> the Bombing Survey, there has been little systematic study of the German war economy, and historians have been slow to quarry among the patchy, although massive, documentation on the subject.[17]

One of the 'notable economists' was Klein, whose book *Germany's Economic Preparations for War* (1959) had already shown that the degree of preparation of the Nazi economy for war by 1939 was very much less than had been believed by the Allies at the time. Klein had effectively destroyed the widely held belief that Hitler had armed Germany to its full extent for the purpose of waging the kind of war that the Second World War represented. In agreement with Klein and the other authors of the USSBS, Alan Milward showed—in both his first article and monograph—that Germany was not operating a full-scale war economy in 1939, or in the first two years of war. This did not mean, however, that the Third Reich was not preparing Germany for a major war; it simply meant that

> Germany *was* preparing for war, but for a war of a special kind—*Blitzkrieg*—which demanded not 'armament in depth' [armament producing permanent military potential] but the less burdensome 'armaments in width' [ready weaponry the provision of which could be increased right before each military campaign].[18]

Where Milward disagreed with Klein and the USSBS was in assessing the actual level of mobilization of the German economy, both before and throughout the war. Indeed, in challenging the wartime assumptions of the Allies, Milward argued that the authors of the USSBS had 'weighed the balance down on the other side rather than correcting it'.[19] He maintained that the main reason why Klein and the other USSBS authors had underestimated the degree of preparation for war of the German economy by 1939 and overestimated the change after 1942 was because they had accepted 'very uncritically the description of the German war economy given by the most co-operative, the most intelligent, and certainly the most knowledgeable of the Allies' prisoners, Albert Speer, the former Minister of Armaments and Munitions.'[20]

In the United States, Speer, who was at that time serving a twenty-year sentence in Spandau prison in West Berlin, having escaped the death penalty at the Nuremberg trials because he acknowledged his guilt in Nazi war crimes, was given, according to Alan Milward, too much credit for having reformed the administration and direction of the war economy. Speer had

---

17. 'Guns and Butter', anonymous review of *The German Economy at War*, 772.
18. Forsyth's review of *The German Economy at War*, 124.
19. Milward, 'The End of the Blitzkrieg', 499.
20. Ibid., 500.

taken with him many extremely valuable documentary records relating to the wartime German armament effort which he was to use, at a later stage, toward his own public rehabilitation. In American eyes, had Speer not come to power as a result of the accident in which his predecessor, Fritz Todt, was killed in an air crash on the Eastern Front on 8 February 1942, 'the German economy might never have been geared to the long war of attrition and mass production forced on her by the overwhelming defeat at Stalingrad'.[21] For Klein and the USSBS, the German defeat in Stalingrad in February 1943 was the turning point in the war. Up until that point they believed that Germany was following the military tactics of the Blitzkrieg. After Stalingrad, the Third Reich would have had to switch tactics and mobilize the economy for a full-scale war. Had they switched tactics earlier, as Speer and others were to argue, then the Germans, under the steady direction of the Minister of Armaments and Munitions, might have won the war.

Alan Milward disagreed with almost all of this. Having worked with the same official German statistics as those used by the USSBS he was much more skeptical of their veracity than were the U.S. officials. In fact, he considered that, before the creation of the German Statistical Service in 1942, it was almost impossible to get reliable statistical information from which to analyze the weight of armaments production in the German economy for the critical years 1939–1941. Even after the creation of this office, he demonstrated how misleading were the indices of armaments production compiled by the *Statistisches Amt* during the war. In order to help get around the problem caused by the inadequate statistics, he investigated the 'politics and personalities' because he believed that 'the political framework in which the economy of National Socialist Germany operated was extremely important.'[22] His reading of the official documentary record of important wartime bodies of the German state caused him to challenge with some authority Klein's and the USSBS's understanding of the Blitzkrieg and of when it was abandoned.

He considered it a mistake to view the Blitzkrieg, as the bombing survey had done, solely in terms of military tactics which ran aground during the five long months, between July 1942 and February 1943, of hand-to-hand fighting in Stalingrad, which killed almost two million people. It was Alan Milward's firm view, first of all, that the Blitzkrieg, as we have already underlined, meant much more than military tactics, and second, that the Blitzkrieg strategy had proven a failure long before the battle of Stalingrad had begun. The Führer-command 'Armament 1942' of 10 January 1942, he maintained, was the break with the economics of the Blitzkrieg and the beginning of a new program of military expansion which committed Germany to sustaining a long-term war effort on a large scale, which in turn

21. Ibid., 501.
22. Milward, *The German Economy*, v.

implied a more effective centralized control over industrial production. Todt, the *Reichsminister* for Armaments and Ammunition, was the main critic of the Blitzkrieg strategy after the campaign against the Soviet Union had required scaling up the military requirements of Germany's overall war effort quite significantly. It was Todt who had already persuaded Hitler of the need for change, and it was Todt who had designed the numerous administrative innovations—central control, rationalization of mass-production of armaments, and the system of authoritative industrial committees—which would be central to the economic organization of the German economy operating on the basis of a long war in search of greatly increased efficiency levels from 1942 onwards, all of which, as we have seen, Speer (and the Allies) would attribute to Speer himself after the war.

By examining what he called 'the machinery of administration' of the German war economy, Alan Milward concluded that 'it was the failure of the first Russian campaign, rather than the catastrophe of Stalingrad, that caused Hitler to abandon the Blitzkrieg.'[23] According to Hugh R. Trevor-Roper, considered by many at the time as one of the most distinguished academic authorities on Nazi Germany, Hitler himself had insisted on the invasion of Russia, arguing that such an operation made sense 'only if we smash the [Soviet Union] heavily in one blow'.[24] The consequence of the failure of this strategy was that the Third Reich became entangled in a long war of attrition against a combination of countries—the United States, the Soviet Union, and those in the British Empire and Commonwealth—with superior forces and military potential, which was precisely what the Blitzkrieg strategy had been designed to avoid. In the colorful language which was to become one of his trademarks, Milward wrote '[a]s the German advance squelched to a halt on Russian mud, and as, for the first time, serious losses of equipment, losses which were exceeding production, made themselves felt, the advocates of "armament in depth" were heard with louder voices.'[25] 'The Blitzkrieg is over', Milward affirmed, quoting a memorandum of 15 January 1942 written by General Hermann von Hanneken, the chief of resources, energy, and mining in the German Ministry of Industry. 'As for the economy,' the memorandum ran, 'it is a matter of the first priority that it should clearly be reconstructed on the basis of a long war.'[26] As Milward summed up,

> there can be no doubt that the decisive change in the administration of the German war economy came in February 1942 with the creation of a powerful civilian Ministry of Armaments and Munitions with control over service departments. And this was clearly the response to the

23. Milward, 'The End of the Blitzkrieg', 507.
24. Trevor-Roper's review of *The German Economy at War*, 61.
25. Milward, 'The End of the Blitzkrieg', 509.
26. As quoted in ibidem.

> failure of the Blitzkrieg offensive against Russia, and the necessity to rearm for a longer struggle than had at first been envisaged.[27]

In case anyone was left in any doubt about where he disagreed with Klein, Milward concluded his 'The End of the Blitzkrieg' article insisting that 'economically the Blitzkrieg ended in January 1942. Stalingrad merely convinced the unbelievers.'[28]

He also strongly disagreed with all those who at that time saw the Nazi regime as a firm-command style economy: '[T]he whole structure of the German administrative body was one of competing individuals and competing machines which by 1942 represented a powerful collection of vested interests each unwilling to relinquish its control of its own small part of the war economy.'[29] While he agreed that private businessmen exercised considerable power in the committees used by Speer, he argued that there were 'strong centrifugal forces in the National Socialist Party, which found the whole idea and system of the Blitzkrieg immensely more attractive than a full-scale war economy which would need centralized direction.'[30] Even after Speer had firmly defeated those in favor of Blitzkrieg, Milward identified 'an equally determined struggle, involving different questions of principle, between the Speer Ministry and the *élite* of the National Socialist movement, the SS.'[31] The *raison d'être* of the Blitzkrieg economy had been the possibility of avoiding an overall economic centralization of power and decision-making, allowing for the maintenance of independent economic empires responding to different, even opposing objectives despite operating under the supreme authority of the Führer. According to Alan Milward, the kind of central planning and command that 'armaments in depth' entailed inhibited the very economic flexibility on which Hitler's strategy so much depended. It was precisely the need for flexibility which made the Blitzkrieg economy suit the structure of the Nazi state. The end of the Blitzkrieg thus meant the end of the perfect symbiosis between war, the independence of the Nazi party leaders, and a sufficiently high level of popular support for the regime.

The final issue over which Alan Milward disagreed with Klein and the USSBS was that of why Germany ultimately lost the war. In the fall of 1944, Alan Milward argued, 'to all but fanatics the war was economically lost'.[32] We have seen that he refused to accept that the first mistake was the adoption of the strategy of the Blitzkrieg itself. Nor did he accept Speer's suggestion that 'their economic edifice would never have fallen down had

27. Ibid., 512–513.
28. Ibid., 518.
29. Milward, *The German Economy*, 10.
30. Ibid., 11.
31. Ibid., 155.
32. Ibid., 163.

the Allies not first bombed the roof off and then occupied the rooms'.[33] While he did agree that the Allied bombs had played a part, he insisted that '[t]he complexity of the economy of so highly-industrialized a country as Germany proved greater than the plans for strategic air warfare allowed.'[34] Of equal importance for the defeat he listed the chronic labor shortage in Germany as well as shortages in vital raw material supplies. Since in his view 'Germany had circumvented her raw material shortages very shrewdly throughout the war, by conquest and by substitution, although in theory they were her greatest weakness', the Allies' conquest in turn of those parts of Europe on which Germany depended was a major blow.[35] Finally he included the tensions between the central economic organization and the central political organization as a cause of equal importance for the defeat of Germany, since they determined the quality and quantity of the German war production.

'Personal rivalries', as one reviewer summarized Alan Milward's findings in this respect, 'prevented a satisfactory solution for the maximum and efficient use of German and foreign labour and for the best allocation of materials and components.'[36] Central authority over the whole of the German economy never existed, apart from Hitler's personal supreme (and contradictory) command. It was not until August 1944 that Speer gained authority over armaments production for all the armed forces, but even then Hermann Göring's industrial empire escaped the Armaments and Munitions ministerial authority, and the *Schutzstaffel* or S.S. under Heinrich Himmler continued to constitute a 'state within a state' with its own industrial empire. In spite of everything, German armaments production reached its peak in July 1944, and in January 1945 it was still more than twice as high as it had been three years earlier.[37] 'The Allies were fortunate'—another reviewer concluded—that the Germans began to display centralized efficient planning 'only when it was too late to do more than postpone the inevitable collapse.'[38] In fact, most reviewers of *The German Economy at War* concurred in underlining the novelty and excellence of Alan Milward's treatment of the damaging consequences, for the coherence and consistency of the German war effort, of the personal and institutional rivalries within the Third Reich.[39] The careful analysis of the relationship between the economic, strategic, and political factors, which Alan Milward deployed for the first time in *The German Economy at War*, would

33. Ibid., 165.
34. Ibid., 166.
35. Ibid., 165.
36. Hillmann's review of *The German Economy at War*, 677.
37. Nicholls' review of *The German Economy at War*, 874.
38. Neil's review of *The German Economy at War*, 217.
39. The sole recorded exception is Birkenfeld who in his review of *The German Economy at War* disagreed with almost all of Milward's main theses.

constitute another permanent feature of his scholarly work, a further component of what could be defined as the Milwardian method.

The main merit of the book was seen to lie in its attempt to understand and explain for the first time the economic rationale underpinning the Nazi military strategy. Alan Milward's evidence was seen to challenge, on the one hand, the belief of those who had argued that the German economy was so fully extended by 1940 that the British bombing policy could quickly bring about its collapse and, on the other, the view of the appeasers who minimized the extent of German rearmament.[40] Trevor-Roper went further than Alan Milward's conclusion that 'under Blitzkrieg economics Germany achieved one of the most remarkable periods of conquest in modern history' by saying that 'one more victory in the series might well have established the New Order on a lasting base.' For Trevor-Roper, '[i]t was by such methods, after all, that Prussia, which was not a great power in its time, became the German Empire, which was. By the same methods, a new German Empire might have been the super-power of today.'[41] Likened by Michael Hurst to an Emmental cheese which, '[d]espite the holes that can be found in it [ . . . ] is of a very high quality', *The German Economy at War* was to become the standard text for many years for a study of the preparation for and wartime efforts of the German economy.[42] Hurst was not mistaken, but whether it remains Alan Milward's finest book, as John R. Gillingham suggests in Chapter 2 of this volume, is a matter of some dispute.

## THE NEW ORDER AND THE FRENCH ECONOMY (1970)

The origins of the Third Reich's Blitzkrieg strategy and the ultimate outcome of the German war effort were both related, in Alan Milward's view, to the concept of a New Order in Europe. This referred to the place which occupied territories—and the subsequent policies for their control—had in the overall German war effort and postwar planning for the establishment of a revolutionary socioeconomic system on a continental scale. For Alan Milward, the Blitzkrieg strategy encompassed the occupation of some parts of Europe and the subsequent control of their resources in order to achieve the Fascist objectives of a New Order in Europe which was neither Capitalist nor Communist, while the failure to make the best use of the occupied

40. Makins' review of *The German Economy at War*, 386.
41. Trevor-Roper's review of *The German Economy at War*, 63. The original Milward quotation is taken from *The German Economy at War*, 8.
42. Hurst's review of *The German Economy at War*, 57. One of the 'holes' was seen to be the absence of any discussion of the contribution of the occupied countries to the German war economy.

territories represented a fatal blow to the overall efficiency of the German economy in the later phase of the war.

As he pointed out in the early 1960s, the effects 'of German occupation on the economies of the occupied countries are still unknown except in the broadest outline, certainly less well known than the political effects of occupation.'[43] Almost fifty years later, we can observe that this is still the case. What he wanted to understand was what the New Order in Europe might have looked like if the Nazis had not been defeated and to what extent their defeat was due to the failure of their occupation policies. In two subsequent monographs on the German occupation of France and Norway he provided some answers to those questions. He started with France, the most significant of all the economies which Germany controlled during the Second World War.[44] The official French account of the Occupation was that it had failed because the majority of French people had resisted rather than collaborated with the Nazis. Raymond Aron's distinction between the good Vichy of Marshall Henri Philippe Pétain, the Verdun hero and aged head of the Vichy *régime*, which sought to soften the impact of Nazi policies on France, and the bad Vichy of Pierre Laval, deputy president of the first Council of Ministers from June to December 1940 and premier after April 1942, which collaborated willingly with Nazi Germany, went largely unchallenged as most public records in France for the Vichy period were closed.[45] Alan Milward, basing his research on France primarily on captured German documents located in Britain and the United States and on published French records of war damage and of negotiations at the Armistice Commission meetings, was interested in the purpose of occupation and the extent of French collaboration.

On the first question, he quite typically rejected as too simplistic the view that the primary purpose of occupation was to loot and punish. What he set out to do was to assess the rationale behind the various measures which the Germans devised in order to extract economic benefit from an occupied territory; in the French case, from the fall of Paris in June 1940 to the invasion of Normandy four years later. Anticipating that there was more to the various forms of German pillage of France's resources and treasuries—which included seizures of stocks of raw materials and of cash, extraction of occupation costs, levies, the use of an overvalued currency (*Reichskreditkassenscheine*) for the purchase of goods and services by the occupation forces, capital penetration in French industry, and forced transfers of French labor and foreign holdings to German factories—than pure plunder or punishment, he measured the extent of French collaboration. This enabled him to answer the bigger theoretical question of whether the

---

43. Milward, *The German Economy*, v.
44. Milward, *The New Order and the French Economy* (1970).
45. Azéma, 'Vichy' (1995), 1084.

Nazi policy of uniting Europe by force could have worked had the ultimate outcome of the war been different.

The way in which he formulated his questions is clearly set out in an early essay, published in 1967:

> The tendency has been to assume that Germany's policy towards the French economy was merely to 'exploit' it in her own interests. This view of the problem is certainly too simple. What exactly were German interests? And which of the many different ways of 'exploitation' should Germany choose? Should Germany invest in the French economy, particularly in the agricultural sector, in the hope of increasing output and thus the share which she herself could take? Or should she merely loot the French economy taking what she could as booty? Owing to deficiencies in investment in armaments industries before 1942 Germany's own armaments-producing capacity was fairly low until 1943. Should she therefore use French plant to increase this capacity? And if so, should she do this only when it was absolutely necessary and as a temporary measure? Or should she incorporate the economy of occupied France, and even Vichy France, into her own war economy, forming what Jean Bichelonne, secretary of state for industrial production in the Vichy government after April 1942, was to call the 'European war economy'? Or should she transfer, in as large quantities as possible, the factors of production from France to Germany, turning France into a rump state, a primary producer like the General-government of Poland? What fate was reserved for France in the 'New Order'?[46]

As he saw it, the German occupation of France went through three main phases. During the first one, which followed the fall of Paris, he argued that the economics of Blitzkrieg did not require much pressure to be imposed on France's economic resources, apart from on aircraft, stocks of military equipment, transport, and raw materials. The second period, which started in the fall of 1941, at the height of the Russian campaign, was when the needs of the Blitzkrieg strategy were greatest, necessitating a more substantial contribution to be made by France in terms of ammunition, consumer goods, and labor. This period of increased exploitation was dominated by the policies of Fritz Sauckel, the Commissar-General for Labor, who demanded the transfer of French (and other foreign) workers to Germany's basic and arms-producing industries in order to speed up production. It was during this period that the new era of a continental European Order under German dominance appeared within reach. It was to serve not only the interests of the German wartime political economy but also lead to

46. Milward, 'German Economic Policy towards France, 1942–1944' (1967), 423–424.

the postwar reorganization of the whole European political economy. The final phase was dominated by the consequences of the collapse of the Blitzkrieg strategy in favor of, first, a more efficient mobilization of all available resources for a long-term war effort and then, the simple exploitation of the conquered economy in the context of an emergency total-war effort within the wider context of a European war economy.

Alan Milward's analysis encompassed German as well as French views on the future role of France in the New Order. As he had shown in *The German Economy at War*, the German state, far from constituting a monolithic administrative and political entity, was riven with divisions, initially over the purpose and degree of control and exploitation of conquered territories, and subsequently over the degree of administrative centralization that followed the end of the Blitzkrieg economy. In the case of occupied France, the most prominent dispute was between Speer, who favored expanding the production of armaments and consumer goods in France in order to meet both the needs of the German armed forces across Europe and civilians at home, and Sauckel, who preferred to force French labor to work in factories in Germany where their level of productivity was higher. Whereas Speer followed a policy of progressive economic rationalization on a pan-European basis, Sauckel was emotionally linked to the early revolutionary doctrine of National Socialism for which the *Grossraumwirtschaft* (the economics of large areas) would be based on the creation of a self-sufficient continental-wide economic system in which the industrial regions of western and central Europe pivoting on the Third Reich would be surrounded by a periphery of countries acting as suppliers of foodstuffs and raw materials. For the old National Socialist guard, Speer's centralist policy represented 'an attack on the National Socialist ideas of the New Order'.[47]

Once again, as Alan Milward had shown in *The German Economy at War*, under the façade of a monolithic organization, Nazi Germany's leadership was actually quite divided, lacking a clear sense of direction over which were the most effective policies to win the war and establish the New Order in Europe. Against the backdrop of conflicting and ever-changing demands from the Nazi masters, there were, as Alan Milward saw it, fundamental differences of opinion within the Vichy state over what the future of France should be in the German New Order for Europe. Marshall Pétain had at the time of the Armistice, in June 1940, readily accepted a role for France as a supplier of food and raw materials to Germany as offering a 'means to France's social and spiritual regeneration'.[48] On the other hand Laval, on returning to power as Prime Minister in April 1942, welcomed Speer's plans as a way for France to avoid the fate of the eastern territories and retain the possibility of having an industrial future.[49] All these

47. Milward, *The New Order*, 146.
48 Milward, 'German Economic Policy towards France', 427.
49. Ibidem.

divisions and changes made Alan Milward's calculation of what Germany managed to extract from France all the more surprising.

He used five case studies—coal, iron ore, bauxite and aluminum, wolfram (the ore from which the strategic metal tungsten is made), and agriculture—which together constitute the main body of *The New Order and the French Economy*—to show how the interaction of all these factors influenced what Germany was able to extract from the French economy. As he demonstrated, by 1942 'France had become an integral part of the German war economy.'[50] Toward the end of 1943 the general level of exploitation was between 40 and 50 percent of French capacity as France became 'the most important supplier of raw materials, foodstuffs, and manufactured goods to the German economy.'[51] Expressed in other terms, 'the total value of goods and services' which Germany was able to obtain from France during the war 'was roughly equal to one-quarter of [France's] own Gross National Product on the eve of the war.'[52] To the value of raw materials, food, production, and labor Alan Milward added the value to Germany of its trade with France. He showed that during the occupation, the prewar trend in which the countries of south-eastern Europe had become the most important source of German supply was broken, and their place was taken by France, with Belgium and the Netherlands in a subordinate role.

The failure of the Blitzkrieg on the Eastern Front turned attention from the New Order to the organization of a total-war economy on a continental-wide basis, which resulted in France becoming by 1943 the most important supplier of the German economy for a wider range of industrial products as well as food. As a consequence, the relative importance of south-eastern Europe to the German economy declined, and long-term plans were designed to reduce the German dependence on eastern supplies even further. How was France to fit into those longer-term plans, he asked. But it was a question which, as he himself admitted, could not be answered in wartime: 'Indeed the answer seemed to recede as the war progressed'.[53] What he was anxious to settle in *The New Order and the French Economy* was whether the 'startlingly' high level of exploitation of the French economy could have been sustained had German domestic economic policy not changed and with it the economic policy in occupied Europe. On this he felt there was no room for liberal complacency: 'In so far as German policy had to be changed in autumn 1943 this was not so much because it was, economically, a failure. Rather it was because events in Germany, the changes in economic policy which had taken place there in 1942, spread

50. Milward, *The New Order*, 137.
51. Ibid., 282–283.
52. Ibid., 277.
53. Milward, 'German Economic Policy towards France', 424.

their implications to occupied Europe.'[54] If Alan Milward was interested in the effects of occupation on individual economies he saw the even more important theoretical question to be whether the Nazi conquest of continental Europe could have worked economically had Germany not been defeated militarily. Was the liberal theory that war and conquest did not pay disproved by the Nazi experience in the period of 1939 to 1942 when it controlled the resources of most of continental Europe? As he wrote,

> [t]hat conquest, in the long run is not profitable, is too satisfyingly moral a lesson to draw. Each conqueror has his philosophy of conquest and can only act within the bounds of that philosophy. Seen in historical perspective the National Socialist conquests were an attempt to solve the political and economic problems of Germany by solving those of Europe on the same principles. The New Economic Order was ultimately essential if National Socialist Germany was not always to face overwhelming economic problems in a hostile world. The economic developments in Germany after the National Socialist revolution were meaningless in the long run if confined to one country; conquest was inherent in them.[55]

As far as he was concerned, to understand the National Socialist theory of conquest and the nature of National Socialism, which he insisted was a variant of Fascism rather than of totalitarianism, it was necessary to 'think ourselves out of the weight of the two hundred years of thought which fascism itself rejected'.[56] Rejecting both the Liberal-Capitalist and the Marxist theories of Fascism, Alan Milward argued, at that time, the following:

> The philosophical starting-point of fascism was the rejection of what fascists called the 'Greek idea', the idea of the individual's growth to emancipation and maturity. It was this particular conception of human destiny, they argued, which was recaptured from Greek philosophy during the Renaissance and thus became the basis for Smith's 'economic man'. Fascism therefore attacked liberal economic thought at the very base of its trunk. The emancipated individual, who was both the producer and the product of capitalism, was disruptive to society, selfish, and an enemy to the community. Conversion to fascism was a revolt against interpreting the world from an individualist and materialist standpoint. Communism, in this light, was merely the last and latest form of materialism, the ultimate liberal heresy. The fascist philosophy imposed drastic restrictions on the 'rights' of the individual and the

---

54. Milward, *The New Order*, 111.
55. Ibid., 295.
56. Milward 'French Labour and the German Economy, 1942–1945' (1970), 350.

> group. Capital was a public trust. Instead of the class-ridden state of the materialists fascism proposed the ethical state, the spartan virtues of whose inhabitants would be far removed from those of the capitalist entrepreneur or consumer. Philosophically, fascism represented a search, not for further economic development in new and more difficult international circumstances but for a point of economic equilibrium, a haven from the pressure of social and economic change.[57]

Berating liberal historians for dismissing the New Order as 'windy rhetoric, a verbal disguise for conquest', he also criticized Marxist historians—such as Wolfgang Schumann and Gerhard Lozek—for interpreting it as 'the subjection and looting of the occupied territories by German bankers and industrialists in whose interests the war had been prepared and carried out.'[58] Alan Milward's view was that

> the conflicting strains of economic thought in National Socialism spanned the whole range from anti-capitalist, or even pre-capitalist, millenarianism to the ruthless advocacy of the businessman's right to dominate all economic policy. These gross differences of opinion were never better shown than in German economic policy in occupied countries.[59]

If *The New Order and the French Economy* had two main levels of analysis, it was only his analysis of German economic policies toward occupied France from 1940 to 1944 which found favor. All reviewers without exception praised Alan Milward's ability to analyze the existing evidence from that new perspective. The second level of analysis was not seen to be as successful as the first. Richard Tilly and Hans Umbreit, while acknowledging the wealth of data which Alan Milward had produced on the French economy, were not convinced that the New Order was a useful way to interpret the economic aspects of Nazi occupation policy in France.[60] Arthur Schweitzer was more critical: 'While the factual investigation is competently done, limited mainly by the inadequacy of available information, the same cannot be said for the efforts to interpret either the occupied economy or the Nazi empire.'[61] Indeed Schweitzer had also written a caustic review of *The German Economy at War*, and was not sympathetic to Alan Milward's apparent adventurism in formu-

57. Ibid., 338.
58. Ibid., 339 for the first quotation. The second is Milward's own direct quotation from Schumann and Lozek, 'Die faschistische Okkupationspolitik im Spiegel der Historiographie der beiden deutschen Staaten' (1964).
59. Milward, 'German Economic Policy towards France', 425.
60. Reviews of *The New Order and the French Economy*, by Tilly and Umbreit.
61. Schweitzer's review of *The New Order and the French Economy*, 126.

lating wider interpretations of National Socialism.[62] Schweitzer was not alone. Charles P. Kindleberger, one of the earliest reviewers of *The New Order and the French Economy*, found it 'futile' to use the French case to generalize about the benefits of military conquest. For Kindleberger, the controversy between liberal theory and the revolutionary doctrine of National Socialism was 'pressed too hard' and unpersuasively.[63] Urs Brand referred to the book's section on the Liberal and Fascist theories of the profitability of conquest as 'historical digression'.[64]

It has to be said that Alan Milward never shied away from an argument, and in his analysis of the operation of the Nazi economy during the war, he was taking on two very powerful theories, those of Liberalism and Marxism, at the same time. In trying to understand the theoretical underpinnings of the Nazi war economy and of the New Order for Europe he was anxious to avoid what he considered to be the dangerous complacency which their oversimplified views created. Many reviewers considered that his determination to understand the politics and economics underpinning Nazi policy in the Second World War in some way indicated his tacit support for the Nazi regime. Two reviewers intimated that he would have welcomed the establishment of the National Socialist New Order. 'Might an imposed economic order have been better for Europe than present bickerings and divisions?' Arthur L. Funk asked rhetorically, after which he added, 'Milward's argument in favor of force as a possible (and presumably legitimate) method of imposing a supranational economic system is a tortuous one.'[65] Volker Wieland, in turn, saw 'expressions which suggest a certain sympathy [of Milward] with National Socialism.'[66] Nothing could have been further from the truth, but it was easier to insinuate that Alan Milward might have had secret sympathies for the Nazis than to consider whether the National Socialist New Order in Europe might have been seen as a viable long-term solution to the socioeconomic problems faced by Germany and the rest of Europe in the interwar period.

Although Alan Milward based his views of war on those of the nineteenth-century Prussian general, Carl von Clausewitz, rather than on the more fashionable game theory as developed by Thomas C. Schelling in

---

62. Schweitzer's review of *The German Economy at War*, 173.
63. Kindleberger's review of *The New Order and the French Economy*. Milward's views on the liberal theory of war were also introduced in his pamphlet on the economic effects of the two world wars on the British economy which he was to publish also in 1970; Milward, *The Economic Effects of the World Wars on Britain*.
64. Brand's review of *The New Order and the French Economy*, 202. Translation by the authors from the German original. The authors of this introduction provide all translations from languages other than English.
65. Funk's review of *The New Order and the French Economy*, 314 (all quotations).
66. Wieland's review of *The New Order and the French Economy*, 865.

1960, his views were quite similar to those of Schelling. On the first page of his influential text Schelling had argued that 'rational behavior' is associated with morality and goodness, while 'irrational behavior' is associated with pathological behavior: 'Among diverse theories of conflict [ . . . ] a main dividing line is between those that treat conflict as a pathological state [ . . . ] and those that take conflict for granted and study the behavior associated with it.'[67] Alan Milward was certainly among those scholars who operated on the assumption that rational behavior was 'motivated by a conscious calculation of advantages, a calculation that in turn is based on an explicit and internally consistent value system.'[68] As Larry Neal puts it, in Chapter 3 of this volume,

> a scholarly appreciation of the rationality of the German war effort under Adolf Hitler had to be kept subordinate to the characterization of the Nazi ideology as irrational and consequently doomed to failure. Otherwise, some other dictator could arise and succeed in perfecting a fascist economic system.[69]

Alan Milward wanted, through his research, to discover exactly why the Nazi system of occupation had failed rather than accept the official version of events. In France the official explanation which had been carefully controlled since the end of the war was that it was the resistance of most French people to the occupation which was responsible for the defeat of Germany. This had received a near-fatal blow in 1969 with the release in cinemas of the documentary film *Le chagrin et la pitié* (*The Sorrow and the Pity*), which showed the speed of the collapse of the French state under German military pressure.[70] While this was attributed to poor French military strategy and the deep political divisions within the Third Republic, the film also exposed the degree of popular support enjoyed by Marshall Pétain. This was reflected in the large numbers of French volunteers who were recruited to fight Communism both at the front and in the German armaments factories, as well as in the anti-British and anti-Semitic sentiments held by many—and not exclusively Vichy politicians—in France. Although what the documentary film portrayed was not dissimilar from what some French authors had already published in the 1960s, as with many of the accounts of the history of France in the period from June 1940 to August 1944, particularly if produced by foreigners, it was subject to the

---

67. Schelling, *The Strategy of Conflict* (1960), 3.
68. Ibid., 4.
69. Chapter 3, this volume, 159.
70. The 1969 documentary film *Le chagrin et la pitié: Chronique d'une ville sous l'occupation*, by Marcel Ophüls, which was an account of ordinary life during the occupation, was shown in cinemas in France rather than on television as originally intended.

policy of a selective combination of memory and amnesia, a sort of 'Vichy syndrome'.[71]

*The New Order and the French Economy*, which was published a few months after the release of the film, received few reviews in France and was not translated into French.[72] As a result it was neither debated nor perhaps read. If Alan Milward had shown that the conquest of France was profitable to the Third Reich and that there was extensive voluntary cooperation between many French businesses and officials with the occupying forces, his overall conclusion to the question of whether the New Order in France could have proved viable was that it was the behavior of labor during the occupation which diminished the importance to Germany of the acquisition of France:

> The study of individual industries and the relative failure of German policies of exploitation suggests that that failure was due not only to the contradictions of German policy but also to the falling rates of labour productivity in the French economy. It is the behaviour of the French labour force during the war, and, indeed, the whole history of the French resistance movement, which assert that the economics of conquest cannot wholly be calculated in terms of cash.[73]

Indeed, Alan Milward was one of the first to make the distinction between the Resistance movement, which he did not consider had made a significant contribution to the outcome of the war, except in a few isolated cases, and the passive resistance of French labor which led to the general decline in French productivity particularly in 1944.[74] This distinction is one among many now accepted by historians who refer to 'passive resistance' as dissent to distinguish it more clearly from 'Resistance' as a political movement.[75] In using the term 'resistance' to apply to both dissent and organized opposition, Alan Milward left himself open to considerable criticism. Kindleberger was quick to challenge him for sidelining the role of the resistance: 'How much was the German eventual military defeat'—he asked Alan Milward—'a result of invasion on the one hand, or the impossibility of holding down a conquered people on the other?'[76] Another reviewer was frustrated because Alan Milward did not investigate 'the cost of conquest

71. Expression borrowed from Rousso, *The Vichy Syndrome: History and Memory in France Since 1944* (1991).
72. The link between *Le chagrin et la pitié* and *The New Order and the French Economy* was first mentioned by Funk in his review of *The New Order and the French Economy*, 313.
73. Milward, *The New Order*, 288.
74. Ibid., 295.
75. Kershaw, *The Nazi Dictatorship*, 183–218, discusses the debate over the meaning of resistance in Germany.
76. Kindleberger's review of *The New Order and the French Economy*, 161.

and the far greater cost of subjugation' with as much emphasis and energy as he 'applied to the calculation of [conquest's] benefit.'[77]

What Alan Milward sought to assess in his hard-headed treatment of the contribution of the resistance to the defeat of Germany was the military value of the resistance. He had an opportunity to debate the issue with the recipient of one of the highest military honors which the French state could give, the *Croix de Guerre*, bestowed on the historian Michael R. D. Foot, Professor of Modern History in the University of Manchester, for his activities in the Special Operations Executive in France in 1944. Since Foot had subsequently written extensively about the positive role played by the Resistance during the Second World War Alan Milward suggested to him that

> [t]he wealth of historical study on the resistance movement in all countries, including Germany, has usually tended to dodge the issue of whether or not resistance was effective. That resistance was widespread, brave and well organized has been demonstrated over and over again. [ . . . ] of course there must come a point where resistance is the only conceivable strategy and the obvious example is that of a state or community, such as Poland or the Jews in 1939, face to face with virtual annihilation [but] does it necessarily follow that such resistance will have any strategic value however inevitable it may be?[78]

And he went on to argue:

> The choice of resistance both as a tactic and a strategy, except in the extreme example of the threat of annihilation, is also a decision against other tactics and strategies. The correctness of the choice can be judged by, in the widest sense, its opportunity-cost; resources invested in resistance could always be deployed in a different way. But in this case the calculation of opportunity–cost must be more than a merely financial one. It must involve as far as possible all the factors including the psychological and social ones which go into the choice of a correct strategy. The history of the Second World War illustrates this excellently. There were in fact very few situations in those years when resistance was the correct strategy if the choice is assessed on economic grounds; in almost every case the resources could have been better invested

77. Wenden's review of *The New Order and the French Economy*, 313.
78. Milward, 'The Economic and Strategic Effectiveness of Resistance', in *Resistance in Europe: 1939–1945*, edited by Hawes and White (1975), 188–189. Contrast this with the chapter by Foot in the same volume, 'What Good Did Resistance Do?' which provided a much more favorable appreciation of the Resistance's contribution.

> elsewhere. But the social and psychological value of resistance was so strong as to make its choice sometimes the correct one.[79]

He gave two examples where resistance had clearly made a difference. The first was in sabotaging the mining of wolfram in France, and the second was the attack on the heavy water plant in southern Norway. Both acts of resistance, he asserted, struck in areas of strategic importance and short supply for Germany. But his general conclusion was that 'as an individual act resistance was liberating, satisfying and necessary; on a coordinated level it seems to have been seldom effective, sometimes stultifying, frequently dangerous, and almost always too costly.'[80] By 1986, as François Bédarida made it clear in summarizing what he saw to be the core of the Foot–Milward controversy, Alan Milward's efforts to distinguish between economic, political, and military factors in order to clarify why Nazi Germany had been defeated had not been appreciated in France:

> On an economic level, A. Milward believes that neither the German war machine nor the wartime strategy were seriously affected by the, albeit very costly, opposition of resistance organizations, except in the case of some very specific and timely operations. In fact, to reduce the effectiveness of the resistance solely to its military dimension is to completely misunderstand the very nature of the Second World War. In a conflict in which the psychological, ideological, and political factors are closely intertwined with the military and strategic factors, the confrontation between the Allies and the Axis must be analyzed in its entirety, without artificially compartmentalizing the various elements. If no one can deny that it was the defeat on the Eastern and Western battlefields that caused the collapse of Nazi Germany and its allies and that on their forces alone the clandestine movement would have been quite incapable of destroying the war potential of the enemy, such evidence can not devalue either the actual results of resistance action or the effectiveness of its contribution to the defeat of the Axis.[81]

In the years following the publication of *The New Order and the French Economy* a considerable amount of research was published which proved conclusively that the Vichy state officially collaborated with Nazi Germany, but the focus was almost entirely on the political aspects of that collaboration. According to the well-known business historian from the *École des hautes études en sciences sociales* in Paris, Patrick Fridenson, the 'considerable gap in historical research' between the politics and economics of the

79. Milward, 'The Economic and Strategic Effectiveness of Resistance', 190.
80. Ibid., 202.
81. Bédarida, 'L'histoire de la résistance: Lectures d'hier, chantiers de demain' (1986), 86.

Vichy period is mainly due to 'the feeling that this shameful moment in French contemporary history did not deserve research which would necessarily undermine French prestige.'[82] Outside France the most recent research carried out by a team of neoclassical economic historians into the German occupation of France has, as Neal points out in his contribution to this volume, confirmed Alan Milward's conclusions that the occupation was of considerable importance to Germany economically. What Filippo Occhino, Kim Oosterlinck, and Eugene N. White argue is that the extent to which conquest can be made to pay depends on the degree of cooperation from the defeated country. France, they reaffirm, collaborated willingly, offering much more to Nazi Germany than was required, in the belief that a German-dominated Europe was preferable to one dominated by Great Britain. 'The economic support of the Reich's vassal states was crucial', they argue, on account of Germany's severe shortage of foreign exchange reserves to pay for vital imports of raw materials and labor shortage.[83] However, while they confirmed Alan Milward's argument that the economic value of the occupation of France to Nazi Germany was very considerable, they stopped short of agreeing with his conclusion that ultimately the occupation could not have been sustained because of the falling rates of labor productivity in French industry and agriculture when the policies of occupation changed.

## THE FASCIST ECONOMY IN NORWAY (1972)

If the Nazi occupation of France was ultimately unsustainable because of the actions of French labor, was the occupation of Norway, a country which the Nazis felt was racially closer than France, any more successful, he asked. *The Fascist Economy in Norway*, published in 1972 and based mainly on the archives of the Economic Department of the *Reichskommissariat*—the highest governing body of the Third Reich in Norway—as well as on those of the German Ministry of War Production, which he had already consulted in London, in addition to many other sources, addressed that question.[84] One immediate consequence of his research was that the archives relating to the German occupation of Norway were moved from London to Oslo.

But once again, as in the case of his previous book on France, the reception of *The Fascist Economy in Norway* was mixed. While reviewers were ready in general to praise the author's capacity to illuminate the actual operation of the economy of occupied Norway, they were reluctant to engage

---

82. Fridenson, 'French Enterprises under German Occupation, 1940–1944' (2002), 259.
83. Occhino, Oosterlinck, and White, 'How Much Can a Victor Force the Vanquished to Pay?' (2008), 5.
84. Milward, *The Fascist Economy in Norway* (1972).

with his wider discussion of the nature of National Socialism. According to many, Alan Milward should have limited himself to detailing the facts, rather than elaborating on the theories supposedly underpinning them. 'The word Fascist in the title is misleading', wrote one reviewer, since what Alan Milward detailed was 'the story of the Norwegian war economy, 1940–45, mainly as it served or (increasingly) failed to serve German needs.'[85] A French reviewer, Pierre Mougenot, commented that 'we feel uncomfortable because we would have preferred the term "Nazi" to "fascist" [ . . . ] we would have liked to see the book entitled *The Nazi Economy in Norway*.'[86] Michael F. Cullis struck the same note, regretting that Alan Milward had used the term 'fascist' in the title, rather than opting for something along the lines of 'The New Order and the Norwegian economy'. He even suggested that Alan Milward's insistence 'point[s] to an underlying polemical, even ideological, purpose that is never made explicit'.[87]

Alan Milward was in fact quite explicit in his argument that in Nazi Germany economics could not be separated from the political and ideological nature of the regime, just as the political nature of the regime could not be understood without recognizing the nature of the economic problems which it faced. The term 'fascist' in the title was deliberately chosen to emphasize that in his view National Socialism, although it was the product of a long history of social tensions in Germany, was not something unique to Germany. Since it had parallels elsewhere in Europe he considered that it was fundamentally a form of Fascism and needed to be understood as such. In the Preface to *The New Order and the French Economy* he had already stated that as he saw it,

> fascism was no cancer in the body politic but a normal stage in the historical and economic development of Europe, and that it cannot be ultimately comprehended on a merely political level. Its form of economic expression and its form of political expression cannot be meaningfully separated, the final end of both was the New Order.[88]

The reorganization of the European economy into the New Order, on which ultimate safety for the National Socialist revolution depended, could only be imposed through force. The purpose of war, Milward insisted, and the purpose of the Nazi exploitation of European economies, was to fit them into the broader framework of the European economy based on Fascist ideology.

Alan Milward's argument in *The Fascist Economy in Norway* is straightforward. Even though Norway may have seemed better suited on racial grounds to be incorporated into the Nazi New Order this was misleading.

---

85. Ellersieck's review of *The Fascist Economy in Norway*, 458.
86. Mougenot's review of *The Fascist Economy in Norway*, 484–485.
87. Cullis's review of *The Fascist Economy in Norway*, 505.
88. Milward, *The New Order*, v.

Because it was, 'of all occupied economies, the most open and the most dependent on international factor mobility' it was in fact 'the least suited to incorporation in the fascist system.'[89] The invasion of Norway on 9 April 1940 was prompted by certain strategic needs, particularly to assure the inflow of iron-ore supplies from Sweden during the winter months and to prevent the Royal Navy from finding safe havens along the Norwegian coast.[90] But once the country had been occupied it had to be administered. The ultimate intention of German occupation policy was to exploit the country in Germany's interests and at the same time to force, 'in the name of the fascist revolution', its future pattern of economic growth to fit the needs of the *Grossraumwirtschaft*.[91] This was also the intention of some Fascist theorists, chief among them the *Reichskommissar* Josef Terboven, who tried to impose Fascist ideology on the Norwegian economy and society. One original feature of Alan Milward's book is the striking contrast between the theoretical place reserved for Norway in a future New European Order and the reality imposed by the needs of the war, particularly after 1941.

The evidence which he put forward was to prove the far-reaching nature of German planning for the economic and social restructuring of the Norwegian economy. The expansion of agriculture and fisheries and the development of Norway as a producer of raw materials and basic metals benefiting from cheap hydroelectricity were designed to retain population in the primary sector as well as provide food and crucial raw materials to the German population (and the European population in the longer term). This was to be accomplished, if necessary, at the expense of industrial expansion. The overriding aim was for Norway to become a primary producer with its industrial development wholly subordinated to German needs. It is within this framework that German plans for the industrialization of Norway are presented in the book. According to Alan Milward,

> the evidence from German policy in Norway confirmed that the New Order was an attempt to force a particular philosophico-economic view of the world on to [Norway] as on to other European countries. That view of the world was anti-materialistic, antagonistic to economic growth, concerned with the creation of a society which would be stable enough to resist the hitherto relentless pressures of social change.[92]

He exposed the tensions between the interests of German businesses and those of the Nazi state and between German and Norwegian business inter-

89. Milward, *The Fascist Economy*, v.
90. For the importance to Norway of Swedish iron ore, and the overall relative importance of the latter to Nazi Germany's armaments industry in 1940, see Milward, 'Could Sweden have Stopped the Second World War?' (1967).
91. Milward, *The Fascist Economy*, 293.
92. Ibid., 290.

ests. In line with his previous work on the German economy during the war and the occupation of France, he also showed that whatever original plans the Nazis may have had in occupying Norway, they had to change them due to the circumstances of the war and the experience of occupation. In fact, *The Fascist Economy in Norway* is 'a close and detailed analysis of what the Germans *planned* and what they actually *did* with their Norwegian conquest after 1940.'[93] The revolutionary National Socialists in the spirit of the New Order were more concerned with social engineering, with an emphasis on (the much idealized) Norwegian peasantry (and fishermen) and with a more limited emphasis on industrial expansion under German control. They soon met with insurmountable obstacles in trying to retain these ideological priorities. As in France, labor productivity was the main problem. In the case of Norway, the labor demands that the *Wehrmacht* requested for communication and defense construction diverted manpower from the primary sector and provided little room for social experimentation. From the winter of 1941–1942, with the end of the Blitzkrieg strategy, as elsewhere in occupied Europe, the Germans gave priority to the needs of a war of attrition against the materially much stronger Allies. '[A]fter the collapse of such strategy', as Alan Milward had already established in the case of France, 'the New Order could only be built by mobilizing the occupied economies [ . . . ] in such a way as to change the shape of the New Order itself.'[94]

The chapter devoted to the Norwegian aluminum industry reveals the gap between Nazi plans and the political and economic conditions in Norway. In view of the need to develop and expand the German air force, immediate Nazi plans assigned to Norway an output target of 250,000 tons of aluminum when its actual production had been no more than 31,000 tons in 1939. The Nazi aim of making Norway a major European producer of aluminum was not shared by the German aluminum and other light metal firms who feared future Norwegian competition in view of the size of the planned investment. Nor was it shared by the *Wehrmacht*, which wanted immediate results even at the cost of depriving the *Luftwaffe* of its increased supplies of Norwegian aluminum in the future, nor by the Norwegian government which had its own economic demands.

It was the lack of attention which Alan Milward paid to the interests of the Norwegian firms themselves which was the main point of criticism of one reviewer: '[*The Fascist Economy in Norway*] shows only the occupying power's policy, not that of the occupied state.'[95] Certainly, if judging by its title some readers might have been disappointed by the relatively short analysis of the Norwegian corporate state and business. As Helge

93. Mitchell's review of *The Fascist Economy in Norway*, 1105 (emphasis added).
94. Milward, *The New Order*, 296.
95. Loock's review of *The Fascist Economy in Norway*, 547.

Pharo commented, Alan Milward's research on Norway 'should be able to provide the starting point for further detailed studies of German economic policy in Norway, and also for studies of the Norwegian business relations with Germany during the war, a heretofore neglected field of research.'[96] This is the task that Hans Otto Frøland has carried out in Chapter 4 of this volume, focusing in particular on the expansion of Norwegian aluminum production, where he shows in detail how the Norwegian firms themselves welcomed the opportunity to expand aluminum output. Using Norwegian records to which Alan Milward did not have access forty years ago, he documents the willingness of Norwegian firms to exploit the opportunity which the Nazi plans seemingly offered them, an opportunity which included protecting themselves against any future competition in the sector.

Ultimately, as Alan Milward showed, the Nazi occupation of Norway failed since Norway produced few commodities that were of value to Germany and had been too integrated into the international economy to survive in a German-directed European economy. He maintained that '[t]here were only two possible ways of carrying out such an enormous project as the aluminium plan. One was to do it with the full and free consent of the conquered territory, the other to do it by ruthless and total subjection of it.'[97] The peculiar situation of Norway, occupied but ruled by its own Fascists who very much depended upon their German counterparts while at the same time disagreeing with them, allowed for neither option.

Notwithstanding the failure of Nazi planning to make Norway contribute to German needs in the long term, it is evident that Norway had to pay a high price for meeting the German wartime needs in the short term:

> The German exploitation of occupied Norway, like that of occupied France, was successful to a degree which most western economists would have denied was possible. The level of exploitation in each case was very similar and in each case very high. The standard of living of the occupied country was drastically reduced and its resources, capital, land, and labour were all ruthlessly diverted to German use. Seen in this light, German policy in Norway was a remarkable example of how far such policies can be carried out.[98]

German plans for Norway's future represented for Alan Milward the evidence which testified that the New Order was 'more than windy rhetoric'.[99] The problem which he faced and for which he was criticized by reviewers was that because the New Order never became a reality his research attributed to the German occupation policy a degree of rationality which

96. Pharo's review of *The Fascist Economy in Norway*, 100.
97. Milward, *The Fascist Economy*, 206.
98. Ibid., 280.
99. Milward, 'French Labour and the German Economy', 339.

was greater than seemed to be merited by a policy characterized by local improvisation.[100] Notwithstanding the seriousness of the purpose that Nazi planners pursued in France and Norway, the conclusion of Alan Milward's research into the occupation of Norway was that '[t]here was very little in fascist economic policy in Norway which offered much chance of converting the population to support for the fascist regime'.[101]

At the time economic historians showed little interest in the issues raised by Alan Milward's work on the Nazi occupation policies. This may be due in part to the fact that it was many years before economic historians became interested in the study of war at all, preferring to focus on what Vera Zamagni, in Chapter 5 of this volume, calls 'normal' periods. As she explains, economic history as a discipline, beginning in the United States in the 1960s, was increasingly moving in the direction of cliometrics. With the expansion of what was then called the 'New Economic History', economic historians became increasingly interested in applying econometric techniques to the wealth of new economic data covering long time periods which was being generated. Their exclusive dependence on neoclassical economic theory to explain historical change left little room for the study of a period in recent history when neoclassical theory was of little use. In Britain and continental Europe where the New Economic History was slower to develop, historians focused on the politics of war and occupation but showed little appetite for following what was seen to be the politically dangerous path opened up by Alan Milward of assessing the occupation of Europe in the economic and ideological terms defined by the Nazis.

## THE ECONOMIC EFFECTS OF THE WORLD WARS ON BRITAIN (1970)

Alan Milward started his career as an economic historian in Britain at a time when the subject, along with all the social sciences, was expanding. In fact in the boom years of the 1960s the British government decided to invest in building six new universities. It was in one of these new universities, the University of East Anglia (UEA) that he sought to advance his academic career. Within a few months of arriving in 1965, however, he received an invitation from Stanford University to spend the 1966–1967 academic year in the Economics Department there. On returning to UEA, he was happy to accept an offer from Stanford to become a tenured associate professor of economics starting in 1969.

While he was at UEA and working on *The New Order and the French Economy* he received an invitation from his former colleague in Edinburgh

---

100. Reviews of *The New Order and the French Economy*, by Tilly and Umbreit.
101. Milward, *The Fascist Economy in Norway*, 300

University, Professor Michael W. Flinn, to write a pamphlet on the effects of the two world wars on the British economy. This was to be part of a new series which the Economic History Society was publishing to present the results of the ever-expanding research in the subject in an accessible form. The invitation provided Alan Milward with an opportunity to think about the impact of war from the perspective of a victor in both world wars. The short pamphlet, published in 1970 with the title *The Economic Effects of the World Wars on Britain*, was the first time that he focused his writing on the British economy.[102] Despite the fact that the aim of the initiative was to provide 'a balanced summary rather than an exposition of the author's own viewpoint', many of the issues raised in this short pamphlet (only 42 pages long) provide us with an understanding of Alan Milward's personal approach to the history of twentieth-century Europe: 'What changes in the economy have historians and economists laid to the account of the two world wars? And what changes may justly so be laid?'[103]

With the argument that the system of state control or intervention in the economy in Britain had already been dealt with adequately for both wars, he was to focus on the long-term changes produced by the two wars on Britain. This justification fit well with his interpretation that it was the long-term changes generated during the two wars which were the more significant. His conclusion was that the large-scale transformations which the world wars produced on Britain, and particularly on the international framework in which the national economy was to operate after both wars, could not be properly assessed by focusing only on the 'cost' of war.

The starting point of Alan Milward's analysis was the liberal theory of war. To those who had read *The German Economy at War* and *The New Order and the French Economy* this was familiar territory. As he explained, the liberal theory of war, the child of the Enlightenment, saw war as 'an almost unmitigated disaster' and as 'a loss to the economy, of cash, of production, of capital and of people' the consequences of which were not limited to the duration of the war but also impacted years later in terms of depression or the late adjustment to the inflationary tensions inevitably produced by wartime financing, as in 1920.[104] That the theory was also seen to have a moral dimension was illustrated by him in quoting the budget speech made by the then Chancellor of the Exchequer, William Gladstone, in the British House of Commons on the eve of the Crimean War: 'The expenses of a war are the moral check which it has pleased the

102. Milward, *The Economic Effects of the World Wars on Britain* (1970). The same pamphlet was reprinted in 1973 with a more specific title, *The Economic Effects of the Two World Wars on Britain*, and a slightly longer second edition was published in 1984. All subsequent references to this pamphlet refer to the 1973 reprint.
103. Milward, *The Economic Effects*, 9.
104. Ibid., 11 (quotations) and 12.

Almighty to impose upon the ambition and the lust of conquest that are inherent in so many nations'. This, however, as Alan Milward with his customary irony pointed out, 'did not absolve the public from the duty to suffer the same moral chastisement when resisting an aggressor.'[105] Leaving conventional morality aside, the challenge for those upholding the liberal theory of war was to measure the extent of the loss in terms of output, people, cash, and capital caused by the war and ultimately to make the vanquished pay for the cost of the war.

The most difficult calculation for the cost of war was to fix a financial figure to the millions of people killed and maimed in war, in other words to the 'human capital' lost. This was a debate which after the Second World War, because of the holocaust of the Jews, could not be confined within the boundaries of rational accounting since it turned out to be considered, essentially, a moral dilemma. How could anyone dare, Wieland had already asked Milward, to measure the costs of the war in terms of human beings?[106] As Alan Milward explained, it was a French actuary, Alfred Barriol, who, on the eve of the First World War, had devised a method of calculating the cost of war which came to be adopted in the final reckoning after that war. Barriol had quite dispassionately worked out the different value of a dead soldier from many countries basing the differences on the cost of his education and training as well as his future productive capacity. 'The differences in value', Alan Milward explained, 'represent roughly the differences in the level of economic development of the countries concerned, the general conclusion being that the effect of war on a highly developed country such as Britain was likely to be much more serious than on an under-developed country.'[107] Although Barriol's methodology was adopted after the First World War in Britain and elsewhere, it was found to be flawed insofar as it ignored the very wide differences in class which existed in the British armed forces and which made all the assumptions about average cost of education, training, life expectancy, future employment, and productive capacity quite suspect. Also, the wide changes in purchasing power and in the relative prices of the different currencies, apart from the very concept of 'war expenditure' in budgetary terms, made it very difficult to calculate the exact cost of a war. But it was not only an academic problem since the demands for reparations from Germany after the First World War, which were to have such disastrous consequences for Germany and the rest of the world, rested on making just such a calculation.

In Britain, it was not the total cost of the war but the differential impact of the wars on the British economy and society which, Alan Milward

105. Ibid., 12 (quotations).
106. Wieland's review of *The New Order and the French Economy*, 865.
107. Milward, *The Economic Effects*, 14.

observed, was to dominate academic debate.[108] By measuring the impact of the wars on different industries and on different groups in society, war was not seen only as a loss but, in certain cases, as producing some gains:

> Indeed the events of the First World War, more than anything else, dealt a death-blow to the classical liberal tradition. The introduction of conscription, the full-time employment of a large part of the population that had not previously experienced regular employment, the beginnings of aerial bomb attacks on civilians, the Allied blockade and Germany's unrestricted submarine warfare directly involved a far larger proportion of the population in the war than in other modern wars. In this light, the liberal interpretation seemed insufficiently comprehensive to explain satisfactorily the impact of war on the economy. War was not only a loss, it was also a force for change, change which in some cases might be construed as gain.[109]

He was to contrast how war was perceived and interpreted in Britain with the United States in this respect. Whereas in Britain, after the First World War, social scientists began to show a greater concern with groups and with society as a whole than with individuals, and social thought moved away from 'mechanical accounting' to 'less strictly defined aspects of the human condition', in the United States, the prevailing view as late as 1940 was to consider the main effect of war to be 'its tendency to promote economic instability and to produce either a downturn in the trade cycle or a severe crisis outside the normal oscillations of that cycle.'[110] Some credit for the change in British perceptions of war was, he suggested, due to the careful statistical analysis of the economist Arthur L. Bowley whose work on the effects of the First World War 'are a fine example of the superiority of research over opinion.'[111] It was this belief in the overwhelming value of research which underpinned Alan Milward's unflagging commitment to it and his contempt for opinion which was not backed up by research. Bowley was interested in measuring the effect of the First World War on income distribution and savings and identified three trends in particular: the tendency of the war to eliminate 'remediable poverty', to diminish 'excessive wealth', and to lead to 'a more equal distribution of incomes'. 'Wise words', said Alan Milward, but he felt that

> Bowley made little of one force which has since received much attention, which was certainly present during the First and Second World Wars, and which operated in such a way as to cause a permanent change in the structure of jobs within the factory and thus in the structure of the

---

108. Ibid., 14–16.
109. Ibid., 16–17.
110. Ibid., 17.
111. Ibidem. Bowley, *Some Economic Consequences of the Great War* (1930).

> wage pattern. This force was the tendency of certain industries to move to a much higher level of productivity than in peacetime.[112]

Not only did the two wars stimulate scientific and technological discovery and lead to the development of new industries, such as the whole of the aircraft industry which had scarcely existed in 1914, but the pressure of producing on a much greater scale than in peacetime 'led to new methods of doing old jobs, new methods of factory layout, new methods of management and more intensive mechanisation.'[113] It led to unskilled workers and women replacing skilled and semiskilled workers. Women, he concluded, became a new industrial proletariat.[114]

If Alan Milward drew on the work of economists to measure changes in the British economy caused by the wars, he looked to sociologists, Stanislaw Andrzejewski and Richard M. Titmuss in particular, to explain the major changes in British society.[115] Here the debate focused on whether the two wars had drawn British society closer together, creating a new degree of social unity which found its expression in the establishment of the welfare state after the Second World War, or whether different groups participated in the war effort to varying degrees and therefore had different amounts of influence over policy after the war. Titmuss, for example, argued that the provision of social welfare for all, as opposed to the restriction of provision to specific groups such as widows or orphans, was a direct consequence of both the greater needs of the state in the Second World War and the democratic effect of war on society. If the population as a whole shared the war suffering—'[t]he bomber did not discriminate' among particular groups or classes—the population as a whole should benefit after the war from a more democratic and cohesive society.[116] This was a view to which the social historian Arthur Marwick subscribed. For Marwick the two world wars had created greater homogeneity between social classes in Britain, a trend which was reinforced by technological developments in methods of communication, such as the motor car and public broadcasting in the interwar period, all of which tended to draw society together.[117] On the other hand Andrzejewski emphasized the differential impact of war on society. In his *Military Organisation and Society* he developed the idea of a 'military participation ratio' based on the theory that there was some specific connection between the number of

112. Milward, *The Economic Effects*, 33.
113. Ibid., 34.
114. Ibid., 36–37.
115. Andrzejewski, *Military Organisation and Society* (1954) and Titmuss, *Problems of Social Policy* (1950) and *Essays on the 'Welfare State'* (1958).
116. Milward, *The Economic Effects*, 22 (quotation).
117. Ibid., 23. Marwick, *The Deluge* (1965) and *Britain in the Century of Total War* (1968).

people required to fight in a war and the degree of social welfare provided by the state.[118]

These views did not go unopposed. Philip Abrams, for instance, argued that the 'military participation ratio' did not imply any automatism in social change: any social group involved in the war would have to make sure to force upon policy-makers its demands for change and reform.[119] In line with Abrams, Alan Milward's own view was that certain groups whose services became much more important in war were able to use this opportunity to improve their position more rapidly than it had been improving in peacetime and to retain their advantages in the long run after the wars. The change in the position of the farming sector was one such example. In general he felt that both Titmuss and Marwick exaggerated the extent of social unity produced by the wars, citing as evidence the fact that 'it was during, not after [the Second World War], that the practice of rearranging financial affairs so as to pay as little as possible of the tax burden developed on a large scale.'[120]

However what struck him most forcefully was that the social and economic effects of both wars on Britain were not very great, and were certainly not on the scale of the changes experienced in other European countries. Indeed he went even further and argued that it was only by recognizing the nature of the changes which the world wars had produced outside Britain that the impact of the wars on Britain could best be understood. The international indebtedness that Britain suffered as a consequence of the foreign loans which it received to finance its war efforts both in 1914–1918 and 1939–1945 produced more far-reaching consequences than any of the internal changes that the world wars had produced in Britain. It changed the relationship between Britain and the rest of the world, including the United States and India, as much as it disrupted the central role played by Britain in the international economy since the mid-nineteenth century. The readiness to impose import controls during the Second World War and, most particularly, to retain them long after the end of military hostilities 'reflected as much as anything else the greatly changed position of Britain in the international economy' that had occurred since 1914.[121] Perhaps the most drastic effect on Britain of the two world wars was that Britain changed from being a structural creditor on a vast scale to being a structural debtor on the same scale. 'The consequences of Britain's international indebtedness were much more far-reaching than those of the domestic indebtedness which [some authors] bemoaned.'[122] In 1970, Alan Milward asked rhetorically:

---

118. Milward, *The Economic Effects*, 21–23.
119. Ibid., 22–23. Abrams, 'The Failure of Social Reform, 1918–1920' (1963).
120. Milward, *The Economic Effects*, 39–41.
121. Ibid., 44.
122. Ibid., 46.

> Were not the effects of the world wars on the international economy more serious for the British domestic economy than their effects on the purely domestic scene? There has been very little historical discussion of this question. The explanation might lie in the still rather parochial nature of economic history studies in this country, or in the fact that many of the contributions to the debate here considered have been made from the sidelines by scholars pursuing some other discipline. The unfortunate result is that this particular aspect can be treated only very briefly in this pamphlet, but the size of its treatment should not be taken as an indication of its importance.[123]

The changes, outside Britain, which he considered to have been the most significant were that

> [t]he world of the gold standard could never be restored after 1918. The immense distortion of currency relationships, of which the British inflation was but a pale reflection, the movement away from liberalism in international trade and domestic policy, of which the similar movement in Britain was also but a pale reflection, the creation of numerous small states with high tariffs, especially in Europe, all led to the emergence of a new and less satisfactory pattern of trade and an inadequate system of international economic arrangements. [ . . . ] The ultimate result was the emergence of an absolutely anti-liberal economic creed in certain trading countries, Fascism, which led them to accept the final and most drastic implications of the difficulties in international trade caused by the First World War and its economically disastrous peace treaties and to deny any relationship between economic growth and trade. The Second World War was a war against this particular political, social and economic ideology, and one of its major results was that the victors established a set of quasi-liberal international economic institutions whose purpose was to bring order out of the supposed international chaos of the inter-war period by re-establishing an acceptable system of international trade and payments.[124]

It was an understanding of the changes to the international economy resulting from both world wars, but particularly the Second World War, which was to capture his intellectual energy for many years. But it was to share space with another line of enquiry: how to explain the nature and causes of the economic development experienced by most continental European countries in the nineteenth century. Here again the influence of a former colleague from Edinburgh University, the economic historian S. Berrick Saul, is evident.

---

123. Ibid., 49.
124. Ibidem.

## AN ECONOMIC HISTORY OF CONTINENTAL EUROPE 1780–1914 (1973–1977)

It was while they were both teaching economic history at Edinburgh University that Berrick Saul, as a professor, and Alan Milward, eleven years his junior as a lecturer, were quite independently disappointed with the available textbooks. At that time all the books written in English about the economic development of continental Europe in the nineteenth century, of which there were few, were based either implicitly or explicitly on a comparison with the experience of either Britain or the United States.[125] And all, whether they were based on neoclassical or Marxist theory, saw nineteenth-century capitalist development as a global phenomenon. Skeptical of the explanatory value of emphasizing the similarities rather than the differences in the nature of economic development, Milward and Saul set out together to write a textbook which would analyze the nature of the European experience by focusing on each individual economy.

The result of their collaborative effort was the publication of two voluminous studies of the 'long' nineteenth-century development of the European economies.[126] The two volumes could and should be taken as a two-volume textbook on economic development in continental Europe covering the period from 1780 to 1914. The purpose of what was unanimously recognized as a daunting task was twofold: first, to set down a factual account of the process of economic development in those economies, about which so little then was known, and second, on the basis of those facts, to see whether there were common economic and social patterns in the European development process. It was, therefore, not until the last chapter of the second volume that they drew their general conclusions about the nature of growth and development. The fact that the second volume was published four years after the first (due to editorial problems linked to the actual size of what was expected to be a one-volume textbook for students) meant that the readers of the first volume, *The Economic Development of Continental Europe 1780–1870*, were obliged to draw their own conclusions. Indeed, as Professor Saul confirms, this was exactly their intention. Although the book was written entirely for students, it was to reach wider audiences, which included economists and many future representatives of the New Economic History for whom an underlying theory was seen as essential for

125. Good examples of the main literature at that time in the field were Rostow, *The Stages of Economic Growth: A Non-Communist Manifesto* (1960) and Gerschenkron, *Economic Backwardness in Historical Perspective* (1962). It was not until 1973 and 1975 that Cipolla's *The Fontana Economic History of Europe*, vol. 3, *The Industrial Revolution* and Rostow's *How it All Began: Origins of the Modern Economy*, respectively, were published.

126. Milward and Saul, *The Economic Development of Continental Europe, 1780–1870* (1973) and *The Development of the Economies of Continental Europe, 1850–1914* (1977).

explaining the evidence drawn from history. Since Milward and Saul deliberately avoided any such theoretical statement, they were left open to the sort of criticism leveled by Douglass C. North, the Nobel Prize–winning economist, who complained about 'the vast sea of facts and figures only loosely organized in [a not] explicit framework.'[127]

The explicit emphasis of their research was on the impact on European societies of the great changes taking place in national economies throughout the nineteenth century. Convinced that economic development constituted 'the very basis of change in modern society', they set out to measure the increase in the factors of production and their deployment in a more productive way, which produced sustained increases in income, output, and welfare.[128] Subscribing to no particular model of economic development, they wrote

> [w]e have deliberately used no single model of analysis because it was obvious to us that the variety of experience was so vast that to attempt to place the process of European development within a single framework would involve an unacceptable distortion and simplification of historical reality.[129]

The existing models of economic development—such as those of Marx, Lenin, and particularly Rostow and Gerschenkron—were seen to be relevant but inadequate for the task to which they were committed. In their view, there was no model of European economic development in existence which actually matched the rich and varied reality of the European experience. What they concluded was that each country followed its own unique path to development based not only on its particular endowment of natural resources but more importantly on its social and institutional structures which, they argued, determined a country's degree of receptiveness to change, including technological change:

> It is indeed the basic tenet of our work that processes of development would vary more widely in accordance with national historical backgrounds than with anything else. Countries with different structures, in different geographical circumstances, with different timing of change, were bound to have different patterns of development. It is for this reason above all that we have paid scant regard to the thesis of the so-called *globalité*, or unity, of European development. The fact that natural resources such as coalfields and forests spanned political

---

127. North's review of *The Economic Development of Continental Europe*, 910.
128. Milward and Saul, *The Economic Development*, 20–21 (quotation 20).
129. Milward and Saul, *The Development of the Economies of Continental Europe*, 518.

> frontiers gave an international dimension to the growth experience, but the differences were far more important than the similarities. Indeed, it might well be argued that eighteenth-century society was more pan-European than it was in the nineteenth.[130]

In their view, the almost exclusive emphasis of many economic historians on the role of industrialization in economic development did not fully explain the major changes which had taken place in European economies and societies as a whole since the late eighteenth century.[131] Their insistence on the importance of understanding the social, political, and institutional context in which economic changes were taking place was to distance them increasingly from the direction in which economic history as a discipline was moving from the 1960s onwards. Located in departments of economics in the United States, the New Economic History was using the tools and techniques of economics rather than those of history to explain the past. For Milward and Saul, quantitative data should both illuminate and be explained by the social, political, and cultural context of each single historical experience. In other words, as Rostow himself expressed it, 'the authors belong to [an] intellectual tradition [ . . . ] which, while using quantitative data, emphasizes the uniqueness of the historical cases in their political, social, geographic, and institutional settings.'[132]

In Alan Milward's view data compilation and quantitative sophistication should not be a substitute for sociopolitical explanations but should be placed within the framework of such explanations. His dissatisfaction with developments in the discipline of economic history was already apparent while he was at Stanford University, which he shared with his coauthor Saul who was visiting on a one-year Ford fellowship. As Alan Milward prepared to leave Stanford and the United States in 1971 to fill a new chair in European Studies at UMIST, he set out his views in a long letter to the Director of the Center for International Studies:

> At the present moment economic history in the United States is undergoing a minor resurgence in the form of 'The New Economic History'. This essentially consists in applying econometric methods to historical problems. [ . . . ] Its proponents sometimes tend to claim that it supersedes previous methods of teaching and research (a rather unsatisfactory attitude for historians). This is not at all the case, it is simply one more valuable research weapon amongst many in the economic historian's armory. Unfortunately it is a weapon which is particularly pleasing to departments 'training' professional economists. The development of the

130. Ibid., 526.
131. Milward and Saul, *The Economic Development*, 23.
132. Rostow's review of *The Development of the Economies of Continental Europe*, 727.

> 'New Economic History' can only improve the quality of research in the subject. But if the object of teaching economic history is to broaden the knowledge and outlook of students (particularly students of economics who are in some ways dreadfully ignorant) 'The New Economic History', however pleasing it may be to economics departments, is not especially satisfactory. Similarly, if high quality research in economic history is to be produced it will not be produced by a concentration on these 'new' methods alone, especially if the graduate students who undertake it have previously only had the very narrow education which economics graduates receive. [ . . . ] The teaching of economic history is bound to prosper where economists become more interested in problems of the real world rather than their own mental world.[133]

Notwithstanding Milward's own views about the New Economic History revolution, one of its protagonists—as coeditor with Douglass North of *The Journal of Economic History* in the early 1960s and future president of both the Economic History Association and the Agricultural History Association in the 1970s—Professor William N. Parker, saw great merit in the Milward–Saul enterprise: 'Others have talked about comparative economic histories; they have written them. Others have promised to link the new income and output data to the literary accounts; they have provided the integration. [ . . . ] Surely economic historians should not complain.'[134] This was no little compliment coming from one of the chief pioneers of the systematic use of quantitative data and statistical methods; Parker shared with Milward and Saul a view of the purpose of the new quantitative approach in economic history.[135]

The choice of the year 1780 as the starting point of Milward and Saul's economic history may have been 'an arbitrary one', but it served to describe European society and its modes of production before the French Revolution.[136] The first chapter of the eighteen-chapter two-volume work is an analysis of the kind of European society—the *ancien régime* or the old regime—that was about to be subject to a profound change due to the French Revolution. But 1780 was also considered at the time to be the starting point for another revolutionary process, the Industrial Revolution, which marked a turning point in European economic and social history. 'The coincidence in time' between the economic, social, and political changes spreading from both revolutionary events 'finally persuaded' them to begin their analysis on the eve of both.[137]

---

133. Excerpt from Milward's letter to Professor Carl Spaeth, 3 June 1971; private papers of Alan S. Milward.
134. Parker's review of *The Development of the Economies of Continental Europe*, 800.
135. Wright, 'William Nelson Parker: Biographical Memoirs' (2007).
136. Milward and Saul, *The Economic Development*, 19.
137. Ibid., 20.

If their main objective was to explain the process of change, the distinctive feature of their interpretation was to stress that change was a gradual and not a sudden revolutionary process, that it was not limited to one sector of the economy, as the term 'industrial revolution' used to describe the changes taking place in England implied, and that each country had to find its own path to change and development. What they concluded was that there could be no economic development without a prior or concurrent change in the agricultural sector, however slow, and conversely that 'the simple pressure of industrial development was never of itself enough to force significant change upon agrarian society.'[138] Their reduced emphasis on the industrial character of 'industrial revolutions', which they compensated for with a greater insistence on the significance of growing efficiency in agriculture and service activity, was convincing to many scholars.[139]

Milward and Saul saw the continental 'industrial revolutions' more as a long-term process of change toward economic activities involving higher productivity than sudden, abrupt, revolutionary phenomena. The speed with which this new form of economic activity was established in different European countries was seen to depend on their ability to respond to the forces of change and their willingness to meet the associated social costs. Social rather than technological factors ultimately determined the rate of growth in the eighteenth and nineteenth centuries. The scholarly approach of Milward and Saul owed little to the entrepreneurial approach of Joseph Schumpeter:

> The historical evidence presented here [ . . . ] strongly suggests that in explaining European economic development much more emphasis should be given to the role of demand. The role of inventiveness and of the heroic entrepreneur [ . . . ] was of little importance compared to the development of the market. [ . . . ] [T]he evidence suggests that differences in demand were more important in determining the nature and the complex pattern of European economic development than differences in supply.[140]

A second distinctive feature of their work was their interest in the interaction of politics with economics. As they wrote

> [i]t is often argued that the most powerful dissolvent of the eighteenth-century economic structure was the tremendous social change which

138. Milward and Saul, *The Development of the Economies of Continental Europe*, 530.
139. See, for example, Ashworth's review of *The Development of the Economies of Continental Europe*, 349.
140. Milward and Saul, *The Development of the Economies of Continental Europe*, 516.

> accompanied industrialisation. [ . . . ] Such an argument would suggest that it was the events of the industrial revolution in Britain which changed the structure of eighteenth-century European society by making industrialisation necessary.[141]

Such an argument, they complained, represented 'a dreadful simplification of history.' Many countries resisted adopting the new technologies simply because 'their societies were incapable of assimilating such changes.' In their view '[a] much more powerful dissolvent of the society of the old régime was the series of political events in France between 1789 and 1815, the French Revolution, the counter-revolution and the reign, both as king and emperor, of Napoleon Bonaparte.' Even if the French Revolution 'did nothing to change the economic base of society [ . . . ] it did create a society in which such economic changes were much easier.'[142] Milward and Saul show this in their detailed analysis of France, of those countries which shared the French experience of industrialization (Germany, Italy, and Switzerland), as well as of those which combined industrial change with the institutional changes brought about during their occupation in the Napoleonic era. But what they showed was that whatever changes Napoleon imposed on continental Europe they were reversed after 1815. This led them to the further conclusion that change could not be imposed upon countries from outside either through force or by applying foreign institutions, laws, or models.

The 'continental system' erected in 1806, after Napoleon's conquest of Prussia was meant to become a protective system for French industry which would encompass most of the continental European market. 'It was partly an automatic response to the loss of the colonial trade in wartime,' Milward and Saul wrote, 'partly a policy of economic warfare against Britain and partly a plan for the development and encouragement of French industry. [ . . . ] [I]t is fair to categorise it as an attempt to reserve the whole of Europe for French manufactured goods while using it as the prime source of supply of raw materials to France.'[143] In similar language to that used by Alan Milward when referring to the *Grossraumwirtschaft* basis of the New Order in his earlier work, they continued their analysis of the continental system by saying:

> Military occupation by the French was primarily a form of economic exploitation of the occupied territories for the benefit of the French treasury. The ties of political sympathy between the small groups of revolutionaries who created the Helvetic Republic in Switzerland and the Batavian Republic in the United Provinces and the revolutionaries

141. Milward and Saul, *The Economic Development*, 248.
142. Ibid., 250 (for all quotations).
143. Ibid., 268.

> in France did not long survive the reality of a military occupation of this kind.[144]

After the pan-European changes introduced by the French Revolution and Napoleon's continental system, it was the national framework, with its highly individual political and social systems which, they argued, determined the nature of economic development until 1914. Economic development was determined by the different ways in which factors of production were combined in each country. Development was a national rather than a global phenomenon. Because Milward and Saul were arguing against an entrenched body of opinion which saw capitalism as a global phenomenon in the nineteenth century they needed to prove through detailed studies of almost every country in Europe that each country had followed its own path to economic development. This is the reason why the Milward–Saul volumes are a collection of country case studies which, if they reveal some features common to most countries, are even more revealing of the significant differences.

Milward and Saul's economic history of continental Europe 1780–1914 was above all 'an able synthesis' of the stock of knowledge that economic historians had generated at the time.[145] Although there were other compilations, the Milward–Saul volumes were regarded by many as particularly successful, not only for the superficial reason that the style was more uniform than in other multiauthored projects but also because they often brought a fresh interpretation to existing knowledge. Thus, in the case of France, they rejected the commonly held view that the nineteenth-century French economy was in some sense backward. Indeed, they argued that from a strictly continental standpoint, by comparing the French economy with the rest of the continental economies rather than with Britain and the United States, France appeared as the largest and most dynamic economic power on the continent, at least up to 1870:

> More than other developed economies France revealed by 1870 the relentless force of historical change in promoting economic development while showing, in spite of the Revolution, over how long a time that historical change must necessarily take place. It was both this process of historical change and the Revolution itself that caused French institutions to be so much copied abroad. Other developing countries felt they could cheat history, or perhaps omit some of it, by borrowing from a land where so much social and economic change had taken place. By lifting institutions from France and incorporating them in their own structures they tried forcibly to modernize their own societies

144. Ibid., 290.
145. Cameron's review of *The Development of the Economies of Continental Europe*, 712.

> and speed up their own histories. Such attempts were seldom successful because to produce such institutions France had had herself to undergo so violent and profound a revolution. The temptation was still very great and it makes the economic history of France an integral part of that of all other European lands.[146]

And Milward and Saul were determined to cover all these other European lands. Parker was impressed by the scale of the undertaking which

> travels not only through England's neighbours and trading partners on the Continent, but through every country from Lapland to Sicily, and the Bay of Biscay to the Urals. Only Portugal, Andorra, Liechtenstein, Montenegro and Turkey in Europe have been left untouched. And this was done by a pair of scholars, not in an edited and uneven multi-authored collection or in a huge foundation-supported series but in a single two-volume work of dimensions and price that permit use as a text.[147]

They paid particular attention to the Low Countries and the main Scandinavian countries demonstrating that in small countries small-scale production in both agriculture and industry had the advantage of being able to adapt quickly to changes in the international economy so that despite the differences in resource endowment, access to transport, industrial and agrarian history, or the natural size of its domestic market, any nation could find 'something to do' in terms of income growth.[148] In fact as Simon Kuznets calculated, the rate of growth of national income of these smaller nations—Belgium, Denmark, the Netherlands, Norway, Sweden, Switzerland, and Saxony and Würtemburg and Baden in Germany—was between 15 and 25 percent per decade in the period 1850–1900.[149]

In an essay written in 1979 Alan Milward discussed the importance of change in the agricultural sector for economic development in nineteenth-century Europe.[150] But although he could see a general pattern emerging in which the primary sector was able to respond to stimuli from other sectors and then interact with other sectors in such a way that productivity levels were driven up, he was very reluctant to define it as a model for development which could be copied in less successful economies. Indeed, as we see in Chapter 6 of this volume, Iceland made the mistake, according to

146. Milward and Saul, *The Economic Development*, 362.
147. Parker's review of *The Development of the Economies of Continental Europe*, 800.
148. Parker, 'Europe in an American Mirror: Reflections on Industrialization and Ideology' (1991), 84.
149. Kuznets, *Modern Economic Growth: Rate, Structure, Spread* (1965), table 2.5, as referred to in ibidem.
150. Milward, 'Strategies for Development in Agriculture: The Nineteenth-Century European Experience' (1979).

Guðmundur Jónsson, of trying to follow the very successful example of Danish agricultural change in the nineteenth century but found that the Danish model did not travel.

In spite of their considerable evidence that there was not one common path to economic development in Europe but many different paths the critics were not convinced. Many scholars continued to insist that the central feature of modern European history was the unity of the experience in terms of the development of nationalism along with industrialization which marked Europe out from the rest of the nineteenth-century world, more than its diversity. This was a view shared by the Marxist historian Eric Hobsbawm, who thought that '[p]erhaps there is more to be said for seeing capitalist development as a global process than this book allows.'[151] Nevertheless, Hobsbawm saw certain advantages in approaching the subject from the standpoint adopted by Milward and Saul, since in their belief that processes of development varied essentially in accordance with national historical backgrounds, they could also stress 'growing regional disparities within as well as between member states'. But for Hobsbawm the 'compare and contrast' method of Milward and Saul stopped them from seeking 'general patterns of European or global economic change.'[152] Striking the right balance between global, national, and regional approaches was as difficult then as it is today. Some, like Sidney Pollard, challenged the national approach arguing that economic development was a regional rather than a national process.[153] Milward and Saul agreed that regional inequality was a research question 'of vital importance' not only in the twentieth century, but also in the nineteenth century, when 'examples of extreme regional inequality [ . . . ] were normal rather than exceptional'; but they argued that it was most probably produced by a pattern of national economic change which failed 'to make substantial improvements in income in regions which remained essentially agricultural.'[154] Thus in their view nation-states provided a better theoretical framework for historical analysis than regions. How, Milward asked years later, was a region to be defined?

> The nation defined itself in history as the social unit by its frontiers with their attendant controls, by its government with its particular policies, and by collecting data relating to the territorial area defined by the frontiers. The collection or reconstruction of satisfactory regional

151. Hobsbawm's review of *The Development of the Economies of Continental Europe*, 693.
152. Ibid., (692 for both quotations).
153. Pollard, *Peaceful Conquest: The Industrialization of Europe, 1760–1970* (1981).
154. Milward and Saul, *The Development of the Economies of Continental Europe*, 65 and 64 (for the two quotations respectively).

> data relating to the past is almost impossible and for both the past and the present the meaningfulness of such data is often questionable.[155]

If for most of the nineteenth century France represented a model for economic growth and modernization, however inappropriate that model was for other countries, 'by 1914 Germany had displaced France as the most powerful of the continental economies'.[156] This was certainly not without consequences for the entire continent:

> Seen in perspective the successful development of the German economy was the decisive phase in the development of the continent. By its geographical situation, by its close economic connections with the neighbouring economies, by the relative unimportance until the last two decades of its extra-European connections, Germany was the most European of the major economies. The centre of the continent had now achieved the same level of development as the western periphery. What was more, by its size and power the German economy now dominated intra-European exchanges. The view was already widely held by liberal economists in Germany that the European economy would have to be dominated by the national German economy if the German economy was to find its own domestic equilibrium and that this would mean that a new European economic structure would have to evolve. Conservative and nationalist circles took the view that this 'new economic order' guaranteeing Germany's economic and social equilibrium would have to be created by force. Few believed that the future nature of the German economy could now be determined without determining the nature of the economy of the whole continent. In our century this has proved to be so.
>
> It was not, however, only the fact that the development of the German economy demanded fundamental political and economic adjustments by the other European powers which commanded the interest of contemporaries and still commands the interest of historians and economists. It was also that the events in Germany seemed to indicate more clearly than those elsewhere what the future nature of European capitalist society would be. Whereas in the early nineteenth century economists, statesmen and social reformers in the less developed countries in Europe sought for clues to the future of their own society by analyzing that of Britain and France, by the end of the nineteenth century this interest has rightly become focused on Germany [ . . . ]. The locus of economic power and interest in Europe had shifted as decisively as it had during the sixteenth century.[157]

155. Milward, 'Comments on Some Theories of Historical Change' (1985), 163.
156. Milward and Saul, *The Development of the Economies of Continental Europe*, 17.
157. Milward and Saul, *The Development of the Economies of Continental Europe*, 65–66.

This was the beginning of the 'German question' which dominated twentieth-century Europe and beyond. It was through his research on Germany in the twentieth century that Alan Milward was to develop his implicit theory of historical change.

The pioneering work of Milward and Saul on the economic development of nineteenth-century Europe and their fundamental thesis that there was not one pattern of development but *patterns* of development was to stimulate considerable interest among economic historians in the subject.[158] But it was not only economic historians who were interested. When the theory of economic development became one of the primary spheres of interest for economists, an unusual dialogue between the two disciplines was generated. That such a dialogue was possible was explained by Kocka and Ránki in the way that each discipline had changed in the postwar period: economics having 'lost its image established in the nineteenth century as a purely abstract science, [while] history writing has changed its value system as well and moved slowly from ideographic descriptions to generalization and abstraction.'[159] Invited to comment on a set of articles on the character and role of theory in the research and writing of economic history, which had originally been presented as papers at the eighth international economic history congress in Budapest in 1982 (at which Alan Milward had also co-organized a session on agriculture and food supply during the Second World War), Milward remained critical of both disciplines:

> Any economic theory which is to be of general value in historical analysis must be dynamic. It must explain the process of change. Most economic theory does not. What is more, much economic theory, like that which assumes a closed economy, as well as a large part of international trade theory, applies to situations so absolutely a-historical as to have virtually no value even as a methodological tool.[160]

It was clearly the task of economic historians to explain long-run social and economic change. But here too he was critical of economic historians who used the logical propositions of neoclassical economics as a methodological tool for explaining the process of economic development. In the final passages of *The Development of the Economies of Continental Europe 1850–1914*, which in fact was the concluding section of the Milward–Saul textbook on the economic history of continental Europe in 1780–1914, we read:

158. See for example, Trebilcock, *The Industrialization of the Continental Powers, 1780–1914* (1981) and Sylla and Toniolo, *Patterns of European Industrialization: The Nineteenth Century* (1991).
159. Kocka and Ránki, 'Introduction' to their *Economic Theory and History* (1985), 7–8.
160. Milward, 'Comments on Some Theories of Historical Change', 157.

> The historical evidence [ . . . ] suggests that there has been much too close an identification in European history between industrialisation, modernisation and economic development. At the heart of this misconception lies the idea of the 'industrial revolution', that the fundamental process of economic and social change in modern history is related to a cataclysmic change in the mode of industrial production. The greatness of Marx comes from the way in which he was able to elaborate the profound consequences of this change and in so doing develop a powerful analytical tool for explaining the process of development on a wide but unified historical, political and economic front. But subsequent model builders have been unable to escape entirely from this view of economic development even when they have been mainly concerned to refute Marx's conclusions.[161]

Within this category of 'cataclysmic change theories', which he rejected, Alan Milward referred not only to Marx but also to Rostow and Gerschenkron. His personal views on the matter had not changed ten years later: 'Almost all the theories of historical change [ . . . ] concentrated on a central transformational period in the history of the social unit in question, when some form of cataclysm changed irreversibly its economic structure and social characteristics.'[162] All, he argued, failed to explain the process of historical change in many countries. Such a process, he maintained, was gradual rather than cataclysmic, depended on change in the agricultural rather than in the industrial sector as the motor for development, and depended on central government action to remove the obstacles to change.[163] Alan Milward himself went on to consider other theories to explain economic change, considering the value of growth theory in particular:

> The attraction of growth theory was not merely that it set aside the concept of a central transformational experience and declared the whole time-span of historical change to be an equally interesting field for enquiry, but also that it allowed economic history, at least initially, to return to an explanatory base constructed by fitting together in different permutations the familiar 'factors' of neoclassical analysis.[164]

However, without a very detailed historical analysis on a case-by-case basis he found growth theory unable to answer the most fundamental question of *why* factors were combined in such a way as to lead to economic growth. Indeed, he argued, had growth rates in the developed world not been so

---

161. Milward and Saul, *The Development of the Economies of Continental Europe*, 536.
162. Milward, 'Comments on Some Theories of Historical Change', 158.
163. Ibid., 159–164.
164. Ibid., 160.

high in the 1950s and 1960s, growth theory would not have exerted the influence which it did.[165] How should economic history fill the theoretical stagnation in which it found itself, he asked. Rather than join 'that avidly-conservative school, now coming into fashion again, which regards history as no more than a genteel, humanistic exercise which tells us something about some people and some events, but can tell us nothing about society as a whole', he felt that perhaps any theory was better than none.[166] It is interesting in this respect to quote North's views ten years after Alan Milward had published his criticisms of neoclassical and Marxist theories:

> Economic history is about the performance of economies through time. The objective of research in the field is not only to shed new light on the economic past but also to contribute to economic theory by providing an analytical framework that will enable us to understand economic change. A theory of economic dynamics comparable in precision to general equilibrium theory would be the ideal tool of analysis. In the absence of such a theory we can describe the characteristics of past economies, examine the performance of economies at various times, and engage in comparative static analysis; but missing is an analytical understanding of the way economies evolve through time.
>
> A theory of economic dynamics is also crucial for the field of economic development. There is no mystery why the field of economic development has failed to develop during the five decades since the end of the Second World War. Neoclassical theory is simply an inappropriate tool to analyze and prescribe policies that will induce development. It is concerned with the operation of markets, not with how markets develop. How can one prescribe policies when one doesn't understand how economies develop? The very methods employed by neoclassical economists have dictated the subject matter and militated against such a development. That theory, in the pristine form that gave it mathematical precision and elegance, modeled a frictionless and static world. When applied to economic history and development, it focused on technological development and more recently human capital investment but ignored the incentive structure embodied in institutions that determined the extent of societal investment in those factors. In the analysis of economic performance through time it contained two erroneous assumptions: first, that institutions do not matter and, second, that time does not matter. [ . . . ]We do not have [ . . . ] a theory [of economic dynamics comparable to general equilibrium theory].[167]

165. Ibid., 161.
166. Ibid., 164.
167. North, 'Epilogue: Economic Performance through Time' (1996), 342–343.

That neoclassical growth theory continues to retain its influence in the absence of such theoretical breakthrough is evidenced in the multiauthored 2010 *Cambridge Economic History of Modern Europe,* funded by the European Union, in which the economic growth of Europe in the nineteenth century is seen as a pan-European process, and not as separate national paths defined by different national institutions and different national histories. While the authors accept the Milward and Saul argument that growth was a gradual process rather than a cataclysmic one by explaining it in pan-European terms they fail to provide adequate explanations for the continuing backwardness in the nineteenth century of some countries on the periphery of Europe, such as Portugal and Greece.[168] This is a question which Pedro Lains addresses in Chapter 7 of this volume.

## WAR, ECONOMY AND SOCIETY (1977)

It was an invitation from Germany, where his research was of most interest, to write an economic history of the Second World War as part of the series of books on the 'History of the World Economy in the Twentieth Century' under the overall direction of Professor Wolfram Fisher, which gave Alan Milward an opportunity to return to the subject of the Second World War and to consider its role as an engine of change.[169] Originally published in German, *War, Economy and Society* was to be a reassessment of his own research on the war in Europe combined with the research of those who had worked on the war in the Pacific.[170] No single scholar had dared to write an economic history of the Second World War from a global perspective before, and no scholar, apart from György Ránki whose book was published posthumously in 1993, was to dare to do so again.[171] At forty years of age, with the right combination of ambition, knowledge, and youth, Milward rose to the challenge.

In his preface, Alan Milward openly admitted to doubts that it was possible to write an economic history of the Second World War, partly because of how little was known of the economic history of the Soviet Union (in spite of 15,000 Russian volumes written on the Second World War) or indeed of Italy during the period. But, in attempting to write about the Second World War from the perspective of all participants, he was unrepentant in his focus on the economics of war:

---

168. Broadberry and O'Rourke, *The Cambridge Economic History of Modern Europe*, vol. 1, *1700–1870* (2010).
169. Milward, *War, Economy and Society, 1939–1945* (1977) was the fifth volume of this collection.
170. Milward, *Der Zweite Weltkrieg; Krieg, Wirtschaft und Gesellschaft, 1939–1945* (1977).
171. Ránki, *The Economics of the Second World War* (1993).

> If there are any as infuriated as myself by the seemingly countless works on military history in which armies and navies come and go, commanded by greater or lesser figures deciding momentous historical issues, and nothing is said of the real productive forces which alone give such events meaning or, indeed, make them possible, they will surely sympathize with my attempt to simplify by looking at the war as an economic event.[172]

It was in his writing about Germany, the occupation of Europe, war as strategy, its impact on labor and on agriculture that he was most authoritative. In many other areas he was constrained by the absence of data or of sufficient research done by others. As a reference work Milward's survey was intended to remain provisional until further specialized studies, particularly on Italy, Japan, and the Soviet Union, would provide reliable data on which to build a new and more accurate historical narrative. It was over twenty years before a complete multiauthored reassessment of the wartime economic experiences of the major powers directed by Mark Harrison was to appear.[173]

One of the central questions which Alan Milward raised in his book was whether the Second World War would lead to the disaster which was widely predicted by the western powers and involve 'a heavy loss of human beings and capital, acute and prolonged inflation, profound social unrest, and almost insuperable problems, both domestic and international, of economic readjustment once peace was restored' or whether 'it lay in the hands of government to formulate strategic and economic policies which could to some extent determine whether or not a war would be economically a cause of gain or loss.'[174] This was very much how Keynes had formulated the question in his 1940 publication *How to Pay for the War* in which he wrote that a properly managed war economy could generate much beneficial social change to counteract the unavoidable cruelties and miseries. Years later, Milward would explain:

> The Second World War became for Keynes one more historical accident which he sought to use to further his mission to rescue liberal capitalism. The insights into the relationship between war and social change which this way of thinking offered changed the historiography of war. Out went public finance, battles, and the accountancy of loss as the prime subjects of scholarly attention. In came production planning, technological innovation, improvements in the living standard of particular social groups, and growth accountancy.[175]

172. Milward, *War, Economy and Society*, xii.
173. Harrison, *The Economics of World War II* (1998).
174. Milward, *War, Economy and Society*, 16–17.
175. Milward's review of Ránki's *The Economics of the Second World War*, 669.

This was the approach used by Alan Milward in *War, Economy and Society,* but his objective was not to 'rescue liberal capitalism' but to understand the more profound ways in which the lessons of the war had led to the replacement of liberal capitalism in Europe after the war. On the one hand, he dealt with the traditional economic analysis of war (its cost and overall burden for postwar recovery, as well as the technological spin-offs) and, on the other, he presented the innovative and creative effects of war; the 'positive' economic effects—a controversial terminology which he retained even though he had been criticized for using it in *The Economic Effects of the World Wars on Britain.* His primary concern was with war as an economic process, an engine for change and in some cases for progress, and a turning point in the economic and social history of many countries. Given the frequency of war, Alan Milward refused to see it as an abnormality.[176]

His initial view of the German war economy remained unaltered by the histories subsequently written by scholars in the Democratic Republic of Germany and the Soviet Union which saw Fascism as 'a stage of capitalism in decline, when it can survive only by a brutal and determined imperialism and through a monopolistic control over domestic and foreign markets by the bigger capitalist firms backed by the government.'[177] Indeed, he reaffirmed his argument that the National Socialist movement was driving towards a different horizon from that of the business world, a horizon both more distant and more frightening. It was in some ways a movement of protest against modern economic development and became a centre of allegiance for all who were displaced and uprooted by the merciless and seemingly ungovernable swings of the German economy after 1918. National Socialism was as much a yearning for a stable utopia of the past as a close alliance between major capital interests and an authoritarian government.[178]

Nor was he convinced by Timothy W. Mason's argument that Hitler was forced to go to war in 1939 in order to solve a domestic political crisis arising from the squeeze in living standards due to the expenditure on armaments:

> [I]t is hard to make out a case that the Nazi economy was in a greater state of crisis in the autumn of 1939 than it had been on previous occasions particularly in 1936. Most of the problems which existed in 1939 had existed from the moment full employment had been reached, and some of them, on any calculation, could only be made worse by a war—as indeed they were.[179]

---

176. Milward, *War, Economy and Society*, 3.
177. Ibid., 10.
178. Ibid., 13.
179. Ibid., 14. Mason, 'The Primacy of Politics—Politics and Economics in National Socialist Germany' (1972) (original German version, 1966).

Building on his rejection of both the Marxist (orthodox and revisionist) and the Liberal theories of Fascism, he developed his own understanding of the Second World War, seeing it as a policy based on a 'strategic synthesis' of each country's vital interests and which ultimately brought both losses and gains:

> The construction of a correct strategic plan requires a correct assessment of the potentiality of the economy for waging war. But warfare is not simply an economic event and a strategic plan is a synthesis of all other factors which it is necessary to take into account, political, military, social and psychological. The more factors which are correctly assessed the greater its chances of success. [ . . . ] The economy does not in wartime function in the vacuum in which it often seems to be considered by economists and strategists alike. It functions in a complicated mesh of social, military, political and psychological considerations which are as much and perhaps more constraining in wartime than in peacetime.[180]

He drew a distinction between an 'economy's absolute potential for warfare' and 'a more useful and operative' concept (in most cases), whereby such potential 'may be defined as the extent to which economic priorities must be re-ordered as to attain the desired strategic objectives.'[181] Therefore the 'correct strategic synthesis will be that which only makes exactly those demands on the economy which are sufficient to achieve the strategic purpose.'[182] Thus Germany's drive to war in 1939 took account of the political and economic situation in which National Socialist Germany found itself. As Alan Milward summarized this situation, the First World War had shown that long wars were self-defeating; thanks to the Treaty of Versailles Germany was surrounded by a ring of weaker powers, which in Hitler's view included the Soviet Union, which could be broken either through force or the threat of force; too thorough a commitment of the economy to war would have reduced the diplomatic and strategic flexibility which Hitler needed; the Blitzkrieg strategy, by reducing the amount of administrative friction, suited the working methods of the National Socialist party very well; it suited the domestic political situation and social policies of the party in as much as it could not count on the support of a majority of the population and therefore had to win its allegiance through bringing an improvement in its living standards; and finally it corresponded to the economic realities of Germany's position since the Treaty of Versailles. This economic reality, as he spelled out, was that

180. Milward, *War, Economy and Society*, 19.
181. Ibid., 19–20.
182. Ibid., 21.

> within its post-Versailles frontiers Germany was no longer economically a great power in the sense in which the United States was and had control over less raw materials and labour than in 1914. Coal was the only raw material essential for war with which Germany was well-endowed. She had no natural rubber and no oil supply. Her armaments industry depended on an extremely high annual quantity of imports of iron ore from Sweden. She had practically no domestic supply of non-ferrous metal ores such as chrome, nickel, tungsten, molybdenum and manganese, essential for the manufacture of armour plate. Copper and tin supplies depended on imports. Many of these vital imports came from outside Europe, and could not be provided within the German trading bloc. A strategy which implied a continued high level of imports of such materials had to be avoided. The *Blitzkrieg* strategy however could be based on stockpiles of raw materials adequate for a short campaign [ . . . ] Where stockpiling could not serve the purpose, as in the case of oil, investment was directed towards producing high-cost synthetic products.[183]

Thus, as Paul M. Hohenberg summarized it, 'the Blitzkrieg made sense in the context of Germany's position, and it led to certain economic choices regarding the development and production of armaments and other matters, from material supply to labor mobilization.'[184] These sets of choices proved dysfunctional after the Blitzkrieg failed, but at that point, as Milward argued, no alternative strategy held much promise to the German cause in any event.

Alan Milward then applied the same 'strategic synthesis' argument to the other powers, omitting France and the Soviet Union since no research had been done on their rearmament or strategic planning. Thus, he showed that British strategy was based on giving

> priority to the production of the most technologically sophisticated and the most costly of available modern armaments, the larger planes and warships. [ . . . ] it was a decision taken with an awareness that the economic resources of Britain could not match those of the possible aggressors and that an adequate defensive strategy could only be sustained by capitalizing on the major advantages of a highly developed economy, research, innovation and modern productive methods.[185]

But it was always assumed that Britain would be able to draw on the resources of the Empire and the Commonwealth and ultimately 'within financial and legal limits the economic resources of the United States could

183. Ibid., 28–29.
184. Hohenberg's review of *War, Economy and Society*, 547.
185. Milward, *War, Economy and Society*, 40.

also be drawn on.'[186] As far as the United States' own strategic thinking was concerned, he argued that

> from September 1940 onwards the United States was moving towards acceptance of a strategy in which, if she were involved in war, the war would be won through industrial production. The strategic assumption was that over a long period of time the United States must ultimately be victorious if war came to a battle of production, however that production was deployed. And there were powerful arguments for deploying American production in the hands of the Allies.[187]

The detailed consideration of the strategies which the major belligerents pursued (or sought to pursue) showed 'how wide the number of effective economic strategies' was.[188] The choice of economic strategy made in 1940 was to have far-reaching consequences for the postwar world:

> The great increases of production in the United States, the changes in the world trading system, the revival of trade and production in the underdeveloped world, the structural changes in the European economies, did not have their origins in 1945 but in 1940. They were the result of the particular economic strategic choices made by the powers in the face of war. [189]

The conclusion therefore was that there were 'no economic priorities peculiar to a "war economy"'.[190] The range of options was wide and governed by a multiplicity of factors, some internal, some external. 'Nevertheless certain common economic problems did emerge' quite irrespectively of the strategic synthesis adopted, and it was to the role of each of these—production, bureaucratic direction and conduct of the economy, the economics of occupation, technology, population and labor, agriculture and food, and economic warfare—that he devoted specific chapters.

In Alan Milward's view the economic potential of the belligerents depended on output, and the battalions that counted most were those on the production line and in the fields. Total available resources came from domestic production and trade, or through the occupation and exploitation of conquered land. He maintained that the contribution made by conquered European countries to the German productive effort was considerable. Even if not every conquered territory was profitable he showed that 'the

186. Ibid., 42. This argument has recently been repeated in Edgerton, *Britain's War Machine* (2011).
187. Milward, *War, Economy and Society*, 50.
188. Ibid., 53.
189. Ibid., 54.
190. Ibid., 54.

conquered territories as a whole were.'[191] Their value lay both in the cash which they transferred to Germany, as well as the production of strategic materials and agricultural output which they were able to offer. Ultimately, though, the occupation was unsustainable with Nazi Germany collapsing economically before it was defeated militarily.

If the National Socialist racial policies distinguished the Second World War from the First, making it very difficult to talk about any positive aspects of the war, he did nonetheless argue that the impact of the war on employment and on the movement and productivity of labor did have a positive dimension. As he showed, in all the western countries, the prewar unemployed were now employed 'not short-term as in the First World War' but in activities linked to 'an economic change which would last for a quarter of a century.'[192] The United Kingdom, which was the only country where the government took full powers to conscript women, was also the country in which women accounted for the largest increase in employment. This contrasted sharply with Germany where in spite of 'the insatiable demand for labour [ . . . ] the social ideas of the National Socialist party prevented any fuller mobilization of women'.[193] Because of the Nazi attitude toward women, Germany's labor demand could be met only by the employment of foreigners: 'The war began the influx of immigrant labour into the central manufacturing core of Europe which was also to be one of the most economically significant aspects of the post-war world.'[194]

Another lasting effect of the wartime production effort was the increase in the productivity of labor and capital but, as he showed, this was true only in those industries where 'substantial technological and organizational changes could be made.'[195] It was only then that the benefits derived from investment in new plant, economies of scale, the exchange of information, and the will to win the war were able to come into play. But in sectors such as coal mining, where labor productivity levels had been in decline, 'no amount of goodwill could improve the position.'[196] The shortage of labor, a fact of life everywhere apart from in the United States where it was not apparent until 1944, led to increases in overtime pay and thus income, to a greater concern for pay differentials within the workplace, but more generally to important shifts in social aspirations and political opinions. All these changes, he maintained, 'went far towards making the post-war economic world a very different one from that of the 1930s.'[197]

---

191. Ibid., 137.
192. Ibid., 219.
193. Ibid., 220.
194. Ibid., 221.
195. Ibid., 230.
196. Ibidem.
197. Ibid., 235–244 (quotation 244).

One unforeseen consequence of the increases in earned income was that demand for food increased. The two countries, the United Kingdom and Switzerland, which faced the greatest challenge in organizing food supplies to meet this demand during the war on account of their dependence on imports, achieved in his view the most remarkable success. British success, which lay in increasing the total net output of calories from British agriculture from 14,700 million in 1938–1939 to 28,100 million in 1943–1944, while conserving shipping space, was due, as he demonstrated, to the conversion from livestock to arable farming and to the new support prices and firm markets guaranteed by the state both during and after the war.[198] The situation facing German agriculture was very different:

> The National Socialist party had inherited a situation in which German agriculture, which still employed 26 per cent of the labour force in 1939, closely approached the desired goal of self-sufficiency. But the strategy of territorial expansion meant that this goal had to be achieved for a larger area of Europe. Planning was not on a national but on a continental scale and where agricultural production did not suffice to meet the future needs of Greater Germany the solution was sought in a restructuring not of Germany's but of Europe's agriculture.[199]

The purpose of the bilateral trade agreements which Germany had signed with the countries of south-eastern Europe in the 1930s were the foundations for guaranteeing strategic safety for German food supply. But since the foundations of the *Grossraumwirtschaft* were to be built in Russia '[t]he stage was already set for a profound clash of political ideas about the nature of human society to be fought out in terms of agricultural policy as collective agriculture came into collision with the National Socialist idea of a society of peasant freeholders.'[200] It was the impact of the war on agriculture just as much as on industry which meant that the Second World War was a force for change. The full importance of the changes in agriculture which stemmed from the war and which in the Second World War were very different from the First World War was a subject which he felt was often overlooked by historians. In western Europe farmers

> realized after 1942 that the new marketing and price structures [imposed by the Vichy regime] were only temporary because Germany would lose the war. The investment climate for European farmers was very poor. They were being asked to change their operations to meet what they perceived as only a temporary situation and patriotism combined with commercial wisdom to make them resist German pressures.

198. Ibid., 249–251.
199. Ibid., 259.
200. Ibid., 263.

> Their reluctance to invest was greatly reinforced by the immediate economic difficulties which European agriculture experienced throughout the war.[201]

Therefore, Alan Milward concluded that, in spite of

> the inherent tendency of war to raise both the output and the productivity of agriculture, the complicated realities of the war reduced both. One result of the Second World War was to reduce the world's total available food supply and make it difficult for world agriculture to regain its former output levels. Of the main outputs of agriculture only grains were still produced in quantities close to the pre-war levels. The devastation of battles, the deterioration of capital equipment, the loss of labour (for large numbers of former agricultural workers were either unable or did not choose to return to their previous employment), the loss of draught animals and the delays in retooling factories to produce agricultural machinery all played their part. And even in countries where output had gone up, a certain percentage of this rise had been due to a concentration on short-term gains which, because of soil exhaustion, could not be sustained in peacetime.
>
> As incomes improved and people's expectations rose it became clear that the war had been the turning point between the apparent food surpluses of the 1930s and a new situation in which, in terms of human expectations, food shortage was to become a permanent feature of the post-war world.[202]

The opportunity to debate the impact of the Second World War on the agricultural sector at the International Economic History conferences held in Edinburgh in 1978 and in Budapest four years later led to a highly acclaimed book which Alan Milward edited with Bernd Martin.[203] The first comparative study of its kind, it revealed the very different impact which the war had on agriculture in the western and eastern hemispheres, but also the great differences between Western and Eastern Europe. It was the further knowledge about the impact of the war on agriculture in Western Europe which was of greatest interest to Alan Milward in his search to understand the changes brought about by the war.

In Western Europe the increase in the demand for foodstuffs put an end to the agricultural stagnation that had characterized the prewar period. The war increased farmers' incomes in almost every country, gave birth to forms of public intervention that were on the whole perceived as successful

201. Ibid., 268–269.
202. Ibid., 293.
203. Martin and Milward, *Agriculture and Food Supply in the Second World War* (1985).

and thus difficult to put aside when hostilities ended, undermined the social position of elites opposed to the modernization of the primary sector, and speeded up the rationalization of units of landholding. When in the immediate postwar years the demand for food remained high and world production levels stayed low, the role of food producers had to be recognized by policy-makers. In the six years that it took for agriculture in Western Europe to regain prewar levels of output, farming producer organizations were able to exploit their power over governments and to define the terms for intervention in West European agriculture which were to last for many years. The Second World War, both Martin and Milward wrote in their preface, accelerated the 'speed of social and political change in the agricultural sector'.[204]

If agriculture provided an example of how state intervention in the economy could have positive results Milward drew the more general conclusion that in an economic sense, 'the legacy of the war was a consciousness that the economy could be directed into the desired channels, some knowledge of how to direct it, and the acquisition of a great store of facts about the economy'.[205] A subtle argument underlying his wide comparative view was that democracies might well be unprepared to wage war, but once they are at war they are much more successful in organizing themselves in order to win the war. Germany and Japan, 'the two belligerents who decided to use war as an instrument of economic gain', concluded Neal after reading *War, Economy and Society*, 'found that the same political forces that led to the decision for war also prevented the rational organization of their wartime economies.'[206]

It was not until the 1980s that Alan Milward's understanding of German policy during the Second World War, particularly his interpretation of the Blitzkrieg strategy, came under attack from a new generation of historians in Germany and Britain. In Germany, Ludolf Herbst, arguing from a political standpoint, claimed that the Blitzkrieg was the invention of historians and had never existed.[207] At the same time, in Britain, Richard J. Overy was arguing that from an economics perspective

> the concept of *Blitzkrieg* economics [ . . . ] in most respects [ . . . ] does not fit with the actual facts of German economic life between 1936 and 1942 [ . . . ] Hitler's plans were large in scale, not limited, and were intended for a major war of conquest to be fought considerably later than 1939. The fact that the large armament failed to materialize was not due to any *Blitzkrieg* conception, but to the fact that eco-

204. Martin and Milward, 'Preface' to Martin and Milward, *Agriculture and Food Supply* (1985), 1.
205. Milward, *War, Economy and Society*, 130.
206. Neal's review of *War, Economy and Society*, 441.
207. Herbst, *Der totale Krieg und die Ordnung der Wirtschaft* (1982).

> nomic preparations were out of step with the course of foreign policy; a dislocation that was exacerbated after 1939 by a combination of poor planning, structural constraints, within German industry, and weaknesses in the process of constructing and communicating policy. The intention was large-scale mobilization. Hilter's object, in the long run, was European conquest and world hegemony.[208]

Where Milward argued that Hitler chose to launch a war in 1939 because it fitted the strategic synthesis of Blitzkrieg, Overy denied that the Blitzkrieg as a strategy had ever existed; it had been invented *a posteriori* by historians.[209] Instead of a synthesis between economic and political objectives, Overy argued that there was in fact a disjuncture. The crux of the matter thus lay in the explanation of Alan Milward's early-1942 turning point. According to Overy, the increase in arms production after 1942 was not due to any specific decision but to the natural maturity of the heavy investment in war-related industry since 1936.

But Overy's views failed to convince many historians. Harrison and Mark Roseman continued to accept the Blitzkrieg thesis.[210] So did Marwick and Clive Emsley, while lamenting that '[l]ike most historians challenging an orthodoxy Overy does tend to make his target appear rather less substantial than it was: Alan Milward's original research in this area was both pioneering and persuasive.'[211] Ránki also agreed that the Blitzkrieg strategy 'corresponded to the economic realities of Germany's position. I regard this', he wrote, 'as the most decisive point in the discussion.'[212] Ian Beckett considered that the Milward–Overy debate was unsettled.[213] As far as Alan Milward himself was concerned, Overy's arguments could not be proven: 'If, in order to give a definitive answer to this problem, we must know exactly what Hitler's personal intentions were,' he was to write in 1995, 'then the debate will never end, for it is unlikely that we will discover much that is new.'[214] Indeed, in spite of the new research produced after the publication of *War, Economy and Society 1935–1945* in 1977, he did not feel the need to update the volume for its paperback editions in 1979, 1984,

208. Overy, 'Hitler's War and the German Economy: A Reinterpretation' (1982), 272–273.
209. Overy, *War and Economy in the Third Reich* (1994), 254.
210. Harrison, 'Resource Mobilization for World War II' (1988), 173; Roseman, 'World War II and Social Change in Germany', in Marwick, *Total War and Social Change* (1988), as reprinted in Emsley, Marwick, and Simpson, *War, Peace and Social Change in Twentieth Century Europe* (1990), 302–303.
211. Marwick and Emsley, 'Introduction' to *War, Peace and Social Change*, 19.
212. Ránki, *The Economics of the Second World War*, 64.
213. Beckett, 'Total War', as reprinted in Emsley, Marwick, and Simpson, *War, Peace and Social Change*, 36.
214. Milward, 'Économie de guerre' (1995), 182. The latter provides a useful summary of the theses presented in *War, Economy and Society, 1939–1945.*

or 1987 (see Appendix 2 of this volume) or, by the mid-1990s, to alter any of his main theses on the war economies.[215] At that time, Alan Milward concluded that greater accuracy in production indexes for the major combatants had permitted refined comparisons of their strategic choices leading to the minor change that

> the long-running historical argument over whether there was a sharp contrast in the period 1938–42 between Britain's commitment to total war and Germany's avoidance of that commitment through the choice of a more flexible Blitzkrieg strategy ought properly to be limited to the years 1940–1.[216]

In 1998 Werner Abelshauser pronounced that both Milward and Overy were wrong. Characterizing Milward's Blitzkrieg synthesis as a 'peacetime economy in war' (*friedensähnlichen Kriegswirtschaft*, a term coined not by Milward but by Speer's chief statistician, Rolf Wagenführ) was just as misleading, he said, as Overy's 'war economy in peacetime'.[217] The National Socialist economic system, according to Abelshauser, had elements of both wartime and peacetime economies. The war economy had to contain elements of a peacetime one in order to stabilize the political system, but they were not intentional. In fact, he argued, a decision for a war economy was taken early on but it was not implemented until 1942. 'This explains', he said, 'for one thing, the "production miracle" under the auspices of Armaments Minister Albert Speer after 1942, which was made possible by stepping up the war economy.'[218] In 2001, Raymond E. Frank Jr., contrasting Milward's and Overy's theses, concluded that making sense of their conflicting views is 'difficult for those less familiar with the subject' since their 'disagreements as to facts and differences of interpretation' remained unsettled.[219] One of Alan Milward's former students, J. Adam Tooze, who had written his doctoral thesis on official statistics in interwar Germany, challenged Abelshauser's conclusion by analyzing the economic statistics compiled by Wagenführ, which Alan Milward in his 1964 *EHR* article had cautioned would probably have underestimated the scale of armaments production

---

215. Overy, in his review of the 1987 paperback edition of *War, Economy and Society, 1939–1945* (158) expressed disappointment with Milward's unwillingness to update his 1977 'classic'.
216. Milward's review of Ránki's *The Economics of the Second World War*, 670.
217. For Wagenführ's concept see Deutsches Institut für Wirtschaftsforschung: *Die deutsche Industrie im Kriege, 1939–1945* ('The German Industry in War, 1939–1945') (1954), 25.
218. Abelshauser, 'Germany: Guns, Butter, and Economic Miracles' (1998), 150–151.
219. Frank's combined review of Milward's *War, Economy and Society* and Overy's *War and Economy in the Third Reich*, 482–485.

in the period 1938–1942 and overestimated them after that date. Tooze showed that his supervisor's caution was justified and that the statistics grossly understated the level of armaments production in 1939 and the level of labor productivity in armaments-producing industries.[220] Rejecting the argument of Overy and Abelshauser that Hitler had not planned to go to war in 1939, Tooze, like Milward, argued that the decision to go to war in 1939 was planned.

In the most recently published work on the topic which we have found, Jonas Scherner maintains that at least two questions, namely 'How well was the German economy prepared to wage war at the end of the 1930s?' and 'How fast did it mobilize at the beginning of the 1940s?' remain controversial.[221] Even though Scherner questions 'the older *Blitzkrieg* account', it is apparent that the new statistical evidence which he produces, which was not available to Alan Milward in the early 1960s, does not invalidate his conception that the economic policy designed in Germany in the 1930s was derived from the specific nature of the Nazi party and the German economy. The fact that the new statistical evidence proves that the investment boom beginning in 1936–1937 was higher than Alan Milward was able to acknowledge at his time of writing and consequently reduces the gap between the 'armaments miracle' of 1942–1944, with respect to 1938–1939 production levels, confirms rather than questions the crux of Alan Milward's argument that, however extensive Germany's preparations for war were in 1939, the intention of Hitler and the Nazi party leadership was not to increase it substantially in order to avoid the social and political disturbances that a total-war effort would have provoked.

It seems that a basic disagreement between Alan Milward and other scholars revolves around the question of whether rearmament was conceived for total war. Alan Milward argued that the level of German rearmament reflected the structural limitations of the German economy and the political limitations of the Nazi state. By planning a series of wars which would expand the territorial base and provide new resources, Germany would not necessarily confront the combined might of the USSR, the United States, and the British Empire at the same time. Where many see Nazi Germany as an evil power intent on provoking an irrational world war, Alan Milward described a strategy which in the ideological vision of National Socialism was a comprehensible answer to the socioeconomic problems facing Germany but one which turned out to be unworkable. The strategy which had led to German control over most of continental Europe by 1941 had to be changed in view of the unexpected resistance of the population of the USSR and the unexpected military power that the Soviet Union was able to generate after the German invasion. Once it was changed it lost its 'strategic synthesis' so

220. Tooze, 'No Room for Miracles' (2005).
221. Scherner, 'Nazi Germany's Preparation for War' (2010), 433.

that Nazi Germany collapsed economically before it was defeated militarily. These differences in how the Second World War was interpreted were to lead to very different interpretations of the postwar period as well. Those who argued that Nazi Germany had to be defeated militarily because it did not collapse economically were to argue that the postwar arrangements to integrate West Germany into Western Europe were primarily about security because the Nazi occupation of Europe had been an economic success. Germany could unite Europe by force unless it was prevented from doing so by integrating it into the institutional structure of a united Europe. Alan Milward argued that the Nazi occupation of Europe, while initially quite successful, had ultimately failed because the Nazi system was no more successful than the liberal system which it replaced in addressing the socioeconomic problems of continental Europe. The lesson of the Second World War was that Germany could not unite Europe by force.

Alan Milward concluded *War, Economy and Society* by arguing that the most serious legacy of the war, the one which made the problems of economic reconstruction 'so difficult to solve in spite of the rapid recovery of output in the separate national economies', was its 'redistributive effects [ . . . ] not its "cost"'.[222] In the United States economic activity increased by more than 50 percent between 1939 and 1945 (expressed in 1939 values)—an unprecedented increase over so short a period of time—and consumption by 12 percent, which altogether led to an historically high standard of living. That country suffered no physical damage and the loss of life, while to be regretted, was comparatively low (around three hundred thousand lives as opposed to over twenty million in the Soviet Union). Average levels of industrial productivity rose by 25 percent due largely to the fact that factories were operating, for the first time since 1929, at full capacity. In the United Kingdom national income expanded by 64 percent; in Germany it had expanded by 10 percent until 1943 and then declined. It fell in the Soviet Union, Italy, and Japan. In full recognition of all the difficulties of defining and then calculating that part of production which was specifically for war purposes, Alan Milward suggested that in Britain and the United States it was between 45 and 55 percent, in Germany and the Soviet Union between 60 and 75 percent, and in Japan between 35 and 45 percent. Ultimately, the Allied victory was due to the fact that the Allies were able to produce more armaments than the Axis powers. This was achieved not through any major changes of political or economic power but simply by the modern bureaucratic state clearly defining its priorities and assuming sufficient controls over the domestic economy and over trade to achieve those priorities. The rapid transformation during the war of the economies of the United Kingdom and the United States showed what could be achieved in advanced economies over a short period of time.

---

222. Milward, *War, Economy and Society*, 336.

But Allied victory was also due to the United States transferring to Britain and the Soviet Union, under lend-lease arrangements, armaments on a scale which was never fully admitted. It was the Allied counterpart to what Nazi Germany had forcibly extracted from its occupation of European countries. Even though Germany had benefited considerably from its occupation of western European countries, particularly from France, the Netherlands, Denmark, and Belgium, its occupation of eastern European countries, which were to have provided Nazi Germany with its *Lebensraum* or 'living space', had not been beneficial economically. In some cases, most notably Greece, the cost to Germany of the occupation was greater than the benefit. Finally, it was due, as Alan Milward argued, to the Allies being able to mobilize their domestic populations by offering them the hope of a better world after the war, one of increased employment opportunities, higher living standards, and a system of social protection organized by the state in contrast to the racist and paternalistic family model of Nazi Germany. In both Britain and the United States, he said, '[p]eople's new aspirations were built on nothing more than a job and more money, because for most people in both economies these had been the real economic changes in the war.'[223] Winning the allegiance of the population was of paramount importance.

Whether there was any automatic connection between the demands made by the state on its citizens during a war in which human resources were fully mobilized and social change after the war, Alan Milward was more cautious:

> It is tempting to argue that the consequences of 'total war' must always be to produce a significant volume of social change because the state must retain the allegiance of its citizens, and the greater the demands it makes on them the more they will seize the opportunity to make demands on it. But this process depends on the governmental arrangements and it would be nearer the truth merely to say that the economic, social and psychological experience of war produces a change in the climate of social consciousness. [ . . . ] [S]ocial equality was now more widely accepted as a desirable end.[224]

For the governments of the United States and the United Kingdom fulfilling their domestic objectives in the postwar world was seen to depend on the reconstruction of an international economic system which would increase the level of world trade and, as Alan Milward said, avoid '[t]he self-adjusting mechanisms of the pre-1914 gold standard [which] had operated through creating periodic deflation and unemployment.'[225] The

223. Ibid., 343.
224. Ibid., 341 (343 for the last sentence of the quotation).
225. Ibid., 345.

main outlines of such a system were finally agreed at an Allied conference which took place in Bretton Woods, a small town in New Hampshire, in July 1944. What was to become known as the 'Bretton Woods system' was an international exchange system which, like its two predecessors, the gold standard and the gold exchange standard, was based on the principle that currencies should be freely convertible into gold at a fixed rate of exchange. One innovation was that governments should have the facility to borrow over the short term from a newly created international pool of currencies, the International Monetary Fund (IMF), which would in principle mean that they would not have to deflate domestic demand or devalue their currency in the event of a deficit in their balance of payments. A second innovation was the creation of the International Bank for Reconstruction and Development which had a double task, the immediate one of financing 'reconstruction'—without knowing exactly what that actually meant—and the longer term one of financing development projects in poor countries. Keynes, negotiating on behalf of the British government, had argued that, given the huge imbalances in the international economy caused by the war, in order for the system to work as intended it would have to be symmetrical, requiring corrective action by both creditor and debtor countries, while providing funds on a sufficiently large scale to cover the needs of debtor countries without forcing them to deflate their economies.

Britain and the Soviet Union had both incurred considerable debts to the United States during the war, under lend-lease, while Britain also had debts with the countries in the sterling area. That countries incurring a structural surplus in their balance of payments should bear the same burden of adjustment in the international payments system as that traditionally attributed to countries running a deficit would have meant in practice that the United States, expected to be the main surplus country in the postwar period in view of its dominant economic position at the end of the war, would have to take measures to reduce its surplus, either through an expansion of imports or allowing discrimination against its exports, while being the main contributor to a large IMF. Harry Dexter White, negotiating the agreement on behalf of the U.S. government, preferred the burden of adjustment to fall on the deficit country, thereby necessitating a much smaller IMF. The largest obstacle to the operation of White's system was the British Empire and the Commonwealth whose members conducted their trade in sterling, which was not freely convertible into gold or dollars, and offered Britain preferential tariffs on trade. The whole thrust of the commercial policy of the United States had since 1936 been to reduce all forms of discrimination against U.S. exports of which Commonwealth preferences were the most objectionable. On the other hand, these preferences were seen to be critical to the British government not only to protect the British balance of payments and therefore the value of sterling but also to protect its domestic manufacturing industries from foreign competition. Keynes, as Alan

Milward was to argue, defended protectionism for both reasons.[226] Unable to reach agreement over the issue of Commonwealth preferences or sterling convertibility, the two issues were postponed in July 1944 at the time of the Bretton Woods conference. All that Keynes would concede in the subsequent difficult negotiations with White to wind up lend-lease was that, in return for a postwar loan from the United States to the United Kingdom, the British government would make sterling convertible into dollars within one year. With no resolution of the issue of Commonwealth preferences the United States refused to ratify the terms of the International Trade Organization (ITO) in 1947. This meant that the liberalization of international trade, to which both governments were nominally committed, was left to be negotiated within the less binding framework of the General Agreement on Tariffs and Trade (GATT).

The Soviet Union chose not to ratify the Bretton Woods agreements in 1944. Victory in the Second World War was interpreted as a vindication of the Soviet Union's model of economic planning and autarky. The agreements which it reached during the wartime conferences at Yalta and Potsdam with the United States and the United Kingdom to settle the terms of the peace in Europe rapidly disintegrated in the growing hostility over many issues including the future of Germany. The U.S. government did not extend its lend-lease to the Soviet Union into a postwar loan. Therefore, by 1947 '[i]nstead of an epoch of universally expanding trade what emerged [ . . . ] was an epoch dominated by the two greatest military powers facing each other with an implacable economic and political hostility.'[227] If the cold war marked the end of the wartime alliance between the United States and the Soviet Union, the failure to restore the convertibility of sterling in July 1947 marked, as Alan Milward saw it, the end of the plans to create a multilateral order, based on a system of fixed exchange rates and progressive trade liberalization worldwide, on which depended the hopes of a new world based on full employment and greater social equality.

## THE RECONSTRUCTION OF WESTERN EUROPE (1984)

What was missing from the last chapter of *War, Economy and Society* was any mention of western continental Europe. This was itself a reflection of the two most important features of the postwar period, first, that the planning for the postwar international economic settlement was a purely Anglo-American affair, and second, that the continental European countries were

226. Milward's specific views on Keynes' positions on the design of the postwar international economy, which we have used in the previous paragraph, can be found in his 'Keynes, Keynesianism, and the International Economy' (2000).
227. Milward, *War, Economy and Society*, 364.

in a relatively weak political and economic position. But Alan Milward was already thinking about the postwar and the conflicting explanations for the unprecedented period of economic growth and prosperity enjoyed by Western Europe.[228] According to the prevailing liberal historiography, at the end of the conflict a short restocking boom was followed by an economic recession, as had been the case after the First World War, from which Western Europe was saved by two separate but related initiatives: the idealistic offer of material assistance from the United States and the ideas of creating a federal Europe held by enlightened individuals in Europe. A combination of American and European idealism thus put Europe on a new path toward peace and prosperity based on liberal economic principles. Marxist historiography, following the official analysis offered by the Soviet Union's leadership, saw the assistance program that the U.S. Secretary of State, General George C. Marshall, offered on 5 June 1947 and the creation of integrationist institutions in Western Europe as the product of American imperialism in the context of its struggle against the Soviet Union. In the Stalinist perspective Marshall Aid served to secure markets for the United States and the survival of a reactionary capitalism which stifled the hopes for radical social and economic change after the war. The drive to create a federal Europe was thus generally seen as a self-serving initiative of the United States designed to achieve its economic and political objectives in Western Europe.

As *War, Economy and Society* went to press Alan Milward was to receive another invitation from a German historian, this time to write about the history of European integration. It came from Walter Lipgens, the first professor of modern European history at the EUI, the academic institution financed by the European Community and its member-states to provide postgraduate teaching and research in the four social science disciplines of economics, history, law, and political science as they related to the European Community, which opened its doors to students in September 1976 in Fiesole (Florence).[229] A committed federalist and Catholic opponent of Nazi Germany, he had devoted his professional life to explaining that the roots of the European Community lay in the federalist thinking of the non-communist resistance to Nazi Germany. By 1977 he had traced and documented the various strands of federalist thinking in the Resistance during the war and up to 1947.[230] It was in that year, Lipgens suggested, that gov-

228. Throughout this Introduction 'Western Europe' refers to the set of countries which participated in the pattern of institutionalized economic interdependence after 1947, while 'western Europe' includes Spain and Finland and refers to all those countries which did not become part of the Soviet zone of influence.
229. A brief but vivid account of the EUI's first days is Hans Daalder (first head of the Department of Political and Social Sciences at the EUI, 1976–1979), 'In Memory of Max Kohnstamm' (2010).
230. Lipgens, *Die Anfänge der europäischen Einigungspolitik, 1945–1950* (1977).

ernments in both Europe and the United States became interested for the first time in the idea of uniting Europe. To help him explain these changes at national governmental level, Lipgens invited a group of historians from all nine member-states of the European Community (EC) to a meeting in Florence in March 1977 at which he proposed that they would collaborate with him in writing the next stage in the history of European integration. According to Professor Donald Cameron Watt from the LSE, who had been invited to the meeting along with Alan Milward,

> [Lipgens] demanded that all present subscribe to a collective declaration on the desirability and inevitability of the establishment of a federal united Europe. The British representatives [Milward and Watt] [ . . . ] resisted the idea as both inappropriate and limiting in that it would enable the inclusion or exclusion of themes, incidents, ideas and fields of study which were certainly germane to the study of European development, but which Professor Lipgens regarded as heretical. The declaration was in fact issued, but the dissenters were not excluded.[231]

Nonetheless, Alan Milward accepted the invitation and chose to write the history of the response of European governments to the offer of Marshall Aid in 1947, which was to form part of his next book about the history of the postwar European economic boom.[232] The one condition nominally attached to Marshall's offer of aid was that the European recipients would cooperate with each other to produce a coordinated response which, by breaking down national barriers, would lay the basis for them to establish a United States of Europe, along federal lines. Alan Milward's approach, as it had been throughout all his earlier writing, was to base his research on the recently opened government archives in multiple countries, including the United States, as well as on the statistical economic record. He set out to understand each country's position in terms of its own history, emphasizing national differences rather than seeing all countries as part of a global system, indistinguishable one from another. Although he no longer used the term 'strategic synthesis' to explain government policy this was in fact how he continued to analyze policy—as a synthesis of domestic economic objectives and foreign policy, the means by which national governments tried to achieve domestic objectives within an increasingly interdependent world.

Alan Milward's understanding was that Marshall's offer was motivated by politics and not economics: that it was a product of the cold war and not—as David W. Ellwood maintains in Chapter 8 of this volume—of a much longer lineage. The Marshall Plan was 'in the first place a practical

---

231. Watt's review of Lipgens, *Documents on the History of European Integration* (3 vols., Lipgens and Loth for the 3rd vol.), 393.
232. Milward, 'The Committee of European Economic Cooperation (CEEC) and the Advent of the Customs Union' (1982).

response to Washington's perception of the danger to its own strategic interests, whatever genuine chords of idealism it might cause to vibrate in America and Europe.'[233] That its motivation was primarily political and not economic was because, as Alan Milward was to argue later, not only was there no economic crisis or depression in Western Europe in 1947 but it was questionable whether the European Recovery Program (ERP, the official name of the Marshall Plan) met the wider needs of the U.S. economy. The challenge facing U.S. policy-makers was how to reconcile the strategic objectives of ensuring that Western Europe, including the western zones of Germany, remained under the influence of the United States rather than falling within the Soviet sphere, with the economic objectives of a multilateral international system as set out at Bretton Woods in 1944:

> [T]he extraordinary growth of output and exports during the war in the United States had convinced American governments that a thriving post-war world and a prosperous America's place in that world depended on the creation of an efficient multilateral trade and payments system in which the international debts and surpluses of countries could be offset against each other in a comprehensive world balance, much as they had been before 1914. Such a system would alone permit American foreign trade and domestic output to exist at the new, much higher levels they must maintain in order to support the prosperity which the war had brought. As the plans for a peaceful post-war world order collapsed, these ideas were still seen as fundamental to a prosperous Western bloc.[234]

Whether Marshall Aid would lead to the coming into force of the Bretton Woods system and to that comprehensive world balance, he very much doubted. This was because by focusing exclusively on the Western bloc the U.S. government had undermined the possibility of reestablishing a dynamic and balanced world economy as it had existed before 1914. This issue of whether Marshall Aid was a step toward the multilateral system of Bretton Woods, as the majority of historians and economists maintained, or a step toward quite a different world, as Alan Milward argued, continues to be disputed. It was his view that the U.S. goal of using Marshall Aid to enable Western Europe to reach an equilibrium in their trade and payments with the dollar area within four to five years, when Western Europe's deficit with the United States represented only half of the world's dollar shortage, was losing sight of the true causes of the fundamental structural imbalance in the international economy of which Europe's dollar shortage was a mere reflection. Recycling dollars through Marshall Aid was, first and foremost,

233. Ibid., 508.
234. Ibid., 524.

an acknowledgement of the global dollar shortage but was an insufficient response to the problem. The United Kingdom, the only economy in Europe which carried out considerably more of its trade with the rest of the world than within Europe, was particularly aware of the global nature of the problem. The U.S. attack on imperial preferences and Washington's refusal at the same time to reduce its own tariff levels, combined with its willingness to construct a purely Western-European bloc for strategic reasons, did not offer the United Kingdom much relief to its financial difficulties.

The new strategy of the United States represented by Marshall's offer posed a different set of problems for France. The plan to replace the original Potsdam agreements on the level of industry in Germany—which the French government considered to be its 'level of security'—with a higher level of industrial output in specific sectors in the Bizone and ultimately to incorporate 'western Germany' into an integrated Western Europe, was already clear by the time of Marshall's speech. The French government saw as its main task, according to Alan Milward, to oppose and delay the process as much as possible while at the same time working toward defining the conditions and terms of a possible solution to what was referred to as *the German question*. This was to enable it to accommodate the many interests involved while defending France's fundamental security interests in both economic and defense terms. The response of the French and British governments to Marshall's offer was to take joint control over the European organization created under American pressure to coordinate the European response. Both governments were determined to lead the recovery of Western Europe but according to their own broad interests rather than to concede to U.S. pressure to unify Western Europe. Alan Milward's careful archival reconstruction led him to conclude that 'before the [Paris] conference began the stage was set for a fundamental opposition between the far-reaching hopes of the United States and the machinery of the conference [on European Economic Cooperation], which had been designed to thwart these ambitions.'[235] The significance of the Paris conference was that '[f]or the first time questions about the reconstruction of Europe were to be handled outside the framework of the great-power conferences.'[236] Furthermore, for the first time the United States was to listen to the views not only of the British and French governments but of all the European governments that had accepted the offer of aid. It was, he argued, the belated recognition that different countries had different interests which meant that '[f]rom the moment the conference met there began a learning process in Washington which was to forge a more realistic set of political aspirations there.'[237] As he explained:

235. Ibid., 513.
236. Ibid., 514.
237. Ibid., 513.

> When sixteen countries ultimately sent delegations to Paris on 12 July [1947] for the conference which took to itself the name Committee of European Economic Cooperation (CEEC), their heterogeneity must surely have impressed at least as much as the similarities in their position. Five had colonial empires, two had less than one million inhabitants, two had important armies, one was occupied by two of the others, and two had been neutral powers for more than a century. Two had per capita national incomes clearly exceeded only by that of the United States, four were still underdeveloped economies. Some had based their recovery on planning and stringent controls, others had been ardent advocates of decontrol and a *laissez-faire* economy. Some had a world-wide pattern of trade and investment, for others their international economic connections were overwhelmingly with the European Continent. The one country [Germany] whose affairs had more than any other been responsible for the conference was not represented there at all.[238]

Without attending the Paris conference, Germany occupied the center of the stage. France, which had not been invited to either the Yalta or the Potsdam conferences, left no one in any doubt that

> any settlement in Germany had to be by agreement with France, and any progress towards a joint European agreement on the use of American aid in reconstruction had to depend on the settlement in Germany. [ . . . ] The Franco-German problem at last occupied the centre of the stage; European integration would only become a part of the play in so far as it was related to solving the dilemma of the main actors and the main plot.[239]

The differences over what should happen to Germany divided Western European countries just as much as it divided the four powers occupying Germany. As Alan Milward went on to explain, the exclusion from all decision-making about Germany was resented by many of the small Western European countries. The Benelux countries wanted a rapid increase in German output and

> the Italian delegate supported the Benelux position on the grounds that Germany was the major market for Italian exports as for Benelux exports. Even the Norwegian representative, while insisting on restrictions being maintained on those areas which competed directly with Norwegian interests—fishing, whaling, shipping, and shipbuilding—

238. Ibid., 517.
239. Ibid., 520.

> spoke in favour of an accelerated German recovery and for much wider consultations with the smaller powers about policy in Germany.[240]

Since it was clearly isolated, all the French government could do was to insist that any recovery of German output must not endanger French security. The crux of the problem lay in how Germany's industrial heartland in the Ruhr would be controlled. Alan Milward summed up the three possibilities for control which were discussed in mid-1947:

> Would it be an international board with direct management powers in the works themselves, or a remote international control board with few direct executive powers? There was a third possibility which briefly emerged in these talks and which was eventually to provide the solution after three more years of dispute, viz. an internationally supervised cartel which would include the French and Benelux firms.[241]

This was his first reference to the origins of the French plan which would eventually lead to the establishment of the European Coal and Steel Community (ECSC), although it was an interpretation which he was to modify subsequently in the light of further research. What he did not find in any of the debates within European bureaucracies and governments, between them and the Economic Cooperation Administration (ECA)—the body set up by the United States to oversee the implementation of the Marshall Plan—, within the CEEC and its permanent successor, the Organization for European Economic Cooperation (OEEC), was any evidence that political movements in favor of European unity had anything other than an insignificant impact on international political and economic agreements. Those gatherings of officials acting on behalf of the governments were not building a unified Europe but solving what they perceived as being their most immediate problems. Furthermore, the evidence which he had been able to gather while collaborating with Lipgens showed that the 'committee system', as conceived and agreed upon by the British and French when they set up the CEEC, was designed to split the main issues into technical details, each one of which would be dealt with by separate teams of experts so that '[w]ider questions of European unity would be entirely out of place'.[242] Participants in the technical committees, as some federalists argued at the time, by working together in such enterprises

> acquired a wider comprehension of the common nature of European economic problems and even developed not only a certain feeling of affinity with each other, but also a degree of solidarity against their

240. Ibid., 519.
241. Ibid., 521.
242. Ibid., 511.

> own national governments at moments when these governments did not show the same comprehension.[243]

The problem, as Alan Milward noted, was that these participants had little power or direct influence over their governments. With the exception of the Italian representative, the other governments appointed as their representatives 'senior civil servants who were already closely involved in the formulation of national reconstruction policy, but who remained only the executants and advisers of their ministers.'[244]

Ultimately, Alan Milward's research method and findings were so much at odds with those of Lipgens that he did not contribute to Lipgens' further publications (*Documents on the History of European Integration*). Whereas Lipgens saw weak states whose hold on power was to be weakened still further, Milward saw many discredited states in Western Europe, apart from the British, determined to rebuild their strength and legitimacy by extending their control over the economy.[245] In spite of their differences, Wilfried Loth maintains in Chapter 9 of this volume that Lipgens and Milward shared a number of assumptions about the nature of the nation-state in postwar Europe. While Alan Milward did not reject the evidence of federalist thinking which Lipgens produced, he was more interested in understanding its significance for the course of postwar European history. What he wanted to know was

> through what political mechanism the idealisms which supported Western European integration actually influenced governmental policy-making in the nation states, unless it be through the vague suggestion that men like Adenauer, Schuman, Sforza, and Spaak, who themselves shared these enthusiasms, were able to override the massed cohorts of government and bureaucracy whose task it was and is to define and uphold the national interest before all else.[246]

Skeptical of the role played by the Resistance in helping to defeat Nazi Germany during the war, he was equally skeptical that the federalist ideas held by the Resistance groups had had anything more than a marginal impact on government policy in Western Europe after the war. The emphasis placed by Lipgens and others on the role of the resistance, in his view,

---

243. Ibid., 512, summarizing the views expressed by Ernst H. van der Beugel, one of the Netherlands delegates to the Paris conference, in his *From Marshall Aid to Atlantic Partnership* (1966), 71–72.
244. Milward, 'The Committee of European Economic Co-operation', 512–513 (quotation 513).
245. Milward, *The Reconstruction of Western Europe, 1945–51* (1984).
246. Ibid., 492.

> strengthened the pervasive political myths in some countries, especially France and Italy, that moral and physical resistance to Nazi Germany had laid a new moral foundation for post-war republican governments and thus given them a particular political legitimation. [ . . . ] The inability to demonstrate that political movements in favour of European unity had anything other than an insignificant impact on international political and economic agreements leads, however, to the conclusion that these explanations are no more than observations of a minor albeit interesting phenomenon.[247]

Not only did Alan Milward reject Lipgens's argument that it was the ideas discussed by federalist individuals and groups active in wartime resistance which explained the creation of supranational institutions in Western Europe after the Second World War but he also questioned the central role attributed to the United States, first, in saving Western Europe from economic collapse in 1947, and second, in providing vital support for European integration. The conclusion of the first documented history of the Marshall Plan written by Imanuel Wexler and based entirely on U.S. sources was that the Marshall Plan was 'one of the great economic success stories of modern time'.[248] Milward disagreed completely and instead of writing his next book about the great European economic boom he focused exclusively on the period of the Marshall Plan.[249]

As he announced boldly in the opening chapter of *The Reconstruction of Western Europe 1945–51*, Marshall Aid did not rescue Western Europe from an economic crisis in 1947 because Western Europe was not experiencing an economic crisis at the time. Making the distinction between an economic crisis and a payments crisis, he explained that what Western Europe was experiencing in 1947 was a temporary payments crisis for four interrelated reasons. The first was the fact that the dollar, as the only currency which was convertible into gold at a fixed price at that time, was in great demand; the second was the surge in imports of investment goods to Western Europe from the United States in the first half of 1947; the third was that since the traditional supplier of such goods, Germany, was operating at very low levels of economic activity (not because of wartime damage but due to the restrictions placed by the Allies on its industrial output), those investment goods had to come from the United States; while the fourth was that in the absence of a functioning international system of trade and payments European countries had no means of earning in third countries the dollars necessary to pay for imports from the United States. The payments crisis was therefore caused by the strength and vigor of the

247. Milward, 'The Origins of the Treaty of Rome' (1988), 3.
248. Wexler, *The Marshall Plan Revisited* (1983), 255.
249. Milward's review of Wexler's *The Marshall Plan Revisited*.

recovery of European economies and was not an indication that they were on the verge of collapse.

Since European reconstruction plans had not been conceived simply in terms of recovery from the war and occupation but as ambitious programs of industrial modernization able to sustain the new social obligations for full employment and comprehensive welfare programs, the Western European states continued to encourage imported capital goods even after prewar levels of production had been reached. By the end of 1947, the whole of Western Europe, except for Austria and Germany, had completed their recovery in terms of reaching prewar output levels. In view of such an achievement, it was wrong, Alan Milward argued, to describe as an economic crisis a time when, in every West European country except Germany, investment was higher absolutely and as a ratio of GNP than in any year since 1919, and when production was rising more rapidly everywhere than it had for twenty years. The so-called 1947 crisis was limited to the temporary difficulty of paying for dollar imports caused by the vigor of the economic recovery rather than by any fall in production and consumption levels. 'It was the success and vigour of the European recovery, not its incipient failure' which had caused a payments problem with the United States.[250] There was thus no economic need for Western European economies to be rescued by the United States.

While Marshall Aid allowed the recovery to be continued it was not, he insisted, the primary cause of the strength of the European economic recovery which had begun in 1945, well before Marshall's offer of June 1947, and well before the arrival of dollar aid. Had the United States not supplied dollars through Marshall Aid he calculated that it would only have been in France and the Netherlands that recovery would have been slowed down at least until West Germany resumed its role as a supplier of capital goods to Western Europe. But, he insisted, France would not have collapsed economically had there been no Marshall Aid, since over the whole ERP period France spent a larger proportion of Marshall Aid on importing machinery and vehicles than any other recipient, while going to great lengths to switch its food imports to the franc zone. The main contribution of Marshall Aid was to pay for those imports necessary for industrial modernization rather than for staving off hunger, social revolt, and political collapse. 'Indeed', as one reviewer of *The Reconstruction of Western Europe* asserted, 'Milward contends that if sheer economic recovery from the war had been the only issue, most European countries could have done without Marshall Plan assistance as early as 1948.'[251]

Where his critics argued that in the absence of Marshall Aid Western European governments would have had to deflate the level of economic

250. Milward, *The Reconstruction*, 463.
251. Schwartz's review of *The Reconstruction of Western Europe*, 667.

activity which, in the tense political climate of the cold war, would have caused coalition governments to collapse, Alan Milward argued that not only was there no evidence that any government apart from that of Italy was prepared to deflate but more importantly they did not need to do so. It was the governments of the United States and the Soviet Union which, each for their own political reasons, wanted to present the countries in Western Europe as being on the verge of an economic crisis. It was important in the United States in order to win Congressional approval for a program of assistance to Europe while it was important for the Soviet Union to encourage trade union opposition to the Marshall Plan.[252] The extent of the success of the Soviet Union in this respect in Italy is analyzed by Maud A. Bracke in Chapter 10 of this volume.

As Alan Milward maintained, the reason that no European government was prepared to deflate the level of economic activity in response to the payments crisis in 1947, as they would have done at any time before the Second World War, was because the balance of political power within Western European states had changed after 1945. The effects of the Second World War in political terms were the most important factor in determining the nature of the postwar economic recovery. The shift in political power was due to the fact that the restored national governments in Western Europe—most of them multiple-party coalitions—needed to regain the political legitimacy which states had lost in 1940 or even earlier. What the speed of the capitulation to Nazi Germany demonstrated was how little allegiance many people in Western Europe owed to their own liberal regimes. He saw this as the result of the failure of the liberal state in the 1930s to address the problems of unemployment and falling living standards, as analyzed by Eamonn Noonan in Chapter 11 of this volume. If the Western European states were to restore their credibility after the war, they had to do more to regain the confidence of voters. This meant taking control of the economy, administering trade and capital movements, offering agricultural protection, increasing wages, subsidizing industries, and generally becoming more responsive to the wishes of voters.

Most European governments, he showed, with the exception of Belgium and Italy, adopted extensive economic planning as a reaction against the failure of the *laissez-faire* policies of the interwar period.[253] Because the political parameters within which politicians could maneuver had been altered so much as a result of the war, had Marshall Aid not arrived, most governments would have extended their controls over the economy even further in the short term rather than abandon their expansionary programs,

252. Milward, 'The Committee of European Economic Cooperation', 544.
253. Milward organized a specific session on economic planning in the post-1945 period for the tenth international economic history congress, Leuven, August 1990, the papers of which were published as Aerts and Milward, *Economic Planning in the Post-1945 Period* (1990).

he maintained. What the European governments had not resolved was how they would continue to pay for their domestic expansionary programs once dollar aid came to an end. At the start of the Marshall Plan they did not necessarily agree that the rules of the Bretton Woods system were a good idea or that they could not be broken. In any case, since those rules were premised on the system operating internationally with countries achieving an equilibrium in their global balance of payments, it was not at all clear that the Marshall Plan was preparing Western Europe to operate within the Bretton Woods system. Those potential problems were postponed as the U.S. government focused on its new policy of preparing Europe to reach equilibrium in its balance of payments with the dollar area alone:

> For the first three years of the ERP the United States was able to reconcile the existence of Marshall Aid to American ambitions for the world-wide multilateral payments system embodied in the Bretton Woods agreements by the argument that in promoting a recovery in Western Europe's output, Marshall Aid was closing Western Europe's dollar deficit with the United States and thus preparing the way for a re-establishment of the principles agreed at Bretton Woods. But the concentration of dollar outflows on Western Europe made it even less likely that this would be the case.[254]

The country for which the new direction in U.S. policy was most damaging was Britain. But, as Alan Milward showed, the alternative way offered by Britain of recycling dollars via the sterling area in order to stimulate international trade would not have satisfied the strategic objectives of the United States in Europe:

> From the standpoint of the British government the Sterling Area was an expansionary force in world trade and a way of overcoming the international structural disequilibria. It offered the possibility of multilateral settlements to a group of nations representing a significant part of total world trade. British imports in 1947 were by themselves almost the equivalent of United States imports. What was more, most British purchases of primary goods were carried out through bulk purchasing agreements over several years and Britain thus offered what underdeveloped primary exporters most required, guaranteed longer-term markets.[255]

It was not until 1949 when, following the recession in the United States' economy, which affected British trade much more than the trade of the

254. Milward, *The Reconstruction*, 466.
255. Milward, 'The Committee of European Economic Cooperation', 526–527.

other West European economies, the British government devalued sterling and threatened to retreat into the sterling area completely, that the United States realized 'that its real interests were more affected by the world-wide ramifications of British and sterling area trade than by Britain's role in Europe.'[256] It was only then that Washington finally recognized that

> [n]o durable reconstruction could have been possible unless the future terms of co-existence of the sterling area, Western Europe and the dollar trading zone had been defined. So long as they were defined in terms of dismantling the sterling area and forcing Britain into an integrated Western Europe nothing could be achieved.[257]

From this recognition came the acceptance that the United States would have to provide dollars to cover the inclusion of the sterling area in a new payments system in Europe—the European Payments Union (EPU)—and that the EPU would not be an institution for uniting Europe. By definition, the EPU represented a settlements mechanism among the seventeen OEEC member-states extremely favorable to debtors, in a way which has never happened before or indeed since. In terms of its automatic settlements mechanism, it was closer to Keynes' wartime proposals for an international fund than to the rules of the IMF. The EPU allowed participating European countries to discriminate against dollar exports while giving incentives to debtor countries to continue to run domestic expansionary programs on the basis of foreign and automatic credits rather than correct those deficits through domestic deflation. It could not have worked, Alan Milward argued, had the United States not been forced to recognize that no multilateral clearing mechanism in Europe could operate successfully without the inclusion of the sterling area, and had the views of the U.S. State Department not prevailed over those of the U.S. Treasury. For both reasons, he insisted, the EPU was not a step toward the convertibility of European currencies within the framework of the Bretton Woods system:

> The Union [the EPU] was unable to eliminate the disequilibrium in intra-Western-European trade and payments not merely because it lacked the power over national monetary and fiscal policies to do so. An equilibrium in intra-Western-European payments could only have been achieved at the expense of the expansion of world trade. The same applies to another goal of the Marshall Plan, a payments equilibrium between Western Europe and North America. Disequilibrium within Western Europe and between Western Europe and North America had always existed and always been resolved in a

---

256. Milward, *The Reconstruction*, 473.
257. Ibid., 473–474.

> worldwide framework. It was a serious inherent weakness of the regional emphasis of the Marshall Plan that it ignored the previous hundred years of the history of international trade. [ . . . ] The account of Britain's ultimate adherence to the EPU fails to emphasize that this could only be obtained by sacrificing most of the ECA's further hopes and ambitions. It was partly for that reason that the agreement was so fiercely attacked elsewhere in Washington. In that struggle, too, even a liberal French minister of finance, Maurice Petsche, tacitly sided with the British, leaving the American negotiations in a very weak position.[258]

Thus, at the end of the ERP, it was neither the Bretton Woods system nor a purely European system which was responsible for regulating payments within Western Europe but the EPU, an institution partly funded with Marshall Aid for financing (on generous terms) deficits in intra-OEEC trade and between Western Europe and the sterling area.

Nor was the United States any more successful, as he showed, in using dollar aid to encourage the West European governments to dismantle their barriers to trade and create one large market. In his view, since the Marshall Plan was primarily an instrument of the cold war, the liberal economic theory which it drew upon was to provide an ideological justification, although it was of very dubious relevance to the Western European countries themselves:

> as America's needs for a militant ideology of its own became so acute from 1947 onwards, the theoretically greater economic efficiency of a large market and a multilateral payments system came to be seen by many in Washington as a fundamental aspect of political democracy and "a free society".[259]

But for Western European countries the crux of the problem was how to earn dollars in third markets to pay for imports from the United States. Creating a large market in Europe would do little to solve that problem:

> The American view that a fundamental change in the mechanisms of intra-European trade would produce an immediate benefit in terms of increased European output [ . . . ] ran directly counter to the view of many European countries that such changes, although no doubt theoretically and practically desirable in the medium term, would in the short term be useless and dangerous unless the fundamental structural disequilibria in world trade were first corrected, a responsibility which

---

258. Milward's review of Wexler's *The Marshall Plan Revisited*, 342.
259. Milward, 'The Committee of European Economic Cooperation', 525.

> fell heavily on the United States and of which recycling dollars through Marshall Aid was but a first and insufficient acknowledgement.[260]

In any event, Alan Milward showed that the United States failed to achieve the liberalization of trade in Europe under the Marshall Plan, contrary to the claims made at the time or subsequently.[261] Such claims were based on a common misunderstanding of the rules of the OEEC trade liberalization program proposed by the British government in 1948. Rather than reflect that proportion of each member-state's overall trade with the rest of its OEEC partners which was entirely determined by market forces, the OEEC code measured the quantitative restrictions on private trade which were removed, as a percentage of all the quantitative restrictions on private trade in 1948. It did not measure tariff protection and it did not include the high proportion of trade which was under government control.[262] The resulting percentages were therefore misleadingly high. In OEEC terms, for example, 100 percent liberalization in 1959 meant in reality that only 14 percent of West German imports from the rest of the OEEC in 1959 were *liberalized*. Furthermore the progress that was made in 1949–1950 was reversed in the face of an external payments problem:

> By the end of 1951 there were more quantitative restrictions than at the end of 1950. Tariffs remained little changed so that the levels of import penetration in most Western European countries in 1955 were not much higher than in 1950 and still lower than in 1913. The first and most vigorous ten years of Western Europe's largest boom, in spite of all American efforts to change the world, were in fact experienced under a protectionist system.[263]

In focusing on the policies pursued by the governments of Western Europe Alan Milward demonstrated that the United States through Marshall Aid had no more than a marginal impact on the agreements reached in Western Europe. 'Marshall Aid', he concluded 'was not in fact important enough to give the United States sufficient leverage to reconstruct Western Europe according to its own wishes.'[264] It was the new institutional structure, in particular the EPU and the ECSC, put in place by some of the European governments themselves which, he claimed, was ultimately responsible for the success of the postwar settlement in Europe and for laying the basis for its unprecedented period of peace and prosperity.

---

260. Ibid., 526.
261. These claims were made by Wexler in 1983 as well as, among many others, Kaplan and Schleiminger, *The European Payments Union* (1989).
262. This is one of Milward's direct criticisms of Kaplan and Schleiminger; see his review of *The European Payments Union*.
263. Milward's review of Wexler's *The Marshall Plan Revisited*, 342.
264. Milward, *The Reconstruction*, 469.

Alan Milward thus concluded that not only did Marshall Aid not need to save Western Europe from economic collapse, nor did it lead to the elimination of the dollar deficit and the operation of the Bretton Woods system, but nor to European integration within a large monetary or free-trade framework. Quite apart from the payments difficulties which meant that the entire sterling area had to be brought into the EPU, '[t]he opposition between French policies towards Germany and those of Britain and America were so profound that no worthwhile decisions about European economic co-operation, much less integration, could be taken in the framework of the CEEC or its successor [the OEEC].'[265] But what Milward did accept was that the United States was able to put pressure on the French government to change its policy toward Germany in the direction of a Franco–German association.

Integration came about not from the original American promotion of a customs union in the OEEC but from a European solution to the German question, which at the same time solved specific European domestic problems. The French proposal of 9 May 1950 was a response to the U.S. pressure in favor of the 'normalization' of Western Germany at a time of rising conflict with the Soviet Union, but it was also, as Alan Milward demonstrated, the outcome of over five years of attempts to address the reasons for France's collapse in 1940. One constant element of French policy since the liberation of France had been a determination to strengthen France as an industrial power by expanding and modernizing its basic industries, including its capital goods industries. As recognized by the provisional government of France's fourth republic, headed by General Charles de Gaulle, this depended on France having access to certain German raw-material resources—above all coal and coke from the Ruhr and the Saarland. In political terms, modernization and industrialization became synonymous with national security, territorial integrity, and economic independence. Modernization and industrialization were seen to be the only path for the future viability of France as an independent nation. In one of his last acts before leaving French politics for twelve years de Gaulle had, in January 1946, created a body to plan the reconstruction of France, the *Commissariat général au plan* under Jean Monnet's leadership. Central to what became known as 'the Monnet plan' was the objective of expanding the industrial base of the French economy, and the steel industry in particular, using coal and coking coal from the Ruhr as well as imports of investment goods from the United States, financed with U.S. dollars. It was a plan to make France rather than Germany the main industrial power in continental Europe, but it failed to take account of the needs and aspirations of other West European countries which depended on a reconstructed German economy as a supplier and market, or of the British need to finance its zone of occupation in Germany, which included the Ruhr. Following the breakdown in relations with the

265. Ibid., 467–468.

Soviet Union, it conflicted with the strategic needs of the United States to strengthen the western zones of Germany economically.

While the Marshall Plan was designed to fund the expansion of the economies of both France and the western zones of Germany, it risked undermining the Monnet Plan and by extension French security by offering France no permanent guarantee of supplies of coal and coking coal from the Ruhr in sufficient quantities and at a price which did not discriminate against French industry. With the establishment of a unitary and independent West German state at the six-power London conference on Germany in June 1948, the French government was forced to begin the search for such a permanent guarantee which would be acceptable to the new German state:

> Until mid-summer 1948 [ . . . ] France's aims in European reconstruction were concentrated on a partition and permanent weakening of Germany and on acquiring a guaranteed access to German coal and coke resources. [ . . . ] From June 1948 onwards the Ministry of Foreign Affairs began the task of moving ministers, governments, parliament and people towards the alternative policy of a Franco-German economic association.[266]

The result of this process was the innovative supranational concept announced to the press by Robert Schuman, the French minister of foreign affairs, on 9 May 1950. It was to take yet one more year of negotiations before the French were able to secure through the Schuman Plan and the ECSC one of the key objectives of the Monnet Plan. Although Alan Milward provided a pragmatic rationale for the French policy which culminated in Schuman's press statement, this did not mean that he did not appreciate the value, the revolutionary nature, and the overall importance of 'supranationality'. On the contrary, he considered that the supranational solution constituted the very last and crucial element in the reconstruction of Western Europe, the one that became a substitute for a peace settlement with Germany.[267] He showed that the new supranational structure was crucial, not only for the future of national planning in France, but for achieving the national objectives of the Benelux countries and Italy. Instead of free trade or the re-creation of the prewar industrial cartels run by the industries themselves, the European states were able to retain control over sectors seen to be vital for their national economic security. The form that European integration took was to be a highly regulated market not within OEEC, as Washington had expected, but among six countries and in the two sectors of coal and steel. In Chapter 12 of this volume Ruggero Ranieri

---

266. Ibidem.
267. It was not until September 1990 that a final peace settlement was signed between Germany and the Allies.

sets Alan Milward's new interpretation of the Schuman Plan within the context of the existing explanations and within the context of Milward's later research.

The greatest contrast between what the United States wanted to achieve in postwar Western Europe and what the West European governments produced themselves was that whereas the United States looked for a liberal solution to Western Europe's problems and to its own security concerns in the form of creating a single large market in Western Europe, the West European governments looked for a state-directed solution to a very specific problem. The basis of the U.S. international economic policy-making was, in Milward's view, 'the unquestioning assumption that the history of the United States itself provided some higher guide to the path of economic development'.[268] In other words, the larger market of the United States could be replicated in Western Europe. By contrast, Western European governments believed that their security needs could not be left to the market or to the most powerful private business concerns. If nationalization was perhaps an answer to the problem posed by the control which the most powerful industry, that of steel, had been able to exercise over the domestic economy in the interwar period, to have put the German steel industry under the control of the German state would have been seen to undermine European security. On the other hand, for Italy, which wanted to develop its own steel industry, free competition within Europe was not possible. The problem of the coal industry was quite different. It was an industry in which productivity was in decline. Nowhere was this more serious than in Belgium. Managing that decline in a way which did not cause unemployment on a large scale was a challenge of a different sort. The solution to both challenges was negotiated by all six governments which signed the Treaty of Paris. As Tobias Witschke in Chapter 13 and Charles Barthel in Chapter 14 of this volume clearly show, the establishment of the ECSC, however supranational its High Authority was to be, did not mean that the European states intended to lose control or indeed lost control over the regulatory framework that affected their coal and steel industries. The Western European governments without exception were determined to maintain their sovereignty and their ambitions to pursue specific national economic strategies. Key to the successful pattern of institutionalized economic interdependence was, Alan Milward affirmed, that it served 'the separate national interests of the countries concerned'.[269]

Initial reviews of *The Reconstruction of Western Europe* were positive, acknowledging its stimulating and provocative nature, but also its intrinsic complexity.[270] Apart from those who found the detailed arguments 'rather

268. Milward, *The Reconstruction*, 285.
269. Ibid., 470.
270. 'Stimulating and provocative' is the verdict of Frederick J. Breit's review of *The Reconstruction of Western Europe* (188) and 'provocative and

indigestible' there were others who criticized his focus on 'bread and butter issues' when they expected him to discuss the cold war.[271] As Federico Romero explains in Chapter 15 of this volume, Alan Milward accepted the cold war as the historical context in which Western Europe was reconstructed but argued that it did not explain the nature of that reconstruction. As Alan Milward was to explain later:

> [t]he greater importance which western Europeans states placed on social and economic recovery rather than very high levels of military expenditure as a barrier against Communist aggression meant that the United States had no choice but to accept that to press Europe for a contribution equal to its own to the military security of Europe was so divisive as to weaken rather than strengthen security in both senses. This conclusion remains supported by the historical evidence of the Marshall Plan period.[272]

David F. Good concluded, perhaps prematurely that '[i]n the end his arguments persuade. After this, who can doubt that it was the pursuit of national self-interest and not the heady idealism of European romantics that ultimately shaped the economic and political institutions of reconstructed Europe?'[273] As Jan van der Harst reveals in Chapter 16 of this volume or Zamagni's personal interpretation in her contribution to this volume of the reasons for Italy's joining the Schuman Plan show, the European romantics have not lost their influence completely.

In the years following the publication of *The Reconstruction of Western Europe* Alan Milward's views stimulated considerable research and debate toward the end of the 1980s, as Anjo G. Harryvan illustrates for the Netherlands in Chapter 17 of this volume.[274] Milward was to observe though that many historians had simply not understood his arguments. He was particularly disappointed to see that in Michael J. Hogan's scholarly history of the economic diplomacy of the Marshall Plan, his arguments had been entirely rejected.[275] On the basis of archival research in the United States and Britain, Hogan had argued that through the Marshall Plan the United States had transmitted the politico-economic compromise of the American

---

stimulating' but 'ultimately convincing' that of Schwartz's review (666). The review by Marks leaves no hint of doubt that, in her opinion, Milward's book is a 'massive' study (408).

271. Wightman's review of *The Reconstruction of Western Europe* and N.P. Ludlow, *European Integration and the Cold War* (2007), 3.
272. Milward's review of Schain's *The Marshall Plan*, 208.
273. Good's review of *The Reconstruction of Western Europe*, 546.
274. For a presentation of the subsequent, mainly European historiography of the Marshall Plan see Burk, 'The Marshall Plan: Filling in some of the Blanks' (2001).
275. Hogan, *The Marshall Plan* (1987).

New Deal as amended by the Second World War to Western Europe: that this in turn had produced the stability and prosperity which characterized post-1947 West European corporative neocapitalism, and led to the integration of Western Europe into one single market, and ultimately made the Bretton Woods system operable. Without Marshall Aid, Hogan affirmed, 'a serious crisis in production would have come with the collapse of critical dollar imports'.[276] Without the Marshall Plan, the economic recovery of Western Europe and thus the favorable conditions for its transformation into a Golden Age would have not been possible.

In this Hogan was accepting the economic arguments of the Marshall planners at face value. When invited to write a review of Hogan's book Alan Milward used the opportunity to set out his arguments once again.[277] What Milward was at pains to demonstrate was that many of the arguments of Marshall planners were politically motivated and had no foundation in economic reality. Not only did he doubt that the ideology underpinning the Marshall Plan originated in the New Deal but he was convinced that the political consensus in postwar Western Europe predated the Marshall Plan and was 'more the outcome of shifts of political power which imposed policies on frequently reluctant politicians and civil servants than the outcome of changes of intellectual outlook by policy-makers or of any coordinated international attempt to overcome the manifest weakness of the international economy.'[278] As he had argued in *The Reconstruction of Western Europe,* given the political and economic conditions in Western Europe there was no evidence pointing to an economic collapse had the U.S. government not supplied dollars through Marshall Aid. He went on to address the second claim made by Hogan, that the alternative policy options which the absence of the Marshall Plan would have made necessary were 'not available to the fragile coalitions that presided over many of the participating countries, none of which could retreat from already low levels of consumption and hope to survive'.[279] This argument, Milward elaborated,

> needs to be emended in one respect where Hogan has perhaps not understood the statistical implications of the contrary argument. No government needed to *reduce* the levels of food consumption of 1947 to implement the alternative policies, and most could have increased them. Of the six countries in question, four could still have obtained dollar capital goods and raw material imports in the same value as under the Marshall Plan and have had a margin of extra gold/dollars

276. Ibid., 431.
277. Milward, 'Was the Marshall Plan Necessary?' Review of *The Marshall Plan*, by Hogan (1989).
278. Ibid., 237.
279. Hogan, *The Marshall Plan*, 431.

> for food imports above the 1947 level. Only France and the Netherlands would have had to stay at that level.[280]

Accepting that emendation Alan Milward presented the alternative course of action that several governments had considered when the conditions attached to U.S. assistance appeared initially as too intrusive. Considering the case of France, the country which perhaps best fits Hogan's 'fragile coalition' definition, Alan Milward insisted that the French government would not have collapsed for economic reasons had there been no Marshall Aid. It was a convenient tactic for the government to warn of a political collapse. The country which was most dependent on Marshall Aid was Britain, not an example of the sort of weak coalition government to which Hogan was referring. It was in Britain that the new direction taken by the United States in proposing Marshall Aid and abandoning a global solution to the problem caused by the dollar shortage could have been most damaging economically, had dollar aid not been extended belatedly to include the sterling area in the EPU. Was the Marshall Plan necessary? On balance, Alan Milward's answer was that, 'eminently successful policy though it was, the postwar European world would have looked much the same without it.'[281]

After the collapse of the Soviet empire, attention in the United States focused on whether a Marshall Plan for Eastern Europe would be an appropriate vehicle for introducing capitalist methods into those countries and for closing the gap in economic performance between Eastern and Western Europe. In 1993 J. Bradford DeLong and Barry Eichengreen concluded that in fact Milward was correct to argue that Marshall Aid was not large enough to 'significantly stimulate western European growth by accelerating the replacement and expansion of its capital stock', nor to finance reconstruction which was completed by 1948. But they maintained that Marshall Aid did make a difference to Western Europe and that difference was in altering the environment in which economic policy was made. In their view, the ERP meant a careful, managed return to markets after the market failures in the Great Depression. Had it not been for Marshall Aid, they asserted, Western European governments would have continued to control imports in order to cope with their deficit in external payments. Marshall Aid therefore helped them to restore the market and to move to the multilateral system of Bretton Woods.[282] Alan Milward's warning that historians should not assume that the period of 1948 to 1958 was 'only a journey back' to the Bretton Woods system was rejected.[283] His demonstration that trade in Western Europe continued to be controlled in the 1950s was also

280. Milward, 'Was the Marshall Plan Necessary?' 242.
281. Ibid., 252.
282. DeLong and Eichengreen, 'The Marshall Plan' (1993), 190–191.
283. Milward, 'Was the Marshall Plan Necessary?' 237.

dismissed. Significantly though, the United States did not offer a 'Marshall Plan' to Eastern Europe.

Alan Milward's own view almost twenty years after he had first analyzed the ERP was that the Marshall Plan

> cannot be said to have been economically necessary to the continuation of the boom, but it did, of course facilitate its continuation. It made the international imbalances of the European countries less acute in 1948 and 1949. More important than the Marshall Plan was the decision to divide Germany and to create the Federal Republic as a west European state. The role of the Federal Republic in the intra-west-European trade network became a major contribution to stabilising the international economy.[284]

It was precisely the contribution of the West German economy to the trade and payments of Western Europe in the 1950s and to the decision of the six ECSC member-states to form a common market which was to occupy Alan Milward's intellectual energies for the next few years.

## THE EUROPEAN RESCUE OF THE NATION-STATE (1992) AND THE FRONTIER OF NATIONAL SOVEREIGNTY (1993)

In writing *The Reconstruction of Western Europe* Alan Milward had explained that his original intention had been to write a history of the great European economic boom. What he wrote instead was a history of the first seven years of that boom. Returning to his original question he now wanted to know what had enabled the postwar European boom to continue after 1951 and last for so long. Why, he asked rhetorically, had the economic recovery in Western Europe not been thrown into reverse by the recessions originating in the United States in the 1950s and, as had happened in the 1920s, been transmitted to Western Europe. Another puzzle was to explain the fundamentally contradictory tendencies whereby the state was to cede some of its enhanced powers to the new supranational institutions in the European Community. His search for explanations of the great European boom thus involved an analysis of the reasons for the further integration of Western Europe.

As ever, he began his research just at the time that the governmental records for the period in question (in this case for the period leading up to the Treaties of Rome in 1957) were being opened in many countries. This time, however, Milward was fortunate in directing a research project, 'Challenge and Response in Western Europe: The Origins of the Treaty of Rome' at the EUI, where he had been appointed to the chair in contemporary

284. Milward, 'Keynes, Keynesianism, and the International Economy', 233.

European history in 1983.[285] He was able to draw on the research of the many scholars either working on the subject at the EUI or invited there as visitors. In a number of publications (articles and chapters in collective works) Milward referred to the work of these scholars as providing the basis for further thought about the role of Western European nation-states in the first decade after the end of the Second World War and, particularly, the motives behind their choices for interdependence and integration. In the preface to the 2003 paperback edition of *The Reconstruction of Western Europe*, which incorporated several important changes to the original edition, Milward paid tribute to this research group by announcing that

> four more years of research [at the EUI] have convinced me that the historical evidence from the 1950s demonstrates that there was indeed an imperative towards wholly new forms of interdependence and to the transfer of national 'sovereignty' to non-national institutions, which the nation-state had to follow to make itself once more an accepted and strong unit of organization. It would now be possible to replace the theories rejected in the last chapter [of *The Reconstruction*] and formulate a historically-convincing intellectual foundation for the process of European 'integration', although it would be equally disappointing to federalists and their associates.[286]

When he returned to Britain to fill a chair in Economic History at the LSE, he retained his links with the research project at the EUI, now directed by a former colleague from UMIST who had become Professor of Economic History at the University of Amsterdam, Professor Richard T. Griffiths. On the occasion of Alan Milward's resignation from his chair at UMIST, the Senate of the University of Manchester passed a lengthy resolution of thanks to their former professor, founder of the Department of European Studies and of the Bachelor of Science degree program in European Studies and the Master of Science degree program in European Community Studies, noting among other things that

> [h]is participation in staff seminars, whether hosted by the Department of European Studies or held elsewhere in the University, was always extremely stimulating, and revealed the breadth and catholicity of his academic interests and knowledge, often easily over-stepping artificial disciplinary boundaries.

They went on to say that

---

285. He was able to persuade the High Council of the EUI to create a chair in the History of European Integration in 1984 on a permanent basis.
286. Milward, *The Reconstruction* (2003 reprint), 'Preface' to the paperback edition, xix.

> [h]e was always keen to foster good staff-students relations in the Department. One of the ways in which he did this was on the cricket field, where he was a fast bowler of fearsome appearance and awesome reputation, and was a member of the legendary European Studies X1 which, astonishingly for such a small Department (and one in which male students and staff are in a minority) won the UMIST inter-departmental knock-out a few years ago.[287]

The mid-1980s was a time of renewed popular and political interest in the historical dynamics of European integration stimulated by the ratification of the Single European Act in 1986. It was a time when the classical theories of integration were enjoying a resurgence of support and when the prospect of political union in Europe returned to excite and divide opinion. It was in Britain where Milward prepared his next book, *The European Rescue of the Nation-State,* which was to be published in the year in which the Treaty of Maastricht promising 'ever closer union' was signed.[288]

Alan Milward was one of the first historians to consider European integration to be a subject of sufficient importance to merit historical investigation. He initially based his research on the theoretical explanations offered by other disciplines, most notably economics and political science.[289] In his view, most economic theory saw the integration of markets as the direct outcome of their growing interdependence. Questioning whether European economies were any more interdependent in the 1950s than they had been under the gold standard between 1896 and 1914, he argued that there was nothing inherent in the nature of economic development which led to the erosion of the state and national frontiers in the interests of maximizing profits and incomes. Indeed, as he pointed out, interdependence could also lead to the growth of separatist movements and the creation of new nation-states rather than the opposite. Although integration was generally considered to have a positive economic effect, economists had great difficulty in measuring those dynamic effects since their assumptions were based on static equilibrium analysis, he said. If he did not agree that there was any automatic connection between economic interdependence and integration, nor did he agree with the argument that 'the growth of markets inevitably generated economies of scale in manufacturing and retailing which in turn generated higher rates of productivity improvement which in turn generated higher rates of national income growth, thus enabling governments to satisfy many of the

287. University of Manchester, 'Resolution of Thanks to Former Professor' adopted by Senate at its meeting on 6 November 1986 and by Council at its meeting on 3 December 1986, private papers of Alan S. Milward.
288. Milward, *The European Rescue of the Nation-State* (1992).
289. See Milward, *The Reconstruction*, 494 ff. In 'The Origins of the Treaty of Rome' he summarized why he was not convinced by those theories.

stronger political pressures on them after 1945.'[290] This was an argument frequently advanced in the United States to justify the purpose of Marshall Aid, and which spawned a number of European 'productivity missions' to the United States in the late 1940s and early 1950s. It formed the basis of Maier's argument that it was by promoting the growth of labor productivity that Western European governments were able to overcome the social tensions of the prewar period. But, since he did not accept the proposition that growing markets inevitably led to improvements in productivity, Milward found Maier's 'politics of productivity' a sophisticated intellectual argument but not an explanation for the growth which occurred in Western Europe.[291] Not content with Keynesian explanations which focus on the role of the state in promoting high rates of economic growth in Western Europe, Milward wanted to know '[b]y what precise political mechanism did the organisational unit of the state, so feebly incapable even of fulfilling its primary task of protection in 1940, come to play such a role in the vast improvement in human life which took place'.[292]

He was equally skeptical of the value of the various theories which had been put forward by political scientists to explain integration. There was no evidence, he suggested, to support Karl W. Deutsch's theory that Western capitalist economies were becoming more similar both in their economic policies and political objectives and had devised institutional methods of cooperating with each other which built on their common sense of purpose and community.[293] There was plenty of evidence of conflict between national objectives, Milward asserted, some of which was generated by the new institutions themselves and which required action by national governments to resolve.[294] He also found the neofunctionalist theory developed by Ernst B. Haas problematic for different reasons. Haas, a refugee from Nazi Germany, who—as Ben Rosamond points out in Chapter 18 of this volume—had a personal wish to see the power of the nation-state eroded, argued that if integration was chosen as a framework to permit a greater degree of interdependence between countries, since national governments would then have to compete with other interest groups for the loyalty of their citizens within the new integrated institutions, the common interest would prevail over national interests resulting in further integration.[295] Even though Haas had rejected the functionalist division between low-level technical issues and high-level political ones, seeing all issues as political, he did not in Milward's view offer a convincing explanation as

---

290. Milward, 'The Origins of the Treaty of Rome', 6.
291. Ibidem. Maier, 'The Politics of Productivity' (1977).
292. Milward, *The European Rescue*, 24.
293. Deutsch *et al.*, *Political Community and the North Atlantic Area* (1957).
294. Milward, 'The Origins of the Treaty of Rome', 4.
295. Haas, *The Uniting of Europe: Political, Social, and Economic Forces, 1950–1957* (1958).

to why nation-states opted for integration rather than interdependence in the first place. And he disagreed, in the second place, that, having chosen integration, it would lead to further integration, citing the results of recent research into the history of the ECSC which suggested that 'nation states actually weakened the integrative powers of the High Authority as soon as they began to operate inside its ambit.'[296]

As a historian, the main difference which he saw between the 1950s and earlier periods, when the degree of economic interdependence in Western Europe was as high if not higher, was that in the 1950s states believed that they could further their national interests permanently through growing and state-controlled economic interdependence and looked for ways to ensure that the arrangements which were in place in the 1950s would not be dismantled.[297] It was thus to the changes in the nature of the state itself in postwar Europe, in political parties, and in national economies that Alan Milward turned first for explanations of the boom and of the integration of the European economies. At that time, for both supporters and opponents of a federal Europe, the process of integration was seen as one in which the supranational institutions of the European Community were replacing those of the nation-state. Milward, questioning whether such an antithesis between the two existed, was to reach the paradoxical conclusion that integration, far from weakening the nation-state, was a policy choice designed to strengthen it, enabling it to implement the domestic policies for which there was a consensus within and among states and which could not be implemented by more traditional methods. Starting from the assumption that after 1945 the governments of democratic Western Europe considered that performing those policies was essential to legitimate the new postwar nation-state and to regain the allegiance of their citizens after the capitulation of all but Britain to Nazi Germany, Milward applied the very visual concept of the 'European rescue of the nation-state' to the decision taken by European states to surrender a degree of sovereignty to supranational institutions in order to strengthen the power of the state over the market, when it was seen to be necessary for political, economic, and strategic reasons. As he explained

> [o]ne of the inherent instabilities of the political economy of the postwar nation was that it had to be internationalized at certain points if it was to survive. All history is movement, and in its rescue the European nation-state was laying the basis of a new international order for the continent. Yet the feasibility of that order was, and continues to be, determined by the evolution of national economic life. [ . . . ] Although therefore the European rescue of the nation-state was necessarily an

---

296. Milward, 'The Origins of the Treaty of Rome', 6.
297. Ibid., 11–12.

> economic one, it is at the point where that economic rescue intersected with the problem of Germany's future in Europe that the common policies of the European Community developed.[298]

He strongly believed that because the real reasons for the creation of the European Community had been misunderstood by those who saw it either as a purely diplomatic solution to the problem of European security or as a liberal solution to Europe's lack of competitiveness, this misunderstanding was taking the European Union in directions marked most of all by a lack of humanity. It was to warn people that the European Union had not been built on an abstract idea of a united Europe, which could be applied indiscriminately to any issue, but was the result of creative decisions taken by the postwar state 'to improve the material conditions and happiness of large numbers of people' as well as providing security against a resurgent Germany, that he felt compelled to write *The European Rescue of the Nation-State*.[299]

Contrary to the prevailing political science theories which, he observed, focused on 'the creation of the institution more than the nature of the problem with which it was supposed to deal', he analyzed integration in terms of the challenges facing the postwar state in Western Europe.[300] His starting point was the impact on the Western European state of defeat and occupation in the Second World War. Drawing on his research into the Second World War, he concluded that '[d]efeat and occupation were not merely a collapse in the face of overwhelming military superiority; in most cases they were also a collapse of internal morale.'[301] As he had previously argued, individual acts of resistance may have been important for restoring individual morale during the occupation, but, contrary to the national myths cultivated by postwar governments, they did not provide the basis for restoring the nation's collective morale after the war. The basis of Milward's argument, which he set out in a number of case studies in *The European Rescue of the Nation-State*, was that there was a recognition among the ruling *élites* in Western Europe that 'the post-war state had to be constructed on a broader political consensus and show itself more responsive to the needs of a greater range and number of its citizens if its legitimacy was to be accepted.'[302]

Political parties had to change from being 'clubs of like-minded individuals associating to vote together at the parliamentary centre' to becoming 'a machine for discovering the demands coming from below in society

298. Milward, *The European Rescue*, 44–45.
299. Ibid., xi–xii
300. Ibid., 12.
301. Ibid., 26.
302. Ibid., 27.

and transmuting them into policies'.[303] While he acknowledged that 'force was to remain as it always had been the core of the state', he concluded that 'one of the characteristics of the new power structure of the post-1945 state in western Europe was that it needed to have less recourse to force than did its predecessors.'[304] In place of repression, the postwar state was based on a much wider political consensus than before the war, responsive to the demands of labor, agricultural producers, and 'lower and middle income beneficiaries of the welfare state'.[305] This resulted in a much larger state commanding budgets in which expenditure on defense, housing, industrial modernization, and, in the 1960s, education, were all growing.[306] Not only was the effect less inflationary than its critics maintained, with rates of inflation in the 1950s lower than in the twenty years of anti-inflationary policy after 1973, but the contribution of government policy to growth was much less than the changes that occurred in Western Europe independently of the state and its activities. These changes were the great increase in manufacturing in Western Europe which drew people in their hundreds of thousands out of the agricultural sector. It would come to be seen, he predicted, as the culmination of the great wave of European industrialization which began in the seventeenth century.[307] What characterized the period in Western Europe both historically and in comparison with the experience in Eastern Europe was the rapid increase in purchasing power which led to the very rapid growth of production, trade, and ownership of objects. It was, he maintained, the vast choice and ability to purchase consumer goods which was held up as 'the superiority of Western Europe over the undemocratic governments of Eastern Europe, with missiles and sputniks but without washing machines and cars.'[308] The fact that the postwar political consensus resulted in such rapid economic change was, he argued, 'largely coincidental, both in thought and action.'[309] He was therefore arguing that the origins of both the European boom and European integration lay in the political priorities set by some national governments rather than being driven by purely economic factors or ideas about uniting Europe.

In what Andrew Moravcsik was to describe as an 'oblique research strategy', Alan Milward drew the evidence for his explanation of integration from a number of different countries and sectors of activity in the 1950s which ranged from coal mining in Belgium and trade in manufacturing in Western Europe to the protection of agriculture and the British government's unilateral plans to restore the convertibility of sterling. What

303. Ibid., 28.
304. Ibid., 24–25.
305. Ibid., 27.
306. Ibid., 36.
307. Ibid., 40.
308. Ibid., 129.
309. Ibid., 33.

Moravcsik found 'frustrating' however was the lack of a single explanation of integration which applied to all countries.[310] Instead of a theory of integration he complained that Milward had offered a set of observations in search of a theory and by referring to political science theories of integration which were already 'old hat' Milward had ignored the more recent developments in political science. Moravcsik's criticism strongly resembled the sort of comment made by economists when reviewing Milward and Saul's interpretations of European development and growth in the nineteenth century.

Even before *The European Rescue of the Nation-State* had gone to press Milward had already embarked on another book, in collaboration with some of his former research students and colleagues.[311] The introduction to the collective volume *The Frontier of National Sovereignty,* which he wrote with one former student, caused some outrage by describing neofunctionalism as a theory of the cold war and 'the intellectual foundation for a hegemonic foreign policy architecture' in the United States.[312] The cold war was, Milward and Sørensen argued, 'first and foremost a war of propaganda'.[313] They likened the teleological theories of integration, such as those of functionalism, neofunctionalism, and federalism, which proliferated in the 1950s and 1960s, with Rostow's stage theory of economic growth, which Rostow had explicitly called a *Non-Communist Manifesto.* Such teleological integration theories, they claimed, were equally driven by ideology, but more covertly. They were, they maintained, 'essentially models of social engineering for the containment of communism and the promotion of economic growth.'[314] When the end of the Vietnam War punctured the confidence which underpinned such integration theories in the United States, political scientists replaced them with interdependence theory, leaving Europeans without an adequate theoretical explanation for the creation of the supranational institutions of the European Communities. Interdependence theory, even though it was to become popular as a description of the way that the EC operated in the 1970s and early 1980s did not explain, to Alan Milward's satisfaction, why interdependence had been replaced by a degree of integration in the 1950s or indeed in the 1980s and 1990s. He had set out to provide such an explanation for the past, but also one which would predict whether the degree of integration would be maintained in the future, extended, or even reversed. It was a vital part of his implicit

310. Moravcsik's review of *The European Rescue of the Nation-State*, 127 (both quotations).
311. Milward, Lynch, Ranieri, Romero, and Sørensen, *The Frontier of National Sovereignty: History and Theory, 1945–1992* (1993).
312. Milward and Sørensen, 'Interdependence or Integration? A National Choice' (1993), 3.
313. Ibid., 1.
314. Ibidem.

theory of historical change. It rested on his conviction that for integration to be successful it had to be based on consensus. Nazi Germany, as he had demonstrated in his previous research, had not succeeded in uniting Europe by force. The German occupation of Europe was not working economically even before Germany was defeated militarily. Integration could not be achieved through force, but was the policy chosen by European nation-states who held similar domestic objectives and similar concerns about protecting themselves against a resurgent Germany. It had to be achieved through consensus from both within and among nation-states. It was for that very reason that all member-states had to be democracies. Turning the federalist theory on its head he argued that the end of integration would mean the end of the nation-state.

What all six countries which signed the Treaties of Rome in March 1957 shared was a determination to 'reassert the nation-state as the fundamental unit of political life as vigorously and securely as possible.'[315] In order to regain the legitimacy which had been diminishing in the eyes of voters since the Great Depression and had evaporated completely in 1940, they adopted a set of policy objectives, some of which could be met through traditional channels and some of which required new structures outside the nation-state. Put another way, some of these policies were within the power of the state to deliver but others, particularly if they were not shared by other states, risked being undermined by them through competition. Although in general terms many of these objectives were shared by all six governments which signed the 1957 Treaties of Rome, such as the provision of social welfare, agricultural protection, full employment, and the promotion of industrialization, the policies required to meet these objectives could and did vary enormously. In the case of Belgium, to which Alan Milward devoted an entire chapter of *The European Rescue of the Nation-State*, where 10 percent of total industrial employment was in coal mining in 1950, full employment meant finding a way of protecting those jobs in the face of competition from the more efficient coal-mining industry in West Germany and the United States.[316] Whereas interdependence, in the form of trade liberalization, would have thrown the full cost of job protection or welfare onto the Belgian state, integration offered a means for the Belgian government to negotiate financial assistance through the new supranational institutions, which in fact meant that the West German government was the main paymaster of the declining Belgian coal industry. As Alan Milward was to calculate

> [w]ithout counting the opportunity costs of using high-price domestic coal instead of cheaper imports, the cost of preservation of so much

315. Ibid., 5; fuller treatment in Milward, *The European Rescue*, 1–20.
316. Milward, *The European Rescue*, 46–118.

> employment in coal-mining in subsidies alone was $141.42 million between 1953, when the common market in coal opened, and 1958. But $50.08 million of this sum was contributed by other Community members, mainly by the German Federal Republic. The integrationist solution was used to sustain levels of welfare and employment in Belgium which would have been much less easily sustainable within a system of interdependence.[317]

Belgium exemplified the way in which a small country could act to protect its vital interests. Again, by even considering the position of small countries within Europe he distinguished himself from the majority of scholars who focused only on the major powers, which in the case of continental Europe meant France and Germany. As Alan Milward had previously explained when writing about the reconstruction period, '[t]here is not much a small power can do to influence the course of history. If the moment is well chosen and the interplay of national interests correctly judged, however, the small power is not helpless.'[318]

For the Netherlands, a small economy which was highly dependent on foreign trade and on the sort of trading networks which had been instituted by Germany during the Second World War and on which its prosperity was increasingly seen to depend after the war, the priority was to ensure that the Federal Republic of Germany would not turn toward Eastern Europe for its imports, as it had done in the 1930s. Its interests were therefore in creating some sort of institutional structure governing trade in Western Europe which would lock the Federal Republic of Germany into it. Many governments, Milward observed, turned to foreign trade as an engine of economic growth even though the macroeconomic evidence on which that was based was very uncertain.[319] Increasing trade liberalization too quickly could threaten some elements of the postwar consensus. For this very reason, Alan Milward argued, the 'insistence on policies of national economic development through industrialization produced a mixture of liberalization and protection of manufactured trade which was highly selective.'[320] The national tariff, which until the Great Depression of 1929–1932 had been the mechanism through which parliaments rewarded or penalized particular social groups, had come to be replaced by other forms of protection developed on an *ad hoc* basis in the 1930s, and after 1945 on a much more coherent and systematic basis, enabling governments to combine commercial policy with industrial policy.[321]

---

317. Milward and Sørensen, 'Interdependence or Integration', 11; extended elaboration in Milward, *The European Rescue*, 116–117.
318. Milward, *The Reconstruction*, 446.
319. Milward, *The European Rescue*, 127.
320. Ibid., 130.
321. See Milward, 'Tariffs as Constitutions' (1981), for his view of the theoretical underpinning of the relationship between international trade policies and

Integration was primarily the first choice of smaller European powers to ensure that the economic gains which they had made in the 1950s would be irreversible. In general, all five European governments shared a concern to lock West Germany into the pattern of trade and payments which had developed in Western Europe since the division of Germany in 1948. As Alan Milward explained 'the tendency of the pre-war Reich to form a trading web with the smaller trade-dependent economies of central and south-eastern Europe was replaced after 1948 by the tendency of the Federal Republic to form a trading web with the smaller trade-dependent economies of Western Europe.'[322] Whereas before 1939 the highly protectionist Third Reich was characterized by exporting manufactured goods in return for food and raw materials, the postwar Federal Republic was increasingly engaged in an intrasectoral exchange of manufactures. The German economy proved to be a much more stable market than that of the United States where fluctuations in demand and the arbitrariness of U.S. commercial policies affected European exports. It was a combination of long-run development trends and the new policies adopted in Western Europe and in the Federal Republic of Germany which made the latter essential for the stability of Western Europe. The legitimacy of the European nation-state, he argued,

> had come to depend on a country that was not really yet a country, without full national sovereignty until 1955, an artificial creation whose future was highly uncertain, still the subject of a possible deal between America and Russia, and still deeply distrusted. [ . . . ] It was commercially, as the pivot of West European trade that West Germany had to be bound in place, and it was this necessity, particularly as the trade boom accelerated after 1953, that gave increasing force to the idea of the customs union.[323]

After the Second World War the historical pattern, which had persisted since the late 1870s, of a low-tariff group of small countries in Western Europe and a group of relatively protectionist larger economies reemerged with, as Alan Milward observed, the difference being that Britain was now on the protectionist side.[324] Low-tariff countries had little bargaining power in GATT and none in OEEC where, under the control of Britain and France, trade liberalization took the form of reductions in quantitative restrictions on trade, not in tariffs.

The organizations which had been envisaged by Allied postwar planners, such as the IMF and the ITO (for which GATT was the substitute),

---

political evolution from 1850 to 1980.

322. Milward, *The European Rescue*, 139. Theme anticipated in Milward, 'The Marshall Plan and German Foreign Trade' (1991).
323. Milward, *The European Rescue*, 167.
324. Ibid., 177.

were worldwide and lacking in any powers to determine the direction of trade whereas, as Alan Milward showed, the Netherlands and other European countries needed some precise mechanisms in Europe which would link the expansion of foreign trade to the rapid growth of national income. The challenge for Western European states was to find some means to safeguard their national development policies by means of establishing a new and more sophisticated mix of liberalism and protectionism within the new international economic order.[325] Rather than seeing the decision to create the EEC as the result of the cold war and the new strategic position of West Germany, Alan Milward was at the time unique in arguing that it was primarily the political economy of the postwar European nation-states which explained the need for integration. The cold war and the division of Germany were the context in which decisions on integration were taken, but they did not explain those decisions. Under repeated challenge to explain why he had completely ignored the role played by the cold war in explaining European integration, he was to say that he had 'deliberately under-emphasised [it] for purposes of creative exaggeration' because 'where foreign policy considerations mattered—and in the cause of keeping our bit of Germany under control they certainly did—there could only be such consensus about them because of the similar political economies of the separate nations.'[326]

If any clear starting date for the history of the EEC had to be chosen, he argued that it was when the Dutch foreign minister, Johan Willem Beyen, first proposed a customs union in 1950 rather than the Messina conference in 1955, the date chosen by most historians.[327] Alan Milward maintained that

> [i]t was [ . . . ] always the Dutch official position after summer 1950 that only supranational constitutional machinery with real executive powers could in fact guarantee that the liberalization of the international sector would be an irreversible process (unless by some entirely unlikely event the United Kingdom changed its foreign policy and agreed on the same outcome enforced by OEEC).[328]

It was the French who changed their policy and finally agreed to a common market in Europe. However, whereas diplomatic historians underlined the fundamental importance of international political crises, such as that of the Suez fiasco and the Hungarian uprising in 1956, to explain the French decision to sign the Treaties of Rome, Alan Milward explained it in terms of the political economy of the French Fourth Republic.[329] It was the recognition in France, he argued, that the protectionist policies incorporated in the

325. Ibid., 130–134.
326. Milward, 'Approaching Reality: Euro-Money and the Left' (1996), 58.
327. Milward, *The European Rescue*, 196.
328. Milward, 'The Origins of the Treaty of Rome' (1988), 11.
329. Milward, *The European Rescue*, 215.

first two modernization plans had failed to limit the expansion of imports in the 1950s that explained the decision to liberalize trade within Western Europe.[330] Although France had a much smaller share of its total trade with Western Europe than most other European economies, the Federal Republic was its biggest outlet for the increase in its exports at a time when empire trade, the biggest share of total trade, grew only sluggishly.[331] It was also the Dutch position, as he showed, that the production, price, and exports of the agricultural sector should be regulated in common rather than left to national control.[332]

In his research into the origins of the common agricultural policy, Alan Milward was anxious to lay to rest many persistent myths, of which the two most prominent were, first, that it represented a Franco–German deal in which Germany, in return for a market for its industrial exports in France, conceded to France a market for its agricultural exports, and second, that it was based on the desire to retain the family farm as the model for European agriculture, as Kiran Klaus Patel maintains in Chapter 19 of this volume. Both myths, he argued, failed to take account of the very great changes in the position of agriculture and in French political priorities which the Second World War had brought about. To take the first myth, he argued that the priorities of successive postwar French governments, as exemplified in the first instance by the Monnet plan, had been to strengthen France as a modern industrial power in opposition to the romantic notion held by a section of the Vichy regime that France was and should remain primarily a producer of food surpluses. The EEC Treaty of Rome was to provide a framework which would secure the continuation of French industrialization within a wide, protectionist regional framework, which would check somewhat the competition of German industry. France also needed a market for its agricultural surpluses, but would have been content with negotiating long-term purchase contracts for them, he argued.[333] The second common error, in his view, was to confuse the rhetoric of preserving the family farm and of farming as a way of life with the reality of European government policy toward the agricultural sector in the very changed conditions after the Second World War. His coedited collection of research papers on the impact of the Second World War on agriculture across the world confirmed how different the position of agriculture was in Western Europe in 1945 in comparison with 1918. After the First World War

330. Milward, *The European Rescue*, 133.
331. Ibid., 204.
332. Ibid., 283.
333. Milward, *The European Rescue*, 283. See also Griffiths and Milward, *The European Agricultural Community, 1948–1954* (1986).

> [l]ow levels of world demand for foodstuffs and other primary products, low levels of investment in agriculture, high levels of protection for a low-productivity, low-income sector employing very large numbers of people at levels of marginal productivity close to zero, created [ . . . ] a set of social and economic problems which [ . . . ] had a strong influence on the politics of the 1930s.[334]

In the aftermath of the Second World War rising incomes led to an increase in the demand for food which called for a rapid and persistent increase in investment and productivity in the agricultural sector. Because the defeat of Germany and Japan was followed by the largest continuous industrialization boom in modern history, the relative weight of the agricultural sector in most economies rapidly declined as people moved out of the sector. But because demand for food expanded this was to increase the political power of farmers bringing agriculture into the postwar political consensus on which political stability depended. After the war governments adopted a whole series of measures designed to increase incomes in agriculture, but they did so in the context where the two acute problems of the interwar period, the low level of demand for primary products and the inability of political society to come to terms with economic change in the agricultural sector, had been cured by the war. It was the war which removed two serious obstacles from the way governments determined to raise per capita incomes by industrialization. The economic events of the war left agriculture in Europe, North America, and Asia in a position to contribute to the large increase in national product after 1945 in a way in which it could not have done before 1939. The Second World War thus undermined the position of those opposed to the modernization of the agricultural sector and accelerated the rationalization of units of land-holding. If governments in all developed economies continued to use the rhetoric of protecting the family farm as a way of life, it was, in Alan Milward's view, only to disguise the dramatic changes which were taking place in the sector worldwide. A combination of rapid industrialization and subsidized investment in agriculture in the context of rapidly increasing incomes was to transform agriculture into a profitable sector in which returns to capital and labor were increasing rapidly while the numbers employed in the sector shrank dramatically. The one thing which was certainly not protected was agriculture as a way of life with the family farm at its center.

The post-1945 world, in striking contrast to the pre-1939 world, was one of food shortage. The coincidence of high demand and low supply after the war naturally led to the persistence of the idea that some form of management of agricultural markets on the national and international levels was

334. Milward, 'The Second World War and Long-Term Change in World Agriculture' (1985), 5.

practical and desirable. By 1950 the first Western European plans for the international management of agricultural markets through a 'green pool' were being discussed at the highest levels, and there is a distinct connecting thread between intervention in the management of agriculture and food supply in the Second World War and the Common Agricultural Policy (CAP) of the EEC, whose tentacles were soon to extend to the control of food supply into Europe from other parts of the world.

If the objective of preserving the family farm and of farming as a way of life was judged by Alan Milward to be part of a myth cultivated by national governments and then repeated by the European Commission in defense of their common sectoral regulation another equally powerful myth, which he sought to expose, was that European integration was the result of a change in political thought. As a historian, he saw the need to establish 'in what way the political movements in favour of European unity had anything other than an insignificant impact on international political and economic agreements'. Unable to establish any direct impact of such groups on the creation of the ECSC he viewed such explanations as 'no more than observations of a minor albeit interesting phenomenon.'[335] But in recognition of the continuing hold on opinion which 'the idea of Europe' had and of the influence of those who subscribed to it, he returned to the question in a chapter provocatively entitled 'The Lives and Teachings of the European Saints'.[336] Here he argued that the 'great men' commonly acknowledged as the 'founding fathers of Europe' converted to the cause of European integration only when it was seen to be necessary to preserve the nation-state. Quoting Robert Schuman, '[o]ur European states are a historical reality; it would be psychologically impossible to make them disappear. Their diversity is in fact very fortunate and we do not want either to level them or to equalize them.'[337] Of the German Chancellor Konrad Adenauer, he said 'Adenauer was unswerving in his idea that western European integration must be the basis of the Federal Republic's security and that it was ultimately the only chance of German reunification.'[338] Jean Monnet, as he reminded readers, was the architect of French national economic planning and was initially opposed to the common market, seeing the atomic energy community (Euratom) as more important. Monnet was also, as Milward pointed out, the least democratic of the founding fathers, never having had to fight an election. It was due to Monnet's influence, Milward said, that the EEC Treaty of Rome paid little attention to democratic accountability.[339] The challenge which Alan Milward threw down to those who continued to believe that it was the 'idea of Europe' itself which had determined postwar

---

335. Milward, 'The Origins of the Treaty of Rome', 3.
336. Milward, *The European Rescue*, 318–344.
337. Ibid., 329.
338. Ibid., 198.
339. Ibid., 336.

integration was to explain how an abstract idea came to be translated into policy. 'Was the idea,' he questioned, 'just floating in the air around the élite true believers, a bottle from which in deadlock they could take a swig of Eurospirit?'[340] However, as Rosamond explains in his contribution to this volume, 'ideational' approaches have become increasingly influential in political science since the mid-1990s, with one of the key issues being the role played by ideas in explaining political outcomes.

It was clear from the early reviews of *The European Rescue of the Nation-State* that what critics on both the right and the left found hard to accept was Milward's focus on domestic politics in Europe as the mainsprings of integration rather than on the cold war and the support given by the United States to the unification of Europe. Anthony Hartley defended the conventional view in asserting that '[t]o ignore the political motives of the "founding fathers" and, above all, of the United States for backing European integration is to fail to understand European politics in the 1950s and perhaps also in the 1990s.'[341] Roger Morgan found little new in Alan Milward's argument about the primacy of the nation-state, suggesting that it was what many political scientists had been arguing since Stanley Hoffman had first suggested it in the mid-1960s.[342] Derek Urwin was unconvinced by the 'rescue thesis', but for different reasons. More would need to be said, he thought, about why other European countries, particularly those in Scandinavia, played such a minor role in European integration in the 1950s.[343] In Chapter 20 of this volume Johnny Laursen addresses this very question.

The longest and one of the most thoughtful reviews came from an expert in European Community law for whom Alan Milward's explanation of the origins of European integration made the current legal complexities and apparent contradictions of the European Union, and of its law, intelligible for the first time.[344] Most lawyers, as Ian Ward explained, had been disappointed by the failures of the Single European Act and the Maastricht Treaty to resolve the perceived constitutional inadequacies of the Treaty of Rome:

> The European Constitution [ . . . ] remains somewhat ill-defined and under-developed. It is clearly something more, at least in practice, than what is stated in the rhetoric of the Treaty framework. Yet, at the same

---

340. Milward addressed this challenge to Parsons, *A Certain Idea of Europe* (2003) in his collective review article 'The European Union as a Superstate' (2005), 101. See Appendix 2, Book Reviews, item no. 210, p. 548, this volume.
341. Hartley's review of *The European Rescue*, 20.
342. Morgan, 'European Integration and National Interests' (1994); Hoffman, 'Obstinate or Obsolete? The Fate of the Nation-State and the Case of Western Europe' (1966).
343. Urwin's review of *The European Rescue of the Nation-State* (1994), 112.
344. Ward, 'The European Constitution and the Nation State', review of *The European Rescue of the Nation-State* (1996).

> time, as the European Court has reined back from its earlier more aggressive integrational impulses, the constitutional vacuum appears all the greater. It remains ill-defined simply because there remains a residual political uncertainty as to how the new Union should be determined. This is not to mean that the individual Member States are uncertain. Everyone has their own opinions. The problem is that there is a corporate uncertainty. It is this problem, and more accurately the origins of the problem, which Alan Milward's book addresses.[345]

As far as Ward was concerned, Alan Milward had exposed as fiction the notion that the member-states had ever wanted a genuine European constitution, and it was the Community's ideological rhetoric which had fooled everyone. The one measure, he maintained, which 'could effect a genuinely free market and represent a corresponding economic and political diminution in national sovereignty, tax harmonization, has remained strikingly absent'.[346] The conclusion that in the mid-1990s he extracted from Alan Milward's work continues to be relevant today: 'There will be no further progress towards a European constitution unless it becomes clear that such a step is unavoidable to the interest of the nation-states.'[347]

Although Alan Milward was not the first to emphasize the resilience of the European nation-state, he was the first to argue that integration was a positive choice taken by EC member-states primarily, although not exclusively, for domestic social and economic reasons. It was a nonliberal solution to a number of problems facing the European nation-states which neither governments nor markets could solve on their own. It was the challenge of many of his arguments which captured the interest of a leading Marxist intellectual, Perry Anderson. Marx, as Alan Milward pointed out, had not predicted that integration would be a stage in the development of capitalism. 'When the European Community started in 1950–52 there was nothing in the dried tea-leaves of Marxist analysis that referred to it.'[348] Anderson's own conclusions were fundamentally different from those of Alan Milward. In opposition to Milward, Anderson argued that Nazi Germany had to be defeated militarily because it did not collapse economically, and it was this fact which explained why France opted for integration. As Anderson wrote,

> It was the memory of this incommensurable record during the war—of the scale of German military supremacy, and its consequences—that shaped European integration quite as much as the commensurate tasks of rebuilding nation-states on a more prosperous and democratic basis

345. Ibid., 165.
346. Ibid., 171.
347. Ibid., 174.
348. Milward, 'Approaching Reality' (1996), 56.

> after the war on which Milward concentrates. The country centrally concerned was inevitably France.[349]

While Alan Milward did not disagree with the importance of providing military security in the postwar world, he argued that it did not explain the new phenomenon of European integration. 'There were other diplomatic arrangements by which an effort could have been made to bind west Germany to western Europe', he wrote.[350] The creation of the North Atlantic Treaty Organization (NATO) may have been a precondition for the Schuman Plan but, in his view, the need to provide security against Germany did not entirely explain the decision to integrate the coal and steel sectors of the economies of the six signatory states of the Treaty of Paris. The lessons which Western European states had drawn from their defeat by Nazi Germany was that not only did they need to increase their levels of armaments to provide for the physical security of their populations but, even more importantly, they had to win the allegiance of their populations by providing for their economic security. If in order to provide military security economic security was undermined then military security would be without meaning. Controlling the coal and steel industries, including those of West Germany, through integration was a means of enhancing the economic security of Western Europe. Had Western Europe not enjoyed ten years of peace and prosperity by the mid-1950s, the Treaties of Rome would have been unimaginable. Whereas providing economic security required a degree of integration military security did not. The one attempt to combine military and economic security, that of the European Defense Community (EDC), ended in failure. Indeed, as Alan Milward reminded readers, to have integrated West Germany into a defense community was seen by many, particularly in France, as a threat to European security. But Milward's insistence that it was the popular demands for economic security which explained national governments' choice of integration was rejected by Anderson, for whom 'the federalist vision of a supranational Europe developed above all by Monnet and his circle, the small group of technocrats who conceived the original ECSC, and drafted much of the detail of the EEC' was a more convincing explanation.[351]

Alan Milward had a further difficulty in accepting the view of Anderson that at the center of the process of European integration was an agreement between France and West Germany based on military security, which incidentally was also the view of most British diplomatic historians. If this was so, why was the United Kingdom not a signatory to the Treaties of Rome in 1957? The United Kingdom, as he pointed out, had been 'closely involved with western Europe's reconstruction and security throughout the

349. P. Anderson, 'Under the Sign of the Interim' (1996), 13.
350. Milward, *The European Rescue*, xi
351. Anderson, 'Under the Sign of the Interim', 14

war and also from the moment it ended. To judge from the volume of documentation in the Foreign Office archives, no question was considered more important to Britain's future than that of Germany's future.'[352] But since, as he also explained, the United Kingdom had many of the same domestic political priorities as Western Europe, such as a commitment to full employment, the welfare state, and protection of agriculture, the question which he needed to answer was why the British state did not perceive the need to surrender a degree of sovereignty to ensure the implementation of these domestic policies as well as addressing the problem of Germany. Did his 'rescue thesis' not apply to Britain?

In a final chapter of *The European Rescue of the Nation-State* he suggested that the key to understanding why Britain did not need the supranational Community institutions was to be found in the policies pursued after 1950:

> Just as it is the Beyen Plan which more than any other single event illuminates the common foundations supporting European integration, it is through the example of British attempts to establish the free convertibility of sterling into American dollars on international exchanges between 1952 and 1955 that we can most sharply perceive the incompatibilities separating British ambitions from European interests and American hopes.[353]

As far as the British state was concerned, the Bretton Woods system, of which Britain was an architect, had been put to one side temporarily while the Marshall Plan was being implemented. After that, Britain's overriding interest was in reestablishing sterling as one of the two international currencies, even if that meant letting the exchange rate float in the early 1950s rather than participating in the soft currency area of the EPU. For Britain it was more important to try to earn dollars directly in the market of the United States rather than indirectly through exporting to Western Europe. But what Britain apparently failed to recognize was that, in the internal divisions within the U.S. administration, it was the view of the State Department prioritizing the need for European integration which had the support of the president and which better came to reflect the ambitions of the United States.[354] This meant that even though the U.S. Treasury and the Federal Reserve remained committed to one-world multilateralism, this had to take a back seat as long as the majority of European participants in the EPU needed special support to achieve their domestic policy objectives. Indeed, had the British government implemented its policy of restoring the convertibility of sterling when most other European currencies

352. Milward, *The European Rescue*, 346.
353. Ibid., 347.
354. Ibid., 348.

remained nonconvertible, it would have reduced Western European trade substantially. In these circumstances, the United States was never going to give its support to a unilateral decision by Britain to restore the convertibility of sterling. 'For all the Western European states any progress towards convertibility which might involve even a temporary loss of trade was to be rejected, and especially anything which jeopardised their common commercial arrangements.'[355] In retrospect, Milward concluded,

> the view of the US financial authorities looks mistaken. The Bretton Woods agreements, while they had devoted much effort to making an international system of trade and payments which was compatible with full employment policies, had taken no account of how the system of fixed exchange rates which they introduced could be maintained when so many other policies and policy instruments were going to be employed at will by national governments.[356]

He thought that the British government had made a policy error in assuming that the French government and industry would be fearful of competing with German exports within a European common market and would therefore never agree to sign the Treaties of Rome. 'The startling absence of genuine comparison with any other European country in the many memoranda and analyses of Britain's economic position gives the impression of a hermetically sealed system with so little outward vision that no understanding of European developments could be possible', he concluded.[357]

## BRITAIN'S PLACE IN THE WORLD: A HISTORICAL ENQUIRY INTO IMPORT CONTROLS, 1945–60 (1996)

In the second edition of *The European Rescue of the Nation-State,* published in 2000, Alan Milward was more understanding of the reasons behind British policy in the 1950s. This was because in 1993, shortly after the publication of the first edition of *The European Rescue*, he had accepted an invitation from the British Cabinet Office to write the Official History of the Accession of the United Kingdom to the European Community and its subsequent relations with the Community up to the mid-1980s. The work, commissioned in two volumes, was to be based on unrestricted access to British government records for the period in question. That an economic historian, and one who had been critical of some aspects of British policy, should have been chosen to write the official history was, as James Ellison recounts in Chapter 21 of this volume, deeply resented by British diplomatic

355. Ibid., 367.
356. Ibid., 350.
357. Ibid., 431.

historians, whereas Charles Maier considered it an inspired choice by the British government.

When he accepted the invitation to write the official history Alan Milward was already working with George Brennan on a topic which he felt had long been overlooked by historians and economists—namely the impact of quantitative import controls, more often referred to as import quotas, on the British economy and on British policy-making in the fifteen years after the end of the Second World War.[358] As the title of the book indicated this was to be much more than a technical study about an unfashionable topic, but was to address a central question and one of Alan Milward's long-term research interests, namely how trade should be regulated in the interests of the modern state. If tariffs had in the nineteenth century served as an instrument of state building in many countries, insofar as they provided the money for government expenditure, supported the objectives of foreign policy, occasionally protected and encouraged manufactures and trades that were considered essential to the state's welfare, and served the constitutional purpose of balancing and compromising the economic and political interests of large and influential social groups, it was Milward and Brennan's argument that many of these functions were performed by quotas in the twentieth century. Quantitative restrictions, in the form of import quotas or state-controlled foreign trade, became a new instrument to be used by modern states to achieve a number of economic, political, and social objectives.

One big disadvantage of quotas was that, unlike tariffs, they were not a source of revenue for the government but their one big advantage was seen to be that they could be imposed quickly in response to an economic crisis without having to endure lengthy parliamentary debates. Whereas it had taken almost twenty years before the Méline tariff, imposed on imported grain from North America, was passed by the French National Assembly, quotas on imports of food from central and eastern Europe were imposed within two years of the 1929 crisis.[359] Furthermore, at a time when prices were falling steeply, they proved to be a more effective form of protection than *ad valorem* tariffs. Their proliferation across Europe in the 1930s and 1940s coincided with the increasing refinement of government statistics, and along with a plethora of other controls over the economy, they became difficult to dismantle after the war. In fact, as Milward and Brennan showed, many countries based their postwar national reconstruction plans on the retention of quotas, thereby posing a direct challenge to the U.S. government's ambitions of creating a nondiscriminatory multilateral regime of trade and payments. Even though the United States insisted in 1947 that quotas should be permitted only in exceptional circumstances

358. Milward and Brennan, *Britain's Place in the World: A Historical Enquiry into Import Controls, 1945–60* (1996).
359. Ibid., 19.

when justified on grounds of national security, to protect domestic agriculture, or to correct a temporary crisis in the balance of payments, it was clear that the West European governments interpreted the exceptions more widely. In early 1950 Hugh Gaitskell, soon to become the British Chancellor of the Exchequer, insisted that import controls would be needed to ensure full employment and economic reconstruction.[360] Indeed in Britain, as they showed, quotas served a variety of purposes ranging from national defense, regional policy, and macroeconomic policy to straightforward protectionism. Because they did not have to be debated by parliament their specific purpose could be kept secret. But, in spite of their secret nature, Milward and Brennan found only one instance where private interests were able to influence government policy on quotas; that exception was the British car industry.[361] It was in the United States where tariffs retained their importance because, as they suggested, imported goods accounted for such a small part of domestic consumption. Since tariff levels had to be agreed by the U.S. Congress one problem which this posed for Western European governments was that in negotiating tariff reductions in order to boost their exports to the United States, any concessions made by the U.S. negotiators could be reversed if a two-thirds majority in the Congress demanded it.

Faced with the U.S. enthusiasm for the creation of a customs union in Western Europe which, in the opinion of the British government could only hurt the British economy, the British government looked for alternative ways to take a leadership role in integrating Europe which would not undermine its central objective of restoring a one-world trade and payments system: 'Only a worldwide, multilateral, commercial and payments framework offered the United Kingdom the chance to pursue a common commercial policy towards the Commonwealth, the USA and Europe, the three areas on which its central place in the world was thought to depend.'[362] The British government wanted to reduce trade barriers between Western European economies, but only as a step toward reducing them between Europe and the United States. Since the tariff that the British government most wanted to force down was that of the United States, it wanted to retain its existing tariff levels in Europe in order to be able to use them as a future bargaining counter in tariff negotiations with the United States. At that time British tariffs were among the highest in Western Europe, capped only by those of the two most protectionist states, France and Italy.[363] Since any tariff reductions, unless they formed part of a customs union, would have to be negotiated through GATT, it would not be possible for the United Kingdom to present them to the United States as a European initiative. The advantage of proposing that the liberalization of European trade should take the

360. Ibid., 27.
361. Ibid, 33–34
362. Ibid., 188.
363. Ibid., 45.

form of a widening of import quotas was that it would extend to all the countries in OEEC and would make it harder for them to reduce tariffs or remove them altogether in a customs union.[364] If a 'nondiscriminatory' world meant for the United States the end of the preferential arrangements of the Commonwealth and the sterling area, the British tried to prove that a first step toward that world was the gradual removal of quantitative restrictions on OEEC trade.

Initially, the strategy seemed to work as Britain intended. Whereas with the cushion of import quotas West European governments had agreed to a first round of tariff reductions within the new framework of GATT in 1947, there were to be no further reductions in tariffs within Western Europe or between it and the United States after Britain took the lead within the OEEC to organize the widening of import quotas. But the United Kingdom soon found itself in a very weak position, since any relaxation of import quotas on intra-European trade, in line with the OEEC-sponsored trade liberalization program and facilitated by the EPU's automatic credit facilities, almost invariably resulted in balance of payments difficulties and a new postponement of the ultimate goal of sterling convertibility. This was to change after 1957 when, strengthened by the boom in intra-European trade, six European governments agreed to reduce tariffs and widen quotas within the regional arrangement of the EEC and to contemplate for the first time weakening their quota protection against imports from North America, 'although their demands for reductions in American tariffs were incessant all through the decade.'[365] Trade liberalization, Milward and Brennan stressed, followed rather than caused the great expansion in European trade which had taken place in the 1950s. Even when quotas became less important in trade between developed countries, they reappeared as a way of protecting indigenous manufacturing industry against imports from developing countries. The EEC Treaty of Rome, as they pointed out, was deliberately vague in this respect. Britain was left with little option but to form the European Free Trade Association (EFTA) which gave it little bargaining power with Washington. By contrast, the six EEC member-states were able to control tariff bargaining with the United States through the new European Commission, as Lucia Coppolaro shows in Chapter 22 of this volume.

In comparison with all of Milward's previous books, apart from *The Economic Effects of the Two World Wars on Britain*, the reviews of *Britain's Place in the World* were few in number. As so often, reviewers found the detailed complexity of the arguments quite a challenge. This time it was Andrew Gamble, a professor of political science, who was most stimulated by the arguments of the book. In his view the essential question which

364. Ibid., 42.
365. Ibid., 28.

it raised was whether British governments were ever correct to believe that they could protect British interests outside a regional arrangement in Europe. As Gamble put it,

> [i]f Milward and Brennan are right the failure of the British economy to modernise successfully in the 1960s and 1970s and to perform as well as the other European economies was directly related to the policy mistake of backing liberalisation in the 1950s and shunning the protection which would have been provided inside the EEC.[366]

Alan Milward, anticipating perhaps the conclusions which he was to reach in his official history, explained in his reply to Gamble that Brennan and he had deliberately avoided specifying such an argument since 'it seemed to us that many other things were at stake, some of them still waiting for good historical analysis.'[367] The crux of the problem for Britain, as he saw it, was that the period of 1948 to 1956 represented a time, perhaps, he thought, the last time, that Britain had a coherent framework for its foreign policy and foreign economic policy. That framework was the one-world system, a goal which Britain would find it impossible to achieve. The best hope for Britain was that the alternative of the EEC would prove to be equally impossible to achieve.

## THE UNITED KINGDOM AND THE EUROPEAN COMMUNITY: THE RISE AND FALL OF A NATIONAL STRATEGY (2002)

In agreeing to write the Official History of Britain's relations with the European Community, Alan Milward looked forward to explaining why, despite being a victor in the Second World War, Britain ended up in a much weaker position than other Western European countries.[368] His conclusion to the first edition of *The European Rescue of the Nation-State* was that Britain had made a mistake in withdrawing from the negotiations which led to the Treaties of Rome for which it was to suffer both economically and politically.[369] His exasperation with the policy-makers and the universities which had produced them was palpable. Determined to explore every nook and cranny of the British state which might help to explain Britain's policy toward Europe, he looked not only at the by-then familiar records of the Foreign Office, Cabinet, and Treasury but also at those of the ministries

366. Gamble's review of *Britain's Place in the World*.
367. Milward's reply to Gamble's review, available at: http://www.history.ac.uk/reviews/review/38/response (last accessed on 31 May 2011).
368. Milward, *The United Kingdom and the European Community, vol. 1, The Rise and Fall of a National Strategy, 1945–1963* (2002).
369. Milward, *The European Rescue*, 433.

of Transport, Fuel and Power, the Commonwealth Relations Office, the Northern Ireland Public Record Office, the Dominions Office, and the Free Trade Office, which had not been much disturbed by diplomatic historians. He also had privileged access to the notes written in shorthand by the Cabinet Secretary which identified who said what in Cabinet discussions.

The tone throughout the five hundred pages of volume 1 of the Official History was carefully measured and impartial. He made it clear at the very beginning that he did not accept the view of many historians, that it was the British government's deluded ambitions to remain a global power, when it no longer had the resources to underpin such ambitions, which explained why it had not participated in the moves to integrate Western Europe in the 1950s. Although he had argued in the first edition of *The European Rescue* that the British government had made a mistake, in the revised second edition he concluded that '[l]ooking at the evidence for the 1950s it is difficult to see how it could have been otherwise.'[370] The argument, which he finally reached after many years of research, was that the state in postwar Britain did have a realistic national strategy which it pursued consistently, but it was one which did not work. As he explained,

> the UK emerged from the war with many great but short term advantages. Adjusting to the post-war world meant cashing in those advantages while they were still there in return for a stable international framework which would guarantee the two main objectives of post-war governments, military security and domestic prosperity. By and large that was the strategy pursued, with remarkably little difference by the two great political parties when they were in office[.][371]

He set out to explain why that national strategy had not worked. This involved understanding how policy and economies changed in Western Europe, the United States, across the British Empire, the Commonwealth, and beyond in the years after 1945. In terms of its global reach it was a sequel to his earlier work on the Second World War, but in terms of the requirements of writing an official history, it was a very different type of history. While he had unrestricted access to British government archives, he did not have similar access to the archives of those countries whose actions affected British policy.

What Milward was required to do was document and explain the evolution of Britain's relations with the European Community and their prehistory. That he chose to do so within the framework of a national strategy was no surprise. His unique approach to writing the history of twentieth-century Europe was to view the role played by the state in terms of its

370. Ibid. (2nd ed., 2000), 424.
371. Milward, *The Rise and Fall*, 2.

seeking to fulfill the twin objectives of military security and domestic prosperity. He used the term 'national strategy' as he had used that of 'strategic synthesis' to analyze the interplay of domestic and foreign policy: it was how he viewed the modern state's attempt to secure its place in the world. Where better to view British policy toward the European Community than from the Chair in the History of European Integration at the EUI which he had helped to found and to which he returned in 1996?

The advantages which he demonstrated that the United Kingdom enjoyed at the war's end included

> its ability to build its own nuclear weapons with their independent delivery system; its tariff preferences on extra-European Commonwealth markets; the former importance, which it hoped to restore, of London as an international capital market; its strategic usefulness to the USA as an offshore European naval- and air-base more secure against invasion than anywhere on the continental mainland; its large colonial empire, which gave it political influence over extensive areas of Africa and the Caribbean; its large armed forces, which were seen from the Pentagon as the only large [ . . . ] force on which the USA could rely for help as an ally.[372]

British strategy, Alan Milward insisted, was not based on a will to exercise worldwide power but rather as 'a medium-sized materialist democracy' to provide both military and economic security for its population.[373] Military security was seen to depend on a continuation of the wartime alliance with the United States, strengthened by NATO and Britain's own atomic weapons, while economic security was seen to depend, among other things, on a return to an older world, the world of the pre-1914 gold standard when Western Europe had provided the largest market for British exports. The recourse to many forms of trade protection in both Western Europe and the United States as a way out of the Great Depression of 1929–1932 had led to a redirection of British exports to the markets of the Empire and the Commonwealth where they enjoyed preferential tariffs. These trade flows had persisted during the Second World War, with the result that in the post-war period a much higher proportion of British exports went to Australia, Canada, and New Zealand than to Western Europe or the United States. In 1951, for example, Australia was the largest market for British exports taking 12% of its overall total in comparison with 5.1% of exports going to the United States and 1.9% to the Federal Republic of Germany.[374] The challenge facing British policy-makers was to find a way of using imperial preferences to force down tariffs in Western Europe and the United States.

372. Ibid., 3.
373. Ibid., 4.
374. Ibid., 188.

Indeed, as he stressed, 'it is as a part of that adjustment to the post-war world at which national strategy aimed that relations between Britain and the European Community should be understood, rather than in the framework of the simplistic question of whether the United Kingdom should have joined the European Communities or not.'[375]

It was the Foreign Office official, Orme Sargent, who, in Milward's view, clearly expressed Britain's position and objectives in July 1945: 'The United Kingdom could make itself treated as an equal in the post-war world by the two emergent superpowers if and only if it also retained the leadership not only of the Commonwealth but of western Europe.' As Milward put it '[t]o be a leading influence in each of those areas—Washington, the Commonwealth, and western Europe—depended on retaining a leading influence in the other two.'[376] The essence of the strategy pursued by the United Kingdom until it finally had to be abandoned in 1962 was to steer some sort of European bloc along with the Commonwealth into a trading world with the United States in a way that would guarantee military and economic security at home. It was 'the one-world policy', in the jargon of British officials. The country whose policy Britain most needed to influence was the United States. Although the Americans had made a commitment in the agreement reached at Bretton Woods in 1944 to the restoration of a liberal world order based on free trade and currencies freely convertible into gold, dollars, and sterling at a fixed rate of exchange, their failure to ratify the ITO and to make a serious commitment to reduce their tariffs in order to enable Britain and the rest of the world to earn dollars by exporting to the United States was seriously undermining confidence in Britain that the United States was indeed committed to the multilateral principles agreed in 1944.

British confidence in the credibility of that commitment had already been shaken by the insistence of the U.S. Treasury that in return for a postwar dollar loan Britain should remove all capital controls and restore the convertibility of sterling in August 1947 without regard to whether the recovery of the British economy had been completed or not. The offer of Marshall Aid, which Milward had already argued in *The Reconstruction of Western Europe* was an instrument of the cold war motivated by the political necessity of ensuring that the western zones of Germany and Western Europe would remain in the United States' sphere of influence, was not a step in the direction of Bretton Woods, nor was it intended to be. But if its motivation was political, Marshall Aid in itself did not commit the United States to the defense of Western Europe. Indeed, in his view, it was not until December 1950, almost two years after the agreement to form NATO, when General Dwight Eisenhower was appointed Supreme Allied Commander in Europe,

375. Ibid., 6.
376. Ibid., 16 (both quotations).

that the U.S. commitment to defend Western Europe took on any operational meaning. Until then, as Alan Milward wryly remarked, 'the only true impediment which the North Atlantic Treaty raised against an attack by the Soviets was the number of committees in their way.'[377]

It was one thing to define the grand strategic objectives, as Sargent had done, but quite another, as Milward showed, to work out what the practical international policies should be to realize those objectives. Obtaining consent to them in Washington was hard, but '[f]itting France, with its own national ambitions, into this framework was [ . . . ] impossible.'[378] The British government was trying to use the political and economic weight, which its temporary leadership over the Empire and the Commonwealth gave it, to end the protectionism of both the United States and Western Europe, in a way which did not undermine its own domestic economic interests, and at the same time persuade the United States to make a long-term commitment to defending Britain and its interests worldwide. It took seventeen years to recognize that such a national strategy had failed. By 1962 it was clear that the EEC had become a preferential trade bloc which, particularly through the CAP, would discriminate against the food exports of the most important countries in the Commonwealth and against the poorest countries in the world.

Could Britain have played its hand better when faced with a series of initiatives from the United States and France which undermined its long-term objective of restoring a multilateral world order based on domestic full employment? Sparing no detail and refusing to gloss over the full complexities of the issues, Milward documented the internal debates within the British government which followed every shift in tactics by the United States and France over the period of 1945 to 1963, as they too sought to implement their national strategies. Critical turning points, with their possible implications for British strategy, such as the announcements of the Marshall Plan in June 1947, the Schuman Plan in May 1950, the Pleven Plan for a European army in October 1950, the creation of the organizational structure of NATO in December 1950, and the plans to create Euratom and the EEC, which resulted in the Treaties of Rome in March 1957, were all assessed. He made few references to the secondary literature except where they related to key issues of political debate in the United Kingdom. He also examined critical issues which politicians and historians should have debated, such as that of national sovereignty, but did not. Internal policy debates and international negotiations were set in the context of a changing international economy, in which levels of production, investment, and trade affected and were affected in turn by those debates.

377. Ibid., 34.
378. Ibid., 16.

Starting in 1945, he underlined how Britain was the only partner of similar weight to the United States on the Security Council of the United Nations, with a currency used in trade across the world and which shared the U.S. strategy of reconstructing an international economic order along the lines of the Bretton Woods agreement. This was to mean that Britain would have to dismantle its own system of preferential tariffs on trade with its Empire and Commonwealth which had been introduced in response to the Great Depression and was, as a condition of a dollar loan negotiated with the United States in 1945, to make sterling freely convertible into gold and dollars in August 1947. As Milward showed, '[u]ntil summer 1947 British-American relations were dominated, not by the question of European reconstruction, but by that of the reconstruction of an international economic order.'[379] On the other hand France was seen to be the only partner in Europe capable of assisting in the defense of Britain once the United States had withdrawn its troops from the continent as soon as the occupation of Germany had come to an end:

> At the best, common action with France in reconstructing Europe might offer alternative strategic possibilities to succumbing to American pressures which might preclude any choice of an international commercial and economic framework other than one dictated by the USA's own national strategy, as had happened with the USA's absolute insistence, against all evidence that it would not succeed, on the over-hasty move to sterling-dollar convertibility.[380]

What Britain needed to do in order to attain its national strategic goals was use its leadership of the Commonwealth in order to strengthen its bargaining position with the United States and ensure that the latter would make a greater commitment to restoring an international order, most notably by reducing its own tariffs, while at the same time exploiting its leadership of Western Europe in order to ensure that the United States would make a more effective commitment to the security of Britain than was possible through the United Nations. This was how Milward explained one question which had long puzzled historians, namely how to interpret Foreign Secretary Ernest Bevin's call in January 1947 for a study into the implications for the United Kingdom of forming a customs union with France, or with the French Union, or with Western Europe. Did this represent a recognition that Britain's future might lie in a closer association with Western Europe rather than with the United States? Milward was clear that Bevin's intention was to bind Western Europe more closely to the United Kingdom 'as

379. Ibid., 11.
380. Ibid., 13.

part of an Anglo-American duumvirate'.[381] It was thus motivated primarily by foreign policy considerations:

> From mid-1946 onwards, with de Gaulle gone from office and centre-left coalitions in power in Paris and as yet with little to indicate that US policy would change from the course Roosevelt had set, Foreign Office eyes turned increasingly towards the prospects of Franco-British association as the core of security and stabilisation in Europe, although economic ministries showed little enthusiasm for what they thought might prove a burden.[382]

Many in the British economic ministries feared that a possible customs union would be 'a road to nowhere, starting with discrimination against the USA, perhaps involving discrimination against the Commonwealth and in favour of Europe, and ending with loss of control over instruments of domestic policy.'[383]

This remained their position even when it became the policy of the United States to promote the formation of a customs union in Western Europe backed with Marshall Aid. A wiser course of action, which was agreed upon after two years of further deliberation, was seen to be the removal of quantitative restrictions on trade in OEEC while maintaining tariffs as a future bargaining counter with the United States. The proposal to liberalize intra-European trade by widening quotas, to which Milward had devoted an entire book, was 'intended to be the limit of the United Kingdom's commitment to the leadership of western Europe. It was not an act of cooperation with France but more an attempt to prevent any French leadership of western Europe by exposing the protectionism of the French state.'[384] As he showed, it remained the position of the United Kingdom that the support of the United States was vital for the security of Britain, the Commonwealth, and Western Europe. In October 1949, as a discussion in Cabinet confirmed, the Commonwealth was 'not a strategic unit', and 'it must be clear to other Commonwealth members that their defence cannot be assured without United States support'.[385] The same was to hold true for Western Europe:

> the fact remains that the military and economic situation of the Western European nations is now such that there can be no immediate prospect of welding them into a prosperous and secure entity without American

---

381. Ibid., 21.
382. Ibid., 17.
383. Ibid., 24.
384. Ibid., 40.
385. Ibid., 41, quoting from CAB 128/16 [CM (49), 62nd meeting], Conclusions, 27 October 1949.

> help; and even with American help it is uncertain whether this can be achieved for some time to come.[386]

Britain's military security could only be guaranteed by the United States. For Britain itself, the installation of U.S. bases in the United Kingdom for the U.S. Strategic Air Command nuclear bomber 'introduced a brutal demarcation between the United Kingdom's national security and that of its continental neighbors. One objective of national strategy, the physical security of the national territory, had been attained.'[387]

The announcement of the Schuman Plan, which in retrospect has been seen to have changed the course of European history, did not greatly alter the way in which the pursuit of British national strategy was perceived. It was not, Milward insisted, a Machiavellian plot to exclude Britain, as some politicians and historians were to argue. Nor were either Schuman or Monnet third-force neutralists. With the nationalized coal industry opposed to it and the steel industry broadly in favor, the British government's interest was in one way or another to find a way of living with it. One thing seemed certain, a future European supranational organization would be preferable to the International Authority for the Ruhr, which was so opposed by the Federal Republic of Germany. British ministers, he revealed, were not opposed to the principle of giving up some power over the coal and steel industries to an international body if it would benefit the British economy, but they were not in favor of doing so for a foreign policy which did not fit into Britain's national strategy.[388] Of course that strategy could be changed but, as he showed, the argument of the Foreign Office at the time was that for Britain joining what was to become the ECSC 'would reduce its independence from, and thus its status and influence with, the USA, while at the same time weakening its links with the Commonwealth and thus even further reducing its influence over the USA.'[389] The speedy decision which the government was forced to make by the French on 2 June 1950 was not the 'fatefully wrong step in Europe for which it was to suffer politically and economically for twenty years.'[390] But, as he made clear, to have accepted Schuman's offer 'would have meant a commitment of political support over the long run to a reconstruction of the pattern of political power in Europe in which the United Kingdom, unless its strategy changed, could not share.'[391] There was no compelling need to make such an important

386. Ibid., 42, quoting from CAB 129/37 [CM (49) 208th meeting], 'European Policy', memorandum by Bevin, 18 October 1949.
387. Ibid., 35.
388. Ibid., 73.
389. Ibid., 75.
390. Ibid., 61.
391. Ibid., 62.

decision in 1950 and, moreover, it would not have meant that Britain would necessarily have signed the Treaties of Rome in 1957.

Instead of joining the ECSC the British government was eventually to sign a Treaty of Association with it in September 1955. That treaty, as Milward showed, produced only two results: 'a UK/ECSC agreement on iron and steel tariffs which did not come until November 1957 and a 1959 agreement to widen German coal import quotas in favour of the United Kingdom.'[392] The point of devoting over forty pages to an analysis of the steps leading to such an inconsequential treaty of association was to demonstrate how poor a model it provided for any future relationship between Britain and the EEC. Nonetheless, it was a model which was proposed (but never successfully implemented) for the plans for an EDC, a European Agricultural Community, and a European Political Community (EPC) which were debated by the six ECSC member-states in the period 1950–1954. The general issue which all such proposals was seen to pose for Britain was whether it would be possible to form some sort of association with whatever organization materialized, without being part of its political machinery. Harold Macmillan, who later as Prime Minister was to take the decision to apply for British accession to the EEC in 1961, was, as Minister for Housing in 1952, certain of what the British position should be: 'Britain's ties with the Commonwealth and with the United States make it impossible for her to join a [European] Federation. She could, however, become a full member of a Confederation, organised on Commonwealth lines.'[393] He opposed the plan of Anthony Eden, the Prime Minister, which was nonetheless accepted by Cabinet in March 1952, which was to associate the United Kingdom with the emerging supranational institutions in Europe of the ECSC, the EDC, and the emerging EPC by placing them all under the Constitutional Assembly of the intergovernmental Council of Europe, of which Britain was an enthusiastic member.[394]

The collapse of the EDC in the summer of 1954, and with it the EPC and the Dutch plan for a customs union, the Beyen plan, left Britain's program for liberalizing trade in Europe by widening import quotas intact. By 1955, as Milward showed,

> quotas on intra-European foreign trade became more liberal than at any time since 1934, and even as eyes in the Treasury and the Bank [of England] focused on 1955 as the year for the reintroduction of sterling-dollar convertibility and a leap to the one world system, the customs union of the Six, regional, regulated and Eurocentric, emerged

---

392. Ibid., 168.
393. Ibid., 108, quoting from 'European Integration', memorandum by Macmillan, 16 January 1952.
394. Ibid., 110–111.

> unscathed from the débris of the European Political Community into which Beyen had inserted it.[395]

How should Britain have responded to the challenge posed by the continental common market, Milward asked. Although it was a question which would divide opinion in Britain for many years, and on which consensus still proves elusive, at the time that the decision to withdraw from the negotiations which were to lead to the Treaties of Rome was taken, it was not even debated in Parliament and scarcely discussed in Cabinet or noticed in the press. Clearly the advice from the Foreign Office that France would not sign up to a common market with Germany proved to be wrong. On the other hand, in providing some details of the secret offer made to the British government by the French Prime Minister, Guy Mollet, in September 1956, on the eve of the Suez invasion, that France and Britain should form an economic and payments union with the sterling and franc areas to keep France out of the common market with West Germany, the great difficulty facing the Foreign Office advisers was made more understandable. Yet Milward remained critical: 'It was the business of diplomats to make accurate forecasts.' Because British policy toward the common market was based on the false premise that the EEC, like the EDC and EPC, would not be agreed to by the French government '[t]here seems good reason to say [ . . . ] that the existing policy was mistaken, irrespective of the question whether Britain should have been pursuing membership in a European customs union.'[396] Unlike most historians, who argue that it was the different foreign policy reactions of both the French and the British governments to the defeat of the Suez invasion which explained their different response to the common market, Alan Milward showed that, even had their Middle Eastern policy been successful, the British government did not see it as being in its interest to form a protectionist economic bloc with France and the payments area using the French franc. Suez was irrelevant.

In dissecting the reasons for the failure of policy in the mid-1950s he pointed to the way that decisions were made within the British state. As an example, he referred to the divisions within the British Treasury which meant that currency convertibility and the commercial policies linked to it were the responsibility of the Overseas Finance Division. Currency came first in that division, and commercial policy was only the consequence of decisions made about convertibility.[397] But the dilemmas faced by those responsible for making commercial policy, even had they been the top priority of the Treasury, were stark: 'The United Kingdom did not have such an obvious commercial interest in joining a European customs union, although it faced obvious danger in being excluded from it if it came into

395. Ibid., 125.
396. Ibid., 181 (both quotations).
397. Ibid., 182.

existence.'[398] In the mid-1950s the three richest Commonwealth countries, Australia, New Zealand, and Canada, with their comparatively small populations, took nearly 20 percent of all British exports, whereas Europe of the Six took just over 11 percent.[399] With the countries of the Commonwealth opposed to Britain's participation in a European customs union Britain had to continue to try to find a means of leading both Western Europe and the Commonwealth toward a world of nondiscriminatory trade. There was, as Milward clearly documented, no way left of associating with a European customs union which would be acceptable to the Six, the Commonwealth, and the United States. Neither a Free Trade Area between the rest of OEEC and the EEC nor a free trade area independent of the EEC (EFTA) solved the dilemma. Consequently, on 21 July 1961 the decision was taken to apply for membership in the EEC, since the government saw it as the only way left to open negotiations and persuade the EEC to recognize the claims of the Commonwealth.[400]

'It was not the potential loss of parliamentary sovereignty and independence of national policy, but rather the effort to preserve the United Kingdom's political and economic links with the Commonwealth, and through those links its continuing influence in the world', which Milward was to show, dominated most of the negotiations for accession.[401] At a meeting in the Prime Minister's country house, Chequers, in June 1961, ministers insisted that exports from the three most developed Commonwealth countries should not suffer as a result of Britain joining the EEC. In return for losing their preferential access to the British market they were to be assured of 'comparable outlets' in the markets of the EEC. Over the period of 1958 to 1961, for instance, between 70 and 75 percent of New Zealand's food exports went to Britain. But at the same time Britain was not to give up its preferential access to the markets of the Commonwealth. They were to be reserved as a bargaining counter for something more important than access to the Community, to be exploited when the United States returned to active tariff bargaining in GATT, as it was to do after the Congressional passage of the U.S. Trade Expansion Act in 1962 which authorized the White House to conduct mutual tariff negotiations and eventually led to the Kennedy Round of GATT in 1964–1967.[402]

The nature of the preferences was, as he showed, as varied as the economies in the British Commonwealth. On the Australian market, which next to that of the United States was the most important one for British exports, the preferences given to the car industry enabled British cars to dominate the Australian market. Canada gave preferences only to those goods which

398. Ibid., 178.
399. Ibid., 188.
400. Ibid., 351.
401. Ibid., 352.
402. Ibid., 352–356.

it did not produce itself. Pakistan and Nigeria offered Britain no preferences at all.

> Beset by the condition that they must try to maintain the agricultural exports of Australia, Canada and New Zealand even with Britain inside the Common Agricultural Policy, and under strong pressure to safeguard the European market for Canadian manufactured products and raw materials, they faced a negotiating task with few, if any, chances of success. On to that was superimposed the problem of persuading the Six to commit themselves to a trading policy which would help in the economic development of the world's largest and one of its poorest democracies. To that was added the obligation to provide also for the economic development of newly independent ambitious and quarrelsome African states the more important of which already regarded the Treaty of Rome's arrangements for francophone Africa as mere window-dressing for French colonialism and two of which, South Africa and Southern Rhodesia (now Zimbabwe), were governed by white minorities and were in open political conflict with other Commonwealth states. And behind all those great territories with their unforeseeable futures came a large flotilla of colonial mini-territories, scattered in poverty across the world and four richer ones, three of them in Europe, Cyprus (scene of a bitter ethnic conflict and a guerrilla war against British occupation), Gibraltar (claimed in its entirety by another west European country) and Malta. There was also a Chinese city, Hong Kong, whose manufactured exports were among the most rapidly expanding in the world and which had already aroused western Europe and the USA to impose non-tariff barriers against them.[403]

It was to be a difficult task to negotiate on behalf of such a collection of economies, particularly since some of the exports for which the British were to find 'comparable outlets' in the EEC were for the most part directly competitive with European agriculture. Edward Heath, the conservative minister delegated to lead the negotiations, set out to achieve a general solution for all Commonwealth trade as a way of preventing individual countries from trying to negotiate on their own behalf:

> While for Britain the Commonwealth and empire had to be considered as an entity, to the Six they were only a loose bundle of third countries, some butter exporters, some grain exporters, some meat exporters, and so on. Moreover, the three that were obviously in question were rich. While governments of the EEC member-states no doubt saw advantages to the West in retaining the Commonwealth as a political

403. Ibid., 369–370.

> association, they did not believe that to be any particular responsibility of the Treaty of Rome.[404]

Moreover they made it clear that they were not going to discuss what if any preferences they would give to agricultural exports from Australia, New Zealand, and Canada until they had reached agreement on the terms of their own agricultural protection. Only once agreement on the principles of the CAP had been hammered out, in December 1961–January 1962, could discussions begin on the price and the terms on which the EEC would accept imports from the three Commonwealth countries. By early August 1962 when it appeared as if some agreement might be within reach with the other five EEC member-states, the French sprang a trap which made it obvious to the British that de Gaulle, who had returned to power in France in May 1958 as a consequence of the Algerian crisis and become president of the Fifth Republic in December 1958, would never accept the British terms. It was clear that they had come to the end of the road with their national strategy of creating a one-world system.[405] It would not be possible to reach an arrangement between the EEC and the Commonwealth acceptable to both. It would not be possible to use British membership in the EEC and the Commonwealth to strengthen its bargaining position with the United States in the forthcoming round of tariff bargaining in GATT. Five months later de Gaulle brought the negotiations to an abrupt end.

The question which the British government raised at the time and which historians have subsequently debated at some length was why exactly de Gaulle had exercised his veto. What had gone wrong? Did de Gaulle oppose the British application because of the economic terms demanded by the British government, particularly those relating to imperial preferences? The conclusions reached by the team led by Christopher Audland, who carried out the postmortem analysis for the British government, was that de Gaulle's veto had nothing to do with the economic issues. No economic concessions offered by the British negotiators would have altered the outcome, since de Gaulle opposed British membership for political reasons. The reason why he allowed the negotiations to continue for so long were entirely due to his need to consolidate his position domestically by settling the future of Algeria, which he did by putting the question of its independence to a referendum in France and then in Algeria, and then securing his own reelection. Alan Milward, while acknowledging the limitations of an official history which was about Britain's relations with Europe based only on British government archives, did not accept the conclusions of the Audland report. But nor did he accept the alternative explanation, more popular with historians and which accorded more closely with the timing

404. Ibid., 379–380.
405. Ibid., 390–391.

of the veto. This was that de Gaulle was reacting to the announcement of the nuclear deal reached between Britain and the United States in Nassau in December 1962 and communicated to France one week before he announced his veto. Not only was the U.S. government agreeing to supply Britain with Polaris nuclear missiles, but it was also taking its proposals for creating a multilateral nuclear force to the North Atlantic Council without discussing it with de Gaulle beforehand. Notwithstanding the recognized hostility between de Gaulle and the United States, which was to lead to France's withdrawal from the military command structure of NATO in 1966, that the close military ties between Britain and the United States were the reason for de Gaulle's veto of the British application to join the EEC, thereby ignoring three years of deadlock between Britain and France in economic negotiations, seemed to Alan Milward to be 'perverse'.[406] Rather, in his view,

> [t]he essential point of difference between Britain and the Six remained that which the French had relied on to keep their treaty partners on their side when they broke off the free trade area negotiations. France and its partners had conceived of the EEC as a European preference area. It was not possible for them to amalgamate that conception with a Commonwealth preference area. Too large a part of Commonwealth exports to the UK competed with the Community's intended market for its own agriculture.[407]

The decision of the Six to form a preferential trade bloc in Western Europe marked their clear rejection of Britain's one-world policy.

> With the Treaty establishing a common market between the Six, the fundamentals of the United Kingdom's post-war strategy were directly repudiated by its European neighbours. Through its economic objectives and its longer-run political purpose a European common market had to be an instrument of regional trade discrimination; the Six rejected incorporation into the one-world strategy.[408]

It was disappointing for Alan Milward that no one in the rest of Europe reviewed his major reassessment of Britain's relations with Western Europe. It was confirmation of the parochialism of the EEC which he had criticized and which Barry Supple picked out in his review.[409] Quoting Alan Milward:

---

406. Ibid., 472.
407. Ibid., 358.
408. Ibid., 177–178.
409. Supple's review of *The Rise and Fall of a National Strategy*.

> The United Kingdom's application arrived still wrapped and garlanded in Britain's long international mercantile and imperial history, the history that had made it briefly a world power. Before it could succeed, Britain would have to become as parochial as the European Community, without particular intimacy with the Commonwealth, with no significant colonies, with only the last dying vestiges of a Sterling Area. The pity is that the awareness of and sensibility to the wider world which the United Kingdom brought into the negotiation did not rub off onto the European Community.[410]

In Britain the only aspect of the argument which left some reviewers unconvinced, because it was not backed up by documentary evidence, was his interpretation of European policies and particularly those of France.[411] However until such time as the French open all their archives for the postwar period the debate about French policy will continue. Sadly for everyone, Alan Milward did not live to complete the second volume of the official history.[412]

## POLITICS AND ECONOMICS IN THE HISTORY OF THE EUROPEAN UNION (2005)

Alan Milward's work as Official Historian and his research on the United Kingdom's relations with the Community was pursued in conjunction with two other projects which he carried on at the EUI after his reappointment there, in 1996, to the chair of the History of European Integration. One was an interdisciplinary research project to study allegiance to nation and 'supranation' in Western Europe; the other was a study of each successive expansion of the European Communities/European Union. The first project, which explored the political programs—welfare, high employment, social security, agricultural protection—by which postwar European states reestablished themselves, led him to propose an ambitious Europe-wide research program which he announced in 1995 in the inaugural article of the *Journal of European Integration History,* a journal edited by the European Union Liaison Committee of Historians.[413] The cool reception of historians and political scientists to Alan Milward's proposal is explained by Mike Newman in Chapter 23 of this volume. Because it was launched at a time when popular support for the European Union was in decline the concept of allegiance was not seen by many scholars as a useful one

410. Milward, *The Rise and Fall of a National Strategy*, 420.
411. N.P. Ludlow's review of *The Rise and Fall of a National Strategy.*
412. The second volume of *The United Kingdom and the European Community* is being written by Sir Stephen Wall.
413. Milward, 'Allegiance: The Past and the Future' (1995).

for understanding the process of integration or for questioning whether it would be reversed in the future.

The British government's decision to apply for membership in the EEC had implications not only for the Commonwealth but also for those non-member neighboring states which relied on Britain for a significant amount of their foreign trade and which were partners of Britain in the recently formed EFTA. Were the British application to be successful, their exports of manufactured goods, instead of having duty-free access to the British market, would face the hurdle of the common external tariff of the EEC. Although the Republic of Ireland was not a member of EFTA it nonetheless depended almost entirely on Britain for its foreign trade. The Irish government, along with the governments of Denmark and Norway, therefore decided to apply for membership in the EEC at the same time as Britain and linked their applications to the outcome of the British application. Thus in little over four years after the Six had signed the Treaty of Rome, four neighboring states had applied for accession to the EEC. They were to be followed by many more. When the British application was finally successful so too were the applications of the other three, although Norway, uniquely, was to turn down the EEC's offer of membership in a national referendum. In less than fifty years the EEC was to expand itself from six to twenty-five members. Why, Alan Milward asked, did countries want to join the EEC? He used an invitation from the University of Graz to give the annual Joseph Schumpeter lectures as an opportunity to consider the underlying dynamics of European integration and of this expansion.[414] His interest was in analyzing the relationship between the European Community and the wider international economy. As a first step, in his Graz lectures, he focused not only on the impact which the EEC had on its neighbors in Europe but also on its dependents in Africa. As he emphasized, since the first expansion of the European Community in 1973 included not only three European states but also many British dependencies throughout the world, it marked the beginning of the internationalization of the Community: 'The European Community had entered the world, as well as the United Kingdom entering the Community.'[415]

Social scientists held fundamentally different views about what motivated countries to seek association with or membership in the EEC. At one extreme were those who argued that the motivation was essentially economic, based on reaping the benefits which membership in a rapidly expanding high-income market would bring. At the other were those who stressed the foreign-policy benefits of belonging to a united Europe in a world dominated by superpowers. Taking as his starting point Jacob Viner's pioneering study of customs unions which measured the net welfare

---

414. Milward, *Politics and Economics in the History of the European Union* (2005).
415. Ibid., 102.

effect of their formation in terms of whether they led to trade creation or trade diversion, Alan Milward questioned the very idea of trade creation. 'The concept of the outside market as uninfluenced by, even independent from, the common market, is [ . . . ] historically dubious', he asserted. As an example he demonstrated that '[i]n the first twenty years of the common market, at the least, the growing share of exports by other member-states to Germany was partly dependent for its dimensions on Germany's exports to non-member states.'[416] He felt that a more useful question to consider was why it was that 'regional' trade institutions, of which the EEC was but one example in the postwar world, had become more effective instruments for liberalizing trade than the international institutions initially conceived by the United States.[417]

The EEC had, simply by virtue of its own territorial expansion, been responsible for much of the trade liberalization in the postwar period. According to Richard E. Baldwin, this was due to the pressure which its increasing integration put on other economies. It was, in Baldwin's view, the growing economic liberalization in the early 1980s culminating in the Single European Act, followed by the collapse of the Soviet bloc in Eastern Europe, which had put pressure on Eastern European countries to seek membership in the Community. As a general rule Baldwin maintained that more integration or 'deepening', which he termed 'an idiosyncratic shock', led to territorial expansion or 'widening' of the European Union (EU). But it was an argument which did not stand up to Alan Milward's historically based scrutiny. 'There was no idiosyncratic shock from the common market which led to the UK's application for membership. The applications by Denmark, Ireland and Norway were largely determined by the importance to them of the British market, that is to say, by a shock emanating from Britain', he pointed out.[418] It was, he maintained, precisely because additional states were seeking membership that explained why the EEC/EU 'intensified its internal coherence' at specific times, rather than the reverse.[419] Therefore he felt that Baldwin's argument, that it was integration which drove expansion of the EEC/EU, was not correct when tested against the record of history. It was certainly not the case that the most significant example of integration, that of the CAP, had been responsible for Britain's application for membership in the EEC. What, he asked, explained why Ireland and Denmark had applied to join the EEC?

Although Ireland and Denmark were two small, agrarian countries which applied for membership at the same time as the United Kingdom, their motives for doing so were, as he showed, very different. For the Republic of Ireland he maintained that '[o]ne of the deepest wells of support for

416. Ibid., 7 (both quotations).
417. Ibid., 11.
418. Ibid., 12. Baldwin, 'A Domino Theory of Regionalism' (1995).
419. Milward, *Politics and Economics*, 12.

Ireland's entry into the EC was the political wish to be recognised in nature rather than name as an independent country.'[420] The Irish request for Community membership involved a break with Ireland's most immediate past, in terms of agrarian and industrial protectionism. Although the Irish government had rejected the option of joining EFTA through the fear of losing more than 50,000 jobs as a result of competition with the British manufacturing industry and a further contraction in the population as emigrants left for Britain, to continue the protectionist policies inherited from the 1930s was seen as no strategy for promoting economic development either. Alan Milward's answer to the puzzle of why the Irish government could consider joining the EEC when it had rejected EFTA was that whereas 'EFTA was only about trade; the EEC was also about similarities in general economic policy.'[421] Accession to the EEC offered the promise of markets not only for Irish agricultural exports at guaranteed prices but also for the manufacturing industry which the government was determined to promote through a mixture of financial incentives and exposure to competition.[422]

Denmark was a much richer economy with potentially more options for promoting national development. Torn between the agrarian interests which depended on the British and German markets for their exports, and the manufacturing interests which looked to the Scandinavian market in EFTA, the Danish government had concluded a trade deal for some of its agricultural exports with Britain within EFTA rather than join the EEC. Britain's decision to apply for membership in the EEC in one sense held the advantage of bringing Denmark's main single markets, Britain and Germany, within the same trading regime but it still left those in Denmark who, for a variety of reasons, preferred closer links with Scandinavia, dissatisfied. Denmark, even though it opted to join the EEC, was to remain one of its most critical and dissatisfied members. Greenland, which subsequently negotiated separate home rule from Denmark, was to be the first territory—and the only one so far—to secede from the EC in 1985.

Britain's accession to the EEC in 1973 had an impact, as Alan Milward showed, not only on its European neighbors but also on many countries outside Europe including Britain's own dependencies scattered across the globe. Britain's accession was a global affair, he insisted. This meant that the history and politics of the European Union had to include some understanding of how it was designed to preserve 'Europe's position and importance in the world'.[423] It was in its commercial bargaining that the EU exerted real power and leverage; it was as a common market that it had global weight. One purpose of Britain's accession to the EEC 'was to put the Community on a level of equal power with the USA in international

420. Ibid., 50–51.
421. Ibid., 51.
422. Ibid., 54.
423. Ibid., 81.

trade disputes.'[424] That meant above all cooperating with France inside the European Community. 'The British', he insisted, 'did not want to overthrow France's position in the Community; they wanted to share it.'[425] However the way in which British dependencies would be associated with the EEC was to bring Britain up against the system put in place at the insistence of France for associating its former colonies as well as those of Belgium and the Netherlands with the EEC.

France saw Britain's membership in the EEC as an opportunity to reinforce Europe's position in Africa and to provide financial assistance for the economic development of the continent. Under the terms of the Yaoundé Convention signed in the capital of the Cameroon in 1963, the sub-Saharan former colonies of France and Belgium were offered preferential access to the markets of the EEC for their exports, apart from those agricultural products which competed with European agriculture, in return for giving the EEC states reverse preferences in their markets. It was this principle of reciprocity which distinguished the French-inspired system from the one offered by Britain to its dependencies. Although the United States was opposed to all forms of discrimination in international trade, it was not until, as Alan Milward showed, it became apparent that with Britain's accession to the EEC the Community preferences would be extended to markets in the Caribbean that it aired its objections. The real reason for the United States' hostility, he suggested, had little to do with the Caribbean, but with its desire to win more important concessions on the CAP from the European Community during the negotiations in GATT.[426] The challenge for Britain was to find a way of presenting a united front with its partners in the EEC in order to bargain with the United States in GATT while opposing the principle of reciprocity on which the successor agreement to that of Yaoundé was to be based. The difference between Britain and France, Alan Milward argued, was not one between trade liberalizers and protectionists but was 'over the extent to which African economies could respond to globalised trading rules and the extent to which they needed special provision.'[427]

Since the countries themselves in Africa, the Caribbean, and the Pacific (known as the ACP) made clear their opposition to the principle of reciprocity, preferring to be free to find markets wherever they could in the world, this made it difficult for France, supported only by Belgium, to uphold its claim to be the voice of the underdeveloped in Africa, and it had to drop its insistence on reverse preferences.[428] Thus, the successor to the Yaoundé Convention, which was signed in Lomé, the capital of Togo, and

424. Ibid., 96.
425. Ibid., 101.
426. Ibid., 88–89.
427. Ibid., 105.
428. Ibid., 102.

renewed three times, provided duty-free access to the EEC markets for most exports of manufactured goods and of tropical agriculture while providing subsidized loans and technical assistance to the African economies without any reciprocal arrangements.[429] Although the francophone states continued nonetheless to direct their exports to France, the more developed economies in West Africa expanded their exports to non-European markets, finding increasing outlets in the United States. But as Alan Milward showed, the Lomé states became increasingly marginalized in world trade and the trade of the whole ACP countries with the EU declined as a proportion of total EU trade, amounting to less than 2 percent of EU exports and less than 2 percent of its imports in 2000.[430] If this was the responsibility of the EU Commission it was, he argued, quite beyond its competence to do anything about it. To have changed the terms of the Lomé agreements and their successors would have called for the Commission to reach an agreement with France and Britain and then with the other member-states. The history of the Lomé agreements demonstrated that France and Britain simply agreed to pursue their own separate national policies in Africa and 'to legitimate' their decision by constituting a common EU trade framework for EU-African trade linked to a common but small EU aid program backed by a European Development Fund.[431] 'The Franco-British agreement on which the Lomé Conventions rested,' in Alan Milward's words, '[did] not seem to have been designed for change.'[432] It was in his search for a theory of historical change that he remained interested to the end of his life.

## Alan Milward's Implicit Theory of Historical Change

Alan Milward was neither a Marxist nor a Liberal. He came closest to being a Keynesian, but he rejected the protectionism which he saw as underpinning the general theory of Keynes. In his lifelong search to find a theory of historical change he combined the historian's method of conducting detailed research into as many relevant archives as were accessible at the time of writing with the economic historian's method of consulting the statistical record. Against the resulting historical narrative he tested social science theories, those of economics, political science, and sociology. The result was an economic history—of nineteenth-century Europe, of the Second World War, and of the great thirty-year Western European economic boom that followed it—which challenged much conventional wisdom.

Although he did not live to acknowledge that he had developed a theory of historical change, or to make it explicit, it has become clear to us that over the course of his lifetime's research he had developed such a theory.

429. Ibid., 79–80.
430. Ibid., 80.
431. Ibid., 112–113.
432. Ibid., 115.

The lessons of history which he drew upon in formulating his theory was that for change—social, political, and economic—to be sustainable, it had to be a gradual process rather than one resulting from a sudden, cataclysmic revolutionary event occurring in one sector of the economy or society. Benign change depended much less on natural economic endowment or technological developments than on the ability of state institutions to respond to changing political demands from within each society. State bureaucracies were fundamental to formulating those political demands and advising politicians of ways to meet them. Since each society was different there was no single model of development to be adopted or which could be imposed successfully by one nation-state on others, either through force as France and Germany had tried to do under Napoleon Bonaparte and Adolf Hitler or through foreign aid as the United States had tried to do under the Marshall Plan. Nor could development be promoted by following the example of a more successful economy, as Iceland had tried to do in copying Denmark. Since there was no single model of development each nation-state had to find its own response to the political demands from within its own society. It was how nation-states responded to those domestic political demands rather than to any external pressures arising from a supposedly greater degree of economic interdependence that determined the nature of historical change.

If the gold standard at the end of the nineteenth century had met the demands of the restricted group of voters who held the franchise and for whom price stability was more important than employment, the gold exchange standard which replaced it after the end of the First World War was ill designed to meet the political demands of a wider group of voters whose livelihood and economic security depended as much on employment in all sectors of the economy as on price stability. How to provide such security was a challenge which neither the liberal democracies nor the Fascist states were able to meet before the Second World War. It was a challenge which those who created the 'Bretton Woods system' in 1944 equally failed to address adequately. It was the defeated states in Western Europe, which drew from the experience of occupation the lesson that they had to provide economic as well as military security for the majority of their electorates if the nation-state was to survive as a democratic organizational unit in the postwar world, who created the new institutional arrangements which provided such economic security in postwar Europe. The new supranational institutions of what was to become the European Union were not designed to replace the nation-state but to enable it to achieve domestic objectives which it could not achieve through more traditional arrangements, while at the same time providing security to Western Europe against a resurgent Germany. The Treaty of Paris signed in 1951 establishing the ECSC was designed to offer security to the six signatory states, including the new democratic West German state, through a form of joint state control over the strategic sectors of coal and steel. The Treaty of Rome signed in 1957 establishing the EEC was designed to offer to the Six member-states of the ECSC economic security through a commercial treaty which provided for the gradual liberalization of trade in manufactured goods, combined with continued protection for the rest of the economy, including agriculture, while at the same time locking West Germany into that trading structure. The Single European Act signed in 1986 was designed to provide for economic security through the gradual liberalization of trade in services as employment in the service sector increasingly replaced employment in manufacturing and in agriculture as Western Europe faced increasing competition from Asia. The Treaty of Maastricht signed in 1992 was designed to lock the new unified Germany into Western Europe by controlling German monetary policy within a European Monetary Union (EMU). But he warned that EMU would work only if the nation-states retained political control in order to address the social and economic consequences of monetary union rather than relinquishing such control to an independent European central bank. 'Domestic politics in Europe will determine the Euro's fate, not central bankers', he predicted on the eve of the creation of the new European currency.[433] For Alan Milward the drivers of benign historical change in a democracy were domestic politics rather than external pressures arising from the international economy or the work of diplomats.

433. Milward, *The European Rescue* (2000), 434

# 1 Nation-states, Markets, Hegemons
## Alan Milward's Reconstruction of the European Economy

*Charles S. Maier*

Sometimes after many years, even decades, of productive intellectual work, the author himself, or his readers, discern underlying questions that have driven his investigations across apparently diverse fields of inquiry. Alan Milward, to the immense sadness of all who have known him, will not be able to carry out such a work of retrospective reflection. But as a historian who shared some of his inquiries and took pleasure in the originality of his thinking I should like to attempt that task. This essay seeks to present the major studies from the 1960s until about 2005 as part of an unfolding historical reflection on the political context of recent European economic history.[1] Alan was of course an economic historian, ready to interpret and deploy the usual quantitative data the profession draws on, but it was the world of national states, large and small, that generated the numbers.

A word first about our relationship: I met Alan at a major conference in Bochum in June 1973, which was organized by Hans Mommsen, Dietmar Petzina, and Bernd Weisbrod on 'Industrial System and Political Development in the Weimar Republic'. This meeting sought to bring together the exciting work in the political economy of Weimar then being opened up thanks to the new availability of firm archives as well as public papers and statistical

---

1. This chapter cites the following of Alan S. Milward's books, listed here according to the date of initial publication (American editions when published in both the United States and the United Kingdom): *The German Economy at War* (1965); *The New Order and the French Economy* (1970); *The Fascist Economy in Norway* (1972); *War, Economy and Society, 1939–1945* (1977); *The Reconstruction of Western Europe, 1945–51* (1984); *The European Rescue of the Nation-State* (1992); *The UK and the European Community*, vol. 1, *The Rise and Fall of a National Strategy, 1945–1963* (2002); *Politics and Economics in the History of the European Union* (2005). When it is clear which book is under discussion, I have identified particular citations simply by page numbers in parentheses following the quotations.

material.[2] Among notable historians present were Tim Mason, who died in 1990, and Gerald Feldman, who passed away in 2007, both of them close to me. It was an exciting moment of research. I still possess a photo of several of us—Alan sporting a very large beard—in sooty coal-miner suits following a descent into one of the last functioning Ruhr mines. But in fact my intellectual collaboration with Alan rested more on our shared interests in post-1945 inquiries, which we took up later in the 1970s, in particular on the history and impact of the Marshall Plan. These issues involved us in several debates around the time of the fortieth anniversary of General Marshall's famous speech of June 4, 1947, and they provided a reason for Alan to invite me a couple of times to the European University Institute (EUI) in Florence to address his seminar or serve as an external examiner. Both of us—Alan eventually in far greater detail and with a much wider range than I—sought to remove the mythology and reverence that surrounded the Marshall Plan. Not that we believed it was insignificant or ungenerous, only that we shared a commitment to studying its role soberly and without sentimentality. We collided occasionally with Charles P. Kindleberger, a tremendously productive and likeable economic historian at the Massachusetts Institute of Technology with whom I maintained a personal friendship, but who felt, I fear, that we were attacking an episode into which as a young economist he had poured heart and soul and intellect. I admired Kindleberger tremendously, but he always thought Alan and I wanted to reduce the Marshall Plan to insignificance. In any case, these years saw a close collaboration between Alan and me, and he wrote an important chapter for a volume Günter Bischof and I edited on Germany and the Marshall Plan.[3] We both continued our research into postwar political economy, but at the EUI, Alan was in a position to encourage a new generation of talented students to work in detail on related themes and to produce in 1992 an important summary of this research: *The European Rescue of the Nation-State*. I was diverted to different themes whereas he continued as the preeminent historian of Western Europe's economies in the decades after the devastation of World War II.

I am not in a position to review systematically the fields Alan researched with his ferocious archive-based specificity, lucid intelligence, and remorseless questioning of accepted pieties. It has been over two decades since we explored the same area although there were conferences and meetings together into the 1990s, and I followed the work of the students I had come to know at the EUI. This essay, though, attempts to think about the underlying themes Alan found important throughout his publishing career. His early scholarly publications concerned the performance and sacrifices of national economies in the Second World War—Germany's

2. Conference results were published in Mommsen, Petzina, and Weisbrod (eds.), *Industrielles System und politische Entwicklung in der Weimarer Republik*.
3. Milward, 'The Marshall Plan and German Foreign Trade'.

and two countries under the German yoke from 1940 to 1944—following which he wrote one of the surveys of the economic history of World War II in the celebrated series produced by the University of California Press. From there he went on to examine the topic where our work intersected: the recovery of postwar Western Europe and Germany during the cold war, at a time when the United States played a significant if not hegemonic role. That period coincided with his repeated service in Florence. Finally, as official historian of the United Kingdom's entry into and participation in the European Economic Community, he published an authoritative opening volume which appeared in 2002. His final published statement was a distillation of several of the major historical issues he had been addressing in this long-term project, which he compressed in masterly fashion just five years ago into the Schumpeter lecture series at the University of Graz.

## A RECURRING ARGUMENTATION

Each of these chronological segments—the economics of World War II, the sources and nature of the European economic recovery after that war, and the United Kingdom's relationship to the Franco–German initiatives that went from the Coal and Steel Community to the Common Market—drew Alan into detailed studies on a diversity of subjects any of which alone might occupy a scholar for life. Surveying the forty-year achievement as a whole, we can discern several recurring themes, some argued very openly, but one largely implicit and to be interrogated in retrospect. All these themes are embedded in Alan Milward's continuing engagement with the argumentation already in print: the explicit weighing of explanations and models, and efforts to find more adequate explanation remained characteristic of his approach throughout.

The overtly explicit theme, which Alan himself identified as his continuing leitmotif at the outset of his final major study, *The Rise and Fall of a National Strategy*, was the continuing concern with the ongoing vitality of national politics and national communities. Nation-states play an irreducible historical role vis-à-vis both nonpolitical market forces and against supranational or potentially imperial political visions. From the first work on the wartime economies to the final reflections on the political input into the enlargement of the European Union (EU), Alan Milward always insisted on the power and persistence of national political motivations. For roughly half of Alan's career, he lived and worked in an academic milieu, which, one can safely generalize, tends to downplay the value and contribution of 'pure' market forces. Alan's work shared some of that overall stance but on historical and not ideological grounds. He did not indict market principles for their unequal outcomes or their alleged entailing of authoritarian enforcement, as, say, Karl Polanyi had done at a moment when Milward would have been a schoolboy.[4] But perhaps as a serious student of German economic development, Alan always understood the power of state institutions to shape market forces. What contributed particular force to these postulates was that they persisted during the second half of his career, that is, during the decades when social scientists and political leaders alike emphasized anew the power and indeed the beneficence of market forces.

Alan's work retained instead the conviction that the political framework and political motivations remained the formative, and at least after World War II, decisive influences upon economic outcomes. The individual studies contributed to a continuous demonstration that politics and economics could not really be disentangled. Economic outcomes depended not primarily on structural conditions (or perhaps he took them for granted as background givens) but on economic policies—a finding that sounds trite but is not really so. Economic policies in turn—both under fascist and democratic regimes—were the outcome of politics.

But the politics remained the politics of the nation-state. Even as Alan insisted on the role of national political choices vis-à-vis market logic, so too he argued for the persistence of national calculation and interest in the face of any supranational commitment. He structured one of his books on the postwar era, *The European Rescue of the Nation-State*, as an extended explanation of how national policy-makers had managed to shape supranational institutions precisely to render postwar nation-states viable in the turbulent postwar conditions. He maintained, convincingly I believe, that the emerging European Economic Community could be crafted precisely because it advanced the national interests of each of its members. The argument in itself does not seem remarkable, but it had to be asserted in the face of a vast sentimentalizing of the European construction, which was and remains generally celebrated as the path that prevented a resumption of war in Western Europe. Europeanist sentiment may have played a more important role than Milward wanted to admit, especially in the emerging Christian Democratic parties, but he was certainly correct in that the European Communities were hardly needed to preclude a renewal of the French-German warfare. With the Soviet domination of Eastern Europe on one hand and a powerful United States on the other—a United States moreover committed to a long-term military alliance and to West European 'integration' no matter how fuzzy the British found the concept—and the deep division of Germany, there could have been no resumption of the constellation that had led to the two wars of 1914–45.

Obviously the Soviet and American roles in Europe meant that the influence of supranational economic commitments emanated not just from the European Coal and Steel Community (ECSC) and then the post-1957 Communities. It was inherent in post-1945 bipolarity. As a historian of the

4. Polanyi, *The Great Transformation.*

wartime economies, Milward was familiar with a far more oppressive effort to impose a supranational hegemony, namely the German *New Order*. This meant that his historical investigations covered two sources and indeed two eras of hegemonic design, albeit very different in intent and structure. The first sprang from the ambition of Fascism, in particular as represented by the case of the National Socialist regime with its aspirations for a New Order in Europe which really meant a German economic empire. The second emanated from a source that Alan certainly beheld as far more benevolent—the American effort to preserve a primacy through European multilateral institutions. The United States spoke for the virtues of extended markets and had contested Nazi policies. But by its size, its immunity in the war, its technological virtues and agricultural bounty, it too represented a hegemonic force that the Europeans needed to contest even as they drew upon it. At the end, Milward's argumentation was one that confirmed the cunning of history. The nation-state prevailed in the face of the universalizing market and the power of economic hegemons. It did so because as a hegemon the United States had an interest in expanding international market regimes and ended up helping to advance the market and sustain the nation-states. The remainder of this essay will try to fill out this argumentation.

*
* *

The underlying condition of international economic life, Alan suggested from the outset, was the search for nation-state viability. And domestic economic systems had to be studied in light of their political constitution and administration. Milward's early analysis of *The German Economy at War* emphasized this throughout. This study, now forty-five years old, would have to be modified today in some respects, in particular its emphasis on Hitler's preparation for a short war but his insufficiencies for a long struggle. Richard J. Overy and Adam Tooze have demonstrated the seriousness of Hitler's rearmament effort for a long or short struggle; however, there was no way Germany could maintain its effort against both the United States and the Soviet Union.[5] In fact, Milward hardly thought differently. 'No nation had ever previously spent so vast a sum in peace time on preparations for war' (27). Still, the economic agencies of the Reich were a tangle of conflicts and priorities and often totally unfeasible quotas. In spite of them, 'Germany overran half of Europe with an economic system which [General Georg] Thomas, quite justifiably, called "a war of all against all"' (27).[6] He went on to argue in this early book that 'there was

5. Overy, *War and Economy in the Third Reich*; Tooze, *The Wages of Destruction*.
6. Editorial note: General Georg Thomas headed the War Economy and Armaments Office of the Supreme Command of the Armed Forces or

a complete absence of systematic planning in the German "New Order"' (30). The Reich was to serve as the center of heavy industrial production; consumer goods and foodstuffs would be supplied from the occupied territories. Milward's brief book shows how this calculation had to be set aside in early 1942, but with the survival of the Soviet Union and the entry of the United States, no German economic strategy could have worked. Albert Speer's organizational talents were remarkable—a view that Tooze harshly contests—but he could not work miracles and understood by early 1945 if not earlier that the war was lost with the overrunning of the Ruhr and Upper Silesia (188–189). German economic strategy—whether the original concept of provision for a successful Blitzkrieg or the later reorganizations effected by 1942–43—still presupposed that conquests had to be retained to supply the armed forces needed to retain them.

Milward largely retained these views a dozen years later in his general economic history of the Second World War, *War, Economy and Society, 1939–1945*.[7] After careful calculation of payments, exports, and redirected labor, the 1977 account likewise reaffirmed the earlier findings that Germans had massively exploited French economic resources. But Milward also went on to estimate military output and efforts in the other belligerent powers as well as to devote attention to technological change, labor and population, and the comparative regulation of wartime economies. In the three decades since the work appeared other economists have provided more systematic comparative estimates and have relied less on the early U.S. Strategic Bombing Survey.[8] Still valuable, though, is Milward's concept of a strategic synthesis, which demonstrated how military planning and the economic calculus of conquest were fatefully interdependent at each stage of the long struggle. Happily Hitler got it wrong.

The same lesson is derived from Milward's studies of the French and Norwegian wartime economies, *The New Order and the French Economy* and *The Fascist Economy in Norway*. These books appeared in close succession in 1970 and 1972. They showed that Alan was wrestling with several overarching ideological issues as well as the more narrowly economic questions that he also set out to answer. Was the National Socialist concept of a European New Order anything more than a pretense for German economic exploitation of its conquests? Was the meaning of a European-wide Nazi rule anything more than just German economic administration? The French economic situation was the easier to understand. Through the conscription of French labor and the forced sale of French coal and iron at quasi-confiscatory prices, the French economy was pressed into service for wartime Germany. The lesson of the French study was that conquest

---

*Oberkommando der Wehrmacht* (1939–1942).

7. *War, Economy and Society, 1939–1945*, esp. 23–30 for Germany, and 132–68 for 'the economics of occupation'.

8. See in particular Harrison, *The Economics of World War II*.

might pay, and Alan began his book in fact with a review of German ideas of how conquest might be made to pay. With some subtlety he showed that although the Hague Conventions of 1899 and 1907 protected individuals in occupied lands from depredation, they did not allow for the protection of national and collective resources. For Milward, this omission indicated the 'illusions of liberal thought' (14), as did the pre-1914 notion identified with Norman Angell's *The Great Illusion*, that modern war must cost more than it was worth.[9] After all, if the expense of modern war proved far greater than anticipated, the costs must just make the conqueror more anxious to extract resources from this victory. The Nazi experiment flew in the face of all liberal thinking since the eighteenth century; but that was the point. State needs, not those of welfare maximization, were the determinants of economic life. Fascism in particular ruthlessly subordinated any concerns with individual welfare to that of the collectivity. And in the case of Nazi policies, state needs were to be met through war and occupation.

In fact, Alan argued, the idea of an integrated New Order had to wait until after 1942, because French assets were to be integrated not systematically but in terms of their utility for the invasion of Russia. The demands of Blitzkrieg, rather than the optimal architecture of an integrated but subjugated Europe, meant French resources were to be tapped sector by sector. Of these iron ore was the most important. By the time of the Speer-Bichelonne agreements of October 1943, the concept was changing: France would not be encouraged to produce military goods for Germany but consumer goods so that Germany might increase military production inside the Reich.[10] This implied, though, that Speer must acquiesce in Fritz Sauckel's demand for conscripting more foreign workers to labor in German factories.[11] As Milward notes, both Speer and Sauckel faced limits because of French resistance. But his major conclusion was that there were too many internal disagreements even among Nazis to settle on a coherent vision for the New Order (179–180).

The lessons derived from Norway's wartime economy were less direct but perhaps more intriguing. Discovering that key Norwegian wartime economic archives had been brought to Britain, Alan was the first historian to use the trove until his own publication led to their return to Oslo. Underlying his interpretation was the fact, which he emphasized at the outset, that occupied Norway had a ruler committed to Nordic Fascism. Plans for the

9. Editorial note: Norman Angell, *The Great Illusion* (New York: G. P. Putnam's Sons, 1913).

10. Editorial note: The agreement of October 1943 between Speer and Jean Bichelonne, the minister of economic affairs of the Vichy government, implied transferring a greater proportion of armament production to France.

11. Editorial note: From March 1942 until the end of the war, Ernst Friedrich Christoph Sauckel was the General Plenipotentiary for Labor Deployment (*Generalbevollmächtigter für den Arbeitseinsatz*) under Hitler's Four-Year Plan Office.

Norwegian economy—a small one in the scheme of things, but important for its hydroelectric resources—had to be understood, he argued, in the context of Hitler's plan to integrate Vidkun Quisling's enthusiastic regime into a National Socialist Europe. Norway was too small to subsidize the German war effort to the significant degree that France could, but Nazi planners devoted considerable effort to thinking how its economy might be reconstructed within the larger New Order. Milward thus used the Norwegian study to discuss German economic plans as a whole, and he returned to elaborate the idea of the *Grossraumwirtschaft*, with German manufacturing at the core, and food and raw materials produced by the conquered periphery (3–4).

His study revealed, however, what a hard morsel Norway was to assimilate because its earlier specialization in agriculture, fishing, mining, and forestry, coupled with a highly developed merchant marine fleet modernized significantly after heavy shipping losses in World War I (33ff.), had strongly oriented it before April 1940 toward international trade, above all with Britain. German conquest would require that the Third Reich supply what trade with Britain had yielded. In contrast to occupied France, 'All German economic plans for Norway should be seen in this light, as plans for a long-term transformation of the economy and of society. [ . . . ] from the moment of the occupation she was to be an integral part of that New Order' (67–68). Nazi Germany's original interest in Norway had not been an economic one. 'It seems to be the case that this primacy of economic affairs was only unwillingly tolerated by Hitler. For him the idea of a fascist reconstruction remained paramount' (278). In the long run it might be reoriented into a continental economic sphere but during the years of occupation, it contributed little economically to the German war effort in comparison to other conquered occupied areas. The problem was that Norway had little to supply the New Order unless its lands and aluminum were developed, and this meant that a land of poor agricultural emigrants would require labor imports to gear it up for a net contribution to the New Order.

The paradoxes of the Norwegian case, Alan admitted, had led him to revise his earlier views of Fascism. Reviewing the theories of Fascism which so many of us earnestly debated in the 1960s and 1970s, Alan opted for one with which I agree: '[As far as Norway was concerned] the New Order was an attempt to force a particular philosophico-economic view of the world on to her as on to other European states. That view of the world was antimaterialist, antagonistic to economic growth, concerned with the creation of a society which would be stable enough to resist the hitherto relentless pressures of social change' (290). Fascism was anticommunist, but also antiliberal; the New Order was a European-wide concept for the defense of the fascist revolution. And, Alan suggested most startingly, the Nazis were right. A fundamentally antiliberal revolution could be carried out only on a European-wide scale.

Milward's work on the wartime economies of Germany, France, and Norway is today less prominent than the contributions to postwar Europe and the role of the European Communities and European Union.[12] But in fact, I think, the historical problems with which he was wrestling provided a fundamental preparation for the works on the postwar. The relationship of political concepts to economic reasoning, the primacy of politics, the effort to compare the logic of individual welfare, national welfare, and the overall prosperity of supranational spatial units all were critical for his books on wartime. These works rested, moreover, on careful interpretation not only of statistics, and outcomes, but of political memos and in-fighting. As with everything Alan wrote, they revealed a taste for paradox and irony. In effect, Alan carried forward his units of analysis—he just had to develop his history in the knowledge that Fascism had failed, and a new—or rather old—system of values had prevailed through the war. Liberal democracy, acceptance of change, and the independence of organized labor movements all came out on top in 1945. The United States would play a hegemonic, if not all-powerful, role. The ideological bases of American ascendancy had to be taken seriously, but perhaps the results would also be at partial cross-purposes with Washington's aspirations. 'Integration' replaced the New Order as a watchword for Washington in the late 1940s. But the real winner, Alan emphasized, would be renewed national autonomy.

## THE PARADOXES OF THE POSTWAR

*The Reconstruction of Western Europe 1945–51* (1984) followed from Alan's reflection on the sources of European recovery. This was the theme that occupied us both in parallel although he made it the basis for a far more sustained argument. He was fortunate, too, in being able to carry out his investigations with a team of first-rate young researchers in the EUI of the 1980s—Ruggero Ranieri, Federico Romero, Frances M. B. Lynch, and Vibeke Sørensen among others.[13] We both wrote on the limits of the Marshall Plan. Alan demonstrated that the European Recovery Program (ERP) appeared urgent in the spring of 1947, not because the European economy was in ruins, but because it faced a crisis of expansion. The postwar framework of bilateral trade increased the need for U.S. commodities, far beyond the dollar reserves available. The Bretton Woods arrangements were becoming a straitjacket rather than a facilitator of international trade. By overcoming the foreign-trade bottlenecks, Marshall Plan aid also

12. Editorial note: In his chapter in this volume, John R. Gillingham makes a strong case for greater prominence to be restored to Milward's earlier work on the wartime economies.
13. See their essays in Milward, Lynch, Ranieri, Romero, and Sørensen, *The Frontier of National Sovereignty* (1993).

contributed to the high rate of European capital formation especially during its first two years. For about a decade, there was a group of scholars rethinking the United States' role in postwar West European recovery and seeking to get beyond either the uncritical accounts of American generosity that had marked early publications or the harsh criticism of neocapitalist imperialism that dominated some of the critical historiography of the 1960s and 1970s. Alan was writing his study at a time when I was also examining the Marshall Plan, and he contributed to the volume I had been asked to edit on Germany and the Marshall Plan, which appeared after some delay in 1991. The other major American contributor, Michael J. Hogan, whose major synthesis came out in the same period, emphasized the neocorporatist ideological presuppositions, particularly among British and American policy-makers, a theme I had touched on for my article on 'The Politics of Productivity', in 1977.[14]

Alan, Hogan, and I all concurred that the United States had a vision of 'integration' that derived from its own depression and wartime economic experience of government intervention in an industrial economy to secure high output. Paul Hoffman, the Economic Cooperation Administration (ECA) administrator, had called for 'integration' in a celebrated speech of October 1949.[15] What it meant in practice might be rather fuzzy, although advancing toward monetary convertibility seemed a key component, and one that Washington was willing to help fund. The timing of the speech suggests that Hoffman was trying to find a renewed mission for the ERP to secure renewed Congressional funding for the remaining two years of the program, which was a commitment for four years but required annual appropriations. It was clear from the documents (Alan discussed this in the early chapters of *The Rise and Fall of a National Strategy 1945–1963*, the first volume of *The United Kingdom and the European Community*) that during the years 1948–49, British politics resisted integration, whereas French policy-makers found the American notion attractive for their own purpose of locking Germany into institutions that would limit its economic recovery but contribute to French industrial modernization. Coal was the key industrial issue for a couple of years; movement toward currency convertibility the major trade and financial innovation. The institution building of 1949–50, which led both to the European Payments Union (EPU) in September 1950 and to the Treaty of Paris of April 1951 by which a European Coal and Steel Community was to be established in 1952, was crucial.

---

14. Hogan, *The Marshall Plan* and 'European Integration and German Reintegration'; Maier, 'The Politics of Productivity'. See also Maier, 'The Two Postwar Eras'.
15. The text of Hoffman's statement is accessible at the Centre Virtuel de la Connaissance sur l'Europe website (www.cvce.eu) (last accessed on 12 December 2011).

These arguments, developed in conferences, articles, no doubt the classroom, and finally in Milward's memorable volumes, revealed how Alan viewed the interlocked forces of national politics and the role of markets. His two large-scale studies of European recovery and the development of the European Community and then the early chapter of his final major work on the United Kingdom and the European Community paid particular attention to the potential and limits of postwar customs unions—the early one of Benelux, then the emergence of the European Free Trade Association and the contrasting nature of the European Economic Community (EEC). Not that Alan believed these arrangements magically expanded the volume of international trade overall, but they provided enough intra-European growth, especially after the Treaties of Rome, to decisively impact—so Milward would argue in *The Rise and Fall of a National Strategy*—on de Gaulle's capacity to resist the British government's belated search to enter the European Communities. Markets facilitated political room for maneuver; politics provided the decisions that opened the way for market dynamism. As Milward put it in his final lectures in Graz, *Politics and Economics in the History of the European Union*, history trod the path of realistic analysis and corrected the early political-science theories of 'spillover', which had contended that an automatic momentum would lead the European Community to regulate ever-wider tasks. In its early years the EEC was about trade regulation, but it envisaged tasks beyond that of lowering tariffs. 'If customs union theory with its clear propositions seems too narrow and mechanistic a tool for explaining why countries join the common market, political theory seems quite the opposite' (29). In fact *raison d'état* and not automatic spillover was decisive for the development of the European Communities. On the other hand, just to attribute the emerging Europe to intergovernmental bargaining over trade, he admitted in his late reflections, was to underestimate the basic fact that supranational institutions came to exist, whether first as a rather feeble ECSC and later as an EEC.

At the end, he suggests the EU counts for something. A court of justice made a difference. '[M]ay not the arena in which the two-level game has to be played give rise to some integrative momentum?' (36). History, Alan suggested, did not invalidate general theories *per se*, and it also underlined the powerful attraction of a customs union in the area of the globe that has more contiguous, high-per-capital income economies, all of them highly dependent on international trade, jostling together than any other. 'No earlier European institution was joined by so many states, paying the price for the peace which has brought the economic benefits they have reaped. Retaining the concept of a national political economy has been, so far, a way of reducing that price' (37).

This mature, surprisingly irenic resolution of so many disputes followed closely upon Alan's close study of his own country's turbulent relations with the early European Community. I have no problem ranking *The Rise and Fall of a National Strategy 1945–1963*—Alan's massive and dense first volume of the official history of *The UK and the European Community*—as a great piece of work. It proceeded from the archival documentation that was made available in the British historical series, follows the protagonists' argumentation, thoroughly explores the relevant might-have-beens, and imposes a comprehensive structure. It must have represented a major emotional exercise in academic discipline, for the author yoked himself to the task of assuming a certain sympathy with the British historical actors even when in his previous personal attitudes he could be scathingly critical. The irony and wit that lay so readily to hand had to be curbed, although occasionally signs of his ready acerbity flash through, as when, discussing de Gaulle's minister of information, Alain Peyrefitte, Milward wrote: 'Like most ministers of information, Peyrefitte was not a man to weaken a good story in the telling by clinging pedantically to the truth' (480).

Alan admitted at the outset that the narrative confirmed his long-held views that the emerging structure of Europe did not result from 'an emotional and political programme' to replace national states with a supranational federal governance, but from 'a set of stochastic, high-level, political bargains between some of those states whose primary purpose was to enhance the position of the nation-state itself' (x). He would use the term 'stochastic' again in his 2004 lectures on *Politics and Economics in the History of the European Union* (36). He anticipated some of his conclusions by dissenting from the most widespread criticism of British policy—but then Alan always dissented—that it was 'mistakenly grandiose, the result of lingering fantasies of the United Kingdom as a world-wide major power' (x). Rather British policy was pragmatic though not always wise: 'Where pragmatism made mistakes it was more through ignorance, or through the pressure of party politics, than through conceit.' He expressed hope that the book would demonstrate 'how heavy and numerous these problems were to eliminate simplistic condemnation or approval of what was done' (x).

At moments, I think, the self-imposed duty to understand British choices (which involved understanding the contending preferences of major bureaucratic actors—Treasury, Foreign Office, Board of Trade—and political leaders such as Ernest Bevin in the late 1940s and Anthony Eden and Harold Macmillan in the mid 1950s) led Alan to greater justifications of policy than a historian without such responsibilities might have drawn. Still, it greatly strengthens the authority of his account that he so thoroughly examines options that were open and realistic. In *The Rise and Fall of a National Strategy 1945–1963*, he specifically addressed in a subchapter the question, 'Should participation in the Schuman Plan have been rejected?' and decided that 'Ironically,'—of course Alan was a man of irony—'therefore, it seems wisest to conclude that although the United Kingdom could have entered the European Coal and Steel Community without as damaging an effect on its foreign policy as it predicted, there was no compelling reason for it to do so, and that had it done so the course of subsequent relations between

Britain and the European Communities would not have been changed.' (77) In fact, London's decision to reject full participation was taken from a mistaken belief that crucial attributes of sovereignty must be surrendered, whereas Alan's earlier volume showed precisely how the European nation-state rescued sovereignty through the Community's architecture.

Of course the argument that nothing much would have turned out differently can safely be made for many decisions; we never know about paths not taken. But was the unwillingness to wager on full participation in 1950 really so inconsequential? The British government spent much of the next decade or more coping with the wake of that decision, which was to haunt it again at the end point of the volume, when Milward subjected the 1963 de Gaulle veto of the British application for EEC membership and its reason to a similar rigorous examination. Yes, 1950 was not catastrophic, but in *the long run* almost all decisions can become inconsequential. In the long run France's decision to surrender in 1940 did not mean catastrophe (or at least not for its compliant non-Jewish citizens). In the long run forty years of Communism in Eastern Europe will represent just an episode. Perhaps such long-run Olympian judiciousness comes with the territory of official history, even when full access to documentation is provided. Nonetheless for the brilliance of his bringing out the implications of alternatives, the patterns of argument that different government agencies mustered, the long-term implications in terms of costs and benefits, national security and prosperity, and the fate of domestic social programs, Milward's volume is a masterly achievement.

Alan identified only the most salient and explicit of his assumptions—the persistence of nation-state calculations—in his preface. The second assumption, which permeates all his work and which this essay has also sought to emphasize, is the inextricable relationship of policy choices to outcomes, even if sometimes indirect or, as Alan said, in a 'stochastic' manner. By stochastic, Alan did not mean purely by chance, but rather that in light of the way other powers must react, the results could not often be foreseen. He elaborated on that complex interrelationship in his Graz lectures. I am not certain that he fully formulated his method and premises. Alan was not a cliometrician. Economic developments often explained political choices as he demonstrated that they did in the case of de Gaulle's 1963 veto, where he showed how important the EEC had become to its member states' surge in export growth. But they did so because they affected policy, which in turn had further impacts on economic outcome. The dimensions of action were so recursively intertwined that no historian should separate them.

## THE LIMITS OF HEGEMONY

This was the case, too, for the third of his underlying factors in shaping multinational economic development—the pressure of the hegemon. Alan did not reflect specifically on this theme across the body of his work, but the reader who surveys the books as a whole will note that the theme recurs under radically different conditions. What should be the structure of Europe? Those who were powerful have always asked, whether they were mighty within or outside the Continent. Nazi Germany had imposed the choices and sought to create a European economic empire that differentiated core and periphery. But Western Europe had not simply liberated itself after 1945; rather it had accepted a new power that was less oppressive but also potentially hegemonic, the United States. One must be clear here: Milward did not believe the United States to be an exploitative power; he appreciated its aspirations. Indeed in his essay in the volume Bischof and I edited on *Germany and the Marshall Plan*, he argued that American aid had knowingly helped the Federal Republic of Germany to recover the German vocation as an exporter of industrial goods even though this development must ultimately mean significant competition with U.S. commercial interest.[16]

Paradoxically, in fact, American choices turned out to have less effect than American policy-makers liked to believe, a view that may explain why Kindleberger took such exception to Milward's views. The United States, Milward explained, was hardly a feckless giant, neither was it merely a self-regarding bully (as left-wing historians might have had it), at least not in Western Europe. It is just that Europe applied its own tremendous economic energies to postwar reorganization as in the construction of the EPU and then the ECSC. Perhaps Alan might have stressed more how helpful American policy had been at decisive moments even of European initiatives. U.S. policy-makers, after all, put the pressure on Konrad Adenauer, the first Chancellor of the Federal Republic of Germany, to resist his own industrialists' opposition to the concessions West Germany would have to make on domestic cartel behavior to win French acceptance of the emerging ECSC deal. In the same period they devoted significant slices of ERP aid to funding the initial reserves that made EPU possible.

The final historical drama that Alan wrote about in narrative form was Charles de Gaulle's 1963 veto of British membership in the EEC. As he showed in a dense but brilliant examination of the decision, de Gaulle did so because he remained convinced that Britain was serving, willingly or not, as America's Trojan Horse. (And he was able to do so because of the prosperous expansion that the Treaties of Rome had already brought about.) It was precisely to show the nature of American power that Milward devoted so much attention in the chapter on de Gaulle's veto to the background of the nuclear sharing issue, including the ramifications of Skybolt and Polaris for both the United Kingdom and France.[17] After exploring

16. Milward, 'The Marshall Plan and German Foreign Trade'.
17. Editorial note: At that time, the U.S. government had developed the Polaris missile, carried by and fired from nuclear-powered submarines, and the air-to-ground Skybolt missile.

the timing of these developments at length in some wonderfully incisive diplomatic history, Milward dismissed them as de Gaulle's motivation for the veto. The British national strategy foundered on the stubbornness of the French national strategy. Paris's national strategy was in turn based on the politics (but a politics dependent on economic developments) of resisting a hegemon—no longer Berlin, but Washington.

Another irony: Alan provoked Kindleberger by his minimalist reading of the Marshall Plan. But he never took up directly, so far as I know, the theme for which Kindleberger's work was most noted (at least until the recent flurry of interest in financial crises)—namely the need for an economic hegemon to preserve open markets, assure monetary liquidity, and be a lender of last resort. (The argument was one of negation: the catastrophe of the Great Depression was magnified because, in Kindleberger's famous formulation, the United Kingdom could no longer play the role of hegemon, and the United States was not yet ready to.) In effect Alan's work argues against that idea. The European Community was, it turned out, a political way of resisting outside hegemony, even friendly hegemony. It was an associative arrangement that was designed to give the Europeans economic weight. Yet, as Alan also understood, the development of the European Community was in the United States' own interest, which was one condition for its prospering. Kindleberger had an implicit point: the EC could develop not because the United States organized it, but because Washington's patterns of mutual assistance from 1947–50 (when it actively sponsored inter-European clearing schemes and later the EPU) helped create the conditions for Europe's own schemes for a common industrial and financial governance. Alan would have argued that his view of Europe disproved Kindleberger's notion of the virtue of a hegemon; Kindleberger would have argued that it confirmed it.

The issue of hegemony thus remained important for Milward, even after its most destructive incarnation—National Socialist *Grossraumwirtschaft*—had been defeated. It did not disappear as a historical theme. But it remained an issue that fully embodied the cunning of history that Alan Milward treasured. For hegemony to function, the hegemon must have a genuine commitment to the welfare of his clients. Hegemony rewards by the fact of leadership itself; the effort to draw rents from economic preponderance ultimately leads to backlash and collapse. Of course, Alan wanted to stress the inventiveness of Europe vis-à-vis the economic power of the United States. This was the message of both *The Reconstruction of Western Europe 1945–51* and *The European Rescue of the Nation- State*. And Britain, for all its reservations, remained part of Milward's Europe even if its leaders never wanted to admit the full logic of the connections. In this sense Milward was a cosmopolitan. It was fitting that he trained so many non-British students at the European University Institute, and that his formidable intellect was free of national prejudices. Those who selected Alan Milward to write the official economic history of the United Kingdom and the European Communities made a choice wiser than they probably understood. For they chose a historian free of national prejudices, open to the achievements of continental policy-makers, a deep believer in Europe (even while a friendly evaluator of American efforts). But they also chose a sometimes contrarian historian who fully understood how contingent, fragmented, political decisions could appear and did his best to understand the complex reasons for which they were adopted. Following the progress of Alan's work from his study of the most brutally exploitative economies, through the hard work of recovery, to the complex building of institutions leaves one admiring—and of course saddened that it was interrupted so prematurely.

# 2 The Early Milward

## An Appreciation

*John Gillingham*

In a volume analyzing the life's work of Alan S. Milward, especially in one weighted to the field of contemporary European history, it is appropriate that the first half of his career, in which he wrote extensively about European history prior to 1945, be fully recognized. Arguably he may be best and longest remembered for the writings of this early period. As a comparatively young man—and long before embarking upon the books for which today he is best known—Milward had to his credit a prodigious scholarly output of great originality, which, though often controversial, has had substantial impacts on no less than three separate fields of historical study: the nineteenth-century European economy, the Third Reich, and World War II. Taken as a whole, these books evince a remarkable precocity, a gift for mastering new subjects, a striking conceptual boldness, and the courage to tread new ground. The result is a corpus of writings which, though seldom definitive, opened vast new areas of research for those with the gumption to seek them. A brief review of the most important of his early books should shed light on his development as a historian.

It is not a story of unbroken success. In producing his great body of work in his early career, Alan Milward tried repeatedly, but without much luck, to develop a theory of historical causation like those of Marx or Hayek or, on a lower level, Kuznets or Rostow, that would guide research, not only with reference to his particular topic, but more generally: that would provide the logic and setting to enable historians to make order out of the seeming chaos of the modern era. The evidence he presents in his books and the conclusions he draws from them are thus often at variance with one another. Although his greatest ambitions may arguably never have been fully realized, his career was, however, anything but a failure. No analytical school bears his name, but Alan Milward left a large legacy.[1] It includes dozens of pupils as well as a broader community of scholars, both

1. Editorial note: Several authors in this volume hold different views about the pertinence of referring to a *Milwardian* approach or school.

present and future, who all draw in many ways from his scholarship and who will remain deeply indebted to him. As an economic historian, he will be remembered as one of the giants of his generation.

Even if never quite realized, I believe that Alan Milward's determination to develop an integrative organizing principle to make sense of our age is what drove his research forward, equipped him to tackle big new subjects, and prompted him to advance fresh, provocative, question-raising new hypotheses, all of which stimulated the work of others. One can trace the source of this lifetime achievement back to Milward's early university career as a Lecturer in Economic History at Edinburgh and East Anglia (1960–68), a tenured Associate Professor of Economics at Stanford (1969–71), and, finally, as Professor of European Studies at the University of Manchester Institute of Science and Technology (1971–83).

## THE GERMAN ECONOMY AT WAR

*The German Economy at War* (1965) was Milward's first and perhaps his finest book. It is an elegant piece of work of less than 200 pages which, even today, can be read with pleasure and profit. The book was translated into German and Italian. It changed the way historians—indeed, the lay public—think and write about the Third Reich. Previous scholarship on the subject had rested on various political theories, many of them generated by exiles, most of them deeply colored by ideological presuppositions, and nearly all of them focused to the point of obsession on tracking down the source of the radical evil incarnated in Hitler.

In this hothouse atmosphere, the economy of Germany in the 1930s got short shrift. It was seldom studied within the walls of academe, and almost never discussed in the offices of history professors. The ongoing chatter of the day, more theology than social science, turned on the question as to whether the Nazi phenomenon should better be considered as fascist or totalitarian. More than any other single figure, Alan Milward was responsible for guiding the subject away from this increasingly sterile debate and opening the economy and society of the Third Reich to more promising historical research.

The publication of Burton H. Klein's *Germany's Economic Preparations for War* (1959) was a first step in this direction. Klein's book summarized the voluminous and exhaustive analyses by the United States Strategic Bombing Survey (USSBS) of the American air war in Europe.[2] Klein demonstrated that, contrary to general supposition, Germany entered World War

2. Milward was familiar with the USSBS material, having made extensive use of it in his doctoral dissertation, 'The Armaments Industry in the German Economy in the Second World War', London School of Economics and Political Science, 1960.

II with an economy that was only partly mobilized. His evidence seemed to call into question the existence of Hitler's design for Europe's conquest.

Milward reconciled the seemingly irreconcilable. The term Blitzkrieg commonly applied to Hitler's method of warfare, he argued, also fit the dictator's approach to diplomacy and governance. It enabled him to move rapidly, efficiently, and opportunistically, be it to manage potential enemies and contestants for power both at home and abroad, or to reallocate resources as required by strategy. Economically, the Blitzkrieg approach strategy enabled Hitler to wage war on the cheap and simultaneously maintain high standards of living within Germany. Hitler's kinetic exercise of this power-wielding strategy was a secret mainspring of his authority, and the technique worked brilliantly until the failure of the Russian campaign in December 1941—a year earlier, actually, than Klein had indicated. Only then did Germany shift to a footing of total war.

This would be far from painless. As Milward demonstrated by means of instructive case studies, all-out economic mobilization unleashed an ongoing, no-holds-barred bureaucratic struggle over strategic resource allocation between Nazis, traditional interests, and hybrid combinations of the two. His account, in a word, made it no longer possible to apply the word monolithic to the Third Reich; indeed, the term pluralistic, if understood in a weird sense, seemed better suited to it. Milward's bold insight into Germany under the Nazis awakened an abiding new interest in the powerful but peculiar economic and political institutions of Hitler's thirteen-year empire. He also added fuel to a longstanding scholarly debate between adherents of two different conceptions of the Third Reich: those on one side who regarded it as a vicious form of populist radicalism and those on the other side who cast it as an antisocial, greed-driven reactionary revanchism. The disagreement still flares up in the present.[3] Its technical details need not concern us here. Exhibit No. One on both sides of this contentious dialogue is still Milward's book of 1965.

## THE NEW ORDER AND THE FRENCH ECONOMY; THE FASCIST ECONOMY IN NORWAY

Milward could have spent the remainder of his career fighting the battle he started—which remains a central issue in British historical studies, as elsewhere—but decided instead to examine the broader question as to the significance of Nazi plans for the future of Europe. It soon resulted in a second important publication, *The New Order and the French Economy*

3. Overy, 'Germany, "Domestic Crisis" and War in 1939', and James' review of Overy's *War and Economy in the Third Reich.*

(1970). This was another path-blazing book, the first economic study of a nation under Nazi occupation. The example was well chosen.

France was, of course, the second industrial and agricultural power in Europe, and the young, now Associate Professor Milward demonstrated beyond the shadow of a doubt by means of a meticulous analysis of German policy and French production that the subject nation provided an immensely valuable economic adjunct to Hitler's war effort, more important, for example, than the Soviet Union, or, for that matter, the USSR, Eastern Europe, and Italy put together. At the same time, Milward also underscored the point that the net yield from France, however great, could, with more effective administration and less internal conflict, have been greater still. His detailed account remains perhaps the best single study in any language of wartime French industry, finance, and labor.

*The New Order and the French Economy* drew attention to a major subject which up to then historians had virtually overlooked, and it inspired a growing number of increasingly specialized books on other highly industrialized occupied and (eventually) neutral European nations: Belgium, the Netherlands, the Czech 'Protectorate', Sweden, Ireland, and Norway—the latter by Milward himself.[4] Thanks largely to this pioneering book, the history of Europe during World War II could no longer be divided into two separate parcels, Germany and the rest. Although sometimes dragged into the New Order struggling and screaming, occupied Europe was very much a part of what must be considered, until military events turned the tide, a going concern.[5]

Yet the results of his French study troubled Milward. He found little evidence in France of what he had sought to find: a Nazi attempt to reverse the course of modern European history. He explains his underlying concerns as follows:

> [t]he economic origins of fascism [ . . . ] lie in the philosophical basis of fascist economic thought. The philosophical starting-point of fascism was the rejection of what fascists call the 'Greek idea', the idea of the individual's growth to emancipation and maturity. It was this particular conception of human destiny, they argued, which was recaptured from Greek philosophy during the Renaissance and thus became the basis for Smith's 'economic man'. Fascism therefore attacked liberal economic thought at the very base of its trunk. [ . . . ] Conversion to fascism was a revolt against interpreting the world from an individualist and materialist standpoint.[6]

4. Milward, *The Fascist Economy in Norway* (1972).
5. Tilly's review of *The New Order and French Economy*.
6. Milward, 'French Labour and the German Economy, 1942–1945: An Essay on the Nature of the Fascist New Order', *The Economic History Review*: 338.

Unable to uncover evidence of a grand design for Nazi policy in France, and with plenty of information to demonstrate that it resulted instead from a succession of wartime expedients, Milward turned in frustration to a second New Order project, to Norway, with the explicit purpose of demonstrating in a single compelling case study that the economics of Fascism was something real and distinctive, which would, if successful, have diverted the course of European history from progress and enlightenment to stagnation and hierarchy, resulting in something like a Morgenthau-Plan-world with jackboots. As Milward himself put it, 'fascism represented a search, not for further economic development in new and more difficult international circumstances but for a point of economic equilibrium, a haven from the pressure of social and economic change.'[7] 'In place of growth,' he added elsewhere, 'the fascists dreamed of a state of [ . . . ] equilibrium in [which] the growing material disadvantages would find compensation in spiritual consolation.'[8] Such a condition of stasis seems far removed from the political dynamism of the Third Reich, its remarkable economic growth, and the victories of its armed forces in the early stages of the war. To demonstrate that such a remote aim drove policy under such different conditions would be no easy job.

Yet Norway would seem to provide an ideal setting as a laboratory of Fascist economic policy. It was, according to SS experts, populated by purebred Nordics, and, as a young, still preindustrial nation, was unvexed by the historical complexities of a modern society like France. It was, furthermore, a place whose survival under German occupation required far-reaching adaptation: Norway was remote, long and narrow, thinly populated, resource-poor, and more trade-dependent than any other European state. Its great asset, a world-class merchant fleet, was lost, and thereby also the wherewithal to pay for vital food imports.

It was not by accident, according to Milward, that the tough *Gauleiter* (Nazi party leader) of Essen, Josef Terboven, took office as Norwegian viceroy instead of the more secular military governors appointed to fill similar offices in France and Belgium. Yet Terboven proved to be no less a realist than his counterparts in Western Europe. He had little rapport with the leading local collaborator, Vidkun Quisling, a vintage true-believing Fascist of the 1920s stripe, who in any case had negligible support within the population. Instead, as *Reichskommissar*, Terboven operated within the strict constraints of Germany's wartime requirements and Norway's potential to meet them.

He followed a hands-off policy by necessity and limited his economic interventions to matters of critical importance. Thus Terboven raised wage levels in agriculture and opened new lands to cultivation, as Milward

---

7. Ibid.
8. Milward, *The New Order and the French Economy*, 21.

shows, in order to increase food-deficient Norway's degree of self-sufficiency but not, as he unnecessarily also insists, in pursuit of misconceived *Blut und Boden* ('Blood and Soil') ideology. He devotes a chapter to the special case of aluminum, an ambitious German program which barely got off the ground. Here the *Reichskommissar* ordered a huge increase in hydroelectric and refining capacity, not however, to serve as a showpiece of *Blut und Boden* ideology, but as something needed for the build-up of the future *Luftwaffe*.[9] Such ostensibly suspect schemes, as well as several others which Milward discusses in *The Fascist Economy in Norway*, were (with the single possible exception of a never-built coastal highway running south from Trondheim) elaborations on prewar Norwegian policy, as Milward himself admits.

Unlike France, Norway became an economic liability for the Third Reich. If the Germans were prepared to bear the costs of occupying the country, it was not in the vain hope of prolonging a mad, Fascist dream. Their strategically necessary objective was one that, on my reading, Milward did not emphasize enough: to protect the northern flank of *Festung Europa*—the 'Fortress Europe' that the areas of continental Europe occupied by Germany constituted.

In the absence of the missing ideological framework, Milward cannot satisfactorily account for the overall success of economic policy in Nazi-occupied Europe. A lack of source material from the subject nations is partly to be blamed for this shortcoming. Once it became more readily available, the economic significance of *la collaboration*—which included producers as well as policy-makers—soon became apparent. A shift in research focus from Nazi policy to the response to it soon began to take place. The new emphasis led, in turn, to the exploration of backward linkages, and in particular to the cartel-like arrangements, both domestic and foreign, that characterized the 'organized capitalism' of the interwar period. Milward later recognized the importance of the new research trends, which he, in fact, had set in motion, and altered his views accordingly to take account of them.[10]

## THE ECONOMIC DEVELOPMENT OF CONTINENTAL EUROPE

In 1971, Alan Milward returned to Great Britain after a two-year stint as an associate professor in the Economics Department of Stanford University to become the first Professor of European Studies at the University of

9. Editorial note: For a detailed study of Nazi planning on Norwegian aluminum see Chapter 4 by Hans Otto Frøland in this volume.
10. Milward's review of *The Economics of the Second World War*, by György Ránki, *The English Historical Review* 109: 432 (June 1994): 669–670.

Manchester Institute of Science and Technology (UMIST). It would be difficult to argue that anyone had a better claim to the chair. It was while in Manchester that Milward cowrote with S. B. Saul of Edinburgh University two massive studies: *The Economic Development of Continental Europe, 1780–1870* (1973) and *The Development of the Economies of Continental Europe, 1850–1914* (1977). Although four years stand between the publication dates of the two books, they were conceived of as parts of the same overall project. The purpose behind it was to expose economic history students in the 'anglosphere' to the relevant non-English economic literatures and therefore to industrial, agricultural, and financial histories of the nations of the European continent in the 'long nineteenth century'. Their remit went far beyond the Great Powers and included virtually all of the minor ones (larger than Andorra) as well.

Milward–Saul undertook a staggering task from the standpoint of language alone, but one that seems even more daunting in light of the deep differences in the numerous traditions of national historical writing as well as in their states of development, in addition to which, of course, were the variations in the historical experiences of the nations themselves. The two volumes should not be compared, in other words, to single books but to whole series, such as the edited, multiauthored and multivolume *Fontana Economic History of Europe* or the *Cambridge Economic History of Europe*. Even critics of the Milward–Saul joint enterprise recognize that no other two contemporary scholars would have dared to embark together upon such a monumental task, let alone have produced equally impressive results.

And critics there were indeed, rather nasty ones in fact. Rondo Cameron, himself author of a nineteenth-century economic history text, 'would have preferred a briefer, more synoptic history, as well as one more accessible to students.'[11] William Parker attacked Milward–Saul for having challenged the Whig version of history without, however, introducing the central character in the play—for having written the Prince of Denmark out of *Hamlet*.[12] In language even stronger than the previous critics, the future Nobel Prize–winner Douglass North found the work emblematic of 'the disarray of European economic history. Without any extant body of theory,' he added, 'the authors have relied on a combination of hypotheses, implicit or explicit, perceived or subconscious, consistent or inconsistent, as the bases for the material presented. The results cannot help but resemble the union of a catalogue and an encyclopedia.'[13] A more charitable reviewer might have found that, although lacking overall design, the results better resemble exquisite miniatures, each of which can be enjoyed for its own sake.

11. Cameron's review of *The Development Economies of Continental Europe*.
12. Parker's review of *The Development of the Economies of Continental Europe*.
13. North's review of *The Economic Development of Continental Europe*.

Arguments between theoretical 'lumpers', like the Milward–Saul critics, and empirical 'splitters', like Milward and Saul remain, of course, unresolved. The duo could have admittedly increased the attractiveness of their volumes by providing a theoretical introduction, or at least a better roadmap to their contents, instead of tacking on an unsatisfactory critique of existing economic developmental theory as an afterthought to their two-volume study. One must add, however, that by inspiring a new generation of genuinely European scholars, Milward substantially increased the utility of the exhaustive studies coauthored with Saul. Perhaps one among them will, by gaining new insights into the complex material which they present, achieve the theoretical breakthrough, the new paradigm, that still eludes economic historians. For Milward himself, the research that went into the massive paired studies of the economies of nineteenth-century Europe laid a broad and durable foundation for his subsequent work.

## WAR, ECONOMY AND SOCIETY; AGRICULTURE AND FOOD SUPPLY IN THE SECOND WORLD WAR

Milward's extraordinary intellectual range and path-breaking originality reached an epitome in *War, Economy and Society, 1939–1945* (1977), a survey originally published in German.[14] Here was yet another pioneering Milward book, the first one in English to treat World War II as an episode in the history of the world economy. It is a landmark in a literature which, up to then, had been limited almost entirely to analyses of high politics and warfare as written largely from the perspective of the victorious Western Allies. Milward's book would open a whole new range of research challenges, including those concerning the economic strategies of the belligerents and their effectiveness; the major social and economic changes resulting from them; the shifts in global power they entailed; and the wartime determinants of the post-1945 international contexts of trade, finance, and diplomacy.

The impact of *War, Economy and Society* has been gradual. It did not provoke immediate controversy, unlike Milward's earliest three books, but over the past generation has rather had the effect of nudging research into new fields of inquiry, as scholars have digested the vast quantities of data which Milward marshaled and, over time, they have imposed a structure upon it. Over the long run, *War, Economy and Society* has contributed

14. *War, Economy and Society, 1939–1945*, vol. 4 of the series 'History of the International Economy in the Twentieth Century', edited by Professor Wolfram Fischer in 1977. The book was originally published as *Der Zweite Weltkrieg: Krieg, Wirtschaft und Gesellschaft, 1939–1945* also in 1977. Italian and Spanish translations have been published.

to a fundamental reinterpretation of the war as something other than a morality play and helped establish it instead as a historical episode in its own right which, in common with all others, involves compromises, leads to tragedies as well as triumphs, and can be located as an event on the narrative arc of change.

The process of revision could hardly have been faster under the circumstances: Milward was, in terms of his methods of gathering and assimilating data, quite simply too far ahead of the pack, as the book's better reviewers noted at the time.[15] Its impact, however, might have been felt earlier, if the factual material presented in *War, Economy and Society* had been framed by an overarching thesis like the Blitzkrieg concept developed in his first and greatest book, in other words, if his account had been driven by a powerful leading idea that would have compelled a rethinking of the war's historical meaning. In the absence of such an organizing principle, the reader must make explicit what the book merely implies, a necessarily somewhat subjective exercise.

Like *The German Economy at War*, Milward's survey of World War II rests on the available patchwork of official histories (in addition to his own extensive research). And, as with the earlier work, it would also challenge historiographical convention. His account thus does not end at VE or VJ Day but instead discusses post-1945 economic recovery and reconstruction as a corollary to wartime demobilization and reconversion. *War, Economy and Society* would also break new ground for Milward himself. For the first time he would delve seriously into the histories of the United States, Asia, the Middle East, and other regions outside of Europe. In the best of all possible worlds, the book might even have laid the basis for future international history as opposed to specifically European studies, a trend driven by globalization.

As in earlier books, Milward's evidence in *War, Economy and Society* led him in directions he apparently preferred not to go. The missing protagonist in this drama is the United States. The work's driving, though unacknowledged, theme—a recurring powerful *Leitmotiv* in its pages—is the rise of American hegemony. The United States, as he might have argued more explicitly, not only waged war on a much vaster scale than the Axis enemy (and did so while supplying its allies and feeding much of the world) but did so in an organizationally superior manner, in which yardsticks applied to other belligerents (as attempted by Milward in this book) were simply not adequate.

The United States waged war not largely on the ground like Hitler's Blitzkrieg, but in three dimensions—air, land, and sea—on a global as opposed to continental scale: and with technologies like atomic weaponry of almost unimaginable destructiveness that did not exist prior to the war.

15. Reviews of *War, Economy and Society* by Wolfe and Sharp.

There was in fact not one World War II, but two of them, as measured not in lives or sacrifice, but in terms of raw power: the lesser one begun by the Nazis and the greater one ended by American might. The contemporary era can be said to have begun not with the defeat of Hitler in 1945 but with the American entrance into the war in December 1941.

This outcome did not depend, as one can infer from Milward's evidence, on any deep-seated or overall strategy but on immense size and rich resources, openness and mobility, democratic tradition, and a new relationship between science and the State cemented by the promotion of education as a national strategic priority. A new, more modern, and in ways frightening, kind of society, though perhaps still protoplasmic, in fact took form during the American struggle against the Germans and Japanese. It would assume shape and structure over the next half-century. Alan Milward can be excused for not fully grasping the significance of his evidence. No American historian had done so at the time, and, not surprisingly, he cannot find any of them to cite. Milward was, after all, far ahead of the pack on both shores of the Atlantic.

The implications of the emergence of the embryonic American superpower for the writing and understanding of Europe's contemporary history are obviously vast, though surely less significant over the long-run, than parallel changes unfolding in the non-Western world. It is to Milward's great credit that his study of World War II included the 'Pacific Theater' (as the Japanese war was still customarily called in the United States at the time of writing) in the same analytical framework as that of the 'Atlantic Theater'. For it now seems evident that over the past hundred years the most momentous world changes have occurred in an Asia returning to historical equilibrium with the West and that in the epochal reversal of relationships still under way, World War II was a critical event.

The most consequential recent reinterpretation of the war, Niall Ferguson's *The War of the World: Twentieth-Century Conflict and the Descent of the West* (2006), presents the second collective bloodbath of the twentieth century along a continuum that originates with the 1931 Japanese invasion of Manchuria and ends, at least provisionally, with the 1953 Korean armistice. Milward produced a work that should be considered an essential precursor of what Ferguson has written. At the same time, he produced a work that is an essential precursor to the younger historian's sweeping study of the last century as an age of warfare, hatred, and European decline.

*Agriculture and Food Supply in the Second World War / Landwirtschaft und Ernährung im zweiten Weltkrieg*, which Milward coedited with Bernd Martin and published in both German and English, was the final book project which he undertook concerning the Second World War period. Conceived at the 1978 international economic history conference held in Edinburgh, the project bought together a young team of Asian and European historians to examine (by means of national case studies) still another all but virgin topic. Though not often enough yet cited, the findings of the volume are striking. Nowhere in Europe, they suggest, did Fascist ideology really shape thinking about farm policy, even in France, where under the Vichy regime, romantic pastoralism became a surrogate national religion. Next, policy-making itself—chiefly a rag-bag of expedients—had only a limited influence on production and distribution. Everywhere but in the Reich, thriving black markets provided the essential margin of survival. Finally, and counterintuitively, modernization was the common thread in the history of wartime agriculture (as Milward now recognized), although the process began and ended at different points. In the global farm economy, the United States was, once again, the main driver of change. U.S. wartime food aid restored international trade, and eventually competition, in agricultural products.

Taking the whole of his production on the pre-1945 period, Alan S. Milward could look back upon what amounted to a lifetime of achievement. Though he had few peers among economic historians, comparison is in this respect unnecessary: the young Milward was a force unto himself. A relentless researcher and fearless linguist, an inexhaustible assimilator of data, and a tireless engine of production, he was an overpowering presence, a veritable force of nature. To say that at an early age he had made his mark as a scholar is trifling. His impact was immediate, and his legacy is very much alive. Milward pioneered in everything he wrote, exhibiting a few of the weaknesses but many of the strengths associated with the role of ice-breaker. He seldom failed to learn from what he had written or to build upon what he had accomplished. This is no incidental matter. In spite of his immense accomplishments while still a comparatively young man, Milward's career had just really begun.

# 3 Alan S. Milward and the European Economies at War

*Larry Neal*

When I was first approached to participate in this volume to assess the work of Alan Milward, I was a bit surprised to be asked to cover his early work as a historian. It took me a while to come to terms with how much older I am than Alan's students and followers, having come to know Alan personally in the mid-1970s when we were both quite young and under-appreciated. In reviewing Alan's curriculum vitae in preparation for this paper, however, I realized that when I came to know him in the mid-1970s, he had already moved on to the work for which he is best known today, the origins and later development of the European Union. I had invited him to be a visitor at the University of Illinois in the late 1970s, which is now a very long time ago and well before most of the participants in the volume knew him personally. But he was then already a well-established scholar, Professor of European Studies at the University of Manchester Institute of Science and Technology (UMIST), a position he had held since 1971.

Prior to then Alan must have been a scholar errant after his Ph.D. in Economic History at the London School of Economics and Political Science (LSE) in 1959. His first appointment was as an Assistant Lecturer in Indian Archaeology at the School of Oriental and African Studies at the University of London, before moving up to the University of Edinburgh in the department of Economic History for five years, to the School of Social Studies of the University of East Anglia for two years, to Stanford University for another three years, and after 1971 to UMIST. It was during this period (1965–79) that his seminal books on the economics of World War II appeared, taking advantage of archival materials that were just being made available to scholars. This was to prove a fruitful research strategy for the rest of his career: set the research agenda for future scholars by framing provocative hypotheses about the events exposed in recently opened archives. In this contribution, I will focus on his early work as a historian, but especially on his path-breaking studies of the economics of World War II.

Using the materials collected by British and American occupation forces in postwar Germany, Alan quickly produced four major works on World War II. He began with Germany, followed that with France under German occupation, moved on to examine Norway as well under German occupation, and then capped off his credentials as the preeminent economic historian of World War II with a synoptic volume bringing together the effects of the war on the economies and societies of all the major belligerents.[1]

Each book received outstanding reviews, and it is clear that Alan could have continued as the preeminent economic historian of World War II for the rest of his career. Now I can see that it was not the economics or finance of war as such that fascinated him so much as the complex interaction of bureaucrats and entrepreneurs when they were called upon to respond to exogenous shocks. Like most economic historians, he then enjoyed explaining the unintended consequences that, more often than not, emerged from the combined actions of bureaucrats and entrepreneurs as events ran their course. In a wartime setting, entrepreneurs had to organize factors of production to meet the logistical demands of the bureaucrats rather than simply try to make a living by satisfying the demands of a civilian economy. Bureaucrats could exert even more control directly upon entrepreneurs by using the military power at their disposal, but ultimately they too had to bow to the economic constraints that fixed technology and scarce resources placed upon their ability to meet both civilian and military demands. While armed forces were demobilized after hostilities ceased, the bureaucracies that had risen in power during the war proved to be entrenched. It was this hysteresis of planning that had arisen during the war in the respective government bureaucracies of Europe that continued to fascinate and motivate Alan's historical research agenda, in my opinion, and shaped the rest of the career that other authors will discuss in this same volume.

This basic insight of Alan's in examining the economics of World War II brought together an analysis of both economic and political forces as they interacted to reshape the organization of the government and the economy in each belligerent power. Early reviews lauded this adventurous attempt, although senior scholars at the time did chide him if he had not cited their own or favorite work. Sidney Ratner at Rutgers, for example, huffed that Alan had simply reinforced the view of Burton H. Klein that Germany had not managed to rearm massively before or even in the first years of the war.[2] Alan's contribution, of course, went well beyond that assertion as he explored in detail the domestic political constraints that inhibited the Nazi regime from achieving its desired rearmament. Ratner did, however, appreciate the detail of Alan's explanation of how Germany managed to shift

1. Milward, *The German Economy at War* (1965); *The New Order and the French Economy* (1970); *The Fascist Economy in Norway* (1972); and *War, Economy and Society, 1939–1945* (1977). The latter was originally published as *Der Zweite Weltkrieg: Krieg, Wirtschaft and Gesellschaft, 1939–1945* (1977). Milward treated Sweden summarily in one article, 'Could Sweden have Stopped the Second World War?' (1967).
2. Klein, *Germany's Economic Preparations for War*. Sidney Ratner's review of *The German Economy at War*.

from Blitzkrieg to total war planning as Albert Speer perfected the bureaucratic organization begun by Fritz Todt. A reviewer from St. Antony's College, Oxford, also appreciated the argument, but strongly recommended another book also published in 1965.[3] This was by an Oxford colleague, Hannah Vogt, which clearly described the evil of the Nazi regime and was intended to be read by German school children.[4] Apparently, a scholarly appreciation of the rationality of the German war effort under Adolf Hitler had to be kept subordinate to the characterization of the Nazi ideology as irrational and consequently doomed to failure. Otherwise, some other dictator could arise and succeed in perfecting a Fascist economic system.[5]

Another reviewer concluded that Alan's description of the bureaucratic battles waged by Speer to implement Todt's vision of total war was yet 'another effective demonstration that behind the façade of monolithic, super-efficient dictatorship, Nazi Germany was actually a chaotic mess.'[6] A more dispassionate reviewer noted that Alan demonstrated that Germany 'was preparing for war, but war of a special kind—*Blitzkrieg*—which demanded not "armament in depth" but the less burdensome "armament in width".'[7] One now has to remember the intense emotions generated about the Nazi regime during the war and the cementing of those biases by the well-publicized Nuremberg trials. The most negative review was by Arthur Schweitzer, Professor of Economics at Indiana University. In his review, Schweitzer was still upset that no one at the Nuremberg trials had paid attention to his discovery of the German document that clearly laid out an extensive four-year plan for massive rearmament beginning in 1937. He had published his analysis in 1957, showing that the plan had been realized in large part from mid-1937 through 1941, but by looting the resources of conquered countries beginning with Poland in 1939. After flailing against all aspects of Alan's appreciation of the Blitzkrieg, Schweitzer grudgingly concluded, 'The second half of the book handles competently the full-fledged war economy.'[8]

Alan followed up his controversial analysis of the economic planning and rationality of the German war effort by examining just how the resources of the major industrial power conquered early in 1940, France, were exploited under Albert Speer's economic plans. In this effort, Richard Tilly's review was most favorable as he acknowledged the force of Alan's demonstration of the 'enormous economic importance of France for Nazi Germany's war effort', but then he took issue with Alan's argument that

3. Nicholls' review of *The German Economy at War.*
4. Vogt, *The Burden of Guilt.*
5. The rise to power of the Shah of Iran in the 1960s, and the economic advice he received from Hjalmar Schacht after his release from prison—the Reich Minister of Economics from August 1934 to November 1937, tried and acquitted at the Nuremberg trials—would be a worthwhile study in this regard.
6. Neil's review of *The German Economy at War.*
7. Forsyth's review of *The German Economy at War.*
8. Schweitzer's review of *The German Economy at War.*

Nazi anticapitalist ideas about the 'New Economic Order' were important in shaping and executing German policy toward France. On that point, Tilly noted that the *Grossraumwirtschaft* ideology in its pure form required deindustrialization of France to keep Greater Germany autarkic economically, but that the continental autarky of the German conquests in Europe was forced upon them by the success of the Allied blockade strategy.[9] A reviewer with less at stake in the argument over Nazi ideology, however, stated that Alan had, indeed, made these very points. But this reviewer then worried that perhaps Alan was too sympathetic to the idea that a self-sufficient economy could be erected within Europe by force, when he stated, 'At that moment when the Blitzkrieg in Russia had almost achieved its ends the shape of the National Socialist New Order may be seen. But the moment is a brief one, and once over, official silence falls' (269). The reviewer asks 'Does one sense here a tone of wistful regret? Might an imposed economic order have been better for Europe than present bickerings and divisions?'[10]

The most entertaining, if somewhat eccentric, review came from Charles Kindleberger, who served as a staff officer with General Omar N. Bradley's intelligence services and who recounted his hazy memory of an intelligence report from the Resistance in France,

> a chart from an aircraft factory—which one I forget—showing the progress in manufacture of large reconnaissance aircraft for the Luftwaffe, either Dornier 24's or Focke-Wulf 200's—again, I forget. The vertical axis represented stages in production from bottom to top, going from beginning to completion. The horizontal axis showed the passage of time by days. The chart measured 8½ inches in height and 30 feet plus in width, with no airplane having been completed over the more than twenty-four months since the first had been started.[11]

All this personal recollection was to make the point that there had been, in fact, an effective internal resistance to German occupation within France despite the quantitative evidence marshaled by Alan to show how much France did contribute to sustaining the German war effort. Kindleberger concluded by asking, 'How much was the German eventual military defeat a result of invasion on the one hand, or the impossibility of holding down a conquered people on the other?'[12] Another reviewer, however, noted that Alan's appraisal of the effectiveness of German control of the French economy was corroborated by the just-released movie, *Le Chagrin et la*

9. Tilly's review of *The New Order and the French Economy.*
10. Funk's review of *The New Order and the French Economy.*
11. Kindleberger's review of *The New Order and the French Economy.*
12. Ibid., 161.

*pitié* (The Sorrow and the Pity).[13] Recently published research also supports Alan's original findings over Kindleberger's impressions.[14]

Kindleberger would become a much harsher critic of Alan's work when he argued against the necessity of the Marshall Plan for the economic reconstruction of Europe after World War II. Alan took this in stride, commenting once to me that after all, the war and the economic reconstruction of Western Europe under the tutelage of the United States had been the high point in the careers of the participants. None of them would take lightly any downplaying of their heroic efforts. And then, of course, Professor Schweitzer was annoyed at Alan's acceptance of Speer's obviously self-serving notes designed to save him from execution along with the other Nazi war criminals. In his equally acerbic review of Alan's book on France, Schweitzer asserted that there was no real difference between the goals of Fritz Sauckel, focused on forced labor, and Speer, emphasizing industrial production. 'The relevant documents support only the conclusion that Sauckel's and Speer's policies constitute different methods for the same Nazi policy of exploitation, which were both sanctioned by Hitler.'[15]

Alan's next book was to look at a purer case of Nazi ideology in action, its occupation of Norway, which was clearly appropriate for incorporation into Greater Germany. The descendants of the Vikings were good Aryan stock, fishing and dairy farming appropriate for maintaining food supplies for German industry and customers for German industrial exports—a perfect member of the New Economic Order. Strategic demands for the war effort, however, trumped all this, not to mention Norwegian desires to industrialize based on hydroelectric power and rich deposits of wolfram and bauxite. Alan's conclusion, that 'the Norwegian people proved as flagrant an example of opposition to the new system as could be found in Europe,' won general approval by reviewers.[16] His attempt to make a test case for the viability of Fascism, however, caused some reviewers to challenge his interpretation of Nazi economic policy as 'fascism'. One of them wondered what subtext was really on Alan's mind,

> Mr. Milward's constant repetition of the word 'fascist', and his evident preoccupation with 'present-day European fascist parties' ('many of them'—but who in fact are they?) along with a tendency towards over-emphatic language in places, and one or two suggestive footnotes, do point to an underlying polemical, even ideological, purpose that is

13. Funk's review of *The New Order and the French Economy*.
14. Occhino et al., 'How Much Can a Victor Force the Vanquished to Pay?'
15. Schweitzer's review of *The New Order and the French Economy*.
16. Reviews of *The Fascist Economy in Norway* by Clausen and Hayes.

> never made explicit, and is indeed otherwise kept below the surface of his scholarly text.[17]

Schweitzer, if he had reviewed the book on Norway, no doubt would have grumped that the German 'New Economic Order' was just a briefly touted propaganda ploy by the Nazis, which was cut off after the military victories in 1940.

By this time, Alan's reputation as the preeminent economic historian of World War II was secure, and he was the natural person to write up the overall economic history of the war efforts by the belligerents for the series of volumes initiated by the University of California Press on the economic history of the twentieth century. Dudley Baines, later to be a colleague of Alan's at the LSE Economic History Department, assessed the series overall as variable in quality, with Kindleberger's *The World in Depression, 1929–39* as the best and Alan's *War, Economy and Society, 1939–45* as outstanding.[18] Widely reviewed, the book was generally applauded as a masterful synthesis, only lacking perhaps in detail over the economic efforts of Italy and Japan, according to a German reviewer, which was odd, as the Russian archives remained untouched.[19] One reviewer presciently noted with approval Alan's conclusion that 'the legacy of the war was a consciousness that the economy could be directed into the desired channels, some knowledge of how to direct it, and the acquisition of a great store of facts about the economy' (130).[20]

Several reviewers, myself included, picked up approvingly on one of his themes, namely 'that the amazing resiliency and flexibility of modern advanced economies in general explains more about Nazi economic accomplishments than does the totalitarian nature of the Nazi system in particular.'[21] While I approved of this conclusion, especially in light of the popular press bewailing both the shortage of oil and the danger of pollution to the environment, other reviewers found Alan's conclusion worrisome. 'More troubling is his [Milward's] argument that this war, like all others, represented no economic abnormality, no hiatus in economic development—that it was a potentially profitable venture for the combatants.'[22] Of course, this was, and remains, Alan's great contribution to modern economic history, treating the economics of war as part of the history of economies in general rather than as an abnormal disruption to the process of long-run economic growth.

---

17. Cullis's review of *The Fascist Economy in Norway*.
18. Baines' review of *War, Economy and Society*.
19. Petzina's review of *Der Zweite Weltkrieg: Krieg, Wirtschaft und Gesellschaft, 1939–1945*.
20. Heath's review of *War, Economy and Society, 1939–1945*.
21. Wolfe's review of *War, Economy and Society, 1939–1945*.
22. D. S. White's review of *War, Economy and Society, 1939–1945*.

When I reviewed Alan's final work on the economics of World War II, *War, Economy and Society*, I concluded that 'Milward's authorship of an economic history of World War II that "could not be written" will be a stimulus for worthwhile research for years to come.'[23] Mark Harrison's subsequent career at the University of Warwick bears out this assessment in good measure, as does the work of Geofrey Mills and Hugh Rockoff, Susan Linz and James R. Millar, and many others.[24] I still like the lesson I drew from Alan's study of the German war economy, which showed that production of war materiel continued to rise even during the course of round the clock strategic bombing by U.S. and British air forces. This was that the complexity of modern industrial economies makes them less, not more, vulnerable to exogenous shocks, an inference that held up nicely during the subsequent oil shocks of the 1970s, but seems less robust after the global 'great recession' of 2007 onwards.

While this review was only published when Alan was already present at the University of Illinois as a visiting professor in 1978, I had come to appreciate both his scholarship and his collegiality earlier. I had assigned his article on the end of the Blitzkrieg as one of the few economic analyses of the German war effort, and found his book on *The New Order and the French Economy* enlightening personally. Alan's demonstration of the exploitation of the French economy under Nazi occupation helped clarify in my mind the strange habits of French gendarmes, *haut fonctionnaires*, and Parisians that had puzzled me during two years of employment at the Organization for Economic Cooperation and Development in Paris from 1970 to 1972. While on sabbatical leave in Wales in 1976, I had finished up a paper that had grown out of my lectures on European economic history, dealing with the economics of Nazi bilateral trade agreements before World War II. The paper was eventually published in *The Economic History Review*, but only after receiving a favorable 'heads up' review from Alan, which he kindly sent to me directly.[25] This was a welcome event, indeed, for me as the paper had previously been rejected by Rondo Cameron at *The Journal of Economic History*! To this day, I am convinced that Rondo used Schweitzer and Tilly as referees. So it is small wonder that my work, which helped strengthen Alan's general case about the weakness of the Germany economy under Nazi governance, and worse, analyzed it in rational, economic terms rather than as representing a demented ideology of racial superiority, would be rejected out of hand by the same scholars who had criticized Alan's work.

Needless to say, Alan and I became fast friends thereafter. (Richard Tilly and Rondo Cameron also became friends, but later and on different

23. Neal's review of *War, Economy and Society, 1939–1945*.
24. Mills and Rockoff, *Sinews of War;* Harrison, *The Economics of World War II*; and Millar and Linz, *The Soviet economic experiment*.
25. Neal, 'The Economics and Finance'.

terms.) I am happy to say that all later work, at least in my opinion, confirms my findings in that article. Indeed, Alan himself wrote a favorable review of a study of the Romanian trade with Nazi Germany that demonstrated the bargaining power of Romania, due to Germany's extreme need for foreign oil, gave it the upper hand in its negotiations with Nazi Germany over the terms of the bilateral trade agreement. Alan's opening salvo was 'Another well-aimed blow is delivered by [Marguerat] at the persistent historical myth that German international economic policy before 1940 exploited the economies of central and south-eastern Europe.'[26] Work by Albrecht Ritschl, taking advantage of the archives of the *Reichsbank* when they became available after 1990, also largely confirmed our findings.[27] An ongoing Ph.D. dissertation at the LSE is exploring the relations of Germany with Spain, concluding as well that Spain benefited greatly from its trade relations with Germany even during the war.[28] A 2008 article in the *Scandinavian Economic History Review* makes the same case for Sweden, confirming again the earlier, but at the time controversial, conclusion that Germany's policy was exploitive, but the Nazi regime could not take advantage of its larger size; the same conclusion reached by Alan in his initial article on Sweden, also published in that journal.[29] In sum, despite the visceral rejection of Alan's early view on Nazi trade policy and of my later work on the nature of the economic incentives at work in those highly controversial trade policies of Germany during the Nazi regime, the empirical evidence continues to support our position.

In 1971, when negotiations had been reopened yet again between Britain and the European Community, Alan had initiated an effort to begin training British students for eventual employment in the European Community. With his usual pessimism about his academic environment, wherever it happened to be, he described to me the obstacles he encountered from obdurate administrators at every turn, until one day, for reasons that remained a mystery to him, there were no obstacles and everything he asked for, save for the leave of absence to come to Illinois for a term, seemed to be granted. I suggested that Britain's actual entry into the European Communities, two

26. Milward's review of *Le IIIe Reich et le pétrole roumain, 1938–1940*, by Philippe Marguerat, in the *English Historical Review* 94: 371 (April 1979): 472–473.
27. Ritschl, 'Nazi Economic Imperialism and the Exploitation of the Small: Evidence from Germany's Secret Foreign Exchange Balance, 1938–1940',
28. Golson, 'Neutrality for Self-Benefit? Spanish Trade in the Second World War', paper delivered to LSE Ph.D. thesis seminar, Lent 2010.
29. As mentioned before, Alan treated Sweden in 'Could Sweden have Stopped the Second World War?' As far as I can see, this topic has been avoided until very recently when two graduate students published an exhaustive analysis of Sweden's trade with Germany prior to and during World War II: Hedbert and Håkansson, 'Did Germany Exploit its Small Trading Partners?'

years after his tour of duty began at the University of Manchester, or his obvious success in placing students in jobs in Europe, had something to do with it. Alan waved these aside as superficial and implausible reasons. More likely, in his opinion, was the inevitable turnover in administrators, which had removed his anonymous persecutor in favor of another individual; this new administrator then focused on tormenting some other faculty member instead of Alan. It was this experience at Manchester, however, that finally turned him from his controversial but definitive studies on the economic effects of World War II to focus instead on the economic history of the European Communities as they emerged from the postwar reconstruction efforts in Western Europe.

It was this expertise as well that led us at Illinois to make him an offer to become head of the Office of West European Studies and Professor in the Economics Department, mainly to replace me with someone of much greater stature. It was an offer he eventually turned down, remaining at Manchester another five years. No doubt he feared the same initial problems in developing a program at Illinois that he had eventually overcome at Manchester, but the distance of Illinois from his research archives was probably the determining factor. Even the presidential libraries of Harry S. Truman and Dwight D. Eisenhower were too distant for scholarly convenience. While Alan's initial claim to fame was to tackle the daunting problem of the economics of modern warfare, exemplified by the total war effort eventually exerted by Nazi Germany, his fascination with trying to weigh the competing economic and political interests of Western European nation-states as they coped with the challenges of World War II drove him to explore what motivated them as they negotiated the terms under which they agreed to participate in what has become the European Union.

As Alan's work moved into the postwar settlements that followed the end of World War II, it seems clear to me that his analysis of the respective war efforts by the belligerents shaped his thinking about the way they made the transition back to peacetime. He was still struck by how entrenched the substantial bureaucracies that each country created to administer its war effort—whether at the direction of the German occupiers or in opposition to the Axis powers—had become. Resurgent nationalism, seen repeatedly in Europe's history during previous great conflicts such as World War I and the Napoleonic Wars, was now made operational through large-scale bureaucracies of central governments remaining from the war effort. Ultimately, he came to argue that the Western European response to the U.S. governments' initiatives in the first decade after 1945 was to 'rescue the nation-state' as the legitimate form of government within Western Europe. Americans, understandably, took this as a rescue of postwar Western European governments from the threat of American hegemony, given the manner in which Marshall Plan aid was distributed by the Organization for European Economic Cooperation (OEEC).[30] Alan's perspective, however, dwelt more on the peacetime control over the civilian economies by the bureaucracies now devoted to economic planning, but with distinctly national rather than transnational motivations. This was a phenomenon I observed firsthand while serving in the Secretariat of the Organization for Economic Cooperation and Development (OECD; the successor to the Marshall Plan's OEEC) in 1970–72.

From an American perspective, Alan's view of the Marshall Plan was a harsh verdict on the unprecedented efforts made by U.S. policy-makers to 'get things right' this time. In their view, reflected in works by Herbert Feis and Charles Kindleberger, they were determined to avoid the mistakes made by the United States after World War I. According to this view, the United States' indifference to the European postwar settlements, especially in its refusal to participate in the League of Nations, bore a good deal of responsibility for the disaster of World War II. Alan obviously enjoyed puncturing this inflated view of the importance of the United States in first bringing Europe into the cauldron of World War II, but especially the standard view of the importance of the Marshall Plan in bringing Western Europe into economic recovery and the economic miracles of the 1950s and 1960s. My own view was that American advisors for the Marshall Plan bore some responsibility in restoring the importance of national bureaucracies by insisting that each country's government presented a coherent plan for its intended use of Marshall Plan aid before dispensing any funds. This is a view forcefully articulated in the Italian case by Vera Zamagni.[31] Even Barry Eichengreen, in defending the virtues of U.S.-led international institutions such as the World Bank and the International Monetary Fund, has acknowledged that it was European initiative that led European governments to reject devaluation of their currencies to solve the so-called dollar shortage problem after World War II and instead try to emulate the German example of strong currencies to reduce the price of imported wage goods.[32]

Alan's obsession with the self-serving power of national government bureaucracies, however, did lead him to miscalculate on the likelihood of these staunchly nationalistic bureaucrats accepting a common currency in the euro. I recall several lunches at the LSE where he admitted he had made

---

30. See Chapter 2, 'A Dispute over Origins: The European View versus the American Perspective' in Neal, *The Economics of Europe and the European Union*, 22–40.
31. Zamagni, *The Economic History of Italy*.
32. Eichengreen, *The European Economy since 1945*.

bets that the euro would never appear as an actual currency in the form of notes and coins. I have no idea how many and how large were his wagers or with whom, but he was worried in 2000. He could take some satisfaction, however, in noting that regardless of the number of countries adopting the common currency, each maintains its existing printing plants and mints with the capacity to return to its legacy currency in case of war, as I learned recently from an official of the Banca d'Italia. It would be great fun to hear his evaluation of Jean-Claude Trichet, the paragon of French *haut fonctionnaire* mentality while in the French Treasury, and now more German than the German bankers as head of the European Central Bank. Perhaps, just perhaps, Alan would see government bureaucracies as the ultimate legacy of World War II, rather than the European nation-state as such, but then he would tell me no doubt that there is no difference between them.

# 4 Nazi Planning and the Aluminum Industry

*Hans Otto Frøland*

Having published *The New Order and the French Economy* in 1970, in which he explored the Nazi exploitation of the French economy in the context of German ideas of a *Grossraumwirtschaft* (the creation of an economic bloc under German dominance across the European continent) two years later Alan S. Milward published a corresponding examination of Norway's economy, *The Fascist Economy in Norway*.[1] Milward viewed his studies as test cases of fascist economic thought and theory in practice.[2] Since the 1970s however, historical research has rejected the notion of one fascist conception implemented in occupied and reorganized Europe. On the contrary, research has emphasized the singularity of Nazism and the *ad hoc* pragmatism of Nazi occupation policy. Yet no historian would deny that notions of a *Grossraumwirtschaft*, so central to Milward's analysis, existed among German government and business circles. Milward argued that in spite of the existence of these ideas of *Grossraumwirtschaft*, the nature of German foreign economic policy before 1939 based on bilateral trade agreements with the countries of south-eastern Europe did not represent Nazi exploitation of these economies. In fact he argued that it was quite the reverse.[3] It was the conquest of territory from 1939 that forced into the Nazi polity different notions of what the 'New Order' might really become.

The aluminum industry was an obvious case when elaborating on the New Order. The *Wehrwirtschaftlicher neuer Erzeugungsplan* (New Production Plan for the Wartime Economy), developed in 1938 under the *Vierjahresplan* (the Nazi four-year plan for war preparation), defined aluminum as a strategic raw material to build up the *Luftwaffe*. Production targets increased after the war broke out and reached their peak in the Göring Plan in June 1941. Germany lacked bauxite as well as energy to reach the new

---

1. Milward, *The New Order and the French Economy* (1970) and *The Fascist Economy in Norway* (1972).
2. See Milward, 'Fascism and the Economy', in Laqueur, *Fascism: A Reader's Guide*, 379–412.
3. Milward, 'The Reichsmark Bloc and the International Economy', in Hirschfeld and Kettenacker, *Der „Führerstaat": Mythos und Realität*, 377–413.

targets. Unsurprisingly therefore, in the book on France Milward devoted a chapter to German exploitation of French bauxite and alumina, and in the book on Norway he devoted a chapter to the German plan for expanding aluminum production. The Norwegian plan, developed in 1940–1941, took the abundance of cheap hydropower as the point of departure, and aimed at its height to expand electrolytic smelting capacity in Norway sevenfold. But as Norway had no bauxite this had to be imported, and not only from France. Milward concluded: '[o]nly with the full and unfettered achievement of the *Grossraumwirtschaft* could there be any chance that the necessary quantity of bauxite and alumina would be available to the Norwegian factories. It was not really a plan for Norway which was under consideration but a plan for Europe.'[4] He was right indeed.

Milward's account of the aluminum plan was in fact a study of relations between the German government and German industry. He declared:

> no other wartime episode is so revealing about the nature of the relationship between the National Socialist government and the industrial circles which supported it, a relationship very much more complex than has usually been admitted by historians of fascism. The history of the aluminium plan shows the German industrialists as much more ardent supporters of most of the government's foreign economic policies than most western historians have been prepared to admit.[5]

He showed how industrialists in their pursuit of strategic influence adjusted to political objectives and how they were integrated into the Nazi government's machinery of exploitation. It was in itself no novel interpretation that German industry was integrated into the obscure Nazi polity. Yet in 1972 Milward's study was pioneering. Surely the aluminum plan had been touched upon by Dietrich Eichholtz from an economic history perspective and Hans-Dietrich Loock from a political history perspective. While Eichholtz saw German 'state monopoly capitalism' continuously aspiring to dominate Europe and entrusted to prepare for aggressive war, Loock saw political negotiations and personal intrigues among political ideologists of the 'fascist revolution'.[6] Milward was right when claiming, first, that his analysis revealed far more complexity 'than has usually been admitted by historians of fascism' (e.g. Eichholtz), and second, that industrial circles were 'more ardent supporters of most of the government's foreign economic policies than most western historians have been prepared to admit' (e.g. Loock). By analyzing the combined actions of government agencies and

---

4. Milward, *The Fascist Economy in Norway*, 206.
5. Ibid., 171.
6. Eichholtz, *Geschichte der deutschen Kriegswirtschaft*, and Loock, *Quisling, Rosenberg und Terboven.*

industrial circles, Milward disclosed the dialectics of the political economy of the aluminum plan:

> Had there been any harmony of interests between the Reich's government and the German firms on the details of what was to be done, [Josef] Terboven [the appointed *Reichskommissar* for Norway] would no doubt have been overridden. But the firms themselves were engaged in bitter rivalry and were each supported in their rivalry by different branches of government.[7]

Hence he concluded that the New Order was a series of politico-economic compromises void of coordination: 'In such circumstances planning was impossible'.[8]

The rather wishful aluminum plan started to crumble even before the Blitzkrieg was replaced by the European war economy. Milward admitted that the aluminum plan, like the New Order itself, only came close to being implemented as the German Blitzkrieg, on which the New Order depended, was replaced by a European war economy from 1942. Admittedly his wider Blitzkrieg thesis, developed in his *The German Economy at War*, has been much contested.[9] Yet Milward saw the aluminum industry as one of those industries which, because of their war strategic value, were not wholly planned on the concept of the New Order but also for the war itself. Hence the fate of the wider Blitzkrieg thesis has no implication for his arguments about the relations between the Nazi government and the German aluminum industry.

Today we know more about the emergence and character of the aluminum plan than appears in Milward's narrative. Richard J. Overy and Rolf-Dieter Müller have provided information on Hermann Göring and Albert Speer and their politico-economic empires.[10] Peter Hayes and Gottfried Plumpe have broadened the understanding of IG Farben's (IGF) role while Fritz Petrick and Lutz Budrass have done so for the role of *Junkers Flugzeug und Motorenwerke* (JFM).[11] The two former scholars have also furthered our knowledge about the role of the *Reichswirtschaftsministerium* (RWM or Reich's Economics Ministry) and the *Vierjahresplan*, while Budrass in

7. Milward, *The Fascist Economy in Norway*, 188.
8. Ibid., 208.
9. Milward, *The German Economy at War* (1965). The book was translated into German and Italian.
10. Overy, *Goering: The Iron Man*; Müller, 'Albert Speer und die Rüstungspolitik im Totalen Krieg'.
11. Hayes, *Industry and Ideology*; Plumpe, *Die I.G. Farbenindustrie AG*; Petrick, 'Zwei Schlüsseldokumente zur faschistischen "Aufteilung der europäischen Aluminiumindustrie"'; Petrick, *Der ‚Leichtmetallausbau Norwegen', 1940–1945*; and Budrass, *Flugzeugindustrie und Luftrüstung in Deutschland, 1918–1945*.

particular has done so for the *Reichsluftfahrtministerium* (RLM or Reich's Air Ministry). Petrick also came up with much new evidence on the role of *Vereinigte Aluminium Werke* (VAW), for which, regrettably, no in-depth study exists as of today.[12] Cornelia Rauh has also provided some new information on VAW's role in her analysis of *Aluminium-Industrie-Aktiengesellschaft* (AIAG).[13] These contributions have provided much more accurate knowledge of the politico-economic compromises of Nazi aluminum planning and proved Milward wrong on several points. Although Milward emphasized the primacy of the state, as opposed to the widely accepted notion of a '*privatizierte Wirtschaftspolitik*' (a political private economy) at the time, he still found that the German aluminum industry's expansion abroad 'was regarded as a fixed, finite affair'.[14] With regard to IGF this has been modified by Hayes and Plumpe.

Like Milward, the above-mentioned scholars have focused on the German actors and ignored indigenous contributions to aluminum planning through economic collaboration. Contrariwise, historical research on Norwegian economic collaboration has broadened the understanding of Nazi aluminum planning well beyond the above-mentioned contributions. Robert Bohn has analyzed the *Reichskommissariat* and Lars Thue the policies of Vidkun Quisling's government to expand hydroelectric power capacity.[15] They have confirmed Milward's overall conclusions that Nazi aluminum planning was 'void of coordination' but have more accurately disclosed the ambiguous relations between Norwegian and German authorities.[16] From the perspective of business interests, Ketil Gjølme Andersen has studied the role of *Norsk Hydro* (Hydro) while Hans Otto Frøland and Jan Thomas Kobberrød have studied the role of *Norsk Aluminium Company* (NACO).[17] These were the two largest Norwegian companies involved in the Norwegian aluminum expansion program. Their accounts show how the two companies contributed voluntarily and proactively. Arguably, German aluminum planning in Norway was far from the 'fixed, finite affair' that Milward observed.

In keeping with recent Norwegian historiography, and focusing on NACO, the purpose of this chapter is to disclose the active collaboration of the Norwegian aluminum industry. I argue that NACO played a more

12. Some information can be derived from the business history of VIAG. See Pohl, *VIAG Aktiengesellschaft, 1923–1998*; and Schneider, 'Die Vereinigte Industrieunternehmungen AG (VIAG) und der Vierjahresplan'.
13. See Rauh, *Schweizer Aluminium für Hitlers Krieg?*
14. Milward, *The Fascist Economy in Norway*, 173.
15. Bohn, *Reichskommissariat Norwegen*; and Thue, *Statens kraft, 1890–1947*.
16. Bohn also canvasses Milward's Blitzkrieg thesis.
17. Andersen, *Flaggskip i fremmed eie: Hydro, 1905–1945*; and Frøland and Kobberrød, 'The Norwegian Contribution to Göring's Megalomania: Norway's Aluminium Industry during World War II'.

active role in the Nazis' aluminum plan than accounted for by Milward, Hayes, Petrick, Plumpe, and Budrass. After a brief presentation of the Norwegian expansion program in the context of the 'New Aluminum Order', the chapter then elaborates on NACO's integration into the Norwegian program. The evidence allows for wider reflections on indigenous business contributions to the Nazis' aluminum planning.

## THE REICH'S ALUMINUM PLAN FOR NORWAY IN THE NEW ORDER

The Third Reich needed to produce 50,000 airplanes a year to fight a war successfully on two fronts. For this reason, on 23 June 1941, Göring decided that Europe's aluminum production should reach 1,000,000 tons per year (t/a) by 1944. An overview of the overall plan is presented in Table 4.1.

Norway would become the largest producer after the Reich. While in 1940 the country's capacity was 38,000 t/a aluminum and 12,000 t/a alumina, by 1944 it would be around 240,000 t/a aluminum and 178,000 t/a alumina.[18] The abundance of hydropower allowed for this. The *Reichskommissariat Norwegen* anticipated that Norway could produce 10–12 billion kW a year, equal to Germany's annual consumption.[19] As Norway had no bauxite, this would be imported mainly from France, Hungary, and Croatia. As the smelters would need twice as much alumina to produce aluminum, the plan also assumed Norwegian alumina imports

*Table 4.1* The Göring Plan for Aluminum Expansion (thousand tons per year) in Europe

| | Reich | Norway | France | Switzer-land | Italy | Croatia | Hungary | Rumania | Greece | Soviet Union |
|---|---|---|---|---|---|---|---|---|---|---|
| Aluminum | 350 | 240 | 95 | 35 | 100 | 40 | | 50 | | 100 |
| Alumina | 676 | 178 | 465 | | 200 | 200 | | 100 | 50 | 350 |
| Bauxite | | | 1250 | | 400 | 700 | 700 | 200 | 411 | 700 |

*Source*: Bundesarchiv-Militärarchiv, Freiburg (Ba-Ma), RL 3/915, *Die Aluminiumnot in der Luftfahrtindustrie und massnahmen zu ihrer Bekämpfung*, unsigned and undated presentation (probably by Heinrich Koppenberg, July 1941).

18. As with the larger Göring Plan different versions also existed of the Norwegian part of it. For a version of the Norwegian expansion plan at its peak, see Ba-Ma, RL 3/914, Leichtmetal Norwegen, unsigned and undated presentation (probably by Wilhelm Moschel, September 1941). Different versions of the plan are presented in Milward, *The Fascist Economy in Norway*, 178; Bohn, *Reichskommissariat Norwegen*, 398; and Petrick, *Der ‚Leichtmetallausbau Norwegen', 1940–1945*, 107, 122, 123, 153, and 168.
19. Bohn, *Reichskommissariat Norwegen*, 389.

of 403,000 t/a. In addition to supplies from Gebrüder Giulini's alumina plant at Ludwigshafen, which would be extended by 50,000 t/a, new alumina refineries in Croatia, Greece, and Vichy France were supposed to furnish the Norwegian smelters with 250,000 t/a. The remainder was to be taken from the Soviet refineries in Kandalakscha on the Kola Peninsula and Tischwin near Leningrad. Their combined capacity was more than 100,000 t/a in 1940.[20]

It is clear that by 12 November 1940 Göring had already adopted a plan to expand Norwegian aluminum and alumina production. At that point in time targets were established at 150–180,000 t/a for aluminum and 310,000 t/a for alumina.[21] Hence in the version of June 1941 the aluminum target was raised while for alumina it was reduced. The former plan had targeted much lower imports of alumina because it was assumed that the Norwegian industry would develop its own alumina on the basis of domestic labradorite, for which two Norwegian methods of production existed. Hydro had developed a process using nitric acid while NACO had developed the Pedersen method. Although the Pedersen method demanded much more energy than the more widely used Bayer process, energy was exactly what Norway could offer. Its main advantage was that it could exploit harder clay with less alumina content than the Bayer process. Labradorite contained only 30% alumina as opposed to the 60% usually found in bauxite. Yet bauxite would still be imported as it was expected in the long run that alumina would be produced by 1/3 labradorite and 2/3 bauxite.

The main German aluminum player in Norway after the invasion on 9 April 1940 was Heinrich Koppenberg, and the plan of 12 November 1940 was often referred to as the Koppenberg Plan.[22] Koppenberg was General Director of JFM and his ambitions reflected those of the company. He had already attached the manufacturer Dürener Metallwerke (DM), famous for its duralumin technology, to JFM, and with the endorsement of the RLM he wanted to secure a metal base for JFM in Norway and transform it into a vertically integrated European concern. In May 1940 the Luftwaffe Director-General of Equipment or *Generallufzeugmeister*, Ernst Udet, had appointed Koppenberg as *Treuhänder* (Trustee) for the aluminum industry in Norway, and in July 1940 his appointment was extended to cover the

---

20. Eberhard Neukirch, 'Die Entwicklung des Leichtmetallausbaues im Vierjahresplan mit besonderer Berücksichtigung der Zeit des grossdeutschen Freiheitskampfes', unpublished manuscript written in 1943, 416ff., located in Bundesarchiv (BA), Berlin-Lichterfelde, R 3112/150–152. Specifically on alumina imports, see Ba-Ma, RL 3/913, Letter from Heinrich Koppenberg to Karl Krauch, 26 July 1941, and RL 3/2702, Letter from Erhard Milch to Koppenberg, 16 September 1941.
21. Ba-Ma, RL 3/883, Besprechung Herr Reichsmarschall Göring—Dr. Koppenberg, 12 November 1940.
22. His personal biography is presented in Budrass, 'Unternehmer im Nationalsozialismus'.

aluminum industry in Belgium, the Netherlands, and occupied France as well. His responsibilities as trustee also covered aluminum trade with Vichy France and Switzerland.[23]

In 1939 under an existing cartel agreement, VAW controlled about 70 percent of German aluminum production, with Aluminiumwerk GmbH in Bitterfeld (AB), jointly owned by IGF and Metallgesellschaft, controlling 18 percent, and Suisse AIAG controlling 12 percent.[24] It is a well-established fact that the New Order in Europe disrupted this cartel agreement and that IGF and VAW saw in Koppenberg's initiatives a new large multinational company dominating the New Order in Europe. But it is wrong to assume, as Milward and even more so Petrick have done, that the two companies were themselves anxious to expand their business into Norway.

It was the Koppenberg Plan of 12 November 1940 and not the invasion of Norway, or for that matter of France, which initiated the disruption of the Reich's aluminum business arrangements. Koppenberg triggered a period of disarray which lasted until 23 June 1941, when the German actors finally agreed on the structure of the Norwegian program. Göring had decided to build up the Norwegian industry as 'a sort of in-house industry for the Luftwaffe'.[25] On his order of 16 November 1940 the German company Nordische Aluminium AG (NA) was established to implement the Koppenberg Plan. As this would favor the ambitions of Koppenberg and JFM, it provoked a hostile reaction from VAW and IGF who, with the support of RWM, soon intervened, since they were not willing to see their influence reduced within the New Order. Karl Krauch, who was *Generalbevollmächtigter für Sonderfragen der chemischen Erzeugung* (General Plenipotentiary for Special Issues of Chemical Production) in the *Vierjahresplan*, was recruited from IGF, and Eberhard Neukirch, responsible for light metals within the *Chemischer Erzeugungsplan* (Chemical Production Plan), came from AB. They would have liked to see IGF and VAW participating in the Norwegian program, not least because they had the competence and experience that NA was lacking.

Rivalries among the companies unfolded throughout the spring of 1941. Negotiations dragged on and were further complicated as the Quisling government and *Reichskommissar* Terboven demanded that the companies and power stations were run according to Norwegian law. But herein also lay the solution. On 3 May 1941 NA set up the Norwegian filial company, A/S

---

23. In April 1941 Koppenberg failed to have the authorities extended also to the Balkans. See Ba-Ma, RL 3/913, Letter from Koppenberg to Udet, 19 April 1941.
24. According to the agreement of January 1937, VAW and AB would together have 86% of production and AIAG 14%. See Pohl, *VIAG Aktiengesellschaft*, 166.
25. 'Aktenvermerk über die Sitzung im Staabsamt am 23. Juni 1941', printed in Petrick, 'Zwei Schlüsseldokumente zur faschistischen', 260–263, quotation 260.

Nordag, in Oslo. The RLM would have a 51 percent stake while 49 percent would be reserved for Norwegian interests. To avoid confusion NA took the name of Hansa Leichtmetall (HL) and was integrated with Junker-Aluminium-Büro, which Koppenberg had set up in August 1940. HL opened offices in Athens, Paris, Oslo, and Riga to secure bauxite and alumina for Nordag. While Nordag would bear responsibility for about 90 percent of the Norwegian expansion program, A/S Nordisk Lettmetall (NL) would be responsible for the other ten. This company, in which Hydro, IGF, and Nordag each had a third of the stakes, was set up on 2 May 1941. Technically, NL was linked closely to IGF's aluminum and magnesium plants in Bitterfeld. VAW had failed to share the spoils in Nordag, but it expanded in the Reich. The General Director of VAW, Ludger Westrick, agreed to take over the RLM's shares in Nordag only after the war. The solution gave IGF a much larger say in the Norwegian program than Göring had assumed when he adopted the Koppenberg Plan. Wilhelm Moschel, who came from AB and led the metal commission of IGF, was appointed chairman of the Board of Directors of Nordag, NL, and HL. This would constrain Koppenberg's room for maneuver and reintroduce confidence among the actors without weakening Koppenberg's position as *Aluminumtreuhänder.*[26]

While the Berlin meeting on 23 June 1941 settled the Norwegian question, on 4 December 1941 the German actors involved finally settled the basics of the New Order.[27] While NL, and partly Nordag, would exploit Norwegian labradorite to produce aluminum, HL and VAW were given different European territories from which they would take their supply of bauxite and alumina. VAW would expand its capacity without challenging the European supplies to HL. The bitter race between Westrick and Koppenberg for European bauxite, revealed in Milward's two books, was ended.[28] No further company was to be allowed into the industry, a decision which was later overturned.

The Norwegian expansion program, like the larger Göring Plan, was a wishful dream and a complete failure. Koppenberg postponed construction

---

26. Petrick, *Der ,Leichtmetallausbau Norwegen', 1940–1945*, 98–119; Plumpe, *Die I.G. Farbenindustrie AG*, 416–422; Hans Claussen Korff, 'Norwegens Wirtschaft im Mahlstrom der Okkupation', unpublished manuscript written in 1949, 44–99, located in Riksarkivet (the Norwegian National Archives, henceforth RA), Oslo, Private Archive 951, box 2.
27. Aktennotiz über die Besprechung bei Herrn Generalfeldmarschall Milch am 4.12.1941, printed in Petrick, 'Zwei Schlüsseldokumente zur faschistischen', 264–268.
28. Milward, *The New Order and the French Economy*, 86–89 and 235–243; Milward, *The Fascist Economy in Norway*, 189–194. Their rivalry in Croatia has been confirmed by Sundhaussen, *Wirtschaftsgeschichte Kroatiens im nationalsozialistischen Grossraum, 1941–1945*. Rauh's *Schweizer Aluminium für Hitlers Krieg?* reveals how rivalry also spilled over into AIAG's sphere of influence.

works on several plants as early as December 1941. His position was gravely weakened during the spring of 1942. Erhard Milch, who had replaced Udet as *Generalluftzeugmeister*, in October 1942, relieved him of his duties as *Treuhänder* of JFM as well as of the aluminum industry, and ordered Ludger Westrick to take charge of a downsized version of the program. Even this proved to be difficult. Producing about 2,000 tons of alumina in 1944 was the only output of the grandiose expansion plan. Annual Norwegian aluminum supply to Germany 1941–1944 was between 14,000 and 17,000 t/a, less than half of Norwegian capacity in 1940.[29]

## NACO IN PURSUIT OF INDEPENDENCE

When Norway was occupied on 9 April 1940, all the aluminum companies apart from NACO were 100 percent owned by the major international firms in the industry. While the Nazis regarded the latter companies as *Feindvermögen* (enemy property), NACO retained much autonomy during the Occupation although Alcoa had a 50 percent stake. This was mainly a result of collaborative actions by NACO, whereby the management deliberately used its commercial and technological competence to influence the Nazis' aluminum planning in Norway.

NACO was founded in 1915 by Sigurd Kloumann, who was director of the company well into the 1940s. From the outset his ambition had been to develop a vertically integrated aluminum concern that was not controlled by foreign capital. NACO set up an alumina refinery and an electrolytic aluminum smelter as well as a manufacturing subsidiary, AS Nordisk Aluminiumindustri A/S (NAI), over the following years. As Norway has no bauxite NACO bought a bauxite deposit in France and established the *Société anonyme de bauxite et alumines de Provence* (SABAP) to extract it, but it failed to run the deposit profitably. In 1923 Kloumann was forced to establish a 50 percent co-ownership with Alcoa, which subsequently supplied the alumina refinery with bauxite. In the 1920s NACO financed the development of Professor Pedersen's smelting method for producing alumina. As we have seen the advantage of this method was that it could exploit harder bauxite of inferior quality as well as other forms of clay found in Norway (labradorite) and Sweden (andalucite). However, as the latter forms yielded less profit Kloumann decided to import bauxite for NACO's alumina refinery but still used the Pedersen method.[30] In 1931 Kloumann reached an understanding with the international aluminum cartel, Alliance Aluminium Compagnie, that NACO would supply the Scandinavian market while the other Norwegian aluminum companies,

29. Korff, 'Norwegens Wirtschaft im Mahlstrom der Okkupation', 58.
30. Kobberrød, 'Norwegian Alumina—A Key to Success in a Global Economy?'.

which were entirely owned by the members of the cartel, would control the export market.[31] In order to defend its position in the domestic market in Scandinavia, NACO decided in 1933 to set up the first Swedish aluminum smelter, A/B Svenska Aluminiumkompaniet (SAKO), which was supplied by NACO's alumina refinery in Norway. In 1934 NACO also bought a manufacturing plant in Denmark, Dansk Aluminium Industri A/S (DAI), to which aluminum was supplied by NACO's Norwegian smelter.[32] In this way by the time that Norway was invaded NACO had established a commercial stronghold in the Scandinavian market. The alumina refinery had a capacity of 12,000 t/a, which supplied NACO's Norwegian and Swedish aluminum smelter. The Norwegian aluminum smelter had a capacity of 8000 t/a, which, together with the 2000 t/a Swedish smelter, supplied NACO's two manufacturing plants in Norway and Denmark. NACO still owned SABAP's bauxite deposits in France and was in control of the Pedersen technology for producing alumina from alternative sources of clay. While the other aluminum companies were pure smelters and were run by foreign management installed by the foreign parent company, NACO's management represented the only advanced technology base in Norway.

When Koppenberg arrived in Norway after the invasion to get hold of aluminum, it comes as no surprise that the Norwegian civilian authority appointed Johan Mürer, NACO's technical director, as spokesman for the Norwegian aluminum industry. Mürer took care of NACO's Norwegian interests. He followed Koppenberg on his journeys to inspect Norwegian smelters and kept in close contact with Werner Miehle, Koppenberg's deputy. NACO's major concern was to maintain its supremacy in Scandinavia under the new constraints set by the Nazis. The Swedish position was strengthened during the war. As Koppenberg prevented NACO from supplying SAKO with alumina, Kloumann was able to procure provisional supplies from Alcoa.[33] With the support of the Swedish government, in 1941 he established *Svenska Aloxidverken AB*. When it came onstream in 1942, it used the Pedersen method to produce 7000 t/a alumina based on Swedish andalucite. This allowed SAKO to double its aluminum capacity during the war.[34]

In Norway, NACO largely succeeded by means of collaboration. However, this might not have been the case had not VAW been pushed aside at an early stage. Krauch had already on 10 April 1940, the day after the invasion, asked VAW to elaborate how Norway's aluminum industry could be kept going.[35] Koppenberg also admitted after the war that before the invasion, his

31. Storli, 'Out of Norway Falls Aluminium', 273–301.
32. Fasting, *Norsk aluminium gjennom 50 år*, 155–165.
33. RA, Landssviksak (treason case) 4226, box 6, Interrogation of Sigurd Kloumann, 19 August 1948.
34. *Svenskt aluminium under tio år*, 19–47.
35. Neukirch, 'Die Entwicklung des Leichtmetallausbaues im Vierjahresplan', 416.

knowledge of the Norwegian industry was based on information provided by VAW.[36] Hence it is no surprise that VAW was represented in Koppenberg's group when he arrived in Oslo on 14 April 1940. His expert advisors were from VAW and DM. Koppenberg found it easy to reach an agreement with the Norwegian industry, in which he bought aluminum stocks in exchange for alumina. Back in Berlin, and contrary to Göring's demand of 9 February 1940 that the aluminum must be reserved for the *Luftwaffe*, Koppenberg however anticipated that VAW might keep much of the metal for itself. Hence Udet convinced Göring that VAW must not be allowed to intervene in Norway. Göring issued a decree on 8 May 1940 giving Udet right of disposal of all existing and future aluminum in the country.[37] Thus it was neither IGF nor Krauch who pushed VAW out of Norway; it was Udet because he was persuaded by Koppenberg that VAW might cheat.

It is true that Koppenberg had little knowledge about aluminum technology, as maintained by Milward, Hayes, and Plumpe, and would seek the assistance of IGF after VAW was pushed aside. It is however wrong, as maintained by Petrick, that Krauch in liaison with the IGF was responsible for the Norwegian expansion plan. Nor was it DM on whose technological competence Koppenberg could rely, as Budrass wrongly argued. The Koppenberg Plan was initially developed by NACO and the critical technology was the Pedersen method for developing alumina, about which the German companies had no experience at all. Actually, VAW in 1941 approached NACO to lease the Pedersen method, but NACO was in a position to reject the request.[38]

## NACO'S DEFENSE OF ITS SCANDINAVIAN MANUFACTURERS

After the invasion of Norway, NACO's concern in the short term was to keep its plants operating.[39] When meeting Koppenberg, the tactic was to convince him that NACO's manufacturers remained onstream. NAI was located in Norway and supplied canned packing and electric cables for the domestic market. DAI was located in Denmark and specialized in making milk pails and cans for the domestic agricultural industry. In negotiations on 19 April 1940, NACO was able to secure short-term aluminum supply contracts for both plants. While the supply of independent Swedish

36. RA, Landssviksak 4226, box 8, Interrogation of Koppenberg, 20 August 1946.
37. Budrass, *Flugzeugindustrie und Luftrüstung in Deutschland*, 608.
38. RA, Landssviksak 4226, box 7, Interrogation of Johan Mürer, 20 April 1948.
39. RA, Riksadvokaten (Office of the Attorney General), div. saker (miscellaneous cases), serie D, box 19, Protocol from meeting of NACO's Board of Directors, 12 April 1940.

manufacturers was rejected, NACO was allowed to reserve a quota of 150 tons per month for NAI and of ten tons per month for DAI.[40]

NACO's success was due to the particular interest of DM as NAI was setting up a rolling mill for duralumin. The alloy was particularly useful for aircraft, and DM worked closely with JFM to increase its supply. Hence Koppenberg wanted NAI to be onstream. But there was no need for him to use force, as NACO immediately saw DM's interest as an opportunity. Mürer immediately invited DM representatives to visit the sites of NAI, and offered to have the duralumin mill working within three months if DM could provide the necessary assistance.[41] An overriding motive was to have the plant going to avoid newcomers challenging NAI's (hence NACO's) position.[42]

To sustain DM's long-term interest NACO knew that NAI's capacity must increase. Hence NACO informed NAI that the capacity of the rolling mill must be largely expanded.[43] NAI also needed know-how from DM, and in the summer of 1940 NAI and DM exchanged technical experts to this end. Already in August 1940 the two companies had agreed on the principles of cooperation, which were then formalized in a *Werkshilfevertrag* (consultancy agreement) on 2 October 1940. DM would provide technical support so that NAI would supply DM with 600 t/a of duralumin. If DM requested it, NAI was obliged to increase the annual duralumin output to 1200 t/a. As payment for the technical support, DM would receive shares in NAI. Hence the share capital of NAI was slightly raised while DM would have a 25 percent stake. Although NACO would have preferred to have paid DM in cash, the agreement was perceived as securing NACO's strategic interests in keeping DM attached to NAI. But some wider interests were also accommodated. NACO had inserted into the contract a proviso saying that if DM produced manufactures that might have been produced at NAI or DAI, then in that case NACO should supply the aluminum.[44]

The capacity of NAI's rolling mill would be expanded from 3600 to 7000 t/a. As hoped for by NACO, Koppenberg expanded NAI's aluminum quota to allow for duralumin production as well. NAI optimistically started to produce duralumin sheets in November 1940. However, production was always behind schedule. Output tended to be between twenty

40. Ole Borge, 'Innberetning til Oslo Politikammer vedrørende A/S Norsk Aluminium Company og Nordisk Aluminium Industri A/S', 85, located in RA, Riksadvokaten, div. saker, serie D, box 19.
41. RA, Riksadvokaten, div. saker, serie D, box 1, Letter from NACO to Koppenberg, 24 April 1940.
42. Ibid., Protocol from meeting of NACO's Board of Directors, 25 April 1940.
43. Ibid., Letters from Mürer to Brodtkorb, 27 April 1940 and 3 July 1940; Borge, 'Innberetning til Oslo Politikammer', 102
44. RA, Riksadvokaten, div. saker, serie D, box 19, Contract (Werkshilfevertrag) between Nordisk Aluminium Industri and Dürener Metallwerke, 2 October 1940.

and thirty tons per month and by October 1941 only 237 tons had been produced. Technical problems remained unsolved while new ones emerged. Already in February 1941 NACO decided that the solution to the problems must be to integrate further with DM and urged DM to send more technical experts and retain them for longer periods at NAI's plant. Furthermore, it proposed to expand the capacity for traditional production as well as for duralumin even further. The annual output target for duralumin would be 1200 tons.[45] Hence it was NAI and not DM that requested an expansion of the output target. Directors of NACO and NAI visited DM in June 1941 to discuss the technicalities of the proposed expansion. DM was willing to finance further investments in NIA to improve efficiency and capacity. A large capital injection took place in 1942, in which DM contributed 25 percent.[46] This allowed NAI also to expand the output of its traditional produce. Again, NACO's efforts with DM met with success.

However, neither of these measures turned out to meet the expectations. The technical problems were never really solved. Of the 4,280 tons of duralumin produced in 1941–1944, 58% were of inferior quality, which DM did not accept. DM continuously complained that NAI's supplies of high quality duralumin were too low. In August 1944 NAI's works were also exposed to sabotage, which caused a reduced monthly output of duralumin for the rest of the war. The sales of duralumin to DM turned out to be unprofitable although DM in March 1944 accepted a 5 percent price increase for metal supplies beyond fifty tons per month. On the other hand NAI was largely able to supply Norwegian civilian customers with its traditional produce, thereby making considerable profits.[47]

NACO also kept a close eye on DAI, but did not have to push for its integration into the Nazis' new aluminum regime, as it did with NAI. The reason was that DAI's director Erik Sommerfeldt was a Nazi himself, who maintained close contacts with German authorities and worked to facilitate exports to the Reich and its larger *Lebensraum* market.[48] As early as May 1940 he had agreed to deliver 4000 milk pails, and a month later a further 25,000 pails. In July 1941 he informed NACO that the German authorities had asked for another 100,000 pails. This meant aluminum imports from NACO, which guaranteed all sales and allowed for extra investment when necessary. This applied significantly to the contract which DAI made with the German aircraft producer Arado Flugzeugwerke in May 1942, in which

45. Ibid., Protocols from meetings of NACO's Board of Directors, 10 and 13 February 1941
46. Borge, 'Innberetning til Oslo Politikammer', 113.
47. RA, Riksadvokaten, div. saker, serie D, box 19, Chr. Nicolaisen: Rapport over regnskapsundersøkelse hos A/S Nordisk Aluminiumindustri, 2 June 1948, and Chr. Nicolaisen: Rapport over regnskapsundersøkelse hos A/S Nordisk Aluminiumindustri og A/S Norsk Aluminium Company, 18 January 1949.
48. Ibid., Letter from Sommerfeldt to NACO, 20 May 1940.

a specific quantity of tinsmith work on the duralumin helms of the aircraft was outsourced to DAI. The latter informed NACO that this would provide 250 new temporary jobs, and that large investments were needed. NACO was supportive as long as the contract did not replace existing production, was long term, and would yield profits.[49] It was implicitly assumed that NAI might supply the duralumin in the future. DAI was exposed to sabotage in February 1943, but NACO decided to resume production to fulfill the contract with Arado. Production was not resumed after a new sabotage in July 1944. Although NAI made net profits and NACO was allowed to supply aluminum, during 1943 NACO had second thoughts about integrating itself too closely into the Nazi arms production.[50]

## NACO'S CONTRIBUTION TO THE KOPPENBERG PLAN[51]

While from April 1940 NACO used NAI's scheduled duralumin plant to establish a close cooperative relationship with Koppenberg, from July 1940 it also worked deliberately to be included in Koppenberg's still ambiguous expansion goals. It is necessary to understand the rivalry in Norway between NACO and Hydro to explain NACO's actions and the subsequent emergence of the Koppenberg Plan.

The only threat to NACO's Scandinavian monopoly in the 1930s was Hydro, which had developed a nitric acid process of making alumina also from labradorite. Hydro, partly owned by IGF since 1927, had always wanted a joint venture with IGF in order to start aluminum production in Norway, but IGF had repeatedly turned down the proposal. Hence in 1939 Hydro suggested to NACO setting up a joint company in Norway, but the proposal was turned down by NACO. In April 1940 Hydro was still eager to start up alumina production.[52]

As the invasion caused an acute shortage of bauxite and alumina, on 15 May 1940 and independent of Koppenberg's activities in Norway, the Norwegian Association of Industry suggested that Hydro and NACO build an alumina plant capable of supplying the entire Norwegian aluminum industry.[53] Hydro's engineer Øistein Ravner, the expert of the company's

49. Ibid., Letter from Mürer and Foss to DAI, 12 March 1942, and memorandum by Mürer after visit to DAI in Mai 1942, 22 May 1942.
50. Ibid., Knut Arnesen: Oversikt vedr. fremstilling av flydeler for ARADO Flugzeugwerke ved Dansk Aluminium Industri med approbasjon av Norsk Aluminium Company, 17 November 1948.
51. This section is largely based on Frøland and Kobberrød, 'The Norwegian Contribution to Göring's Megalomania'.
52. Andersen and Yttri, *Et forsøk verdt: forskning og utvikling i Norsk Hydro gjennom 90 år*, 136–139; Storli, 'Out of Norway Falls Aluminium', 302–304.
53. RA, Landssviksak 4226, NACO, box 1, Letter from Norges Industriforbund to NACO, 15 May 1940.

labradorite experiments, stood behind the Association's proposal, and he later also confirmed Hydro's support.[54] In all likelihood Ravner had discussed the issue with Eberhard Neukirch, who had followed Koppenberg on a journey to Norway. Neukirch informed Krauch of Hydro's attempts after he returned to Berlin.[55] Krauch immediately considered setting up a 25,000 t/a alumina plant at Hydro's site at Herøya. Krauch sent Johannes Fahrenhorst, a member of his staff and former director in the IGF, to Oslo on 11 June 1940 to further elaborate the idea with Hydro. On 1 July 1940 Hydro submitted a memorandum to Fahrenhorst, in which, obviously in response to Krauch's idea, they suggested that Hydro quickly establish an alumina production of 20,000 t/a based on labradorite.[56] It was not until the end of September 1940 that Krauch, who had not yet considered Hydro's alumina option in depth, sent Neukirch to Norway to further elaborate Hydro's proposal.

Meanwhile NACO used its privileged position and intervened with Koppenberg. Rightly, Mürer and Kloumann saw Hydro's suggestions as another attempt to challenge NACO's monopoly.[57] First Kloumann suggested to Axel Aubert, his counterpart at Hydro, that the two companies cooperate in their relations with the Germans. Aubert, who also represented Hydro in IGF's shareholders' committee, declined.[58] He obviously preferred Krauch's idea to Kloumann's. This made Kloumann on 1 July 1940 write a first letter to Koppenberg, in which he volunteered his assistance as the foremost Norwegian expert in the field. He argued that NACO needed its own metal for its Norwegian manufacturing plant and that metal for Germany should be supplied by the other Norwegian smelters.[59] Kloumann obviously wanted to secure NACO's position and prevent Hydro from entering alumina production.

While Hydro's proposal was under scrutiny with Krauch, Kloumann submitted several memoranda to Miehle, in which NACO presented practical solutions to Koppenberg's needs while simultaneously sustaining NACO's domestic position. These demonstrated both how hydroelectric power could be expanded as well as possible locations for power stations, alumina refineries, and aluminum smelters. They proposed that, apart from NACO, all the existing smelter companies, including some which might be expanded, should be merged into one. As this new metallurgical society

54. Ibid., Letter from Norsk Hydro to Norges Industriforbund, 22 May 1940.
55. Ibid., Eberhard Neukirch's report on his journey to Norway 16–21, 23 May 1940; Neukirch, 'Die Entwicklung des Leichtmetallausbaues im Vierjahresplan', 416–418.
56. RA, Landssviksak 4226, box 1, Memorandum by Aubert and Kielland: Herstellung von Tonerde, 1 July 1940.
57. Ibid., Letter from Kloumann to Mürer, 21 May 1940.
58. Andersen, *Flaggskip i fremmed eie: Hydro, 1905–1945*, 367.
59. RA, Landssviksak 4226, box 1, Letter from Kloumann to Koppenberg, 1 July 1940.

would be in constant need of alumina, they suggested that a large new alumina plant using the Pedersen method should be set up. NACO should then become a minority owner in the alumina company in exchange for its supply of technical expertise.[60] NACO's efforts escalated on 9 October 1940, when Miehle received a set of detailed memoranda, in which NACO drew up two alternatives which would expand Norway's aluminum production capacity from 36,000 t/a to 60,000 t/a within two years. The main supplies of alumina would come from the proposed alumina plant, but NACO now assumed explicitly that Hydro would also produce alumina at Herøya.[61] Kloumann had obviously given in and included Hydro in his plan.

Koppenberg built on NACO's memoranda when, on 11 October 1940, he informed Udet about his expansion plan for Norway. However, Koppenberg had raised the aluminum target to 120,000 t/a. While NACO's proposal was basically about exploiting existing plants and power stations, Koppenberg's extra output capacity implied building five new power stations on virgin soil. In spite of this it was to be completed by spring 1943.[62] The extra 60,000 t/a wished for were added by Miehle's office without consulting NACO, the *Vierjahresplan,* or the German aluminum producers. No matter how, it was only possible because NACO had fed Büro Miehle with full and detailed information about the specific potential of power expansion and alumina production in Norway based on labradorite.

There was much wishful thinking in Koppenberg's plan before it lay on Göring's table on 12 November 1940. Still, Göring ordered Koppenberg to raise the aluminum target even further. The capacity of 60,000 t/a was to be reached by the end of 1941, 120,000 t/a by the end of 1942, and between 150,000 and 180,000 t/a by the end of 1943.[63] The 310,000 t/a alumina capacity would largely be based on labradorite, which meant that NACO's Pedersen process and Hydro's nitric acid process were to be applied. According to Hans Clausen Korff, who from fall 1940 headed the department of finance in the *Reichskommissariat,* Göring's decision was reached 'without taking into account either the views of the Ministry's officials or the Four-year plan.'[64] It was not only Koppenberg who had reverted to dreams. Even under the favorable condition of a successful Blitzkrieg the

60. Ibid., Letter from Kloumann to Miehle, 24 August 1940, and memorandum by Kloumann: Kraftforhold og utvidelsesmuligheter på de steder, som av oss er foreslått til aluminium- og aluminiumoksydfabrikk, 30 September 1940.
61. Ibid., Memorandum by Kloumann: Vorschläge für den Ausbau der norwegischen Alu-Industrie unter gleichzeitiger Errichtung entsprechender Tonerdeproduktion für die Versorgung der gesamten Elektrolysen, 9 October 1940.
62. Ibid., Letter from Koppenberg to Udet, 11 October 1940.
63. Ba-Ma, RL 3/883, Abschrift Besprechung Herr Reichsmarschall Göring—Dr. Koppenberg, 12 November 1940.
64. Korff, 'Norwegens Wirtschaft im Mahlstrom der Okkupation', 64.

timetable was wishful thinking at best. Already with the Göring Plan the alumina target was reduced considerably.

## NACO'S DEFENSE OF THE SWEDISH MONOPOLY

NACO was concerned that the Norwegian expansion program might establish a surplus after the war that would challenge the company's monopoly position. The best way for NACO to secure its future position was by getting influence over the expanded industry. During the collaboration with Koppenberg in the fall of 1940 an objective of the NACO management was to secure such influence. In exchange for technical know-how and consultancy NACO demanded the maintenance of the Scandinavian monopoly.[65]

The *Beratungsvertrag* (consultancy agreement) between Nordag and NACO, under which NACO would provide the patent of the Pedersen method as well as technical know-how, was agreed upon in January 1941 but formally concluded two months later. NACO provided technical consultancy well before the agreement was signed, and fulfilled its obligations to Nordag. Anticipating a close cooperative relationship with Nordag, NACO also obtained rights to quarries of labradorite, limestone, and fluoride in Norway. Nordag would need these raw materials for its production, and the purpose was to offer Nordag a leasing contract. Hence NACO would increase its leverage when negotiating the *Beratungsvertrag*. The legal expert who, after the war, investigated NACO's involvement in the German expansion program, maintained that the *Beratungsvertrag* was negotiated on NACO's initiative and under no German constraint whatsoever.[66]

What counted for NACO was that the *Beratungsvertrag* confirmed NACO's Scandinavian monopoly. This met with success. In the following ten years, NACO and SAKO together were allowed to produce 16,000 t/a for the Scandinavian market, while Nordag would export to the German market. A clause also stated that, as a revision would be due in 1951, negotiations would be based on the principle that Scandinavia was the natural marketing area of NACO and SAKO. In effect, NACO was allowed to sell 900 tons of aluminum per year to Sweden.[67] NACO would also receive a cash payment from Nordag of 3,800,000 Norwegian Krone, but this was of less importance to NACO.[68]

65. RA, Landssviksak 4226, box 1, Protocol from meeting of NACO's Board of Directors, 30 October 1940.
66. Borge, 'Innberetning til Oslo Politikammer', 149–152.
67. RA, Landssviksak 4226, box 7, Interrogation of Erling Foss, 12–14 April 1948, and Interrogation of Johan Mürer, 20 April 1948.
68. RA, Landssviksak 4226, box 1, Letter from NACO to Koppenberg, 8 January 1941.

As the IGF was included in the Norwegian program, it turned out that NACO's technical assistance was needed less than had been assumed. The director of Nordag and NL, Wilhelm Moschel, came from AB and was an expert himself. This led HL, in which Moschel was also a director, to ask for a cash rebate in November 1941 as well as a renegotiation of the Scandinavian market clause.[69] Only in September 1943 did the parties agree on a revised *Beratungsvertrag*. NACO agreed to reduce the cash payment but successfully resisted any change of the market clause.[70]

The reason why HL had wanted to revise the market clause related to financial problems. To finance imports of machines from Sweden to NL as well as to Nordag, during the fall of 1941 Hydro and IGF had negotiated a loan with Skandinaviska Enskilda Banken (SEB) in Stockholm on behalf of NL. Another loan was negotiated in the spring of 1942. As neither German nor Norwegian authorities allowed any drawing on their bilateral clearing accounts with Sweden, on Hydro's initiative the parties agreed to pay for the loans in aluminum.[71] Hence the agreement might lead NL and possibly also Nordag into the Swedish market, which was exactly what NACO had worked continuously to avoid. It is not clear whether Hydro's initiative reflected a strategic decision to intervene in the Swedish market or simply was a practical solution to an unexpected problem. However, as the deal would violate the Scandinavian market clause of the *Beratungsvertrag*, NACO was not kept informed about the negotiations.

Only in October 1942 did Kloumann become aware of the deal. The delayed information fitted well with recent experiences. First, during the negotiations on the revision of the *Beratungsvertrag* Moschel had refused to state explicitly that NL was also covered by the Scandinavian market clause. Second, in April 1942 Koppenberg had also denied NACO the option of transferring technology to its Swedish subsidiaries. Hence in Kloumann's mind Hydro was again challenging NACO's supremacy in Scandinavia. On Kloumanns' initiative NACO acted swiftly to avoid any watering down of the monopoly. While demanding that the Scandinavian market clause remain unchanged in the negotiations with Nordag, Kloumann demanded of Moschel that NACO should provide the aluminum that SEB required, and that this must appear as an order from Koppenberg himself. Hence the order of the *Treuhänder* would implicitly confirm the Scandinavian market clause of the *Beratungsvertrag*. Moreover, Koppenberg must issue a formal decision saying that Nordisk Lettmetall was also constrained by the Scandinavian market clause. NACO threatened not to hand over fluoride

69. RA, Riksadvokaten, div. saker, serie D, saksarkiv, box 19, Copy of protocol from meeting in the Aufsichtsrat of Hansa Leichtmetall, 17 November 1941; Borge, 'Innberetning til Oslo Politikammer', 61 ff.
70. Borge, 'Innberetning til Oslo Politikammer', 64.
71. Andersen, *Flaggskip i fremmed eie: Hydro, 1905–1945*, 392–395.

quarries to Hydro unless Nordisk Lettmetall also formally complied with the market clause.[72]

The issue was resolved in March 1943 in such a way that NACO's tactics were largely successful. While keeping the Scandinavian market clause intact, on the order of the *Treuhänder* NACO delivered the aluminum to SEB without drawing on the export quota of 900 t/a. NACO's sales manager negotiated the delivery scheme with the stockpiling agency of the Swedish government. An agreement was also reached between NACO and NL that the latter would not challenge NACO's position in Sweden.[73]

## NAZI PLANNING AND NEW ORDER: ECONOMIC COLLABORATION

Nazi Germany's attempt to establish a New Order for the European aluminum industry developed *ad hoc* and reached its height of ambition with the Göring Plan in June 1941. Based largely on the information provided by the Koppenberg Plan of 12 November 1940, the Göring Plan targeted a massive expansion program for Norway.

While Milward emphasized the rival actions among German government agencies and companies, this chapter has given evidence that NACO deliberately entered into collaboration as Koppenberg's presence held out prospects of a New Order. On NACO's initiative its manufacturing subsidiaries were involved in the Nazis' arms production. NACO's management provided Koppenberg with the detailed information he needed to work out an expansion program for Norway. On NACO's initiative a technical consultancy agreement was established between NACO and Nordag. Through aluminum deliveries to Swedish creditors NACO voluntarily became involved in the funding operations of the Norwegian expansion scheme. Admittedly, NAI's involvement in the arms production largely failed, the Norwegian expansion targets were raised far beyond what NACO had proposed, and IGF came to play a more significant role than was assumed when the Koppenberg Plan was adopted. Still, NACO's contribution was important in the absence of VAW. Yet it was not decisive as, counterfactually, it is not difficult to imagine Hydro and IGF playing an equivalent role in the absence of NACO.[74]

72. Borge, 'Innberetning til Oslo Politikammer', 64–85.
73. RA, Landssviksak 4226, box 9, Henrik Helliesen: Tyskernes utbygging av lettmetallindustrien i Norge, 25 February 1946.
74. This is indicated also by Wilhelm von der Bey, 'Direktor der IG Farben Industrie AG über seine Tätigkeit in Norwegen', unpublished manuscript, 1945, located in RA, Landssviksak 4226, box 8. Von der Bey came from IG Farben and was a member of the board of Nordisk Lettmetall.

NACO was an obvious case of business collaboration with the occupying government. Its motives were purely economic. Under the new constraints the management of the company worked to keep its factories operating and make the usual profits. However, it also anticipated a German Blitzkrieg victory in Europe and worried about the possible effects of an expanded industry after the war. Hence NACO's monopoly position in Norway and Scandinavia was at stake, and the company entered into economic collaboration to influence the character of the New Order in Scandinavia. Subsequently, as victory was long in coming and the anticipated New Order crumbled, NACO became less committed. Having replaced Koppenberg as *Treuhänder*, Ludger Westrick wanted NACO to let SABAP, its dormant French bauxite company, start up production in 1943. NACO refused, which it probably would not have done in 1940–1941.[75]

Milward maintained that '[t]here were only two possible ways of carrying out such an enormous project as the aluminium plan. One was to do it with the full and free consent of the conquered territory, the other to do it by ruthless and total subjection of it.'[76] This also largely fits with Christoph Buchheim's observations of the behavior of German (non-Jewish) business. Their strategic interests were to survive as autonomous organizations, and they tended to position themselves for the future reintroduction of a more liberal market economy. Their involvement in the arms effort was not a result of force.[77]

While Milward's account of the aluminum plan has been modified on several points with regard to the German industry, transnational and comparative studies of the responses of the European aluminum industry to the prospects of the New Aluminum Order are still missing. The issue of business collaboration during World War II was neglected for decades, but since the 2000s relevant accounts have appeared, particularly in France.[78] Like this chapter, they analyze collaboration from a restricted national perspective. Hence the trans-border study of private business collaboration under the New Order is still an underdeveloped field of historical research, and a first publication to address the issue in some depth was also organized as national chapters.[79] The aluminum plan is well suited for a systematic

75. NACO in 1940 considered putting SABAP onstream because Koppenberg set too high a price on imported bauxite. RA, Landssviksak 4226, box 6, Interrogation of Sigurd Kloumann, 19 August 1948.
76. Milward, *The Fascist Economy in Norway*, 206.
77. Buchheim, 'Unternehmen in Deutschland und NS-Regime, 1933–1945'. See also Scherner, 'Das Verhältnis zwischen NS-Regime und Industrieunternehmen', which reveals how companies could successfully resist government pressure even in the aluminum industry.
78. See the website of the French research program 'Les entreprises français sous l'occupation' (http://gdr2539.ish-lyon.cnrs.fr/) and Lemmes, 'Collaboration in Wartime France'.
79. Lund, *Working for the New Order.*

and comparative study of the character of and motives behind business collaboration with the Nazis. Only such a comparative study can actually test Milward's wider argument that the Nazis' New Aluminum Order was doomed to fail.[80]

80. Milward, *The Fascist Economy in Norway*, 208.

# 5 Economic History and the Political Economy Approach

*Vera Zamagni*

The book in which this essay is published deals at length with Alan S. Milward as an economic historian, although he was certainly more than an economic historian. But stating that Milward was an economic historian could today be challenged on the grounds that economic history is a branch of economics and Alan was no economist.[1] This chapter discusses first how economic history is no longer recognized unanimously as an autonomous discipline and which are the threats deriving from this. In the second part of the chapter, Milward's approach to economic history—a 'political economy' approach—will be highlighted. The conclusion will be that economic history today encompasses more than one methodological approach and must preserve its richness, which is typical of any historical subdiscipline. Historical specializations, even more than specializations in other social sciences, must be seen as complementary and not as exclusive, because the historical events to be explained are complex and contain variables that cannot be separated out, unlike most experiments done in the field of natural sciences.

## HAS ECONOMICS SWALLOWED ECONOMIC HISTORY?

I start with a very illuminating essay written by John Hicks in 1941 on 'Education in Economics'.[2] In discussing the university education to be offered to students of economics, Hicks was firm on two main tenets. The first one was that an economist should get a multifaceted education. In his own words, his reasons for such a statement:

> In the field of economics, over-specialization is doubly disastrous. A man who is a mathematician and nothing but a mathematician may live a stunted life, but he does not do any harm. An economist who is

---

1. Editorial note: Alan Milward's 1956 Bachelor of Arts degree was in Medieval and Modern History at University College, London.
2. Hicks, 'Education in Economics'.

> nothing but an economist is a danger to his neighbours. Economics is not a thing in itself; it is a study of one aspect of the life of man in society. It scarcely ever happens that the decision on what policy to adopt on any practical issue can be made (or at any rate should be made) on economic grounds alone. Other things—political questions (internal or foreign), administrative questions, educational questions in a broad sense, moral questions and so on—always come in as well. Now, it is quite hopeless for an economist to pretend that he can give advice on purely economic grounds, and that some other specialist will put in an appearance to fill the gaps. Generally that other specialist isn't there, and even if he is, who is to compose their views into unity? Presumably some harassed politician or businessman, who won't have time to understand what is being said to him, and who cannot be expected, at the moment of decision, to give proper weight to a number of quite different opinions, based on quite different grounds. No, if the economist is to be of any use in the world, he must be more than an economist. [ . . . ] The economists of the Ricardian epoch knew very well what to advise: their advice was sometimes wrong, but it was not a narrow advice; it was not based solely upon economic reasoning, but on a social philosophy as well. The economist of to-morrow [ . . . ] will also know what to advise, *on economic grounds*; but if, through increasing specialization, his economics is divorced from any background of social philosophy, he will be in real danger of becoming a dodge-merchant, full of ingenious devices for getting out of particular difficulties, but losing contact with the plain root-virtues, even the plain economic virtues, on which a healthy society must be based. Modern economics is subject to a real danger of Machiavellism—the treatment of social problems as matters of technique, not as facets of the general search for the Good Life.[3]

Among the five subjects that Hicks considered essential for the education of an economist—who would not be only an economist—there was Economic History, quite clearly recognized as a separate subject (the other four were Economics, Statistics, Politics, and Commerce). Hicks deals at length with the distinction between Economic History and 'Descriptive Economics' (which he also called 'Applied Economics', the expression in use today), a distinction that he finds in the primary responsibility of the economic historian: 'to scrounge for his information in odd corners'.[4] Hicks acknowledges the benefits to be derived by economic history adopting some of the techniques of applied economics, but he is convinced that 'the technique of economic history remains a very different technique from the technique of

3. Ibid., 6–7.
4. Ibid., 11.

descriptive economics; in the latter, scrounging for facts has become a very minor matter.'[5] For these reasons, Hicks insisted on the fact that economic historians should be trained both as historians and economists.

In 1954, in his *History of Economic Analysis,* Schumpeter manifested a similar view, with an even more flattering consideration of economic history, no doubt due to Schumpeter being an economist interested in growth. He wrote:

> What distinguishes the 'scientific' economist from the other people who think, talk, and write about economic topics is a command of techniques that we class under three heads: history, statistics and theory [later he added economic sociology] [ . . . ] Of these fundamental fields, economic history is by far the most important. [ . . . ] And this on three grounds. First, the subject matter of economics is essentially a unique process in historic time. Nobody can hope to understand the economic phenomena of any, including the present, epoch who has not an adequate command of historical *facts* and an adequate amount of historical *sense* or of what may be described as *historical experience*. Second, the historical report cannot be purely economic but must inevitably reflect also 'institutional' facts that are not purely economic: therefore it affords the best method for understanding how economic and non-economic facts *are* related to one another and how the various social sciences *should* be related to one another. Third, it is, I believe, the fact that most of the fundamental errors currently committed in economic analysis are due to lack of experience more often than to any other shortcoming of the economist's equipment.[6]

In the 1950s it became largely established, especially in Britain, that economic history was a discipline *different* from applied economics, necessary for the adequate formation of an economist and cultivated in economic history departments; at the same time, it also became a shared view that economic history could improve its interpretative power by applying quantitative techniques. Economic historians started to be trained both as historians and economists, so much so that the world-class Italian economic historian Carlo Cipolla wrote a book entitled *Tra due culture* ('Between Two Cultures'), meaning history and economics, where he pleaded the case for an education of the economic historian that would offer all the basic economic tools of analysis.[7]

The message of modernizing economic history through the use of economic theory and of the most up-to-date statistical techniques started to be applied in the United States in the 1950s in an especially intensive and

5. Ibid., 12.
6. Schumpeter, *History of Economic Analysis*, 10–11.
7. Cipolla, *Tra due culture.*

technical way.[8] The movement, which became known as 'New Economic History', officially started in 1957 with a conference in Williamstown (Mass.) devoted to 'Trends in the American Economy in the Nineteenth Century', but became established through the 'Clio (or 'Cliometrics') Conferences' held annually at Purdue University for a decade after 1960. Conferences moved then to Wisconsin and continued thereafter in other places until the present. A 'Cliometric Society' was founded in 1983 and has published its *Newsletter* since 1985. Since then, the term cliometrics has become the established label of this approach to economic history. In Europe, the movement was more widespread in Britain and less so across the continent, but it has become everywhere more and more assertive, though never as hegemonic as in the United States.

But what exactly does cliometrics mean? It is hard to answer this question for three main reasons. In the first place, the cultural hegemony of neoclassical economics over the past thirty years turned the attention of most quantitative economic historians to the use of a theoretical framework, thus narrowing the range of issues to be analyzed. Second, applied economics too has changed profoundly over the past thirty to forty years with the advent of more and more sophisticated econometric techniques, challenging the capability of any single scholar to apply such techniques and still have time and interest for something else. Third, the production of longer-term series of data on the part of economic historians (Angus Maddison in the forefront) has proceeded at such a rapid pace as to attract the attention of plain economists to the use of long-run time series, blurring the time-honored boundary between economic history (long term) and applied economics (short term).[9]

When in 1993 the Nobel Prize in Economics was granted to the economic historians Robert Fogel and Douglass North 'for having renewed research in economic history by applying economic theory and quantitative methods in order to explain economic and institutional change', the 'new economic history or cliometrics' was defined as 'research that combines economic theory, quantitative methods, hypothesis testing, counterfactual alternatives, and traditional techniques of economic history, to explain growth and decline'.[10] Economic history was still in the domain of 'two cultures' and its practitioners were still recognized as economic historians, although

---

8. The best detailed account of the developments sketched below is to be found in Lyons, Cain, and Williamson, *Reflections on the Cliometric Revolution.*

9 Editorial note: At the University of Groningen Growth and Development Centre website (http://www.ggdc.nl/maddison/ - last accessed on 12 December 2011), the interested reader would find access to Professor Angus Maddison's work in terms of compilation of quantitative date for most world economies and much more.

10. See The Royal Swedish Academy of Sciences' press release of 12 October 1993 at http://nobelprize.org/nobel_prizes/economics/laureates/1993/press.html (last accessed on 11 November 2010).

the economic side of this two-faced Janus was given more and more weight. Fogel and North, and their colleagues of similar age, were beyond doubt historians, interested primarily in historical issues. North, especially, had soon become very critical of neoclassical economics, because he considered it too static a theory, which did not take into account transaction costs and, above all, made use only of instrumental rationality, forgetting about *intentionality*. He developed this profound dissatisfaction with mainstream economics because he was basically interested in explaining historical facts and not in using whatever time series was available to apply a standard econometric model with the aim of reaching conclusions applicable to present day problems.[11]

But North's position was by no means hegemonic among cliometricians, and the 'melding' of quantitative economic history with mainstream applied economics proceeded in the United States at a very fast pace.[12] Departments of economics started to appoint economists to teach economics and economic history interchangeably. Researchers dealt with long-term or short-term issues using similar models and reaching results that were used for policy purposes. Economic history journals became more and more demanding in terms of econometric techniques, some of them ending up by not publishing a single essay that did not display an econometric model.[13] Indeed, economic history had become a branch of economics, but one in which very few young scholars would specialize, because an economist is seen as somebody who must give advice for future action, and history never repeats itself.

At this point it is useful to reconsider Christina Romer's article, just mentioned, which is significantly entitled *The End of Economic History?* She considered this result positively, because 'economic history has come back to being a part of all of economics, rather than just a separate piece'.[14] She reviews many fields in which the 'fusion' between economic history and economics has led, according to her, to important interpretative results, and concludes that:

> the bringing together of researchers with different perspectives has not only stimulated exciting research, it has also meant that the lessons of history have been incorporated into other fields. In this way, the end of economic history has really been just the beginning of better and richer economics.[15]

---

11. Zamagni, 'What is the Message', 157–163. I will later on return to the concept of *intentionality*.
12. Romer, 'The End of Economic History?'
13. Di Vaio and Weisdorf, 'Ranking Economic History Journals'.
14. Romer, 'The End of Economic History?' 50.
15. Ibid., 64.

It must be admitted that Christina Romer has a point: indeed, it has by now become quite common for economists to write essays where they use long-term data, sometimes very long term, particularly when they are interested in development issues, and such essays are often appealing and intriguing, but *very seldom* do they contain anything relevant from an historical point of view.[16] In such works there is no production of 'economic history', rather whatever historical data are available are employed to highlight economic issues. However, many have reached the hasty conclusion that this is economic history, or rather the only type of economic history worthy of cultivation by economists, and this has weakened economists' interest in having economic history taught at all by 'specialists'. Economists can cover the field themselves if and when they deem it necessary. To counter the downgrading of cliometrics to occasional work done by mainstream economists, it is not enough to claim, as a recent essay by Jean-Luc Demeulemeester and Claude Diebolt does, that cliometrics must deal not only with economic variables, but with institutions and cultures, to broaden the standard views of economists beyond what neoclassical theory can offer.[17]

We reach here the core of the issue which I want to bring to the fore in this essay: if economic history is no different from applied economics, as Romer purports, then she is right in heralding the end of economic history. The kind of economic history that economists are interested in can be produced by them autonomously and embodied in economics *tout court*. On the other hand, if economic history is still preserving features specific to such a discipline, then it is worth going beyond what Demeulemeester and Diebolt argue and ask the following questions:

1) Can the cliometric exercises that are mostly practiced today be properly considered 'economic history'?
2) Is economic history a discipline based on one single methodological paradigm?
3) What is the usefulness of economic history today for the education of an economist?

The answer to the first question is simple: the primary role of any historian—no matter which specialty he/she cultivates—being to uncover past facts that are not yet well established, most of the cliometric papers published today cannot be considered economic history contributions, because they do not embody historical research, but use existing data to test models. If the two things—producing new data and using models for interpretation—can be done in conjunction, so much the better, but there

16. An excellent example is Acemoglu, Johnson, and Robinson, 'The Rise of Europe'.
17. Demeulemeester and Diebolt, 'How Much Could Economics Gain from History'.

is no economic history if there is no effort to uncover new facts and offer new interpretations. As a long-term practitioner in the field, I might point out in this connection that historical research takes a long time, is messy, and is quite demanding in terms of consultation of sources and elaboration of data, so that a good historical researcher is seldom in a position to be an excellent cliometrician also, because econometrics too is complex and needs long hours of application. Indeed, econometricians often correctly criticize very technical cliometric papers on the grounds that they are not sufficiently refined. Collaboration among specialists in different fields might be the best solution to this problem, a point that I will raise in the conclusions.

The second question is more difficult to answer and needs a more detailed discussion. Cliometricians take for granted that the only interesting economic past is the one dealing with economic variables at the macrolevel. Not by chance does this coincide with the neoclassical view of a self-contained *homo œconomicus* who acts rationally maximizing his/her utility function. A confirmation of this comes from the fields surveyed by Romer as the ones having produced more interesting results from the use of econometric techniques. They are all macrofields: cycles (the 1929 crisis, the post-1945 economic miracles); labor markets; the functioning of monetary regimes and financial markets; growth models. But the microlevel is also an extremely important field of analysis: the behavior of single firms and individual entrepreneurs has at least the same relevance to the understanding of the performance of an economy as the evolution of the aggregate variables. In this context, biographies are sometimes quite interesting, as the recent biography of Siegmund Warburg shows: bankers of the prefinancial innovations period were very different from the present ones, had cultural and political dimensions, and worked for more than profit maximization.[18] Here I am not trying to establish which of the two levels—macro and micro—could be considered foundational, which is still an intriguing issue, but simply to underline the fact that the two exist. There is today another branch of economic history—business history—devoted to the task of studying the microlevel, with dedicated journals and a large number of practitioners. It is to be noted that the relations between cliometrics and business history are almost nonexistent, although some economic historians are eclectic enough to encompass both.

Besides, there is the question of institutions and contexts, as Demeulemeester and Diebolt have argued, that show substantial differences across countries and over time. In the world of hard sciences, an international community of researchers is by now an established fact. Take for example myeloma, a terrible blood cancer existing in the whole world *with the same features*: the international community of scholars who study it exchange

18. Ferguson, *High Financier: The Lives and Time of Siegmund Warburg.*

their views in a *lingua franca* (English) aiming at applying the best available clinical treatment all over the world. But it is impossible to apply the same policies to different societies, because what is useful to improve the lot of one society might not be viable for another society, although there is scope for cross-fertilization. Moreover, nature is deterministic, and the problem is to understand its logic. Societies are always changing and there is no determinism in them, so that they can be turned in one or the other direction according to the different views of their members. This means that in hard sciences progress is cumulative and unidirectional, while in the social sciences alternative options coexist: cycles, declines, reinterpretations. Take for example Marxism and Communism: they appeared for some time to be a strong alternative to Liberalism and Capitalism; then Communism failed. It is therefore extremely important that economic historians include in their work an analysis of contexts and institutions.

In addition, there is one other crucial point to be discussed. I made a passing reference above to the concept of *intentionality*, which is the most novel addition that Douglass North has made to his list of criticisms of neoclassical theory.[19] His view is that the concept of rationality—on which neoclassical models are based—is too narrow a concept to understand how a human world functions. Instrumental rationality can only explain a small portion of the actual choices made by people, even in the field of economics. Cultures (including ideologies and religions) and environments matter, in the first instance because they shape institutions providing formal rules, informal norms, and enforcement mechanisms that allow a society to make decisions, but also because they shape political systems, international relations, peace and war decisions made by states—all factors affecting the economy. The immediate implication of this is that the strict separation of economics from politics appears unwarranted, and the study of 'political economy' too becomes crucial to the understanding of economic developments.[20]

## ALAN MILWARD'S POLITICAL ECONOMY APPROACH

It is at this point that we come to the kind of economic history practiced by Alan Milward. What exactly is meant by 'political economy' is not univocal, but basically the expression points to the relevance of the structure of governance of a polity for the shaping of institutions. 'Such issues as constitutional versus authoritarian regimes, the extent and the working of democracy, party coalitions and political competition, monopoly of coercion by

19. North, *Understanding the Process of Economic Growth*.
20. It has recently been argued that a 'political economy' approach can usefully be introduced also in business history: see John, 'Bringing Political Economy Back In'.

the State or participation of civil society to enforce rules are at the core of understanding how institutions work', as I wrote elsewhere.[21] This is exactly the field of enquiry in which Alan Milward has excelled, producing first a number of innovative pieces of work on the way the German, French, Norwegian, and British economies operated during the Second World War, and concluding this research project by collecting his broad knowledge of the period in a comparative book on the Second World War.[22] The functioning of a war economy was a rather original topic for an economic historian to approach at that time since the preference of the practitioners of such a discipline had generally focused on 'normal' periods. However in more recent times interest in the two world wars and their wider impact has grown.[23] Milward showed from the very start his unconventional approach to economic history, one which was never separated from political events. The numerous translations of these earlier works of his bear witness to the considerable interest raised by his work.[24]

Meanwhile, he had engaged with Berrick Saul in a major endeavor, that of writing a comprehensive and detailed history of the economic development of continental Europe in the 'long nineteenth century' in two volumes. Its translation into Italian and Spanish allowed it to become one of the most widely used university textbooks in the 1980s in both countries, when it was still possible to adopt books of this size (the Italian version by *Il Mulino* had around 1500 pages).[25] The approach of the book was holistic, with a few chapters dealing with general issues and most concentrating on national cases, revealing the comparative vision that Milward always preserved in his scholarly work. Basically, the book shows the authors' firm belief that the 'national' dimension has been of overwhelming importance

---

21. Zamagni, 'What is the Message', 160.
22. *The German Economy at War*; *The New Order and the French Economy*; *The Economic Effects of the Two World Wars on Britain*; *The Fascist Economy in Norway*; *War, Economy and Society, 1939–1945*.
23. Harrison, *The Economics of World War II*. The book has a much more quantitative approach, but the works by Milward are widely quoted. There is now the companion volume: Broadberry and Harrison, *The Economics of World War I*.
24. Editorial note: The interested reader should consult the list of publications in Appendix 2 of this volume.
25. Editorial note: The Italian translation by Franco Bassani was entitled *Storia economica dell'Europa continentale: 1780–1870* (Bologna: Il Mulino, 1977). The Spanish translation by María José Triviño took two more years to be published as *El desarrollo económico de la Europa continental* (Madrid, Tecnos, 1979). *The German Economy at War* was also translated into Italian by Marcello De Cecco (*L'economia di guerra della Germania*, Milan: Franco Angeli Editore, 1971) and *War, Economy and Society, 1939–1945* as *Guerra, economia e società, 1939–1945* (Milan: ETAS libri, 1983). In Spanish the latter received the misleading title of *La Segunda Guerra Mundial, 1935–1945* (Barcelona: Crítica, 1986).

in shaping the evolution of the European economies and that 'inter-national' relations clearly had nations as actors shaping and directing markets.[26]

But in my view, Milward's masterpieces concern the process of integration in Europe in the post-1945 years.[27] These constituted a long-run research project which can be seen as a continuation of his earlier interest in the period of modern European history that was marked by a true discontinuity, that of the Second World War, which destroyed much of the earlier achievements and opened Europe up to a peace process escaping (at least partially) from path dependency. It is not the purpose of this essay to highlight the achievements of Milward's scholarship in this field, because numerous other contributions to this volume are aimed precisely at such a treatment. Rather, what will be done here is to extract from Milward's work the paradigm of political economy he has practiced.

First of all it must be recognized that Milward ended up by concentrating his attention on a very crucial topic—European integration is now unanimously considered the major positive novelty of the 'short' century (the twentieth century, starting only after the First World War)—and he did it on a grand scale, producing works that are milestones that no one teaching the subject can avoid. Milward's approach can be summarized along three main lines: the actors, the shape of institutions, and the economic impact.

Milward's first major preoccupation was to identify the actors and their interactions. His actors are the 'nations' of Western Europe, which, facing up to the novel approach of the United States according to which war was removed as an instrument for state competition in Western Europe, saw economic integration as the only viable road to a sustainable growth path.[28] Among the many documents that prove this American approach, the one I have always found intriguing is the speech that Paul Hoffman, the Administrator of the Economic Cooperation Administration, delivered at the meeting of the ministerial council of the Organization for European Economic Cooperation (OEEC) on 31 October 1949 in Paris. Milward notes how frequently Hoffman referred to 'integration' in his short speech (in around 2,200 words the exact word appeared sixteen times but the concept even more). In face of the obvious difficulties of the OEEC to come to an agreement on how to distribute Marshall Plan money, Hoffman relaunched and pressed hard toward having 'ready early in 1950 a record of accomplishment and a program which together will take Europe well

26. This makes a startling contrast with the recent two-volume textbook edited by Stephen Broadberry and Kevin O'Rourke, *The Cambridge Economic History of Modern Europe*, in which the national dimension has almost completely disappeared.
27. *The Reconstruction of Western Europe, 1945–51*, and *The European Rescue of the Nation State*.
28. Further elaboration of this thesis will be found in Eichengreen, *The European Economy since 1945*.

along the road toward economic integration'.[29] He was well aware of the fact that the European Recovery Program (ERP) could close the 'dollar gap' only temporarily. Thus, the need for the European economies to recover their external balances as soon as possible was overwhelming. This goal could only be reached by integrating the European economies, following the example of the United States' federation:

> The substance of such integration—Hoffman said—would be the formation of a single large market within which quantitative restrictions on the movement of goods, monetary barriers to the flow of payments and eventually all tariffs are permanently swept away. The fact that we have in the United States a single market of 150 million consumers has been indispensable to the strength and efficiency of our economy. The creation of a permanent freely trading area comprising 275 million consumers in Western Europe would have a multitude of helpful consequences. It would accelerate the development of large scale, low-cost production industries; it would make the effective use of all resources easier; the stifling of healthy competition more difficult.[30]

While the United States was the innovative actor, in my view, the European nations acted as subjects stubbornly aiming at maximizing their domestic interests, with very little inclination to accommodate ideal targets of 'common good', as could be seen in intra-OEEC negotiations. According to the well-known interpretation by Milward, the European Communities were born out of the effort on the part of nation-states to 'rescue' themselves from part of their difficulties, and the inner governance structure of the present EU can be understood only by recognizing the primacy of the governments in decision-making: the EU was born partially as an intergovernmental structure, partially as a supranational one, although over time this initial dichotomy has been somewhat blurred, with resulting incoherencies in its architecture.[31] I personally think that Alan Milward exaggerated this and underrated other factors that have contributed to the process of European integration, but he was essentially right on the predominance of state action. The national-governmental dimension is still prominent in the EU at the time of writing this essay, more than fifty years after the beginning of the process of European political integration.

Notwithstanding the importance of the national-governmental dimension, there were—and there are today—other factors at work. For example, one important additional factor explaining the changes of approach by

---

29. The text of Hoffman's statement is accessible at the Centre Virtuel de la Connaissance sur l'Europe website (www.cvce.eu) (last accessed on 12 December 2011).
30. Ibid., 3.
31. Milward, *Rescue.*

some European nations immediately after the end of the war can be found in the interesting literature on continental Christian Democratic parties, which I have recently surveyed.[32] This literature shows that leaders of such parties, starting back in 1946, met secretly in Switzerland to discuss which projects for the reconstruction of Western Europe they could share: full reconstruction of the German economy; enhancement of European security through the diffusion of welfare (this was a field of collaboration with Social Democratic parties, which were also sponsoring the welfare state, though from a different angle); a strong social dimension to the market-based European economic system (the well-known German approach to a 'social market economy') that was to different degrees shared by all the Christian Democratic parties in Europe; the *organic interlocking* of French and German basic industries (the chemical industry was even included in the first instance) as a solution to French security; and the building up of a 'common market', an idea that had circulated already in the 1930s.[33] The most active leaders in these meetings were Georges Bidault, Robert Schuman, and Konrad Adenauer. The role of Christian-Democratic leaders was strategic in shaping the partnership in the new institutions that came into being. For instance, Italy's membership in the European Coal and Steel Community (ECSC)—the latter being the first important result of such meetings—can be explained, in my opinion, by the excellent relations entertained by Alcide de Gasperi, head of the Italian Christian-Democratic party, with Adenauer, more than by any *interests* of Italy, a nation that had a very modest steel industry distant from the core productive area.[34] From this I am inclined to think that indeed national interests were still the main driving force toward continental Europe's economic integration, but coupled with some openings toward novel cooperative solutions mostly produced by the commonality of views shared by the many Christian Democratic parties in power in continental Europe.

The one nation-state that remained cut off from these developments toward economic integration was Britain, and I think Milward was right in emphasizing in this case the predominance of its *national* interests, which were seen as lying mainly outside continental Europe.[35] Milward has very harsh words on the British position in several of his works. I am convinced that his views on the whole process of European integration owe much to

32. Zamagni, 'The Political and Economic Impact of CST since 1891'.
33. Kaiser, *Christian Democracy and the Origins of the European Union*.
34. It is worth recalling that Italy did have plans to enlarge its steel industry, as Ruggero Ranieri has amply shown in his works (starting with his Ph.D. thesis, 'L'espansione alla prova del negoziato'), and it became second only to the Federal Republic in the output of steel.
35. See Milward's detailed account of the United Kingdom's policies toward the European Communities from 1945 to 1963 in his *The Rise and Fall of a National Strategy, 1945–1963* (vol. 1 of the Government Official History Series of the United Kingdom and the European Community).

the experience of the United Kingdom. There is one passage that I never fail to quote to the students of my European Economic Integration classes, because of its literary effectiveness. It is the following:

> The Franco-German association which [was] created was in many respects a shotgun wedding. The German bride, although her other choices were not very enticing had nevertheless to be dragged protestingly by her aged father to the altar while numerous members of her family staged noisy protests on the way and an equally large number of the bridegroom's friends and relations prophesied disaster. Yet the knot once tied, this surprising union soon settled into a safe bourgeois marriage in which the couple, rapidly becoming wealthy and comfortable as passions cooled, were held together, as such couples are, by the strong links of managing their complex joint economic affairs. To all those associated with the marriage and brought into the house the same bourgeois prosperity was vouchsafed. The UK was left in the position of a prim spinster who, having earlier rejected the bridegroom because of the lack of promise of his stormy adolescence, was later allowed into the household on not very flattering terms as a rather acidulous baby sitter. If she leaves, it will not make much difference, except to her. But if the marriage breaks up it will be the end of the peace settlement and perhaps of us all.[36]

Beside actors, Milward studied the functioning of institutions and the advantages and disadvantages of the shape they were given. Among the many examples of this, the explanation of why most of the earlier new European institutions were devised—by the U.S. planning group within the Economic Cooperation Administration—at a technocratic level seems to me really brilliant. After having seen the failure of the OEEC because it was too political an organization, it was:

> better to design institutions which would be on no higher a level than the bureaucratic and technocratic and allow them to be operated by non-political actors, who would then see themselves as solving technocratic problems in unison rather than as representing a particular combination of purely national interests. [ . . . ] If by an act of political will Western Europe could put one or two such institutions in place they would, like yeast, work their own ferment.[37]

The European Payments Union was one such institution. The idea came from the Keynesian proposal of a Clearing Union and is today considered a

---

36. Milward, *Reconstruction*, 420.
37. Ibid., 285.

very effective mechanism of financial diplomacy.[38] It also helped to liberalize trade from quantitative restrictions, and by putting in place a routine of international negotiations that would result in mutual benefit, it showed the advantages of cooperation.[39] The ECSC was another such institution but at the supranational level. It involved lengthy technical negotiations with the Americans also, who were worried that the new institution would conceal a new steel cartel. So, Jean Monnet was careful to shape his guidelines for the statutes of the institution in such a way as to avoid the danger of the resurrection of cartels, against the will of most European steel producers. Indeed, articles 65 and 66 of the ECSC treaty embodied the most advanced American antitrust thinking of the time. For Europe it was a major innovation, later to become the basis for the antitrust legislation of the Community.[40]

In the third place, Milward studied the impact of new institutions. One of the best examples of this effort is the study he did of trade, multilateral and bilateral, and of international payments in Europe from the end of the 1930s to the 1950s. Through this analysis it was possible to clarify the deeper causes for the launching of the Marshall Plan: the problem was not starting reconstruction in Europe, something that had been going on rapidly since the end of the war, but preventing the halting of its momentum by the dollar gap. This is why U.S. intervention was planned over the span of four years, because the solution of the dollar gap could not be a matter of a few months. The solution to this problem went through the crucial revival of the West German economy, and the Marshall Plan was instrumental in achieving this as well, insofar as it granted France the full support that the country was expecting, contributing to the change of approach that France showed toward the 'German question'.

Having encompassed more than one actor and institution, Milward also tried to connect the various steps of integration to one another, to produce a grand picture. Here is where his views have been mostly questioned, as for instance in relation to his scaling-down of the role of the Marshall Plan (often not correctly understood) or with the downgrading of the achievements of the European Union. But the general picture emerging from Milward's scholarship is still solid today and is best summarized in his words:

> By rejecting the task of first regulating the major political questions concerning Western Europe, and then rejecting the constraints on national economic recovery imposed by the agreements signed at Bretton Woods,

38. Kaplan and Schleiminger, *The European Payments Union: Financial Diplomacy in the 1950s.*
39. Eichengreen, *Reconstructing Europe's Trade and Payments: The European Payments Union.*
40. Gillingham, *Coal, Steel, and the Rebirth of Europe*; Killick, *The United States and European Reconstruction.*

> and finally rejecting the ultimate implications of American policy in Western Europe after 1947, Western Europe made its own peace settlement. In place of the major peace settlement that never came it created an alternative pattern of reconstruction, a restricted but workable institutional framework for economic interdependence which has proved more effective than any previous peace settlement.[41]

Beyond the conclusions reached by Milward, some of which could today be questioned, one of the lasting achievements of his scholarly work has been to show that there is no escape in a political economy approach from coming to terms with actors of policies and their targets, the shape of institutions and their economic impact, which are the basic lines of research that a sound political economy approach must undertake. Only when the analysis is centered on the economic impact of institutions might there be scope for introducing more quantitative techniques, but the consultation of archives and the detailed description of the chain of events are the necessary prerequisites to carry on meaningful research on actors of policies and shape of institutions. The predominance in economic history of quantitative models is the reason why Milward's achievements in the analysis of the process of European integration, though always quoted, have not been widely discussed among economic historians, whereas political and diplomatic historians, as well as political scientists, could not pass over Milward's work because they too were concerned, though from different angles, with actors and shape of institutions.

## ECONOMIC HISTORY AS A MULTIVALENT DISCIPLINE

From what has been discussed above I draw five main conclusions:

1. Economic history has the primary duty of unraveling the secrets of past economic activities, and as such it cannot become a branch of mainstream economics. Economic historians are there to search for facts that are still obscure.
2. Past economic activities can be studied at the macro, and microlevel. As the evolution of institutions is key to understanding the relative economic success of certain societies and the failures of others, institutions are also an integral part of economic history.
3. Institutions are molded by political authorities and therefore the study of those governance structures that promote institutions is also an integral part of economic history, as I have argued in discussing Alan

41. Milward, *Reconstruction*, 476–477. Editorial note: This was written before the Allied Settlement with Germany in 1990.

Milward's political economy approach to economic history. Of all the approaches to economic history this is the one most closely connected with the use of archival material, because it deals with negotiations among many partners, the outcome of which is due more to power relations and ideal goals than to any economic rationality. On the other hand, as institutions provide the rules within which markets function, it is of the utmost importance to understand why and how they are shaped, to be able to analyze appropriately their economic impact, their limits, and their possible modifications.

5. From 1, 2, and 3 it follows that there is more than one method to be employed by economic historians to interpret the facts they uncover with their research. Econometrics is only one among these. Due to the demanding nature of each tool of analysis there is more than one type of specialization possible within economic history, but none of these specializations can claim to be the only admissible one. A footnote to this conclusion is that there could be cliometricians who prefer to belong to the applied economics field, and this is not only acceptable, but also very positive. To have economists convinced of the importance of the long-run view is always useful, although often this interest is cultivated by them in a less than adequate way. Such cliometricians can avoid being concerned with researching historical facts and can belong fully to the category of mainstream economists, with a special interest in long-run issues, but cannot be mistaken for economic historians.
6. Economic history does not differ from other types of history in its role: avoiding excessive simplification of theoretical models; showing the lack of determinism of human choices; building chains of causes and effects; identifying major historical actors; analyzing advantages and disadvantages of specific institutions, and finally, recognizing the long-term roots of the present (the so-called *path dependence* phenomenon).[42]

To reduce economic history to the running of econometric models is not only unfair to the discipline, because it narrows it down unduly, but in the end it is useless to economics itself since it will learn little from such exercises. As Robert Solow once remarked: 'this sort of economic history [cliometrics] gives back to the theorist the same routine gruel that the economic theorist gives to the historian.'[43] If today mainstream economists do

42. As is well known, the concept of path dependence has been worked out mostly by Paul David. See the summary statement of his work done by David himself, 'Path Dependence: A Foundational Concept for Historical Social Science'.
43. Quoted in Lyons, Cain, and Williamson, *Reflections on the Cliometric Revolution*, 40.

not recognize the need for a multifaceted cultural preparation where economic history is included as a distinct component, along the lines indicated by Hicks and Schumpeter, in the future things might change, and other schools of thought might be friendlier to history. Economic history must resist adapting too much to the brand of economics mostly practiced at any one time and leave ample openings to variety.

Moreover, there is great scope for collaboration among different specialists, for instance, between economic historians and econometricians, but the basic requirements of such collaboration are twofold: each partner should maintain its own distinctive line of research, and no one should try to encapsulate the other in its domain.[44] Even more basic to the success of any possible collaboration is the awareness of 'the limited nature of any type of interpretation or causation', an acquisition that according to Leontief should push all the social scientists to give up any pretension of 'sovereignty'.[45]

44. Patrick K. O'Brien has harsh words for those economists who are not respectful of economic history and have 'reduced too many younger economic historians (when they employed them at all) to the status of serfs on their estates, laboring to recover meaning from the past, expressed in their language and congruent with the theoretical expectations of Deans and Heads of Departments'. Quoted in Lyons, Cain, and Williamson, *Reflections on the Cliometric Revolution*, 442.
45. Leontief, 'Note on the Pluralistic Interpretation of History', 619 and 624.

# 6 The Impossible Dream

## Transferring the Danish Agricultural Model to Iceland

*Guðmundur Jónsson*

The rapid but uneven spread of industrialization in nineteenth-century Europe created divergent paths of growth and development in different countries. As a result, the more backward economies had the opportunity to benefit from the accumulated knowledge and technologies of the more advanced economies. At the same time, they were confronted with difficult decisions of choosing strategies, types of production, organizational structures, and institutional frameworks that would best enhance their productive capacity. Models successful in one time and place might not be as effective in others.

The relationship between changes in agriculture and the process of modern economic growth is a frequently visited theme in Alan S. Milward's writing, especially during the 1970s, as demonstrated in the two popular textbooks he wrote with S. B. Saul on the economic history of Europe between 1780 and 1914, but also in later works on the effects of the European integration process on agriculture in the post-1945 period. In an insightful article from 1979, in which Milward deals specifically with the strategies of agricultural development in nineteenth-century Europe, he critically examines the different responses from the agricultural sector to pressures from other sectors of the economy in the early stages of 'sustained development', and asks the question: what were the determinants of a satisfactory response?[1] The answer to this question is important, he maintains, not only in relation to the successful economies, but perhaps even more so in understanding what went wrong in those that were less successful. National choices are influenced by examples sought in a country's own historical legacy as well as the experience of other countries. Milward rightly points out that 'countries sought the guiding path into the future from the history of the successful', although these historical images tend to be distorted and therefore provide unsatisfactory guidance toward choosing an appropriate strategy. The central problem was to identify correctly what

---

1. Milward, 'Strategies for Development in Agriculture: The Nineteenth-Century European Experience', in *The Search for Wealth and Stability*, edited by Smout, 21–42, here 39.

was useful in the national legacy and what could be learned from the experience of others.

Milward mentions Denmark as the most frequently cited example of the successful transition of the agricultural sector in the late nineteenth century, a theme that will be explored in this chapter in relation to the role which that country played as a model for agricultural development in Iceland during the agrarian transition in Europe of the late nineteenth and early twentieth centuries. The focus will be on the search for new types of farming and production in response to critical problems emerging in the farming sector, manifested on the one hand in the rapid shift of labor from agriculture to other sectors after 1880, and on the other hand in the difficulties of entering foreign markets for those selling traditional produce in the 1890s. Inspired by the successful transition of Danish agriculture at the time, Icelanders increasingly looked to the Danish model as an example to follow. Ties between the two countries were close, Iceland being a dependency (*biland*) of Denmark until 1918 and Copenhagen its traditional gateway to the wider world. The emerging Danish agricultural model seemed to offer Icelandic farmers a way out of the impasse: small- and medium-scale animal husbandry on intensively cultivated farms, dairies, slaughterhouses, and distribution networks organized on a cooperative basis, production geared toward exports of butter and cheese to Britain as well as to the fast-growing home market. Was it not possible to make the Danish model work in Icelandic agriculture as well?

Economic historians have long been occupied with identifying and analyzing the obstacles to a successful transition of the agricultural sector of nineteenth-century Europe. The list of obstacles is long, from poverty, risk-aversion, lack of specialization, and inappropriate government policies to institutions that generate poverty and backwardness. Some institutional economists contend that economic growth depends on two types of complementary technologies: production technologies and social technologies.[2] Production technologies have characteristics of public goods, that is, goods that are nonrival in consumption and available to all, and are therefore considered highly transferable. However social technologies, defined as 'social models that describe how social institutions create social outcomes', do not typically travel well, as their evolution is rooted in a specific cultural context.[3] As production technologies are not effective unless complemented by social technologies of at least minimal quality, the unsuccessful transfer of the latter is a critical barrier to economic growth.

The distinction between production and social technologies is useful in our context. Scholars working in the field of new institutional economics tend to see the problem of applying new social technologies as the key

2. See, e.g., Nelson and Sampat, 'Making Sense of Institutions', and Eggertsson, *Imperfect Institutions*.
3. Eggertsson, *Imperfect Institutions*, 25–26.

barrier to economic growth. Here the argument is developed, however, that Iceland in the beginning of the twentieth century presents a case of agricultural development in which a new agricultural strategy adopted from outside proved successful as far as new social institutions were concerned, whereas the development of new products was much less successful. We use a broad definition of the term institution, to include organizations as well as standard and expected patterns of behavior. A cooperative system for the processing and marketing of agricultural goods and the underlying technologies associated with it was successfully adapted in Iceland. However, the introduction of new production met with limited success, primarily because of the unsuitability of the strategy as a whole, a strategy that was selected on the basis of bad judgment about the potential of Icelandic agriculture and its possibilities in foreign markets.

## ICELANDIC AGRICULTURE AT THE CROSSROADS

A well-known Danish agriculturist, Peter Feilberg, visited Iceland in 1876–1877 to study the state of agriculture and advise the Danish Royal Agricultural Society on how to expand and improve cultivation on Icelandic farms. Feilberg came to the conclusion that the most serious deficiencies of Icelandic agriculture were lack of capital and practical knowledge among farmers. Icelanders were 'one of the most intelligent people' in Europe and had produced great literary works in linguistics, history, and poetry, but practical knowledge, which is a prerequisite for modern development, had not thrived.[4] Iceland's problems were rooted in cultural norms that only Icelanders themselves could change, primarily through practical experiments, good examples, and education. Outside help could be useful, but only in the form of education and training to promote cultural change. Feilberg adamantly believed that farm improvements should be grounded in the national experience. In a debate with a fellow countryman many years later he remarked: 'Experiences from other countries are of little importance—the agricultural knowledge that will be of use to tackle the difficulties on the island [Iceland] cannot be imported; it must develop in the country itself like the plants that are to grow there', adding to clarify his point that the distance between Zealand (in Denmark) and Iceland was equivalent to the distance between Zealand and northern Italy.[5]

The typically Danish idea of reform through education and practical knowledge was well known in Iceland but little practiced. Iceland was predominantly an agricultural economy with rudimentary specialization and hardly any manufacturing base. Farming was still bound up in primitive

4. Feilberg, *Om Forholdene paa Island*, 19–20.
5. Feilberg, 'Kulturarbejeder i Island', 144.

pastoral traditions where peasant farmers, for the most part very poor, eked a living from land-extensive sheep rearing, supplementing their earnings with cattle farming, fishing, seal hunting, birding, and, during the winter, producing woolen knitwear. Grain had been grown until the fifteenth century but was discontinued because the climate became colder, and vegetable cultivation was insignificant until after 1890. Most of the land was meadow or marshland of varying quality and wasteland not fit for any use, and cultivation was mainly limited to producing hay for winter fodder on the small hay fields around the farmhouses. The peasant farmers relied more on winter grazing than improving the hay fields or making use of more efficient farming methods to increase the herds, which would ultimately have returned more stable and higher growth. They used basically the same technology as their forefathers had done for centuries, and little improvement was made in hay harvesting techniques before 1900. Expansion of the hay fields was a slow process due to the difficult terrain, lack of capital and fertilizers, as some of the manure was used as fuel and chemical fertilizers were not introduced until after 1920.[6]

Interest in farm improvements, however, was slowly increasing after 1880, and greater public efforts were made to promote education and training. Three agricultural schools were established in the 1880s, and the number of agricultural societies rapidly increased with the introduction of a government grant scheme for farm improvements. Advisers were employed by the societies to promote 'practical knowledge' in the rural communities. 'The reformers' advocated a new type of farming in which increased cultivation of farmland, more use of modern techniques, better feeding practices, and selective breeding were seen as the principal means for the advancement of agriculture. Increasing the hay crops by extending and improving the hay fields in various ways was seen as the key factor in achieving a more stable and higher growth and as a precondition for any significant advance in dairy farming. Before 1900 there were noticeable improvements in farm practices, for example in the extension of hay fields, better outbuildings, and increased vegetable production. However, these changes proceeded at a slow pace, hampered not only by a shortage of capital and education but also by widespread tenancy and the insecurity of leases that did not guarantee the tenant the benefits of his improvements on the farm.

In Europe, the greatest challenges facing agriculture in the late nineteenth century were brought about by the 'grain invasion' from North America and Russia after 1870. As Iceland was one of the few countries not growing grain at all, the sources of its problems lay elsewhere. One major challenge was the structural change taking place in the economy after 1880, with a great surge of people leaving agriculture in the wake

6. Guðmundur Jónsson, 'Institutional Change in Icelandic Agriculture', 101–102.

of a colder climate and depressed agricultural prices, leading to a sharp downturn in output and incomes. At first, most of the migrant population went to America, but increasingly after 1890, the flow was to the expanding fishing towns on the coast. These changes were happening rapidly, with the rural population declining from over 90 percent of the total population in 1880 to 46 percent in 1930.

Agriculture faced increasing competition from fisheries and other urban industries for labor and capital. With the abolition of labor bondage in 1894 and other liberal legislation introduced around the turn of the century, agriculture effectively lost its privileged position on the labor market. Luring labor with higher wages was not enough to stem the flow of people to the towns. The landless rural poor wanted to have a plot of their own land and establish families—to lead an independent life. Strong demands were therefore made for better access to land for the landless poor at the same time as the rural population was dwindling.

Another more immediate challenge emerged in 1896, when the British government suspended imports of live sheep on the pretext of disease control, bringing the most important export article for Icelandic farmers to a halt. In the preceding decades, the export of live sheep had been instrumental in bringing Icelandic farmers into the cash economy as their production was increasingly geared toward the market. By the turn of the century, the share of agricultural production sold on the market, mainly abroad, had risen to 47 percent.[7] Since other traditional exports such as unprocessed wool, low-quality salted mutton, and live horses had little or no growth potential, it was necessary to redirect agricultural production and find alternative export opportunities.

## THE DANISH AGRICULTURAL MODEL AND ITS INFLUENCE IN ICELAND

As one of the most influential politicians in Iceland during the interwar period, Jónas Jónsson, an MP for the Progressive Party and a government minister from 1927 to 1932, put it:

> Icelanders must make substantial changes to their agricultural production. Stop prioritizing the production of meat, wool and horses. Export instead butter, cheese, pork and eggs. In short: they must largely abandon what might be called Icelandic farming and adopt Danish farming. This may not be very loyal to the nation's traditions. But necessity is the mother of invention.[8]

7. Guðmundur Jónsson, *Hagvöxtur og iðnvæðing*, 173.
8. Jónas Jónsson, *Komandi ár*, 164. Author's own translation.

In the intensive search for ways out of the impasse, farmers, and politicians soon turned to Denmark, where the radical changes which had been taking place in agriculture over the previous decades had earned it an international reputation. In Denmark, the sector had been transformed into a modern, efficient industry specializing in livestock products, focusing on exports of butter, cheese, and eggs to Britain and other countries. By the turn of the century, agricultural produce still accounted for about 90 percent of all exports, and agriculture continued for decades to make a unique contribution to the growth of the Danish economy.[9]

The initial driving force behind these changes had been the grain invasion in the 1870s. This was to pose a great challenge for Denmark as a major grain exporter with only an insignificant part of its exports being dairy products and live animals to Germany and Britain. Denmark did not impose a tariff on grain but instead diverted its production increasingly to animal products, taking advantage of cheaper grains as animal feed and the comparatively good prices for livestock products. The difference in price trends gave an advantage to intensive livestock farming.[10] Many countries of north-western Europe were starting to move from grain production to meat and dairy farming as a response to the agrarian crisis.[11] However, a number of factors gave the Danish transformation the distinctive character that made it so successful. Compared to other European countries, Danish agriculture was already in a favorable position in terms of efficiency when the crisis came; 'progressive' farmers were embarking on improved farming methods by using grain and fodder as the basis for intensive dairy farming as early as the 1860s.[12] However, it was the spread of agricultural cooperatives after 1880 that was to become the distinctive feature of the Danish transformation, changing agriculture into a highly integrated sector of production, processing, distribution, and marketing based on the cooperative system.

The agricultural cooperatives were initially confined to dairies (creameries), which were instrumental in increasing the output and quality of dairy production, using new techniques (such as the steam-driven cream separator) that greatly increased efficiency and encouraged cooperation of farms in creameries. Importantly, the cooperative organization of creameries allowed the dominant small- and middle-sized farms to benefit from economies of scale in processing and marketing. Later, other types of

9. Further elaboration in Henriksen, 'The Contribution of Agriculture', 143–144; Tracy, *Government and Agriculture*, 107–115; Henriksen, 'Avoiding Lock-In'; and Bjørn, *Det danske landbrugs historie*, vol. 3, especially 313–381.
10. Henriksen, 'The Contribution of Agriculture', 127, and Tracy, *Government and Agriculture*, 110.
11. Peltonen, 'Agrarian World Market and Finnish Farm Economy', 28–32.
12. Bjørn, *Det danske landbrugs historie*, 313–325.

cooperatives were set up, such as for the purchase of animal feed and for egg exports. Cooperative bacon factories were established in response to the restriction and eventual ban on the import of live pigs into Germany in 1887–1896, which led to a major redirection of Danish production into bacon for the British market.

As Icelanders closely watched these changes in Danish agriculture, acutely aware of how backward their own farming was, many farmers and policy-makers came to see Danish agriculture as a model to follow. Danish influences were already seeping in: agricultural societies were modeled on their counterparts in Denmark; agriculturists went to Denmark for further education; research, advice, and educational materials were provided by the Danish Royal Agricultural Society, although not on a permanent basis.[13] And although Danish farming practices had hardly made any inroads in Iceland, where environmental and economic factors were very different, Icelanders were becoming more receptive to new methods based on practical and scientific knowledge. Above all, the example of Danish agriculture had greatly contributed to a change in Icelanders' notions about agriculture, as they came to realize that, instead of utter reliance on nature's gifts, the expansion and improvement of cultivated farmland was the way forward to higher and more stable growth. The ideas of cooperative dairy farming and slaughterhouses modeled on Danish agriculture gained great popularity in Iceland around the turn of the century.

In 1901, eighteen years after the first cooperative creamery was set up in Denmark, a small group of farmers in southern Iceland established a creamery to produce butter for the British market. One of its founders, a small farmer, recalls the difficulties in farming in those years with falling prices for sheep products, the 1896 earthquake in the south, and bad weather for three consecutive years at the end of the century.[14] Many creameries were set up in the following years, small operating units scattered around the countryside, exporting at the peak of their operation in 1913 around two hundred tons of butter from thirty-one dairies, involving 1,200 farmers.[15] A dairy school was established in the area of Borgarfjörður in 1900 with the assistance of the Danish Royal Agricultural Society, headed by a Danish expert and promoting similar training and production techniques (cream separator and steam-driven butter beaters) as in Denmark. However, the small size of the Icelandic creameries and their use of ewes' milk for the production made them different from the Danish ones. The creameries received substantial support from the government in the form of investment credit and export subsidies, the latter a novelty in Iceland.[16]

13. Sigurðsson, *Landbrug og landboforhold i Island*, 150–162.
14. Helgason, *Endurminningar*, 141.
15. Pálsson, 'Rjómabú', 78–79, and Sigurjónsson, 'Útflutningsverzlun Íslendinga', 228.
16. Guðmundur Jónsson, 'The State and the Icelandic Economy', 142–143.

The creameries were the first significant step toward more advanced dairy farming, transferring a large part of the production outside the homes and turning it into a higher-quality export commodity processed with new techniques and organizational structures. However, these creameries were only a transitional stage in the development of the dairy industry toward the large-scale dairies established in the 1920s and early 1930s. During the First World War, the creameries started to decline for a number of reasons. Farmers in the vicinity of Reykjavík and other urban areas made more profit by selling fresh milk and even homemade butter directly to the market at more favorable prices. Moreover, the production of ewes' milk, an important supply of the creameries, plummeted as a result of labor shortages, rising wages, and greater emphasis on the production of lamb meat.[17] The shift from mutton to lamb accelerated a change in sheep rearing, leading to the near-disappearance of ewes' milk in the marketplace, since lambs were now reared on their mother's milk over the summer to gain weight before they were slaughtered in the autumn.

In public debate, dairy farming was frequently associated with smallholdings, in line with popular ideas of cottage farming (*husmandsbrug*) in Denmark at the time. In Iceland, prominent farmers wanted to see agriculture move away from land-extensive sheep rearing with reliance on grazing to a dairy production for the domestic and foreign market, operated on smaller intensively cultivated farms, with the processing and distribution organized on a cooperative basis. It was argued that dairy farming on small and intensively worked land would be more efficient than land-extensive sheep rearing; it would require less land, and labor would be used in more efficient ways, reducing the need for hired labor. In addition, the cooperative organization of processing and distribution would strengthen the competitive position of the small farmer. Dairy production and smallholder farming were linked together and perceived by many not only as a strategy for growth but also as an effective way of stemming the flow of people out of agriculture.[18]

Another consequence of the English import ban on live sheep was the establishment of cooperative slaughterhouses after the turn of the century, which had an even greater economic significance than the creameries, since mutton was one of the most valuable agricultural products. Traditionally, farmers sold live sheep to merchants in towns who took care of the slaughter and the export of the meat, primarily in the form of cheap, low-quality salted mutton to Denmark. The first cooperative slaughterhouses were founded in 1907, one in Reykjavík by farmers in the south and another in Húsavík in the north, soon to be followed by other areas. By 1912, slaughterhouses were found in all the major ports in Iceland. Modeled on Danish

---

17. Pálsson, 'Rjómabú', 78.
18. Guðmundur Jónsson, 'Á slóðum Bjarts í Sumarhúsum'.

practices, the slaughterhouses were organized and run by the farmers themselves on a cooperative basis, and standardized methods of slaughtering and processing were introduced that greatly enhanced the quality of the meat. New types of production and processing allowed for a shift in production from heavily salted mutton to lightly salted lamb, which was soon to become the most valuable agricultural export, mostly for the Danish and Norwegian markets. Sporadic attempts were made to export chilled or frozen lamb before the First World War, but no significant change occurred until the late 1920s.[19]

## THE AGRARIAN OFFENSIVE OF THE 1920S

The decline of the creameries was a serious albeit short-lived setback for the dairy industry. After the First World War, agriculture gained unprecedented political support. In the *Althingi* (parliament), a strong desire was felt across the political spectrum to provide agriculture with legislation, public money, and credit institutions that would bring the sector into the modern age and provide a real counterweight to the movement from country to town. With structural changes in the economy going at a fast pace and the rural population in steep decline, some of the advocates of stronger agriculture genuinely believed that the urban population was soon about to reach its upper limits, and only agriculture was capable of accommodating future population growth.[20] The rise of agrarianism was not just about strengthening the economic power of agriculture; for many it was a matter of preserving the economic independence of Iceland and the culture and national identity of its people.

A strong feature of the interwar agrarianism was the idea of economic modernization based on small-scale production with agriculture forming the core of the economy. Farming, it was felt, should be organized as a family operation while linked industries should be run on a cooperative basis. The cooperative movement enjoyed wide support among farmers and spread quickly during the 1920s, receiving firm political backing from the two largest political parties. Iceland's second largest town, Akureyri in the north, was the stronghold of the cooperative movement and became a showcase of the successful integration of primary production (farming and fishing), manufacturing production (dairies, woolen mills, tanning, slaughterhouses, food processing), and retailing within the same cooperative organization. During the rural Progressive Party's time in power between 1927 and 1942, the agrarian ideology was resolutely promoted.

19. *Sláturfélag Suðurlands, 1907—28*, and Sigurjónsson, 'Útflutningsverzlun Íslendinga', 229–230.
20. This resolute ideology is excellently explored in Ásgeirsson, *Iðnbylting hugarfarsins*.

In the new agricultural offensive, cultivation was the keyword that was to transform agriculture from land-extensive sheep rearing into a more diversified sector in which dairy farming would be a major activity. Its advocates spoke of the need for radical change from centuries of neglect, decline, and exploitation of nature's resources to a modern, technologically advanced sector based on greatly increased hay production and horticulture. This was the message of a commission appointed by the Federation of Agricultural Societies to prepare legislation on government support for farm improvements, leading to the landmark Cultivation Act of 1923.[21] The commission report contended that Icelandic agriculture had not taken advantage of the enormous advances in agriculture made possible by science and knowledge over the last century. As a consequence, Iceland had fallen behind, sticking to old habits of exploitation instead of cultivation, hardly making use of machines, fertilizers, and modern feedstuffs, its produce fetching, as a result, lower prices in international markets. Yet, the report claimed, Icelandic agriculture had enormous potential with more than 20,000 $km^2$ (two million hectares) of arable land, which could allow an increase in the number of farms in the country from 6,000 to 50,000, supporting 300,000 people (from the then-current population of around 100,000). According to the report, agriculture not only had a great growth potential, but farming would improve the individual mentally and physically better than any industry: 'The core of the nation should be born and bred in the countryside, whence the strength of the nations is renewed.'[22]

The fantastic opportunities for Icelandic agriculture were further elaborated in another report by an influential committee preparing legislation on reorganizing the Cultivation Fund. The report claimed that agriculture had enormous potential for increasing the quality of hay to the extent that it could provide fodder for half a million cattle instead of the then-existing 24,000. 'We once exported 200,000 kg of butter. That could be 20–30 million kg. Our butter was considered good. With the most advanced production and distribution technology, we should be able to produce butter that is as good as the highest quality butter of other nations.'[23]

These were the kind of ideas that were to guide agricultural policy in the 1920s. Huge sums of public money were poured into agriculture, on average 8 percent of the government budget between 1921 and 1930, excluding infrastructural investments and a part of government support

21. 'Frumvarp B.Í. til atvinnumálaráðuneytis 19 Des 1922', *Búnaðarrit* 37 (1923): 124–125. The bill on farm improvements was passed in the parliament the following year and published in *Stjórnartíðindi* [Government Bulletin] 1923 A, 179–186.
22. 'Frumvarp B.Í. til atvinnumálaráðuneytis 19 Des 1922', 125.
23. National Archives of Iceland, Reykjavík, Skjöl Búnaðarfélags Íslands [The Agricultural Society's Collection], 'Lánastofnanir fyrir landbúnað' [Credit Institutions for Agriculture], 25 January 1925, 12.

for agricultural credit.[24] Central government, the agricultural societies and the agricultural schools were the key institutions in implementing the new agricultural policy. The government launched several massive farm support programs aimed at increasing hay production and encouraging farm improvements. The Cultivation Act of 1923 offered farmers grants to improve their hay fields, increase vegetable cultivation, renovate farmhouses, and purchase tools and hay harvesting machines. In 1925, another program was launched with the reorganization of the Cultivation Fund, founded in 1905, with the injection of large sums of public money to provide credit to farmers for cultivation improvements and renovation of rural housing. The new money came largely from export duties on fish products, a decision reached with wide support in parliament and seen as a 'helping hand' from the fisheries sector. In 1928, a new government grant scheme was introduced for the agricultural societies, promoting mechanization on the farms by providing credit for the purchase of machinery.

The most ambitious public plans to encourage cultivation were a number of irrigation projects in the south of Iceland undertaken between 1910 and 1930, with the aim of greatly increasing hay crops by irrigating vast areas of meadows and marshlands with mineral-rich water from rivers via a vast network of canals and dikes.[25] When these costly projects were finished, the irrigated land covered 17,000 hectares involving 205 farms and was expected to increase the home field hay crop by a third.[26] However, the hay yields fell far short of the target, and hence the increase in agricultural output was much lower than expected. The poor results were partly due to the irrigation networks not being fully utilized, as farmers were turning away from hay production on irrigated land to production on cultivated home fields, using artificial fertilizers and harvesting machines that increased output and productivity. The Great Depression was also starting to have an impact when the last of these projects was finished, discouraging farmers from taking full advantage of the irrigated land.

The cultivation projects were seen in conjunction with, and were indeed a prerequisite for, the advance of the dairy industry that was to lead the export drive. In the 1920s, the industry emerged as a modern, mechanized activity. An ambitious program to establish dairies was set in motion, with the new government of the rural Progressive Party in 1927 giving substantial public financial support on condition that the dairies operated as cooperatives.[27] The aid covered all initial costs, a quarter by direct grants and the rest with credit. In the following years, six technically advanced dairies

---

24. Guðmundur Jónsson, 'The State and the Icelandic Economy', 256–265 and 396–399.
25. Sigurðsson, *Búnaðarhagir*, 121–54, and Kjartansson, 'Áveiturnar miklu á Skeið og Flóa', 330–360.
26. Kjartansson, 'Áveiturnar miklu á Skeið og Flóa', 333.
27. *Alþingistíðindi* [Parliamentary Papers], vol. 1928 A, 1120–1122.

were established under the scheme, all enjoying generous government support. Direct support was increased further by a law in 1933 allowing the government to cover 50 percent of the dairies' initial costs.[28]

## THE END OF EXPORT-ORIENTED FARMING

The big question lurking behind the strategy of export-based agriculture was how economically viable it was. The success of the bold agricultural schemes of the 1910s and the 1920s depended in the final analysis on foreign markets, since the domestic market could not absorb a substantial part of the expected increase in production. Was Icelandic agriculture in any position to significantly increase its agricultural exports given, on the one hand, the country's relatively poor natural resources, unfavorable climatic conditions (short and cool summers), difficult terrain, small size of farms, low level of technology, low-quality products, high trade costs due to rudimentary infrastructure, and distance from markets and, on the other hand, increasingly competitive international markets? The topography, the climate and the economic realities were stacked against a strategy of export-oriented agriculture in Iceland.

The advocates of the export strategy acknowledged some of the comparative disadvantages of Icelandic agriculture. Surely, there were great differences between Icelandic and Danish agriculture, but they believed Iceland was facing similar problems to those Denmark had faced thirty or forty years earlier, having to adapt to difficulties in foreign markets for grain and live animals. Iceland had abundant, relatively fertile land, its vast pastures were ideally suited for sheep rearing and its milking cows were of good stock; what the country needed now was capital, technical skills, and active government intervention to make use of these comparative advantages.

The breakthrough in agricultural exports did not occur. In fact, their share of total exports rapidly declined in the 1920s to 10–15 percent compared to 20–25 percent before 1914. This decline was exacerbated by the simultaneous export boom in the fishing sector.[29] Butter exports came to a halt during the First World War and did not recover in the 1920s; cheese exports were promoted but were of little economic significance. Traditional produce such as wool and hides continued to dominate exports, but even the value of these commodities shrank because of falling prices during the 1920s. Exports of salted lamb had increased significantly after the import ban on live sheep in England in 1897 and had become the most important agricultural export. The market, however, was narrow and fragile, with Norway as almost the only outlet, where prices were

28. *Alþingistíðindi* [Parliamentary Papers], vol. 1933 A, 1116–1117; *Stjórnartíðindi* [Official Journal], vol. 1933 A, 281.
29. Guðmundur Jónsson and Magnússon, *Hagskinna*, 539.

depressed because of rising tariffs to protect Norwegian mutton and the entry of Argentinean salted mutton in 1925–26.[30] Icelandic farmers and their associations responded by diverting some of the meat production over to lamb carcasses to be sold refrigerated or frozen in the British market. They were backed by financial support from the government. The Confederation of Icelandic Cooperatives, which spearheaded the initiative, was promised compensation in the Finance Acts from 1924 onwards if lower prices were fetched in foreign markets for refrigerated or frozen lamb than salted lamb. Government support was to come in various ways, such as giving grants to the Icelandic Steamship Company in 1926 toward the purchase of a cold-storage freighter.[31] Government subsidies were, however, not needed, as the sale of the frozen lamb proved reasonably successful. In the following decade, frozen lamb replaced salted mutton as the main meat export produce, but export volumes did not reach the same levels as before the Great Depression.

The international economic environment changed radically during the Great Depression. The crisis was transmitted to Iceland by a fall in commodity prices in international markets starting in 1929. By 1932, export prices had dropped by over 40 percent on 1928 prices, lamb by 47 percent, and wool by 68 percent.[32] The price fall was followed by protracted market problems at home and abroad. As agriculture was especially hard hit, the grand agrarian schemes crumbled away. The leaders of the farming community soon realized that the struggle ahead was about avoiding the impact of serious cuts in exports and the need to concentrate on the domestic market. Despite the difficulties, agriculture fared relatively better than the fisheries during the 1930s, as a result of improvements in international markets after 1934. More importantly, the sector was saved from the worst vagaries of the Depression by various public measures, including a rescue plan for indebted farmers in 1933. Iceland abandoned its long-standing liberal trade policy by putting up trade barriers in 1931, followed by a comprehensive import-substitution policy in 1934, in which imports of most foodstuffs were banned or severely restricted. In response to increasing competition and price falls in the domestic market, legislation in 1934–1935 introduced regulation of the milk and meat market for the benefit of the farmers, ensuring them minimum prices. Competition was all but eliminated, and marketing boards were set up to regulate supply and set prices with little regard for efficiency or proximity of farms to markets.

---

30. Agnar Kl. Jónsson, *Stjórnarráð Íslands, 1904–1964*, vol. 2, 625–631, and Guðmundsson, *Samband íslenzkra samvinnufélaga, 1902–1942*, 145–146.
31. Guðni Jónsson, *Eimskipafélag Íslands tuttugu og fimm ára*, 172–177.
32. Birgir Kjaran, 'Íslenzk utanríkisverzlun milli tveggja heimsstyrjalda', 19, and Valdimarsson and Bjarnason, *Saltfiskur í sögu þjóðar*, vol. 1, 123.

## THE DECEPTIVE MIRROR OF THE SUCCESSFUL

Thus, under the conditions of the 1930s, the strategy of export-oriented agriculture *à la danoise* was effectively no longer pertinent. Frequent attempts were made after 1945 to boost agricultural exports, primarily lamb meat, at considerable cost to the Icelandic taxpayer, but these were in the main a catalogue of failures. Icelandic farmers had looked into the mirror of the successful Danes, to use Alan S. Milward's figure of speech, and been lured into believing that they had found the optimal strategy to follow.

The argument might be developed that the great agricultural export drive during the first three decades of the twentieth century was a victim of unfortunate timing, the farm improvement schemes and restructuring of production only starting to bear fruit when international markets crumbled in 1929. Considering the multiple disadvantages of Icelandic agriculture mentioned above and the fierce competition in international markets, this argument is difficult to sustain. Iceland did not have any serious chance of becoming a significant butter or meat exporter in the increasingly intensified international market, when even well-established European countries were losing out to newcomers like Australia and New Zealand on the international dairy market as early as the 1890s.[33] The competitive position of Icelandic sheep farmers was only slightly better: in spite of having a sizeable stock of sheep by European comparisons and large pastures, Iceland was late to introduce freezing technology, its processing and marketing structure was rudimentary, and, crucially, its output volume was too small compared to the big producers in the international market. All these factors made it extremely difficult for it to find a niche in the market that would allow it to grow.

However misjudged the agricultural export drive may have been, one must not forget that the development strategy pursued so forcefully during the first three decades of the century was not just about exports. These policies were an essential part of the farm improvement schemes, notably the irrigation projects and cultivation support schemes, and powerful justifications for securing public money for various programs. But looking at the wider picture, the development strategy can be seen as a major private and public effort to transform Icelandic agriculture from primitive pastoralism into more diversified livestock farming based on the cultivation of the land and the use of modern technology. Substantial progress was made in several key areas. The expansion and the improvement of cultivated land, resulting in hay fields more than doubling in size between 1890 and 1930, was a prerequisite for the advance of the modern dairy industry that was to provide the fast-growing urban population with milk and dairy

33. Grigg, *The Agricultural Systems of the World*, 203–209, and Peltonen, 'Agrarian World Market and Finnish Farm Economy', 31.

products. The introduction of new techniques in hay harvesting, dairy production, and slaughtering increased efficiency on the farms and improved the quality of the produce. The number of milking cows increased by over 40 percent and milk production by more than 70 percent between 1890 and 1930, increases that were mostly absorbed by the expanding home market. Perhaps the most important legacy of the development strategy was the diffusion of the cooperatives, which radically altered the organization of processing and marketing of farm produce and allowed the smaller farmers to benefit from economies of scale.

# 7 The Burden of Backwardness

## The Limits to Economic Growth in the European Periphery, 1830–1930

*Pedro Lains*

'[T]he real problem was in starting.'[1]

Convergence of levels of productivity and income per capita is a major feature of European economic history during the period of industrialization from about 1830 to 1930. Yet by 1930 parts of the Continent still remained behind, and catching-up was far from complete.[2] The experience of the forerunners crucially shows that the main drivers of growth and backwardness can be related, among other factors, to social and political capabilities to grasp the opportunities for growth. Thus, we need to understand better why such capabilities did not develop sufficiently in the backward areas. That is the purpose of this chapter.

We begin with a survey of the two main growth theories that best help us to understand backwardness. However since these theories are essentially based on the successful experiences of the forerunners and early developers, in the section titled 'How it all began' we go back to the drawing board in order to see whether a closer look at how industrialization spread across the European continent provides further clues for the study of backwardness. Industrialization did spread to the periphery, and its economies were certainly transformed, but that did not happen rapidly enough. In the section 'The burden of backwardness' we argue that the delay was due to the fact that the economic climate in the periphery was simply too adverse, and the bridge over the income and productivity gaps was not crossed with the necessary speed to allow for the full convergence of the Continent at the

---

1. Milward and Saul, *Development of the Economies of Continental Europe, 1850–1914*, 528.
2. See Gerschenkron, *Economic Backwardness*; Landes, *Unbound Prometheus* and *Wealth and Poverty of Nations*; Bairoch, *Commerce extérieur*; Milward and Saul, *Economic Development of Continental Europe, 1780–1870*, and *Development of the Economies of Continental Europe, 1850–1914*; Pollard, *Peaceful Conquest*; Berend and Ránki, *European Periphery and Industrialization*; Teich and Porter, *Industrial Revolution*; Maddison, *World Economy*; and for recent surveys, Broadberry and O'Rourke, *Cambridge Economic History of Modern Europe.*

end of the period under scrutiny.[3] We thus conclude that backwardness was not so much the outcome of bad policies or intrinsic social shortcomings, but of the fact that in some countries the burden of backwardness was too heavy to be overcome in the period before 1930. In the section 'The inter-war years' we deal with the period from 1914 to 1930 when the periphery began to catch up, and we explain this convergence by looking at the economic policies of peripheral states.

## MODELS OF GROWTH AND BACKWARDNESS

After one hundred years of growth and industrialization in Europe, levels of factor productivity and income per capita still varied considerably. The situation in 1930 could be compared with that at the beginning of the nineteenth century. The major difference was that a significant number of countries which were in the middle of the industrial ranking in 1830 were by 1930 at the top of the list of levels of productivity and income. That group includes countries that had large agricultural economies and which were transformed into efficient industrial and service economies, namely, the Scandinavian countries, Switzerland, and, to some extent, Austria. The most striking similarity between 1830 and 1930 is that the countries at the bottom of the league were largely the same. These were the Balkan states, Poland, Portugal, and, to a lesser extent, Spain and Hungary.[4]

Models of European economic growth for the nineteenth century have largely been based on the analysis of the causes of industrialization which took place in the forerunners, particularly in England. This analysis has changed in scope since the beginning of the discussion of growth models in the 1950s. The first models were based on an analysis of the British industrial revolution during the period from about 1780 to 1830 and focused on the impact of technological innovation in the coal, iron, and textiles industries on the rest of the economy. Some attention was also given to the performance of the agricultural sector and to the impact of the productivity increase in agriculture and the consequent 'release' of labor and capital on the levels of investment and demand in the manufacturing sector. Thus, according to those models, the way that Britain industrialized was successfully replicated in some parts of Europe and not in others depending on the availability of the appropriate range of natural resources and according to the entrepreneurial capacity to absorb the British way.[5]

3. O'Brien, 'Do We Have a Typology for the Study of European Industrialization'.
4. See Maddison, *World Economy*, and Lains, 'Southern European Economic Backwardness'.
5. See Rostow, *Stages of Economic Growth*, and Landes, *Unbound Prometheus*.

A second generation of studies searched for alternative models of growth which focused on domestic capabilities and on each country's openness to international markets.[6] As historical reconstruction of data on growth was being crafted, it became evident that there was also growth in other parts of Europe since the beginning of the nineteenth century and in earlier periods. In some cases the rates of growth were quite similar to those of the United Kingdom during its industrial revolution, which were not exceptionally high. Yet growth on the European continent was not necessarily driven by coal, iron, or textiles. After all, successful growth depended on developments in a large array of sectors, and the mix of successful sectors varied substantially, depending on the structure of supply as well as demand of any given country. Thus, countries with low levels of rainfall, poor soils, or far from the main routes of international trade had necessarily poorer conditions for growth. This second generation of studies highlighted the fact that more factors, which were specific to the backward countries, are needed to understand their failure to catch up, and '[t]o explain [ . . . ] differences in development merely in terms of the presence or absence of factors which caused the industrial revolution in Britain [ . . . ] is hopelessly unhistorical'.[7]

In view of the large number of successful cases the explanations offered by economic historians for output and factor productivity growth and industrialization in nineteenth-century Europe became more complex. It was shown that growth could occur in countries like England or Belgium, well endowed with natural resources such as coal and iron, but also in predominantly agricultural economies, such as the Netherlands or Denmark.[8] Growth could also occur in the context of high population density and rates of population growth, such as Britain and the Netherlands, but also in countries with low rates of population growth such as France. It could occur in countries with large imperial legacies, namely Britain and France, but also in countries with no significant colonial power at the time of industrialization, as was the case of Sweden and Germany. The wider perspective on growth stemming from this second generation of studies provided the grounds for more accurate interpretations of the causes of industrialization and sustained growth. The new evidence shed light on the many different relationships between investment in physical and human capital, technology, and institutional development and economic

6. See Gerschenkron, *Economic Backwardness.*
7. Milward and Saul, *Economic Development of Continental Europe, 1780–1870*, 39. The authors analyze the economic development of continental European countries in their own right rather than by taking the industrial revolution in England as a model. See also S. Pollard, *Peaceful Conquest*, O'Brien and Keyder, *Economic Growth in Britain and France*, and Mokyr, *Economics of the Industrial Revolution.*
8. On the role of agriculture, see Lains and Pinilla, *Agriculture and Economic Development in Europe.*

growth. Concomitantly, they help to explain the persistence of backwardness or slow growth in those parts of Europe that remained behind in certain particularly relevant periods, such as that of 1830 to 1930.[9] The research agenda for understanding backwardness was directed to study why rates of investment persisted at relatively low levels, why technology was not sufficiently developed or sufficiently adapted from experiences abroad, and why the institutional framework was also not sufficiently developed in order to allow for higher levels of growth and catching-up with the forerunners.

Backwardness was too hastily associated with absence of growth which, in turn, was then associated with the absence of the factors of growth that were detected in the industrializing countries, leading to a variety of possible causes of backwardness, such as lack of entrepreneurial capacity, low levels of education of the workforce, insufficient financial intermediation, poor performance of governments in conducting economic matters, poor overall institutional framework, and low levels of expectation regarding development prospects.[10] These factors were certainly present in backward areas of Europe, and growth in the developing parts of the Continent is certainly related to the overcoming of such negative factors, but we need to go beyond establishing correlations and analyze causal links properly if we want to explain the true causes of backwardness.

## HOW IT ALL BEGAN

Many economic historians argued that industrialization was not a national feature in nineteenth-century Europe, as the growth of manufacturing sprouted in different regions across nations.[11] By the same token, the role of the central state should not be overemphasized, as there was not 'a clear path to economic development which could be pursued by the diligent and determined government'.[12] The diversification of the supply of goods that comes with industrialization implies that regions specialized according to their natural endowments. Thus, fertile plains would produce grains, and the woodlands would specialize in a larger range of production, including husbandry and handicrafts. Regional specialization was to some extent also the outcome of the existence of different

---

9. See Sylla and Toniolo, *Patterns of European Industrialization*, and Broadberry and O'Rourke, *Cambridge Economic History of Modern Europe*.
10. See Bairoch, *Commerce extérieur*, and Berend and Ránki, *The European Periphery*.
11. See, for example, Pollard, *Peaceful Conquest*, and Pounds, *Historical Geography*.
12. Milward and Saul, *Economic Development of Continental Europe, 1780–1870*, 114.

growth facilitators, such as transport, commercial, credit, and information networks. Growth facilitators could be regionally concentrated for a while, and certain regions worked as hothouses of new developments, new ideas, and new investments.

The first regions to industrialize were located in England and in the northern part of Europe across the English Channel, during the period from about 1780 to 1830. Several factors contributed directly to the growth of manufacturing in those areas, namely, the existence of abundant sources of nonanimal energy, essentially coal, the availability of labor, and a certain level of demand for industrial products, such as textiles, bricks, or industrial tools. Regions with higher levels of labor productivity in agriculture were more prone to industrialize, as higher productivity allowed the release of labor to industrial occupations, and higher income implied higher levels of purchasing power. The existence of coal was also relevant, because coal was at the time the best source of energy, although in some places the existence of abundant water was important for agricultural but also for industrial use. But other factors intervened crucially at a national level in determining in which regions industrial growth would emerge. Among such factors, we need to consider the existence of a favorable institutional setting that protected investors, manufacturers, and traders, the absence of war or at least of prolonged wars, an integrated communications network, and adequately developed financial instruments.[13] Such a set of characteristics was however more widespread across Europe than the availability of coal and technological knowledge.

Regions could be increasingly industrialized and specialized for long periods of time before becoming fully integrated with the rest of the national economy. That happened for example in the west Midlands, west Yorkshire, and north-west England, regions that 'created a critical mass of manufacturing, service and transport upon which sustained development was dependent'.[14] The proximity to urban areas with higher levels of purchasing-power capacity was a major element in such developments. Accordingly, regions which were more densely populated and closer to cities, roads, waterways, and other networks were in an advantageous position in relation to regions which were further away. These favorable conditions are the outcome of some virtuous circle, because the growth facilitators were there in the first place as the regions had some initial advantages relative to others, namely in geographical location, quality of land, or levels of rainfall. But the fact is that there was a regional differentiation in levels of economic potential or in the capacity to increase output per capita. Some of those regions would turn to manufacturing more quickly if they had an additional set of advantages, namely, the availability of certain natural

13. See North, *Structure and Change.*
14. Stobart, *First Industrial Region*, 3.

resources, such as 'coal pits and salt works, rivers and fast-flowing streams, agricultural supplies, and sources of skilled labor'.[15]

Market infrastructures were clearly less developed in most of southern Europe at the time that industrialization began than in northern Europe. Significant periods of development had taken place in southern Europe in the past, such as during the heyday of colonial trade in Portugal or Spain, or at the time of the substantial trade in livestock that developed later on in the seventeenth and eighteenth centuries in Hungary, Saxony, and around the large cities of southern Germany and Switzerland. But in none of these cases could such episodes of trade expansion be compared, in terms of growth potential, to the intricate network of commerce within the populous areas of northern Europe. According to Pounds (1985), 'it was the absence of a market in much of pre-revolutionary France or in eastern Europe in the first two-thirds of the nineteenth century which, more than any other factor, inhibited economic growth'.[16] The absence of that legacy is a major element in explaining why industrialization did not sprout in the early phases, although it became less and less relevant as substitutes could be imported from abroad, and as innovation, replication, and diffusion of new technology became widespread. But the presence of such commercial networks was certainly a major element in explaining the early development of markets for manufactured products. Fossil fuel was relevant, but the size of domestic demand may have been as important if not more so.[17] That was because whereas the capital needed for industrial development was still relatively small and could come from many sources in agriculture and trade, markets on the other hand, because of low purchasing power and the lack of commercial networks which rendered transactions more costly, were not available everywhere. This was the case in the early stages of industrialization but changed as requirements for industrial investment increased with technological sophistication.

Moreover, the expansion of international trade meant that industrial producers also had to compete successfully with suppliers from other regions. The spread of the use of fossil fuels was very slow as charcoal remained for a long time a better alternative. Apart from England, only in the Saint-Étienne region in the Loire and in Upper Silesia was coal relevant in the early stages of industrial development. Although it is hard to establish what the necessary and sufficient conditions were for speeding up the development of manufacturing, it is important that we pay attention to the possible list of conditions because it would help us to define further the industrialization process. The exercise that we are proposing

15. Stobart, ibid., 219–221.
16. Pounds, *Historical Geography of Europe*, 2–3. See also Milward and Saul, *Development of the Economies of Continental Europe, 1850–1914*, 516–517.
17. The role of demand should not be overemphasized, though. See Mokyr, 'Demand vs. Supply in the Industrial Revolution'.

here calls our attention to the possibility that the conditions that favored the spurt of industrialization may be local, confined to relatively well-defined regional spaces.

The above is fundamentally different from the perspective where the nation is the framework, and industrialization is the outcome of the will of governments to make their elites and their subjects or citizens better-off within their national territories.[18] Under that perspective, industrialization appears as the outcome of government action, in the form of tariff protection, concession of monopolistic rights, or public investment, competing in the international arena for raw materials and markets. The national perspective predicts that industrialization sprouts in countries which are dominant in the international economy and that have powerful and well-established governments that can fully manage the domestic economy. We have however to recognize that such a predictor is not a very accurate one, because of a number of imperial powers with strong governments that failed to industrialize in the nineteenth century. It is also a perspective that has undergone a number of considerable theoretical and empirical revisions, as we advance in our knowledge about what really happened on the ground.[19] The regional and national perspectives on industrialization are not mutually exclusive, although we need to sort out which is more in tune with the historical facts in each case in question.

The west Jutland region was sparsely populated and poor, although maybe not as poor as sometimes described. Yet there was change, despite 'stubborn peasants and rigid institutions'.[20] One such change was the enclosures during the last quarter of the eighteenth century. Enclosures represented an important institutional change, which implied considerable amounts of investment, and although there the impact was not as large as in England, they led to the development of the markets for land, which would have a large impact in west Jutland in the nineteenth century. From the 1860s onwards, the landscape of the region changed considerably, and the moors were transformed into grain fields. That transformation also led to an increase in the population and to the increase of investment in other areas such as the woodlands. These were important structural transformations that apparently had a large impact on output and productivity levels. How this was achieved sheds light on the advantages of being a poor region within an otherwise relatively wealthy country. We have to take into account that such transformations need not only institutional improvements, which can be relatively cheap and feasible in areas where there is some sort of social consensus which translates into

18. See Gerschenkron, *Economic Backwardness*, and Landes, *Unbound Prometheus* and *Wealth and Poverty of Nations*.
19. For the revision of the role of central states in economic development, see S. Pollard, *Peaceful Conquest*. See also O'Brien and Keyder, *Economic Growth*.
20. Eliassen et al., 'Historical Regions and Regional History', 273–274.

the ability to take political action, but they also need investment in physical capital and require know-how and a minimum level of literacy and connection to worlds with better practices. In west Jutland, the needed investment to transform the agricultural landscape came in fact from other parts of Denmark, particularly through an incorporated company, the Danish Moorland Company (det Danske Hedeselskab), that 'provided the farmers with expertise and professional help in their struggle against the wilderness and the manifold activities of the company meant that the moorlands were cultivated at the speed no one had ever imagined'. This was then followed by the immigration of 'enterprising' laborers from the rest of the country.[21]

But not all poorer regions in Europe experienced benefits from the contact with richer regions within the same country. In his analysis of long-run regional inequality trends in France, Brustein (1991) looks for causes of the increasing disparities between the northeast, on the one hand, and the west and the *midi* on the other. One major point the author makes is that the sources of regional inequality date back to the early Middle Ages, following what happened elsewhere under feudal regimes when some areas went through a considerable process of change in agricultural production because of better climatic conditions and technological change.[22] Moreover, 'the commercial importance of north-western Europe in the medieval and early modern times had left a legacy of roads and navigable waterways, a system of financial and commercial houses and an economy based on money and exchange'.[23]

During the nineteenth century, industrialization spread throughout the Continent, under different formats. By the end of the century, every European country with no exception whatsoever had a manufacturing sector based on large-scale production in factories and using steam power. There was not a single country that did not produce textiles with the help of at least part of the machinery that had been invented a century earlier and improved since then. Railways, the largest symbol of the new modern age, had reached all the major cities on the Continent and connected all the capitals. Also in every country of the Continent, there were a large number of people living in urban areas, often in deprived conditions, working for a wage in manufacturing. However, the spread of industrialization was highly uneven, and there were big differences in the levels of intensity of the elements mentioned above. There were countries with large geographical areas where these elements dominated, and countries where they could be found only very sparsely. It could be argued that the best predictor for the timing and pace at which the backward areas of Europe adopted or reinvented the new techniques are not national boundaries but the geographical or economic distance of any given region from the pioneers. The

21. Eliassen et al., ibid., 280.
22. Brustein, 'An Endogenous Explanation', 96–97.
23. Pounds, *Historical Geography of Europe*, 3.

pioneers were located in north-western Europe, namely north-west England, the southern Low Countries, the lower Rhineland and parts of northern France, as well in parts of northern Italy or the Czech lands, all of which entered the industrial era more rapidly than did southern France, eastern Germany, or southern Ireland. If we take this regional perspective, we can even detect differences in productivity levels, which are of course much higher than those that we may find between national averages. By the mid-nineteenth century, central Belgium, the lower Rhineland, and the Swiss plateau were as far apart from mountainous Romania and Macedonia, or the forests of eastern Poland or northern Scandinavia, as developed countries are from third world countries in the present times. Distance was not a matter of importance only in the nineteenth century, as it affected also the development of some of the conditions for industrialization that were mentioned above, particularly those related to communications infrastructure, like roads and waterways, communication networks, and financial intermediation. The lack of development of basic physical and institutional infrastructures was a considerable part of the problem of being backward. Peripheral states contributed to the development of the needed infrastructural framework when industrialization was under way, from the mid-nineteenth century onwards.

## THE BURDEN OF BACKWARDNESS

The difficulties that backward countries or regions had to face at the start of their industrialization periods were certainly considerable, and harder to overcome than in the case of the earlier developers.[24] Those challenges were both domestic and international. Domestically, the list included the nonexistence of the growth facilitators that existed in the more developed regions of Europe, which have been mentioned before. Internationally, backward countries had to face increasingly more competitive nations which exported cheap manufactured and agricultural goods. The tasks which backward countries faced are particularly evident in the Balkan region in the nineteenth century. As the nations in the area became independent, in the period from the 1820s to the 1870s, they had to create a series of basic national institutions virtually from scratch, including the three levels of power: executive, judiciary, and legislative. Such a task was by itself greater in the nineteenth century as the set of institutions which those nations had to replicate in order to become politically integrated into the Continent was more complex than the political institutions of earlier times. And the task was made even more difficult because it had to be carried out in a context of overall backwardness where resources were scarcer and dearer than in the

24. See Berend and Ránki, *European Periphery and Industrialization.*

more developed areas of the Continent. Moreover, peripheral economies were 'overwhelmingly agrarian, had little capital and inadequate technical and communications infrastructures'.[25] In the decades from about 1870 to 1910, the Balkan countries had to create governments, parliaments, and judicial systems for which they had access to a relatively small tax base and a population with a high degree of illiteracy.

Let us look more closely at Greece to see how those problems materialized. Greece started its existence as an independent country carrying the burdens and the benefits of the Ottoman heritage. The vicissitudes of geography had made the population living in the region dispersed and isolated. As Gerasimos Augustinos states:

> The infrastructure needed to build a national economy was largely missing. Roads, ports, and post facilities were in a primitive state. Banking services would take decades to develop, primarily through investment by Greeks from outside the country. Agriculture, the main productive sector of the economy, was handicapped by poor techniques, abandoned and underdeveloped land, complicated and inexact legal relationships, fractionalized and insecure landholding, and a primitive distribution network that kept it localized. Industry was at the proto-industrial stage with small artisanal and craft enterprises. Commercial wealth was to be found mostly outside the state frontiers among the Greek communities in the major urban centres of Europe and the Near East. The development of political life also reflected the historical conditions from which Greece emerged. Like other subject peoples who were part of the Ottoman imperial world, the Greeks had maintained limited contact with the political authorities through a few communal intermediary bodies controlled by their religious leaders and notables.[26]

The author concludes that because of the size of the task, 'political unification was achieved without social integration'.[27]

In 1833, at the onset of independence Greece was a destitute country ravaged by poverty and lack of infrastructure. McGrew contrasts the hopes that bear on the newly arrived young king, Otto of Bavaria, and the state of the country after twelve years of wars and 'brutal' military invasion that left the country 'ruined physically, its economy in shambles and its population in misery.'[28] The wars had been particularly violent, with thousands of deaths and widespread use of scorched-earth tactics. When the forces sent by the Ottoman Empire left, the Christian forces took revenge, prolonging

25. Augustinos, *Diverse Paths*, 3. See also Berend, *History Derailed.*
26. Augustinos, 'Development through the Market', 89.
27. Ibidem.
28. McGrew, *Land and Revolution*, 1.

the agony of the country. Virtually everything had to be rebuilt from scratch: houses, entire villages, vineyards, and olive orchards. The reconstruction task was even greater because there was a lack of basic infrastructure such as roads and ports, which required the attention of the government, and also a lack of financial and human resources. To aggravate all this, the reconstruction of the old and the construction of the new had to be accompanied by the building of the basic national institutions.[29]

But the problems were also felt deeper on the ground. Because of the Ottoman occupation, a large share of the Christian population lived in the mountains with a poor quality of land and with poor communications. The population was scarce and unevenly distributed, with different degrees of density not reflecting differences in soil productivity. Peasants were mostly self-sufficient and lived on a poor diet of barley and maize bread, olives, and a few vegetables and milk products. Most clothes were homemade, and most tools were wooden, including those used in agriculture. Very little use was made of any artificial fertilizers, the use of manure was far from widespread, and land irrigation was rare. The incentive to increase the levels of investment in the land was reduced, because unused land was abundant, as large parts of the territory were abandoned. The lack of financial capital and financial intermediation further hindered investment in land, new cultures, tools, and animals. The only exceptions to this dim scenario were some stretches of land along the coastline which produced currants, figs, unprocessed olive oil, and other basic foodstuffs for export. The production of manufactures for domestic commercialization was limited to a few coastal areas too, and consisted mainly of silk and leather goods.[30] The abandoned prairies and river valleys had turned into disease-prone swamps and marches. Plague was not unknown down to the end of the eighteenth century, and malaria was still common in the early nineteenth century.

That dim situation was hard to change for many reasons. The main potential factor for change was the distribution of land. The state however was unable to intervene with consistent policies because there was no national register of land ownership, and the peasants seized the lands left by the Turks hoping to gain full possession in the future. The state did not oppose the squatters for lack of means, but it also saw unlicensed cultivation as a major source of taxation. These changes after independence led to a scenario of low population densities, imperfect landownership, and small undercapitalized plots, three factors that militated against the transformation of the agricultural sector. The sector did not attract capital from outside and was even a source of tax revenues which funded the existence

---

29. Ibid., 3–5.
30. The situation may have been slightly better in previous times, before the Ottomans left, as there are testimonies of abandoned land and infrastructures from the eighteenth century. See McGrew, *Land and Revolution*, 7–8, and Palairet, *Balkan Economies*.

of a 'large number of well paid state employees' in the cities.[31] During the decades down to the 1880s analyzed by McGrew there were many changes, but agriculture remained backward, and industrialization did not gain momentum. According to the author, critics accused the Monarch of failing to impose changes in the structure of property. But the author concludes in a more cautious tone: 'The monarchy of King Otto bears only limited responsibility for perpetuating the wretched state of Greek agriculture. Nominally absolute, its powers in reality were subject to severe constraints. It would have been impossible under prevailing circumstances to carry out any land reforms which required public capital investment, strong administrative controls or adequate property records.'[32] The major source of change would come, however, from population shifts from the mountains to the plains in the last quarter of the nineteenth century as safety conditions improved, and as the demand from foreign markets increased business opportunities along the coast.[33]

In the Balkans, Greece was not necessarily the most destitute country, but the description is quite telling of the high barriers imposed by backwardness on industrialization and economic prosperity. The conditions further north in the Balkan peninsula were worse, as the area was more distant from the economic center of the Continent, had more difficult access to the sea, became independent a few decades later, and was also not connected to the rest of the world by an entrepreneurial emigrant community which, in Greece, was a source of capital, knowledge, and overseas contacts. The descriptions of backwardness we may find for the regions that became Bulgaria and Romania are even more striking in what they reveal of the widespread levels of deprivation, poverty, and lack of infrastructure. Deprivation of food, shelter, or security, is not the only reason for peasant revolts, as peoples also revolt for lack of political rights. On some occasions, political confrontations exploit peasant revolts, as happened around 1846–1848 in many parts of Europe. Revolts can occur also when levels of satisfaction have been severely affected by rapid changes in overall economic conditions, leading to the reaction against the decline in living conditions and not against absolute levels. Yet peasant revolts do indicate the general feeling of the population regarding the level of satisfaction with their conditions, and the fact is that in the nineteenth century peasant revolts happened above all in the poor regions of Europe, with varying degrees of violence.

In Romania, as late as 1888 and 1907, there were two bloody peasant revolts that 'shook all of Europe'.[34] The problems with Romanian peasants began early with the emancipation conceded following the coup d'état by Prince Cuza against the boyars, the landowners, in 1864. Emancipation

31. McGrew, *Land and Revolution*, 221.
32. Ibid., 213.
33. See also Petmezas, 'Agriculture and Economic Development'.
34. Gunst, 'Agrarian Developments', 29.

also implied the sale of the land to the peasants and distribution of land by the state. The area which peasants received depended on how many draft animals they had. Peasants had to pay for the land at a price fixed at the time of transfer, but they did receive some help from the state in the form of 15-year loans. However when those payments became a burden, the new proprietors, unable to sell the land for a period of time, found themselves imprisoned in the process. Moreover, the land received was in many circumstances not enough for a livelihood, and peasants had to supplement their earnings by working on the land of the former landowners. In Wallachia, the poorest part of Romania, peasants paid one-fifth—and by the end of the century one-third—of their crop as rent. This was less of a burden for peasants who owned tools and animals, but for the others it was a heavy price to pay.

As the land which they had purchased so dearly became insufficient to sustain them and their families, the peasants' demand for land increased. At the same time the land which was kept in the hands of the landowners was probably underused, as can be deduced from the fact that they had difficulties in hiring enough labor. Such imbalances could not be solved by the market itself, apparently, because they were the outcome of the change in the laws governing landownership and the functioning of the labor market. According to Gunst the problem was more acute in Wallachia, 'where landowner self-managed farming prior to 1864 was not as developed as in Moldavia', and so they did not have the necessary tools and animals to till the land. The author, however, concludes that 'compared to European conditions, Romanian peasants lived in unbelievable poverty and could be considered basically vegetarians, since they could rarely eat meat'.[35] This resulted in revolts as the price of grain fell and the debt burden increased. The creditors were in many cases tavern-keepers as, unlike in the case of Hungary, the Romanian landowners were undercapitalized and had no money to lend. This meant that the peasants' anger turned against the small shopkeepers and led to the uprising of 1907.

As we move westwards in Europe, the level of backwardness declines. The situation of the peasants in Hungary was better than in Romania partly due to the fact that in Hungary the proportion of peasants who owned the land was smaller. What this meant essentially was that Hungarian peasants were not as indebted as the Romanian peasants who had had to pay for the land they tilled. A further reason was that in Hungary the production for the market was more developed, as was the number of wage-earning laborers. Moreover, in Hungary as industrialization gained momentum it relieved the population pressure on the land, although it was not until the end of the nineteenth century that the agricultural population started to decline in absolute numbers. Hungary also started to build a transport

35. Ibid., 33 for both quotations.

network earlier, which had a positive impact on the rural areas by providing both better communications and an additional source of employment for agricultural labor. Exports of grain to the west, namely to neighboring Austria and southern Germany, expanded, which had a positive impact on the growth of output, the increase in the scale of production, and ultimately mechanization, particularly threshing and later on harvesting.

The narratives about backwardness and poverty in the European periphery are all too common. National historiographies have to a great extent contributed to the description of the difficulties which the peoples of those regions faced in terms of bettering their economic prospects. We still however lack a convincing explanation for why these countries did not enter the stream of industrialization at the same time as the rest of Europe. The range of possible explanations is wide and includes both domestic and international factors. Domestically, probably the most common factors to be presented as causes of backwardness are the set of national institutions, including public and private, from excessive government intervention and the role of landowners.

However, when we consider the whole of the poor periphery of Europe, the shape of domestic institutions alone does not explain backwardness. The diversity of historical experiences, institutional developments, and policy options was relatively large in countries such as Portugal and Bulgaria, or Spain and Romania, and there is not a common pattern which will tell us what exactly went wrong in their institutional development. For example, Portugal was a protectionist country, and its state accounts were unbalanced throughout most of the nineteenth century, whereas Bulgaria was a free-trade area, and its state finances were balanced in the same period, and yet both remained backward.[36] Thus the causes for the persistence of backwardness have to remain elsewhere.

By the mid-nineteenth century, Portugal was arguably the most backward country in Western Europe.[37] That should come as no surprise if one thinks about its peripheral position within the Iberian Peninsula which was already a peripheral region of Europe. Portugal's peripheral status was reinforced in the nineteenth century by the end of the trade monopoly with Brazil, in 1808, and ultimately with the independence of the former American colony, in 1823. Besides that, the first half of the century was disrupted by the French invasions and the military and political instability that ensued up to the *Regeneração* coup in 1851. The *ancien régime* ended formally in 1820, but it took almost half a century for the new parliamentary monarchy to be consolidated. The bulk of the liberal reforms that were designed in the aftermath of the 1820 revolution, concerning land ownership, the civil and commercial codes, economic liberalization, infrastructure building,

36. See Lains, 'Southern European Economic Backwardness'.
37. See ibid.

and other features of a nineteenth-century type of state, were only fully achieved by well into the 1860s and 1870s. Crucially, the timing of institutional change did not differ substantially from what was happening in the other extreme of the Continent, where new nations were being created, following the demise of the Ottoman Empire in Europe.

Thus, by 1850, the Portuguese economy was profoundly backward in many respects. Vast areas of its territory were not put into productive use; large parts of land were left fallow, despite the fact that a large proportion of the labor force was still employed in the agricultural sector, and little use was made of fertilizers, either natural or chemical, or of animal power. Similarly the industrial sector was characterized by the predominance of traditional activities and limited use of mechanization based on coal or other sources of nonanimal energy. Roads were bad, ports were scarce, and there were no economically useful waterways. The two main cities, Lisbon and Porto, were not connected by railways until 1877, and before that the best link between the country's two largest cities was by sea. By the same token, the state was relatively inefficient, constrained by political instability and scarcity of financial resources, which implied low levels of investment in infrastructure and education. The central state gained full control over the southern province of Algarve only in the 1860s as until then the region was ruled by militias.

Portugal's extreme backwardness was partially overcome in the years from 1850 to 1913. In agriculture an increase in the area of land under cultivation, at the expense of fallow land, and changes in the structure of output led to improvements in labor productivity. Land productivity levels did not change in significant ways, as the introduction of new cultivation processes and techniques was relatively slow.[38] In the industrial sector, there were also some productivity gains and changes in structure, which were associated with higher levels of protection. Yet due to highly protective tariffs, both in the domestic and the colonial markets, at the outbreak of the First World War, Portugal had a relatively large share of its industrial labor force occupied in the textile sector, which was relatively inefficient. Moreover, notwithstanding tariff protection, the degree of internationalization of the Portuguese economy increased from at least 1870 to 1914, as foreign trade, capital imports, and emigration expanded faster than the rest of economy. Such developments however came to a halt with a balance of payments crisis that culminated in the abandonment of the gold standard in 1891 and partial default by the state in 1892.[39]

The slow pace of economic growth in the decades up to 1914 went together with the slow development of institutions and infrastructures. But there were some positive signs in institutional development too. First, the

38. See Lains, 'New Wine in Old Bottles'
39. See Lains, 'Growth in a Protected Environment'.

control of the state over the territory increased significantly and was universally achieved by the eve of the Great War. Second, literacy rates rose in significant ways and, at the same time, mortality fell and urbanization increased. Third, the financial system became more developed and widespread. Finally, there was an important effort in building railways, roads, and other infrastructure, mainly up to the 1890s. Such developments were made possible by increasing government deficits that were financed either domestically or in the international capital markets. Such positive economic and institutional developments were nevertheless insufficient, and Portugal failed to catch up with the levels of income per capita of the forerunners.

But at the same time the constraints on industrial growth in the periphery were numerous. For a start, access to capital was difficult, as savings levels and the development of banks were inadequate, and industrialists frequently had to compete on the capital markets with governments that in some cases in the periphery resorted more to debt; demand was stronger in the lower level of quality of manufactures; and it was also the case that domestic producers had to compete with more efficient producers from more industrialized foreign countries, both in the domestic and the international markets. Furthermore the labor force had less experience, had lower levels of literacy and in-job training, and thus was less adapted to work in industry. Finally the level of investment in social overhead capital was also lower. There were however some favorable factors. Among those possibly positive factors was the fact that there was already a pool of foreign technological innovations that could be imported and adapted; industrial capital could also be imported more easily; and finally there were also some export markets for industrial goods which could be exploited by the industrialists in the periphery.

## THE INTERWAR YEARS

The First World War was highly disruptive for the countries that were directly involved and for the development of the international economy. The huge losses in human life and capital of the countries that entered the war were accompanied by the end of the world economy as it was known by 1914, where free trade, free movements of capital and people, and the gold standard ruled. The peripheral countries in Europe were also affected on these two accounts. Paradoxically, however, in some parts of the periphery, economic growth resumed and eventually reached unprecedented rates in the years following the end of the war, up to about 1939.[40] Thus, Portugal, Spain (up to 1936), Greece, and Romania had rates of growth which were historically high in the 1920s and 1930s (growth rates of real income per

40. See Aldcroft, *Europe's Third World*.

capita above 1.5% per year), and they caught up partially with the levels of income of the more developed areas of the Continent. Catching-up was facilitated by the fact that core countries were not expanding rapidly.

A major consequence of the First World War in the periphery as elsewhere was the increase in levels of protectionism, as well as in the role of the state in the economy, either by imposing a more regulated economy or by promoting investment in the agricultural and industrial sectors, and in social overhead capital. The increased role of the state went together with the implementation of fascist-type dictatorships, replicating Nazi Germany or Fascist Italy, the 'revolution of the right', in Janos's words, which extended across the periphery.[41] This stronger interwar state contrasted with the weaker nineteenth-century liberal state, but they were intrinsically linked. To a certain extent, the twentieth-century dictatorships in the periphery were the zenith of the liberal state that had progressively developed in the previous century, in the sense that it would have been much harder to implement totalitarian or authoritarian regimes without the institutional framework and the state infrastructure that were built, sometimes with some pain, particularly in the last three or four decades before World War I. The same may be stated in regard to the economies that developed under protection after the mid-1920s, which were certainly a result of the slow but persistent growth of industry, agriculture, and services throughout the nineteenth century. To a large extent, the Gerschenkronian state that developed in Germany, after 1871, and which helped to develop the German economy and was also dependent on the German economy, was replicated in the periphery later on and under the form of dictatorial regimes.[42]

Peripheral states in the interwar period were truly developmental regimes with significant success, as their policies promoted the levels of domestic savings and investment, and the institutional setting for the expansion of a string of modern sectors in the economy. Investments led by the state ranged from road building and electricity supply in Portugal to land conquest in Greece or agrarian reform in Romania. States did not work alone, as they were followed by investments by the private sector, and this is the time when larger conglomerates developed also in the periphery, in the industrial, agricultural, and financial sectors, namely, in cements, chemicals, energy, and banking.

Patrick O'Brien has argued that the periphery was partially transformed after 1850 or 1870, but that the period up to 1914 was too short for a full transformation into industrial societies akin to those of the European core to take place. While Janos has seen that process of transformation extending into the interwar period and up to 1945, it could be argued that the golden age of growth following the Second World War was the continuation

41. Janos, *Politics of Backwardness.*
42. See Good, 'The State and Economic Development'.

of the process begun after 1850.[43] It certainly is an irony that such positive events occurred under Fascism, autarky, and ultimately Communism. This conclusion is certainly not optimistic regarding the role of democracy, free trade, and the open society. However the conclusions drawn from history need not be generalized, as the conditions change over time.

## CONCLUSION

Once it was thought that the catching-up of backward countries with the levels of productivity and income of the forerunners was dependent on the prior development of new attitudes by industrialists, landowners, and governments, who would introduce modern machinery, new methods of exploiting the land, and wise policies. Those developments were certainly an important component of the catching-up history of parts of the European continent, but only to a limited extent. A deeper look at how the technological and organizational developments of the forerunners were related to solving opportunities and constraints showed that replication was not what catching-up was all about. Soon it was found that other parts of Europe that eventually caught up followed different paths toward prosperity. Those different paths led large parts of Europe to industrialization in the century of free trade that came to an end with the outbreak of World War I.

But by 1914 there still remained large strips of the Continent which were left out of the convergence club, and we still need an explanation for those economies that failed to follow the industrialization road. It was in the context of that search for explanations for backwardness that educational and more general institutional explanations sprouted. The rationale for that string of explanations remained unchanged. Accordingly, if backward economies of Europe followed the institutional developments that could be observed in the core countries, the road to prosperity would have been followed much more quickly. Yet, such optimistic counterfactuals fail to take into account that institutional developments in the forerunners were also related to their specific sets of domestic problems.

However it has to be said that in the nineteenth century domestic problems were less important as the development of the international economy made national developments increasingly interconnected. And what happened in the core certainly was a source of inspiration for the backward periphery, which to a great extent took advantage of the wide circulation of ideas, goods, capital, and people across the Continent, and across the globe. The reasons why the backward areas did not import the favorable institutional developments are similar to the reasons that they did not import advanced technology, namely, that their domestic settings were simply not

43. See Janos, *Politics of Backwardness*, 322–323.

fit for such developments. It was therefore not because people in the periphery were less ingenious or less entrepreneurial, but simply because the overall environment was much too backward and the conditions for new ways of doing things were too adverse.

During the second half of the nineteenth century, domestic conditions in the periphery changed, and the institutional and infrastructural setting was slowly implemented in the periphery, albeit at a rhythm that did not allow catching-up. Following those positive developments, paradoxically or not, in a period of autarkic authoritarian regimes, the new conditions were set for the first time ever since industrialization began one century before, and catching-up finally took place. It is important to understand the timing of such developments. Things could have been different at all levels, but by looking closely at the constraints imposed by extreme backwardness, we have to conclude that they could not have been much different.

# 8 Was the Marshall Plan Necessary?*

*David W. Ellwood*

The Marshall Plan came from afar. Its immediate causes are well known and have been rehearsed time and again: the apparent financial crisis of many European nations, the cold war escalation in all its forms, the political weakness of so many governments, the Franco–German question, doubts about the United States' occupation policies, and so on. But its rationale went back much further than the contingent emergencies of early 1947.

In 1939 Vera Micheles Dean, journalist, political scientist, and international relations expert, had written that what Nazism and Communism shared was a

> [ . . . ] revolt of the dispossessed classes against industrial capitalism and such remnants of feudalism as the aristocracy, the officer class and a politically minded church. Both [ . . . ] sought to provide the masses with material opportunities and a taste of power hitherto reserved for a social elite. [ . . . ] Both, paradoxical as it may seem, represented an effort to realize the promises held out by the political democracy of the $19^{th}$ century, which the possessing classes had too often failed to translate into terms of economic democracy in an age of mass production.[1]

*This* was the key American perception and understanding of the roots of the world wars, of the Great Depression, of totalitarianism, which fed the determination of that nation's government to place the peace of the world on a different, non-European footing, after the Second World War provoked by Europeans in twenty-five years. This chapter will argue that the thinking which eventually produced the European Recovery Program (ERP, the Marshall Plan's formal title) came from a lineage of American reflection about

---

* This chapter has been conceived as a reassessment of the controversial views on the subject that Alan Milward summarized in 'Was the Marshall Plan Necessary?' (1989), and based in part on chapters in Ellwood, *The Shock of America. Europe and the Challenge of the Century*, Oxford University Press (forthcoming).

1. Dean, *Europe in Retreat*, xv–xvi.

the relationship between prosperity and democratic progress which stemmed from that nation's experience in World War I and at the Versailles peace conference. It was further developed as totalitarianism took hold in Europe in the context of the wars, threats of wars, and the Great Depression of the 1930s.

These ways of looking at Europe then went into the great debate about the United States' role in the postwar world which started across that country even before the war broke out, informed the planning effort which started in and around the State Department from 1940, could be seen in the long series of economic conferences organized by the Roosevelt administration during the war, and then profoundly colored attitudes toward the spread of Communism in the Old World, in the ruins left by the war.

None of this explains the precise form which the Marshall Plan eventually took or its fairly chaotic and contradictory evolution in reality. Nor does it explain why the Plan emerged exactly when it did. As we shall see, the origins of the Plan were at the same time philosophical, political, and psychological. The gathering cold war was its immediate context and gave the operation an urgency which intensified over time, to the point where, after the Korean War emergency, military priorities took over entirely, and the Economic Cooperation Administration (ECA, the agency running the Marshall Plan) gave way to the Mutual Security Agency. The East-West confrontation was not an affair of numbers, and its pressures were far more important in determining that something like the Plan happened than the dire balance of payments situation of Western Europe, which was the short-term, formal prompt for Congressional action. In the end it was politicians, technocrats, businessmen, and journalists who thought up the Plan and made it happen, not treasury people or central bankers, not the staff of the International Monetary Fund (IMF), the World Bank or the Export-Import Bank, and certainly not the kind of public-private financier like Dawes and Young who had been so inventive in finding ways to save Germany in the 1920s. The most extraordinary thing about the Marshall Plan was not how key élite elements in the United States and Europe decided it was necessary—on that the political consensus at the time was strong—but that it did in fact happen.[2] The perceived dangers of the cold war explain a lot: but not everything. The Marshall Plan was also a product of the depth and longevity of a debate in the United States about the malignancies of Europe, and what the United States could do about them.

## ECONOMICS MAKES THE WORLD SAFE FOR DEMOCRACY

'Hunger does not breed reform', Woodrow Wilson told U.S. Congress in his address announcing the armistice of 1918, 'it breeds madness and all the

---

2. The story is told once more in heroic terms in Behrman, *The Most Noble Adventure*, part 1.

ugly distempers that make an ordered life impossible. [ . . . ] Unhappy Russia has furnished abundant recent proof of that.' So the moral was clear: 'Nations that have learned the discipline of freedom' should now rule, 'by the sheer power of example and of friendly helpfulness.'[3] Wilson of course was no economist, and did not escape the disdain heaped by Keynes on the peacemakers of Versailles, who had neglected all the unappealing material realities which in his view were the key elements in restarting the life of the war-torn Continent.[4]

But there was one man at the peace conferences who struck the Cambridge economist quite differently. This was Herbert Hoover, an American mining engineer with experience across the world whose specific contribution after 1918 was to invent another new means for projecting American power into Europe: large-scale humanitarian relief organizations. On the basis of prolonged experience in attempting to bring relief to Russians, Hoover had turned into a militant anticommunist. He later explained:

> [The Communists] found so receptive an audience in hungry people that Communist revolutions at one time seized a dozen large cities and one whole country—Hungary. We sought diligently to sustain the feeble plants of parliamentary government which had sprung up in all of those countries. A weak government possessed of the weapon of food and supplies for starving people can preserve and strengthen itself more effectively than by arms.[5]

Hoover told Wilson that 'a foundation of real social grievance' fed the revolutionary movement in Russia. The Bolsheviks were able to gain leverage from 'the not unnatural violence' of masses who had 'learned in grief of tyranny and violence over generations. Our people, who enjoy so great liberty and general comfort, cannot fail to sympathize to some degree with these blind gropings for better social conditions'.[6]

Hoover left a series of important traces in the U.S. attitude toward the problems of economics, democracy, and modernity in Europe. His pronouncements reinforced a long-held U.S. official view, traceable at least back to Jefferson, that considered historical Europe a world of nationalistic hates, autocratic miseries, revolutionary disorders, and power politics of the most imperialistic sort, between and within nations.[7] Wilson of course shared many of these convictions. But the president had possessed

---

3. Address of 11 November 1918 in Baker and Dodd, *The Public Papers of Woodrow Wilson*, vol. 5 *(War and Peace)*, 300–302.
4. Keynes, *Collected Writings, vol.* 2, 134 and 211.
5. Hoover, *Memoirs of Herbert Hoover: Years of Adventure*, 301.
6. Letter to Wilson of 28 March 1919 in ibid., 412.
7. See Harper, *American Visions of Europe: Franklin D. Roosevelt, George F. Kennan and Dean G. Acheson*, 44–47.

an unlimited faith in the redemptive potential of the history of the United States and, so armed, had set out on a 'gigantic crusade to impose American ideas and ideals upon Europe', as Hoover recalled.[8] The result was that all but a few of the valorous aspirations which Wilson had brought to Paris had been 'variously violated or distorted by the time they came out from under the millstones of the best European diplomatic thought.'[9]

As president, Hoover and his reputation were destroyed by the great crash and what came afterwards. Following his defeat by Roosevelt in 1932, Hoover retired to write his memoirs. There we read that Europe was to blame for the slump, meaning in his view a generalized European shiftlessness which in the course of the 1920s had learned how to exploit the weakness and greed of the United States' banking system.[10] For its part, the Roosevelt administration knew that whatever the rights and wrongs of European financial and trade behavior, it had played a major role in precipitating the great crash and then aggravating the depression when the backwash from Europe's crisis hit trade, industry, and employment in the United States.

In this context, both Roosevelt and his Secretary of State, Cordell Hull, explained the rise of the dictators in overwhelmingly economic and deterministic terms. They took seriously the arguments the Nazis and Fascists liked to make about the grievances which the 'have-not' nations felt toward the 'haves', and casting their perceptions of Japanese imperialism back onto Europe, they took for granted that a fair share of world trade and access to raw materials was what they all wanted underneath. But that still left to be explained how tiny extremist groups such as the Fascists and the Nazis (and the Bolsheviks for that matter) could become mass movements and take over great nations. Here again it was Hull who spelled out the rationale which would sink deepest into official minds in the United States. By the time ideological and psychological dimensions had been added to it, it would go on to become one of the key orthodoxies of the cold war, and beyond. Hull told the British ambassador in early 1936:

> The most incomprehensible circumstance in the whole modern world is the dominating ability of individuals or one man to arouse the mental processes of the entire population of a country, as in Germany and Italy, to the point where overnight they insist upon being sent into the frontline trenches without delay. When people are employed and they and their families are reasonably comfortable and hence contented, they have no disposition to follow agitators and to enthrone dictators.[11]

---

8. Hoover, *Memoirs of Herbert Hoover: Years of Adventure*, 469.
9. Ibid., 471.
10. Hoover, *Memoirs of Herbert Hoover: The Great Depression*, 89–90.
11. Hull, *The Memoirs of Cordell Hull*, vol. 1, 521. This was very much the message of Lippmann's tract, *The Method of Freedom*, which insisted that 'the

Hull had already berated the Italian ambassador for the invasion of Ethiopia, asking him why Mussolini had not invested $100 million in the country instead of conquering it and spending far more. Now he told the British diplomat that if only Italy had been able to keep up her pre-crisis exports, there would probably have been no military campaign. As for the future, if only a $20 billion increase in international trade could be engineered, and investment to provide work for twelve to fourteen million people, then this might make the whole difference between war and peace in Europe.[12] In his memoirs, published in the year in which the Marshall Plan started, Hull enlarged on the lessons that he saw in his long experience:

> A people driven to desperation by unemployment, want, and misery, is a constant threat of disorder and chaos, both internal and external. It falls an easy prey to dictators and desperadoes.
>
> In so far as we make it easier for ourselves and every one else to live, we diminish the pressure on any country to seek economic betterment through war.
>
> The basic approach to the problem of peace is the ordering of the world's economic life so that the masses of the people can work and live in reasonable comfort.[13]

In the long term this meant developing in systematic fashion the promise of mass consumption that pioneering thinkers had signaled in the 1920s, and even before, to be the unique contribution of the United States to humanity's material progress. New Deal thinkers in business, government, and economic research now began to take on this challenge with specific organizations built for the purpose.[14]

## A VERY PHILOSOPHICAL WAR

In his intellectual history, *Why the American Century?*, Olivier Zunz points out that by the time the shadow of the coming war fell over the United States from the late 1930s onwards, businessmen, researchers, university leaders, foundation trustees, and government officials in that country had quietly constructed 'a vast institutional matrix of inquiry', a system whose purpose was to turn knowledge of the universe in all its forms into concrete

modern state cannot endure unless it insures to its people their standard of life', and hoped for a permanent expansion of the middle class as the key to political stability; Lippmann, 36 and 97–100.

12. Hull, *The Memoirs of Cordell Hull*, vol. 1, 439 and 521.
13. Ibid., 364.
14. Donohue, *Freedom from Want*, 182–197; Zunz, *Why the American Century?* 88–90.

economic, social, and scientific projects which could, potentially, challenge existing arrangements in any part of the world.[15]

When the United States entered the conflict directly in late 1941, this energy was directed to one theme above all: the postwar world and the United States' place in it. A vast panoply of public and private organizations across the nation had taken it up. The *Bulletin of the Commission to Study the Organization of Peace*, a compendium and guide to all this activity, listed at this time no less than ninety-one private organizations dedicated to it, supplemented by thirty-two universities and other 'learned societies', seventeen religious groups, and twenty-eight government agencies. Another forty-one foreign or international groups also supplied information and analyses. In stark contrast with the behavior of nearly every other country, belligerent or neutral, comments the specialist Carlo Santoro, 'this almost obsessive interest in the future [ . . . ] indicated a kind of unconscious or premonitory sensation that the business of decision regarding the future world order lay indeed with the United States itself.'[16]

In his celebrated 'American Century' article (February 1941), the publisher Henry Luce said that when the American people finally faced up to the challenges of their time, they would see that these were to make their nation 'the dynamic leader of world trade', a land 'which will send throughout the world its technical and artistic skills', one which would feed hungry people everywhere with its boundless produce.[17] By the beginning of 1942 every leading speaker in the great debate had been obliged to promise at least a new world organization to construct the peace, a transformed global trade system, and a democracy based on rising purchasing power. The Four Freedoms declaration, the Lend Lease Act and the Atlantic Charter—all of 1941—had made very clear just how serious were the United States' government's intentions about these promises, all revolving around the three principles of a revised collective security system, multilateral trade liberalization, and raising living standards everywhere, what for long was called 'development'. The uncertain, unsettled United States of the 1930s, half in the international system, half out of it, had turned into a revolutionary, even evangelical nation.

Much of the effort of the great debate inside the United States was dedicated to exploring just how the perceived U.S. experience of the connection between economic progress and democratic liberty might be translated into empirical, universally applicable recipes. Among the favorite models was always the Tennessee Valley Authority, the great New Deal system of dams, hydroelectric plants, and irrigation projects which had transformed the prospects of a once-backward rural region. Former Under Secretary of

---

15. Zunz, *Why the American Century?* xi–xii.
16. Santoro, *Diffidence and Ambition*, 34.
17. Luce editorial of 17 February 1941, reproduced in Hogan, *The Ambiguous Legacy*, 11–29; discussion in ibid., Introduction, and Chapters 1 to 8.

State Sumner Welles pinpointed the Danube and the Balkans as the most suitable terrain in Europe for a similar scheme.[18]

The talk in these discussions was all of interdependence, the transformation of sovereignty, the moral responsibility of the leading powers and its link to their self-interest, political egalitarianism, the need to think in the long term, the supremacy of just that factor whose exclusion had ruined Versailles: economics, as planning, as business, as *growth*. Roosevelt recited these views for the benefit of Churchill and Stalin at Yalta, following a note from his adviser Harry Hopkins: 'Mr. President: When are you going to spring your T.V.A. for Europe?'[19]

The Americans of World War II had quickly been proved right when they had understood that the war provided a unique opportunity for radical change, and gave scope to impulses and energies in the United States and outside it which could remake the world. They did not have to wait long to see the confirmation of their belief that the end of the European colonial empires was at hand. They had also been the fastest to understand the full implications of 'interdependence' and had been correct when they understood that a revolution of popular expectations had taken place in the twentieth century, which the liberal democracies ignored at their peril, and which the U.S. experiment was—in its unmistakable way—intensely ready to meet. The connection which they made in this way between prosperity and democracy, and the propositions which they derived from this belief, would return to challenge successive generations of believers in liberal freedoms. At the same time their faith in the capacity of the public and private institutions of the United States to invent new ways to project national power would be repeatedly upheld.

But there were just as many facts of international life which the New Dealers of wartime Washington could not and would not face up to. Most obvious was the irreducible persistence in the world of the 'power politics' which they all deplored, specifically the geopolitical realities created by the outcome of the war itself. Nor could they conceive either the scale and depth of the misery which the conflict had brought, nor understand how the more total it had become—with America's armies, weapons, and propaganda playing their special part—the more Europe's 'dread turmoil' (Herbert Hoover) had been aggravated, and the further away it had become from the universe of the Four Freedoms, Bretton Woods, and all the rest.[20] But most importantly, wartime opinion in the United States could not grasp the fact that amidst all the death and wreckage, the

18. Welles, *Time for Decision*, 152–153.
19. Episode recalled in Stettinius, *Roosevelt and the Russians*, 164–166.
20. There is no trace of any of these problems, for instance, in Alvin Hansen's 1945 book, *America's Role in the World Economy*, though Hansen was at the time the leading economist in Harvard and a 'Special Economic Adviser' to the Federal Reserve.

Europeans had worked out their own programs for meeting those hopes and aspirations of decades that the war had brought so compellingly to the surface. In Europe the Left was the great beneficiary everywhere of this surge in popular feeling. Left-wing parties, trade unions, and social movements were swelling on all sides. 'Private enterprise', said so many, had had its day, was not a credible option. And the workings of private enterprise America as a many-faced power system, so enthralling when seen from inside, were understood through quite different, far more pragmatic eyes by all the others without exception.[21]

World War II was the pivotal moment in the history of the American modernizing challenge to Europe in the twentieth century, because the challenge was open, organized, and conscious in a way in which it had never been before and would never be again. As ever, some welcomed it, some dreaded it, but all were forced to come to terms with it. Precisely because the balance of every form of power between the two sides was so skewed at the end of the war, the battle to come over those terms was all the more intense.

## THE MANY MEANINGS OF THE MARSHALL PLAN

In the immediate postwar years the Marshall Plan was the scene of the most explicit and most significant of these confrontations over the modernizing impulse coming from the United States. It is one of the great merits of Alan Milward's best-known book that it throws an unprecedented light on what happened during that experience, setting aside decades of myth-making to focus on the hard transatlantic power struggle which went on all the way through it.[22] Milward was perfectly aware of course that this was not the first such battle of the era. Leaving aside the Anglo-American tensions over the Atlantic Charter, the first of the series took place at the Bretton Woods conference of 1944. Although dominated again by the representatives of the United States and the United Kingdom, that event saw a total of forty-four delegations, including those of the Soviet Union and France (the French delegation was led by Pierre Mendès-France, who left a caustic account of his experience).[23] After this meeting the Europeans in

---

21. The Dutch case is documented in Snyder, 'United States Diplomacy in the New Netherlands', see for instance 152–154, 193, 195, 285, 312, and 326.
22. Milward, *The Reconstruction of Western Europe, 1945–1951.*
23. Some indication of Mendès-France's view of the event can be gained in the letters included in his *Oeuvres complètes,* 2, 44–49, and in his report on the Monetary Conference of Savannah of March 1946, in ibid., 192–195. In these papers Mendès-France hints at the methods the Americans used to build a very heavy hegemony—including reliance on the 'total' [sic] support of the Latin American delegations—on the discomfiture of the British, and the marginalized status of the Europeans, clients of no one.

general—governments in exile, neutrals, liberated territories—as well as the British—were forced to realize the vast scale of the United States' ambitions for the postwar world, which took for granted, among other sweeping developments, the end of their colonial empires. An ever-more open system of multilateral trade and payments would take the place of the empires, a regime managed under the benign sway of the Bretton Woods arrangements, including a new International Trade Organization (ITO), the whole built so as bring about an unlimited, unprecedented expansion of production, consumption, and development around the world.[24]

All of this was predicated on a peaceful, rapid shift to postwar reconstruction, with the hugely expanded U.S. economy looking abroad for markets, raw materials, and trading partners to ensure that none were left behind as government made sure the nation's wartime prosperity would be continued from other sources, now the war was over. The Europeans for their part were barely more realistic. All of those in a position to draw up reconstruction plans did so taking for granted help from the United States, but assuming somehow that it would be unconditional, or little more complicated than a banker's loan. In 1946 the British and the French, each in their own way, discovered most painfully that this would not be the case; in 1947—in the context of the Committee of European Economic Cooperation held to respond to the original offer of assistance by the U.S. Secretary of State, General George C. Marshall—the truth gradually dawned on all the others. The Soviet reaction is the best known.

But by this time the U.S. government was forced to face some unpleasant truths too. The Bretton Woods settlement was completely unworkable in the prevailing circumstances of extreme dislocation and misery which presented themselves after the war in Europe and Asia. The ITO dwindled into the halting process leading to the General Agreement on Tariffs and Trade, not least because most U.S. business was quite unprepared for the diminished sovereignty of 'free trade'. The World Bank was irrelevant, the IMF in no position to force or even help its members to agree on exchange rates that they might have some hope of sticking to. In the United Nations Relief and Rehabilitation Administration the United States supplied most of the money and goods, but were forced to pay lip service to the views of the organization's other members, which included the Soviets. It was quickly wound down.

The Milward view of the Marshall Plan acknowledges all these realities. It ignores, however, the deeper historical analyses of Europe's malignancies

---

Official—skeptical—French reflection on Bretton Woods fifty years later summarized in Lepage, 'La France et les institutions de Bretton Woods'.

24. I have treated these developments in some detail in my forthcoming book, *The Challenge of the Century*, Chapter 6, part 2. There is still (in 2010) much work to be done on how the awareness spread among European elites of what the United States was planning.

which the United States brought to the situation of 1947, and gives almost no attention to the swelling political dynamic of the cold war, without which the Plan would never have passed U.S. Congress. Instead we read that 'the enormous political ambitions of the ERP were based on the exaggerated impression in the United States of the severity of Western Europe's economic position in 1947'.[25] This commitment of the author to an insistently benign view of certain key economic conditions in Europe after the war—down to the point where he set in motion a debate around counterfactuals as to whether the ERP was 'necessary' or not—has distracted attention from the heart of his message.[26]

'The purpose of Marshall Aid', Milward wrote, 'was, through furthering the process of economic recovery in Western Europe, to develop a bloc of states which would share similar political, social, economic and cultural values to those which the United States itself publicly valued and claimed to uphold.' These values, as transmitted through the ERP's own information/propaganda campaign, might be listed as 'the values of so-called 'free enterprise', of entrepreneurship, of efficiency, of technical expertise, and of competition', which were together summed up in the concept which overarched them all: productivity. Higher productivity all round would produce economic *growth*, and growth would in theory promote political stability, or at least reduce political arguments 'to a narrower range'. Here Milward makes explicit reference to Charles S. Maier's well-known formulation of the 'politics of productivity', pointing out, however, that European protagonists possessed their own ideas of what these politics might consist of.[27]

Indeed. The central accounts in *The Reconstruction of Western Europe* demonstrate that right from the start the West Europeans involved in the great experiment, singly, in groups, and together, set out to *thwart* the ambitions of Washington, to blunt the United States' reforming zeal, to water it down and neuter it, all the while imposing their own analyses

---

25. Milward, *Reconstruction*, 113.
26. The positive view of postwar economic conditions was launched in *Reconstruction*, Chapter 1, and highlighted in Milward's review essay of Hogan's *The Marshall Plan: America, Britain and the Reconstruction of Western Europe, 1947–1952*. The essay was published in *Diplomatic History* 13: 2 (Spring 1989): 231–253. The most effective rebuttal came from Sir Alec Cairncross in his review of Milward's book, published in *The Economic History Review*, February 1985: 166–168. The economist Harold van Buren Cleveland had anticipated the argument that all-round deflation could have eventually righted the transatlantic payments situation in a conference paper 'If there had been no Marshall Plan . . . ', later published in Hoffmann and Maier, *The Marshall Plan*, 59–64. The approach was very firmly rejected by the other conference participants—many of them leading Marshall Plan executives—on the grounds of absolute political impracticality: ibid., 65–69.
27. Milward, *Reconstruction*, 123, quotations, and 124. Maier, 'The Politics of Productivity', in Katzenstein, *Between Power and Plenty*, 23–49.

and their own priorities. The Europeans wished to be dominated on their terms, to install a hopefully temporary form of conditional dependence which would ensure the continued flow of U.S. aid, but in ways consonant with visions and necessities identified and managed locally. They exercised all the strength of the weak, in case after case.[28]

In such a setting, the ideal of comprehensive European integration, which the U.S. government embraced so avidly, stood no chance. It was presented as a logical, almost technical development of the need for as wide a market as possible in a situation where everyone would be producing more, exporting more, and importing more. It ended by being the chief string attached to Marshall Aid, as Milward puts it.[29] Much of what Milward has to say on this subject of integration revolves around the clash of conceptions and interests which emerged from the U.S. insistence on this priority.[30] He emphasizes the success of the Europeans in destroying the United States' illusions over the potential of the Organization for European Economic Cooperation (OEEC) to act as the embryo of a future European government, and shows how the European Payments Union had to be seriously modified to take account of a variety of local interests, before it could be made to function. He gives credit to Washington for introducing the Europeans to the reality that *institutionalized economic interdependence* was the key to freer trade and higher living standards for all. But he underestimates the deep political reflection which lay behind the United States' policy, and how intense was the conviction that extremes of nationalism had brought Europe to ruin and war to the United States. As far back as 1942 the Council on Foreign Relations of New York had asked how 'the popular association of sovereignty with national freedom and independence [could] be effectively broken.'[31] Nationalism was Europe's 'evil genie', said a senior foreign policy expert, Harold van Buren Cleveland, later. In the United States all were of one mind on this and had been so agreed for years: if that source of collective madness and malevolence could be caged in a tight federal framework, then there was some hope that the European

---

28. Concept of 'thwarting' introduced in Milward, *Reconstruction*, 92. Three instances cited by the author of the success of European leverage include a rejection of U.S. proposals to allow German trade most-favoured-nation treatment; a refusal to submit exchange rate policy to IMF supervision; and the opposition of Switzerland to joining in the future development of the OEEC: *Reconstruction*, 114–120.
29. Milward, *Reconstruction*, 57–60, 123–124.
30. The refusal of the British to play the role assigned them by the Americans in this vision is the main theme of Hogan, *The Marshall Plan*.
31. Council on Foreign Relations, 'National Sovereignty and the International Tasks of the Postwar World', 31 August 1942, by Walter R. Sharp, document P-B48. This is a comprehensive paper anticipating many themes and objectives of postwar U.S. foreign economic policy.

continent could enjoy peace and prosperity and stop disturbing the rest of the world.[32]

Sixty-five years after the end of the war, these questions are still with us in one form or another, and the 'alternative framework' which the West Europeans built in defiance of the United States' demands of the time—starting out with the Schuman Plan—has shown all its limits. But in the late 1940s this achievement was not so small, and Milward explains its significance in these terms:

> In place of a liberal unified Europe came a closely regulated Little European common market whose twin purposes were to provide for French national security by containing West Germany and to permit its members to continue to pursue a very limited range of common economic policies in a few specific sectors of the economy, which would otherwise have become impossible.[33]

Whatever its defects, this construction 'was certainly better founded than anything devised in the inter-war period.'[34]

So, concluded Milward, what the United States got out of the Marshall Plan was far less than they hoped, and it was only judgeable 'in relation to specific issues and specific countries'. It was 'nonsense' to suggest that the ERP had reshaped the politico-economic future of Western Europe in some radical way. Everywhere the United States met limitations to the exercise of its power and influence, obstacles and restrictions which were 'subtle, complicated, but always present and often narrow'. In the end these limits added up to 'the most striking aspect of the story'.[35]

## THE PARADOX OF THE MARSHALL PLAN

Through the thick and thin of the early postwar era, the French and all the other West European states built political and economic systems which were socially oriented, inclusive, and directed toward dealing with the miseries handed down to their peoples from the past. Milward characterizes national politicians in these times as 'prisoners of a shift of power which imposed new policies on them', of a kind which excluded the deflationary action which sooner or later would have righted the huge payments deficits of many countries.[36] But politicians who got themselves elected after the Second World War knew that a vast head of steam had been building up

---

32. Cleveland, *The Atlantic Idea and its European Rivals*, 105.
33. Milward, *Reconstruction*, 476.
34. Ibidem.
35. Ibid., 125.
36. Milward, 'Was the Marshall Plan Necessary?', 238.

over the Depression and war years, if not earlier, for *radical* social change, starting with the construction of varieties of the welfare state. Hence the great shift leftwards in politics everywhere and the general assumption that *private enterprise capitalism* as a system was comprehensively discredited. Conventional macroeconomic policy-making in such a context, vastly aggravated by conditions of misery, dislocation, semi-starvation in parts, prerevolutionary strikes, not to mention the deepening cold war, became almost impossible, for politicians and bureaucrats alike. The Marshall Plan not only supplied a setting in which such policy-making could be rehabilitated, but supplied a basic measure of *confidence* to capitalists everywhere that their ideology and system would survive.

But the messages of the Marshall Plan offered with unequalled energy and invention a quite different prospect: the model of a good society which was private, consumerist, and oriented toward the future. Explicitly they declared: 'prosperity makes you free'; implicitly they suggested that only the 'American way' could meet the demands of the 'revolution of rising expectations'. How then to reconcile such vastly differing impulses, in such a context as the early cold war, where restoring any sort of faith in the coming years seemed so problematical and urgent?[37]

A typical U.S. response was supplied in an April 1951 article in *Foreign Affairs* by one of the ERP's most influential brains, Richard M. Bissell. At the end of a tightly knit argument about how to reconcile reconstruction and rearmament, Bissell made clear that only structural changes in Europe's economic structure would suffice to restore vigor to its capitalism and hope to its masses. There was recognition, if reluctant, that the European-style welfare system was here to stay. There was of course formal acknowledgment that nothing could be imposed, no matter how great the temptation to do so. But in the end, said Bissell, the United States could lead only by the force of its example and its powerful appeal across all sections of European society:

> Coca-Cola and Hollywood movies may be regarded as two products of a shallow and crude civilization. But American machinery, American labor relations, and American management and engineering are everywhere respected. [ . . . ] What is needed is a peaceful revolution which can incorporate into the European economic system certain established and attractive features of our own, ranging from high volumes to collective bargaining. [ . . . ] [This] will require a profound shift in social attitudes, attuning them to the mid-twentieth century.[38]

---

37. More oral evidence on fears of Soviet invasion, Communist take-over, or Third World War is found in Nicolson, *The Future of the English-Speaking Peoples* (text of speech of November 1948), and Behrman, *The Most Noble Adventure*, 119–121.
38. Bissell, 'The Impact of Rearmament on the Free World Economy', 404–405.

But many Europeans doubted whether the two impulses of social welfare and American-style economic growth could ever be reconciled. André Siegfried, the leading French commentator on the United States before the war, told the readers of *Foreign Affairs* in 1952 that the American universe of making and getting was unthinkable in the 'established and rigid European system.' Siegfried highlighted all the contrasts which put Western Europe at a disadvantage compared to the United States: 'It can be said truthfully that in Europe technical progress does not necessarily "pay". There are too many people and too few raw materials; the social system is too complicated.'[39]

Very soon, much sooner than anyone imagined, Europe's development was to prove such voices wrong, their lack of faith in the future out of tune with the popular mood of the times, and their doubts misplaced. They saw all of the immediate limits of the ERP's operations, but they failed to see how it helped legitimize 'the revolution in which the ordinary citizen [demands] that he share in the benefits of industrialism', as an American critic of European skepticism put it—in other words how it turned the revolution of rising expectations into something like a self-fulfilling prophecy.[40]

Instead what often struck Europeans at the time—and some in the United States—was the sheer utopianism of the ERP, the massive abstractions, illusions, and ideological constructs which characterized so much of the original design. The notion that the European state system could be remade in four years by a new agency in Washington, the Economic Cooperation Administration (ECA), run by private sector management types, is still as hard to believe today as it was then. Did Hoffman, Cleveland, Bissell, and their colleagues seriously believe that the Europeans would do by 1952 what in reality they eventually succeeded in doing, in rather weaker form, only after 1992, with the Treaty of Maastricht? If 'you too can be like us' was the implicit message of the Marshall Plan, the Europeans soon learned from their contacts with the ECA Missions, the propaganda, and visits and exchanges to ask: 'or as you imagine yourselves to be?' As Milward put it: 'Economic integration was seen as a part of the march of history and history as the march of progress with the United States in its vanguard. The real role of integration in European reconstruction was to show how glibly superficial such ideas were.'[41]

And yet who can deny the eventual, long-term success of the Marshall Plan's key exhortations and invitations, its assumption that to catch up with American production and consumption was the only economic policy Europeans should ever seriously apply? Impelled by their reading of history, the challenges of the times, and of course by their own will-to-power, far-sighted elements in the leadership of the United States temporarily chose a

---

39. Siegfried, 'Can Europe Use American Methods?' 663.
40. Quotation from Miller, 'The Reimportation of Ideas', 85.
41. Milward's critique of American abstractions, lack of realism, and 'missionary zeal' in *Reconstruction*, 211.

massive and complex formal intervention with a specially designed, explicit set of objectives, a four-year quick fix to inject sustenance into Europe's sickly capitalism lest it give way and the Communist hordes rush in. The technocrats' attempt to modernize institutions and attitudes on what they believed was the United States' own pattern represented the highest point, the most explicit one, in that twentieth-century trend which superimposed the United States' model of modernization on whatever efforts European societies were making to meet the challenges of mass democracy, mass production, and mass communications thrown into high relief by the First World War. Every participating nation in the Marshall Plan showed examples of how this reformism was blunted, how difficult it was to manage interdependence when the American and the West European sides believed in such different ideas of the road to the future. But on one point all the players were united: if only Europe could grow economically the American way, or some local variation of it, everything might be possible, even political 'stability'. And when the Old World's great boom did indeed finally arrive after 1954 'catch-up growth' would turn out to be the great force driving it onwards and upwards.[42]

42. Crafts, 'The Golden Age of Economic Growth', 445. I have developed this point more fully in *Rebuilding Europe*, Chapter 12, especially 224–248. This book was originally conceived in a seminar run by Alan Milward at the European University Institute, in 1986–1987. It reflects the influence of many of his approaches—and some of those of Charles Maier—but emphasizes the mental and cultural inspiration which U.S. models in all their forms offered in these years, as well as a variety of West European responses.

# 9 Integrating Paradigms

## Walter Lipgens and Alan Milward as Pioneers of European Integration History

*Wilfried Loth*

Paradigms are guideposts in scholarly discussion. They assist in organizing a research field and in structuring the narratives in which the results of research are presented. They make it easier to integrate specific results in specific fields and thus also allow one to gain a rapid overview of a particular area. Given that they necessarily abbreviate and condense the narratives upon which they are based, they also often give rise to controversies—controversies having less to do with expanding knowledge than with opinion leadership, that is, with power positions in the scholarly community. The scholarly fruits of such struggles are generally meager. One should therefore seek opportunities to overcome them.

The following contribution makes such an attempt. When seeking paradigms that have developed in the field of European integration history, it is usually the case that the work of Walter Lipgens and that of Alan S. Milward are contrasted. Lipgens, a German professor of modern history born in 1925, and Milward, a British economic historian born in 1935, are certainly among the pioneers of historical writing on European integration. In the 1960s and 1970s, Lipgens made contributions to the study of the emergence and development of ideas and projects about certain forms of union among European nations in the period from the First World War through the years immediately after the Second World War.[1] In the 1980s, Milward published a foundational work on the economic reconstruction of Western Europe after the Second World War and in 2002 the first volume of an 'official' history of British European policy since 1945.[2] The two scholars' work

1. Lipgens, *Europa-Föderationspläne der Widerstandsbewegungen, 1940–1945*; Lipgens, *Die Anfänge der europäischen Einigungspolitik, 1945–1950: Erster Teil, 1945–1947*, English edition: *A History of European Integration, vol. 1, 1945–1947*; Lipgens, *Documents on the History of European Integration, vol. 1, Continental Plans for European Union, 1939–1945*; *vol. 2, Plans for European Union in Great Britain and in Exile, 1939–1945*; Lipgens, *45 Jahre Ringen um die Europäische Verfassung: Dokumente, 1939–1984*.
2. Milward, *The Reconstruction of Western Europe, 1945–51*, and *The Rise and Fall of a National Strategy, 1945–1963* (vol. 1, *The UK and the*

resulted in opposing views of the interpretation of the integration process. In this chapter I will demonstrate that these interpretations do not exclude one another but can instead be productively combined.

## OPPOSING PARADIGMS

Walter Lipgens was a Catholic intellectual who, after the collapse of the Third Reich, sought the origins of the 'German catastrophe.'[3] This led him to take a critical stance toward the forced unification of the Germans into a nation-state by Otto von Bismarck and also to oppose those who would make the principle of the nation-state absolute in the twentieth century. He was convinced that economic, political, and intellectual developments since the age of imperialism had been driving more and more toward 'large-scale communities.' European nation-states were 'becoming dwarves' and consequently were no longer in a position to 'achieve the common good.' This in turn had brought about the rise of Fascist movements, which intensified nationalism into a 'brutal late form of national imperialism.' The two world powers that had liberated the continent from National Socialist dictatorship had brought about the 'schematic restoration of the nation-states' and divided Europe between themselves into spheres of influence; at the same time, the expansion of the Soviet realm had pushed the eastern boundary of Europe significantly to the west. In place of the European nation-state system, there had emerged 'a bipolar system of global hegemony by the United States and the Soviet Union.'[4]

Borrowing from Arnold Toynbee, Lipgens conceived the European movement for unity as both a 'response' to the 'challenge' of the rise of the new world powers and a reaction to the threat to European culture resulting from the condition of powerlessness that the Europeans had brought upon themselves. He found the beginnings of this movement in the period of the First World War. According to Lipgens, the amalgamation of the European states had already been sought by the 'real spiritual elite of Europe' during the First World War as a precondition for preserving peace. Added to that was the motive of the 'existential necessity of the expansion of economic markets' and the self-assertion of the European peoples that could be achieved only by integration. Moreover, there was also a desire to free the 'realm of European values' from the shackles of a barbaric nationalism. This movement had not however made headway among broader social classes; democratic politicians had not succeeded in getting fundamentally beyond the nation-state system at the time. The way had thus lain open for

---

*European Community*).

3. See Loth, 'Walter Lipgens (1925–1984)'.
4. Lipgens, *Anfänge*, 5 ff.

the seizure of power by Fascist movements that had set as their goal the 're-establishment of uncompromising national sovereignty.'[5]

The experience of powerlessness in the face of National Socialist expansion during the Second World War had then led to a 'sweeping invalidation of the nation-state ideal' in the consciousness of the peoples of continental Europe; against the dominance of Europe by the National Socialists there had arisen an ideological resistance movement that had reactivated dying European traditions and that was seeking the 'voluntary federation of the European peoples.' This movement lacked the power to succeed on its own because, with the liberation from National Socialism, Europe had come under the sway of 'both world powers', the United States and the Soviet Union. Only when in 1947 the United States had decided to promote regional European federation as a means of containing Communism did Europe once again have a chance—and that chance was taken up by the European unification movement—given that some form of unification was now 'a concern of broad social classes within the population.' After vain and ultimately fatal hopes for the participation of Great Britain and the Scandinavian countries, France with Robert Schuman in the lead had taken the opportunity in 1950 'finally to make the first breach in sovereignty, to be able to establish the first supranational authority.'[6]

In contrast, Alan Milward had discovered the subject of Europe in the course of his analysis of economic problems and politico-economic strategies since the First World War. In conscious contrast to prevailing beliefs and also to the work that Lipgens had already published, Milward presented the European integration policies of the 1940s and 1950s as policies of nation-states and national governments. 'The founding of the European Communities,' he asserted, was 'the work of nation-states, that expressly created them in order to preserve and strengthen themselves.'[7] European integration policy was an 'integral part of the reassertion of the nation-state as an organizational concept.'[8] European integration constituted 'a new form of agreed international framework created by the nation-states to advance particular sets of national domestic policies which could not be pursued, or not be pursued so successfully, through the already existing international framework of co-operation between interdependent states, nor by renouncing international interdependence.'[9] After the collapse of most European nation-states from 1929 to 1945, national security, economic prosperity, and the expansion of the social welfare state could only be achieved by means of integration; new

5. Lipgens, 'Die europäische Integration', 25 ff.
6. Ibid., 27–29, 31 and 33.
7. Milward, 'Der historische Revisionismus'.
8. Milward, *The European Rescue of the Nation-State*, 3.
9. Milward, 'Conclusions: The Value of History', in Milward et al., *The Frontier of National Sovereignty*, 182.

legitimacy and citizen loyalty were thus secured for the nation-state after the shock of the Great Depression, National Socialist expansion, and wartime destruction. Hence, the European Communities were and remain the 'buttress' of the nation-state, 'an indispensable part of the nation-state's post-war construction.'[10]

Given this position, Milward is often understood as being anti-Lipgens, as a demythologizer who detects tangible national interests behind alleged European idealism and who destroys the fond dreams of a united Europe by pointing to the continuing reality of the nation-states. In particular, adherents of the 'realist' school of foreign policy analysis are eager to hear this message and embrace it—figures such as Andrew Moravcsik, whose collection of case studies from the origins of the Treaties of Rome to the Maastricht Treaty is subsumed under the thesis that European integration is based on 'a series of rational choices by national leaders' who 'responded to constraints and opportunities stemming from the economic interests of powerful domestic constituents, relative power of each state in the international system, and the role of international institutions in bolstering the credibility of interstate commitments.'[11]

Diplomatic historians who have traditionally stood close to the 'realist' school have scoured national archives in search of national interests in the formulation of European policy. Evidence can be found because policy within national institutions must always be articulated in terms of the nation. Hence, we now have a whole series of studies describing European integration policy as national interest policy. Along with economic interests and the expansion of the social welfare state emphasized by Milward, foreign policy and defense policy considerations have also become objects of investigation. Raymond Poidevin, for example, highlights the French interest in defense against Germany, while Hans-Peter Schwarz points to the desire of the young Federal Republic to regain its sovereignty, and Georges-Henri Soutou emphasizes the national goals of de Gaulle's European policy.[12] Such works neglect to consider that the definition of national interests can also be based on 'European' insights. Likewise, they do not take into account the structural change in the international system that occurred along with integration. European integration policy thus appears as a slightly adapted resumption of the showdown between sovereign nation-states in a new form.

10. Milward, *The European Rescue*, 3. See also Milward, 'Allegiance: The Past and the Future'.
11. Moravcsik, *The Choice for Europe*, 18.
12. Poidevin, *Robert Schuman: Homme d'Etat, 1886–1963*; Schwarz, 'Adenauer und Europa'; Schwarz, *Adenauer: Der Aufstieg; 1876–1952*; Schwarz, *Adenauer: Der Staatsmann; 1952–1967*; and Soutou, *L'Alliance incertaine*.

## COMMON GROUND AND CONVERGENCES

Milward was not completely innocent of this 'national' and static interpretation of his approach insofar as he represented himself as a critic of Lipgens. Milward's 'national' interpreters could however have been warned by the fact that the two historians had worked closely with each other: Milward's first contribution on the topic of the rebuilding of Europe, a comprehensive chapter on the Committee of European Economic Cooperation, appeared as an addition in the English edition of Lipgens' major work, *A History of European Integration 1945–1947.*[13] Both authors conceived of it as an extension of the original German text that was made possible due to the opening of the British archives to historical researchers. Lipgens and Milward also worked productively together in the establishment of the 'European Liaison Committee of Historians.'[14] Their collaboration ended only with the early death of Lipgens in 1984.

Looking more closely at the works of Lipgens and Milward, it can be seen that the two views were not so far apart after all. Milward too saw functional deficits in the nation-state that had arisen due to technological development; he even spoke of a 'collapse' of the nation-states during the Second World War, due to defeat and occupation.[15] Integration was necessary in order to overcome this situation. Without integration, the nation-state would not have been able to offer its citizens the national and economic security that would enable its survival. Likewise, Milward saw that integration implied the reduction of national sovereignty and that this went hand in hand with the development of a second loyalty, that of the citizen toward the European Community. In his most recent work, he also stressed that this process of transferring sovereignty and legitimacy can go further—if the nature of national political decisions allows it: '[T]here is an inherent force within the developed modern nation-state which can tend to integration [ . . . ]. But whether that force does actually tend in that direction depends absolutely on the nature of domestic policy choices and thus on national politics.'[16]

In his *The Rise and Fall of a National Strategy, 1945–1963*, moreover, Milward rejected the concept of 'national interest' as too unclear—a concept that raises the question of who defines the national interest as well as that of the standards used to measure the national interest. Self-critically, he added that 'national interest' is 'a term so heuristically useless that I

---

13. Milward, 'The Committee of European Economic Co-operation (CEEC) and the Advent of the Customs Union', in *A History of European Integration*, edited by Lipgens, 507–569.
14. On the history of the EU Liaison Committee of Historians, see Le Boulay, 'Investir l'arène européenne de la recherche'.
15. Milward, *The European Rescue*, 4.
16. Ibid., 447.

wish I had never used it, but find, sadly, that occasionally in the past I have done so.'[17] Instead, he proposed using the concept of 'national strategy' in analyzing national European policy: 'an overall view of where a country is heading and for what purpose', formulated by the responsible politicians in engagement with divergent opinions and competing influences.[18] Regarding the relationship between national strategies and the European movement, he added by way of qualification that the latter did not play a decisive role in the development of the European Communities 'until at least 1963.'[19]

The contrast between Lipgens and Milward is thereby reduced to the nature of the description: whereas Milward speaks abstractly of states reacting to the needs of their citizens, Lipgens focuses on the citizens themselves acting, having had the same kind of experience in the respective nation-states and their institutions. The process described by both scholars is identical in structure: functional deficits of European nation-states in the age of modern industrial societies led to the establishment of international structures. Lipgens and Milward also agree in regarding the outcome of this process as essentially open: what the former considers a necessary insight into what historically is called for—something that can also fail—is referred to by the other as a 'political choice.' If it is lacking, then the process stagnates or even moves backwards.

The opposition between the two views appears greater than it actually is essentially because of specific weaknesses in each of them. In Lipgens' work, there is no differentiation among various conceptions of European unity and no investigation of the various special motivations, so that the unification movement seems essentially stronger, more unified, and more effective than it has actually been. For his part, Milward reduces the spectrum of possible motivations for unification to the economic sphere and does not formulate things clearly in that realm either. It thus remains uncertain why states with similar economic and social interests react differently to the issue of integration (think of the contrast between Belgium and Denmark or between France and Great Britain, for example). Beyond this, Milward on occasion posits a persistence of the nation-state that contradicts his own theoretical construct; there is no discussion of how factors such as change, statehood, governance, and the international system are experienced in integration.

In addition, there are also differences in the subject matter examined by each scholar's concrete historical research: Lipgens emphasized work in the archives of the European associations in the first postwar years; moreover, his early death in 1984 prevented him from working with government sources. Conversely, Milward and his adherents have from the beginning

17. Milward, *The Rise and Fall*, 6.
18. Ibid., 7.
19. Ibid., x.

concentrated on government actions, which gained greater relevance with the implementation of the Marshall Plan in 1947–1948. The development of public opinion is not taken into account. The exchange of arguments between the two authors was unable to advance beyond its beginnings due to the death of Lipgens. In reality, the two scholars' findings reinforce one another more than they contradict one another.

## THE MODEL OF THE FOUR DRIVING FORCES

It was as a student of Walter Lipgens that I began my own research on European integration. Later, I had the privilege of working with Alan Milward in the EU Liaison Committee of Historians. This personal background may explain why I have aimed to develop a conception that seeks to overcome the weaknesses of the approaches taken by the two scholars.[20] This conception is characterized by the view that in regard to the functional deficit of nation-states that has led to steps toward integration, there are several problem areas to be distinguished, which first, can be of different degrees of urgency and second, can also call for different solutions. It seems sensible to me to distinguish among four types of problems from which driving forces for European integration result. Two of them are old but have acquired new urgency due to technological development in the twentieth century, whereas the other two have emerged directly from this development.

The first problem is that of preserving peace among sovereign states—or in other words, the problem of overcoming anarchy among states. This constitutes the essential motive of the European unification plans of earlier centuries, from Dante to Immanuel Kant and Victor Hugo. The urgency of this problem has grown dramatically due to the development of modern military technology. The vast increase in the number of casualties, the amount of human suffering and economic destruction have strengthened calls for institutions capable of securing peace, especially during and after the catastrophes of the two world wars. Thereafter, the danger of nuclear destruction and self-destruction, as well as the emergence of new nationalisms after the end of the East–West bloc structure, have accentuated this problem in new ways.

Second, the German question must be seen as a special aspect of the preservation of peace. This problem too is older than the twentieth century but has become more pressing with the development of industrial society in Europe. For reasons of population and economic power, a German nation-state in the center of Europe constituted and constitutes a latent threat to

---

20. Formulated for the first time in Loth, 'Der Prozeß der europäischen Integration'. See Loth, 'Identity and Statehood'; Loth, 'Beiträge der Geschichtswissenschaft'; and, most recently, Loth, 'Explaining European Integration'.

the independence of its neighbors. This has resulted in a vicious circle of encirclement and expansion, which could only be broken by integrating the Germans together with their neighbors into a larger community. To have understood this after two calamitous turns of that vicious circle is undoubtedly one of the great achievements of the Europeans in the second half of the twentieth century.

Economics in a narrower sense can be characterized as the third functional deficit: it became increasingly clear that the national markets in Europe were too small for rational production methods. Their independent existence was only sensible on a temporary basis; in the long term, this threatened to result in a loss of productivity and consequently also a loss of the state's legitimacy.

This was linked, fourth, to a loss of power and competitiveness vis-à-vis larger state units—to the United States in economic and political terms, and to the Soviet Union in military terms. Self-assertion in the face of the new world powers thus became an additional motive of European unification policies. Depending on one's perception, it was either defense against U.S. hegemony or against Soviet expansion that stood in the foreground. It was often the case that both were pursued simultaneously—the preservation of the Europeans' freedom of action in an alliance with the United States.

The major point in this model is that these four motives have not always been equally strong, and they have not always worked in the same direction. Hence, it was the case that both the need for self-assertion and the unresolved German question rendered an association of Western European countries after the Second World War quite appropriate; with regard to the goal of preserving peace, however, it became problematic. The common necessity for unification stood against the very different sensitivities and needs of the participating states; the overarching interest in a common market contrasted with the very different economic needs of individual states as well as different interests of individual production sectors. European policy thus could not be a unified policy; it has always been and continues to be embedded in conflicts among different conceptions of order and interests at the European level.

Thus my model is to a certain extent complex. It does, however, also have the advantage of being able to explain an integration process that is itself complex. From the development of these driving forces, we can explain both the timing of specific integration initiatives as well as the decision for specific types of integration, which at the same time are always decisions not to proceed with other conceivable forms of integration.[21]

---

21. For a comprehensive picture based on an enlarged version of my model, see Thiemeyer, *Europäische Integration*.

## STEPS TOWARD INTEGRATION AND THEIR CONSEQUENCES

In looking through the prism of this model of integration history, it becomes clear that the German question in the context of the cold war reveals itself as decisive for the creation of the European Coal and Steel Community, the core of supranational community building in Europe in 1950–1951. This motive was augmented by a certain level of self-assertion and reinsurance vis-à-vis the United States as the leading power—both in the context of the growing significance of economic potential for one's international power position, which Guido Thiemeyer has also pointed out in his study of the beginnings of the European agricultural policy.[22] After worries about a split between East and West had initially prevented many Europeans from promoting unification plans restricted to the Western portions of the continent, such plans seemed to be an indispensable prerequisite for winning back freedom of action after the Soviets had rejected Marshall Aid in the summer of 1947. At the same time, a framework was needed for the long-term inclusion of the West Germans, who now became indispensable allies. The French initiative in the summer of 1948 that led to the founding of the Council of Europe did indeed aim to establish such a structure. This was clearly not successful due to British hesitancy, and so a second attempt became necessary. What was actually new in Robert Schuman's proposal of 9 May 1950 for a coal and steel union was his willingness to begin supranational unification without the participation of Great Britain; he thereby secured the success of the second French attempt at pursuing a European policy.[23]

The European Defense Community (EDC), another integration project that was proposed even before the end of negotiations over the coal and steel union, failed due to the impossibility of reconciling the respective goals of the participants. The Netherlands wanted the creation of a common market as a condition for the initiative, but the French expressed their unwillingness to accept that. Thus, the idea of giving the EDC a strong supranational framework—the European Political Community—disintegrated; French public opinion thereby saw itself confronted with a level of German resurgence that was very difficult to accept. The integration framework as a means of controlling the German contribution to defense then gave way to the U.S. presence in Europe and the prospect of a French nuclear force; membership in NATO took the place of a projected European integration.

Given this background, the Treaties of Rome signed on 25 March 1957 constituted an attempt to salvage what was possible of the European project after the EDC debacle by means of concentrating on a compromise

---

22. Thiemeyer, *Vom 'Pool Vert' zur Europäischen Wirtschaftsgemeinschaft.*
23. On my own contributions to this analysis see Loth, *Sozialismus und Internationalismus*; Lipgens and Loth, *Documents on the History of European Integration*, vols. 3 and 4; Loth, *Der Weg nach Europa.*

acceptable to all participants *in extremis*. It rested on France's acceptance of the economic community demanded by the Netherlands—admittedly, only in the distant future and to be achieved in various stages—while France's European partners swallowed the idea of creating a European nuclear community, a prospect attractive to no one but French technocrats. Decisive for the founding of the European Economic Community (EEC) was the lasting conviction that there was a need to integrate the Germans better and to have greater autonomy vis-à-vis the United States. This view led Guy Mollet on the French side and Konrad Adenauer on the West German side to make compromises that in light of their respective economic interests could hardly be justified. The EEC was thus primarily a political construction, even if that was hardly ever stated publicly.[24]

The fact that the Community of the Six was able to prove itself and expand is largely due to its growing economic attractiveness. Even in its rudimentary beginnings with the Six, the Common Market demonstrated that it was an instrument of socially acceptable productivity increases, something that soon seemed indispensable and that became attractive for an increasing number of membership candidates. It was economics more than the interest in European self-assertion that compelled Great Britain to join the Communities; approval of its accession after long resistance was the price France had to pay for the completion of the agricultural market and the prospect of deepening the Community.[25] With the entry of Britain, Ireland, and Denmark in 1973, the Common Market further increased in economic significance and weight. At the same time, more and more domains of economic activity wound up within the realm of common regulation. Even if one may not speak of a direct and irreversible development toward ever stronger integration—as the functionalist theory of integration would like to suggest—it is a fact that more and more political and social actors made use of the European dimension to pursue their various goals.

This process was disrupted by a lack of agreement on the political goals that lay behind the development of the Community. With regard to the role that the European Community was to play within the West, views diverged greatly; only a few were prepared to accept Charles de Gaulle's conception of a European defense community armed with nuclear weapons within the framework of the Western Alliance.[26] The severe crises resulting from this could only be overcome with great effort.[27] Divergent political interests

24. See Loth, 'Deutsche und französische Interessen' and 'Die Entstehung der Römischen Verträge'.
25. N. P. Ludlow, *The European Community*.
26. Loth, 'De Gaulle und Europa'; Vaïsse, *La grandeur*.
27. Loth, *Crises and Compromises*. On the 'empty chair crisis' of 1965 see Loth, Wallace, and Wessels, *Walter Hallstein*; Palayret, Wallace, and Winand, *Visions, Votes and Vetoes*; and most recently, Bajon, 'Die konstitutionelle Krise'.

and waning awareness of the political dimension of European construction ended up reducing the willingness to compromise on contentious economic issues as well. The search for compromise thereby became an arduous business, and the Community repeatedly failed to develop into a world political actor. The political artistry of Willy Brandt and Georges Pompidou was sufficient to get the 'Europe of the Nine' under way; the ability to act in the political realm was not achieved, however—essentially due to French mistrust of German efforts toward reunification.[28] Valéry Giscard d'Estaing and Helmut Schmidt had to content themselves with pragmatic steps toward further development of the Community.[29]

Behind the impetus toward integration initiated in 1985–1986 by the Single European Act, there stood—as far as François Mitterrand and Helmut Kohl were concerned—the old political goals that had brought together Schuman and Adenauer: integration of the Germans and self-assertion in world politics.[30] The idea of constructing a political Community was clearly still very foreign to the newcomers of 1973, Britain, Denmark, and Ireland; they only signed the compromise because they hoped to improve the performance of their economies in the face of Japanese competition. Additionally, Margaret Thatcher aspired to overcome vested rights in the social welfare state that could not be directly eliminated at the national level by means of deregulation on the European level.[31]

The European Community was nevertheless relatively well equipped when new tasks fell to it in the wake of the end of the East–West conflict and the collapse of the Soviet empire. It was able to—or had to—take over functions to ensure order on the European continent that had previously been the purview of the superpowers and their blocs. Among these were intensified efforts to bind the Germans after the two Germanys had been reunified and the Four-Power responsibilities for the country had ended. Additionally, the Community suddenly became responsible in part for the restructuring of the former Eastern bloc countries. At the same time, the political barriers that had formerly kept the neutral countries of the European Free Trade Association from joining a body more effective for the pursuit of economic modernization had now faded away.

The new tasks can explain why, with the end of the cold war, the Community not only did not break apart—as was feared by many who had too one-sidedly identified the Soviet threat as the main reason for the association's existence—but instead actually took further significant steps toward

---

28. Hiepel, 'Willy Brandt—Georges Pompidou'; Hiepel, 'Willy Brandt und Georges Pompidou'.
29. Guasconi, *L'Europa tra continuità e cambiamento*; Knipping and Schönwald, *Aufbruch zum Europa*; Weinachter, *Valéry Giscard d'Estaing*.
30. Gaddum, *Die deutsche Europapolitik*; Saunier, 'Le tandem François Mitterrand—Helmut Kohl'.
31. Young, *One of Us* and *This Blessed Plot*.

integration. The spillover effect played only a limited role in the completion of the internal market, the introduction of the common currency, and the commitment to enter new political realms; decisive in each case for the implementation was the favorable political context. The acceptance of new integrative steps was made easier because, with the end of the East–West division, the ambivalence of the European project regarding the peace question had disappeared.[32]

Reference to the different driving forces of European integration also explains why certain methods of integration have been successful whereas others have not. In the light of the different ways of conceptualizing a united Europe, there was always a broad majority amongst the member-states of the Community of the Six for a fundamental commitment to a united Europe. At the same time, however, there was never unambiguous support for any form of European unification that was actually feasible. A similar situation may well apply to the larger European Union; in any event, this must be more fully investigated. The discrepancy between what is desired and what is actually achievable in European integration explains first of all the outstanding significance of individual personalities in the decision process on European integration policy, from Robert Schuman and Konrad Adenauer to Jacques Delors and Helmut Kohl. Given the ambivalence of public opinion, strong leaders could set the course, bypass the routine of the bureaucratic apparatus via direct contact with partners, and commit majorities to their projects. Second, these figures explain the success of the coal and steel union and the Treaties of Rome; success was possible for forms of integration that put little value on citizen participation and that withdrew integrated political spheres from public discussion. Only by allowing the implications to remain unclear was it possible to avoid having negative coalitions derail the always controversial steps toward integration.

Third, it becomes clear in this context why the so-called democratic deficit has in the meantime emerged as the most pressing problem of the European Community. In the light of the expansion of the Community's competence and the resulting increase in regulation, majority decisions in the twilight of various ministerial council formations, negotiations within the Permanent Representatives Committee, and the low democratic legitimacy of the Commission are no longer acceptable in the eyes of citizens, independently of the pronouncements of constitutional jurists who make reference to the nation-state model when addressing the subject. The technocratic detour to Europe, first embarked upon by Jean Monnet in 1950 and successfully continued over many years, most recently once again in

---

32. Historians have not systematically investigated developments since 1989–1990, however. For initial analyses upon which I base my thesis here, cf. Rometsch, *Die Rolle und Funktionsweise*; Dyson, *The Road to Maastricht*; Woyke, *Deutsch-französische Beziehungen*; Peter Ludlow, *The Making of the New Europe*; and Rambour, 'Les réformes institutionnelles'.

the launching of the Maastricht program, does not work any longer, as the fierce public debates about the Maastricht Treaty and the difficulties at the moment of its ratification have made clear. This has become fully evident with the blocking of the Treaty establishing a Constitution for Europe. Whether the terms of the Lisbon Treaty will be sufficient to overcome this deficit of democracy and legitimation is an open question.[33]

## CONCLUSION

Alan Milward has correctly pointed out that in writing the history of European integration, it is not only a matter of giving 'a better answer to the question of why the process of European integration has continued.' It also necessarily leads to answers to the question of 'what the European Community / European Union has now become.'[34] In analyzing the integration process with the help of the model of the four forces, it can be seen that the European Union is neither on the path toward a European federal state, as Walter Lipgens envisioned, nor is it an agreement among sovereign nation-states that can be altered at any time, as the 'realist' interpreters of the works of Alan Milward thought. In actuality, there is a two-level system of governance that is developing dynamically. Focusing on the constant crises that are inherent in the system should not obscure the fact that they continually result in 'more Europe.'[35]

---

33. See Loth, 'Mise en perspective historique'; Loth, 'Die Verfassung für Europa'; and Loth, *Experiencing Europe*.
34. Milward, *The Rise and Fall*, x.
35. For an excellent analysis of the condition of the European Union up to 2008, see Wessels, *Das politische System*.

# 10 Competing Utopias?

## The Partito Comunista Italiano between National, European, and Global Identities (1960s–1970s)

*Maud Anne Bracke*

This chapter deals with a unique case of transformation of the political strategy of a European Communist Party vis-à-vis the European Economic Community (EEC). This case, a complex one, refers to the *Partito comunista italiano* (PCI), the Italian Communist Party, and will illustrate the tension created by a sense of belonging to different international spheres. From the 1950s to the 1970s the party's position gradually shifted away from the initial sharp cold war rejection of the Common Market and the EEC toward first accepting and then embracing 'Europe' as a political home and sphere of belonging. A distinction needs to be made between two different understandings of 'Europe' in the PCI.[1] On one level, 'Europe' referred to the end-vision of a political entity that would allow for strong cooperation between (although not the dissolution of) nation-states. Here, teleologically, 'Europe' was understood as continental in terms of its geographical scope and Socialist in terms of its political project. On a more immediate, practical, and policy-oriented level, the PCI started to engage with the EEC, its institutions and policies. A dynamic tension existed between these two concepts and debates in the PCI. This made the PCI's policy toward 'Europe' both conditional and unique: the teleological notion of 'Europe' served as a touchstone and point of reference for the party's interpretation of what the EEC ought to be.

These dramatic changes interacted with the transformation of the party's relations with the Communist Party of the USSR and the Communist world dominated by it. Although up to 1989 a full break away from this sphere of belonging did not take place, before then fundamental shifts occurred in terms of the political and symbolic meaning of the USSR and the Communist world in the PCI's identity and strategy, allowing for a search toward alternative international alliances. I argue that the PCI's links to the USSR and the Communist world led by it included a degree of genuine belief that the fates of Communists in Italy, the USSR, and elsewhere were

1. Due to source availability, the present analysis will mainly be concerned with leadership attitudes and debates.

fundamentally tied, and that Soviet ideological and strategic leadership over the global alliance of Communists was legitimate.[2] Over time however, and particularly since 1956, the party's attitudes vis-à-vis the Soviet-dominated Communist world gradually transformed into a relation that was devoid of actual political meaning, and ossified into a largely identity-based and rhetorical one. A residual connectedness to the Soviet-dominated communist world did nonetheless continue to exist up to the end of the cold war, and this caused a series of contradictions in the PCI's pro-European positions. Indeed, the PCI suffered in the 1960s–1970s from what could be argued was a contradictory multiplication of international alliances.

The PCI's European transformation occurred between 1962 and 1979: initiated in the context of de-Stalinization, this phase coincided with the heyday of European *détente* and the ideological and programmatic moderation that it provoked in the party. A key moment was the Czechoslovak crisis of 1968, which saw the Soviet-led invasion that ended the Prague Spring and the PCI's explicit dissent on this occasion. The debates within the PCI leadership following the events involved a deep and wide-ranging discussion about European *détente* as a new international context impacting on the PCI's domestic political strategies. The shifts in the party's European, and more broadly, international strategies are analyzed here as resulting from two sets of factors: the party's reformism in its domestic strategy on the one hand, and its specific interpretation of the European cold war and the meaning of continental *détente* on the other. I propose that a constant principle throughout this development was the primacy of domestic political strategy, and the ambition to bring the party as close as possible to governmental power.[3] Sections in the party leadership came to perceive linkages between domestic and European political concerns. That is to say, creating a European identity for the party and a constructive approach toward the EEC came to be understood as a useful and indeed necessary strategy for turning the party into an acceptable political actor in Italy. More broadly, the European integration process that Italian Communist leaders started to look upon more favorably during the 1960s was understood as one that would create the conditions for a gradual transformation toward a democratic form of Socialism on both sides of the Continent.

Since Communist archives in Italy, as elsewhere, have become partly accessible in the 1990s, a number of studies have been carried out on questions relating to the PCI and its European strategies. The theme has become

2. Among the vast literature on the PCI's Soviet-oriented 'internationalism' as a matter of identity, political strategy, and ideology, see for instance Aga-Rossi and Quagliariello, *L'altra faccia della luna*, and Urban, *Moscow and the Italian Communist Party.*
3. A historiographic tradition identifying the primacy of domestic politics in the PCI's international strategy exists; see for instance Blackmer and Kriegel, *The International Role.*

a standard one in historical narratives of the PCI during the cold war period.[4] However, relatively more work has been carried out on the initial stage of rejection of the European integration process by the PCI between 1945 and the late 1950s, in the context of postwar reconstruction, the division of the Continent, and German rearmament.[5] The period of interest to us, from the late 1950s to the late 1970s, was marked by an unlocking of the impasse and rigidity created by the early cold war, and by rapid shifts in the international positions of the PCI and to a lesser degree other Western Communists. In the case of larger Western Communist parties such as the PCI, the *Parti Communiste français* (PCF), and the *Partido Comunista de España* (PCE), the post-Stalinist period was characterized by their willingness to participate in domestic politics and the consequent ideological moderation. For the case of the PCI, the important study by Mauro Maggiorani has located the party's changing positions vis-à-vis the EEC in the broader developments of post-Stalinism.[6] However, only comparing the PCI to other Communist parties would allow overcoming the particularism that characterizes some of the Italian historiography. This chapter, while maintaining its focus on the PCI, aims to illustrate both the specificity of this case and the degree to which its development was part of a broader trend; specifically, comparing and contrasting the experience of the PCI with that of the PCF is useful.[7]

The contrast between an instrumentalist and noninstrumentalist, although conditional, approach vis-à-vis the process of European integration, held respectively by the PCF and the PCF, will be illustrated below. In the PCF, I suggest, there never was a shift toward genuine support for the idea of Europe, and when and where the party adopted a more positive stance on the EEC or on European integration, this was always instrumental to either its relations with the USSR or domestic alliances. One set of factors explaining these differences lies in the PCI's traditions of genuinely understanding class conflict to be of a global nature. More specifically, the postwar political set-up in Italy, whereby international interference in Italian domestic affairs had contributed to the PCI's exclusion from government, had made the party leadership acutely aware of the country's

---

4. For instance, Gualtieri, *Il PCI nell'Italia*. This is also the case for autobiographical work, such as Napolitano, *Dal PCI al socialismo*. Giorgio Napolitano became a member of the PCI's *Direzione* in 1964 and was a member of parliament between 1953 and 1996. He has since 2006 been president of the Italian Republic.
5. For the early cold war period see Galante, *Il partito comunista*; Risso, *Divided We Stand*; and Santamaria and Guiso, *La colomba e la spada*.
6. Maggiorani, *L'Europa degli altri*; Maggiorani and Ferrari, *L'Europa da Togliatti a Berlinguer*.
7. For PCI-PCF comparisons see Bracke, *Which Socialism*, and Lazar, *Maisons rouges*. A vast strand of literature exists on the eurocommunist movement of the mid-1970s, written during or shortly after this period.

sensitivity to international developments. This awareness not only distinguished the leaderships of the PCI from that of the PCF, but also political culture in Italy and France more broadly: while in Italy during the cold war it was considered legitimate for political parties to maintain strong international links, thereby linking visions of the nation's future closely to global developments, in France notions of untouched national sovereignty were at all times a key source of legitimation for political actors, especially during the Gaullist period.[8] Thus, comparative work remains essential for a proper understanding of how and why specific policies toward the EEC by Communist parties were forged in specific national contexts.

## SOCIALISM AND REFORMISM IN ITALY

At the start of the cold war, the PCI had, in line with Soviet (and Communist International Bureau or *Cominform*) policy and discourse, interpreted the first stages of European economic integration as an expression of the concentration of capital, of the growing domination of the United States over and interference in Western Europe, and as an acute security danger to the populations of Europe as it allowed for German rearmament.[9] Between the late 1950s and early 1960s sections within the PCI leadership, particularly *Direzione* member Giorgio Amendola and in the final years of his life also general secretary Palmiro Togliatti, started advocating a more reformist and pragmatic attitude vis-à-vis the EEC, arguing for the need to combine a pan-European and a West European strategy. It was a new European reformism that mirrored, and sprang from, the party's reformism in terms of domestic political strategy. The latter consisted of the strategy, adopted at the end of World War II and further developed in the wake of 1956, for a gradual transformation toward Socialism rather than immediate insurrection. The notion of an 'Italian road to socialism' allowed not only for a degree of autonomy vis-à-vis Moscow, but also for a reformist notion of Socialism, based on participation in democratic institutions as well as cultural hegemony. Sections of the PCI leadership, as they started to abandon the sharpest and most hostile cold war positions on European integration, came to envisage the potential for a similar reformist strategy on the level of the EEC. The first concrete step in this process was the sending in 1956 of PCI observers to the consultative assembly of the Council of Europe in Strasbourg.[10]

At the same time, PCI discourse on Europe continued to be partly based on Soviet cold war rhetoric surrounding 'peace' and the 'overcoming' of the division of Europe. Since the late 1940s, the PCI had adhered to the cold war

---

8. Bracke, *Which Socialism*, 23–24; Lazar, *Maisons rouges*, 93–95.
9. Galante, *Il partito comunista*, *passim*.
10. Spagnolo, *Sul memoriale di Yalta*, 202–203.

phraseology that laid the blame for the division of the Continent exclusively on the Western camp, associated the 'forces of peace' with Communist Europe, and proposed an unspecified, propagandistic vision of a unified Europe. Despite a new interest in the EEC, the PCI leadership was still all too easily called back to order by Moscow on matters of European security. In 1957, for instance, the USSR issued a document of fierce condemnation of the Rome Treaties; the PCI responded immediately by toning down its emerging European enthusiasm by affirming the 'fundamentally aggressive' nature of the EEC.[11] It was only in the context of the *crisis* of European integration and of the Western alliance in the mid-1960s—the 'empty chair crisis' and the French withdrawal from the military wing of NATO—that the phrase 'overcoming the division of Europe' became more than a hollow, ritualistic slogan and one that bore actual strategic meaning.

A debate developed within sections of the party's leadership on what European political and economic integration actually meant and how it would impact on Italy. In an article in the party's influential theoretical periodical, *Critica marxista*, Amendola, while reiterating that West European economic integration was an expression of monopolistic capital, argued that the EEC, its institutions and the Rome Treaties *could* be given a dramatically different content, and the process could be led in an 'anti-monopolistic' direction. The eventual goal would be the creation of what was termed 'a democratic alternative in Europe', based on the political power of the working classes and their representatives (the PCI), and paving the way for Socialist transformation.[12] Amendola had a specific view on the political actors and alliances involved, which was grounded in his views on domestic political strategy. While in Italy he proposed an alliance, eventually resulting in unification, between the PCI and the *Partito socialista italiano* (PSI), on the European level this was to be extended into a close alliance between Socialist, Social Democratic, and Communist parties. Support for Amendola at this stage was rather limited. Many in the *Direzione* remarked—rather astutely—that Amendola's concept of a democratic, socialist transformation of the EEC bore little relation to reality, for instance in his perception of an emerging 'European conscience' of Italian workers.[13]

Amendola was influenced by newly emerging debates in the country's largest trade union, the *Confederazione generale italiana del lavoro* (CGIL). The CGIL had historically been connected to the PCI, but since the 1950s it increasingly presented autonomous points of view, thereby pressurizing the party and the Marxist left more broadly. A first key step in the CGIL's reevaluation of the EEC was the recognition of positive effects of the customs union for the Italian economy. Some in the CGIL started to argue that

11. Ibid., 204.
12. Amendola, 'Movimento e organizzazione'.
13. Amendola, 'Unità e autonomia'.

a European strategy ought to be created that would combine trade union mobilization with a policy of structural reforms presented to the European Parliament, which would call for instance, for the nationalization of key industries in a number of countries.[14] Bruno Trentin, leader of the metalworkers' federation (*Federazione impiegati operai metallurgici* or FIOM), was the first in PCI and CGIL circles to argue, in disagreement with both official Soviet interpretations and new left critiques of capitalism, that the recent economic expansion in Western Europe had not led to 'the full integration of the working class into capitalism', by which was meant the loss of political and industrial bargaining power for workers' organizations. At a 1965 conference on 'Tendencies of European Capitalism' organized by the *Istituto Gramsci*, Trentin argued that European economic integration had led to an increase in real wages for Italian workers. Significantly, even the Soviet representatives present at the conference advocated a certain reformism vis-à-vis the European Communities: although they did not understand the EEC as anything different from the internationalization of 'state monopoly capitalism', characterized by the domination of trusts, the European working classes, it was claimed, should operate pragmatically inside the new European decision-making bodies. There was a general consensus that 'one cannot win in *Fiat* if one does not win also in *Peugeot* and *Volkswagen*', although disagreement was revealed over whether the EEC institutions were an appropriate channel for these battles.[15] While Trentin and his supporters were more willing to answer this question with an unproblematic yes, Eugenio Peggio and others adhered to a double strategy of combining 'vast action' on the European level (including entry into the European Parliament) on the one hand, with a 'questioning of the very existence' of the European institutions and the proposal of a 'radical alternative' on the other hand.[16]

In a text from 1963 entitled 'A Democratic Europeanism', Togliatti, while still stressing the monopolistic origins and nature of the EEC as well as the fact that 'the small Europe' of the Six was characterized by a wide gap between the rich and the poor, acknowledged that European integration had had a positive impact on the living conditions of Italian workers. Like Trentin, he called for engagement in political battles on the West European level through trade union action as well as institutional participation.[17] Nonetheless, in the 1964 text of the *Yalta Memorandum*, which is habitually understood to be his political testament, Togliatti made it clear that the party's prime international loyalty continued to lie firmly with the Soviet Union, although he introduced criticisms of the latter's foreign policies. In the memorandum, Togliatti argued that

14. See for example the speech by Lama in 'La relazione, il dibattito', 21.
15. Quoted in Parlato, 'La classe operaia', 24.
16. Peggio, 'Intervento'.
17. Maggiorani, *L'Europa degli altri*, 188; Spagnolo, *Sul memoriale*, 57–58.

Western Europe was rapidly becoming a key 'front' in the global struggle between capitalism and socialism. Division in the Atlantic Alliance was noted, especially in the context of growing French opposition against the United States, which, Togliatti proposed, could be exploited. This, however, required a mass-based workers' movement rather than the 'isolated' positions of most Western Communist parties—a critical note that announced the PCI's ambitions to play a key role in the construction of a broader West European left.[18]

Significant pressures on the PCI toward an engagement with the EEC existed in the dramatically changed domestic political environment created by the *apertura a sinistra* or the opening to the left. In 1963, the PSI entered into a coalition with the Western-oriented *Democrazia cristiana* (DC), thus taking part in a deliberate attempt to isolate the PCI.[19] Up to this point a degree of sympathy with the USSR had existed within the PSI, and while these positions now became marginal, neutralist tendencies remained alive. The PSI's shift toward an enthusiastic embracing of the EEC and strong identification with Europe can be seen as a way to overcome these divisions in the party. PSI leader Pietro Nenni shifted the party's attention toward Europe, in an attempt to unite opinion on the Italian center-left more broadly and to allow for a compromise between those in favor of and critical of the Atlantic Alliance.[20] Also in the DC subtle foreign policy shifts occurred during the mid-1960s: a degree of criticism of the United States' hegemony in the context of the North Atlantic Treaty Organization (NATO) was accompanied with an interest in developing trade and cultural relations with the Communist states. Foreign minister Amintore Fanfani developed a discourse surrounding 'pan-European cooperation' and autonomous European agency in the cold war.[21] All this amounted to a new clustering of opinion across the political spectrum in Italy—with the exception of the far right—in favor of support for the EEC, although with varying degrees of critique. In a further stage, it created a setting in which the PCI also engaged with the pro-Europeanism shared across the Italian political spectrum.

## ITALIAN AND EUROPEAN DÉTENTE

Following Togliatti's death in the summer of 1964 initial disorientation rapidly led to the opening up of new debates. General Secretary Luigi Longo (1964–1972) allowed for a relatively high degree of openness in the internal discussion, and it was in this context that disagreements

18. Togliatti, 'Promemoria sulle questioni', 265.
19. See also Spagnolo, *Sul memoriale*, 218.
20. Nuti, *Gli Stati Uniti*, 477 and 643–644.
21. Ibid., 38–57; Gualtieri, 'Il PCI, la DC', 69.

between the 'left' and the 'right' in the party became visible. Amendola and his supporters on the right now unambiguously argued for a 'third way' strategy in Italy and Europe, that is to say the creation of a system of mixed economy based on broad center-left alliances. Those on the left, headed by Pietro Ingrao, opposed any form of 'social-democratization' and were unwilling to prioritize the institutional strategy, either in Italy or in Europe.[22] Yet significantly, Ingrao and sections of the left came to adopt their own Europeanism in the years following Togliatti's death. They did so from a different perspective and for reasons which had little to do with reformism and pragmatism, but resulted, rather, from an innovative debate on the nature of *détente* and Europe's and Italy's role in it. Here, the PCI started to investigate and understand *its own motives* for favoring the end of the military blocs and the political division of Europe, as distinct from Soviet strategies toward European *détente*. It was this real divergence in international interests between the PCI and Moscow that led to the open conflict between Moscow and the PCI in 1968, as well as allowing the latter to develop a more encompassing European strategy.

Of crucial importance was the new international context of the mid-1960s, in which the bipolar European cold war settlement found itself in crisis. As argued by Jeremy Suri, the stabilization that occurred on the European continent following the Berlin crisis of 1961 led to instability within the two blocs. NATO and U.S. strategies in Europe were profoundly challenged by French President Charles de Gaulle's vision of European *détente* and of a Europe 'from the Atlantic to the Urals', involving in the first instance a strengthening of the Paris-Bonn axis, and subsequently the exploration of relationships with the USSR and East European Communist states.[23] Furthermore, a new European vision was implicit in the early articulation of *Ostpolitik* by the West German Social Democratic Party (*Sozialdemokratische Partei Deutschlands* or SPD) headed by Willy Brandt, as they came to power in the Federal Republic of Germany as part of the Grand Coalition in 1966. An autonomous West German strategy vis-à-vis the Communist states of Eastern Europe was claimed, creating a degree of tension between Bonn and Washington. The PCI debate was reinvigorated by these developments, as Italian Communist leaders understood them to be signs of fundamental shifts in global relations, creating windows of opportunity for change in European countries through reduced U.S. influence. It was, thus, in the context of the *crisis* of the EEC and of NATO in 1965–67 that a majority in the PCI, and no longer only the

22. On the Ingrao left see Amyot, *The Italian Communist Party*. On Amendola, Napolitano, and others on the right, see, apart from the latter's memoirs mentioned above, Matteoli, *Giorgio Amendola: comunista riformista*.
23. Suri, *Power and Protest*; Soutou, *L'Alliance incertaine*; Paxton and Wahl, *De Gaulle and the United States*.

Amendola line, turned in favor of adopting a European strategy, one that was constructively critical of the EEC. It was a debate that was particular to the PCI, and one that in its fresh analyses contrasted sharply with the discourses in the Soviet-aligned Communist world and the PCF, where 'peaceful coexistence' between Eastern and Western Europe continued to be a sterile phrase.

A great deal of the discussions at the 10th party congress in 1966 evolved around these international themes. The Congress theses laid down the party's vision regarding the creation of a 'system of collective security' on the European continent. This concept was taken from USSR discourse and from the Bucharest Declaration of 1966, where it included a call for a European conference on security, and the long-term perspective of the abolition of both military alliances. The PCI transformed these partly propagandistic proposals into an urgent agenda. The PCI's collective security agenda involved the establishment of a nuclear-free zone in central Europe and the withdrawal of all military bases from the Continent, next to the eventual abolition of both military alliances.[24] The need to limit superpower influence over both sides of the Continent was raised on several occasions during the discussions, although the implications of this claim with regard to Soviet power in Eastern Europe were not spelled out as yet. Further, Longo proposed a detailed analysis of the EEC, identifying the contemporaneous, and conflicting, existence of two visions of European integration. One, he argued, was pro-Atlantic and found its origins in the cold war nature of European integration; the other was Gaullist, and existed in conflict with the Atlantic alliance. Longo proposed the possibility of 'another Europe' distinct from these two, based on peaceful coexistence among largely autonomous states and moving toward antimonopolistic economic reform. Longo was opposed to supranational political power when not checked by the democratic mechanisms that existed on the national level.[25] Yet unlike the Gaullist vision, national sovereignty did not figure prominently in critiques of the EEC or in the vision for a future European order.

The PCI leadership was during the 1960s highly active in creating European links, and this occurred in two distinct spheres and stages. In a first instance, it worked toward the creation of a cluster of West European Communist parties whose prime function would be to act as a pressure group within the Soviet-aligned Communist world. The PCI aimed in a first instance to influence the PCF, specifically toward a position less hostile to the EEC, and less subordinated to Moscow. They were the major players at two conferences of 'Communist Parties of Capitalist Europe' held in 1965 in Brussels and 1966 in Vienna. At the Brussels

24. Bracke, *Which Socialism*, 106–108.
25. Maggiorani, *L'Europa degli altri*, 205–207.

conference, the PCI was able to convince other parties to replace in the final *communiqué* the call for the 'cancellation' of the EEC, with a call for its 'suspension'. Contrary to some interpretations, these meetings did not contribute to the development of the PCI's new European strategy; rather, the meetings and especially the attitude of the PCF, acted as a brake on it.[26]

In response to this impasse, the PCI sought European and global alliances outside the Soviet-aligned Communist world. The party coined the notion of *allargamento* (widening) of the world Communist movement as a way to establish links with political actors other than Communist parties, specifically anticolonial liberation movements in the European colonies. This was mirrored on the European level with an intense diplomacy aimed at establishing links with non-Communist parties of the left, specifically the West German SPD and the Scandinavian Social Democratic parties. It was an innovative strategy, and one that was viewed by Moscow with suspicion rather more than the Western-Communist conferences. This was not only because it suggested the PCI's escape from the Soviet-dominated Communist world, but also because if such a network of parties would come about and acquire political and strategic meaning, it might act as a point of reference for reform to Communists and Social Democrats in Eastern Europe. Up to the mid-1960s the chances of developing such a broad West European left strategy had been thin, as in West Germany and elsewhere social democracy had abandoned revolutionary Marxism. However, new areas of convergence between the PCI and the SPD now seemed to be created on issues of European policy and East–West *détente*. Through the PCI's now vivid debate on European *détente*, a future vision was articulated involving a unified Europe, which not only stood 'in between the blocs' but would actively seek their dissolution. Contacts and strategic convergence between state and nonstate actors across the Iron Curtain was the first concrete step in this process, and the PCI considered itself to be in a privileged position in this regard. In the years preceding 1968 the PCI's vision of *détente* was by no means an eccentric one. In fact, *Ostpolitik* as proposed in 1966 was based on a similar notion of East–West European *détente*. As proposed in 1996 by Egon Bahr, who was then considered to have been one of the most important and influential advisors of Willy Brandt and future Secretary of Prime Minister Brandt's Office from 1969 until 1972, then serving as Ministerial Director of the Planning Staff of the German Foreign Office (*Auswärtiges Amt*), NATO and the Warsaw Pact were to be replaced with an entirely new system of collective security and integration in a pan-European context.[27]

26. Bracke, *Which Socialism*, 89–92.
27. Garton Ash, *In Europe's Name*, 55–56 and 80.

Unsurprisingly, the one key aspect about which most ambiguity existed was the PCI's view on Soviet–East European relations. While the party's notion of continental *détente* 'from below' crucially relied on greater East European independence from Moscow, only a few of the party's leaders made this explicit. One exception was Ingrao, who in a text of 1967 entitled 'European Autonomy' explicitly linked the new Europeanism to a critique of Soviet foreign policy. In the article, he proposed for the EEC to be transformed into an instrument for breaking the 'European status quo', that is, the division of the Continent and its political dependency on both superpowers. 'Europe' was here seen as a force that could contribute toward the dissolution of the Western alliance as well as the Eastern bloc. Similarly, during the *Direzione* discussions preceding the 1967 conference of European Communist parties held at Karlovy Vary, in the former Czechoslavakia, Ingrao proposed an alternative to the draft conference resolutions which involved a sharp critique of the Soviet strategy in Europe. While agreeing with the PCI's official line on the creation of a system of collective security in Europe, Ingrao went further in criticizing the USSR for what he referred to as a 'static' understanding of peaceful coexistence and *détente*. He meant by this that it had become a hollow slogan rather than an active strategy for change on the Continent, and one that was too strongly based on the Socialist states. As he put it:

> The struggle for peaceful coexistence has in recent years not had the necessary development and impulse, also because it has been understood by our forces [the world Communist movement] as a struggle to be carried out essentially by the economic and state initiatives of the socialist countries.[28]

The PCI's condemnation of the Soviet-led invasion of Czechoslovakia and the forceful interruption of the reform-Communist experiment that was the Prague Spring caused a watershed in the PCI debate. Significantly, the most innovative discussions taking place in the party leadership between August 1968 and the summer of 1969 did not deal with the nature of the Prague Spring, of Socialism, and democracy, but with the European cold war. The PCI leadership here for the first time criticized the USSR for its European policies. The criticism was based primarily on a different understanding of European *détente*, of why and how Communist parties should contribute to it, and of how its end goal should be envisaged. What the invasion of Czechoslovakia revealed to the PCI leadership was, first, that the USSR continued to rule through violent interference in Eastern Europe and that it did not see this as being in contradiction with *détente*, and second, that radical change in Western

28. Archivio PCI, Fondo Enrico Berlinguer, Movimento operaio internazionale: 35.3. "Nota per conferenza sicu eur. Commenti Pietro Ingrao sul progetto, 18/7/67".

Europe was Moscow's lowest possible concern, illustrated by the fact that it had failed to consider the negative impact of the invasion on Western Communist parties.[29] The European policy that was articulated at the 12th congress of the PCI in 1969 was in fact a continuation of the party's twin notions of the gradual transformation toward Socialism in the West and the democratization of Communist regimes in the East. These developments would go hand in hand with growing unification of the Continent as well as a greater pan-European agency on the global level.[30] The PCI's first sending of a delegation to the European Parliament in Strasbourg in 1969 demonstrated its new commitment to interact with the European-integration institutions.

However, the party's vision of European *détente* through integration ignored the key lesson of 1968: namely, that the invasion demonstrated that the USSR adhered to a static rather than a dynamic concept of *détente*, that is to say, improved East–West relations on the basis of the reinforcement of the blocs rather than their gradual dissolution. The Czechoslovak crisis changed the nature of *détente*, as superpower hegemony was indeed consolidated following 1969. In Eastern Europe this was very clear, as the frictions between Moscow and its allies, which had during the 1960s resulted from the challenge of *Ostpolitik* and Gaullist *détente*, were now once again 'resolved' through Soviet discipline. The Western alliance allowed this. While in the United States the *Sonnenfelt doctrine* explicitly favored 'greater organic unity' between the USSR and the East European states, the Bonn government implicitly accepted Soviet hegemony in the East by first signing a nonaggression pact with the USSR in 1970, before it proceeded to sign the Basic Treaty with the Democratic Republic of Germany two years later.[31] On the Western half of the Continent, the French rebellion against U.S. supremacy developed into a new *modus vivendi* between Washington and Paris, whereby the latter abandoned ambitions to fundamentally upset the balance of forces within the Atlantic Alliance.[32] Instead, France in the 1970s broadly resorted to a nationally based defense strategy, one in which Europe was of limited significance. This created a domestic political context in which the PCF was less pressurized by other parties to develop a strong European profile or policy. The situation was very different in Italy, where the tendency toward a broad pro-EEC consensus noted above was one factor pushing the Communist Party toward constructive engagement with the European institutions.

---

29. For a discussion of these debates see Bracke, *Which Socialism*, 211–217.
30. Ibid., 279–280.
31. Garton Ash, *In Europe's Name*, 57–58; Sarotte, *Dealing with the Devil*, 170–177. According to the 'Sonnenfeld doctrine' the national interest of the United States concerning stability for Europe was best served by the Soviet Union's continuous dominance over the Eastern European countries.
32. Mélandri, 'La France et l'Alliance'.

## THE LATE COLD WAR AND CONCLUDING REMARKS

The 1970s seemed to present the PCI with new opportunities for domestic and European alliances. In Italy, it was in these years that saw its greatest expansion in terms of membership and parliamentary representation, as well as taking hold of local government in a number of major cities.[33] During the years 1975 to 1979 it formed part of the governmental majority, without holding ministerial posts since the PCI had not yet become an acceptable force for government in the eyes of its former enemies. Washington continued to put pressure on its allies in Italy in order to persuade them not to allow the PCI into government.[34] The PCI's cold war impasse was thus reproposed during the 1970s rather than coming to an end. Within the party the tension regarding the nature of European *détente* was reflected in contradictory positions on the EEC and European integration. On the one hand, the new PCI general secretary Enrico Berlinguer held on to notions of a 'third way' Europe, a Europe that would help create the conditions for the ending of the bipolar world order. For instance, in the leadership debates surrounding the alliance strategy with the Christian Democrats, popularly known as the *Historic Compromise*, Berlinguer coined the notion of a Europe that would be 'neither anti-Soviet nor anti-American'.[35]

Eurocommunism, or the converging of the strategies of a number of Western Communist parties during the mid-1970s, was part of this latter European vision, at least from the PCI's perspective. Both the PCI and the Spanish PCE undertook a genuine attempt to turn the convergence of Western Communist parties into a broader West European strategy that would allow Communist parties and their allies to come to power. The central element underpinning eurocommunism was the aim to bring the PCE to government in Spain following the end of the Franco regime and in the transition to democracy in this country. When this failed eurocommunism ceased to exist as a real alliance. It had from the outset been hindered by the PCF's approach, which understood eurocommunism to be yet another tactical maneuver for changing power relations within the Soviet-aligned Communist movement, rather than an alliance that was independent from the latter.[36] The PCI's own 'eurocommunism in one country', as Silvio Pons has aptly put it, involved little more than the continuation of its earlier

---

33. Party membership between 1969 and 1978 rose from ca. 380,000 to ca. 520,000; electoral results in parliamentary elections rose from 26.9% in 1968 to 34.4% in 1976, its highest score in national elections; Bracke, *Which Socialism*, 375–376.
34. Henry Kissinger in the mid-1970s threatened the Italian government with financial penalties as well as possible exclusion from NATO if the PCI became a full member of a government coalition; see Njolstad, 'The Carter Administration'.
35. Berlinguer and Tato, *La politica internazionale*, xii.
36. See Bracke, *Which Socialism*, 345–351.

European strategy, and this was specifically so in two ways.[37] First, the PCI understood eurocommunism as a tool for creating an international context which would support its coming to power in Italy. Second, in what Joan Barth Urban has termed its 'messianic' dimension, the Italian Communists believed that the radical change that was to occur in Western European governments would stimulate democratic change in Eastern Europe.[38] Despite limited actual impact on the political situation in West European countries, the eurocommunist episode did, nonetheless, consolidate the pro-European positions in the PCI leadership.

Simultaneous to the PCI's involvement in the eurocommunist convergence, but to some degree distinct from it, the Berlinguer leadership in 1976 formally ceased to oppose NATO. Marking a fundamental break with the past, this position existed in tension with the PCI's notion of a Europe that was 'neither anti-American nor anti-Soviet'. Berlinguer in a 1976 interview that was to become famous stated that Italy's membership in NATO was beneficial not only to the country's security, but also to the party's domestic strategies. Berlinguer here referred to the future possibility—one which he saw as nigh—of the PCI's entry into government. His statement very clearly went beyond the party's earlier moves toward independence vis-à-vis the USSR. He implied here that the Soviet Union could actually constitute a security threat to a future Italy governed by the PCI and that only NATO membership would protect Italy from this threat. This radical foreign policy shift can only be understood when taking into account the centrality of the domestic strategy and Berlinguer's keen ambition to turn the PCI into an acceptable partner for Aldo Moro's Christian democracy. The shift meant a radical break with the PCI's earlier international strategy and specifically with its line of constructing Europe to act independently from NATO. Strong opposition existed in the party leadership against Berlinguer's positions, especially on the issue of abandoning the ambition to 'overcome' the existing military bloc confrontation.[39]

The end of *détente* in the late 1970s impacted negatively on the party's European strategy on a number of levels. While the party had since 1978 actively supported the DC-led government, in 1979 it withdrew its cooperation. This took place, on the national level, in the wake of the political crisis provoked by the escalation of political violence—exemplified by the assassination of the Italian Premier Moro by the Red Brigades in May 1978—and in a context of rapidly deteriorating economic conditions. The immediate cause for the PCI's withdrawal of support for the centrist government was the announcement of Italy's participation in the founding of the European Monetary System (EMS). The PCI opposed Italy's EMS membership because it did not see this as advantageous to Italy's economic and

---

37. Pons, *Berlinguer*, 162.
38. Urban, 'The Four Faces'.
39. Pons, *Berlinguer*, 47 and 82–83.

financial situation, and, as convincingly argued by Roberto Gualtieri, there were firm arguments in favor of this view. The fact that the DC argued in favor of immediate participation was partly the result of strong international pressure on the Italian government—and was a political decision rather than one taken on economic grounds. The PCI's opposition to Italy's immediate membership was taken as an opportunity by Giulio Andreotti's DC to push the Communists out of the government.[40] The PCI's opposition to the EMS in 1979 was not, I argue, a sign of receding Europeanism; rather, it stood in a tradition of engaging with the EEC in a critical way. The fact that the PCI opposed Italy's EMS participation on substantive rather than ideological grounds demonstrates its genuine engagement with matters of European integration—a situation which contrasts sharply with the attitudes of the PCF during this time.

The PCF had in 1972 agreed upon a *Programme commun* with the *Parti socialiste* in a bid toward forming a government coalition of popular-front type, and this involved a partial, and pragmatic, adoption of the Socialists' wholly positive attitude vis-à-vis the EEC. The PCF remained, despite internationalist rhetoric, a party deeply committed to full national sovereignty and wedded to an outlook that did not go beyond national interests. The question of positions vis-à-vis the EEC was not a significant matter of debate between the two parties of the French Left, and it was not at the root of the rupture between them in 1977.[41] In Italy, by contrast, the PCI at all times understood the international context to be of crucial importance to the party's domestic strategy. To be sure, the primacy of domestic politics guiding its European policy was maintained, but domestic politics were interpreted as highly responsive to international developments.

The events of 1979 did, however, mark the start of a new era for the PCI, one in which it was up until the end of its existence in 1992 to find itself increasingly isolated domestically and on the European level. To a significant degree, this was due to the profound transformation of the center-left political sphere in Western Europe during these years. The majority of the PCI leadership did not welcome the PSI's transformation under Bettino Craxi or the post-Marxist development in the PSF under François Mitterrand. Hostility between the PCI and the two major West European Socialist parties was exacerbated following the Soviet invasion of Afghanistan (1979), despite the PCI's explicit opposition to it.[42] The intense debates surrounding NATO's double-track decision and the placing of Euro-missiles on Italian soil demonstrated the deep divisions that continued to exist between the two parties on foreign policy, despite the PCI's 1979 pro-NATO shift. Through the Euro-missiles debate, the PCI, following the other major Italian parties, relived a phase of cold war rhetoric and temporarily regressed

40. Gualtieri, *L'Italia dal 1943*, 208.
41. Frank, 'La gauche et l'Europe', 465.
42. Pons, *Berlinguer*, 178.

into, as Pons has termed it, the 'alarmist pacifism' of previous decades.[43] Here too, I would argue that this was not a withdrawal of its support for the EEC. What the episode revealed instead was that the PCI's 'détente from below' vision of the 1960s–1970s, which saw the EEC as a potential instrument for undermining the cold war alliances had become anachronistic in the era of the second cold war.

These years also revealed the loss of the most original dimension of the PCI's vision of Europe shaped by *détente*. This was the PCI's 'messianic' ambition in Eastern Europe, and the notion that political change in East and West European countries was an interrelated process. In the context of the Polish crisis of 1980–1981 it became clear that the PCI had no privileged relationship with Solidarity or other sections of the Polish opposition. Hence, its ambitions to influence the situation in Eastern Europe through a European strategy had become of little significance. The attempt to impact on Eastern Europe by offering visions of a democratic-socialist, continental-wide Europe here lost much of its political substance. It could be argued that this was related more broadly to the loss of the utopian dimension in its European vision. If the party's vision for a 'socialist Europe' had been unrealistic and lacking in broad support, it did propose a framework for critical engagement with the European-integration institutions and policies and offered a long-term teleological project as the touchstone for these.

43. Ibid., 165.

# 11 Economy and Society in Interwar Europe

## The European Failure of The Nation-State

*Eamonn Noonan*

Alan S. Milward did not essay a comprehensive overview of the interwar years on the lines of the magisterial *The European Rescue of the Nation State*; nor did he conduct detailed primary research on the interwar economy to match his pathbreaking output on the war economy. Nevertheless his collected writings have much to say on central historiographical controversies—on the Great Depression; on Nazi Germany; on the origins of the Second World War; and on the interwar conceptions of Europe. This chapter attempts a synthesis of his views on these issues, and draws mainly on three different aspects of his prolific output: essays on specific topics, such as the effects of the two world wars; the introductory chapters of his major monographs; and his frequent and incisive book reviews.

An innovative and coherent interpretation emerges from this exercise. It shows many of Milward's strengths as a historian: skepticism toward mechanistic theories and indeed of dogmas of any kind; a clear focus on the economic realities underlying political developments; and a dedication to uncovering the interaction between politics and economic policy. Milward combines traditional and innovative elements in his approach to the sources. He is orthodox in that he focuses clearly on government papers as a leading primary source. Indeed, the papers are at times more revealing than the accounts of leading protagonists, who often had ulterior motives; the former are at the very least an essential counterpart to the latter. He innovates particularly in his close engagement with economic data. Traditional political historians often disregarded this material, with the result that verdicts on key questions were rendered without due consideration to one crucial dimension. Milward frequently rails against the shortsightedness of this kind of history; his mission is to bridge the gap between political history and economic history. Recent history reminds us that economics is far too important to be left to economists; Milward's position has long been that political history must examine critically the relevant economic evidence; it is not enough to assume trends suggested by models of one or other kind.

The virtue of this combined approach—and perhaps the inspiration for it—is that it promises a solution to a phenomenon that has long bedeviled studies of the Great Depression. To paraphrase Wolfram Fischer: economists could explain economic developments and concluded that the problem was politics; political historians could understand political developments and concluded that the problem was economics.[1] Or as Milward put it himself: 'political economy without the economics breeds bad history.'[2] In order to reach more robust accounts of cause and effect in matters of such major importance, interdisciplinary approaches need to be embraced; but it is not obvious that there is greater support for such approaches now than in the 1970s or 1980s.

## THE CHANGING ROLE OF THE STATE

The dominant theme of Milward's writings *tout court* is a sharp appreciation of the changed and changing role of the state. This leads him to approach the interwar period in the context of a spectacular, disastrous denouement: the complete collapse of the vast majority of European states in 1939–40. His contributions on the two interwar decades, though disparate, collectively amount to a sustained attempt to expose and explain the factors which led to this spectacular failure.

The introductory chapters of *The European Rescue of the Nation-State* set the context.[3] The character of the state evolved toward greater weight and greater significance in peoples' lives over a number of centuries. The late nineteenth century saw the emergence of linguistic, ethnic, and cultural rationales; thus the character of the state moved far beyond the original rationales of political expediency and local power. Central parliamentary representation was a key feature, and parliamentary democracy had a national framework. Yet, up to the late nineteenth century, these changes did not entail a significant expansion of the state's functions, powers, or obligations to its citizens.

There was then a change of gear, and this was accelerated by the Great War. The educational dissemination of national history—and myth—promoted collective identity and paved the way for a remarkable degree of loyalty to the state. The war dictated state organization of areas far beyond its traditional activities. It also demanded the acknowledgement of obligations to citizens, as a means of assuring their allegiance, and their willingness to fight a war characterized by unprecedented levels of bloodshed. While many wished the changes in the role of the state as necessitated by the war to be permanent, an opposing view favored the least possible intervention

1. Fischer, *Wirtschaft und Gesellschaft im Zeitalter der Industrialisierung.*
2. Milward's review of *The French Economy, 1913–39: The History of a Decline,* by Kemp, *International Affairs* 49 (April 1973): 274–275, here 274.
3. Milward, *The European Rescue of the Nation State.*

by the state. The view that the universal search for greatest returns produced the best results when the state did not interfere with the market had a long pedigree. Rooted in the ideas of Adam Smith, it was hotly debated in the 1930s. In the Great Depression, the then president of the United States, Herbert Hoover, stood for the then orthodox view, and he cleaved to a policy predicated on waiting out the cyclical process; his successor, Franklin D. Roosevelt stood for an interventionist approach. The verdict on which of the two got it right has been a litmus test for both economists and historians ever since. Those faithful to the free market and to classical economics were in full retreat with both the manifest failure of Hoover's strategy and the manifest success of Roosevelt's New Deal. In the 1980s, however, a reinterpretation of the Great Depression and its aftermath gathered ground, closely related to the emergence of the Chicago school and the renewed political influence of neoliberal economic thought. This debate has flared again in the current economic downturn, driven by the perception that the rolling back of state intervention, notably as a regulator of the financial sector, has contributed to the present-day economic crisis.

Milward notes how state intervention affects the economy:

> the geographical distribution of manufacturing across the European continent, when compared to that of the United States, strongly suggests that the influences of government policy over two and a half centuries has distorted what might have been the pattern of distribution created by the free play of market forces.[4]

He agrees that all states have pushed industrial policies, even if there are many different policies, reflecting different characteristics of the times and of respective governing groups. But the important thing is to identify policies which affect the economy and to develop criteria by which their impact can be measured and evaluated. A central element of Milward's interpretation is the rejection of the theory that in economic affairs the state is to be seen simply as an obstacle to the optimum result.

## THE 'EUROPEAN IDEA'

Milward's major contribution to postwar history has been to elucidate the continuance of the nation-state perspective along the entire trajectory of Western European integration. His analysis of the 'European Idea' as it emerged in the interwar years therefore merits close attention, even if the issue in itself is not a major theme of interwar historiography. He is skeptical

---

4. Milward's review of *European Industrial Policy: The Twentieth-Century Experience*, edited by Foreman-Peck and Federico, *The Journal of Economic History* 60: 4 (December 2000): 1133–1134, here 1133.

about the significance of the earlier generation of 'European saints'. In 1982 he wrote that

> there is one insidious temptation persistently gaining ground [ . . . ] it is to suggest that one European perspective which was glimpsed and which might with more wisdom have been permanently held was the one which came into the central focus after 1947, that is to say the Franco-German alliance and the international control of the French and German coal and steel industries. No settlement of this kind was possible after 1918 because Germany was too strong to need or to accept such an outcome.[5]

Milward cannot take seriously the 'noisy but ineffective' 1920s advocates of European political unity. The European Communities were not rooted in the Pan-European Union, the International Committee for a European Customs Union, or the numerous other ephemeral organizations of this stamp. In his view, these disparate groups cannot be seen as unified proponents of one, indivisible idea. Rather, these early European ideologues believed many different things. The 'European Idea' variously served as a strategy to reconstruct the German empire; as a means to allow Austria to escape from independence; as a defense of the ruling elite's conservative values; as an anti-Soviet front; as a liberal customs union through which German industry could dominate European markets; as a set of cartels protecting France from German economic domination; and as a way to protect European interests from the United States of America.[6]

He is correct to point out that this issue was marginal in the 1920s, in contrast to the central political focus it became after the war. In fact, as he implies in *The European Rescue*, the various contributions of the 1920s were rehabilitated and reevaluated as part of the deliberate effort to create a European myth. This was a curious echo of the earlier creation of national myths by European nation-states; and in his view, 'national consciousness has always been more the consequence than the cause of nation-states.'[7]

His critique of the relevance of interwar Pan-Europeanism goes further. He contends that the origins of the Communities were much more of a defense against a 'European Idea' on interwar lines than a final acceptance of its truth. The basis for this is his finding that the European Coal and Steel Community in its initial disposition was not, as often assumed, a U.S.-sponsored project; rather, it was a response by France to head off

---

5. Milward's review of *Reparation in World Politics: France and European Economic Diplomacy, 1916–1923*, by Trachtenberg, *The Journal of Modern History* 54: 1 (March 1982): 131–133, here 132.
6. Milward's review of *Evolution of the European Idea, 1914–1932*, by Pegg, *The Journal of Modern History* 57: 1 (March 1985): 109–110.
7. Milward, *Rescue*, 25.

a U.S. initiative. The Communities were formed 'precisely to defend the European nation-states against this sweeping solution to which they could not possibly agree.'[8] What Milward considered to be a neglected historical background provides a useful perspective on the current debate on U.S. attitudes toward European integration.

It is easy to agree with Milward that 'the EEC was and is the response to particular historical problems and circumstances. Some of the problems for which European unity was proposed as a solution in the 1920s were not there after 1945; others were but had nothing to do with the process of European integration; and there were also of course quite new ones.'[9] Continuing issues were France's security vis-à-vis Germany and the overwhelming might of the United States; but here the actual responses were different.

His analysis can however be challenged on a couple of points. First, interwar pan-Europeanists did indeed have many different motivations and conceptions; but the same can be said of postwar actors. The difference was that their postwar counterparts exercised political authority, and for that reason had both the opportunity and the need to negotiate a common program. This brought a focus on concrete as opposed to theoretical considerations. The establishment of regular Council meetings created a process for working through differing perspectives and finding ways to cater for different objectives. The proponents of European cooperation in the interwar years never had the opportunity to engage in this kind of negotiating process.

Second, there remains the fascinating episode of Franco–German rapprochement under Aristide Briand and Gustav Stresemann. Both had some conception of political cooperation that went beyond narrowly defined national interests, and both had political significance. As such they can be seen as early exponents of the kind of approach that dominated the postwar scene. The Briand Plan, tabled at the League of Nations in September 1929, foreshadowed to some extent the structures of the EEC—regular meetings of the member-states, a rotating presidency, a separate secretariat, and a specific focus on cooperation in different policy areas, ranging from economics and finance to labor and transport.[10] Admittedly, Stresemann's early demise and Briand's political decline meant that this path was not further explored, and historical inquiry based on counterfactual hypotheses is of limited value.

8. Milward's review of *Evolution*, 109.
9. Milward's review of *Evolution*, 110.
10. Noonan, 'Choosing Confrontation: Commercial Policy in Britain and Germany, 1929–1936', 50–55; and Néré, *The Foreign Policy of France from 1914 to 1945*, 88.

## THE INTERWAR VIA CRUCIS

Milward is an incisive analyst of the *via crucis* that was interwar history. The immediate task in the 1920s was to master the changed circumstances produced by the Great War. In one of his earliest books, Milward described the peace treaties as economically disastrous, giving rise to 'the emergence of a new and less satisfactory pattern of trade and an inadequate system of international economic arrangements.'[11] In this, Milward is in agreement with John Maynard Keynes, who first came to prominence with his attack on the economic consequences of the peace. Keynes set out the case against a punitive approach to reparations: 'If we aim deliberately at the impoverishment of Central Europe, vengeance, I dare predict, will not limp.'[12] After the mid-1970s, when the oil shock cast a shadow over the long postwar boom, admiration for Keynes waned, and Milward defended him against the fashionable criticism that he had exaggerated the flaws of Versailles. But Milward adds nuance to the debate. Drawing on his firm grounding in quantitative analysis, he suggested that the actual amount fixed for reparations was not in itself the problem; rather, the dilemma was that Germany had no opportunity to develop the capacity to pay by generating output, international trade, and income. This in turn was a result of the failure of domestic economic policies everywhere in 1920, and this undermined any attempt throughout the 1920s to reach a settlement on the basis of mutual economic expansion. No great power, including Germany, was prepared to accept the economic and political consequences of an international order in which Germany could have paid reparations on the scale proposed. As for France, Milward acknowledges that reparations were a fallback position, rather than a first choice; for all that, he concluded that French foreign policy was shortsighted and short of realism. He also introduces a still neglected perspective into the debate: the idea that Britain had a stake in continuing Franco–German animosity, and was indeed prepared to insist on tougher repayment terms as a means of blocking rapprochement between the two continental powers. Sadly, he does not elaborate on the evidence for this.[13]

The failure to construct a properly functioning international economic system in the 1920s left the onus on each nation-state to arrive independently at policies which could adequately respond to the difficult circumstances of the time. There were even economists who pointed to the usefulness of welfare rights, a key component of postwar strategies. There were disparate efforts toward employment policy, management of exchange rates, reconstruction policy, welfare policy, labor policy, macroeconomic policy (the term was coined in the wake of the Great Depression), stabilization policy,

11. Milward, *The Economic Effects of the Two World Wars on Britain*, 40.
12. Keynes, *Economic Consequences of the Peace*, 124.
13. The previous two paragraphs are based on Milward's review of *Reparation in World Politics*.

and growth policy. It is tempting to conclude that government after government was trying to find new strategies and instruments in too many areas at the same time.[14] Milward also notes a neglected aspect of the loss of political allegiance to the Republic of Weimar. The tax assessment system led to income and corporate taxes becoming a serious burden for the first time in 1922, leading to wide resistance to taxpaying. This contributed in part to the hyperinflation of 1924, which in turn undermined popular allegiance to Weimar.[15]

The government of Chancellor Heinrich Brüning (March 1930 to May 1932) stands out as the classic case of a failure to solve the challenges of the time. Milward acknowledges that it was no easy task to find a way through depression, reparations, disarmament, eastern frontier issues, and vigorous domestic opposition. But in his view the Brüning government's failings were also of its own making; a case in point was the fixing on such a feeble option as the attempt to form a customs union with Austria. Brüning's own limitations—he was neither able, prescient, nor likeable—were an obstacle to establishing a durable consensus. This was evident as early as September 1930, when the moderate parties suffered heavy losses in the Reichstag election. They were unable to counter critics who derided them as defenders of the Young Plan (which presented a revised scheme for reparations payments), which the court of public opinion considered to be despicable. Without stating so explicitly, Milward implies that the agricultural sector was the one that got away. Having previously lent support to a variety of nonsocialist parties without achieving notable political influence, it was at this election that they first swung behind the National Socialists.[16]

The main thrust of Milward's analysis is the failure of nation-states, which was concurrently a failure of parliamentary democracy. The economic collapse of the Great Depression (acting on 'inherent fissile tendencies') led to the withdrawal of political allegiance of important groups. This was transferred in some cases to new, nondemocratic conceptions of the state (Nazism, Fascism, or Communism).[17] Recovery policies were determined by the history and institutional inheritance of each state, not

14. Milward's reviews of *The Cambridge Economic History of Europe, vol. 8, The Industrial Economies: The Development of Economic and Social Policies,* edited by Mathias and Pollard, *The English Historical Review* 106: 419 (April 1991): 408–412; and of *Multinational Enterprise in Historical Perspective,* edited by Teichova, Lévy-Leboyer, and Nussbaum, *European History Quarterly* 19: 4 (October 1989): 555–557.
15. Milward's review of *Wealth and Taxation in Central Europe: The History and Sociology of Public Finance*, edited by Witt, *European History Quarterly* 19: 4 (October 1989): 568–571.
16. Milward, 'Fascism and the Economy', in *Fascism: A Reader's Guide: Interpretations, Bibliography*, edited by Laqueur, 409–453.
17. Milward, *Rescue*, 25f.

by general theories. But Milward takes a clear position in the enduring debate on the correct response to the Great Depression. The lesson he draws is that countries had to act. To sit and wait for a cyclical upswing was useless and cruel.[18] He adds nuance also in this matter with his analysis that successful responses involved the establishment of a durable political coalition. The fact that state after state in Europe failed to accomplish this had disastrous consequences.

## NAZI GERMANY

Milward's approach does not sit well with the theory of a German *Sonderweg*, that the particular circumstances of German development were decisive factors in the Nazi accession and the catastrophes which followed. The implication of inevitability in this theory is at odds with his conviction that examination of the historical facts must take precedence over general theories. The particular circumstances of Germany resulted in the political crisis coming earlier than elsewhere, as opposed to it being a qualitatively different development than other countries experienced.

Milward sees three key factors in economic recovery after the Great Depression.[19] First, the Nazis were able to build a durable political coalition. Second, they found ways to increase demand through fiscal devices. He points out that initiatives such as incentives for house construction and repairs were successful when judged by the criteria of cost-effectiveness and long-term economic usefulness. By contrast, the economic significance of the much-studied road-building program has in his view been overrated; and other public infrastructure investments have been relatively neglected. Third, an increase in both demand and consumption amounted to systematic aid to agriculture. Germany was one of the few countries to take on the huge costs involved in supporting agriculture in the 1930s, alongside the United States, Norway, and Sweden; only after the war did public support for agriculture become a general policy choice.[20]

Milward rejects simplistic theories of an identification of interests between heavy industry and the Nazi government. '[H]ypotheses [ . . . ] which equate fascism to a stage in capitalism or to the defensive reactions of major capital interests [ . . . ] are inadequate'.[21] His approach is broadly in line with Tim Mason's argument that there was a primacy of politics in

18. Milward's review of *Capitalism in Crisis: International Responses to the Great Depression*, edited by Garside, *The English Historical Review* 111: 440 (February 1996): 264–265.
19. Ibid.
20. Ibid.
21. Milward, 'Fascism and the Economy', 452.

the Third Reich's economic policy.[22] Milward draws attention to sectoral interests that were at odds with certain Nazi economic policies. Steel producers were strongly opposed to the policy of using German iron ore, because of the higher costs involved. IG Farben had to follow an investment path laid down by the government; prioritization of synthetic rubber (*Buna*) and rayon (*Zellwolle*) resulted from heavy government pressure, at the expense of the company's own desire to develop production of PVCs (polyvinyl chlorides). They gained domestic markets and military-related work, but lost ground in most foreign markets.[23] There is however a need to further refine theories of the relation between business and politics up to 1939. The Nazi regime adopted a range of policies which represented a qualitative shift in the nature of state intervention in the economy. One pillar of this new approach was rapid rearmament. This and other initiatives revived domestic demand, at a time when the prospects of exporting industry were increasingly hampered both by increased protectionism and by the failure of Germany to follow other countries off the gold standard. In these circumstances, hitherto export-oriented sectors accepted the opportunities offered by the revival of domestic demand and by rearmament.

On the conceptualization of Nazi foreign economic policy, Milward provides an incisive critique of the idea of *Grossraumwirtschaft*. He considers that the idea of a distinctive, coherent conception has been rebutted. He accepts Alice Teichova's analysis that *Grossraumwirtschaft* meant different things to different people—and indeed that this proved useful for the government. It became an 'integrative political formula, and brought further strands of nationalist, conservative, expansionist opinion into line with Nazi policy. Hitler set guidelines, but there was no sequential economic programme'.[24] The nature and purpose of German trade agreements with eastern and central Europe in the 1930s, for example, merit further investigation. Southeast Europe was a limited market in European terms, and the increasing focus on it was a sign of weakness rather than of strength; it was a reaction to circumstances rather than an a priori policy objective. *Grossraumwirtschaft* as an economic model posited a German heartland producing manufactures and a group of client countries supplying primary products and raw materials and absorbing German manufactures. Based on a close analysis of trade patterns, against a background of the limited convertibility of the Reichsmark used to pay for imports, Milward challenged

22. Mason, *Sozialpolitik im Dritten Reich: Arbeiterklasse und Volksgemeinschaft*. See also Milward's review of *Autarkie und Grossraumwirtschaft in Deutschland, 1930–1939: Aussenwirtschaftspolitische Konzeptionen zwischen Wirtschaftskrise und Zweitem Weltkrieg*, by Teichert, *The American Historical Review* 91: 1 (February 1986): 139–140.
23. Milward's review of *Industry and Ideology: IG Farben in the Nazi Era*, by Hayes, *The American Historical Review* 94: 2 (April 1989): 474–475.
24. Milward's review of *Multinational Enterprise in Historical Perspective*.

the prevailing interpretation that Germany successfully exploited southeast Europe and concluded that the German position within the so-called Reichsmark bloc had significant weaknesses.[25] The southeast was never a viable alternative for the markets that German industrial produce had previously found in Western Europe; and as Milward shows, it was not even clear that Germany could bend the terms of bilateral trade and payments agreements significantly in its favor.

Unfortunately, Milward does not embark on a closer examination of the theory and practice of vertical trading blocs in the interwar period. This would have made for interesting reading, not least in the light of his later engagement with the creation of a Western European trading bloc in the postwar era. The fact is that the vertical integration model contradicted the evidence of contemporary trade statistics: industrialized countries were each others' best markets. The failure to grasp this reality was part of the interwar tragedy.

Because of the Nazi administration's skill in monopolizing credit for rapid recovery from a sharp and steep depression, Hitler accumulated enormous political capital. This greatly enhanced the government's ability to set the economic agenda, and increasingly to bend the country's industrial muscle toward the needs of an aggressive foreign policy.[26] But how sustainable was this recovery? In Germany as in the United States there was greater public expenditure on job creation. This was incremental and piecemeal rather than systematic. The focus was on massaging unemployment statistics rather than creating sustainable employment. The exercise in both countries was not cost-effective in terms of the number and the quality of the jobs created. The conclusion Milward draws is that government action could not do more than alleviate the problem, at great expense; the background was especially challenging, in that the fall in employment coincided with structural changes in the location and nature of employment, and a detachment from international trade and payments systems.[27]

It is tempting to consider the short-term success of recovery policies primarily as a political achievement. It remains difficult to determine criteria by which to judge their economic merit. The high cost entailed a greater detachment from the world economy, and a vicious circle developed. Reviving the domestic economy made reintegration in world markets more difficult (as did the actions of other countries, each focusing on national

---

25. Milward, 'The Reichsmark Bloc and the International Economy', in Hirschfeld and Kettenacker, *Der Führerstaat*, 377–413; Wolfgang Mommsen, 'Einleitung', ibid., 14.
26. Milward's review of *Autarkiepolitik im Dritten Reich*, by Petzina, *The Economic History Review* 23: 2 (August 1970): 390–392.
27. Milward, 'The Reichsmark Bloc', 397 ff.; review of *Capitalism in Crisis*, by Garside; and review of *The Nazi Economic Recovery, 1932–1938*, by Overy, *The Economic History Review* 36: 4 (November 1983): 652–654.

priorities). This in turn favored the continuation and intensification of policies predicated on reviving the domestic economy. A definitive verdict on the sustainability of the Nazi economic recovery is elusive, as their choice for aggressive rearmament and expansionism created a new and ultimately disastrous context: full-scale war. Apparent economic success copper-fastened Nazi political hegemony; this reinforced a strategy predicated on military adventure; and this in turn destroyed the neighboring nation-states and ultimately Germany itself.

## THE KEY TO SUCCESS OR FAILURE

Milward quantifies the European failure of the nation-state in the period 1919–1939. In 1939/40, twenty of the twenty-six then existing states collapsed; ten were occupied, three annexed, four partly occupied, two reduced to a satellite status, and one was occupied by an ally.[28] Germany, the apparent winner in 1939/40, had already failed the test of democracy in 1933. He contends that the other countries' fate owed as much to a loss of internal morale as to the military superiority of Germany; this point alone suggests an agenda for future research, and will no doubt remain controversial.

The key to success or failure, according to Milward, was the creation or absence of a durable coalition of political interests. This was the nature of the New Deal, and it accounts for the adoption of contradictory policies. The rationale was to hold the coalition together. The Nazi case was similar. This also explains why the ideologically preferable choice sometimes had to yield, in order to cater for a specific constituency. France, by contrast, did not establish a durable coalition. A core of administrators operated within traditional parameters. Devaluation and protection were accepted as economic necessities, to protect the status quo, rather than as part of the creation of a coalition capable of bringing political coherence.

The story of the struggle for control of Romanian oil resources in the 1920s—twice discussed by Milward in characteristically incisive book reviews—casts some light on the processes influencing the formation of a durable coalition.[29] In 1924 the National Liberal Party brought in a mining law which stipulated that 80 percent of mining concessions should go to Romanian companies, at a time when foreign companies held about half of the market. This led to insistent and continuing pressure by the United States and the United Kingdom, who linked reform of this law to

---

28. Milward, *Rescue*, 4.
29. Milward's review of *România şi trusturile petroliere internaţionale până la 1929* [*Romania and International Oil Trusts to 1929*], by Buzatu, *The English Historical Review* 99: 393 (October 1984): 929–930.

issues ranging from reparations repayments to the opening of new credits for a hard-pressed economy. The pressure included a well-funded press campaign representing the Romanian government as incompetent. It paid off. The law was repealed in 1928, as a quid pro quo for the provision of a stabilization loan. This was accompanied by the ousting of the national liberals, at the instigation of the king, and the entry of the National Peasant Party to power; a party which had long opposed the mining law, seeing it as favorable to the interests of the bourgeoisie and inimical to the interests of their own constituency. Even here, a conclusion based on the inherent exploitative characteristics of large-scale capitalism would be overly simplistic. Milward provides the characteristic nuance in a review of a book on French investments in Romanian oil, by pointing out that a French-controlled company managed the paradoxical feat of counteracting French interests in the sector while simultaneously making liberal politicians more hostile to France.[30]

The story of the inability of a small state to secure control over national resources is a commonplace one. In this case, it is important not to attribute this exclusively to pressure from outside; there was no national consensus in favor of the disputed law. The episode illustrates Milward's core idea that economic policy is the expression of an aggregate of the interests of contending groups. But it also reminds us that external influences are at play in determining which interest becomes embodied in policy and legislation. This, indeed, would be a fruitful avenue for further research on the interwar economy.

The period of 1919 to 1939 is a striking counterpoint to the period of 1945 to 1968. The earlier decades are characterized by complete economic and political failure; the latter by unprecedented economic and political success. The choices made in the Great Depression—for protectionism and self-sufficiency within vertical trading blocs—proved to be the wrong ones. In exchange for short-term dividends, they set Europe on a path toward economic stagnation, which then became a road to war. Even if there was no inevitability about the cascade of events leading to war, there were lessons to be learned about wrong choices and their consequences. Key postwar actors learned from these lessons. This allowed them to forge a new political consensus in favor of reversing protectionism and coordinating national responses to the central issues of international trade and finance. But that is another story, and one which is well told in Milward's work on the postwar years.

30. Milward's review of *Banque et investissement industriel: Paribas, le pétrole roumain et la politique française, 1919–1939*, by Marguera, *The English Historical Review* 105: 415 (April 1990): 533–534.

## CONCLUDING REMARKS

For Milward, the historian's task is to expose and explain, and to dispel clichés and platitudes. Historical argument is a powerful explanatory device rather than a frivolous and unwholesome exercise of the imagination. The historians he admires, such as Charles Kindleberger, David Kaiser, and Josef Becker and Klaus Hildebrand achieve this wide perspective.[31] A focus on historical evidence triumphs over prejudices and assumptions. His verdicts on those who do not measure up can be scathing:

'Beneath a superficial covering of descriptive narrative large and important areas of historical enquiry lie unexposed and unexplained, presumably because they are questions of interest for "economic" historians or some other breed.'[32] 'Unfortunately, like most books on economic warfare, this sticks to diplomacy and avoids any attempt at economic measurement [ . . . ] So vagueness prevails in all its judgements.'[33] A certain chapter in a collection of essays 'can only have been published for the kindly trance-inducing effects of the tantric illustration on page 736 whose central maze leads to the words 'rubbish' and 'exhaustion''.[34]

Where does Milward stand in relation to the mainstream political ideologies of the past half-century? He is not an obvious cheerleader for dogmatic interpretations, whether socialist or conservative, nationalist or internationalist. He is no devotee of the great-man tendency. He is outside the once influential Marxist school; his disdain for overly mechanistic or predictive models leaves him at odds with key tenets of Marxist theory. He recognizes that the interests of the powerful are a factor in the policy mix, and some of his strongest contributions are devoted to the political significance of key economic sectors. He has a close interest in underlying structures and long-run trends, and combines this with a determination to bring out the role and nature (and interaction) of the interests of different groups. He has some sympathy for the German tradition of *Finanzsoziologie*, the study of society through public finances—a useful corrective to the

31. Milward's reviews of *Economic Diplomacy and the Origins of the Second World War: Germany, Britain, France, and Eastern Europe, 1930–1939*, by Kaiser, *The American Historical Review* 86: 5 (December 1981): 1066–1067; and of *Internationale Beziehungen in der Weltwirtschaftskrise, 1929–1933*, by Becker and Hildebrand, *The English Historical Review* 98: 389 (October 1983): 929.
32. Milward's review of *International Banking in the 19th and 20th Centuries*, by Born, *The Journal of Modern History* 57: 1 (March 1985): 112–114.
33. Milward's review of *Der Stille Krieg: der Wirtschaftskrieg zwischen Grossbritannien und der Schweiz im Zweiten Weltkrieg*, by Inglin, *The English Historical Review* 110: 437 (June 1995): 809–810.
34. Milward's review of *The Fontana Economic History of Europe, vol. 5 (2 parts): The Twentieth Century*, and *vol. 6 (2 parts): Contemporary Economies*, by Cipolla et al., *The English Historical Review* 93: 367 (April 1978): 421–424.

British tradition that public finances were a given, and therefore neutral in a political sense. And while he rails against those who accumulate data for the sake of it, he is strongly fixed on empirical facts, as a sound basis for teasing out cause and effect.

One review of Milward and S. B. Saul's *The Development of the Economies of Continental Europe, 1850–1914* identified a tendency to adopt middle positions on controversial issues; the two were accused of doffing their cap to left and right.[35] No one who has had the privilege of attending Professor Milward's lectures will recognize the timidity implied by this comment. When he had reached a verdict on a given issue, based on consideration of the relevant evidence, he was clear, explicit, and unapologetic. And his judgments are of continuing relevance. Impatience with those who cling to ideal models at the expense of considering the real world is one of his recurring themes. In the wake of the economic downturn following the 2008 credit crunch, this very issue has returned to the forefront of academic and public discourse. Robert Skidelsky has called for economists to return to the real world, away from mathematical models. He urges a return to Keynes's conception of the discipline, as expounded in the 1930s: economics is a moral science, not a natural one.[36] Milward's writings could profitably be cited in support of the case for such a reorientation. He establishes that a predetermined theoretical model cannot account for the many travails of the interwar economy, and their disastrous political consequences; these can be understood only through an examination of the interplay of specific factors at specific junctures, always proceeding from the evidence provided by both political and economic sources.

Since the 1960s, history and other academic disciplines have moved away from 'big picture' approaches, and new branches of enquiry have arisen, often focusing on niche areas and issues. More recently, the pendulum seems to have swung back in the direction of traditional, political histories. Milward's work on the interwar period is closely focused on what the economic data reveals. But he bridges the gap between micro- and macro-history through good handiwork and through his determination to integrate the relevant facts into a coherent interpretative framework. One key to the strength of his analysis is that he argues from the facts to the conclusions, and can therefore dismiss arguments lacking an empirical basis. Another is that he concentrates on the interplay between political and economic factors, rather than following the common practice of specializing in one field to the exclusion of the other. It would be pleasing to report that this approach has become more popular over time, but this is far from obvious. On the contrary, a malignant form of politicization, in which the

---

35. Kemp's review of *The Development of the Economies of Continental Europe*.
36. Skidelsky, 'How to Rebuild a Shamed Subject'.

facts take second place to predetermined conclusions, increasingly threatens the integrity of historical inquiry. In this context, Milward's empirical approach has enduring relevance as a counterweight to the contemporary inclination toward unscientific research.

# 12 Unlocking Integration

## Political and Economic Factors behind the Schuman Plan and the European Coal and Steel Community in the Work of Alan Milward

*Ruggero Ranieri*

The Schuman Plan is quite central to Alan S. Milward's research on Western Europe after the Second World War. The Schuman Plan, as is well known, was launched on 9 May 1950, and was essentially a proposal for France and West Germany to put their coal and steel industries under the joint management of a supranational body, the High Authority. Other neighboring West European countries were invited to join, in what was envisaged to be the nucleus of a future West European federation. In *The Reconstruction of Western Europe, 1945–51*, published in 1984, the Schuman Plan features as the key building bloc of the Continent's reconstruction. In his second major book on postwar Western Europe, *The European Rescue of the Nation-State*, published in 1992, one long chapter entitled 'Coal and the Belgian Nation' is devoted to the Belgian coal industry inside the European Coal and Steel Community (ECSC) throughout the 1950s. Third, in *The Rise and Fall of a National Strategy, 1945–1963*, published in 2002, two substantial chapters are devoted to the attitude of the British government toward the Schuman Plan and the ECSC. The Schuman Plan is also an important paradigm of Milward's larger thinking on the issue of European integration. For example, the initial two chapters of his 1992 monograph, quoted above, one on 'History and Theory', the other on 'The Lives and Teachings of the European Saints' are largely based on material pertaining to the Schuman Plan.[1] We are dealing, therefore, with one of the main topics of Milward's research and also one of his most original and pathbreaking.

It is interesting to observe how remarkably coherent this body of historical writing appears. The core of Milward's historical interpretation is already apparent in his earlier work. After having laid the initial interpretative framework, he proceeded to fill its various parts with historical detail, at the same time pushing forward the frontiers of his interpretation and

1. Milward, *The Reconstruction of Western Europe, 1945–51* (1984); *The European Rescue of the Nation-State* (1992); *The Rise and Fall of a National Strategy, 1945–1963* (2002).

drawing further lessons and implications. His historical methodology is, at the same time, innovative and consistent.

The last chapter of his *War, Economy and Society, 1939–1945*, published in 1977, is devoted to the reconstruction of the international economy after the Second World War; in it Milward discusses some of the issues that will concern him in the following years. The focus here is on the world economy, rather than on Western Europe, but problems surrounding the reconstruction of Germany are also well highlighted. The key difficulty was to make the multilateral trade and payments system envisaged at the Bretton Woods conference of July 1944 compatible with the economic changes brought about by the war, in particular with the expansionary aims of domestic economic policies:

> The low levels of production and employment in the inter-war period were now seen as a needless waste of resources and one which by knowledgeable management of the economy could be averted.[2]
>
> It is tempting to argue that the consequences of 'total war' must always be to produce a significant volume of social change because the state must retain the allegiance of its citizens, and the greater the demands it makes on them the more they will seize the opportunity to make demands on it.[3]

Consequently, the mechanisms that were devised at Bretton Woods to bring this about, but also other proposals, 'never took adequate account of the structural changes in the international economy which the war had produced.'[4]

While the guiding ideas of his later work were already there, including the concept of 'allegiance', it is also remarkable how little Milward had to say in the final chapter of a monograph exploring the war economy in Europe on the actual policies that shaped post-1945 Europe. Obviously he must have been aware of a vast unexplored territory. What was, then, the state of play of the historiography on the reconstruction of Western Europe and more particularly on the Schuman Plan? I will limit myself here to three of the most important contributions that Milward encountered and challenged as he started his investigation.

The first one was Pierre Gerbet's 1956 seminal article on the origins of the Schuman Plan.[5] Relying heavily on memoirs and testimonies from Jean Monnet's circle, this is essentially a piece of diplomatic history, perceptive of many aspects of French foreign policy, but giving other elements a very low priority. There is very little consideration of the role of the Plan for the Modernization and Equipment of the French Economy, known as

---

2. Milward, *War, Economy and Society, 1939–1945*, 339.
3. Ibid., 341.
4. Ibid., 345.
5. Gerbet, 'La Genèse du Plan Schuman'.

the Monnet Plan, in shaping France's international economic policy, and the negotiations over the International Authority for the Ruhr (IAR) are also considerably played down, as are all issues relating specifically to coal and steel. French policy, according to Gerbet, had, by early 1950, reached a dead end, and it was rescued by the imaginative statesmanship of Jean Monnet and Robert Schuman.

A few years later William Diebold's influential book on the Schuman Plan offered a neat, well-informed account of the background and origins of the French initiative and its further development into the ECSC.[6] Diebold, an American scholar with some involvement in policy-making, argued with considerable understanding of the coal and steel question and of the economic motives behind the Schuman Plan. Again, however, he provided little insight into the relevance of the Monnet Plan in French policy-making and, while he understood the IAR as having been a disappointment for the French, he did not probe the issue in any depth and in the end deferred to Gerbet's very partial interpretation of the immediate origins of the Schuman Plan.

Appearing at about the same time, Duncan Burn—the industrial correspondent of the *The Times*—offered a refreshingly different account of the same events.[7] Burn focused on the Monnet Plan and its objectives in relation to the French steel industry as well as on the interdependence between the steel industries of France and Germany. He spotted the difficulties of the Monnet Plan in 1948 and 1949 in the face of the rise in output of West Germany and explored the possible alternative of re-creating an organization similar to the interwar European Steel Cartel (ESC). His work, however, did not attempt to explore the links between economic and international issues, concentrating more on the firm level.

My purpose in this chapter is to highlight some of Milward's key findings and conclusions about the Schuman Plan and the ECSC. In the next section I will examine his seminal chapters in *The Reconstruction of Western Europe*. The next two sections will assess his work first on Belgium and then on the United Kingdom, drawing attention to how these two country studies helped him further to refine his research, empirically and theoretically. Finally I will look at how Milward attempted to conceptualize some of his findings on the early history of European integration.

*

* *

The reconstruction of Western Europe as described in Milward's monograph was complex, intricate, and tortuous. Very schematically it can be seen as resting on a strong base, going through a number of stages; events

6. Diebold, *The Schuman Plan*.
7. Burn, *The Steel Industry, 1939–1959*.

foreseen and unforeseen were often met by national and international strategies, which proved to be wrong and therefore had to be amended, even radically, along the way; and it was finally crowned by the creation of two enabling European institutions, which opened the way to further progress. The base on which the reconstruction rested was the domestic expansionary economic policies undertaken by all Western European states after the war. This is a key point, elaborated upon at different points in the book, starting with the crisis of 1947 which Milward argues was not about an impending collapse, but the result of a generalized investment boom, which opened up a dangerous dollar gap:

> Practically no Western European government would have been content with mere recovery to the level of 1938. Most sought a fundamental reversal of their experience of the 1930s. [ . . . ] High and increasing output, increasing foreign trade, full employment, industrialization and modernization had become in different countries, as a result of their experience of the 1930s and the war, inescapable policy choices, because governments could find no other basis for political consensus.[8]

Of these national expansionary strategies, the French Monnet Plan was the one that had a more lasting effect on the rest of Europe.

The turns and twists of the reconstruction can only be hinted at here. The first casualty was the Bretton Woods agreement, which was inadequate precisely because it was a compromise between projected levels of domestic employment and output, on one side, and international adjustments in the monetary field, which were likely to endanger them, on the other. It had been largely an 'invention of economists'.[9] The Marshall Plan was needed precisely to fill that gap. This was an effective temporary solution, since it allowed Western Europe to pursue its chosen course of expansion, overcoming the payments crisis of 1947. The problems with the Marshall Plan were that the donors and, possibly, its recipients misjudged its real nature: The United States' leverage was not strong enough for them to be able to dictate either the terms of the liberalization of trade and payments or the extent of integration among the Organization for European Economic Cooperation (OEEC) member states, or the steps to be taken to reintegrate Western Germany into the European economy. Compromises had to be reached on all these points between the United States and its main European partners, starting with France and the United Kingdom.

Intervening events—such as the acceleration of the cold war, the postwar recession in 1949, offset in continental Europe by the recovery of West Germany, the resumption of intrawestern European trade—were responsible

8. Milward, *Reconstruction*, 466.
9. Ibidem.

for the timing of the different solutions that were found. Of these, Milward judges two to have been essential, both launched in 1950: the European Payments Union (EPU) and the ECSC. He defines them as 'the pillars of the reconstruction'.[10] There was however a difference between them. The EPU, Milward argues, was not a step toward political and economic integration of Western Europe, as the United States would have wished; rather it performed the very important but limited role of multilateralizing payments within Western Europe and, more importantly, spelled the end of U.S. plans for pushing the United Kingdom to join its continental neighbors in a new integrated economic bloc. Furthermore, it was not, in any way, a supranational body, but rather reflected the choice for what Milward, in his later work, was to define as 'the inherited framework of interdependence', essentially traditional intergovernmental cooperation among nation-states.[11] The ECSC, on the other hand, was a creative European solution to the longstanding Franco–German question, 'the central tie in western European reconstruction which was so conspicuously missing in the 1920s', based on a transfer of sovereignty, that is, 'integration', a new postwar mode in international relations. 'International regulation of the economy was institutionalized as the alternative to the formal diplomatic resolution of [ . . . ] political conflict.'[12]

Inside the greater picture of the reconstruction of Western Europe there is a smaller inner core of events, hinging on the relations between France and Germany, and leading up to the Schuman Plan. These are carefully presented in two dense chapters in *The Reconstruction of Western Europe*: 'France and the Control of German Resources' and 'The Schuman Plan'. The narrative starts from the Monnet Plan. Its aim was to make the French economy more internationally competitive in the future, particularly against German competition.[13] At its centre was the assumption that exports of French steel would replace prewar German steel exports, and that the French steel industry would increase its output well above prewar levels. This could only be achieved by increasing the inputs of German coal and coke into the French economy. This in turn meant maintaining the German economy at very low productive levels. There is no question that, at least in its initial formulations, 'the Monnet Plan was based on the crudest possible expression of mercantilistic principles', and it could only have been realized if some of the most far-fetched aims of French postwar foreign policy, such

10. Ibid., 470.
11. Milward and Sørensen, 'Interdependence or Integration? A National Choice' in Milward et al., *The Frontier of National Sovereignty*, 1–31, here 21.
12. Milward, *Reconstruction*, 418 (for both quotations).
13. See also Milward, 'La planification française et la reconstruction européenne', in *Modernisation ou décadence*, edited by Cazes and Mioche, 77–115.

as the separation of the Ruhr's resources from those of the rest of Germany, had proved realistic.[14] This, however, was far from the case.

There were two obstacles to the French plan. The first and more practical one was a consequence of the pattern of development of the French and European steel industries after 1945. Large investment projects in new steel plants were drawn up not just in France, but in the Netherlands, South Wales, Norway, Italy, and elsewhere, in addition to which much steel investment was going into existing plants:

> Taken as a whole investment in the steel industry was not fitted into a rational programme of action but responded to the immediate situation where order books were full and steel sold at high prices.[15]

Not surprisingly the slackening of demand in 1949–1950 everywhere in Europe except in West Germany was a worrying development for the steel industry, particularly in France where it came on top of a predictable bottleneck in the flow of inputs and was immediately translated into a fall in exports. Nor was the likelihood of a permanently weakened German steel industry realistic, since by mid-1949, despite enduring Allied occupation 'the international bonds which restrained the Promethean strength of Germany's steel industry were already being tested and broken.'[16]

The second major obstacle was diplomatic. France's aims were incompatible with the aims of its Allies, and this had become abundantly clear by June 1947, both in view of the meager results in terms of German coal allocations to France in the Moscow 'sliding scale' agreement, as well as of the Marshall Plan's objectives of the reintegration of Western Germany into the economy of Western Europe. Things looked ominous. It seemed as if France was going to have to face a resurgent Germany in the framework of a liberal integrated Europe, funded by U.S. dollars, and thus be forced to renounce its claims. France, however, was not entirely without bargaining power, and by skillfully deploying it at the right moment, while at the same time partially reconsidering its objectives, was able first to score some limited important points and finally to drag success out of the jaws of defeat.

The scene was the Allied London conference of 1948–1949 on Germany, to which Milward devotes considerable detailed attention. There, it soon became clear that the decision to set up a unitary West German state with important sovereign powers would exact a change in French aspirations, but, argues Milward, only 'in their international aspect'.[17] The problem was precisely to devise a different policy, which would nonetheless support the national economic objectives of the Monnet Plan:

---

14. Milward, *Reconstruction*, 137.
15. Milward, *Reconstruction*, 364.
16. Ibid., 371.
17. Ibid., 468.

> From June 1948 onwards the Ministry of Foreign Affairs began the task of moving ministers, governments, parliament and people towards the alternative policy of a Franco-German economic association. Because such an association would have to cover the question of France's access to German resources of coke and coal as well as that of the future regulation of steel markets it was conceived as beginning in these [ . . . ] important industrial sectors.[18]

In preparation for this important strategic shift by France, there was a clever holding action by French diplomats revolving mainly around the powers and functions of the newly created IAR. The French could draw on their experience of the Ruhr in the 1920s, and they soon realized that what was on offer was a body which was very far from meeting their original hopes. Drawing on evidence from French diplomatic archives, Milward argues that in the final stages of the London conference the French were essentially seeking a number of short-term bargaining advantages, with which later to strike a better deal with Western Germany. Thus the key elements of the policy which would emerge one year later in the Schuman Plan were already being drawn up. The conclusion Milward reaches is that:

> The Schuman Plan did not, as all commentators on it have so far suggested, emerge like a *deus ex machina* from the Planning Commissariat in spring 1950. It was in essence already there at the end of the London conference.[19]

The chapter on the Schuman Plan starts off with two long paragraphs, full of economic detail, focusing on a comparative analysis of the French and German industries. The investigation is conducted with an eye to what was going on inside the French Planning Commissariat in preparing the Schuman Plan. It is a tortuous and intriguing paragraph, full of question marks rather than firm conclusions. Difficult as it was to measure the comparative strengths of the two industries, Milward believes that some of the conclusions that were reached were probably right, such as trying to stop double pricing of German coal exports or raising the productivity in French steel works; others dubious, such as breaking up German business groups or *Konzerns*; and others misconceived, such as the faith in Lorraine steel production. The discussion serves as a kind of methodological counterfactual: the economics of the Schuman Plan should be seen as an essential background factor, but there was much more than that:

18. Ibidem.
19. Ibid., 164.

> The intention of dwelling at such length on such uninspiring subjects is not to insist on the primacy of the economic objectives of the Schuman Plan. Far from it, the objectives [ . . . ] were overwhelmingly political. It is to explain precisely what the real possibilities for political initiative were [ . . . ] and, above all, to show how the Schuman proposals [ . . . ] evolved logically from the consistent pursuit of France's original domestic and foreign reconstruction aims.[20]

In other words there is no primacy, either of political or of economic explanations; the latter, however, have pride of place in fully understanding the former.

Who, then, was responsible for the Schuman Plan? Amid the accurate analysis of the international scene in late 1949 and early 1950, including the shift in U.S. foreign policy which brought Secretary of State Dean Acheson to solicit the French to produce an initiative able to rescue European integration, Milward points to the fact that in early 1950, after the rejection by the French government of 'Finebel', which had entailed more liberal trade and payments relations with the Federal Republic, the initiative to produce something was back with Monnet's Planning Commissariat.[21] Their task was to reinstate the Monnet Plan as a guideline for French foreign policy. If it had not been possible through the joint effort of the planners and the Ministry of Foreign Affairs to advance a solution through the IAR, 'it was up to the planners to think of something else'. This they did, with the result that 'the Schuman Plan was invented to safeguard the Monnet Plan.' But, Milward insists, this does not contradict the evidence that '[t]he first origins of the Schuman Plan were really in the Ministry of Foreign Affairs during the London Conference.' The root of international policy, Milward is arguing here, must lie inside the machinery of nation-states.[22]

After having analyzed the international reactions to the Schuman Plan, including the refusal to join on the part of the British government, Milward deals with the negotiations leading to the Treaty of Paris establishing the ECSC. The account is rather sketchy, since at the time few documentary sources were available. Nonetheless, by focusing on Franco–German economic issues, Milward concludes that France did rather well and was able to exploit the advantage of negotiating from a position of strength.

20. Ibid., 380.
21. Finebel is the acronym for a planned economic agreement between France, Italy, Netherlands, Belgium, and Luxembourg. The agreement was discussed between September and December 1949 and it was designed to achieve a substantial measure of trade and payments liberalization among the participant countries. It was also apparent that West Germany wished to join the scheme and that this was also strongly supported by the ECA and by the Dutch. Ibid., 306–315.
22. Ibid., 395 and 396.

However, the interests of the other member states of 'Little Europe' had to be taken into account, which involved complex adjustments and solutions, exposing the fallacy of 'the more sweepingly simple ideas of the Planning Commissariat . . . that the future could be cleansed of the influence of the past.'[23] The High Authority, with its limited and contradictory powers and its policing of a highly imperfect single market for two industries, did not conform to Monnet's neat technocratic prescriptions.

Despite Milward's often scathing critique of their actions, the whole thrust of *The Reconstruction* is a tribute to the achievement of French policy-makers, able to translate their domestic ambitions into an original and lasting European framework. His conclusions about the initial rejection by national industrial associations of the Schuman Plan and the ECSC go in the same direction. The battle between governments and industrialists was nominally over the Schuman Plan, but effectively it was over the control of economic policy. It was the same battle which private industry had been fighting in various countries against nationalization and economic planning, 'the last fierce resistance to the acceptance of real government power over the mixed economy in western Europe in peacetime'.[24] In fact the ECSC, when set up, proved to be very much in the interest of private industrialists, but that was something they were only prepared to accept later, once the fundamental issue had been settled against their aspirations.[25]

Milward's approach in *The Reconstruction* can be described as starting from the roof. By this I mean that, while he had explored and in fact uncovered the main outlines of the diplomatic settlement that was reached in Western Europe, he had not given much historical substance to the way domestic policies had provided the building blocs of the edifice. This, he seemed to claim, was the task of future research.

*
* *

Milward's second major investigation into the Schuman Plan and the ECSC covered Belgium. He was writing some ten years after *The Reconstruction*, when new documentary evidence on the period had emerged: Belgian archives, in particular, were among the first to be available, together with the official records of the ECSC. Although many actors appeared on the scene, Milward's primary concern was Belgium, a country which had no other option but to join the Schuman Plan:

23. Ibid., 415 (first quotation) and 418 (second).
24. Ibid., 419.
25. The fact that the ECSC worked, ultimately, in favor of business interests rather than against them is a conclusion Milward hints at in *The Reconstruction*, 419. He comes back to this point in 'Conclusions: The value of History' in Milward et al., *The Frontier of National Sovereignty*, 193.

> It was taken for granted that peace between France and Germany was essential for Belgium's security, and that this was the strongest reason for accession to the treaty. After that acceptance it was vital to ensure that Belgium's other national interests were not trampled into the ground [ . . . ].[26]

And this was true both for the Belgian government as well as for the Belgian coal and steel industries.

The emphasis here, therefore, is not so much on the nation itself, although the Belgian government is part of the picture, but on how the ECSC brought about a shift in the balance of private and public management in two key industrial sectors by bringing forward an inevitable process of internationalization. Milward's guiding assumption remains that the ECSC reflected the convergence of domestic choices taken in the different nation-states and that these domestic choices were the result of national strategies of expansion and full employment, which, in the case of Belgium took on a particular meaning:

> The very strength of the Schuman proposals lay in the fact that they were [ . . . ] based on Monnet's perception, blurred but still grasping an essential truth, that international interdependence at a deeper level [ . . . ] would give the peace settlement force and durability. In elevating the interdependence between public national and supranational economic authority to the role of guarantor of the Franco-German peace settlement he forced Belgian industry to accept a role in the postwar mixed capitalist economy [ . . . ] which before 1950 it was still anachronistically resisting.[27]

The starting point for Belgium, inevitably, was the importance of the two sectors, which together accounted for sixteen percent of gross domestic product and a workforce of well over a million. At the same time the two industries were closely linked in terms of supply of inputs, as well as in terms of ownership, both belonging to the intricate, cartelized financial holdings coalescing around the *Société Générale* and the *Banque de Bruxelles*. The Belgian coal industry, inefficient and high cost, approached the Schuman Plan in an embarrassing spirit of autarky and denial. The Belgian steel industry, on the contrary, was efficient and strongly export-oriented, and a longstanding member of all European cartels. Its agenda focused around an anachronistic refusal of any government intervention into its investment and pricing strategies. Because its case was rather hopeless, it hid behind

26. Milward, *Rescue*, 83.
27. Milward, 'The Belgian Coal and Steel Industries and the Schuman Plan', in *The Beginnings of the Schuman Plan*, edited by Schwabe, 437–453, quotation, 453.

the far more popular struggle of the coal industry, which was perceived as a vital artery of the nation to be defended against encroachment by evil foreigners. This was, nevertheless, a diversion, destined to cause much fuss and few practical results. In fact Belgian steel, in the end, could not prevent the establishment of a High Authority with real powers.

Out of the Treaty of Paris emerged the agreement of *péréquation*, which was a system of levies to be imposed by the High Authority on the coal production of those countries whose average production costs stayed below the weighted average in the ECSC and which in fact ended up being used to provide generous subsidies, for at least five years, to the Belgian coal mines, mainly at the expense of the Ruhr. This in fact placed a burden, of quite an exceptional nature, on the West German coal industry, which can only be explained by the Federal Republic's weak negotiating hand at the start of the Schuman Plan negotiations. The subsidies were granted on the understanding, which the Belgian government encouraged, that the Belgian coal industry would rationalize and increase its productivity. Nothing of the kind, however, happened. Despite increasing evidence that the position of the industry was rapidly deteriorating, it preferred to hang on to all the temporary advantages and opportunities that the international coal market still provided in the course of the 1950s. Not only did the High Authority scarcely try to counteract this trend but, on the contrary, it actually went as far, at least on one occasion in 1955 under pressure from Belgium, as to support Belgian coal protectionism quite openly. Here, Milward argues, is clear evidence which contradicts the assumptions of the neofunctionalists who posit the rationalizing influence of the supranational Community. In fact, members of the High Authority were far from being emancipated from their national governments.[28]

Behind the scenes the Belgian government was playing a complex game of survival. On the one hand it was twisting the arms of its two main industries to establish a greater influence on their management. At the same time, it was negotiating on their behalf in the ECSC, occasionally moderating their more extravagant claims, and finally looking beyond them to the perceived advantages of supranationality. These were that genuine restructuring might have been made easier if its political costs, not least in terms of the regional tensions between Walloons and Flemings, could be shared with the High Authority, or perhaps blamed on it. This third option was intermittently used, but never coherently pursued.

As a result, Belgium could not bring itself to make the hard choices that were necessary, given the fast and inevitable decline of its coal industry, within the broader picture of a shift in energy sources. By 1958 the forces of the market had determined the industry's bankruptcy. At this point, the ECSC could have used its emergency powers to enact a Community-wide

28. Milward, *Rescue*, 105.

regime aimed at sharing the burden of painful restructuring among the member states. It was, however, impossible to reach such a consensus at a time when de Gaulle was insisting on the narrowest possible interpretation of the ECSC Treaty provisions. It was only possible to muster what seemed initially a weak understanding on continued subsidies and measures to cushion the blow to southern Belgium in the framework of a regional policy.

Contrary to what many believed at the time, however, this did not spell a defeat for the integration project. The ECSC, through its 'Readaptation Fund' and a variety of other instruments, was increasingly empowered to implement measures to cushion the crisis, much beyond the letter of the Treaty of Paris. What this amounted to was a readiness to supplement Belgium's already fairly generous national social security schemes and sustain incomes in the Walloon province of Borinage. According to Milward, regional policy—a different name given to an employment and welfare policy—can largely be seen as a fabrication designed to provide cast-iron guarantees to particular categories of workers left out of the great economic boom. That all member states should have endorsed this revealed, in Milward's view, a widespread consensus on the scope of the postwar welfare state, which lay at the heart of the integration project, even beyond the letter of the Treaties. The Belgian state was able to guarantee national survival and economic security to its citizens first by shaping the actions of the ECSC on behalf of its coal industry and then by shaping the future course of integration itself.

*

* *

A decade later, Milward approached the history of the Schuman Plan and the ECSC from yet another angle, that of the United Kingdom. He could now draw on a considerable body of new work, which included the semiofficial history of the High Authority by Raymond Poidevin and Dirk Spierenburg as well as further research on single countries and on leading actors, much of it inspired by Milward's own research.[29] The result is that he was now much more confident and detailed in his findings. Furthermore Milward now sheds his former reluctance to move into the fine details of diplomacy and often engages the reader with day-to-day accounts of diplomatic correspondence. Writing about his own country, he deploys a fairly intimate

---

29. Spierenburg and Poidevin, *Histoire de la Haute Autorité*. Among the studies inspired by Milward's work I should perhaps mention my own: Ranieri, 'Assessing the Implications', 'Inside or outside the Magic Circle?', and 'L'espansione siderurgica italiana'. Among the many others: Lynch, *France and the International Economy*; Griffiths, 'The Schuman Plan Negotiations'; Kersten, 'A Welcome Surprise?'; and Warner, *Steel and Sovereignty*.

understanding of its political and economic situation. He also brings into the picture new factors such as military and strategic ones, which he had previously largely avoided, as well as providing detailed insight into the often contradictory positions of the various segments of Britain's bureaucratic machinery. All this said, his work gains interpretative power and strength as an extension and development of his previous analysis of the Schuman Plan. His interpretation is too far reaching, innovative, even at times polemical, to be fully appreciated simply as part of an overall series on British foreign policy. Milward starts by attempting a full and complex analysis of what he believes was a fairly coherent British foreign policy, a 'national strategy', well fixed, and broadly supported by the country's whole political body although open to a number of tactical revisions.

Therefore, the rejection of the Schuman Plan, as later the feeble approach to an association with the ECSC, were consistent with this strategy and not based on misinterpretation or prejudice. In explaining the national strategy, which, in its main lines, emerged in 1945, Milward finds traditional, well-established explanations quite convincing, although he is careful to distinguish between foreign policy and the nation's strategic objectives. The concept of a one-world policy, and of the 'three circles', meant that alliance with the United States, leadership of the Commonwealth, and a guiding role in Europe were all essential to maintaining a position of strong world influence. Britain had a number of short-term advantages (military, colonial, economic) on the world, not the European, scene, which it could exploit, but it was well understood, he argues, that their purpose was not to hold on to world power, as much as to create a postwar framework in which the country could prosper, so 'as to sustain growing incomes at a high level of employment and with a high level of welfare provision'.[30] Britain thus acted on the same premises, following similar political and social realities, as other Western European nation-states; however it held quite different assets, which prevented it from an exclusively European involvement.

After a period of uncertainty between 1945 and 1949, during which the Labor government contemplated forms of closer European involvement, by early 1949 it had ruled out a substantial initiative toward Western Europe and defined its involvement there in very specific and limited terms. At this point, in May 1950, it was confronted with the Schuman Plan, the logic of which it found unacceptable. The French were not hostile to British participation as long as it did not endanger their key objective, which was a binding economic partnership with West Germany. The real inflexibility, argues Milward, was on the British side, and it was on the matter of supranationality.

Milward is keen to dispel the notion, entertained for example by Edmund Dell, that mistakes were made on the British side: that, by a more favorable disposition, Britain could have negotiated away the supranationality

30. Milward, *The Rise and Fall*, 3.

it found so irksome.[31] Such an outcome, Milward argues, was not on offer. He also dispels the notion that British politicians were influenced by the hostility displayed toward Europe by the press and public opinion. This was at most a pretext, since the polls showed a mixture of ignorance or indifference. Despite all the soul searching by contemporary actors and historians, Milward believes simply that the Schuman Plan highlighted what was already becoming clear in the course of the reconstruction: Britain wanted to lead Europe, but most of the Western European partners, and in particular France, had developed their own independent national strategy:

> Britain's refusal to participate in the Schuman Plan negotiations marked a clear, reluctant, mutual understanding in Paris and London that their respective future national visions had different priorities [ . . . ].[32]

More ominously, the emergence of a Franco–German bloc would eventually endanger the entire British strategy.

A substantial chapter of the monograph is devoted to the question of the United Kingdom's association with the ECSC. There repeated attempts at reaching a binding agreement were tried between 1951 and 1954, but no progress was made. Finally an association agreement was signed in late 1954, but its practical significance was extremely limited: it was an agreement to consult and little more, there was certainly no surrender of sovereignty, and even the acknowledgement of economic interdependence between the coal and steel industries of the two sides was on a minimal scale. Again Milward refuses to take these discussions lightly. Association, he argues, was not a tactical smokescreen for British hostility toward the Six, it was a policy which parts of the British government considered important, but which never gained enough traction to be successful. In fact, Milward argues, this was not without consequences, for later Britain faced the same dilemma with the Treaties of Rome and found that it had no credible alternative to either joining or staying out.

Why did association with the ECSC fail? Milward carried out an in-depth examination of the records of the discussions inside the government and between the government and the coal and steel industries. The corresponding chapter in *The Rise and Fall* is a very interesting study of policy-making at the level of sectors, in many ways running parallel to the work on Belgian industry. The details are too intricate to be recounted here. In summary, while coal was always resistant to any move toward Europe, the picture in the steel industry was more mixed, for there were some advantages to be gained from closer links. The government could have forced the issue, not least since foreign policy reasons suggested a positive move

31. Dell, *The Schuman Plan.*
32. Milward, *The Rise and Fall*, 70.

toward the ECSC, especially during 1953. It never, however, was united and purposeful enough to make it, and its commitment to public management, as opposed to corporate cartelized management, was more lukewarm than in continental Europe. The key issue, however, was domestic consensus:

> [T]he government's withdrawal from any battle with the coal and steel interests acknowledged the extent to which the attitude of each industry reflected public expectations of the postwar domestic economic balance. Employment and personal and family security were the greatest weights in that balance. In their protectionism, the NUM [National Union of Mineworkers], the NCB [National Coal Board], and the steel firms were thus on the side of the angels. [ . . . ] The United Kingdom thought of itself as modernised and victorious, whereas the rhetoric of modernisation helped the progress of the Schuman Plan in France [ . . . ] The British public would have been surprised to hear that industries which had won the war needed to be modernised by the force of competition with those of the defeated.[33]

The idea of a British decline, Milward argues, had not yet reached the level of public debate. His whole account of Britain's policy toward the Schuman Plan, while consistent with his overall interpretative framework, has a positively traditionalist, even conservative accent. The postwar world, as already seen in Belgium, was built, he insists, on a set of deeply held notions of socially inclusive protection. While there were arguments and interests which challenged the status quo, Milward tends to dismiss their contemporary relevance.[34]

*
* *

Milward's theoretical reflections should be understood exactly in the way he presents them, as a direct emanation of his empirical research, rather than as an attempt to construct an all-round model. Again, while he holds firm to some key points, others he is continuously changing and elaborating upon. The best synthesis of his understanding of European integration is contained in *The European Rescue*, and it hinges on the rejection of any

---

33. Ibid., 161–162.
34. My own work on the attitude of the British steel industry to the ECSC pointed to the existence of a section of the industry, including some of the more dynamic, export-minded firms, unhappy about the negative position taken by the British Iron and Steel Federation. See Ranieri, 'Inside or Outside the Magic Circle?' Geoffrey Owen has examined the same question from the point of view of British industrial decline, underscoring the weaknesses of the British corporatist pattern and the resulting negative consequences on industrial performance, see Owen, *From Empire to Europe*, 124–132.

antithesis between the European Community and the nation-state. The evidence, he claims, points to the fact that:

> [T]he evolution of the European Community since 1945 has been an integral part of the reassertion of the nation-state as an organizational concept. [ . . . ] without the process of integration the west European nation-state might well not have retained the allegiance and support of its citizens in the way that it has. The European Community has been its buttress, an indispensable part of the nation-state's postwar construction. Without it, the nation-state could not have offered to its citizens the same measure of security and prosperity which it has provided and which has justified its survival.[35]

Because so much weight is made to rest on the nation-state, an essential point of this explanation is to define its nature and its boundaries. This is something Milward repeatedly comes back to. He first talks of a 'national interest', then he moves on to attempting to define a 'national strategy', while at the same time he tries to probe the nature of the consensus behind nation-states—what he calls 'the frontier of national sovereignty' or 'allegiance'—and how it shapes their actions in the process of integration.

I will touch here on three important moments of his analysis. First, in the powerful and much misunderstood Chapter 6 of *The European Rescue*, 'The Lives and Teachings of the European Saints', Milward focuses on a number of key West European statesmen involved in the creation of the Communities. Among others, he looks at the biographies of Robert Schuman, Konrad Adenauer, and Alcide de Gasperi, as well as of Jean Monnet. What distinguishes them, he claims, was not their supposed pro-European-unity idealism. Quite the opposite, they supported the reassertion of their respective nations, but they did it in a modern way, recognizing—in some cases as the result of their Catholic affiliation and of their experience of having challenged the top-down dimension of old prewar elitist policy—the importance of modern grassroot policies and of social welfare in the postwar world. This led them to understand the importance of European integration, that is, of those 'limited surrenders of national sovereignty through which the nation-state and Western Europe were jointly strengthened'.[36]

A second route through which Milward defines his interpretation is by challenging other readings of European integration. In particular, he repeatedly criticizes the neofunctionalists, such as Leon N. Lindberg and Ernst B. Haas, who had analyzed the ECSC and the European Economic Community as the result of a progressive, quasi-automatic, enlightened surrender of sovereignty from the national to the supranational dimension,

35. Milward, *Rescue*, 2–3.
36. Ibid., 319.

a transfer of a functional problem to the European dimension, in order to accelerate its solution. Quite the contrary, Milward argues, '[i]ntegration, in the case of the ECSC, took place precisely because the issues involved could not be reduced to the merely functional level.'[37]

As chosen opponents of his ideas the neofunctionalists were not necessarily very militant: the core of their writing was in the 1950s, and they had, in any case, subsequently renounced some of their original claims. Milward, as often the case with him, is actually acknowledging them at the same time as he is refuting them; he is just as worried about the vapid neofunctionalist common sense creeping into much current thinking about European integration. There is another side of his argument which is worth stressing: his criticism of 'realist' or 'intergovernmental' theories, which explain away the supranational dimension as subordinate and/or largely instrumental. This, Milward argues, underplays 'the supranational symbolism' which was an essential moment for the reassertion of the nation-state.[38] The surrender of sovereignty involved in integration, he argues, although limited, specific, and controlled, is an essential dimension, to the point where it may also have encouraged some momentum of its own, albeit in a narrow framework.

Finally, where Milward's historical method and theoretical ambitions come together in their most persuasive form is his overall discussion of the role and nature of the state in the postwar Western European economy. By providing much empirical evidence on the growth of welfare, on state support of agricultural incomes, on industrial policies and modernization across Western Europe, he builds on former explanations such as the ones by John Maynard Keynes and Andrew Shonfield to advance his claim that the postwar state did not simply influence or even determine, as an exogenous factor, sustained levels of economic growth. The search for a broader, more inclusive, political consensus—what is referred to as the mixed economy—changed the nature of the postwar nation-state, made it something quite different from the past:

> It was the broader postwar political consensus and the political machinery by which it was operated which led to the economic and social policies to which growth theorists point as part of their explanation for the high rates of growth of the period.[39]

In other words, by building the political and social coalitions that ensured its survival, including European integration, the nation-state triggered the

37. Ibid., 15. See also Milward and Sørensen, 'Interdependence or Integration? 1–32.
38. Milward, *Politics and Economics in the History of the European Union* (2005), 36.
39. Milward, *Rescue*, 28.

mechanisms that sparked off the great boom, in what Milward calls 'the economic consequences of the postwar political consensus'.[40] This, I feel, is a theme he would have undoubtedly wished to explore further.

40. Ibid., 33.

# 13 The Evolution of a 'Protoplasmic Organisation'?

## Origins and Fate of Europe's First Law on Merger Control

*Tobias Witschke*

The European Coal and Steel Community (ECSC) is history. If its inception started with the declaration of French Foreign Minister Robert Schuman on 9 May 1950, its life ended fifty years after the entry into force of the ECSC Treaty in summer 1952. The scientific interest in the ECSC's end holds no comparison with its importance in the 1950s. At that time, the ECSC was often seen as a first step toward a European Unity 'project' and was at the origin of the development of specific 'European integration' theories, such as neofunctionalism.[1] With the establishment of the European Economic Community (EEC) in 1957, public attention ceased to focus on the ECSC. In most accounts of European integration, the ECSC is hardly mentioned after the 1950s, while emphasis is laid on the creation of the common market—following a 'winner takes all' approach.[2] Indeed, those who look at developments in the ECSC after the 1950s come to rather harsh conclusions. Most parts of the ECSC Treaty were never enforced.[3] In a recent review of its history, the ECSC is called a 'paper tiger'.[4] This astonishes, as the development of a European legal system in the framework of the EEC—integration through law—is presented as the driving force for the emergence of a 'European polity'.[5] So why did it not work out for the ECSC Treaty? Why is there so little interest in the experience of the ECSC?

This question is even more interesting in terms of competition policy since the ECSC Treaty introduced antitrust and merger control provisions—being the first step of what is now called the 'antitrust revolution

1. See for an overview, Niemann and Schmitter, 'Neofunctionalism'.
2. See for example Sweet, Sandholtz, and Fligstein, *The Institutionalization of Europe*.
3. Spierenburg and Poidevin, *The History of the High Authority of the European Coal and Steel Community*.
4. Alter and Steinberg, 'The Theory and Reality of the European Coal and Steel Community', 90.
5. Cappelletti, Seccombe, and Weiler, *Integration through Law*. For a critical review of these claims, see Rasmussen, 'From *Costa v. ENEL* to the Treaties of Rome: A Brief History of a Legal Revolution'.

in Europe'.[6] However, the ECSC merger control provisions (Article 66) had very limited—if any—impact on successive antitrust legislation or on the wider political and academic debate on antitrust policy.[7] West Germany, which is generally seen as a staunch advocate of antitrust policy, only introduced a merger control in 1973. Classical competition policy textbooks or narratives considering European competition policy as a 'success story' usually ignore the example of the ECSC or treat it very superficially without taking into account its implementation.[8]

It will be argued here that the fate of the first competition policy on mergers can best be understood by analyzing its historical origin in depth. While there was a formal legal mandate for the ECSC's High Authority to forbid mergers with an anticompetitive effect, the Schuman Plan negotiations also set an 'informal' mandate, which was related to the future development of the West German steel industry, which was being 'deconcentrated' by the Western Allies in parallel to the Schuman Plan negotiations.[9] There was some public disagreement between the German Federal Republic and France over the extent to which this deconcentrated structure should be maintained in the future.[10] It was then left to the High Authority to deal with this politically very sensitive question within the framework of the ECSC Treaty as a legal and technical issue, and no longer as an issue of relative political power between nation-states. This informal mandate, reflecting the domestic choices of member-states, was finally decisive for the implementation of the ECSC's competition policy—much more than competition policy theory.

Alan S. Milward's work has been criticized for its 'state-centrism' and its focus on 'intergovernmental bargaining'.[11] However, this article aims to show that Milward's understanding of the role of supranational institutions and supranational law can in fact explain the outcome of policies, even where the role of supranational institutions is very strong, such as in competition policy. The potential role and tasks of supranational law

---

6. McGowan, *The Antitrust Revolution in Europe*. See Cini and McGowan, *Competition Policy in the European Union*, 15–37, for an analysis of the ECSC Treaty merger-control provisions.
7. Gerber, *Law and Competition in Twentieth Century Europe*, 342.
8. See for example, Lyons, 'An Economic Assessment of European Commission Merger Control'; Hildebrand, *The Role of Economic Analysis in the EC Competition Rules*, 72; Jones and Sufrin, *EC Competition Law*, 35; Cini and McGowan, *Competition Policy in the European Union*, 17. For the 'success' approach see McGowan and Wilks, 'The First Supranational Policy in the European Union'; and McGowan, 'Theorising European Integration', 13.
9. Warner, *Steel and Sovereignty*.
10. Palayret, 'Jean Monnet, la Haute Autorité de la CECA face au problème de la reconcentration de la sidérurgie dans la Ruhr', and Witschke, *Gefahr für den Wettbewerb*.
11. Kaiser, 'Transnational Networks in European Governance', 13 ff.

and institutions occupy a surprisingly prominent place in Milward's *The European Rescue of the Nation-State*:

> When states chose to advance policies by integration one of the advantages that resided in that choice was the greater irreversibility of commitment. ( . . . ) It offered a central enforceable law in place of international law which has never been enforced and whose weakness is also a prime weakness of most frameworks of interdependence.[12]

European law is seen here as a series of commitments made by the member-states. Supranational institutions have to enforce this commitment, which gives supranational institutions a central role in the integration process. This relationship can be modeled on the relationship of the 'principal' and the 'agent'.[13] Based on this model, 'principals'—here the ECSC member-states—delegate tasks and specific powers to an 'agent'—here, the High Authority of the ECSC—for its specific expertise and/or to monitor compliance. Both elements for explaining 'delegation'—monitoring compliance of commitments and specific technical expertise—apply in the field of competition policy. However, the principal/agent model also offers some propositions as to why there may be implementation problems of central enforceable law. The agent may develop its own preferences which meet the opposition of the principles. What happens when the delegated tasks are ambiguously formulated, for example due to a lack of agreement among the principals? Principals may also change their minds without changing the formal delegation to the agent. There are a number of possibilities under this scheme of how law may be implemented differently from that initially programmed once it had been delegated to the agent.

This is also reflected in Milward's terminology when calling the ECSC—in the *The Reconstruction of Western Europe, 1945–51*—a 'protoplasmic organization able to take any shape it wished according to the pressures on it from the nation states.'[14] This suggests a nonstatic view of the ECSC, which in fact may open the possibility of explaining why formal agreements are not enforced, or are enforced differently from that initially envisaged. Is there, as suggested, 'little correspondence between how institutions are supposed to function according to the Treaties and how they operate in practice'?[15] All this justifies taking a close look at the origins and the further implementation of a rule or a law. In order to

---

12. Milward: *The European Rescue of the Nation-State* (2000), 429.
13. Pollack, *The Engines of European Integration*, and '*Principal-Agent Analysis and International Delegation*'. See also Eckert, '*Between Commitment and Control*, and Kassim and Menon, '*The Principal-Agent Approach and the Study of the European Union*.
14. Milward, *The Reconstruction of Western Europe* (1984), 420.
15. Olsen, 'Reforming Institutions of European Governance', 592.

understand its implementation one has to look at the nature of the original mandate delegated by the principals to the agent. This means that the question of why the ECSC Treaty contained a merger-control provision has to be answered.

This chapter will therefore proceed as follows. First, it will look at the origins of the ECSC merger control article. Then, it will discuss the implementation of the ECSC merger-control policy during its first decade of existence, a decade which was dominated by merger requests from the steel industry in West Germany.[16] The chapter concludes that Milward's concepts of supranational institutions can be in fact very useful for such a historical analysis of policy implementation.

## THE ORIGINS OF THE ECSC COMPETITION ARTICLES

While there are detailed archival studies on the Schuman Plan negotiations, there are still different views as to why the ECSC Treaty included articles on competition policy, and especially on merger control. According to John Gillingham, the ECSC antitrust provisions were a means of gaining control over the deconcentrated industry structure in the West German steel industry: 'Monnet, in the name of the High Authority, was asserting the right to forbid re-concentration indefinitely.'[17] In fact, only two weeks before Jean Monnet announced the introduction of strong antitrust rules in the Paris Treaty, the Allied High Commission in West Germany, consisting of U.S., French, and British representatives, adopted a regulation in order to liquidate the old *Konzerne*, or trusts in the West German steel industry.[18] However, there are no signs that Monnet was already aware of the link between these two issues—deconcentration policy and the future competition articles of the ECSC Treaty—when calling for the first time during the negotiations for antitrust provisions.[19] Kipping, Gerber, Berghahn, Wyatts, and recently Leucht, interpret this initiative as the result of a common interest between the U.S. government officials, who wanted to introduce strong anticartel legislation in Europe, and Monnet.[20] They all wanted to

16. Spierenburg and Poidevin, *The History of the High Authority*, 293 ff.
17. Gillingham, 'Solving the Ruhr Problem: German Heavy Industry and the Schuman Plan', 422.
18. Griffiths, 'The Schuman Plan Negotiations: The Economic Clauses', 61–66.
19. Monnet to Schuman on 28 September 1950 in Monnet and Schuman, *Correspondance, 1947–1953*, 60–61. See also Kipping, *Zwischen Kartellen und Konkurrenz*, 216 f.
20. Kipping, *Zwischen Kartellen und Konkurrenz*, 214–222; Gerber, *Law and Competition in Twentieth Century Europe*, 342; Berghahn, *The Americanization of West German Industry*, 144 ff.; Wells, *Antitrust & the Formation of the Postwar World*, 173 ff.; and Leucht, 'Transatlantic Policy Networks in the Creation of the First European Anti-trust law'.

make a clear break with the European cartel practices in the steel industry, being convinced that intensive competition and the enforcement of the antitrust rules similar to those of the United States would contribute to a more dynamic economic development in Europe. If the proposed regulation allowed a certain control of the West German industry this would not be rejected although it was not the main aim of the regulation. Gerber and Leucht also point to the importance of the competition concept of *ordoliberalism* thinking which originated in West Germany.[21]

The negotiation history of the wording of the article in fact provides a clear answer to the question of why the ECSC Treaty included articles on competition policy, and especially on merger control. If the initial idea of Monnet in introducing antitrust articles aimed to counter a procartel stance in the negotiations, the antitrust provisions were soon seen as a device to control the further development of the Ruhr's deconcentrated steel industry. Compared with the initial draft of the article, presented by the French delegation on 27 October 1950, the role of the High Authority was substantially weakened in the final version. Moreover, the final text contained a 'non-discrimination' clause, which was introduced following a request of the West German delegation in order to allay fears of a 'Lex Ruhr'. Both elements are overlooked by Leucht and Kipping, who see only 'minor changes' in the wording of the articles during the negotiations.[22]

On the 27 October 1950 Monnet presented two draft articles, concerning merger control and anticartel provision, to the Conference.[23] It is known that American experts, such as Robert Bowie, Professor of Law at Harvard University and at that time legal adviser of the Allied High Commission in West Germany, contributed to the drafting of the articles. Concerning merger control, the proposition was very far reaching and would have meant granting an extremely powerful position to the ECSC supranational institution since all mergers had to be submitted for approval to the High Authority. The latter was to allow these mergers only if they were in the 'general interests of the economy'. Moreover, control of over twenty percent of the coal and steel market by one legal entity was completely forbidden. There was no indication of whether this percentage referred to control over coal and steel industries together, although they were actually quite different branches, or if it applied to each industry separately. The French proposition on mergers went far beyond the antitrust provision prevailing in the United States since the twenty percent clause, for example, would have led to a deconcentration of the steel industry in the United States.

---

21. Gerber, *Law and Competition*, 340 f., and Leucht, '*Transatlantic Policy Networks*', 68. See also, Giocoli, 'Competition vs. Property Rights'.
22. Kipping, *Zwischen Kartellen und Konkurrenz*, 222, and Leucht, 'Transatlantic Policy Networks', 68.
23. Leucht, 'Transatlantic Policy Networks', 64 f., and Witschke, *Gefahr für den Wettbewerb?* 51 f.

However, once on the negotiating table, the draft merger control article was soon brought into the context of the ongoing deconcentration debate of the West German steel industry. In parallel to the Schuman Plan negotiations, the Allied powers were discussing with the Federal government—and finally imposed on it—the deconcentration of the six most important steel groups, which had dominated the prewar German steel industry, as well as their limited ownership of coal mines. Since the French steel industry depended on imports of coking coal from the Ruhr, French industrialists were horrified by the idea that they would have to buy such an essential input from their main competitors. Hence the economic interest in deconcentration. Within the French Ministry of Foreign Affairs, the merger control provision was now seen as a means of maintaining the deconcentration of the West German steel industry. Monnet himself now started to advocate the merger article as a means of maintaining the deconcentration of the Ruhr steel industry—unlike his position at the end of September 1950 when he had qualified deconcentration as noncompliant with the principle of equal treatment of the Schuman Plan.[24] In a letter to Foreign Minister Schuman on 22 December 1950, he affirmed that the merger article would allow the High Authority to maintain the deconcentration of the West German steel industry.[25] Moreover, he also said that a 'reconcentration' of the West German steel industry would present a danger for future peace in Europe. Clearly, he was trying to use the European competition policy as a way of allaying political fears in French public opinion about German dominance of the new Community.

The West German delegation was of course opposed to this line of argument. It wanted to make sure that the ECSC Treaty would not freeze the deconcentrated industrial structure so that a reconcentration would be possible in the future. Ludwig Erhard, Minister of Economics, rejected the inclusion of any competition articles in the ECSC Treaty although he was trying to introduce similar legislation in Germany.[26] It is therefore difficult to identify the 'ordoliberal' influence in the negotiations. Hence, the West German government made clear that it would not accept the draft article proposed by Monnet as long as the result of the deconcentration policy was not fully known. The German position led to the negotiation of the contents of the anticartel provisions during the months of February and March 1951. When a solution advocated by the Allies—and especially by the United States—was finally accepted on 14 March 1951 the West German government also agreed to the antitrust articles during the Schuman Plan negotiations. The ECSC Treaty was thus signed one month later. The most important change introduced in the original anticartel provisions was that the High Authority was now obliged to allow all mergers of firms

24. Monnet to Schuman, 28 September 1950, *Correspondance, 1947–1953*, 60–61.
25. Monnet to Schuman, 22 December 1950, *Correspondance, 1947–1953*, 90.
26. Hentschel, *Ludwig Erhard: Ein Politikerleben*, 143 f.

provided the resulting entity did not fulfill a number of negative criteria (concerning price determination and distribution control). The burden of proof of the noncompatibility of a merger with ECSC law was now on the side of the High Authority. This was much more than a minor change.

Another important change compared to the initial draft was the introduction of the 'non-discrimination clause'. The wording of this paragraph changed several times in the last days of the negotiations, as the West German delegation tried to introduce 'legal arguments' to justify a rapid 'reconcentration' of the West German steel industry, which the French delegation tried to oppose. Therefore, the wording of article 66.2 is interesting—and particularly its second paragraph:

> The High Authority shall grant the authorization referred to in the preceding paragraph if it finds that the proposed transaction will not give to the persons or undertakings concerned the power, in respect of the product or products within its jurisdiction:
> —to determine prices, to control or restrict production or distribution or to hinder effective competition in a substantial part of the market for those products; or
> — to evade the rules of competition instituted under this Treaty, in particular by establishing an artificially privileged position involving a substantial advantage in access to supplies or markets.
>
> In assessing whether this is so, the High Authority shall, in accordance with the principle of non-discrimination laid down in Article 4(b), take account of the size of like undertakings in the Community, to the extent it considers justified in order to avoid or correct disadvantages resulting from unequal competitive conditions.[27]

This clause led to an interesting interpretation during the ratification debate of the ECSC Treaty in the German Bundestag.[28] The German government and the Chancellor Konrad Adenauer himself told the parliamentarians that this would allow the deconcentrated German steel groups to merge automatically to reach the size of companies in the ECSC member-states. As if the wording of Article 66 were only about company size! A totally different interpretation of the article was communicated to the French deputies when debating the ratification of the Treaty. Monnet stated that Article 66 would maintain the deconcentration of the West German steel industry.[29]

---

27. Article 66.2 of the ECSC Treaty (draft English text available at the official web page of the European Union: http://eur-lex.europa.eu/en/treaties/index.htm (accessed on 22 February 2011).
28. Witschke, *Gefahr für den Wettbewerb?* 72–78, and Poidevin, *Robert Schuman: Homme d'Etat, 1886–1963*, 284 ff.
29. Palayret, 'Jean Monnet, la Haute Autorité de la CECA face au problème de la reconcentration de la sidérurgie dans la Ruhr'.

In actual fact two contradictory interpretations were given by the governments of the two largest ECSC founding member-states to their ratifying parliaments: on the one hand the revision of deconcentration policy, on the other its maintenance. These were two politically conflicting goals which had no direct relationship with the actual wording of the merger article. Due to these different interpretations of the meaning of Article 66 we can speak of a formal mandate to the High Authority—consisting of the technical implementation of Article 66—and an 'informal mandate': it would be up to the High Authority to deal with the conflicting views of the two governments and in fact also to assume the responsibility for the future development of the steel industry in the Federal Republic of Germany.

In addition to this, there were other inconsistencies in the ECSC Treaty which raised doubts about whether the final version was really a breakthrough in competition law based on the U.S. influence. One of the criteria of Article 66 assessing the legality of a merger consisted in the future capacity of the merged company to 'determine' prices. This was in fact a surprisingly modern approach, in compliance with current economic thinking on antitrust, unlike that of the European Community merger regulation of 1990.[30] However, what is also often ignored by legal experts and historians is that Article 60 of the ECSC Treaty, dealing with the publication of prices, constituted in fact a basing point pricing system promoting market segmentation instead of market integration, which was illegal in the United States.[31]

Steel companies were legally obliged to publish their prices, which were quoted from a particular geographical location, the basing point, for example Thionville in France. The prices were charged to the customer including transport costs from the basing point. Competitors were not allowed to undercut the prices of companies from another basing point—unless they were quoting the same prices from their own basing point at their home market, excluding transport costs. Such a system enhanced implicit price collusion and market sharing, especially between neighboring countries with large domestic markets such as France and Germany. Companies would rather focus on raising revenue in their home market instead of starting a price war with an ECSC competitor in its own domestic market. In short: while the ECSC Treaty banned price agreements and mergers giving companies increased capacity to raise prices substantially, it also favored geographical market sharing through price collusion. This was of course a

30. Motta, *Competition Policy*, 13 f.; Bishop and Walker, *The Economics of EC Competition Law*, 54 f.; Etter, 'The Assessment of Mergers in the EC', 103–139.
31. Philips, *Competition Policy: A Game-Theoretic Perspective*, 119 f., and Duncan Burn, *The Steel Industry, 1939–1959: A Study in Competition and Planning*, 504 f. The effect of article 60 is not mentioned by Leucht, Kipping, or McGowan. See also Martin, 'Building on Coal and Steel'.

clear contradiction, but the wording of the Article 60.2(b) was so technically complex that its economic impact was probably not clear to everybody around the negotiating table:

> the prices charged by an enterprise within the common market, calculated on the base of the point chosen for the enterprise's price scale must not as a result of the methods of quotation:
> —be higher than the price indicated by the price scale in question for a comparable transaction; or
> —be less than this price by a margin greater than:
> —either the margin which would make it possible to align the offer in question on that price scale, set up on the basis of another point, which procures for the buyer the lowest price at the place of delivery;
> —or a limit fixed by the High Authority for each category of products, after consultation with the Consultative Committee, taking into account the origin and destination of such products.[32]

As the Treaty provisions themselves were contradictory, their implementation constituted therefore a real challenge, one open to pressure from the member-states. Hence, the implementation of the merger control clauses—especially in relation to the West German steel industry—will be analyzed in the next section.

## ECSC COMPETITION LAW IN PRACTICE, 1954–1962: A QUESTION OF INFORMAL DELIBERATION?

At the beginning of 1954, a consortium composed of companies from the French steel industry finally bought a coal mine in West Germany, thereby helping to alleviate their supply problems of coking coal. The real economic need for deconcentration measures from a French point of view had disappeared even before the merger policy of the High Authority became operational in May 1954, which corresponds to the adoption date of the implementation regulations of Article 66.[33] Thanks to this acquisition, the French steel industry also became part of the central selling agency for coal in the Ruhr area which was in fact a cartel and which the High Authority never managed to dissolve. During the first years of the High Authority, the application of the anticartel article against the existing coal cartels was

32. Article 60.2(b) of the ECSC Treaty (http://www.consilium.europa.eu/uedocs/cmsUpload/Treaty%20constituting%20the%20European%20Coal%20and%20Steel%20Community.pdf) (accessed on 22 December 2011).
33. Lefèvre, 'Les sidérurgistes français propriétaires de charbonnages dans la Ruhr'. See also Spierenburg and Poidevin, *The History of the High Authority*, 170 ff.

anything but a successful story; in fact, the coal cartels were never effectively dissolved.[34]

Regarding the merger provisions, the High Authority was soon faced with the question of reconcentrating the West German steel industry. In fact, the head of the competition department of the High Authority soon found that following Allied decartelization, the six biggest prewar steel groups were dissolved into a number of legally independent steel companies but that ownership ties often remained. When the first steel group, Mannesmann, asked for the authorization to reconcentrate, he came to the conclusion that the authorization by the High Authority was in fact not necessary because despite the Allied 'deconcentration' measures the 'independent' companies were still subject to one common ownership control.[35] However, by deciding that the Mannesmann group had in fact never been materially split up, the High Authority would have revealed that large parts of the Allied deconcentration measures had not been carried out, or at least, effectively implemented. Such an open disqualification of the measures carried out by the Allies over a period of several years was not of course politically viable. Therefore, the High Authority took the decision to authorize the merger, avoiding the delicate matter that the companies were already in fact a single entity due to the existing ownership ties.[36] The High Authority however also pointed out that this did not mean that all reconcentration requests would be automatically authorized. This was not a 'legal question', as mentioned in the minutes of the meeting of the High Authority, but a political decision.[37] Instead of investigating in depth the ownership ties in the deconcentrated West German industry, the High Authority legitimized by European law the reconcentration process of the West German steel industry on a case-by-case basis, in line with the implementing provision of Article 66 on ownership control adopted by the High Authority in early May 1954.[38] By 1958 the High Authority had dealt with about one hundred merger applications, nearly half of them coming from the Federal Republic of Germany, and none of them were rejected.[39]

---

34. Spierenburg and Poidevin, *The History of the High Authority*, 86–99.
35. Von Simson, 'Reflections on Jean Monnet's Skillful Handling of Member States and People during the First Years of the Community'.
36. Spierenburg and Poidevin, *The History of the High Authority*, 174 f.
37. Historical Archives of the European Union (HAEU), records corresponding to the High Authority of the ECSC (CEAB) 2/722 Records of the meeting of the High Authority, 22 December 1954.
38. ECSC High Authority Decision no. 24–54 of 6 May 1954 laying down in implementation of Article 66 (1) of the Treaty a regulation on what constitutes control of an undertaking; http://eur-lex.europa.eu/LexUriServ/LexUriServ.do?uri=CELEX:31954S0024:EN:HTML (accessed on 22 February 2011).
39. European Coal and Steel Community, High Authority, *Sixth General Report*, Luxemburg, 1958, vol. 2, p. 104. See also Spierenburg and Poidevin, *The History of the High Authority*, 291 ff.

This was of course contrary to what the French government had affirmed during the ratification process in the French National Assembly. It was Michel Debré, later to become French Prime Minister, but at that time member of the ECSC parliamentary assembly, who questioned the High Authority about the reconcentration. The High Authority stressed that it was applying the existing law according to the 'non-discrimination' principle.[40] Somehow the 'agent' pointed out that it was only executing its 'formal' mandate. It was also not responsible for unilateral statements by national governments during the ratification debate. During the discussion about the ratification debate of the Treaties of Rome in France, the process of reconcentration of the steel industry in West Germany was mentioned as an example of the 'weakness' of supranational institutions to stop German dominance.[41] The French government was also then reminded that the 'maintenance' of the deconcentrated structure of the German steel industry was promised during the debate on the ECSC Treaty. However, the ECSC merger policy had not so far provoked any direct intervention from any of the member-states' governments.

Things changed in 1958 when two groups, the August Thyssen Hütte and Phoenix Rheinrohr, both controlled by the Thyssen family, asked for the authorization to merge. This became the *cause célèbre* of the ECSC merger policy.[42] Both groups together represented the largest crude steel capacity in the ECSC. After long negotiations with the High Authority, the companies withdrew their application due to the unacceptable conditions tabled by the High Authority, which included a far-reaching control over investment. This was the first proposed merger which was not finally authorized by the High Authority. The interesting question is why this happened.

For the first time, the member-states intervened at least informally in the merger authorization process. After the companies had asked for authorization of their merger, the French government requested a discussion of the High Authority's merger policy in the Council of Ministers of the ECSC. At a meeting of the Council the German position was that the matter was of the exclusive competence of the High Authority. Minister Erhard, in a quite polemical way, also argued that the German government did not have to receive lessons in the field of competition policy.[43]

---

40. Diebold, *The Schuman Plan: A Study in Economic Cooperation, 1950–1959*, 369 f.
41. 'Le "Pool" Charbon-Acier, banc d'essai du Marché Commun', *Le Monde*, 23 June 1957.
42. Swann and McLachlan, *Competition Policy in the European Community*, 205.
43. Bundesarchiv (BA) B 102/22304 Embassy in Paris to Auswärtiges Amt (AA) in Bonn, 30 January 1959, B 102/ 22304 Ludger Westrick, state secretary at the Federal Ministry of Economics (Bundesministerium für Wirtschaft) to von Scherpenberg, state secretary at the Ministry of Foreign Affairs (Auswärtiges Amt).

The High Authority did not come to a clear-cut conclusion when assessing the proposed merger since its members were deeply divided.[44] The competition department, while pointing out that none of the 'negative criteria' of Article 66 were fulfilled, stated that it was a political decision to determine whether and under which conditions the so far most important merger in terms of size should be allowed.[45] The real political question was the following: after having allowed all previous 'reconcentration measures' in the West German steel industry could they now allow a West German steel company to become the largest company in the ECSC? Was it not time to set an example and reject a merger for the first time?

As the decision-making process in the High Authority was dragging on, ministers of the West German government wrote letters to their French counterparts asking them to support the merger. Chancellor Adenauer even asked Prime Minister Debré for his agreement.[46] Although the internal technical services of the French foreign ministry could not find an economic reason for a refusal, the conclusion from a political level was different. In January 1960 Debré informed Adenauer that he could not give his support to the merger.[47] Before the committee of foreign affairs of the French parliament, the French Minister of Foreign Affairs, Maurice Couve de Murville, publicly announced that the position of the French government was that it considered the proposed merger as an 'excessive economic concentration'.[48] If the High Authority was to allow this merger, it would also have to adopt other decisions to reduce the power of the new group.

This public statement of the French Minister of Foreign Affairs was criticized by Fritz Hellwig, one of the two German members of the High Authority, as an unacceptable interference from a national government in the High Authority's decision-making process. In any case, the members of the High Authority were deeply divided over the question of how to handle this case and spent a long time (March and April 1960) discussing the possibility of authorizing the merger subject to the Thyssen group submitting any of its future investments to the High Authority for

44. Spierenburg and Poidevin, *The History of the High Authority*, 530 ff.
45. HAEU CEAB 2/1656 Divisions Ententes et Concentrations, 'Rapport concernant la demande présentée par l'August Thyssen-Hütte AG en vue d'obtenir l'autorisation d'acquérir une participation majoritaire dans la Phoenix-Rheinrohr AG—Vereinigte Hütten-und Röhrenwerke du 19 octobre 1958', Luxembourg, 19 August 1959, 59 f.
46. BA B 102/35225 Franz Etzel, German Minister of Finance (and former member of the High Authority 1952–1957), to Antoine Pinay, French Minister of Finance, 14 September 1959, and B 136/8364 Chancellor Konrad Adenauer to Prime Minister Michel Debré, 30 November 1959.
47. Witschke, *Gefahr für den Wettbewerb?* 268 ff.
48. Archives de l'Assemblée Nationale, Commission des affaires etrangères, Séance du Mardi 8 mars 1960, 44.

approval.[49] This investment control of unlimited duration should then prevent the development of excessive economic concentration—although the legal service considered such a condition as noncompliant with the ECSC Treaty. The Thyssen group refused this option as unacceptable interference in the commercial policy and freedom of the company and, by consequence, withdrew the merger request.

The West German press reacted very bitterly when the Thyssen group finally withdrew the application due to the unacceptable conditions proposed by the High Authority.[50] The High Authority's policy was compared with that of the postwar occupation powers. In terms of the principal-agent model, since the Six—or in fact especially two of the member-states—had different, contradictory positions on these mergers, decision-making at the 'agency' level was very difficult indeed.

Mergers relating to the Thyssen group continued to preoccupy the ECSC authorities at the beginning of the 1960s.[51] The reconcentration argument then played a much less prominent role than in the 1950s, as the size of the steel companies continued to increase on the ECSC market. Both governments tried to deal with these questions through formal and informal bilateral contacts rather than through public statements. An essential point for the consideration of the mergers was now the concentration in the fields of flat steel and tin plate, one of the main products of the Thyssen group. The French government feared too strong a domination by the Thyssen group for these products, as West Germany represented an important market for French exports.[52] The final decisions of the High Authority on these mergers were in fact very close to what had been previously proposed in informal Franco–German bilateral contacts at government level, for example when the Thyssen group acquired the majority of shares of the tin plate producer Rasselstein AG.[53] This decision-making practice of the High Authority resembled the Milwardian expression of the 'protoplasmic organisation'.

In terms of competition law, the High Authority also realized that it faced a policy dilemma: one criterion of the relevant article was to assess whether the market power and the capacity to raise prices of the resulting firm had increased. However, steel prices were in fact still—formally

---

49. Witschke, *Gefahr für den Wettbewerb?* 276 ff., Spierenburg and Poidevin, *The History of the High Authority*, 711 ff.
50. The press reactions were the subject of an exchange of letters between the Thyssen group (August Thyssen Hütte or ATH), the High Authority, and the West German government. See documentation in BA B 136/8364 ATH and the ECSC, 27 April 1960, and Piero Malvestiti, president of the ECSC High Authority, to Chancellor Adenauer, 4 May 1960.
51. Spierenburg and Poidevin, *The History of the High Authority*, 534 ff.
52. AN (Archives Nationales, Paris) 331 AP (Archives personnelles) Pierre-Olivier Lapie, member of the High Authority, to Michel Debré, 21 July 1961.
53. HAEU CEAB 2/1317 High Authority, Records of proceedings, 27 September 1961. See also Witschke, *Gefahr für den Wettbewerb*, 294 ff.

or informally—controlled by the member-states, especially in France and West Germany, a practice against which the High Authority had never intervened decisively.[54] Under these circumstances, the High Authority was not able to apply Article 66 to the letter.

In the 1960s the public attitude toward mergers changed, especially in France. Once the reconcentration of the West German steel industry had been completed, the question ceased to be an issue which attracted the attention of public opinion in France or West Germany. With increasing global competition and the rise of exports from third countries into the common market, member-states favored market concentration in order to achieve economies of scale. They also favored price stabilization through cartels and coordination of production and investment. This was often accompanied by public aid, which was also in principle forbidden by the ECSC Treaty. These initiatives were prepared and implemented at the national level—either by governments or by industrial associations but without coordination at the European level. The High Authority refrained from taking any decisive action against these measures.[55] In West Germany, the High Authority tolerated privately organized cartels in the steel industry, and mergers were not subject to difficult approval procedures.[56] In France, there were important public aid programs for the domestic steel sector in order to foster investment.[57] It is quite interesting to point out that during the same period, the EEC competition policy started to develop, especially after the adoption of the antitrust-oriented Regulation 17/1962.[58] For such an important sector as the steel industry, the member-states, however, decided to pursue their own national strategic policies without European coordination and despite the antitrust provisions of the ECSC Treaty.[59]

## CONCLUSION

What does this short overview of the history of the ECSC merger control policy in its first two decades say in relation to the questions initially raised in this article concerning the protoplasmic nature of the ECSC according to Milward? The High Authority did not establish a sort of doctrine on mergers, or guidelines, which could have set an example for the further

54. Spierenburg and Poidevin, *The History of the High Authority*, 525.
55. Ibid., 595.
56. Ibid., 619.
57. Daley, *Steel, State, and Labor: Mobilization and Adjustment in France*, 93 ff.
58. Leucht and Seidel, 'Du Traité de Paris au règlement 17/1962'. As an example of a less successful implementation of EEC competition rules see Ramírez, 'La politique de la concurrence de la Communauté économique européenne et l'industrie'.
59. Mioche, *Les cinquante années de l'Europe du charbon et de l'acier*, 58.

application of competition law. Thus, the application of Article 66 did not result in a lasting contribution to the development of European competition policy and was soon forgotten. However, this does not mean that the merger policy was superfluous. Looking at the initial negotiations of the Schuman Plan, the member-states were not interested in a strong supranational High Authority, and certainly not in strict competition rules. The final wording of Article 66 was the outcome of a Franco–German dispute over the future structure of the West German steel industry rather than of an antitrust doctrine. It is therefore not surprising that Article 66 constituted a mainly Franco–German informal bargaining platform about the future of the West German steel industry. 'Domestic choices'—using Milward's terminology—determined the implementation of the merger control. However, this was probably much better for the European cooperation and integration process than an open conflict between the two governments. Therefore, Article 66 actually reduced the transaction costs for economic cooperation and integration between ECSC members. Although this was not the objective of the legal content of Article 66, this seems to have been the implicit objective of the negotiators.

As illustrated in this chapter, the principal-agent model is very useful both to describe the implementation history of supranational rules and policies and to analyze the respective weight of the member-states and supranational institutions in supranational decision-making. The analysis of the origin of a rule may already have important implications for its future implementation. As Milward pointed out, summarizing the state of the art of historical research on the ECSC, often undertaken by his own students, nearly two decades after the publication of the *The Reconstruction of Western Europe*:

> Not only was the supranational High Authority of the Coal and Steel Community subordinate to the major political interest of its member-states, but it had little or no influence on their policies. It was merely a channel through which national policies flowed. Nevertheless, this literature, whether conceived as political theory or history, does not regard the symbolism of the High Authority and the ECSC as hollow. It emphasises its importance to the achievement of the political goals of the participants. There was very little supranational governance emanating from the ECSC, but the existence of the supranational institution in itself was essential to what was achieved.[60]

Following this, supranational institutions and law represent instruments to coordinate national policies in times of economic and political

---

60. Milward, *Politics and Economics in the History of the European Union* (2005), 31.

interdependence. All this resembles somehow the 'protoplasmic organisation' and may explain why some policies develop and have influence, and others do not. The term may be quite provocative but seems appealing for a research agenda on the implementation of European policies and law.[61] If 'implementation is the continuation of politics by other means', it may be one of the fields where further historical research can make a crucial contribution to a better understanding of the European Union in dialogue with related disciplines.[62] Last but not least: it fits very well with the legacy of Alan S. Milward's scholarship on European integration.

61. For already existing compliance and implementation studies see, for example, Henrich-Franke, 'Gescheiterte Integration'; Mastenbroek, 'EU Compliance: Still a "Black Hole"?'; and Stephenson, 'The Role of Working Groups of Commissioners in Co-ordinating Policy Implementation'.
62. Bardach, *The Implementation Game: What Happens After a Bill Becomes Law*, 85.

# 14 The 1966 European Steel Cartel and the Collapse of the ECSC High Authority

*Charles Barthel*

On Tuesday, 14 December 1965, an unusual meeting took place at the headquarters of the European Coal and Steel Community (ECSC) on Place de Metz in Luxembourg. The ECSC High Authority officials met the envoys of the Steelmakers' Club, who had come begging for help in their fight against the drastic collapse of steel prices.[1] Reinforcing-steel, for example, which had been sold at $98 per ton before the outbreak of the overproduction crisis in 1961–1962, was now being bought at only $71 per ton. The price of other goods such as metal sheets had slumped even more spectacularly.[2] The increasing disorder inside and outside the Common Market was forcing most steelworks to offer their merchandise at below cost price. These multiple losses had reduced their cash flow to the point where they were being forced to postpone modernization of their production sites at a time when they should have been investing massively in order to catch up with their non-European competitors, who were busily engaged in expanding their activities.

The nine members of the ECSC High Authority were fully aware of the problem. Even the most reluctant were eventually compelled to acknowledge the persistent structural discrepancy between the demand for and supply of steel. They were less certain, however, about the remedy. They knew de Gaulle was convinced that the ECSC 'has the big fault [ . . . ] of being a supranational power', and they feared that in view of the French 'empty chair' policy, all initiatives on their part would immediately be blocked by the Council of Ministers.[3] Added to this was a further embarrassment: owing to the Merger Treaty, which had been signed a few months earlier,

1. Created on February 17, 1953, in Düsseldorf, the 'Steelmakers' Club' (*Club des Sidérurgistes*) grouped the national iron and steel producers of France, West Germany, Belgium, Luxembourg, Italy, and the Netherlands. See Funck, *Une Europe*, 1–8.
2. ANLux [Archives Nationales de Luxembourg], ARBED [Aciéries réunies de Burbach-Eich-Dudelange] 12572–12579: Columeta. Conférences des directeurs commerciaux, 1961 to 1968.
3. Spierenburg and Poidevin, *Histoire de la Haute Autorité*, 499.

the High Authority was due to be taken over at any moment by the Commission of the European Economic Community (EEC) in Brussels. This would explain why the ECSC president Dino Del Bo refused to entertain the possibility of proclaiming a 'manifest crisis' (article 58 of the ECSC Treaty) as a preliminary to imposing the market stabilization program drawn up by the Directorate-General for Steel. Nevertheless, his reluctance seemed to be a question of procedure rather than of principle, because he then 'appealed to the producers' self-discipline' and invited them to 'get prepared'. Obviously, he was loath to lay himself open to criticism, preferring the steel barons themselves to introduce 'production quotas without prejudice of what may happen later'.[4]

Although disappointed by the evasions of the High Authority, the industrialists used the rather ambiguous instructions given by Del Bo as an excuse to draw up, within weeks, the most complex and complete cartel that the continental heavy industry had ever witnessed. This flagrant violation of Community law, and its lethal repercussions on the ECSC High Authority's governance, is only briefly mentioned by Raymond Poidevin and Dirk Spierenburg in the last pages of their *Histoire de la Haute Autorité*.[5] The present case study not only tries to fill that gap, but also provides new evidence confirming Alan S. Milward's general interpretation of the real nature of the coal and steel pool.[6]

## THE EMERGENCE OF A CARTEL

The leaders of the Steelmakers' Club were not unprepared to take action, since they had already been trying out different forms of cross-border cooperation for four years. Initially, they had contented themselves with establishing an ordinary commercial committee. Founded in November 1961, it was supposed to transmit mandatory instructions to all the mills regarding export prices. The fixing of general sales conditions and contingents for deliveries to non-ECSC member states had also been at the center of talks started in 1962 with the intention of reviving the Brussels Agreement of 1953.[7] Along with the first attempts to syndicate several products, such

---

4. HADIR-CP [Hauts-fourneaux et aciéries de Differdange-St.Ingbert-Rumelange, Committee of Presidents], Réunion de la Haute Autorité avec les sidérurgistes à Luxembourg, 14 December 1965.
5. Spierenburg and Poidevin, *Histoire de la Haute Autorité*, 499.
6. See Chapter 10, 'The Schuman Plan', in Milward, *The Reconstruction of Western Europe*. For a detailed analysis of Alan Milward's further work on the ECSC topic, see the contribution of Ruggero Ranieri in the present volume.
7. Concluded after the end of the Korean War, when the demand for steel products dangerously slowed down, the Brussels Convention signed by most of the forges from five of the six ECSC member-states (Italian mills were not

as ripped bars, the negotiations finally led to the 'Devillez Memorandum'. Basically, this global settlement was a declaration of intent through which the ironmasters tried to restore order to the internal as well as external markets. While awaiting the implementation of a genuinely restrictive cartel for the casting of crude steel, the heavy industry proclaimed, on 1 November 1964, a 'steel truce' whereby the sales managers of all works having signed the agreement solemnly promised to stop unfair or downright illicit practices such as hidden discounts, the undercutting of the price scales deposited with the High Authority, or cheating as to the true destination of goods.[8]

In spite of the laudable resolutions taken and reasserted during countless meetings between leaders of national steelworking associations, each attempt to subject individual companies to common rules ended after a few months when, failing to see the beneficial effects of the new regulations and in view of the urgent need to fill the order books, more and more firms opted to act independently. Their dissidence explains why Charles Funck, the secretary general of the Steelmakers' Club, had since mid-1965 developed the very unusual idea of appealing to the ECSC in order to 'exceptionally and on a provisional basis allow businesses to conclude agreements intended to restore the Community's overall output [ . . . ] by fixing production limits. These authorizations [ . . . ] can only be targeted at those agreements whose application is controlled by the High Authority [ . . . ] and which would assure a fair distribution of the output among the different plants'. Consumers' interests were to be seriously taken into account as well.[9] But even so, the suggestion of freezing market shares met with a blank refusal by the supreme European coal and steel institution. As indicated above, Del Bo was certainly prepared not to look too closely at possible infringements of article 65 prohibiting cartels; on the other hand, he did not wish to risk lending his support to a guild of capitalists who were eager to use the ECSC to impose a private discipline which they clearly had increasing difficulties in imposing for themselves. The steelmakers were thus thrown back on their own devices when they tried to overcome the ultimate obstacles that were delaying the completion of the 'Outline Agreement' of 1966.

---

involved) only concerned sales outside the Common Market. The combine comprised minimum prices as well as delivery quotas. The creation of a common office in charge of collecting and redistributing export orders had also been envisaged, but never really entered into force. The cartel finally disbanded by the end of the 1950s. See Barthel, 'De l'entente belgo-luxembourgeoise à la Convention de Bruxelles'.

8. For further details on the cartelization process during the first half of the 1960s, see Barthel, 'Une "crise manifeste" jamais déclarée'.
9. HADIR-CP, Projet, June 1965; Note sur les problèmes de l'orientation des investissements, September 1965.

Conceived mainly by Jacques Ferry and his collaborators from the *Chambre syndicale de la sidérurgie française* (CSSF), this contract was endorsed for twelve months starting on 1 January 1966.[10] It is true that on that date, the definitive terms of the cartel had not yet been outlined. They were agreed upon and came into effect retroactively after a myriad of obstacles had been eliminated during endless and often heated debates. Some clauses were not even introduced until the first half of 1967, when the actual entente had already ceased to exist; they were used only for settling the accounts. Other contentious terms were never clarified because the arbitrators from an expert commission, led by Eric Conrot of the *Groupement des industries sidérurgiques luxembourgeoises* (GISL), failed to overcome their differences of opinion, despite the unoriginal character of the deal. In fact, its various components derived directly from the International Steel Cartel of 1926 and from the export sales syndicates of the 1930s, of which they represented a mere synthesis only improved 'on a trial basis' by some innovative elements that were meant, if not to resolve, then at least to mitigate the injustices inherent in the two models of the interwar years.[11]

One of the 1966 Outline Agreement's peculiarities was the normal values used to estimate the production limits to be allowed by the 'ingot steel agreement'. Instead of relying on accurate castings, the steelmakers adopted the average output estimates reported by companies in the Common Market to the ECSC High Authority and to the Organization for Economic Cooperation and Development for the years 1965 and 1966. The rather surprising choice of such 'arbitrary' criteria, which bore no relation to reality,[12] was dictated by the need to take into account the recently changed situation in Italy. Following the start-up of the Taranto plant, Italy, which used to import steel, 'had just become an exporter'. As a result, the *Associazione industrie siderurgiche italiane* (ASSIDER) would have contested the use of any 'historical' data.[13] Thus Ferry was obliged to advocate the adoption of 'available figures' from the statistical yearbooks of the two international institutions, though he regretted the necessity, saying 'We do not have any other'.[14]

Thereupon the classical struggle for production quotas started in a turbulent atmosphere, reminiscent of the time of Emile Mayrisch.[15] Delegates from the six ECSC member-states fought hard to obtain the best possible deals for their respective national groups. For two days, on 29

10. See Ferry's statement in an interview given to Philippe Mioche, in Mioche, *Jacques Ferry et la sidérurgie française.*
11. HADIR-CP, Rapport sur les travaux de la commission spéciale présidée par M. Conrot, February 1966.
12. Ibid., Réunion des présidents, Paris, 29–30 December 1965.
13. Ibid., 'Bericht über die Lage der italienischen Stahlindustrie [ . . . ]', 28 October 1965.
14. Ibid., Réunion des présidents à Bruxelles, 2 December 1965.
15. See for instance Nocken, 'International Cartels'.

and 30 December 1965, the professional chambers of France, Germany, and Luxembourg, which were united in a common effort to bring about a rise in steel prices through a drastic reduction of castings, had to confront the exorbitant demands of Ernesto Manuelli of ASSIDER and of Pierre van der Rest from the *Groupement des hauts-fourneaux et aciéries belges* (GHFAB), both concerned primarily with capturing extra tonnages for their plants. For his part, Pieter Bentz van den Berg of the *Nederlandsche Hoogovens en Staalfabrieken* in Ymuiden did not want to adhere to any kind of agreement that would slow down the production rate of his blast furnaces.[16] Given the very specific situation of the Netherlands, where there was only one big steel company whose output was moreover largely inferior to the local demand, the Dutchman flatly refused cutbacks that would have benefited the competing Walloon works and the German *Wirtschaftsvereinigung Eisen- und Stahlindustrie* (WVESI). A common denominator between the often diametrically opposed positions was thus hard to find. Eventually it was thanks to the talents of the head of *Aciéries réunies de Burbach-Eich-Dudelange* (ARBED), René Schmit, that a compromise was reached: in order to remain below the psychological mark of seven million tons, the absolute threshold for producing crude steel was fixed at 6,900,000 tons per month, shared out on the basis of 42.8% for Germany, 22.4% for France, 15.3% for Italy, 10.6% for Belgium, 5.3% for Luxembourg, and 3.6% for the Netherlands.[17] On the other hand, Hoogovens was exempted from paying the $10 penalty fee for each ton above the common 'tonnage program' on condition that this surplus was entirely geared toward the Dutch home market.[18]

The Italian steelmakers enjoyed similar compensations. The privileges they obtained were not so much due to any gap between the increase of domestic and export sales, as in the Netherlands, but rather an incentive for Manuelli and his fellow countrymen to subscribe to the Paris agreement. ASSIDER, whose output reached approximately 84% of the Italian production, alleged the 'insufficiency' of its quota as an excuse to give its backing to the agreement for three months only. Thereupon Armando Ceretti, the spokesman for the *Industrie siderurgiche associate* (ISA), entered the fray,

---

16. Besides his post as chief executive officer in Ymuiden, Bentz van den Berg assumed the presidency of the *Vereniging de Nederlandse Ijzeren Staalproducerende Industrie.*
17. Percentages in round figures. For the precise quotas, see HADIR-CP, Acier lingots: Décisions prises le 30 décembre 1965.
18. Ibid., Réunion des présidents, Düsseldorf, 1 January 1966. The monthly tonnage programmes constituted a projection that was meant to inform the works about the quantities they were allowed to produce and deliver without running a risk of being penalized. Although the system based on penalties had probably never properly worked, the Dutch group was supposed to pay a fine for its excess supply to other outlets within the Common Market and countries outside the ECSC.

asserting that six factories belonging to the confederation which he represented had 'never provided the High Authority with information regarding their production'. Because the figures transmitted to the ECSC had nevertheless been the basis for estimating the total from which the market shares were calculated, he now requested a surplus estimated at a minimum of 265,000 tons.[19] As his demand was refused, Ceretti promptly quitted the alliance. His termination of the contract was just in time to be used as a pretext by Manuelli to repudiate the intra-Italian solidarity. This meant that ASSIDER, as well as announcing that it would refuse to accept any responsibility for acts committed by ISA and the dissidents from Brescia, required its own market share, different from that laid down for the whole country. The temporary absence of a representative from the rival Italian association enabled him by the way to impose a reevaluation of his own share, henceforth fixed at 86.14%. In addition, he achieved an extra million tons reserved for the entire Italian industry. Without this increase of the global quota, so Manuelli claimed, the pressure put on him by ISA and the Brescians would become intolerable, and thus ASSIDER, facing rising losses, would also have to violate the international agreement. No sooner had he made his request than Ceretti hatched a new plot. In September 1966, ISA informed the president of the Steelmakers' Club that its plants would return to the fold on condition that they too obtained a surplus allowance of half a million tons per year.[20]

The Italian duo's ploy was so blatant that nobody was taken in. This is clear from the reaction of the iron and steel industry's hardliners from France, Germany, Belgium, and Luxembourg. Since the previous autumn, they had openly spoken in favor of breaking away from the troublemakers in Italy and the Netherlands. Rather than continuously exposing themselves to the threats of a minority of nonconformists who were granted generous privileges, they would prefer to continue an '*entente à quatre*', the more so since neither the Italians nor the Dutch had adhered to all the regulations related to the second pillar of the cartel, namely the agreement on rolled material.[21]

The six syndicates created for merchant bars, sections and broad flanged beams, thick and medium plates, metal sheets, hoops and wire rod were initially supposed to function according to uniform criteria set out by the Conrot Commission. But things did not turn out as expected.[22] In their

19. Ibid., Réunion des présidents, Düsseldorf, 28–29 January 1966.
20. Ibid., Rapport [ . . . ] pour la réunion du 12 octobre 1966; Réunion des présidents, Düsseldorf, 12 October 1966.
21. Ibid., Réunion des présidents. Bruxelles, 3 November 1966.
22. Besides the six syndicates mentioned, other cartels existed for some time for tinplates, galvanized sheets, steel sheet piling, and heavy railway material. These organizations had independent structures and were operating outside the outlined agreement of 1966.

haste to overcome grave differences and secure agreements as quickly as possible, the plenipotentiaries nominated for each specific product were prepared to abandon collective general rules in favor of variable norms, with derogations and opting-out clauses given either to particular manufacturers or to some national association. What emerged was a rather confusing patchwork of *à la carte* stipulations sometimes applying to all groups, sometimes to only a few of them. The coexistence of no less than three distinct reference periods to calculate the market shares is one example of the proliferation of divergent rules that governed the six product organizations.[23] This lack of homogeneity makes it impossible to document all the operations. We will therefore focus on a selection of key areas, even at the risk of oversimplifying an extraordinarily sophisticated structure.

A first observation is about the break with the tradition of prewar syndicates regarding the quantities to be taken into account. In the past, steelworks' production figures had been at the center of the industrialists' preoccupations, but now the tonnage shipped to clients was what counted. This new approach lent the agreement 'a character of greater realism'.[24] It simultaneously allowed the steelmakers to remove any unpleasant surprises due to the classic assessment errors prompted by the rerolling of semifinished products or the massive sale of finished goods either deducted from stocks or manufactured inside the ECSC with slabs, blooms, or billets coming from non-Community countries. In previous decades, both practices had engendered the 'sudden appearance' of large surplus tonnage, which ended up thrown on the market.[25]

Apart from this more pronounced market orientation, the 1966 syndicates made a clear differentiation between internal domestic sales: that is, within the area covered by the ECSC ('I'), and exports to other destinations outside the Community ('E'). The distinction was conditioned by the need to proceed to a 'harmonization I + E [which is] as complete as possible', without which GHFAB president van der Rest and his counterpart Schmit from GISL would probably never have joined the cartel.[26]

In contrast to their German and French competitors, the Belgian and Luxembourg works were indeed deprived of a large national home market where they could have sold most of their production advantageously. They were, however, the big winners of the Common Market. A simple glance at

23. The three reference periods were November 1964 to October 1965 for beams; beginning of the second term of 1964 to end of first term of 1965 for wire rod; and the average of a three-term cycle for merchant bars (October 1963 to September 1964, November 1964 to October 1965 and July 1964 to June 1965).
24. ARBED-P[residency], Club des sidérurgistes, 'Essai de contribution à l'étude de l'évolution des prix', September 1969.
25. HADIR-CP, Note [by Funck] sur les moyens d'assurer l'équilibre entre l'offre et la demande, June 1965.
26. Ibid., Réunion des présidents, Paris, 29–30 December 1965.

the statistics shows how during the fifteen years after the implementation of the ECSC Treaty, both GHFAB and GISL had more than doubled their shipments to the Federal Republic of Germany, and trebled orders collected in France.[27] The two smaller partners therefore defended themselves tooth and nail against the projects of WVESI and CSSF, which aspired to provide each group with a 'privileged position' in its home market by making its respective neighbors sign bilateral contracts through which 'interpenetration', that is, trade between countries of the European pool, was fixed at a maximum threshold that was not to be exceeded on pain of heavy fines.[28] Introducing such a *modus operandi* would obviously have driven the Belgian and Luxembourg groups toward increased activity outside the ECSC. However, such trade involved greater risks and generated smaller profits than the more lucrative intra-Community transactions. Before coming to an agreement with Ferry and Hans Günther Sohl of the *Gruppe Walzstahl*, GHFAB and GISL insisted on receiving some assurances.

This is precisely why a global 'I + E' quota was introduced. It was left to 'evolve with a certain flexibility, while a lower limit is fixed, from which coverage is granted. The guarantee comes into play from the moment that the actual share of a group loses a certain percentage (i.e., 2.5%) compared to the reference quota [ . . . ]. From that moment, this group will receive a compensatory tonnage basically allocated in orders taken outside the European Community. The other groups (above all those exceeding their allotment by more than 2.5%) will charge it to their export allocations. This compensatory tonnage will also benefit from special aid in order to allow the group concerned to attain an income corresponding to the average level of its business in the ECSC area and on export sales'.[29] The formula registered in the memorandum leading to the gentlemen's agreement meant that once the actual deliveries of one of the cartel's partners dropped below 97.5% of its theoretical allowance in 'I' and 'E', the other signatories would yield first the 'E' amount necessary to bring the gap down to 2.5% and, second, monetary compensation for the fact that rebalancing a loss suffered from 'I' would be accomplished by recovering less profitable 'E' business.[30] Besides a harmonization of the running of blast furnaces reached through the ingot steel settlement, the regulation of the product syndicates was thus seeking to establish an equitable equilibrium between both the factory outputs and the average revenue received by each company.

So much solidarity was, of course, not to everyone's liking. The Dutch persisted in refusing the least restriction on their home market, and likewise

---

27. Mioche, *Les cinquante années de l'Europe du charbon et de l'acier*, 44–45.
28. Without being generalized, similar agreements did already exist or were being negotiated between different countries.
29. HADIR-CP, Projet de mémorandum commun, December 1965.
30. Ibid., Accord-cadre—produits, janvier 1967, approuvé en principe le 3 mars 1967.

contested the transnational 'I + E' adjustment system. Consequently their participation in the arrangement was minimal. The same was true of the Italians. Because the peninsula 'has a natural geographic protection', the local producers were guarded against a flood of supplies from French, German, Belgian, and Luxembourg competitors.[31] Conversely, these latter suffered from massive competition from the Brescians, forcing them to distribute a growing part of their production in third countries. It is not hard to understand why, under these circumstances, neither Manuelli nor Ceretti were keen to bear the brunt of the damage done by their dissident compatriots. Participating in a mechanism of joint refunds and tonnage distribution which was mainly of benefit to their Northern neighbors was unacceptable, especially because ASSIDER's and ISA's exports were negligible, so that they would profit very little from the monetary compensation.

While the first two facets of the steel pact remained more or less a combine of the four traditional heavy industries, the corollaries designed to improve the cartel's stabilizing action were intended to operate in ways that could more easily be borne by the six national groups. This was the case for instance of a better coordination of export sales strategies through regular meetings between appointed experts within a commercial commission convened to assist the Presidents' committee of the Steelmakers' Club. It was the same with the introduction of 'standard prices' largely based on practices previously in use with the International Rail Makers Association (IRMA). Laying the foundations of a general approach to the trade policy to be followed in the future, these prices were decreed by each national group for its domestic market, and set the minimum that should not be undercut either by national producers or by those European partners who wanted to strike a deal on the territory of another member of the Common Market. As soon as these went beyond a certain preallocated sale volume, they were required to display a 'protection price' higher than the standard. In this way consumers—while still receiving the impression of lively competition—were imperceptibly induced not to buy from mills abroad.[32]

By turning price transparency and the free movement of goods into a farce, the industrialists had committed a 'mortal sin' in the eyes of the heirs of the order created by Robert Schuman and Jean Monnet.[33] Hence, if only to reestablish the legal power of the Paris Treaty and thereby the prestige of a supranational body that was visibly losing momentum, the majority of the representatives at the ECSC High Authority persisted in claiming that the wrongdoers should be punished. The irony of the story, however,

31. Ibid., Réunion des présidents, Düsseldorf, 12 October 1966.
32. HADIR-DC [Dossier confidentiel], Note sur l'organisation de l'exportation, 26 November 1966. Concerning the IRMA price regime, see Barthel, *Bras de fer*.
33. Mioche, *Jacques Ferry et la sidérurgie française*, 139.

is that instead of restoring the image of the first European community, the Eurocrats' crusade for law and order turned into a disaster.

## THE FAILURE OF ECSC ANTICARTEL ACTION

Barely one month after the famous meeting of December 1965 at the ECSC headquarters, MEP Paul Kapteyn set off the powder keg. Through a parliamentary question, this apparently well-informed Dutchman asked for details concerning that gathering: 'Is it true that the heavy industry recommended to the High Authority [ . . . ] the creation of a crisis cartel? Can the High Authority let us know if there have been attempts to promote a production syndicate, if it has worked satisfactorily and for how long it has survived?'[34] Three days later, one of Kapteyn's fellow countrymen took over. Acting as chairman of the Committee on the Internal Market, Cornelis Berkhouwer wanted to know if the people at Place de Metz were aware 'that in the Federal Republic of Germany an entente for steel plates, with production quotas and penalties, has been set up recently'.[35] Somewhat surprised by the judiciousness of the questioning, Del Bo and his teammates denied, or more exactly pretended 'not to be able to confirm the existence of a combine'.[36] The elusive vocabulary of the explanations, far from fooling anyone, offered journalists the scent of a scandal. Meanwhile 'attacks against the High Authority have been launched in the Dutch press which believes that the answers to the questions from Kapteyn and Berkhouwer do not give the impression that respect for the Parliament was close to the heart of the High Authority'.[37]

Pressure from outside ended up locking members of the ECSC executive in a dilemma from which they were unable to escape before they left office in the summer of 1967. Faced with the big question of how they should react to the prohibited activities of the steelmakers, their opinions were divided. What followed was a split within the apparatus of the Coal and Steel Community, with on the one side those that might be called the 'fundamentalists of the legal order' and on the other side the 'pragmatists'. Their discord

---

34. CEAB [Commission européenne, Archives Bruxelles] 2–3069, Question écrite num. 93 de M. Kapteyn, 11 January 1966.
35. CEAB 2–4138, Question écrite num. 94 de M. Berkhouwer [ . . . ], 14 January 1966.
36. CEAB 2–3435, Réponse de la Haute Autorité à la question écrite num. 94 de M. Berkhouwer, 3 February 1966. This was affirmed despite consistent reports received by the High Authority to the contrary; ibid., Note [by Linthorst Homan, the Dutch member of the High Authority] à l'attention de M. Lapie [the French member of the High Authority in charge of investigating the cartel], 14 December 1965.
37. CEAB 2–1367, Procès-verbal [henceforth: P-v] de la 858e séance de la Haute Autorité, 16 February 1966.

became evident to all when the high officials judged the 'Clabecq/Stabstahl-Vereinigung' case.

It so happened that the day after the meeting with the leaders of the Steelmakers' Club, Pierre-Olivier Lapie, who was responsible for the legal investigations of the pool, presented to his colleagues the final report of the enquiries conducted against the Walloon Forges de Clabecq and a syndicate of merchant bars producers associating twelve big German companies as well as the Burbach plant of the Luxembourg ARBED. Routine checks in connection with the construction of the 'Ausweichsitz' (read: bunker) of the German Federal government in the Ahr valley had in fact revealed to the inspectors of the High Authority irregularities committed by the main works in Germany. Firmly determined to exclude foreign competitors from public tenders financed by Bonn, they had entered a coalition to negotiate a contract for supplying reinforcing-steel directly with the main building contractor. Needless to say the terms of the agreement were contrary to the ECSC rules. To this was added a second and no less illegal combination with Clabecq. At that time the Belgian producer prepared a quite suspicious 10% cut of its prices, which were already exceptionally low. As soon as the news spread, the Stabstahl-Vereinigung became involved. Fearing that the new price reduction in the neighboring country would snowball and thereby lead to a worsening of the sales climate all over Germany as well, it bought several lots of ribbed bars and wire for a global amount of 6.79 million Deutschmarks from its Walloon rival, in return for Clabecq's agreement to freeze its official price list.[38]

Investigations by Community civil servants had clearly established the facts, so it only remained to agree on the action to be taken. But there lay the rub. Embittered by the low-profile policy pursued by the ECSC executive since the setbacks it had suffered in the late 1950s when the pool failed to save the collieries, Johannes Linthorst Homan, the Dutch member of the ECSC High Authority, aimed to at least restore 'our authority [ . . . ] regarding the facts that happened behind our backs, or still happen behind our backs, and to maintain our powers to implement the existing treaty'.[39] He wanted to set an example that would show the vitality of the ECSC as a supranational organ that was admittedly doomed to disappear, but was determined not to be led by the nose during the last months of its existence. Linthorst Homan made it into a personal matter. Given that competition lay within his portfolio, he felt directly affected by the intrigues of the industrialists. His obsessive conviction of being the target of the whole affair was further reinforced not only by his egocentric temperament, but

38. CEAB 2–1343, Artikel 65 zuwiderlaufende Absprachen auf dem Betonstahlmarkt, s.d.; CEAB 2–4138, Note à l'attention [ . . . ] des groupes de travail joints 'instruction' et 'concurrence', 28 January 1966.
39. CEAB 8–1386, Note [by Linthorst Homan] à mes collègues, 20 October 1966.

also by the fact that the harshest criticism leveled at the High Authority's pitiful anticartel policy emanated from European parliamentarians and journalists from his homeland.

While Homan was loudly calling for draconian punishments, his two German colleagues, Fritz Hellwig and Karl-Maria Hettlage, proved quite lenient with respect to the companies that had infringed the code of fair trade. 'While not opposing the principle of a sentence', they nonetheless wondered 'whether it would be advisable to exceed a purely symbolic penalty'? In connection with the shady Stabstahl-Vereinigung intrigues, the German members of the High Authority declared themselves in favor of mere 'prohibition' of the association's unauthorized activities. The Belgian Albert Coppé protested immediately. Since the Forges de Clabecq would certainly have to pay a penalty for breaching the price regulation, by what right could the German companies escape without being fined? Hellwig had an answer at the ready: according to the legal texts 'it is not possible to punish a professional association; the High Authority can only forbid its offending activities'.[40] His argument was irrefutable from a strictly formal point of view, yet it poorly veiled other considerations of a more private nature. By showing mercy toward the industrialists from the Ruhr and the Saar, the German certainly had his own future professional career in mind.[41]

Keeping relationships with the steel magnates intact was the tactic also supported by Del Bo. The Italian reasoned like a true politician. He would have preferred to let the storm pass, turning a deaf ear to the criticisms from Strasbourg and from certain media, because he was perfectly clear about two closely related notions. The first concerned the priorities of the High Authority. These did not consist of a punctilious application of a regulatory system invented by his illustrious predecessor, Monnet, but the urgent adoption of an overall emergency plan to combat the poverty that the factories and their employees were suffering from. In this respect the president was wise enough to recognize that his institution had neither the financial means nor the know-how required to achieve a recovery from a situation that had become alarming from the end of the winter of 1965. If they were to make any progress, it was crucially important to seek support from the people with practical experience and to work hand in hand with them. Del Bo's second argument derived from a concurrent aspect of the crisis: faced with the social fallout resulting from the fact that more and more companies were getting into increasing difficulties, each member-state of the Community was beginning to explore on its own ways to avoid layoffs

40. CEAB 2–1368, P-v de la 860ᵉ séance de la Haute Autorité, 2 February 1966.
41. Hellwig was not the only one looking after his future; most of the other members of the High Authority had to find substitute occupations for their posts at the High Authority that were doomed to be abolished.

and job losses. The High Authority was likely to be sidelined as the six governments refused to grant it the full powers without which joint action would be futile.

The proclamation of the 'manifest crises' as a prerequisite to concrete industrial measures orchestrated by the men at Place de Metz would in fact have required an '*avis conforme*', that is, the concurrence of the Council of Ministers. Reaching the necessary 'absolute majority' was, however, by no means a certainty.[42] On the contrary, the experience of the late 1950s, de Gaulle's current intransigent attitude and, last but not least, the feeling of many officials in all six countries that, for 'psychological reasons', it was not wise to openly speak of a 'crisis' (whether in economic or in European political-institutional terms), made it unlikely that the vote would be carried.[43] Del Bo thus inclined to an alliance with the steelmakers because 'if there is a logic in politics, the governments will find it hard to turn down anti-depression measures which the steel industry unanimously accepted and which the High Authority would support'.[44] In his view this was the only possible solution to escape a 'complete disintegration of the general Common Market'.[45]

Yet, instead of determinedly opting for the lesser evil and condoning the secret agreements between the steel companies in order to save the ECSC, the president of the High Authority and his colleagues Hellwig and Lapie thought that they could keep everybody happy by adopting a rather inconsistent approach: in deference to the Paris Treaty's legal principles, they chose to impose sanctions on the offending factories, but at the same time, for tactical political reasons, they avoided punishing the steelmakers properly by fixing fines that were ridiculously small compared to the fraudulent

42. The 'concurrence' of the Council was 'deemed to have been granted if the proposal submitted by the High Authority is approved [ . . . ] by an absolute majority of the representatives of the member States, including the vote of the representative of one of the States which produces at least twenty percent of the total value of coal and steel produced in the Community' (art. 28). Being aware of the various obstacles the proclamation of the 'manifest crises' (art. 58) might have encountered, some members of the High Authority imagined they could circumvent the difficulties by referring to article 95, which related to 'all cases not expressly provided' in the 1951 Paris Treaty. At first sight this alternative procedure seemed to be far more suitable to an initiative launched by the High Authority; it would have given the ECSC officials much more room for maneuver. Wehrer however warned his colleagues that recourse to article 95 required the '*unanimous* concurrence of the Council'. CEAB 2–1383, P-v spécial de la 884e séance de la Haute Autorité, 26–27 October 1966.
43. CEAB 2–4139, Compte-rendu de la réunion tripartite 'sidérurgie' du 6 juin 1966.
44. Réunion de la Haute Autorité avec les sidérurgistes à Luxembourg, 14 December 1965, cit.
45. CEAB 2–1381, P-v de la 878e séance de la Haute Autorité, 14 September 1966.

gains. Only Albert Wehrer dared protest against what was in his opinion a senseless strategy. The Luxembourger knew the steel barons' arrogance and propensity for hairsplitting. His friendship with the ARBED bosses enabled him to anticipate that it would not be the twenty or thirty thousand marks that their companies had to pay that would upset the industry magnates, but the fact that they were reprimanded by bureaucrats who had apparently nothing better to do than annoy an industry in distress with pernickety requirements 'prohibiting what would be useful, without offering remedies'.[46]

Wehrer was right. The chiefs of the national steel organizations invoked the Clabecq/Stabstahl-Vereinigung issue as grounds for refusing any future 'contact with the High Authority'.[47] Instead of participating in a new summit meeting convened for the end of March 1966, they sent representatives holding no real mandate. According to the insinuations in several documents, the delegates even walked out before the end of the conference, since the representatives of the High Authority had no concrete proposals but offered only reproaches.[48] The breach between heavy industry and the ECSC was complete. It lasted until the end of the year, notwithstanding the subsequent abrupt change in direction on the part of most of the nine High Authority members. As if suddenly alarmed by the consequences of their own procrastination, they proposed to 'halt the investigations that had been previously launched' because they now admitted that 'to resolve the crisis, the necessary discipline on the steel market implies the conclusion of ententes between producers'.[49]

Unfortunately the above about-turn came too late. In the meantime Kapteyn and Berkhouwer, in collusion with the Dutch MEP Henk Vredelink, had picked up new rumors spread in the Netherlands about the unorthodox practices of an international cartel for tinplates and the German Schiffbaustahl-Export-Kontor.[50] This time the parliamentarians would not budge. In front of the Strasbourg plenary they had announced that a public debate would be organized. It promised to become 'turbulent'.[51]

This new and unexpected development was undoubtedly grist to Linthorst Homan's mill. Unwilling to change his opinion, the Dutchman drew up five commandments for his counterparts concerning cartels: 'a) We are politically and legally obliged to find out each and every important fact; b) If these are not completely communicated to us, then we have to

46. Réunion de la Haute Autorité avec les sidérurgistes à Luxembourg, 14 December 1965, cit.
47. CEAB 2–1370, P-v de la 861e séance de la Haute Autorité, 9 March 1966.
48. HADIR-CP, Rapport [ . . . ] de la commission spéciale présidée par M. Conrot, 19 March 1966.
49. P-v de la 861e séance de la Haute Autorité, cit.
50. CEAB 2–4139, Note [by Jean Jaeger and Johannes Petrick], 28 April 1966.
51. CEAB 2–1373, P-v de la 867e séance de la Haute Autorité, 4 May 1966.

officially enquire; c) If the articles of our treaty offer a legal basis we have to act on that; d) If there is no legal ground [ . . . ], then we have to inform our member states of our problems; e) A deliberate oversight or failure to carry out checks cannot be an option'. The intimidating allusion conveyed above all by the last injunction is patently obvious; if the trio of MEPs managed to prove their allegations, then anyone at Place de Metz who had closed his eyes and plugged his ears would be unmasked as someone who had 'failed in his duty prescribed by the treaty and this could have, apart from moral considerations, serious *political* and *legal* consequences' (underlined by Linthorst Homan).[52]

The threat of being individually held guilty of serious professional misconduct weighed heavily on the members of the High Authority. It diluted the collective nature of ECSC governance and provided an opportunity for any one member, temporarily, to take his colleagues hostage by imposing a policy that the majority disagreed with but was forced to follow, because Linthorst Homan took every opportunity to 'formalize' his personal convictions by promising the Strasbourg Assembly and the press that he would shortly make known the truth about the cartels. Suffice to say that Lapie's inspectors were obliged to recommence their inquiries inside the steelworks. Their findings quickly revealed the full extent of the phantom ECSC built up by the industrialists; the confiscation of the minutes of 'at least 60 meetings' of managers at a European level and of 'hundreds of preliminary and executive meetings' allowed the officials to paint a true picture not only of the structures and functioning of several specific combines, but also of the crude steel and product cartel itself.[53] Nevertheless, the price paid for collecting these clarifications was very high. Since the industry reacted to the resumption of investigations by 'refusing to provide information', the High Authority, at the risk of losing face, was compelled to respond by prosecuting those companies that declined to deliver accurate data. They thus became more and more mired in a conflict carried on with 'childish glee'.[54]

This could not continue, for various reasons. First, the absurd spiral of measures and countermeasures would bring the ECSC into disrepute. Although the inspectors had plenty of clues about the world of gentlemen's agreements, it would take 'a vast and long procedure of perfecting and completing the checks' in order to obtain irrefutable evidence that would

52. CEAB 2–4138, Aufzeichnung für den Herrn Präsidenten der Hohen Behörde, 9 February 1966.
53. CEAB 2–3436, Rapport intérimaire sur les résultats des contrôles, 12 August 1966.
54. Ibid., Note des membres des groupes de travail 'instruction' et 'concurrence' 5 October 1966.

lead to indictment.[55] Would the investigators find such proof? Would they discover it in time, before the departure of Del Bo and his colleagues? Nothing was less certain. Then, in addition to completely poisoning the atmosphere in Luxembourg where lower-rank employees did not hesitate to vilify the inconsistent and contradictory policy of their superiors, the cartels' issue paralyzed the development of a joint action plan for the forthcoming Council of Ministers on 22 November 1966. The 'special group', for example, which had been created to hasten the development of a series of improvements to help the industry control the crucial problem of excess production capacity, made no progress at all because of the almost permanent quarrelling between Roger Reynaud and Hellwig on the one side, and Linthorst Homan on the other side. While the latter, either on principle or for revenge, bypassed the powerful steelmakers' organizations wherever he could, the Frenchman and the German did not want 'to give up cooperation with the professional associations'.[56] Their growing discord became apparent in the quarrel about production forecasts. Up to then, the quarterly statistics were collected in each country by the respective steel producers' associations (such as WVESI, CSSF, GHFAB, etc.) before they were transmitted to Luxembourg. Linthorst Homan objected to this practice, suspecting that the national associations were abusing their role as mediators to 'operate a distribution of the production by company, which would run counter to the provisions of article 65'.[57] He therefore requested the Community to contact each individual plant directly in the future, although he knew perfectly well that this would take an extraordinary amount of time in the absence of a sufficient number of ECSC civil servants. On the opposite side, Hellwig and Reynaud wished to speed up the publication of such important figures to guide the companies in refining their investment projects.

Last but not least, Del Bo and the moderates feared the rise of a peril that they considered to be far more worrying than the cartel phenomenon: namely the resurgence of the nations. Hellwig, Wehrer, and Lapie were able to see the impending danger for themselves when, as part of the preparations for their meeting with the ministers, they made the round of the capitals of the Six. Everywhere they had warned governments that their restructuring plans, focusing on an isolated industrial region or on a single country, were in flagrant opposition to the spirit and letter of the ECSC Treaty, but nobody had paid much attention to their warnings. Since then the obsessive fear of a 'break-up of the Common Market' had never left the president of the High Authority. Meanwhile Del Bo had found out in

55. CEAB 2–4014, Projet de rapport à la commission du marché intérieur du Parlement européen, 11 January 1967.
56. CEAB 2–1388, P-v de la 903e séance de la Haute Autorité, 12 April 1967.
57. CEAB 2–1384, P-v de la 886e séance de la Haute Autorité, 16 November 1966.

a private conversation with Ferry that most associates of CSSF seemed to 'share his preoccupations'.[58] Was the specter of nationalization able to forge an alliance between the High Authority and the Steelmakers' Club against excessive government supervision?

To ask the question was to answer it. Linthorst Homan was pushed aside without further ado. He was given permission to take out his frustrations on the German Schiffbaustahl-Export-Kontor; on the other hand, the international crude steel regulation and the six product syndicates were declared off-limits. This was the *conditio sine qua non* for the steelmakers' return to the conference table at Place de Metz on 15 December 1966.

## THE OUTCOME OF A FAILED EXPERIMENT

The resumption of the dialogue between the Steelmakers' Club and the High Authority after a silence of 366 days left its mark. Distrust remained on both sides, with good reason. The business leaders' new docility did not proceed from any kind of awareness that they had acted wrongly before. The true reason for their rapprochement with the ECSC was that, all things considered, their cartel arrangements were unlikely to survive. According to the existing contracts, the entente should have been renewed before 1 October 1966. Excessive claims put forward by some companies during the preliminary discussions indicated that the national envoys would at best reach a 'moral commitment' by which the different groups would promise to avoid 'doing anything stupid'.[59] For lack of proper private agreements, it might therefore seem appropriate to place their activity again under the tutelage of Del Bo's team, even if only to throw responsibility for the failure of crisis management onto the ECSC.

'Reconciliation' with the High Authority held a further advantage. After the above-mentioned Council meeting of 22 November 1966, the ministers decided to create an *ad hoc* committee initially composed only of government officials and ECSC representatives. Their task was, among other things, to submit 'concrete intervention proposals' to restore the balance between supply and demand for steel.[60] Would it therefore not be in the interests of the industrialists to move closer to those they had ignored for a year? Their self-exclusion from the European policy-making process may have seemed worthwhile as long as their cartel fortress remained more or less intact; but now they found themselves completely isolated. If they wanted to avoid crucial decisions about the future of their mills being made without their knowledge and support, their only option was to hasten the

58. P-v de la 878e séance de la Haute Autorité, cit.
59. HADIR-CP, Comité des présidents, Paris, 6 July 1967.
60. CEAB 2–4013, Note pour Monsieur le président de la Haute Autorité, 14 December 1966.

'normalization' of their relations with the ECSC staff in order to ensure joint representation within the new crisis management unit. The maneuver was successful thanks to the support of a majority of High Authority members who still believed, somewhat naively, that they could use the steel magnates to defend Schuman's Europe against a Europe of nation-states.

The supporters of supranationalism had unfortunately failed to notice that the views of the business leaders had changed. If, a few months earlier, they had seriously 'preferred common solutions to unilateral government solutions', this was no longer true at the beginning of 1967.[61] Meanwhile the inability of the High Authority to exchange its sterile dogmatism for a real industrial policy had made the steelmakers shift their ground. Especially in the bigger countries, they were now counting on the subsidies granted by national planners in order to keep a maximum number of workers active on a maximum number of sites. Cross-border coordination of plans for modernization and restructuring obviously did not find a place within this kind of thinking. Moreover CSSF, WVESI, and ASSIDER were inclined to use their participation in the *ad hoc* committee as a Trojan horse to undermine those who, in the name of European solidarity, wanted to deprive them of the windfall of public funds. The fundamental challenge facing the Community—overcapacity—still remained unresolved. The steelmakers were unable to find a solution to this problem, nor did they succeed in reviving their cartel practices before the predictable catastrophe of the 1970s.

As for Del Bo and his 'team', they had trapped themselves. Their internecine quarrels over the cartels had cost them the last chance to end their mandate brilliantly. But this distressing result of their European Rescue attempt certainly would not be much of a surprise to Alan S. Milward: after all, fifteen years of European experience had left no noticeable mark on the behavior either of the six governments, or the industrialists, or those at Place de Metz who supposedly acted as supervisors. Aware of its own weakness, the ECSC High Authority did not even try to use the powers provided for in the Paris Treaty. Instead of acting as a form of collective governance, something which remained wishful thinking, the personal quarrels inevitably led to a capitulation in favor of the merely national interests pursued by the steelmakers, whose rather antiquated and ineffective cartel practices in the end paved the way for a return to the very classic attitude of 'every country for itself'.

61. HADIR-CP, Comité des présidents, Bruxelles, 2 December 1966.

# 15 Was It Important?

## The United States in Alan Milward's Postwar Reconstruction

*Federico Romero*

Eager and wary at the same time, I did not know what to expect when I got down to rereading, twenty years or so later, Alan S. Milward's main works on Europe's postwar reconstruction and integration.[1] I must disclose that my reading is inevitably affected by recollections of the countless discussions we had in the years when I collaborated closely with Alan, at the European University Institute and then at the London School of Economics, from 1984 to 1990. Memories appear to provide insights, but how can they be trusted? They emerge through a hopelessly uneven mist. A few images stand out crystal clear, convincingly (or deceptively?) persuasive. But I am aware that they may well be warped, since many more are fuzzy or wobbly. All of them therefore project more than a shade of uncertainty.

At any rate, my early rereading impressions were diverse. Some of his theses and topics obviously look less central today. Several arguments maintain a surprising relevance, or have become so deeply embedded in subsequent historical interpretations that we now take them for granted. More importantly (or perhaps just unexpectedly), threads that did not stand out at the time now acquire an unforeseen visibility, consequently drawing more attention.

As far as the role of the United States is concerned, one has got to go back to the peculiar historiographical context Milward (as well as everybody else, of course) was contending with, at the time when he was writing *Reconstruction*. For well over a decade American historians of the cold war, of U.S. foreign policy, and of U.S.-European relations had been transfixed by the polarized, rigid, and mutually exclusive narratives of

---

1. Alan S. Milward: *The Reconstruction of Western Europe, 1945–51* (1984); 'Was the Marshall Plan Necessary?' *Diplomatic History* 13: 2 (Spring 1989): 231–253; *The European Rescue of the Nation-State* (1992); and (with Lynch, Ranieri, Romero, and Sørensen) *The Frontier of National Sovereignty: History and Theory, 1945–1992* (1993).

orthodoxy and revisionism.[2] The former posited a benevolent projection of American power meant to save the world, and Europe to begin with, from an impending Soviet threat to liberty and democracy. The latter focused on the sources and mechanisms of a U.S. imperialist expansion aimed at rescuing global capitalism, preventing or choking revolutionary challenges, and conquering new markets.

The origins of the cold war and of the postwar Western world were therefore framed by two mirroring abstractions driven by contending morality tales. This was hardly conducive to open-minded historical enquiries on the actual dynamics of reconstruction, the mechanisms of alliance formation, and the complex web of relations and interactions that linked together a multiplicity of actors in the postwar Euro-American world.

By the late 1970s the Vietnam-era ideological battles that had animated that contest were exhausted. Most historians had grown weary of such introverted, self-referential dueling. The increasing availability of archival sources was opening up new possibilities, and a postrevisionist approach gained rapid ground, so much so that by the early 1980s it would be canonized as an innovative, sophisticated synthesis on the origins of the cold war. Postrevisionists (always an uneven galaxy rather than a cohesive trend) accepted a broad, if vague, notion of empire. The American one was, many of them would argue, of a 'defensive' nature, an empire endowed with enormous resources but also an inbuilt 'sense of restraint.'[3] More importantly, it was assumed to be a highly successful and efficient one, as the strategic, economic, and diplomatic record of the postwar period testified. Wary of the pitfalls incurred by the previous generation of American historians, postrevisionists eschewed any exceptionalist rhetoric, but they also avoided comparisons with other experiences of empire. Never openly conceptualized, the assumption that the international projection of U.S. power had such a peculiar, nation-specific character as to be virtually unique was nonetheless ubiquitous and shaped the overall research effort of American diplomatic historians. Their intellectual thrust and research agenda concentrated on the internal determinants of U.S. policies—domestic politics, interest representation, institutional infighting, strategic culture. Very little energy was channeled into studying 'the impact of U.S. policies on foreign societies', which remained a stated but quite elusive aspiration.[4]

These features were quite visible in the emerging studies on U.S. economic policies toward postwar Europe, and primarily on the European Recovery Program (ERP), a subfield that by the early 1980s was growing quite rapidly, and with good reason. The Marshall Plan was perceived as the most effective and enlightened pillar of containment, the key to America's successful waging

---

2. Best exemplified respectively by Schlesinger, 'Origins of the Cold War', and Kolko and Kolko, *The Limits of Power.*
3. Gaddis, 'The Emerging Post-Revisionist Synthesis', 182.
4. Ibid., 187.

of the cold war in Europe. It epitomized a distinctly American approach to alliance formation and to the construction of international hegemony. It was also the most appropriate ground upon which to refute the economic determinism of earlier revisionist writers, because it stood out as the exemplary instance of America's propensity to use economic resources in order to achieve (noble) political goals, rather than the (despicable) imperialist habit of using military might to pursue selfish economic interests.[5]

These new studies were quite removed from the apologetic, almost heroic Marshall Plan narratives constructed by an earlier generation of participants and contemporary observers.[6] But by focusing primarily on origins and intent—on visions, plans, and ideas rather than results and accomplishments—they neither confirmed nor dispelled the inherent assumption that the Plan had been an unrestrained success, which continued to hang around untested, and therefore uncontested.[7] Attempts at measuring not only U.S. power but also the contours and limits of its influence were rare.[8] The insight that, with the advent of the Marshall Plan, the West Europeans had acquired 'the power to frustrate America's traditional vision of a liberal economic order, for their very survival depended on the creation of a regional economic bloc' (and the fate of containment of course depended on their survival and well-being), stood out as virtually unique.[9] American literature of the time was largely oblivious to the role, actions, motives, and influence of European reconstruction's other actors.

It was this scholarly landscape that Milward had in his sight while preparing *The Reconstruction of Western Europe, 1945–51*. He certainly spared no punches in lambasting 'the lamentable standard of American historiography of the post-war period.' His main objection was that 'the more American diplomatic historians insist that the economic dimension was crucial to post-war foreign policy, the less effort, however, they make to understand what the economic problems actually were.'[10] In his view this was much more than a methodological and disciplinary flaw. It was a major intellectual failure, an epistemological sin against his document-based, evidence-driven, knowledge-enhancing conception of history and scholarship.

---

5. For this argument and intent see especially Pollard, *Economic Security and the Origins of the Cold War*.
6. The classic cases are Price, *The Marshall Plan and Its Meaning*, and Jones, *The Fifteen Weeks*.
7. See Jackson, 'Prologue to the Marshall Plan', and Hogan, 'The Search for a "Creative Peace"'.
8. An early, partial, tentative attempt in Rappaport, 'The United States and European Integration'.
9. Barnet, *The Alliance*, 108.
10. Milward's review of *Economic Security and the Origins of the Cold War*, by Pollard, *The Slavonic and East European Review* 65: 3 (July 1987), 493–494 (for both quotations in the paragraph).

There were exceptions, of course, and Milward entertained an open dialogue with them. But quite symptomatically, they pertained to different, if adjacent, fields. Economic historian Imanuel Wexler assessed the Marshall Plan's effectiveness. He restated the standard interpretation of an overall success on the basis of the growth rates, production increases, foreign trade expansion, and investment trends attained in Europe. But he also saw the persistence of trade imbalances, the slow growth of private consumption, and the lack of integration. Thus, Wexler tended to deflate the notion that American aid had reshaped Europe: 'the basic structure of Western Europe's economy and polity [ . . . ] remained essentially the same as it had been at the start of ERP.'[11] Milward had several substantial disagreements with Wexler's views, but quite characteristically he praised his 'pioneering work' as 'the first systematic history based on documentary evidence.'[12]

The second, far more influential exception was the work on the political economy of Europe's postwar stabilization by Harvard historian Charles S. Maier, who saw in the New Deal mix of Fordist production and consumption, social coalitions for growth, and a culture of prosperity the template for the 'politics of productivity' which reshaped western European society by sidelining radical antagonism.[13] Here the recipe emerging from the American experience, and its deliberate projection abroad within the mechanisms of the European Recovery Program, was central. But the very concept of the 'politics of productivity' shifted the focus of enquiry to the local actors, to the type of solutions and compromises that governments, political parties, and interest representation groups would engineer in recipient countries. Therefore it opened a bridge, which many scholars would later try to explore in detail, between the American project and its segmented, mediated, often limited and compromised impact within various, and rather different, national contexts.

Broader in its historical reach and intellectually more sophisticated than most contemporary musings on American influence, Maier's approach elicited a nuanced response by Milward. There was agreement on the model's appeal. 'America became the cynosure of European eyes, a land of plenty, safety and democracy', Alan concludes in *Reconstruction*, and '[w]ith such a model before its eyes and safe only in a close alliance with it, [ . . . ] European political opinion increasingly emphasized productivity and growth [ . . . ] as the answer to political governance in the post-war world.'[14] There was also a common ground in the crucial role attributed to the local coalitions of political, economic, and social actors as the decisive agents of

11. Wexler, *The Marshall Plan Revisited*, 253.
12. Milward's review of *The Marshall Plan Revisited*, by Wexler, *The Journal of Modern History* 57: 2 (1985): 341–343.
13. Maier, 'The Politics of Productivity'; see also Maier, 'The Two Postwar Eras'.
14. Milward, *Reconstruction*, 487.

reconstruction, and therefore as the focal point of historical enquiry. But Milward seemed to conceive of American cultural influence as a factor operating primarily in the public arena, in the realm of intellectual debate and ideological constructions—if not plain electoral posturing—rather than in political and economic decision-making. 'The "politics of productivity" [ . . . ] were every bit as useful to European politicians hoping to back a central political position', he wrote, but 'the forces within those countries pursuing the same goals were usually much stronger and had much more effective weapons to hand than the ECA.'[15]

Here we come to the true bone of contention, that is, agency. Who drove reconstruction, devised its political and institutional recipes, and engineered its compromises? Which actors and factors weighed more decisively in shaping the complex interdependence that defined the postwar Atlantic world? Milward's work never touched upon the strategic and ideological framework of the emerging cold war. Not because he deemed it irrelevant or secondary, but because he took it for granted as the overall determinant of the geopolitical map. He simply assumed that the United States pursued the strategic goal 'to develop a bloc of states which would share similar political, social, economic and cultural values'.[16] But containment was not his topic. Always mindful of its crucial importance, and of decisive U.S. power in the realm of security strategies, he just left its investigation to other scholars.

Nor can it be plausibly argued that he underestimated the enormous might and relevance of the American economy. No economic historian could possibly do that. Besides, he had previously stated that the productive effort in the United States was 'the most influential consequence of the Second World War for the post-war world,' and his earlier discussion of the postwar outlook for the international economy revolved around the centrality of American output, trade, capital flows, and policies for a multilateral order.[17]

Thus, when Milward controversially argued that 'Marshall Aid did not save Western Europe from economic collapse' and that 'Marshall Aid was not in fact important enough to give the United States sufficient leverage to reconstruct Western Europe according to its own wishes,'[18] he was not so much devaluing American power, or undermining the notion of its crucial

---

15. Ibid., 124. A few years later, when reviewing a collection essays by Maier, *In Search of Stability*, Milward argued that the formation of the new postwar coalitions 'preceded the ideology of productivity which justified them' and which should therefore perhaps be seen as 'a later justification of a general shift in the balance of political power in capitalist society'. Book review published in *The Journal of Modern History* 62: 1 (1990): 105–108, here 108.
16. Milward, *Reconstruction*, 123.
17. See Milward, *War, Economy and Society*, 63 (quotation) and 329–365.
18. Milward, *Reconstruction*, 465–466 (first quotation) and 469 (second quotation).

role in the postwar era, as qualifying it and contextualizing it. That is to say, he was historicizing it, and doing so with three major motivations and goals. The first was contingent and related to the contemporary historiographical debate. The second concerned his epistemological and methodological approach to history. And the third one encapsulated his most original (and enduring) interpretative contribution.

Perched on opposite ideological slopes, American orthodox and revisionist writers nonetheless shared a common ground. Its contours were defined by U.S. ideals or power, morality or domestic arrangements, strategic or economic ambition. Outside those boundaries there were adversaries, contained or overpowered, but everybody else appeared only at the margins, passive entities seen either as recipients of America's benevolence or helpless objects of its imperial projection. Even postrevisionist scholars rarely rose above this introverted, inherently exceptionalist intellectual framework. While dissecting the sources, nature, and thrust of U.S. postwar international projection, they assessed agreements, alliances, and multilateral arrangements as tools of America's policy. However, they seldom delved into their inner working and actual dynamics, neglecting their inherently interactive nature. Benevolent, oppressive or defensive, the American empire remained a one-way affair, whose strength and effectiveness flowed outward, seemingly independent from the allies it reached, the feedback it got from other actors, the interactions that ensued.

Milward's *Reconstruction* moved deliberately against this *deus ex machina* approach to postwar European history and overturned it.[19] Instead of a single overpowering force armed with a dazzling model, his scene was dominated by bargaining among multiple actors, mediations and compromises, solutions achieved by detours and give-and-take. Agency was not monopolized but diffused and fragmented, with key political resources distributed unequally but widely. The end result was a complex system of multilateral, internally differentiated interdependence that bore little resemblance to Washington's original plans but could still (and actually better) suit America's main strategic aims precisely because it accommodated the other actors' needs and goals. 'In place of a liberal unified Europe came a closely regulated Little European common market [ . . . ] Western Europe made its own peace settlement. [ . . . ] it created an alternative pattern of reconstruction, a restricted but workable institutional framework for economic interdependence which has proved more effective than any previous peace settlement. There is very little to say that this was not in the end the best solution for the United States too.'[20]

Iconoclastic and occasionally abrasive in his polemical drive, Milward was shifting the focus of enquiry onto the political economy of the Western

19. I am borrowing the simile from Gilbert, 'Partners and Rivals: Assessing the American Role', 178.
20. Milward, *Reconstruction*, 476–477.

European nations. In doing so, however, he was also positing a more nuanced and realistic notion of hegemony in the Atlantic world, which transpires from his texts although he never fully articulated it. U.S. ability to reorder the international economic system, coalesce the Western alliance, and erect a functioning architecture of containment did not flow automatically from its military and economic might, nor from its postwar visions and plans ('long-run dreams which had only an impossibly short term to be turned into realities'). It had to be constructed with flexibility, policy shifts, and adaptations, in a constant dialogue with other governments, until it came to rely on 'a framework acceptable to the European states'. The key to success, then, was interaction, convergence, and adjustment, since 'the leverage which Marshall Aid gave to the United States in matters of grand policy was small unless it were coupled to genuinely powerful political forces in Europe.'[21]

It was a conceptual breakthrough, criticized by American diplomatic historians as a new 'European revisionism' based on an 'implicit trivialization of the American connection with Europe'[22] or uncomfortably recognized with numerous reservations.[23] The wide, controversial, but deep impact it had on historical studies on postwar Europe—in economic and political history, and of course in the history of European integration—need not be recounted in this chapter. Other contributions in this book dwell on it. Suffice it to say that the field, however articulated in a variety of approaches and interpretations, has advanced ever since within the intellectual framework of a negotiated interdependence, while notions of a top-down Atlantic order have become increasingly marginal and ultimately irrelevant.

Milward's breakthrough, and the concomitant flourishing of studies on postwar European reconstruction in the 1980s, indirectly contributed also to the critical reassessing of American diplomatic history that got under way at the end of that decade, when several historians (American as well as European) denounced its 'provincialism' and called for a less self-centered view of international history, capable of integrating the interaction with other actors, their views, and—above all—their agency.[24]

Furthermore, a present-day perspective on the long-term evolution and effectiveness of U.S. international hegemony brings to the fore another epistemological benefit inherent in Alan Milward's scholarly contribution. The interpretative reconsiderations of cold war history brought about by the end of that long conflict have finally made possible—especially in view of the new analyses of the rise and fall of the Soviet project—a comparative

21. Ibid. 501, 472, and 125 (respectively for quotations).
22. Kaplan, 'The Cold War and European Revisionism', 148.
23. For instance by Hogan, *The Marshall Plan*.
24. Lundestad, 'Moralism, Presentism, Exceptionalism, Provincialism'. See also Lundestad, 'Empire by Invitation?'; Marks, 'The World According to Washington'; and Hunt, 'The Long Crisis in U.S. Diplomatic History'.

assessment of the sources of strength and weakness in each superpower. In this respect, one of the key factors that has acquired increasing explanatory relevance concerns their respective ability to forge alliances and manage coalitions. Historians with otherwise deeply divergent interpretations of cold war history now converge in emphasizing the comparative and progressively larger advantage that the West enjoyed in this respect, and its long-term importance.[25]

The Soviets dilapidated their postwar ideological and political influence by the rigidly submissive regime they imposed upon Eastern Europe, suffered more setbacks than successes in managing their allies in the Arab world and elsewhere in the global South, and were strategically weakened by a string of schisms and ruptures in the international Communist movement—from Yugoslavia to eurocommunism—that grew to become strategically disastrous in the case of China. In contrast with Moscow's crippling inability to mediate, include, and adapt, the Western coalition proved to be infinitely more expansive, attractive, resilient, and effective. This depended on its larger economic and financial resources, of course. But it also derived from its internal mechanisms of negotiation and compromise and the much wider margins of flexibility and change they allowed. At the end of the day, U.S. hegemony proved to be proportional to its ability to build alliances that accommodated difference rather than suffocating and suppressing it, to adapt its policies to the interlocutors it dealt with, to recognize and organize coalitions of plural interests and subjects. Where this was not the case, and naked domination prevailed, as in several Third World countries, U.S. influence was more limited, temporary, and embattled. This more adaptable and inclusive character of America's international outreach was already visible and important in the post-world period, and became increasingly so in the 1960s and 1970s. It was one of the key resources of Western superiority throughout the bipolar era, and it became one of the crucial factors that determined the peaceful ending of the cold war.[26]

Alan Milward did not participate in a direct and explicit way in this more recent evolution of scholarly interpretations on the international history of the cold war era. Nor did he partake in the postcolonial rethinking of empire as a set of unequal but interactive relationships. However, the characterization of the Western coalition as plural, negotiated, and adaptable stems in no small part from the well-known dynamics of its founding period in the Euro-American core. It is quite plausible, and indeed probable, that we might eventually have arrived where we are by different routes. But there is no denying that Milward's work pointed this way and that we got

---

25. Two symptomatic examples, among many, are Westad, 'The Cold War and the International History of the Twentieth Century' and Gaddis, *We Now Know*, especially 189–220.
26. For a more extensive discussion of this topic see Romero, *Storia della guerra fredda*, 335–346.

here also by way of his depiction of the 'painstaking and accurate construction of a system of international economic interdependence which built on the few interests which the national economies did have in common.'[27]

Constantly intertwined with his interpretative arguments against narratives centered on America's overwhelming power to reshape Europe at will, a second polemical thread recurs in his texts, concerning the aims and methodology of historical inquiry. Milward's published work rarely engages in open discussions about methodology, but occasional statements and hints interspersed throughout his texts make his assumptions quite explicit.

They convey a stark binary alternative. On the one hand his undisputed, and for him undisputable, 'preference for rational enquiry and assessment based on the weight of evidence,'[28] a veritable compass of his scholarly work (and a yardstick against which many contemporary trends in social and cultural history were harshly liquidated as 'semantic parlour games' if devoid of 'any connections to the pattern of economic change'[29]). On the other hand stands the construction of models and theories unsubstantiated by hard evidence, and therefore subject to the vagaries of predetermined assumptions, especially biases of ideological or political character. The latter were at the receiving end of Alan's intellectual disdain, nowhere more visible than in his harsh criticism of the 'cold war theories of European integration' advanced by American social scientists. Neofunctionalism served, he wrote in a joint essay with Vibeke Sørensen, as 'the intellectual foundation for a hegemonic foreign policy architecture', proving 'how easily theorists can end up promoting the values of their political masters'.[30]

Disagreements with historians were usually couched in a less unforgiving language, but the same intellectual matrix operated in Milward's rejection as 'nonsense' of all the orthodox, revisionist, or postrevisionist accounts of U.S. foreign policy (and especially of the Marshall Plan) that did not see 'the limitations to the exercise of American power and influence' and disregarded the real movers and *loci* of Europe's postwar settlement.[31] Here interpretative contents and method were inextricably fused, because one-dimensional readings of U.S. hegemony were rooted in the weight of preexisting (and prefabricated) ideas as much as in lopsided selections of data, in unidirectional notions of influence and hegemony as much as in the neglect of foreign archives and literature.

---

27. Milward, *Reconstruction*, 464.
28. Milward, 'Conclusions: The Value of History', in Milward et al., *The Frontier of National Sovereignty*, 182–201, here 184.
29. Milward, 'Preface', in Milward et al., *The Frontier of National Sovereignty*, viii–xi, here x.
30. Milward and Sørensen, 'Interdependence or Integration? A National Choice', in Milward et al., *The Frontier of National Sovereignty*, 1–22, here 1 and 3.
31. Milward, *Reconstruction*, 125.

Thus, Milward's appeal for interpretations derived from the painstaking, evidence-based mapping of the dynamics of interdependence was not only rooted in the economic historian's familiarity with data and figures, although that clearly mattered. It was also a larger argument for the complexity of history, and for the historian's task to recognize, explore, and organize it. It was, in an increasingly self-conscious and deliberate way, 'a reassertion of the superior value of historical research to contemporary comment', to less empirical scholarly approaches, to theories in search of proof.[32]

It was also a refutation, in a more discipline-specific manner, of traditional approaches to international history centered only on strategy-making and high-policy relations between chanceries and diplomats. Complexity here operated horizontally as well as vertically. Because the real challenge for 'historical analysis of the postwar world, the attempt to explain its prosperity and stability,' required the opening up of subfields and their interlinking in an effort to correlate economic and social change to political and international transformations, and vice-versa. 'Diplomatic history,' he wrote in his most direct engagement with U.S. historiography, 'is superficial stuff unless it relates to what is actually happening inside countries.'[33]

Assessing the impact that Alan Milward's reconfiguration of the U.S. role in Europe has had on subsequent historiography is not a linear task. Individual interpretations obviously differ and clash. More importantly, his arguments percolated into a variety of subfields, each one with its peculiar emphasis and angle, and were therefore contested or appropriated and arranged in partial, selective ways.

Scholars who focus on security and strategy have little use for them. The indispensable role of America's power of deterrence and the centrality of the German question for peace in Europe drive them to argue that defense and geopolitics were far more relevant than economic arrangements, and that U.S. influence was therefore deeper and more compelling than any reasoning on the Marshall Plan would suggest. Lundestad extends this thesis to embrace European integration as well and argues that the pivotal importance of the integration of Germany in Western Europe gave the U.S. far more leverage than Milward concedes.[34]

Issues of peace and security certainly affected the dynamics of European reconstruction and integration in crucial ways. Milward recognized the problem, particularly in relation to the Franco-German settlement, but did not integrate it in his analytical and interpretative framework, thus exposing its main vulnerability.[35] One cannot fail to notice, however,

---

32. Milward, 'Was the Marshall Plan Necessary?' 253. This article was Milward's review of Hogan's *The Marshall Plan*, cit.
33. Ibid., 233.
34. Lundestad, *Empire by Integration*.
35. See Wurm, 'Introduction' to Wurm, *Western Europe and Germany*, 16–20.

that the most thorough account of the European diplomatic and security settlement, by American historian of strategy Marc Trachtenberg, can do entirely without Milward—who does not even appear in the bibliography—but revolves on a web of endless negotiations that evidence a complex framework of intra-Western negotiation much more than a unilateral American commanding authority.[36] Furthermore, Michael Latham suggests a useful distinction in two spheres that, although conjoined in many ways, and indeed inseparable, operated according to different logics: by providing West Europeans with security, NATO—where American leadership was most pronounced—gave them a space in which to build their own economic coordination and integration.[37]

For economists and economic historians, on the other hand, evaluations of the Marshall Plan and of the many issues correlated to it seem to have irreversibly changed. Claims that 'Marshall Plan dollars saved the world' sound like quaint relics of a distant past.[38] Leaving aside works by Milward's students or by scholars that directly refer to his approach, the main accounts of Europe's reconstruction and growth published since the early 1990s emphasize the domestic factors that drove investment-led growth and the centrality of corporatist patterns and internal institutional arrangements.[39] The nature of European integration is defined by national interests and national projects for growth much more than American prodding, even though American aid is recognized as a relevant contributing factor.[40]

If a consensus of sorts has been reached on the actual impact of the Plan, it reads like this. The European Recovery Program's contribution to the 'pace of private investment' and to 'public investment in infrastructure' was helpful but 'of negligible importance.' Its role in eliminating bottlenecks, especially balance of payment constraints to foreign trade, 'had some but not overwhelming significance.' Most scholars converge, however, in emphasizing that the Marshall Plan played a 'vital'—albeit 'difficult to quantify'—part in facilitating 'the negotiation of a pro-growth 'social contract' that provided the political stability and climate necessary to support the postwar boom.'[41] The most recent attempt to sum up the state of the art concludes that 'Marshall aid did not restart European economic growth, but it allowed European states to continue along a path of industrial expansion and investment,' in order to promote a 'politically essential welfare state.' The Plan's true contribution was that 'in restoring economic choices

36. Trachtenberg, *A Constructed Peace.*
37. Latham, 'Cooperation and Community in Europe'.
38. Kindleberger, *Marshall Plan Days*, 247.
39. See for instance Eichengreen, *The European Economy since 1945*, 61–69.
40. Bossuat, *La France, l'aide américaine et la construction européenne.*
41. De Long and Eichengreen, 'The Marshall Plan', 6. See also Crafts and Toniolo, 'Post-war Growth', 22; Eichengreen, 'Mainspring of Economic Recovery'; and Reichlin, 'The Marshall Plan Reconsidered'.

to Europeans,' away from the deflationary strictures of the 1930s, it 'also restored political choices.'[42]

The focus has thus shifted considerably. American aid had 'a qualitative more than a quantitative impact'[43] insofar as it encouraged and facilitated policies of sustained growth that improved standards of living and supported robust centrist coalitions. Without those policies, 'the decisive change of postwar politics—the capacity to leave behind the politics of the interwar period with its totalitarian appeals on the left and right—would perhaps not have occurred.'[44] Milward's 'reasoning seems hard to refute,' according to Tony Judt; the importance of the Marshall Plan was 'psychological' even more than economic or political.[45] It is certainly no coincidence that the Marshall Plan retains an iconic centrality, and perhaps an overstated importance, only in the studies on the culture of consumption, the area of historical scholarship most thoroughly focused on cultural, psychological, and behavioral change.[46]

Iconic but no longer fundamental, the Marshall Plan (and the amount of American leverage that went with it) has therefore become one factor among the many that combined to assemble a 'transnational economy' of growth, based on a complex coordination among several actors—American and European, governmental and societal, private and public—and a 'collaborative political economy'[47] that embodied a compromise between 'liberal capitalism and social democracy.'[48]

This succinct, incomplete, and entirely personal sketch of the literature is not meant to map the legacy of Milward's work, which would require a broader critical analysis. It is rather conducive to my concluding point, the attempt to highlight the third major impulse behind Alan Milward's effort to refashion America's role and put the European nation-state at the center of reconstruction.

Upon revisiting the output of his long season of research on European postwar recovery and integration I was struck, in particular, by the forceful, pervasive presence of a set of questions that lurk in the background of *Reconstruction*, are more explicitly addressed in *European Rescue*, and nowadays burst through all those texts with fresh strength. They came fully alive just a few years later, in 1995, in a short essay that inaugurated the *Journal of European Integration History*. Alan was outlining the state of the art in integration history and suggesting a new agenda. He centered

42. Hitchcock, 'The Marshall Plan and the Creation of the West', 160 and 165.
43. Maier, 'The World Economy and the Cold War', 58.
44. Maier, 'Introduction to Part II', in Maier and Bischof, *The Marshall Plan and Germany*, 114.
45. Judt, 'Introduction' in Schain, *The Marshall Plan*, 6–7.
46. See for instance the unconvincing chapter on postwar reconstruction in the otherwise illuminating book by De Grazia, *Irresistible Empire*, 336–375.
47. Maier, *Among Empires*, 214 and 206 respectively.
48. Spagnolo, 'Reinterpreting the Marshall Plan', 289.

his appeal for a new scholarly effort to unravel the mechanisms of integration, and understand the transformations of European societies in the second half of the twentieth century, on the notion of 'allegiance'. The economic historian who had worked primarily on trade flows, government policies, and intergovernmental arrangements was recommending a new focus on the 'mutual demands made on each other by government and voters' and on the 'marked change' that intervened after 1945 'in the nature of democratic party politics,' which required 'a wholly different analysis from that used for earlier periods.'[49]

In *Reconstruction* he had related European governments' international policy choices to their new postwar domestic goals and necessities, but the latter were not explored. The 'broader political consensus' to nation-states that needed to be 'more responsive to the needs of a greater range' of their citizens, primarily in terms of economic security and well-being, was brought to bear more directly on the overall argument of *The European Rescue*.[50] And the theoretical ambition of *The Frontier* engaged directly with the notion that integration sprang 'from the evolution of the European nation-state', which after World War II 'has better represented popular will than in the past'.[51]

With 'Allegiance' he was bringing to the surface, and turning into a core concept at the heart of a new research agenda, what had long been the crucial subtext of much of his previous work, the key questions that had propelled his search on reconstruction. How had the nation-state changed in post-1945 Western Europe? What were the roots of its newly found democratic reach and solidity? How did it relate to citizens, interest groups, social classes, voters? What were the new and old forms of public allegiance to the nation-state as well as to new European institutions and the larger Atlantic West?

They had been the premise of his earlier work, the core—unspoken at first and then progressively more recognized—of his unsatisfied intellectual curiosity and sensibility. His effort to qualify and circumscribe America's role in postwar reconstruction, highlighting the crucial agency of the European nation-state, originated also in his sensitivity to the profound change in the postwar fabric and texture of European society, in the values, ideas, and dynamics that had reshaped the relationship between citizens and state, and the very notion of citizenship. International history had to relate to them fully and squarely and therefore broaden into a larger and deeper transnational analysis of the economic, social, cultural, and political factors that make the modern state, if it was to make sense of the postwar world.

---

49. Milward, 'Allegiance', 15.
50. Milward, *Rescue*, 27.
51. Milward, 'Conclusions: The Value of History', in Milward et al., *The Frontier of National Sovereignty*, 182–201, 198 and 186 respectively.

The nature of the new democratic pact between state and citizens, and the sea-change contrast between pre- and postwar Europe in this respect, has now become the crucial subject matter of broad, recent reconsiderations of the Continent's history across the twentieth century. Their interpretative emphasis is on the break with the 'legacy of chauvinism, depression and authoritarian solutions,' the focus of their enquiries is on the endogenous nature of Europe's transformation—albeit in direct relation with world-wide processes—rather than on notions of externally driven change.[52]

Alan Milward's work proceeded by in-depth analyses and daring, occasionally caustic, arguments. His approach to history, and especially to historiography, was that 'of the myth-buster, not the accountant's.'[53] Some of his theses were unilateral and extreme, many others quite robust and immediately persuasive. But they were almost always pathbreaking. They pushed the field forward and simultaneously reshaped its conceptual and interpretative frame of reference. The way we see and think the history of Europe—international, transnational, and domestic—is also, to no small extent, of his making.[54]

52. Judt, *Postwar*, 97. See also Mazower, *Dark Continent*, and Sheehan, *Where Have All the Soldiers Gone?*
53. Zamagni's review of *The Reconstruction of Western Europe*, 132. Author's own translation.
54. Judt, *Postwar*, acknowledges 'a special debt' owed to Alan Milward's 'learned, iconoclastic studies of the postwar economy' by 'everyone who studies modern Europe' (xiv).

# 16 When History Meets Theory
## Alan Milward's Contribution to Explaining European Integration

*Jan van der Harst*

For a long time European integration studies have been characterized by a strictly mono-disciplinary approach. Economists, historians, political scientists, jurists, and others tended to do their own thing. In particular, the dividing wall between the disciplines of history and political science was solid and long-lasting, despite their focus on the same actors and events. According to some observers, the disciplinary divisions still exist today.[1] This is remarkable, especially taking into consideration that in most other research areas of international relations (henceforth, IR) cooperation between history and political science became readily accepted, as shown for example by the influential role of the history-driven 'English School' in explaining the functioning and development of the international society.[2]

This chapter aims to provide a survey of the causes at the root of the differences between the academic disciplines of history and political science in the field of European integration. It also gives an account of the important role played by Alan Milward in bridging the gap between the two. A specific section is concerned with the praise and criticism which Milward's conceptual ideas on explaining European integration have encountered. We end up with a brief overview of the current relevance of Milward's work.[3]

### POLITICAL SCIENCE AND HISTORY

The root causes of the dividing wall between history and political science in addressing European integration were manifold. First, it took time before political scientists recovered from the collapse of neofunctionalism. In the 1960s, neofunctionalists had dominated the theoretical debate, holding high expectations on what—in their original concepts—was called the

1. Kaiser, 'History Meets Politics', 301.
2. See, e.g., Bull, *The Anarchical Society*.
3. Some of the notions put forward in this chapter are derived from Van der Harst, 'Geschiedenis en theorie van Europese integratie: de erfenis van Alan Milward', inaugural lecture, University of Groningen, 21 April 2009.

'automatic logic of integration'. They reasoned that European integration was an incremental but unstoppable process, driven along by processes of functional and political spillover. In their predictions, these would slowly but surely make the nation-state obsolete.[4] Political reality was different, however, as the policies of French president Charles de Gaulle, who during the 1960s proved that nationalism in Europe was still vibrant, revealed. One of the main problems underlying neofunctionalist thinking had been its ahistorical character: history was pushed aside as being a potential threat to positivist-theoretical purity.

Together with the (at least temporary) revocation of neofunctionalism, intergovernmentalism gained ground during the 1970s.[5] Intergovernmentalists focused on national governments who could decide on cross-border cooperation, but on the strict condition that their national sovereignty was safely protected.[6] This approach fitted in well with the actual development of European integration during the decade. The oil crisis of 1973 was followed by a long period of stagnation and economic protectionism. The nation-state indeed seemed to be the dominant actor and the European institutions of secondary importance. At that time, most political scientists were hardly interested in empirical research on European integration. In the absence of prominent historical studies they forced historical facts to fit preconceived theoretical models.

Historians were not doing much better. With their focus on empiricism, most historical researchers successfully suppressed any possible desire to get themselves involved in matters of theory and generalizations. The *histoire événementielle* prevailed. In circles of integration historians, one could discern a persisting influence of 'theory phobia', partly as a consequence of the defects of neofunctionalism (which also had a daunting and discouraging impact on historians), partly because of generalized unfamiliarity with the task of theorizing. Diplomatic historians were trained in the humanities, most of them having little talent for or interest in other social sciences. Model-making and quantitative research aroused suspicion, the more so in a context where one of the renowned IR theorists of the day carried the name 'Modelski', and that was no nickname.[7]

Hence, for a long time theory played only a marginal role in postwar historical research on European integration, with one exception: the enduring fascination displayed for good old federalism. Its main advocate was

---

4. See, e.g., Haas, *The Uniting of Europe*, and Lindberg, *The Political Dynamics of European Economic Integration*.
5. A revival of neofunctionalism was signaled in the early 1990s; see Tranholm-Mikkelsen, 'Neo-functionalism: Obstinate or Obsolete?'
6. Hoffmann, 'Obstinate or Obsolete? The Fate of the Nation State'.
7. Reference is made here to G. Modelski, professor in political science, for a long time employed at the University of Washington; author of 'The Long Cycle of Global Politics and the Nation-State'.

the historian Walter Lipgens, who in 1976 became the first professor in integration history at the European University Institute (EUI) in Florence. Lipgens situated the origins of European cooperation within the antifascist resistance movements during World War II. These movements had instigated the emergence of a European-federalist ideal, even conscience, which sooner or later was expected to come to political fruition.[8] Lipgens also attributed importance to the 'great men who created Europe', individuals like Konrad Adenauer, Jean Monnet, and Robert Schuman, without whose passion, vision, and leadership the uniting of Europe would have not been possible.[9]

Lipgens was confronted with problems similar to those faced by neofunctionalists one decade earlier. He had been too selective in his observations. Whereas neofunctionalists had underrated the impact of de Gaulle, Lipgens encountered the heritage of an early postwar political constellation that was not dominated by federalists but by opposing nationalist forces. Lipgens had overestimated the political will among ruling elites to change the existing international context. Until the start of the 1980s, he kept trying to gain support for his convictions, but was literally overtaken by newly revealed historical facts. Concerning their government archives most European countries follow the so-called 30-years rule, meaning that the embargo on public access to documents is lifted exactly three decades after the date on which they were generated. Hence, around 1980 it was possible for the first time to investigate—on the basis of primary sources—what exactly had happened in European governments and bureaucracies during the early postwar years. This archival research showed a picture which fundamentally contrasted with Lipgens' assumptions.

## MILWARD: CONCEPTUAL THINKING AND FOLLOWERS

One of the first to benefit from access to the new archives and to be ready to undertake a serious attempt to tear down the padded wall between history and political science was the economic historian Alan S. Milward. As Lipgens's successor as the European integration history chair at the EUI in Florence, he put forward a new interpretation of early postwar developments. For Milward integration was not the result of neofunctionalist spillover, or of the activities of the 'great men' and their personal convictions. Integration celebrities like Jean Monnet, Max Kohnstamm, Paul-Henri Spaak, and Altiero Spinelli were treated as *hommes d'action,* rather than as revered figures or 'saints' with powerful abstract thoughts. Many people

---

8. Lipgens, *Europa-Föderationspläne der Widerstandsbewegungen*, and 'European Federation in the Political Thought of Resistance Movements'.
9. Lipgens, 'Der Zusammenschluss Westeuropas', 347. On Lipgens' role and position in the academic debate on European integration, see also Loth, 'Explaining European Integration', 12–16.

found his approach to be lacking in sufficient respect.[10] In one of his EUI lectures, Milward said provocatively that Monnet, soon after launching the European Coal and Steel Community, had become politically speaking a dead person.[11] That was like swearing in the then prominent federalist church, for whom Monnet indeed was a kind of saint. This congregation included not just scholars but also European civil servants in Brussels, most of whom were convinced 'Monnet believers'.

Ideas, visions, and ideals only played a minor role in Milward's conceptual thinking; the emphasis was on *material interests*. On the basis of his research in the then recently opened government archives of the six founding member-states of the European Community (EC) as well as those of the United Kingdom, the United States and the *Fondation Jean Monnet pour l'Europe*, in Lausanne, Milward argued that successful European cooperation was the result of harsh and laborious interstate bargaining. National governments focused on protecting their autonomy and—being averse to idealism or altruism—opted for European solutions only out of enlightened self-interest. Hereby, supranational decision-making was sometimes needed to break down the existing policy barriers. This was particularly the case in commercial-economic areas, as shown in the creation of both the European Economic Community and its customs union. In this respect, Milward found himself close to the intergovernmentalist school of thought, as referred to above. However, differing from traditional intergovernmentalism, Milward did not consider integration as a 'zero-sum game' with unequivocal winners and losers. In his view, the state did not necessarily 'lose' what was delegated to the supranational-European level. On the contrary, because of their EC involvement governments were placed in a position to perform tasks for their citizens which otherwise would not have been possible, as shown for example in the construction of national welfare states in the 1950s. Europe offered the financial leeway, economic benefits and institutional framework to facilitate the establishment of welfare societies within the EC member-states. As a result, the nation-state became more powerful and comprehensive than it had been in the pre-World War II period. This achievement enhanced the citizens' loyalties to their national government. Seen in this way, European integration contributed to strengthening the legitimacy of national governing elites, for whom the principal reason in favor of European integration was the *preservation* of

10. Milward, 'The Lives and Teachings of the European Saints' (chapter six of his *The European Rescue of the Nation-State*).
11. The author remembers this vividly, because he was present at the lecture, which dealt with Monnet's receding influence in the EDC debate. On this topic Milward later would write that after Monnet 'had gone in 1952 to Luxembourg as head of the High Authority, he became increasingly impotent politically' (*The European Rescue*, 334).

their executive capability, rather than its *erosion*.[12] In other words, Europe helped to 'rescue the nation-state', according to the title of one of Milward's most influential works.

With this new interpretation of historical development in post-1945 Western Europe, Milward succeeded in gathering a large community of international followers. In the mid-1980s, the author of this chapter belonged to the so-called 'Milward school', a group of young Ph.D. researchers at the EUI in Florence working on integration history, together with Anjo Harryvan, Ruggero Ranieri, Vibeke Sørensen, and others.[13] His 1988 dissertation on the European Defense Community (EDC) (a failed plan for a supranational European army launched in the early 1950s) fitted neatly in Milward's integration concept. Where Lipgens had analyzed the EDC's failure as a missed opportunity and a black day for European federalism, the dissertation argued that the Defense Community was incompatible with the self-interests of the participating states and as such an unfeasible exercise. With a security guarantee provided by the United States within the framework of the recently established North Atlantic Treaty Organization, a 'European rescue' in the defense realm was—other than in the economic realm—apparently not called for.[14]

To his widespread reputation as an economic historian Milward added a similar reputation as a theorist of European integration. He was one of the very few historians who managed to establish a prominent position in the political science debate on European integration.[15] Milward's status was boosted even further by the chaotic situation in which the IR discipline found itself at the end of the cold war. Hardly anybody had succeeded in explaining, let alone predicting, the sudden collapse of Communism and, as a consequence, the discipline found itself in a temporary crisis.

Although Milward's work kept a strongly empirical focus where the archival research—that is, the documentary evidence—remained crucial, he gathered many followers from other disciplines, mainly economists and political scientists. Andrew Moravcsik—one of the most prominent political-science theorists of the 1990s—based a great part of his conceptual thinking on Milward's earlier insights. Moravcsik's standard work *The Choice for Europe* gave ample evidence hereof.[16] Like Milward, Moravcsik interpreted European integration as the outcome of rational choices of government leaders who pursued economic interests. Moravcsik also considered

---

12. Rosamond, *Theories of European Integration*, 139.
13. Editorial note: A list of completed Ph.D. theses supervised by Professor Milward appears in Appendix 3 of this volume.
14. For the commercial edition of this dissertation: Van der Harst, *The Atlantic Priority: Dutch Defence Policy at the Time of the European Defence Community*.
15. The author of this chapter has already had the opportunity to reveal this in his 'Introduction: History and Theory', 6.
16. Moravcsik, *The Choice for Europe*.

these economic interests as more fundamental than geopolitical and other interests. And, like Milward, Moravcsik downplayed the role played by Monnet and other 'founding fathers'. The challenging quality of Moravcsik's work was that he dared to analyze the European integration development in a diachronic way over a longer period of time. In *The Choice for Europe* he aptly linked the 1957 Rome Treaties to the Treaty of Maastricht in the early 1990s and applied a conceptual framework to his empirical analysis. Moravcsik's work was not to remain unchallenged, however. For a political scientist with historical interest he had shown remarkable inaccuracy in the use of his sources—an indirect criticism of Milward's research methods. He based his research on a random selection of literature and when referring to original documents or statements by policy-makers, these were sometimes difficult to trace, with problematic consequences for the reliability of his firmly expressed assumptions. Moravcsik has been criticized for his research habits, not only by historians but also by his *confrères* in political science.[17] Some time ago, a research group from the University of Nijmegen vigorously attacked Moravcsik's impressionistic use of the sources.[18] It showed all the more how justified Milward's unremitting emphasis on the importance of precise historical-archival work had been.

## MILWARD CRITICIZED

Milward's prominence in the early 1990s was a temporary one. Political scientists and IR specialists recovered from their end-of-the-cold-war-trauma and started to launch new approaches, stimulated by breathtakingly fast developments on the European continent, such as the creation of the European Union (EU), in which the EC became integrated; the introduction of a European common currency; and the enlargement of the Union with countries of Central and Eastern Europe. Processes of widening and deepening produced new dynamics. A clear illustration of this development was the Treaty of Maastricht, with its complex pillar structure and mix of intergovernmentalism and supranationalism. The unity of Europe became inextricably linked to its complexity and IR theorists faced this new challenge with professional gusto. They successfully applied diverging concepts—derived

17. See, e.g., Pine, 'European Integration: A Meeting Ground for History and Political Science?'
18. Lieshout, Segers, and Van der Vleuten, 'De Gaulle, Moravcsik and the Choice for Europe'. Despite repeated requests by the editorial board of the *Journal of Cold War Studies* Moravcsik has not so far been willing to defend himself against the critique from Nijmegen.

from governance, institutionalism, and constructivism—to the actual development of the EU after the cold war.[19]

Historians reacted slowly to the post cold-war changing circumstances. For a long period of time, probably too long, they had focused on Milward's work and ideas, above all the dominant attention for research in national government archives. This had two major drawbacks. First, such a research method tended to produce the most obvious conclusions. The researcher who centralizes the position of national governments and bureaucracies should not be surprised to be confronted with predominantly state-centric outcomes. Doing this type of research is like a self-fulfilling prophecy: the influence of transnational actors, like interest or pressure groups, automatically gets less attention and weight. Milward had written history 'from above', rather than 'from below'.

A second problem was that many historians, in doing their work, stayed literally close to their archival sources. Partly for financial reasons, partly out of sheer indolence, they contented themselves with consulting the documents which were easiest to find, namely in the nearby national government archives. In the Netherlands—the home country of this chapter's author—this was all the more attractive, because of the unusually liberal archival policy for which the country is known.[20] The national research orientation produced a one-sided and—if seen in the broader context—fragmented picture. Truly European research could not be the sum of individually accomplished national studies.

The methodological problems were accompanied by shortcomings regarding content. The concept of national interest—often applied by Milward—is hard to objectify.[21] 'National interest' is also a static concept: possible changes in preferences cannot be adequately addressed. After all, what is in somebody's interest today will not necessarily be so tomorrow or the day after tomorrow. Milward had also put too much emphasis on the national government polity as being an autonomous and indivisible entity. In practice this polity is highly diffuse and multilayered and subject to many contradictory (transnational, transgovernmental, and other) influ-

19. For a 'European' application of the governance approach, see Marks, Hooghe, and Blank, 'European Integration from the 1980s'; for institutionalism, see Pierson, 'The Path to European Integration'; and for constructivism, Risse, 'Social Constructivism and European Integration'.
20. See, e.g., Griffiths, *The Netherlands and the Integration of Europe*, and Harryvan, *In Pursuit of Influence*.
21. In later work, e.g., *The Rise and Fall of a National Strategy, 1945–1963* (2002), Milward used the term 'strategies' for (national) interests, but—as Kaiser and Leucht have observed—this was more a semantic than substantive concession (Kaiser and Leucht, 'Informal Politics of Integration', 36).

ences. As a consequence, nowadays we prefer to speak of *governance* rather than *government*.[22]

Finally, the author of this chapter reached the conclusion that he disagreed with Milward's rejection of the 'great men approach' to European integration history. When he—together with Anjo Harryvan, another of Milward's students at the EUI—wrote a biography of Europe's founding father Max Kohnstamm, they did exactly what their former supervisor had always discouraged them from doing, namely choosing as a case study one of the pioneers of the European integration process.[23] Kohnstamm, who acted as the right hand of Jean Monnet in the 1950s and was a leading activist in the Action Committee for the United States of Europe until the mid-1970s, taught them that mutual economic interests constitute a main driving force behind cross-border cooperation, but such cooperation is doomed to fail if not based on individual incentives, ideas, and ideals. Milward's interpretation was probably overly rationalist or materialist. Milward seemed not to realize that Europe needed to be constructed beyond the workings of markets. *Il faut faire l'Europe*! Moreover, once constructed, 'Europe' was in continuous need of maintenance and overhaul, as is shown also today in times of economic crisis. Kohnstamm's passion for Europe, partly emanating from his personal war experiences, taught Harryvan and Van der Harst that Europe was more than just a normal bureaucratic polity. Apart from an economic community (a material construction), the EU also has the potential to develop into a community of values (a social construction).[24] In this respect, Max Kohnstamm, who died in October 2010 at the age of 96, turned out to be a modern, almost trendy figure.

## NEW GENERATION

Currently, a new generation of integration historians, who share Milward's fascination for theorizing but at the same time tend to accentuate distinct elements in their research, is on the rise. This was shown for example by the 2008 publication of a special volume of the *Journal of European Integration*

---

22. See, e.g., Marks, Hooghe, and Blank, 'European Integration from the 1980s'.
23. Harryvan and Van der Harst, *Max Kohnstamm: A European's Life and Work*. Max Kohnstamm (1914–2010), Dutch civil servant, was commissioner responsible for the administration of the Marshall Plan and for German Affairs (1948–50), head of German Affairs Bureau at the Ministry of Foreign Affairs (1950–52), member of the Dutch delegation to the Schuman Plan negotiations (1950–51), secretary of the High Authority of the European Coal and Steel Community (1952–56), secretary general, later vice president, of the Action Committee for the United States of Europe (1956–75), and president of the EUI, Florence (1974–81).
24. Christiansen, Jørgensen, and Wiener, *The Social Construction of Europe*.

*History* dedicated to the theme of history and theory.[25] In it the historians Kaiser and Leucht explain why a network analysis has more potential to account for the creation of the ECSC than the formerly dominant state-centric approach. The informal contacts between Christian-Democratic politicians in a transnational European setting were especially instrumental in making the ECSC a reality. At the time, the networks proved more powerful than the weakened national governments.[26] In another contribution Rasmussen and Knudsen emphasize the importance of committee structures, such as those of the Committee of Permanent Representatives (*Coreper*) and the Special Committee for Agriculture. Due to these institutional structures, founded in the 1960s, we were faced with an early process of socialization between national and European civil servants, meeting each other on an ever-more frequent basis and giving shape to the uniting of Europe in a consistent but hardly noticeable manner (what is termed 'creeping integration'). As a consequence, a political system has emerged which is more than just the sum of the histories of the member-states.[27] A third and last example concerns a large-scale research project on the Netherlands' postwar political-parliamentary debate on European integration.[28] This project aims to trace the key moments of transformation in the domestic policies on Europe and also attempts to map—through speech analysis—the various discourses which were at the origins of those transformations. The rationale behind the project is to explain increasing manifestations of euroskepticism in the country, especially during and after the European constitutional referendum in 2005. Even the foreign policy elites nowadays handle European integration more and more as an object of fear, with which they no longer want to be identified. The man in the street senses this feeling of insecurity displayed by the leaders and increasingly questions the wisdom of further steps in integration.

The citizen-elites' relationship has been subject to academic research before, particularly by political scientists and jurists, and also by sociologists since the 2005 referenda on the European Constitution held in France and the Netherlands.[29] Historians have so far been reticent in dealing with the topic, which is regrettable because a hermeneutic analysis of

25. *JEIH* 14: 1 (2008).
26. Kaiser and Leucht, 'Informal Politics of Integration'.
27. Rasmussen and Knudsen, 'A European Political System in the Making, 1958–1970'.
28. This research project is done in cooperation by the *Centrum voor Parlementaire Geschiedenis* (Nijmegen) and the *Documentatiecentrum Nederlandse Politieke Partijen* (Groningen) and is expected to lead to a book publication in 2012. The editors are A. G. Harryvan, and J. van der Harst.
29. On the Dutch case, see for example: Aarts and Van der Kolk, *Nederlanders en Europa*; Barents, *Een grondwet voor Europa*; and Besselink, *Grondwet voor Europa*.

the European discourse *through the postwar decades* would have helped to clarify the essence of the problem.

The new generation of historians no longer revolts against political scientists, but rather tries to link their empirical research to the theoretical devices provided by political science. They use the toolbox of theorists in an eclectic way.[30] Kaiser and Leucht—mentioned above—relate their informal networks to the multilevel governance approach; Rasmussen and Knudsen base their socialization thesis on the assumptions of sociological institutionalism; and the political-parliamentary project in the Netherlands makes use of discursive elements derived from social constructivism. With this type of research, one has the best of both worlds: historians transcend government centrism, pay increasing attention to transnational influences, and no longer avoid the possibility of making generalizations. It is also possible to update the research topic thanks to the usage of interviews and the benefits of Internet. Political scientists, in their turn, get hold of relevant and well-structured empirical material and are in a position to draw conclusions having a wider scope than only the last ten or twenty years. To do reliable institutionalist or constructivist research, a right understanding of the time factor (of the actual historical development) is indispensable.[31] Fortunately, this is well understood by an increasing number of political scientists who nowadays make extensive use of applying historical methods to their work, like Mathieu Segers and Craig Parsons.[32]

## THE CONTINUED RELEVANCE OF MILWARD'S IDEAS

Even though some of Milward's theoretical concepts have been called into question recently, and despite the rise of a new generation with different approaches, Milward's work still has substantial relevance for present thinking on the development of European integration. We mention two examples to illustrate this.

First, there is the continued topicality of the 'rescue' thesis, although in an opposite direction from the one originally proposed by Milward. Back in the 1950s, as Milward has argued, the creation of the national welfare state contributed to a strengthening of the legitimacy of national political elites. This development could not have taken place without the achievements of European integration. As a result the allegiance of national citizens to their own nation increased substantially.[33] Following the same logic, a similar phenomenon could be happening within the European Union but only if

30. Kaiser, 'History Meets Politics', 306.
31. Ibid., 301.
32. Segers, *Tussen verzoening en verval*, and Parsons, *A Certain Idea of Europe*.
33. Milward, 'Allegiance: The Past and the Future'.

the latter delivered what the citizen expected it to. As Milward put it: 'If the supranation, like the nation, provides a consistent and effective level of organization, it can count on the loyalty of its citizens.'[34]

Currently, the welfare state in the EU member-states is subject to a process of erosion and degradation. Globalization threats—like the impact of the recent financial-economic crisis—have made it difficult to uphold past achievements and maintain the complex network of social solidarity. Nowadays, national governments seem to be less willing and able to provide the same degree of economic security as they achieved in the first three postwar decades.

Telling examples are the Europe-wide retrenchment operations on pensions, social benefits, and health care. Whereas in early postwar Europe the nation-state had managed to absorb an enormous amount of new tasks and responsibilities, we are currently faced with a contraction of state activities, caused by far-reaching processes of privatization and deregulation. The erosion of the national welfare state has consequences not only for the legitimacy of national government elites (as witnessed by the current tendency to vote out government coalitions at national elections), but also for the public support of European integration. In the present circumstances, both national and European allegiances are subject to erosion. A European rescue of the nation-state is no longer self-evident. Milward himself was the first to admit that such an opposite development could take place. For him, the 'rescue' was a temporary phenomenon.[35]

A second example of current relevance of Milward's work concerns his ideas on the development and level of democracy in the European Union. Milward has published little on this topic, but what he wrote deserves attention:

> The history of national parliaments suggests that important popular demands will only focus on the European parliament if the power of raising taxation is shifted to the Union level. Until then it is within the nation that political parties have to fulfill their task of organizing a democratic consensus. It seems besides the point to denounce the EC for an undemocratic and bureaucratic pursuit of policies which were themselves the choice of national democracies.[36]

Milward's views on democracy have lasting validity. He made his observations at a time when it was still *en vogue* to promote democracy in the EU by increasing the powers of the European Parliament. This has changed substantially in the most recent period, with the emphasis nowadays having shifted to upgrading the position of *national* parliaments (see also the relevant provisions on yellow and orange card procedures in the recent Treaty

34. Milward, *The European Rescue*, 444.
35. Ibid., 438.
36. Ibid., 446.

of Lisbon). Milward's emphasis on the role of national parliaments in promoting democracy is widely shared today, but back in the early 1990s his was a minority opinion. Once again, it was Andrew Moravcsik who took over Milward's argument on the locus of parliamentary power in Europe. In a widely read article published in 2002, nine years after Milward's *The European Rescue of the Nation-State*, Moravcsik wrote that the general concern about the EU's 'democratic deficit' was misplaced for various reasons, among which were fiscal constraints and the Union's limited capacity in the field of taxation. As a result, national parliaments continued to be the major representatives of the public voice in European politics.[37] Political scientist Alfred Pijpers held a similar view, arguing that the EU's high-minded pretensions were misplaced as long as it did not dispose of further-reaching powers and competences. In Pijpers' words there should be 'no representation without taxation.'[38] The same expression was used by Joseph Weiler in his essays on the constitution of Europe. Weiler also proclaimed that European citizens would only start to pay attention to the EU if a system of direct taxation was introduced: a European tax administered and distributed by a European government.[39] Vivien Schmidt in her much-praised book *Democracy in Europe* (2006) shared Milward's position on the status to be attributed to the national and European parliaments respectively. Schmidt wrote: 'The E[uropean] P[arliament] [ . . . ] remains the weakest of representative institutions with the weakest of partisan politics by comparison with national political institutions and partisan politics.'[40] Like Milward, Schmidt held the view that the organization of a democratic consensus was, at the moment of their writings, centered on national governments and parliaments.

Equally relevant for today's discussion on the working of democracy in Europe is what Milward and Sørensen wrote in the introductory chapter of *The Frontier of National Sovereignty* (1992):

> Political parties seeking office continue to present to the electorate the concepts of European 'integration' and 'unification' as grand general ideas, which they either favour or oppose. Would it not be wiser to descend to the detail of the relationship of each specific policy proposal to the available European international frameworks for advancing it and to specify whether it would be better advanced by integration or by more traditional processes? Not only would that be a step towards acknowledging European political realities, but for ardent champions of the cause of European Union [ . . . ] it might actually advance their cause. For the greatest single piece of evidence that the nation-state

37. Moravcsik, 'In Defense of the "Democratic Deficit"', 605.
38. Pijpers, *De mythe van het democratisch tekort*, 36.
39. Weiler, *The Constitution of Europe.*
40. V. Schmidt, *Democracy in Europe*, 158.

> continues to dominate all policy choices is surely that political parties continue to advocate major changes of national policy with scarcely any explanation to the electorate of the international requirements needed to make them possible, even in the European Community.[41]

Milward's observations found confirmation in the campaigns prior to the 2005 referenda on the European Constitution in France and the Netherlands. On these occasions, the champions of the cause of European Union indeed tended to present European integration as a grand general idea and forgot to go into the details of the Constitutional Treaty. They avoided facing their electorates with a realistic political discourse on what the Constitution was all about. The result was the negative vote on the Treaty in both countries. Again, Milward found Schmidt on his side. Schmidt too argued that 'national leaders have chosen not to engage their publics in deliberations about the effects of Europeanization on national democracy' and that European integration is at risk 'because of the lack of new ideas and discourse that address those changes at the national level.'[42]

On one important issue Milward and Schmidt fundamentally disagreed. Whereas Schmidt observed an increasing transfer of competences from the national to the European level (leading to a situation of 'politics without policies' in the member-states), Milward argued that the nation-state continued to 'dominate all policy choices.' This was in line with his predominantly intergovernmentalist or state-centric way of approaching national and European politics. If we compare the views of the two authors, it seems that both of them have taken up too extreme a position, a more nuanced view is needed. Nowadays, it makes no sense to refer to 'politics without policies', if only bearing in mind the central role played by national governments in the financial-economic crisis of 2008, even leading to large-scale nationalizations of commercial banks. Neither, it could be argued, is Milward's statement that the 'nation-state continues to dominate all policy choices' an adequate analysis of what really is at stake in the current EU. This outdated view may have been caused by Milward's expectation in 1993 that a European Monetary Union—one of the most implicating forms of political commitment by the EU member-states—was still something far off and maybe even something that would never happen.[43]

## CONCLUSION

Alan Milward has made an important contribution to explaining the post-war development of European integration, both in an historical-empirical

---

41. Milward and Sørensen, 'Interdependence or Integration?'
42. Schmidt, *Democracy in Europe*, 3 and 265 respectively.
43. Milward, *The European Rescue*, 435.

and theoretical manner. He was one of the very first who succeeded in bringing the traditionally distant disciplines of history and political science together. In the field of European studies, no other historian has had more authority in influencing the IR debate and research. At present there is a new generation of integration historians manifesting themselves, with interesting and fresh contributions to conceptual thinking, but thus far they have failed to have a similar impact to the one Milward wielded in the 1980s and 1990s. Despite the fact that in the course of time Milward's original ideas and methods have become subject to substantial criticism, some of his concepts—including the rescue thesis and his ideas on European democracy—have to a large extent managed to withstand academic scrutiny. With the current state-centric trend in the European Union, this conclusion seems to have even more validity.

# 17 The Significance of the Milwardian Analysis for the Dutch Marshall Plan Debate, and Vice Versa

*Anjo G. Harryvan*

When on 5 October 2006, the Netherlands' *Nationale Conventie* reported to the Hague government on the desirability of changing the country's political system, its chapter on the European context entitled *Het verloren Europese paradijs* ('The Lost European Paradise') outlined the historical importance of European integration for Dutch security, wealth, and welfare:

> The growth of the European common market and the financial means it has generated for the Treasury have contributed to the Netherlands' welfare state. With these funds a solid social security system could be set up and money for education, public housing and a health care system became available. In this way The Hague pleased the nation and preserved the post-war decolonized and weakened Dutch state from decline.[1]

It is hardly surprising to observe in the accompanying footnote the reporting parliamentarians and their policy advisors referring to Milward's *The European Rescue of the Nation State*. It is a telling example of the influence which Milward and his followers have had on Dutch historiography and politics. In this chapter we analyze the forms and ways in which such influence became manifest, concentrating on Milward's *The Reconstruction of Western Europe* and the Dutch Marshall Plan debate.

When publishing *The Reconstruction of Western Europe,* Milward did something which was exceptional at the time and could easily be overlooked today: in his analysis of postwar European cooperation, the smaller countries of the Continent were treated as fully fledged players with problems, traditions, and policy aims of their own. This contrasted with the mainstream tales of reconstruction and integration in which attention was almost exclusively focused on the large powers and more specifically on the Franco-

1. Nationale Conventie, *De Europese Unie als statenverbond*, 9. The *Nationale Conventie* was established by the Dutch government in 2005. This advisory body was to draft proposals for government reform. Quotation translated from the original by the author, as will be the case in the rest of the chapter.

German relationship. The Dutch bore at least part of the blame for this state of affairs themselves. As late as 1982 the authoritative *Algemene Geschiedenis der Nederlanden* observed that 'on the Dutch contribution to European integration so far few studies have been published.'[2] Dutch interest in the European Community, which was regarded as a foreign policy affair, was limited first and foremost to its economic dimensions: the benefits of the EEC's common market for Dutch exports were widely acknowledged, albeit that the country's high rate of dependency on intra-European trade was criticized in equal measure during the 1970s economic recession.[3]

Milward's interest in the Netherlands and other smaller European powers stemmed from his conviction that by concentrating on France, Germany, and the United Kingdom, only part of the story of European integration could be told. To live up to this conviction he was served by his formidable and ever-progressing language skills. Fluent at that time in English, French, and German, and with at least a reading knowledge of Dutch, Italian, and Norwegian, he was possibly the first historian who could digest the national studies and—even more importantly—the primary source material in the national archives of all the original six member-states of the European Communities as well as the British archival sources. Hence *The Reconstruction* is to be regarded as an outstanding example of how European integration history could and should be written: as much as possible on the basis of primary sources and with a transnational viewpoint, that is, paying due attention to all the relevant actors including the smaller powers of the Continent.

If Milward has been important for establishing conceptions of the role of the Netherlands, the reverse is also true. The country provided him and his 'History of European Integration' project at the European University Institute (EUI) in Florence with a unique archival source and a skillful man on the ground in the person of Professor Richard T. Griffiths, whom Milward knew from his earlier years at the University of Manchester Institute of Science and Technology. Since archival policies in the Netherlands were of a more liberal nature than elsewhere, during the early 1980s Dutch researchers enjoyed a comparative advantage in that they had access to more documents and at an earlier moment. Griffiths' contribution to an EUI conference in November 1983 on postwar economic reconstruction, 'Economic Reconstruction policy in the Netherlands and its international consequences, May 1945–March 1951', qualifies as the first specimen of modern European cooperation and integration historiography based on primary source analysis.[4] As Griffiths' assistant at the time I vividly recall

2. Blok et al., *Algemene Geschiedenis der Nederlanden*, vol. 15 (1982). See also the commented bibliographical section in Kersten, 'Nederland en de buitenlandse politiek na 1945'.
3. Messing, 'Het economisch leven in Nederland, 1945–1980', 179–180.
4. Griffiths, 'Economic Reconstruction Policy in the Netherlands'.

the clouds of dust filling the air when the two of us stormed the archives of the Hague Foreign Ministry.

The availability of primary sources as well as the crisis of both the federalist and neofunctionalist explanatory models at times of so-called 'Eurosclerosis' promoted a subsequent series of studies by Milward and Griffiths and a number of young historians. Under their guidance various aspects of the Netherlands' European policies were analyzed and explained in terms of the competing or converging national interests as negotiated in a multilateral intergovernmental European framework. When Milward left Florence for the London School of Economics in 1987, Griffiths as his successor continued the EUI History of European Integration project in much the same vein (arguably '*plus milwardien que Milward*' when it came to highlighting the errors of 'great men who have made Europe' historiography).

A stocktaking conference in Nijmegen in October 1989 distinguished four leading directions in terms of European integration historiography: 1) the classical school, characterized by federalist idealism and emphasis on the thoughts and actions of the pioneers of European unification (the 'European saints' as Milward called them later in *The Rescue*; 2) the Marxist school, analyzing European integration as a byproduct of capitalist exploitation; 3) the diplomatic history school, which had disregarded the subject of European cooperation and integration until the early 1980s when the primary source material became accessible, but now shared such emphasis on primary source analysis with the more radical 4) Milwardian school, the latter being at the time, as I myself described it, 'a loose cooperation framework of for the most part young historians from various member-states of the European Communities who find inspiration for their research in the methods and research findings of Professor Alan Steele Milward of the London School of Economics, previously of the European University Institute in Florence.'[5]

More than twenty years later, I find it instructive to share with today's readers my own views on the then apparent radicalism of the Milward school:

> Identical [in comparison with the diplomatic history school] is the leaning towards primary sources. Printed and published statements by politicians in the press, in national parliaments and autobiographies are treated with suspicion. 'All politicians are liars' is the Milwardian's cautious point of departure. It sees a fundamental difference between the real substance of a policy and the way in which this policy is presented, i.e. the way it is sold to the public.

5. Harryvan, 'De historiografie van de Europese integratie, 1945–1985', 22–45, here 36.

> Whereas the new diplomatic integration historiography criticizes the assumptions and findings of the classic historiography implicitly, Milwardians do so explicitly. In their view the process of European integration is by no means the history of an unstoppable, lofty idea [ . . . ]. [The European treaties] are first and foremost viewed as the outcome of hard intergovernmental bargaining between sovereign states which were aiming at optimal promotion of their national interests rather than realizing European unification. For Milwardians the dominance of national interests counts as the principal explanation.[6]

This goes to show that well before the publication of *The European Rescue of the Nation-State* (1992) and *The Frontier of National Sovereignty* (1993) a Milwardian school with distinct characteristics and concepts of European integration analysis had found recognition.

## RECONSTRUCTING A RECONSTRUCTION

When *The Reconstruction of Western Europe, 1945–1951,* was published in 1984 it had an immediate impact on Marshall Plan historiography, thus marking the start of what Desmond Dinan calls a 'Milwardian onslaught' on the historiography of European integration.[7] Milward's conclusion that 'Marshall aid did not save Western Europe from economic collapse' was as contrary to prevailing beliefs in the Netherlands as elsewhere and sparked a lively debate on the importance and functioning of the European Recovery Programme (ERP, the official name of the Marshall Plan) for postwar Dutch economic reconstruction.[8]

The notion that Marshall Aid had been essential for overcoming the 1947–1948 economic crisis was widespread in Dutch historiography as well as in public opinion. Mainstream Dutch historiography on the Marshall Plan was high in eulogy content. This was particularly the case in (semi-) governmental publications commemorating the Plan and its significance for the Dutch economy and society, such as *Herwonnen welvaart: De betekenis van het Marshallplan voor Nederland en de Europese samenwerking* ('Prosperity Regained: The Significance of the Marshall Plan for the Netherlands and European Cooperation'). In this volume A. H. Philipse summarized the significance of the Plan as follows: 'Thanks to the Marshall Plan the Netherlands has arrived at a position which in the spring of 1948

6. Harryvan, ibid., 37.
7. Dinan, 'The Historiography of European Integration', 310.
8. 'It was the success and vigour of the European recovery, not its incipient failure, which exacerbated this payments problem. Marshall aid did not save Western Europe from economic collapse' (Milward, *The Reconstruction of Western Europe*, 465–466).

it could not have dreamed of achieving in many decades.'[9] The same volume also contains an essay by Nobel Prize–winning economist Jan Tinbergen in which he rather more carefully argues that the impact of the plan is difficult to measure. He deems it likely, however, 'that Marshall aid has provided the decisive upward push.'[10]

What did Milward's revisionist claim regarding the economic significance of the ERP mean for the historical debate and views on the ERP in the Netherlands? Initially very little. The reaction to *The Reconstruction* by historical and other academic journals was tepid. Reviews were scarce and short or shallow. There are a number of reasons for this state of affairs. First, the early 1980s were unhappy days for European integration in that stagnation, also known as 'Eurosclerosis', was rampant, and interest in European cooperation and integration history was a likely victim. Second, although *The Reconstruction* unquestionably qualifies as a highly original and factually rich book and Milward's assertions about the state-centric nature of European integration are convincing, the major drawback of the work—as one observer of singular authority puts it—is 'that it was so badly written: only the most dedicated students of European integration would have the stamina to trudge through it.'[11] Third, for those dedicated students from the Netherlands who did trudge, Milward's ERP analysis was relatively innocuous in that he excepted France and the Netherlands from his general conclusion about the relative unimportance of Marshall Aid. In his reasoning the essential question was one of capital formation: whether without Marshall Aid European economies could have achieved as high levels of capital formation as they actually did. His answer is that 'two of them, France and the Netherlands, could not have done so. The others may have been able to. In its other aspects Marshall aid was of less importance and its importance diminished more rapidly.'[12] Milward's reasoning was based on the differing degrees in which Western European countries' dollar earnings from exports covered the expenses of their imports from the dollar area. Since for France and the Netherlands this was not the case, as well as the fact that these two countries had the most ambitious reconstruction plans, they would have had to reduce their capital imports from the United States and Canada. The other major European capital goods importers could have done without ERP aid, provided that they were prepared to keep their food consumption at the 1947 level.[13] The exception

9. Philipse, 'Het Marshallplan gezien vanuit de Nederlandse ambassade te Washington', 121. Dr Philipse was head of the economic department of the Dutch embassy in Washington and from 1952 onwards a high-ranking officer at the Hague Foreign Ministry.
10. Tinbergen, 'De betekenis van het Marshallplan voor de Nederlandse volkshuishouding', in ibid., 24–29, here 28.
11. Dinan, 'The Historiography of European Integration', 313.
12. Milward, *The Reconstruction of Western Europe*, 469–470.
13. Ibid., 105–106.

Milward made of the Netherlands and France was criticized by Michael Hogan and Jeffrey Vanke.[14] Later in the decade scholarly interest in *The Reconstruction* would increase due to other publications by both Milward (such as *The European Rescue of the Nation State* in 1992) and the EUI and LSE researchers in his circle, where—trudging or no trudging—the book obtained cult status.[15]

In spite of this late general readership, *The Reconstruction*'s central conclusion on the limited significance of the Marshall Plan was picked up quickly and found immediate application in the work of a young historian from Groningen, Pierre van der Eng, especially in his book *De Marshall-hulp: Een perspectief voor Nederland 1947–1953*, published in 1987. In the introduction Van der Eng observed that for too long the causal link between Marshall Aid and the Netherlands' economic recovery had been considered blatantly obvious. A reappraisal was called for. His analysis and calculations led him to conclude that Marshall Aid had indeed enabled the Netherlands to sustain a higher balance of payments deficit and hence a higher level of economic activity than would have been possible in the absence of American aid. Consequently, net national income, which experienced an annual increase of 5.43% between 1947 and 1954, would have been somewhat lower, at 4.65%. This was indeed marginal. By thus stimulating national economic growth between 1948 and 1953, the Marshall Plan had saved the country from a delay in its postwar national income recovery of about a year.[16]

A year's delay forestalled as the essence of the ERP's contribution to national economic recovery was a crushing conclusion, going well beyond the Milward-attributed exception of the Netherlands and light years away from the classic ERP eulogies about a national economic 'position which in the spring of 1948 [the country] could not have dreamed of achieving *in many decades*'.[17]

A lively debate ensued, in which Griffiths and Van Zanden gathered round the flag of Milward's exception thesis. They criticized Van der Eng's model as 'rather simplistic' and questioned the latter's assumption that public spending in the absence of the ERP would have been at about the same level as in the real course of events, as well as his allegedly unwarranted

14. Vanke, *Europeanism and European Union*, 31 ('[Milward] fails to reconcile the incongruence of this interpretation with his thesis') and Hogan, *The Marshall Plan*, 431–432 ('the Marshall Plan provided what Stephen A. Schuker calls the "crucial margin" that made European self-help possible').
15. Leading to a reprint in 2003.
16. Van der Eng, *De Marshall-hulp*, 166–169. For growth in per capita consumption, however, the calculated gap was considerably larger: 0.73% as against 0.14%. Absence of ERP would have brought about a delay of over five years on this variable.
17. Philipse, 'Het Marshallplan gezien vanuit de Nederlandse ambassade te Washington', 121. Emphasis added.

optimism concerning private investment and its impact on employment. Somewhat ambiguously their final blow characterizes the Van der Eng scenario as being of a too light-hearted nature: 'In fact, *even this scenario* [Van der Eng's] makes clear how important the Marshall Plan has been for the reconstruction and industrialization of the [Netherlands].'[18] In his 1984 EUI working paper Griffiths had stressed the importance of overcoming the dollar gap for going beyond the needs of economic *recovery* to targets of *restructuring*, primarily in the direction of industrialization. The ERP was indispensible: 'Riding on the wave of Marshall Aid funds the Dutch economy entered the phase of an investment boom the stated goal of which was to produce such a structural change in the economy as to enable the country to stand on its own feet in its dealings with the rest of the world by the time American aid dried up in 1952.'[19]

Amsterdam historian Frank Inklaar also underlined the ERP's positive contribution to national economic recovery. Without the ERP, the recovery of postwar national prosperity would have taken 'considerably longer.' Siding with Van der Eng, however, he deemed an 'economic malaise' in the absence of American aid improbable: 'It is unlikely that recovery would have collapsed without Marshall Aid, or that serious social problems would have arisen.' Likewise, he argued that

> [i]mportant infrastructure work was accomplished with Marshall funds, but these projects had been budgeted for anyway. It cannot be said that branches of industry were saved from destruction by Marshall Aid. The program though was responsible for giving both government and industry more elbow-room. This has certainly had an indirect, positive influence on the industrialization of the Netherlands. The main economic growth in the Netherlands was not caused by Marshall Aid. This country benefited in particular from favourable international developments like the liberalization of international monetary and trade systems and the reintegration of the German economy. And specific to the Netherlands was the stringent government control of wages. The great importance of Marshall Aid was mainly psychological.

Inklaar stressed the sociopsychological impact of the Marshall Plan—the way in which it advocated the 'American way of life', characterized by mass

18. Van Zanden and Griffiths, *Economische geschiedenis van Nederland*, 195. Emphasis added.
19. Griffiths, 'Economic Reconstruction Policy in the Netherlands', 15 and 21 (quotation). For Griffiths, however, Marshall Aid counted as an important explanatory factor, among others, for the Netherlands' economic growth and transformation. A restructuring of the country's international trade relations and its liberation from 'the stranglehold of bilateralism' were at least as important; Griffiths, 'The Stranglehold of Bilateralism'.

production and consumption and high productivity as well as efficiency, elevating the United States to the position of 'reference society', where one could learn how to operate a modern prosperous society.[20]

Hans Ibelings and others underlined the importance of the ERP's Technical Assistance (TA) program. Functioning as an 'ideas transfusion service' aimed at raising national productivity, TA impacted a wide range of sectors, from Dutch farming to architecture. Where other ERP programs came to an end by 1954, TA continued active in the Netherlands until the late 1950s.[21] In sum, for 'a whole generation', as Marc Dierikx declared on the commemoration of the fiftieth anniversary of the Marshall Plan, 'Marshall Aid came to symbolize the generosity of the United States—the richest, most powerful country in the world, the shining beacon on the western horizon.'[22]

More generally, the 1997 commemoration rekindled the debate on the significance of the ERP for the Netherlands. For instance, Pien van der Hoeven stressed the miraculous nature of postwar Dutch economic recovery, referring to the 200% increase in the country's exports between 1948 and 1952, which transformed the 1947 balance of payments deficit of 1.6 thousand million guilders into a surplus of over 1.7 thousand million guilders in 1952. Accepting Van der Eng's calculations, she wonders whether consumption per head, which according to Van der Eng's model would have suffered a lag of over five years had the ERP not materialized, rather than net national income, should be the variable to judge the significance of Marshall Aid. Would the absence of any growth in consumption over such a long period of time not have led to serious societal unrest? Looked upon in that way, Marshall Aid was considered invaluable for Dutch recovery. Like Griffiths, she stressed the mutually beneficial importance of the ERP and the gradual liberalization of intra-European trade and payments in the period between 1948 and 1954.[23] Martin Fase of *De Nederlandsche Bank* put ERP aid into perspective by relating it to the Netherlands' national income at the time, to which it contributed about 5 percent: a sizable stimulus, but nothing to get excited about.[24]

Richard Griffiths, by then back from Florence and teaching in Leiden, was among the editors of *Van strohalm tot strategie: Het Marshall-plan in perspectief* in which he once again drew attention to the currency shortage of 1947, a shortage which, contrary to the food, housing, and energy shortages, remained 'invisible' for the public at large, but led to despair in The Hague government circles. A rapidly increasing trade deficit with the United States in particular resulted in dollar shortages which threatened to bring the recovery

20. Inklaar, *Van Amerika geleerd*, 30, 423 (quotation), and 424.
21. Ibelings, *Americanism*, 17; Van der Eng, *De Marshall-hulp*, 158, 191–196.
22. Dierikx, *An Image of Freedom*, 7.
23. Van der Hoeven, *Hoed af voor Marshall*, 142 and 144.
24. See Pen, 'Het onderschatte Marshall-wonder', *Het Parool*, 24 May 1997.

of the economy to a grinding halt. The day before Marshall presented his initiative in a speech at Harvard University, the Hague government faced the news that by the end of the year payment for imports would no longer be feasible. Precisely for this reason Marshall's initiative was greeted with relief: instead of harsh austerity measures policies could now be developed based on the hope that financial improvement was in sight.[25]

The revived debate brought some of the former Dutch ERP practitioners to the fore. Venerable economics professor Jan Pen recalled his early days as a civil servant at the Ministry of Economic Affairs. He criticized the Fase analysis on the grounds that the official dollar-guilder rate of approximately 3:1 used in the calculation was a fictional one. In the absence of free convertibility the rate in some of the (black) markets was five times as high: 'Someone could argue that thirty guilders to the dollar would be a better ratio for the significance of those currencies. That would raise the afore-mentioned five percent to perhaps even fifty percent!' Pen pinpointed Milward as the founder of 'the school that says that we would have been all right without those extra dollars.' In Pen's view, Milward reasoned with the typical long-term view of an economist, according to which unstoppable technical progress was destined to raise labor productivity. Such reasoning, however, did not do justice to the exceptional circumstances shortly after the war. A 'disaster scenario' loomed: without the ERP, export and trade could well have remained stifled by currency shortages, industrialization plans would not have come off the ground, and the Netherlands would have missed the upward momentum and the golden age of the 1950s and 1960s. The fact that Richard Griffiths did not discard this 'disaster scenario' and accepted it as a possible counterfactual outcome was worth a compliment.[26]

Jan van den Brink, Pen's former boss at the Ministry of Economic Affairs reacted with slight irritation when confronted with the idea that 'some historians' argue that with or without ERP economic recovery would have materialized: 'They may be right. But I don't feel like fantasizing about what would have happened had Marshall aid not come.' Without the 'ray of light from Washington', Van den Brink stated, he would not have had the courage to accept heading the Ministry of Economic Affairs half a century

---

25. Griffiths, 'Het jaar 1947' in Griffiths et al., *Van strohalm tot strategie*, 5–15. In the same volume an article by Henk de Haan on the impact of the ERP on the Dutch economy stresses the ERP's *indirect* influence, by means of the liberalization of international trade and payments it encouraged, invaluable for an open economy like the Dutch; de Haan, 'De invloed van het Marshall-plan op de Nederlandse economie', in ibid., 114–122. For the role of Marshall Aid in restoring the Netherlands' balance of payments see also Van Zanden, *Een klein land in de 20e eeuw*, 174–179. Of the additional factors a 30% devaluation of the guilder against the U.S. dollar in September 1949 worked wonders for Dutch competitiveness (176).
26. Pen, 'Het onderschatte Marshall-wonder'. And in the same vein: Pen, 'Nieuw Marshall-plan?' *Het Parool*, 5 April 1997.

ago. 'Marshall Aid amounted to an extra four percent of national income for five years. That does not look much, but back then it was a sizeable amount. Look, if one is getting by on limited means, additional funding to the tune of four percent of national income is formidable support.'[27]

Alan Milward himself stuck to his guns. In an interview with *NRC Handelsblad* correspondent Bernard Bouwman he stated: 'In comparison with the recovery and investment programs the European states embarked upon themselves after the war, the entire Marshall aid is no more than a drop in the ocean.' He reiterated the exemption status of the Netherlands and France, since these countries in particular were dependent on capital goods imports. Not that it mattered much: 'According to my calculations American dollars accelerated the Netherlands' growth some seven or eight months and France's growth three. That does not amount to much.'[28]

## CONCLUSION

*The Reconstruction of Western Europe* helped to put the contribution of Marshall Aid to the Netherlands' postwar economic revival into perspective. Due to the exception clause Milward deemed applicable for the Dutch case, his revisionist analysis originally had but an indirect impact. Van der Eng's *über-Milwardian* approach set off the discussion in meritorious fashion, albeit accompanied by criticisms on both Milward's model and interpretations. Traditional historical views, however, acclaiming the ERP as saving the country from collapse, destitution, and Communist uprising are no longer fashionable today. Marshall Aid helped to bridge a serious dollar gap and as such contributed, among other important factors, to the restructuring of the country's international trade relations. Apart from its economic impact the ERP brought forth an important sociopsychological heritage in preparing the country for an Americanization of economic and cultural life. Conversely, the Dutch Marshall Plan debate raised considerable interest in *The Reconstruction* and the Milwardian approach to European integration in general. Belatedly, the book, by 1997 acclaimed as 'path breaking', obtained the readership it deserved.[29]

---

27. Cillekens, 'Minister vd Brink', and 'Marshall-hulp: W-Europa uit klauwen Moskou houden'.
28. Bouwman, 'De Britse historicus Milward zet vraagtekens'.
29. Koper, 'Een Amerikaans plan voor Europa'.

# 18 History, Political Science, and the Study of European Integration

*Ben Rosamond*

Alan Milward's work on the historical origins of the European Union (EU) routinely brought him into direct contact with political scientists. Such encounters between the fields of political science and history have, in the contemporary era of intense disciplinary specialization, become increasingly rare. Naturally, there are regular calls for these respective disciplines to talk to each other more, but the very fact that appeals for rapprochement and mutual learning are needed is indicative of the extent to which such appeals go against the grain.[1] So the acknowledgment of Milward's work in ostensibly 'politics' research circles, texts, and curricula should be taken as something of a tribute to the significance of that work and the compelling arguments that it provides. Desmond Dinan, a political scientist, chooses the phrase 'the Milwardian onslaught' to characterize the importance of Milward's historical research on European integration.[2] The pedagogy of EU studies has become accustomed to drawing upon historical scholarship on postwar institution building as an essential prelude to the analysis of contemporary EU governance, policy-making, and external relations. Students of political objects are not unused to being provided with historical context, but the peculiarity of the EU requires that its origins and evolution are narrated somehow, not least because of the idea that we learn something of the present character of the EU if we understand both why it was created in the first place and what dynamics account for its development. The relative youth of the EU tends to act as another reason for the convergence of historical and political science scholarship. As a phenomenon of 'contemporary history', where the release of government archives under the normal thirty-year rule provides a steady year-on-year drip of new data, European integration is recurrently open to the gaze of historians.[3] Plus, as Milward himself noted, the two disciplines have been united by common interest

1. For example, Kavanagh, 'Why Political Science Needs History', and McLean, 'Political Science and History: Friends and Neighbours'.
2. Dinan, 'The Historiography of the European Union', 310.
3. Kaiser, 'From State to Society?' 190.

in a compelling question: 'the causes of the proliferation of supranational institutions in Europe'.[4]

Despite this obvious point of convergence, Milward's work was periodically critical of the way in which political scientists sought to tackle this question. This chapter begins by suggesting that Milward identified two broad areas of criticism of political science: the theory-driven tendency to generalize (often at the expense of the empirical record) and a sometime tendency to emphasize the ideational over the material. It then examines some of the key themes in the contemporary political science of the EU as a prelude to suggesting some ways in which the two disciplines can feed off one another and work together in the study of European integration.

## 'HISTORY HAS CONQUERED THEORY'?[5]

Milward's oft-repeated claim that historical scholarship on the origins of European integration had undermined much of the political science research on the Communities is as important as it is bold. Not only does such an assertion invite investigation of the specifics of the claim itself; it also poses important questions about the relationship between historical and social science scholarship more generally. In Milward's hands the critique of political science / international relations scholarship on European integration developed around two broad and interrelated themes: a tendency to generalize at the expense of the empirical record and an incipient idealism. For the purposes of what follows I will subsume international relations (IR) scholarship under the broad heading of political science. While some writers have paid attention to the distinctiveness of IR scholarship on the EU, it is nevertheless conventional, within political science in the United States at least, to treat IR as one of the broad discipline's main subfields (the others being comparative politics, political theory, and—tellingly—'American' politics).[6]

## GENERALIZATION AND THE RETREAT FROM 'THE FACTS'

The first of these themes concerns the variance between the findings of political scientists and the empirical record. At its most basic this criticism provides a crude vindication of the historian's method, where facts—rather than propositions derived from theory—provide the basis for accurate interpretation of events. Reviewing David Calleo's *Rethinking Europe's Future*, Milward noted that Calleo's 'books are among the few works on

---

4. Milward, 'History, Political Science and European Integration', 99.
5. Milward, *The European Rescue of the Nation-State*, 18.
6. See Kaufman-Osborn, 'Dividing the Domain of Political Science'.

international relations that historians can read without having to flinch in the face of shallow generalizations or plain error'.[7] Presumed here is a relationship between 'generalizations' and 'error': the tendency to engage in the former invariably yields the latter. Most of Milward's ire was reserved for neofunctionalist integration theory. Neofunctionalists held that the development of European integration represented a major reorientation of the form and scale of political authority in Western Europe. The creation of the European Coal and Steel Community and the European Economic Community in the 1950s would have been driven by the functional imperatives of modern complex economies under conditions of heightened interdependence. The expansion of supranational competence would be driven by a mixture of the expansion of functional tasks and processes of loyalty transference as social and economic actors, operating hitherto within domestic settings, become persuaded of the efficacy operating beyond national borders.[8] Milward was not the first to suggest that such an account had underestimated woefully the importance of national governments in the creation and maintenance of the new supranational order, but he was the first to use the detailed historical record to show this.[9]

The problem for Milward was not so much the conclusions that neofunctionalists drew, but how they came to draw them in the first place. Neofunctionalism, he argued,

> failed the test of history because it did not ask the crucial question about where the locus of power lay in the post-war period and, in its enthusiasm for a theory with predictive value, practically did away with the nation-state as the central unit of political organization.[10]

For Milward this type of thinking begets a kind of teleologism that encourages the researcher to look at only those sources vindicating his or her original position. As he put it, '[t]heory appeals to those who want the outcome which the theory predicts.'[11] For example, there are, throughout the history of Western European integration, plenty of examples of the assertion

7. Milward, 'Europe's New-Old Order', 161. This was a review of Calleo, *Rethinking Europe's Future.*
8. The key early texts of neofunctionalism are commonly held to be: Haas, *The Uniting of Europe*; Haas, *Beyond the Nation-State*; and Lindberg, *The Political Dynamics of European Economic Integration.* For an overview see Rosamond, *Theories of European Integration*, Chapter 3.
9. The two most prominent political science critiques of nefunctionalism from this time were Hoffmann, 'Obstinate or Obsolete?' and Roger D. Hansen, 'European Integration'.
10. Milward and Sørensen, 'Interdependence or Integration? A National Choice', 3–4.
11. Milward, *Politics and Economics in the History of the European Union*, 31.

of national governmental authority or of national preferences scuppering integrationist initiatives. An enthusiasm for the basic idea that the nation-state was withering in significance led these political scientists to treat such episodes not as an integral part of the story of integration, but rather as exceptions to the general tendency toward supranationalism.[12] This, for Milward, was a cardinal error: the simplification of the historical record.

Historians were also prone to such 'first principles' errors that misread, fail to read, or distort the valid evidence. This, after all, is Walter Lipgens' primary mistake as understood by Milward.[13] Such idealist, postnational sentiments were rife in the aftermath of World War II. In the case of neofunctionalist political science, the greater influence—well understood by Milward—was social scientific fashion and in particular the affection of (U.S.) political scientists of the 1950s for systems theory and pluralist theories of politics.[14] Systems theory had the immense virtue of providing comparative leverage by finding a conceptual vocabulary to treat all political systems, regardless of time, space, or ideological inflection, as functionally equivalent. The acquisition of general analytical leverage was thus achieved at the expense of specificity. Pluralist political science operated with a conception of the state as little more than a cipher for the processing of societal preferences.[15] Pluralists had rightly drawn the attention of political analysis to the processes of preference formation and aggregation within society, but in so doing had perhaps done away with the autonomy of the state. This made it easier to theorize the withering of the national form of the state as its functional use supposedly diminished. Armed with a baseline conception of the pluralist polity, neofunctionalists had foreseen its transplantation from national to supranational levels of action. In contrast, Milward had been able to show that power remained with the nation-state, that delegations of power to supranational institutions were tightly circumscribed, and that states were able to assert the primacy of national interest, even in the face of significant pressure from below.[16]

Milward also made it clear that the tendency of political scientists toward deductive approaches based upon flimsy premises was a localized example of a more general social scientific problem. In *The European Rescue of the Nation-State*, Milward blamed 'the persistent hold of economic theory as a basic intellectual map for understanding the universe.'[17] Economic theory is prone to see the nation-state as an aberrant constraint on the operation

12. Milward, 'Historical Teleologies'.
13. See Milward, *The European Rescue*, 16–17, for a particularly coruscating critique.
14. Ibid., 10. On systems theory see Easton, *The Political System*.
15. For example, Truman, *The Governmental Process*, and Dahl, *Who Governs?*
16. Milward and Sørensen, 'Interdependence or Integration?' 4.
17. Milward, *Rescue*, 7.

of markets, yet the history of economic cooperation and customs union formation shows that the exercise of national political will—in direct defiance of the precepts of theories of the perfect market order—can be enough to dissolve any such project. Milward's point, therefore, was that there is no inexorable logic of integration. It proceeds according to national will. It also proceeds when specific circumstances allow. The general theories advanced by Ernst B. Haas, Leon N. Lindberg, and Karl W. Deutsch relied upon the very specific sets of historical circumstances found in Western Europe after World War II.[18]

The apparent obsession with political science treatments of integration from the 1950s and 1960s did have some pertinence in the early to mid-1990s, when Milward's critiques were most sharply articulated. The Single European Act (1986) and the more general *relance* of integration under Jacques Delors' European Commission did yield some attempts to reinterrogate the 'spillover' hypothesis that many associated with neofunctionalism.[19] Milward and Sørensen used this as an opportunity to restate the advantages of the historian's method over that of the political scientist:

> [T]he time has surely come to base any attempt at theory on the accumulating empirical evidence of the history of the European Community. Surely the first step towards eliminating the present confusion about European integration must be to get the historical facts right.[20]

The contrast between political science and history as modes of enquiry can be overdrawn or overly stylized. However, Milward was clearly onto something when he talked about the differences in approach to common subject matter that social scientific and historical accounts of European integration illustrate. In a relatively recent and reflective essay on the topic, Milward initially (and ideal-typically) presented history as the study of the particular, where the possible scope of generalized theoretical speculation is, by definition, limited. Indeed the historian suspects any move in the direction of generalization as equally a move in the direction of inaccuracy. Political science, in contrast, relies upon generalized theoretical statements in order to proceed. The absence of a general theoretical framework from which hypotheses can be derived can only yield thick description, which in turn begets zero academic leverage.[21] Put another way, historians are interested in why $x$ happened at point $t$; political scientists are interested in figuring

---

18. Deutsch et al., *Political Community in the North Atlantic Area*. For Haas and Lindberg, see the references provided in footnote 8 above.
19. See Tranholm-Mikkelsen, 'Neo-functionalism: Obstinate or Obsolete?' and Mutimer, '1992 and the Political Integration of Europe'.
20. Milward and Sørensen, 'Interdependence or Integration?' 5.
21. Milward, 'History, Political Science and European Integration'.

out of what *x* at point *t* is an instance. We will return to the degree to which these stylized depictions of enquiry are incompatible later in this chapter.

## IDEALISM(S)

Before doing so, we need to explore the second general charge against the political science of European integration: that its interrogation of the factual record is skewed by a tendency towards idealism. There is more to this than saying that the neofunctionalists came to the study of the early integration projects with a priori ideological preferences. But that is certainly part of the story. We have already noted that Milward read Haas, Lindberg, Deutsch et al. as carriers of a (perhaps understandable) disillusionment with the possibilities of nation-state forms of governance. There is something in this. In a revealing interview about his life and work, Haas—a refugee from Nazi Germany—made it clear that at an early stage of his academic career he became interested in the possibilities of post nationalism:

> What attracted me to the one theme that underlies everything I've done—that theme is the conditions under which the state as we understand it disappears, disintegrates, weakens, changes—okay, why the interest in the state? Well, because I grew up under a system of an extraordinarily powerful state that victimized me. So my idea was, how in the future do we get rid of states of that kind?[22]

But while this constitutes a normative commitment *par excellence*, it is worth noting that Haas was careful to also locate his search for instances where the nation-state was perhaps withering within a broader intellectual context. Aside from the obvious debts to earlier functionalist accounts of postnational governance, Haas and the neofunctionalists were also part of a move within international relations away from the vice-like grip of realism on the subfield.[23] Realists, it should be remembered, were not simply state-centric in their view of international politics. They also discounted the significance of domestic or commercial sources of governmental preferences, preferring to identify the origins of 'national interest' purely within the domain of strategic/security calculus. Haas and the neofunctionalists offered one route away from IR realism. Milward's historical approach and Moravcsik's version of political science,[24] while state-centric, offer alternative routes from the same set of propositions about the dynamics of international politics. Finally, it is worth reiterating that the basic normative

---

22. Kreisler, 'Science and Progress in International Relations: Conversation with Ernst B. Haas'.
23. Haas, 'Introduction: Institutionalism or Constructivism?' xiv.
24. Moravcsik, *The Choice for Europe*.

commitment of neofunctionalism was polished by a serious commitment to the newly emergent professional norms of political science.[25]

The charge of idealism has two further components. The first of these 'errors' is committed when an analyst overemphasizes the role of ideas in explaining political outcomes. In particular, to explain decisions to integrate in terms of the rhetoric of the most voluble proponents of integration and federalism is to commit a grievous analytical error. If anything, from Milward's point of view, this 'great men/big ideas' interpretation was more of a problem with the early historical studies of European integration than with the efforts of political scientists. Chapter 6 of *The European Rescue of the Nation-State*—pointedly entitled 'The Lives and Teachings of the European Saints'—did not cite any political scientists, but the political scientists' search for new forms of international community and shifts in authority toward a new supranational governance was evidently, from the vantage point of this critique, a species of the same problem. In this chapter, Milward did not argue for the complete insignificance of the so-called 'founding fathers' of European integration. Rather Milward argued that their actions were better explained by national motivations than by the drive of federalist or other forms of postnationalist sentiment.

The second additional component of idealism is one that Milward attributed very explicitly to the neofunctionalist scholars of integration. Writing with Vibeke Sørensen, Milward described neofunctionalism as an example of a 'cold war theory'.[26] 'Once the unity of western Europe became a goal of US foreign policy,' they continue, 'political theories which predicted the likelihood of that goal's being achieved proliferated.'[27] Neofunctionalism became 'in the 1950s and 1960s [ . . . ] the intellectual foundation for a hegemonic foreign policy architecture.'[28] This is quite an allegation, if read crudely. Milward and Sørensen did not provide any evidence to demonstrate these connections (direct or otherwise), and the relationship between U.S. political science and U.S. foreign policy is a topic that deserves detailed attention.[29] The accusation against the neofunctionalists is a serious one. To allow values to so penetrate the research process would be to infringe one of the most basic rules of enquiry.[30] However, they did make another important (albeit underdeveloped) point: neofunctionalist ideas came to be

---

25. See Ruggie et al., 'Transformations in World Politics', and Rosamond, 'The Uniting of Europe and the Foundation of EU Studies'. On the professionalization of U.S. political science in the 1950s, see Riker, 'The Ferment of the 1950s'.
26. Milward and Sørensen, 'Interdependence or Integration?', 1.
27. Ibidem.
28. Ibid., 3.
29. For a highly controversial, but scholarly, study along these lines, see Oren, *Our Enemies and US*.
30. See Mihic, Engelmann, and Wingrove, 'Making Sense In and Of Political Science'.

taken up by European policy-makers.[31] In other words, the charge of idealism in this case is not that political scientists themselves drew upon ideas that were empirically invalid, but rather that they generated empirically invalid ideas that were transmitted to policy-makers, who then acted upon the basis of those ideas. This is a very interesting proposition, which so far has been barely investigated in EU studies.[32]

Milward's critique of the political science of European integration is interesting because it did not preface a wholesale retreat to the safety of historical scholasticism and excessive empiricism. In his work after *The European Rescue of the Nation-State* Milward advanced the idea that his more inductive approach, rooted in the tenets of good historical method, had produced an alternative and rather more plausible 'theory' of integration: that of integration as a 'national strategy'.[33] 'Integration' was not necessarily antithetical to national interests. The rational pursuit of national commercial interests could produce integrative outcomes and institutional forms above the nation-state. Political theories of European integration proceeded from the assumption that integration represented a triumph over national will or that successful assertions of national preference would automatically imply the stalling of integration. Milward's theory implied that hypotheses about the sources of integration could be formulated differently from conventional political science. Methodologically, Milward's position implied that national governmental records could be rich sources of information on the motivations for decisions to integrate. Therefore, Milward's field was not a history that regarded all attempts to theorize as *prima facie* bad. Writing in 1995 in the inaugural issue of the *Journal of European Integration History*, Milward argued that the absence of detailed historical scholarship on the origins of integration in the early years of the European Communities was partly responsible for the failings of that early political science. The founding of a new periodical for historians of integration would provide a space for historians to develop and test their own theories, but by implication the two disciplines should learn to work together.[34]

## POLITICAL SCIENCE AND THE LESSONS OF HISTORY

At first sight, Milward's critique of political science seems decisive. It also raises significantly wider questions for both the relationship between the two disciplines and the conduct of social scientific research. It is, after all, hard to argue with a position that insists upon (a) a clear relationship

---

31. Milward and Sørensen, 'Interdependence or Integration?' 3.
32. For a brilliant exception, see White, 'Theory Guiding Practice'.
33. On the twin risks of pure induction and pure deduction, see Grofman, 'Seven Durable Axes of Cleavage'.
34. Milward, 'Allegiance'.

between conclusions and the factual record, (b) the use of hard primary source material as the basis of that factual record, and (c) suspicion of theoretical or ideological predispositions that lead the researcher toward conclusions at variance with the factual record. In his own writings Milward seemed convinced, based upon citation of more recent political science, that he had won the argument. From the vantage point of the mid-1990s Milward interpreted political scientists as by then being broadly in accord with his position.[35] A decade later he dated the political science retreat to Haas's preface to the second (1968) edition of *The Uniting of Europe* where there is explicit acknowledgment of the early neofunctionalists' failure to take account of the role of national governments in the integration process.[36] If Andrew Moravcsik's hugely influential intergovernmentalist work *The Choice for Europe* (1998) was typical of the new political science of European integration, then Milward's work could be seen laying the groundwork.[37] Moravcsik's work maintains that integration is driven by national commercial preferences and occurs and proceeds when the national preferences of the key member-states converge. So there is an empirical resemblance to the Milwardian account. But there is also a theoretical and methodological affinity. Theoretically, Moravcsik is keen to distance himself not only from neofunctionalism, but also from 'grand' theorizing, associating himself with a determined move within political science toward the 'mid range'. Methodologically, Moravcsik makes great play of the virtues of selecting appropriate source material for research:

> [T]he reliability of a source is a function of the extent to which the activity it documents is one in which it is costly to manipulate or misstate the truth [ . . . ] the greater the difficulty of manipulating or concealing evidence of what really occurred at the time, the more reliable (the 'harder') the source in retrospect.[38]

Moravcsik's work has come under detailed scrutiny on this methodological terrain, the key issue being whether he practices what he preaches. For example his two detailed pieces on Charles de Gaulle's European policy came under detailed scrutiny from a group of distinguished historians, Milward included.[39] The developed form of Moravcsik's liberal intergovernmentalism is possibly the single most important intervention in EU studies over

35. Ibid., 7.
36. Milward, 'History, Political Science and European Integration', 101; Haas, *The Uniting of Europe*.
37. Milward, *Politics and Economics*, 36.
38. Moravcsik, *The Choice for Europe*, 82.
39. Moravcsik, 'De Gaulle Between Grain and *Grandeur*'; Milward, 'A Comment on the Article by Andrew Moravcsik'. For a thorough and much more intemperate critique of Moravcsik's use of his sources, see Lieshout, Segers, and van der Vleuten, 'De Gaulle, Moravcsik and *The Choice for Europe*'.

the past two decades. But it is also probably the most disputed account, and thus the most controversial. To regard his government-centered account of integration as a straightforward point of consensus does not stack up on a reading of the vast contemporary political science literature.

This is not the place for a summary of the anatomy of the political science of the EU.[40] For the purposes of this discussion, it is worth teasing out three themes that will provide some context of the state of political science in relation to EU studies. Mention of these themes will also help us to assemble a case for thinking about how political science and history might work together as EU studies move forward. The three issues are first, the localized question in EU studies of what is the appropriate 'object' of enquiry; second, the debate about proper method in political science; and third, the role of ideas in political analysis.

The first of these issues is the question of what is or should be the 'object' of enquiry. Milward's empirical work on European integration is all about why choices were made to delegate powers, hitherto held by national governments, to new supranational institutions. In short, the puzzle is about *integration*, which—by definition—was also the agenda of classical integration theory. However, political scientists have tended to move quite substantially away from the ground staked out by classical integration theory. In perhaps the most visible and well-articulated move of this kind, Simon Hix makes the point that the maturation of the EC/EU into an identifiable political system means that the *problématique* of 'integration' is no longer particularly relevant.[41] By the 1990s, he maintains, the EU had become a complex political system that could be read and analyzed using the tried and trusted tools of political science. Instead of being seen as the consequence of the prevailing preferences of one of state or societal or supranational-institutional forces, the EU should instead be seen as an arena for the practice of really rather familiar processes: executive, legislative, and judicial politics; cleavage formation; pressure group activity, public opinion formation, party politics, and so on. Of course, by inserting the EU into this tradition, Hix is able to make a case for an EU studies that achieves analytical leverage, reaps the benefits of the comparative method and avoids falling into the $n = 1$ trap.[42]

---

See also Pine, 'European Integration: A Meeting Ground for History and Political Science? A Historian Responds to Andrew Moravcsik'.

40. For a recent overview see Rosamond, 'The Political Sciences of European Integration'.
41. This key argument was first made in Hix, 'The Study of the European Community'. For a more recent rendition see Hix, 'The European Union as a Polity (I)'.
42. The $n = 1$ trap or the *sui generis* problem occurs when the object of study is nothing other than an instance of itself. The only possible knowledge that can be generated in such a case is thickly descriptive rather than explanatory, and theory-building is thus impossible.

Others have been more skeptical about the status of the EU as straightforward comparator to national political systems classically defined. From such a position, the EU is better seen as potentially transcendent of established political orders rather than being viewed simply in terms of their reincarnation at a new level of action. This treatment of the EU as a site for experimental forms of governance and/or as part of a 'multi-level' system of governance does not necessarily require the analyst to abandon the search for appropriate comparators.[43] For example, Giandomenico Majone's characterization of the EU as a 'regulatory state' is deliberately couched in terms of the evolution of state forms across the advanced industrialized world, of which the EU is but one interesting example.[44] The point is that the recasting of the object from *integration* to *political system* (albeit in a variety of contested forms) means that the study of the EU is more about how actors (be they state or nonstate) engage in collective forms of decision-making in institutional settings that cover multiple levels of action.

The second and third issues relate to whether the contemporary political science of the EU continues to suffer from the two principal complaints described in the previous section (the tendency to generalize at the expense of the empirical record, and rump idealism). Both are complex matters. Recently political scientists have been engaged in intense debates about questions of methodological propriety, which open up at a quite fundamental level the question of what constitutes 'good' political science. Also one of the key issues in political science over the course of the past decade or so has been the role played by ideas in explaining political outcomes. 'Ideational' approaches to political analysis have become increasingly significant since the mid-1990s.[45]

Standard texts on political science methodology prohibit the kinds of errors of which Milward accused the early integration theorists. The most-used text in U.S. graduate schools sets very clear benchmarks for what qualifies as good qualitative political science. For Gary King, Robert O. Keohane, and Sidney Verba, the relationship between four components of research design (research question, theory, data, and the use of data) is the key.[46] Theory, from this point of view, 'is a reasoned and precise speculation about the answer to a research question'.[47] Theories that proceed in defiance of the empirical evidence are not proper theories in this sense. The Popperian standard of falsifiability should be applied to theory choice. Such

---

43. For a good summary of this position, see Jachtenfuchs, 'The European Union as a Polity (II)'. On 'multi-level governance', see Hooghe and Marks, *Multi-Level Governance and European Integration*.
44. Majone, *Dilemmas of European Integration*.
45. A recent overview and discussion of ideational approaches is given in Gofas and Hay, *The Role of Ideas in Political Analysis*.
46. King, Keohane, and Verba, *Designing Social Inquiry*, Chapter 1.
47. Ibid., 19.

textbooks on political science research will never instruct the user to pursue theory for theory's sake, but it is certainly the case that one of the principal rationales for conducting research, in addition to developing practical or 'real world' applications out of the findings, is to improve theory.[48] W. Phillips Shively calls this—rather unhelpfully—'recreational research', but it is clear that such theory-oriented work is seen by the mainstream of the modern political science community as the basis of robust explanation.[49] There are several reasons for this preference. The rules of theory building, when properly adhered to, are the most capable of producing robust explanations. If a theory is stated simply, if it is falsifiable, capable of being serviced by a mass of data and attached to questions of relevance, then it is much more likely to yield reliable empirical results. Shively argues that 'to be "new", the research results must either produce totally new theories or lead to some change in the status of older theories'.[50] Given Milward's preference for (or at least nonallergic reaction to) the idea of 'theory', this does seem like a point of significant convergence.

*European Union Politics*, a journal founded at the turn of the twenty-first century, was required, its first editorial team maintained, because of the need to unite study of the EU with the most advanced and sophisticated work being undertaken within political science.[51] However, such claims about what counts and is thus admissible as the 'best' political science is open to criticism from those who would prefer the discipline to be theoretically and methodologically pluralist.[52] In the case of EU studies, there is an additional question of whether a move to harder, more disciplinary forms of enquiry would scupper the interdisciplinary potential of EU studies.[53] Plus what if the EU actually is different? Standards of theoretical propriety and methodological rules of thumb hatched to study the operation of national political systems—that is, historically specific forms of governance—may have perverse effects when applied to the EU. Such 'methodological nationalism' would have the effect of reading a genuinely novel governance form as if it were familiar and 'normal', thus obscuring what might be very interesting abnormalities.[54]

---

48. There is no necessary logical disconnect between political science as policy-relevant and political science as 'scientific'. Indeed the latter was seen in one early statement of intent as a prerequisite of the former. See Easton, 'The Decline of Modern Political Theory'.
49. Shively, *The Craft of Political Research*, 4–6.
50. Ibid., 23.
51. Schneider, Gabel, and Hix, '*European Union Politics* Editorial Statement'.
52. See Monroe, *Perestroika! The Raucous Rebellion in Political Science*, and Rosamond, 'European Integration and the Social Science of EU Studies'.
53. On interdisciplinarity in EU studies see Rumford and Murray, 'Globalization and the Limitations of European Integration Studies'.
54. This argument is made by Beck and Grande, *Cosmopolitan Europe*. These authors criticize the orthodox social science of the EU for insisting upon the

These squabbles about theory and method also bleed into debates about the role of ideas in political outcomes. Milward's work shares with Moravcsik's a view that ideas have not been significant drivers of integration. These are broadly 'rationalist' arguments. Outcomes are explained by actors operating on the basis of their predefined interests. To focus on ideas is misleading because either (a) ideas are no more than strategic or rhetorical justifications for materially motivated action (so they cannot be the root causes of outcomes) or (b) ideas are obfuscatory, if not false, in which case the task of the political analyst is to point to the reality as distinct from the rhetoric or to provide a corrective to the errors and exaggerations of political discourse. The 'ideational' literature contains many strands, and it is probably misleading to portray, as is common, the field of contemporary political science as bisected by a division between rationalist and constructivist camps where the former does not take ideas seriously and the latter does.[55] Nor is there space here for a full-scale discussion of the premises of ideational/constructivist social science other than that ideas are generally seen as the crucial filters though which actors encounter and act upon the social world. Actors' interests and identities, as well as the environments in which they operate, are not fixed exogenously to action. All of these are socially constructed, which means in turn that the social scientist should also ask questions about the processes through which the contexts of action become normalized as 'social facts' and how some actions are thought of as more technically or normatively rational than others.

The constructivist turn has not eluded the study of EU politics.[56] One of the emphases of such work has been the building of various forms of political community in Europe around emergent shared norms. This means that a good deal of constructivist research has brought the question of 'integration' back in to the study of the EU, albeit in a way that is both attentive to integration as a process without preordained outcome and the multiple sites (not just supranational institutions) where such dynamics occur. In his last writings on European integration Haas became very interested in the potential for bridge building between soft

---

use of theories and techniques that were developed to study national forms of governance. By deploying such theories and utilizing such techniques, social scientists reproduce images of European integration that are preprogrammed to neglect or downgrade transcendent or transformative aspects of the process.

55. The rationalist–constructivist distinction occurs at a fundamental ontological level. Constructivists dispute the rationalist claim that the world is materially given, preferring instead to see reality as socially constructed. Broadly speaking this leads constructivists of various hues to the idea that human encounters with the material world are not easily separated from ideas about the world.
56. For a discussion, see Checkel, 'Constructivism and EU Politics'.

rationalist theories like neofunctionalism and the new constructivism.[57] Indeed it is possible to read protoconstructivist themes into some of the classic neofunctionalist literature.[58]

## CONCLUSIONS: TOWARD A HISTORICAL POLITICAL SCIENCE OF THE EU?

From this brief overview, we might draw the following conclusions. First, historical scholarship is central to the enterprise of EU studies. Second, historians have tended to touch base with political scientists in the study of integration dynamics (what explains European integration and the creation of supranational institutions). Third, 'Milward school' historians actually share more with many political scientists than ideal-typical representations of 'history' and 'political science' suggest. Indeed, the claims to distinctiveness made by the historical school are certainly valid in terms of the quality and impact of their findings, but the claim of methodological separation from political scientists working on the EU is exaggerated and relies upon a limited reading of the relevant political science literature. Nevertheless, political science has diversified its encounters with the EU far beyond its initial preoccupation with 'integration'. It disagrees with itself about what kind of polity the EU is and what role ideational (as opposed to material) dynamics play in the politics of the EU.

The relationship between history and political science to date offers ample evidence of the virtues of thinking of EU studies as a site for multiple disciplines to work with one another. Just as legal scholarship on the EU has forced political scientists to take the jurisprudence and the constitutionalizing role of the Court of Justice of the European Communities/Union seriously, so historians have provided important archive-based correctives to some of the key hypotheses that have guided political science research. Indeed, historians are better than anyone at reminding political scientists of the existence of the archive and of its potential to fulfill the role of robust primary source. With the exception of works such as those of Moravcsik and Parsons, there is actually a paucity of work from political scientists that concentrates on defined historical periods of European integration.[59] There are fine theoretically informed studies by historians, but these rarely appear on the radar screens of political scientists, who for professional/disciplinary reasons tend to read and cite work within political science.[60] Thus what is

---

57. Haas, 'Does Constructivism Subsume Neo-functionalism?' and Haas, 'Introduction: Institutionalism or Constructivism?'
58. For example, Rosamond, 'The Uniting of Europe'.
59. Moravcsik, *Choice for Europe*, and Parsons, *A Certain Idea of Europe*.
60. Examples of theoretically informed histories of European integration include Daddow, *Britain and Europe since 1945*, and Kaiser, *Using Europe, Abusing*

needed is something rather more than an articulated call for historians and political scientists of integration to read each others' work. Rather a genuine partnership could be forged whereby political scientists and historians develop clear projects to answer puzzles that can be addressed through access to the archive-based sources of the 1960s, 1970s, and soon enough the 1980s. Such projects require historians to think like Milward: to have an eye on the bigger explanatory picture, but not to be distracted by it.[61] From the other side, they require the practice of what might be termed 'open political science'.[62] As far as this argument is concerned, openness means the avoidance of the exercise of tight disciplinarity and closure around a set of rigid definitions of what is admissible research.

Is it possible to bring together historical work that has tended to find in the archive confirmation of rational interest-driven behavior as a key driver of integration and recent work in political science that takes ideas seriously? They would seem to be antithetical. Here are two suggestions. First, in his 2007 essay Milward agreed with Haas that there is significant merit in looking at 'the sociological theory of how "actors" construct their interests as a result of the historical context shaping their perception'.[63] This is, in effect, to concede to the constructivist point that 'interests' are historical constructions. If interests are constructed, then it follows that what is deemed to be rational is also historically contingent. The striking finding of Milward's studies of European integration is that a rationality predicated on the logic of national interest prevailed over a rationality derived from certain ideas of postnationalism. Not only does it remain important to see whether such a story continues to hold over time, but it is also well worth thinking about *how* and *why* that logic was able to prevail. Recent work by Frank Schimmelfennig has suggested, in contrast, that the logic of national interest was not able to prevent the eastern enlargement of the EU precisely because of the capacity of key actors to deploy norm-based arguments strategically.[64] According to Schimmelfennig, appeals to Community standards of legitimacy (normative arguments) were able to outflank the interest-driven calculus of member-state preferences. Rationalist political science, based upon an analysis of the preferences of key member-states, would not have expected enlargement to occur. In other words, historically informed, archive-based scholarship should also be prepared to look for outcomes based upon the 'logic of appropriateness' (behavior that follows from norms, identities, and

---

*the Europeans.*

61. See Kaiser, 'From State to Society?' for a fuller discussion of how historians should look to generate historical scholarship that is compatible with social science theory.
62. Rosamond, 'Open Political Science'.
63. Milward, 'History, Political Science and European Integration', 101.
64. Schimmelfennig, 'The Community Trap'.

values) rather than or in addition to 'the logic of consequences' (behavior driven by rational calculus).[65]

Second, recall the—almost throwaway—accusation by Milward and Sørensen that neofunctionalism was an erroneous set of propositions that became (nevertheless) influential in European Community policy-making circles in the 1960s. Some historians may balk at the idea that their project is anything other than the adjudication of historical veracity. But the way in which ideas are taken up by and populate institutions—even if those ideas are at variance with the empirical record—is a topic on which historians and political science should have much to say. There is, after all, an emerging sociological literature that shows how economic ideas can have 'reality effects'.[66] Conceptualizations of the world that originate in abstraction are taken up by real-world actors, whose behavior in accordance with the precepts of the abstract model in turn generates a reality that confirms the original abstraction. Equally interesting—and this may apply to the history of European integration—are instances where the take-up of ideas do *not* have these performative consequences. Even if actors can be shown to have internalized, say, neofunctionalist propositions, their failure to realize them—if found—may even prove to strengthen yet further the thesis about the prevailing logic of national interest that guides Milward's historical research.

65. See March and Olsen, 'The Institutional Dynamics of International Political Orders'.
66. See for example Mackenzie, Muniesa, and Siu, *Do Economists Make Markets?*

# 19 Interests and Ideas

## Alan Milward, *The Europeanization of Agricultural Protection*, and the Cultural Dimensions of European Integration*

*Kiran Klaus Patel*

One of the lasting achievements of Alan S. Milward's research is undoubtedly his subtle analysis of agricultural integration in Europe after 1945. As one of the first scholars to do so, he challenged the hitherto dominant interpretation of the birth of the towering common policy of the early European Economic Community, a view that still haunts the world today. According to the standard narrative, the EEC's Common Agricultural Policy (CAP) was created in a sort of compromise—or, more appropriately for the topic, a horse trade—between the Federal Republic of Germany and France. German industry would have access to the French market for industrial goods; in exchange, Germany helped pay for France's farmers and accepted a supranational, protectionist, and expansive CAP.[1]

Milward, in contrast, demonstrated that both governments had a vital interest in industrial trade, whereas French agriculture interests originally had been rather suspicious of the complex creature into which the CAP was to develop. Moreover, Milward argued, the conventional wisdom downplays the role of the Netherlands, an important early contributor to the CAP with a huge impact on its basic structure.[2] Over the past ten years, research has confirmed many elements of this interpretation and added further nuance to it.[3] Milward's work thus remains an indispensable point of reference for any analysis of the topic.

On a conceptual basis, Milward's work focused on the role and the interests of nation-states negotiating and collaborating over European integration. Accordingly, European integration after 1945 was the result of the

---

* This chapter revisits a subject that Alan Milward discussed in 'The Europeanization of agricultural protection', chapter 5 of his *The European Rescue of the Nation-State* (1992).

1. E.g., see http://en.wikipedia.org/wiki/Common_Agricultural_Policy (accessed on 1 December 2010).
2. Milward, *The European Rescue of the Nation-State* (2nd. ed., 2000), 283–284; and *The Reconstruction of Western Europe, 1945–51* (1984), 435–461.
3. E.g., see Knudsen, *Farmers on Welfare*; Patel, *Europäisierung wider Willen*; N. P. Ludlow, 'The Making of the CAP'.

bargaining of 'national interests'. The main motivation behind integration was thus not to transcend or supersede the nation-state; instead, joint projects and institutions stand for a selective Europeanization of domestic welfare policies that the member-states could not have sustained any longer.[4]

For the argument of this chapter, Milward's definition of these national interests is important. In his work, particularly in his studies of the nascent CAP, he emphasized socioeconomic motivations and provided a powerful interpretation of how political and economic considerations played out in the process of European integration. As such, his approach privileged material interests. Having said that, Milward's interpretation also left some room for the role of ideas in the making of Europe's agricultural policy. In the chapter on the Europeanization of agricultural protection in the *European Rescue of the Nation-State*, for instance, he mentioned the 'old rhetoric of nineteenth-century French agrarians, that agriculture was the fabric of "*la France éternelle*"', and that such notions enjoyed 'a splendid revival across the whole of Western Europe' after 1945. For Milward, these ideas were 'surely provoked by the wish to hide reality' and stood for a 'frenzy of concealment'.[5] Overall, Milward certainly did not ignore ideas and culture; nonetheless, they appeared merely as 'ideologies', covering the truly important economic and political processes, or as their sheer replication. Still, these nonmaterial factors seemed to have hardly any causal value.[6]

This is exactly the starting point of this chapter. It argues that in the realm of European integration, as elsewhere, ideas and culture more generally should be seen as explicit factors in their own right. This, however, does not mean that they have a historic significance separate from material factors, as suggested by some historians opposed to the Milwardian approach. Among the latter are those who identify with Walter Lipgens in emphasizing the contributions of the resistance movements, as well as the European movement to the 'European idea', but fall short of demonstrating the precise link from there to interstate bargaining processes.[7] Instead, the argument of this chapter is that particular ideas mattered in particular socioeconomic circumstances: for example, the European family farm provided a particularly powerful image that has shaped the history of the CAP from its inception until today. Mentioned only briefly in Milward's analysis, it shall be discussed here in more detail and weighed in its importance.[8]

4. Most explicit in Milward, *Rescue*.
5. Milward, *Rescue*, 235.
6. This is particularly true for Milward's empirical work on the history of the CAP. Other parts of his work seem to leave a bit more room for culture; see Milward, 'Allegiance: The Past and the Future', even if also there, ideas per se are of little interest.
7. As recent surveys of the state of the art, see Kaiser and Varsori, *European Union History*, and Patel, 'Europäische Integrationsgeschichte'.
8. Revealingly, the index of Milward, *The European Rescue*, does not have an entry on this expression, and family-owned farms are only mentioned

I argue that this image was a central element legitimizing agricultural integration and underpinning concrete political negotiations.[9] Moreover, I show that this concept preceded the birth of the CAP and that it then became an important factor in shaping its political—but to a much lesser extent, its economic—trajectory. The story of the rural image's waxing and waning thus appears to represent an intricate but certain core element of the CAP.

In order to fully grasp the creation of this image, one's focus should go beyond the state actors that dominated Milward's analysis.[10] Admittedly, in his work on agricultural integration particularly, the British historian gave ample room to nonstate actors, notably to potent national pressure groups such as the French *Fédération nationale des syndicats d'exploitants agricoles* or the German *Deutscher Bauernverband*.[11] Milward thus provided a nuanced analysis of the internal disputes within the various nation-states. In his work, national interests do not appear as a given but rather as the outcome of complex bargaining processes involving state as well as nonstate actors. On the international level, however, Milward treated states as the only relevant and consistent actors, fighting for their material interests in intergovernmental bargaining processes. Hence, he attributed little explanatory power to transnational activities of nationally defined nonstate actors, to the role of transnational platforms as well as of newly instituted European bodies such as the European Commission. Upon analyzing the image of the European family farm, it becomes clear that such transnational institutions did have quite an impact on the course and direction of European integration.

At the same time, my line of argument draws a lot of inspiration from Milward's work in at least two further respects. More than many other scholars over the last decade, he highlighted the long-term dimension of European integration. The rather presentist tendency of a good portion of the literature produced over the last fifteen or twenty years—that starts in the postwar era without factoring in longer trajectories—stands in marked contrast to Milward's genuinely historical approach. An additional strength of his work that this chapter tries to adapt is to avoid approaching European integration history only from the perspective of its member-states and

---

in passing in an economic context, e.g., 231–232, 296, footnote 116. See also Milward and Saul, *The Development of the Economies of Continental Europe, 1850–1914* (1977), 228.

9. This phenomenon has not been studied very much so far; see Knudsen, 'Ideas, Welfare, and Values'; Bluche and Patel, 'Der Europäer als Bauer'.
10. For a similar line of criticism, see Kaiser, Leucht, and Rasmussen, *The History of the European Union*; Kaiser, Leucht, and Gehler, *Transnational Networks*; on methodological nationalism more generally, see, e.g., Wimmer and Schiller, 'Methodological Nationalism and Beyond'.
11. See also, e.g., Griffiths and Milward, 'The European Agricultural Community'.

its inner dynamics. Against the reductionism of this 'intrinsic' approach, Milward pointed us in the direction of considering a wide range of 'external' actors and, in doing so, forces one to reconsider questions of agency, namely inclusion, exclusion, and delimitation.[12]

*

* *

The idealization of the peasant as an embodiment of particular social and moral qualities can be traced back to antiquity. A well-known example is Lucius Quinctius Cincinnatus: this fifth-century BC Roman was working on his farm until he was called by the Senate to serve as dictator, an office from which he immediately resigned after completing his task of defeating Rome's enemies. Cincinnatus was soon praised as an example of outstanding leadership, civic rectitude, and modesty. By and large, one finds a long tradition of praising the particular virtues embodied in farming. Certainly one has to avoid overgeneralizing from long-term continuities, and there is also a long and parallel history of criticism of rural life, describing it as barbarian and backward. More important in this context is the fact that since the nineteenth century a combination of modernization of technology and of globalization challenged the basic fabric of the agricultural world, and that as a reaction to these changes the idealization of the family farm gained tremendous force in Western societies. It was lifted from and united beyond the sphere of a sheer economic enterprise and loaded with strong moral and social overtones. In part, these debates were driven by nostalgia for a lost or jeopardized world; in part, they sought to legitimize massive state protection for the sector.

These ideologies, which Heinz Gollwitzer and others have analyzed, became even more important after 1918 when many European countries—particularly in Eastern, Eastern Central, and Northern Europe—witnessed the creation of specific political parties rallied around an ideology of peasantry or farming. In 1929, for instance, the Czechoslovakian politician Karel Viškovský stressed that the peasant was 'the eternal creator and renovator of values, the upholder of life and of the circuit of the basic values of the state'. This ideology saw the rural sector as a source of identity, vitality, and self-assurance vis-à-vis accelerated social change. Despite confessional, social, and political differences, one would find very similar statements in Spain, Norway, or many other parts of Europe, and they had a strong impact on agricultural policies.[13]

Until 1945, the main point of reference of these ideologies was the nation, even if regional affiliations remained important. Accordingly,

12. For details, see Patel, 'Europäische Integrationsgeschichte', 635–641.
13. Speech by Karel Viškovský published in *Bulletin Mezinárodního Bureau*, Prague 1929, 111 (own translation); many other examples in Gollwitzer, *Europäische Bauernparteien*.

it took a strong nation-state to bring farms to full fruition, and in line with the organicist language of the time, the same was true the other way round, too.[14] There were many structural similarities and even convergences between the various forms of agrarian romanticism and rhetoric across the Western world. The years between 1889 and 1919 also saw regular international agricultural congresses with heavy European participation.[15] But contrary to the internationalism of the labor movement, the explicit transnational or European dimension of the rhetoric of the family farm remained rather marginal before 1914.

The interwar years then saw a slight increase in transnational activities, with state and nonstate actors trying to find solutions to the aggravating problems of the agricultural sector.[16] For instance, the League of Nations got increasingly interested in this issue during the 1920s and 1930s. Even if this organization is normally seen as part of what Akira Iriye has called the 'Global Community', much of its work was dominated by European powers and their preoccupations, and particularly in the field of agriculture they sought to find European solutions to transnational and global challenges.[17] For instance, in 1939 the League planned a 'Conference on European Rural Life'. The preparatory work of this conference stressed the central role of the family farm—here seen not merely in a national context but framed as a pan-European phenomenon.[18] The conference itself, however, never took place, for when it was scheduled—in September 1939—the outbreak of war forbade such activities. The fate of this initiative—as well as of the League by and large—is thus quite representative of all attempts to Europeanize the notion of the family farm before 1945.

After the Second World War a Europeanized version of this vision of farming and rural life, and more particularly the idea of the family farm as an allegedly European trait, gained momentum. In the beginning, it was a rather small group of people who advocated such an idea, the most prominent person among them being the Swiss Professor of Agricultural Science Ernst Laur (1871–1964). Laur had already been a leading figure in international agricultural cooperation during the 1920s. After the Second World War he became the first president of the *Confédération européenne de l'agriculture* (CEA), which in 1948, when it was founded, brought together ten—and a few years later as many as 475—agricultural lobby groups from nineteen nations. The CEA, the most important agrarian special interest group in early postwar Western Europe, called the family farm 'their core element and their key plea'. According to Laur, 'European

14. See, e.g., Weber, *Peasants into Frenchmen*.
15. Aldenhoff-Hübinger, *Agrarpolitik und Protektionismus*, 42–70.
16. See Von Graevenitz, 'From Kaleidoscope to Architecture'.
17. Iriye, *Global Community*, 20–23.
18. League of Nations, *European Conference on Rural Life*; for more details, see Clavin and Patel, 'The Role of International Organizations'.

agriculture differed significantly from that overseas'. The European family farm with its diversified economy, its strong share of self-sufficiency, and the prominent role of women and children was epitomized as a specifically European phenomenon.[19] As on the national level, the main idea was that the family farm deserved the utmost attention and protection because it comprised particular qualities of Europe's agriculture and rural economy, but also symbolized the Continent's heritage and culture.

'Othering' was an important factor in this process of Europeanization. Laur, for instance, stressed the threat of 'the communist idea and the elimination of independent and free family enterprises because of state-owned estates, kolkhozes, and similar forms'.[20] Collectivization in the Eastern bloc and, more generally, rising cold war tensions were important factors as to why the family farm was now not only framed in national but also in European terms as an imperiled way of life and production, and as a beacon in the ideological night. Still, it should be noted that the family farm was not perceived as a shared Western idea, but more as a particularly European achievement. It was often also demarcated from the United States' capitalist large-scale farming, even if delimitation was less aggressive and explicit than vis-à-vis the East.[21] Ironically, the United States also witnessed an intensifying discussion of the 'family farm' at the time, and also here close links between collective identity and farming were drawn, thus updating a long-standing element of American political culture, going back to Thomas Jefferson's idea of the 'yeoman farmer'.[22] An additional irony was that despite its eurocentrist proclamations, the CEA also included organizations from countries that most people would probably not call European, such as Lebanon or Tunisia. Intellectual consistency was certainly not the norm.

Therefore, the Europeanization of the idea of the family farm had many different sources. To some extent, it was driven by the cold war. Agriculture was a showcase of Communist policy, with its 'collective farms' offering a clear-cut alternative to the way labor, property, and distribution—but also other issues like gender roles—were organized in the West, under the auspices of capitalism. In the light of this threatening alternative, entrepreneurship, freedom, and self-control were stylized as the 'European'

19. CEA (Confédération européenne de l'agriculture), *Historique, organisation, activité*, 28–29 (own translation); see also ibid., 70–80 and 214; see also Bundesarchiv Koblenz (BA/K), B 136/2562, EEC, Information on CEA Resolution, 5 February 1959; Historical Archives of the European Union (HAEU), BAC 9/1972–1, CEA Declaration, 15 October 1965.
20. CEA, *Historique, organisation, activité*, 29 (own translation).
21. See, e.g., BA/K, B 116/2975, Speech by Walter Hallstein, first president of the European Commission, 3 July 1958.
22. See, e.g., U.S. Farmers Home Administration, *Strengthening the Family Farm*; Schmidt, *The Family Farm*; on these debates, see Jager, *The Fate of Family Farming*, and Vogeler, *The Myth of the Family Farm*.

answer, and the family farm perceived as the quintessential expression of these qualities.

As a second global factor the increasing density of trans- and international organizations connecting Western European countries among themselves and knitting close links to North America must be mentioned. The production and trade of agricultural commodities and the situation of rural societies were discussed not only in forums such as the General Agreement on Tariffs and Trade and the United Nations—particularly its Food and Agriculture Organization (FAO) and its Economic Commission for Europe (UNECE)—but also in the Council of Europe as well as in the Marshall Plan's Organization for European Economic Cooperation (OEEC). The creation of these organizations went hand in hand with the birth of new NGOs, such as CEA and the International Federation of Agricultural Producers. This latest wave of Western internationalism with its alphabet soup of institutions both harmonized positions on important agricultural questions and promoted visions of the transnational solidarity thereof. This justified their existence in demanding joint action, thereby legitimizing the integration of Western European agriculture in the name of the family farm.[23]

Furthermore, economic globalization and the gospel of modernization exerted pressure on the agrarian world and helped to forge transnational, Europeanized rural images. The production and productivity of most European farms lagged behind countries such as the United States or New Zealand. Building on earlier waves of state interventionism—most importantly a first wave after the late 1870s and a second one after the late 1920s—European agriculture sought new instruments in order to survive global competition. These economic challenges were largest in those West European states, such as France and the Netherlands, with huge surpluses because they had to seek markets for their domestic production. Not surprisingly the first plans of creating a European agricultural community came from these two nation-states.[24]

And, finally, the nostalgic and romantic patina of this image also aimed at stabilizing individual and collective identities in times of fundamental change. While these factors had also been played out on national levels for several decades, it was the relative weakness of the nation-state in the early postwar years that explains why the idea of the *European* family farm now gained in influence. Nation-states found themselves in a deadlock: they wished to include the crisis-ridden farmers in the increased welfare statism of the time, yet they also feared the danger of overburdening themselves with the heavy state subsidies which protectionism implied. Therefore they

---

23. See Iriye, *Global Community*, 37–59; Patel, 'Paradefall der Integration?'; on the broader context, see Iriye, *Global Community*, 63–103.
24. See Griffiths and Girvin, *Green Pool*, particularly Griffiths and Guirao, 'The First Proposals'; Tracy, *Government and Agriculture*.

started looking for new means of helping their farmers. 'Europe' seemed to supply the answer.[25]

*

* *

These Europeanized rural images of the family farm would have remained a footnote in history had the 1950s not seen several concrete attempts at integration by political means in Europe. On agriculture specifically, the first part of the 1950s brought the discussion of the '*Pool vert*' project, as a first attempt to integrate the agricultural markets and policies in Western Europe. After several rounds of discussion this project failed; and quite interestingly, the idea of the European family farm as a common denominator was less central to it than it would be to later efforts.[26]

The second attempt at agricultural integration was started as part of what an earlier historiography has called the '*relance européenne*' after 1954, and it featured a European rural rhetoric more prominently. The 1956 Spaak report, which became a central document on the way to the Treaties of Rome, was extremely vague regarding all practical problems of agricultural integration. Still, it stressed that the 'special problems that stem from the social structure of agriculture, based essentially on family farming' demanded strong measures.[27] Two years later, the 1957 EEC Treaty opened the possibility for agricultural integration but left all the important details unsettled. The agricultural ministers of the six original member-states as well as representatives of their farmers' unions then met in Stresa to discuss the problems of the sector and means of integration. In his opening speech the president of the Commission, Walter Hallstein, said:

> In almost all of Europe, agricultural enterprises have the same family structure. Politicians and economists will certainly agree: the

---

25. Milward, *Rescue*, 224–317; Griffiths and Girvin, *Green Pool*.
26. E.g., see the defensive statement of the International Federation of Agricultural Producers, 'Resolution', 4–6 September 1951, or the marginality of the argument during the important discussion in the Council of Europe on 1 December 1951, or the absence of this notion in the *Résolution de la Conférence sur l'organisation des marchés agricoles*, 20 May 1953. Here, the CEA is the exception to the rule, emphasizing the 'exploitation familiale': *Résolution adoptée par l'Assemblé générale de la Confédération européenne de l'agriculture*, 27 September 1951. All these documents are available online via www.cvce.eu (accessed on 1 December 2011). For the broader context and reasons for the project's failure, see Thiemeyer, *Vom 'Pool Vert'*, Griffiths and Girvin, *Green Pool*, and Noël, *Du Pool Vert*.
27. Comité intergouvernemental crée par la conférence de Messine (ed.), *Rapport des chefs de délégation*, 40 (own translation).

> conservation of the family farm with its independent labor and its human values has to march lock-step with the development of modern society.[28]

Also many representatives of the member-states identified the family farm with Europe and stressed its importance. The final resolution of the conference emphasized that 'all means should be taken to support and strengthen these particular enterprises'.[29] Thus, the family farm played an important role in policy documents of the early EEC and became the general orientation and role model of the Common Agricultural Policy, the largest, most expansive and in many respects defining policy of the European integration process in the first decades of its existence. The CAP was conceived primarily as a means of welfare statism, aiming to improve the income of family farms and stressing their place in society. The needs of consumers, taxpayers, or producers outside the Community were considered to a much lesser extent.[30]

A closer scrutiny of the debates reveals that in different parts of Europe the precise content of this rural image varied widely. In France, for instance, the link between the '*exploitation familiale*' and the nation-state was much stronger than in the case of the West German '*bäuerlicher Familienbetrieb*', whereas the anticommunist rationale loomed larger on the Eastern side of the Rhine. In the Netherlands and Denmark, economic arguments played a more important role, whereas the link to cultural identity was weaker. In Italy, one finds similar claims. Furthermore, each society obviously saw a plurality of opinions, corresponding to the different political camps. To paraphrase George Bernard Shaw, one could therefore say that the six EEC member-states were divided by one common point of reference: the European family farm.[31]

Despite the use of similar rhetoric by their politicians, the agricultural sectors of the six original EEC member-states were rather heterogeneous. The family farm did not give an accurate picture of life and work in the European countryside but a highly eclectic, romanticized ideal. There also existed large units of production, some of which used the latest business- and agro-technologies, whereas others relied on labor-intense practices and the remnants of feudal hierarchies. Nor did tenancy, cooperatives, and part-time farming correspond with the propagated ideal. Economic demands, production, and the culture of farming varied widely. Yet all were now

---

28. BA/K, B 116/2975, Speech by Hallstein, 3 July 1958 (own translation).
29. Communauté européenne, *Recueil des documents*, 219–224 (own translation).
30. This is the central hypothesis of Knudsen, *Farmers on Welfare*.
31. Bluche and Patel, 'Der Europäer', 142–153; Knudsen, 'Romanticising Europe', 52; for Denmark and the Netherlands, see Sørensen, 'Denmark, the Netherlands'; for Italy, see, e.g., Laschi, *L'agricoltura italiana*.

latched on to one rural image, which not only resonated well with a long-standing idealism but also with the specific needs of these societies in their search for a balance between modernization and globalization on the one hand and cultural identity and stability (sometimes including very conservative and in some cases also the fragments of fascist ideas) on the other.[32]

Against this backdrop, the Europeanized rural image became so central from the second part of the 1950s onwards precisely because it did *not* provide a clear-cut and detailed plan for political action. Cloaking was an important part of the operation. Due to its haziness, it could be easily latched onto the national discussions over the value of the family farm, which all European countries had since the nineteenth century, thus strengthening the credibility of this new, transnational point of reference. With public spheres still predominantly organized along national lines, each country could have its own version and discussion of the (European) family farm, informed and driven by national traditions, cleavages, and needs.

'Othering' continued to be a key component of this process. The cold war climate of the late 1940s had already led to a reduction of this Europe of the Europeanized family farm to Western Europe.[33] A decade later, the 'European family farm' was applied even more narrowly to those residing within the Europe of the Six. Ironically, Laur, as one of the first propagators of this idea, now found himself and his Swiss co-farmers on the wrong side of the fence. Even if the CEA continued to propagate this rural image, the EEC forum had become the center stage for the discussion, marginalizing—and to some extent usurping—older and larger points of reference. André Genin, the vice president of the most important French farmers' union, the *Fédération nationale des syndicats d'exploitants agricoles*, summed up this position:

> Between the types of agriculture of the Eastern countries and of the American continent, the Europe of the Six shall prove the viability and efficiency of agricultural enterprises of the modern family type by forging a united and organized agriculture.[34]

In the EEC member-states, it was primarily the actors directly involved in CAP politics that further developed the idea of the European family farm. This was true for the European Parliament as well as other Community bodies. What is more, the *Comité des organisations professionnelles*

32. On the situation of agriculture, see Federico, *Feeding the World*, 117–142.
33. As examples for the delimitation from the East, see CEA, *Historique*, 29; as later examples, see, e.g., Politisches Archiv des Auswärtigen Amtes, Berlin (PA/AA), B 20–200/433, Pressestelle Bundeslandwirtschaftsministerium, Speech by West Germany's minister of agriculture Werner Schwarz, 24 August 1960; Archiv für Christlich-Soziale Politik der Hanns-Seidel-Stiftung, Munich, NL Höcherl/39, West Germany's minister of agriculture Hermann Höcherl to journalist Ullrich Breuer, 25 November 1969.
34. Genin, 'Vers l'ère nouvelle' (own translation).

*agricoles* (COPA)—a transnational committee of farmers' pressure groups tailored to the size of the six EEC member-states—stressed the central role of the family farm, and used it in public statements as well as in its communications with the bodies of the EEC.[35] And the *Comité agricole franco-allemand* underscored this in a report of 1958 with regard to European communalities: 'The same family structure with a majority of small and medium-size family farms'.[36] National lobby groups and administrations—but also farmers and others participating in the debate—were less consistent. Much of their rhetoric and policies were directed at the national level; but the European dimension was introduced whenever this wider horizon helped to formulate, legitimize, and propagate particular claims.[37]

Despite the fact that this discussion was led only by a rather narrow group of actors, it continued to be imbedded in and stabilized by wider discourses and practices. Maybe most prominently, the Papal Encyclical *Mater et Magistra* of 1961 dedicated a long passage to agriculture and stressed that the family farm should 'be safeguarded and encouraged in harmony with the common good and technical progress'.[38] Certainly, the reach of the Catholic Church was smaller, yet also much larger than the EEC. But still, *Mater et Magistra* became a point of reference and legitimization for the Europeanization of the family farm as a particular feature of Western Europe and, more precisely, of the EEC.[39]

Simultaneously, other institutions, particularly transatlantic and international ones, supported the European dimension of this vision through discourses and practices. FAO, the ECE, and the OEEC as well as its successor, the Organization for Economic Cooperation and Development, played an important role because they collected immense amounts of data on the situation of European agriculture and its farms. They were supported by lesser-known bodies such as the European Productivity Agency (EPA), a semi-autonomous organization within the OEEC which conducted specific research and publications on the European family farm. All of these

35. See, e.g., Clavel, 'La conférence de Milan'.
36. Centre des Archives Contemporaines, Fontainebleau, SGCI, 771473–127, Rapport du Comité agricole franco-allemand sur les problèmes agricoles de la Communauté Economique Européenne (Session des 21/22 avril 1958 à Bordeaux) (own translation).
37. For the example of Germany, see Patel, *Europäisierung wider Willen*, 156–60.
38. An English version of the Papal Encyclical online: http://www.vatican.va/holy_father/john_xxiii/encyclicals/documents/hf_j-xxiii_enc_15051961_mater_en.html (accessed on 1 December 2011).
39. As an example from the EEC, see Mozer, *'Gastarbeider' in Europa*, 50–51; for a wider notion of European cooperation, see the talk by the Austrian minister of agriculture, in: HAEU, BAC 9/1967–18, Speech by Eduard Hartmann, 1963.

projects thus helped to turn this rural image into a meaningful category of collective identity, economic stratification, and political action.[40]

*

* *

How did this model of the European family farm engage with the interstate bargaining and other core manifestations of European integration? I argue that despite and because of the vagueness of its content, it had an enormous impact on the political trajectory of the EEC's Common Agricultural Policy. It must be stressed that it amounted to more than just the hiding and cloaking of 'hard' economic and political interests—as a Milwardian interpretation would have it. For political negotiations, the Europeanized concept of the family farm helped to legitimize the need for a highly interventionist, protectionist, and costly policy against the resistance of various forces, including parts of the national administrations and paradoxically even the European Commission.

Based on the aforementioned early CAP documents highlighting the centrality of the family farm, concrete negotiations on a common policy started in 1960. There was no single factor that accounts for why, by 1968, after almost ten years of continuous and intensive consultation and a whole series of bargains, a highly interventionist and protectionist policy emerged. Still, the ideology of the family farm goes a good way toward explaining this result.[41] This became particularly apparent when, during the negotiations in Brussels, the question arose as to how this vague image could be turned into concrete political action. In line with the encompassing ideal of the family farm, the Six decided that the CAP should revolve around a price-centered approach. Accordingly, producers would basically receive guaranteed prices for their commodities. Obviously, the level of these prices as well as the precise criteria of this policy would have a huge impact on the degree of protection for EEC farmers. When, in November 1963, the European Commission tabled a proposal that defined three sorts of criteria, the one that came most under fire was the Commission's idea to fix prices so that only 'the agricultural enterprises that are rationalized and economically viable' be able to achieve an 'adequate income'. The other two criteria focused on economic reasoning, too, without taking the cultural dimensions of the family farm

---

40. On the FAO, UNECE, and the OEEC, see Clavin and Patel, 'Role of International Organizations'; on the EPA, e.g., see European Productivity Agency, *The Small Family Farm;* and Boel, *The European Productivity Agency.*
41. On these negotiations and their context, see Knudsen, *Farmers on Welfare,* and N. P. Ludlow, *The European Community.*

into consideration.[42] Hence, the Commission challenged the unqualified support for the European family farm, and the discussion boiled down to the question of whether this model should just be a rhetorical point of reference for the CAP or a true guiding principle. In 1963 alone, the issue of defining the main group of recipients of CAP subsidies appeared on the agendas of no less than ten EEC Council of Ministers meetings.[43]

That the Commission as 'Guardian of the Treaties' challenged the vague rural rhetoric can to a good extent be explained by the background of Sicco Mansholt, the larger-than-life commissioner for Agriculture during the early years of the EEC. Following a strong current in the Dutch debate, he stressed the criterion of viability and thus qualified his support for the European family farm: in one interview in German he did not speak of the *bäuerlicher Familienbetrieb* (family farm) but of the *hochleistungsfähiger Familienbetrieb* (family farm capable of an outstanding performance).[44] Accordingly, the ultimate goal was to lift productivity to a level at which the EEC's agricultural producers would be able to compete globally. Concurrently, the role of European farms as custodians of collective values and of heritage was less important for Mansholt, and he pushed for this vision not only during the formative phase of the CAP but again in the late 1960s. The much-debated memorandum that the Commission tabled in December 1968, often referred to as the 'Mansholt Plan', was yet another attempt to bundle resources on the most competitive enterprises; revealingly, the memorandum did not speak of 'family farms' but of 'modern agricultural enterprises'.[45]

Nonetheless, these attempts to qualify or modify support for the European family farm were doomed. Words mattered, and the fact that the Commission had departed from the semantic consensus was one reason why its proposals triggered fierce criticism in rural Europe. In the early and in the late 1960s—as well as at all other times when the status quo and the ongoing trajectory of the CAP were challenged—the member-states prohibited major changes. They stressed the cultural importance of farming and insisted that the 'European family farm' remain the guiding principle of the CAP: a vague and yet stubbornly defended mantra that stabilized a policy with problematic side effects such as surplus production and high costs. Consequently, the criteria proposed by the Commission in late 1963 and the 1968 Mansholt memorandum suffered a similar fate: their ideas

42. European Commission archives COM (63) 430 (own translation); also see Mansholt, *Die Krise*, 19–20; Knudsen, *Farmers on Welfare*, 267–271.
43. E.g., see HAEU, CM2/1963.
44. 'Europas Brot-und-Butter-plan (Interview with Mansholt)', *Der Spiegel*, 1 June 1960; on Mansholt, see Van Merriënboer, *Mansholt: Een biografie*.
45. See Commission sur la réforme de l'agriculture dans la C.E.E., *Plan Mansholt / Rapport Vedel*, 32–64 (own translation).

were watered down during endless discussions, and basically, the CAP did not qualify its support but aimed at helping all existing farms.[46]

Germany and France spearheaded the group pleading for unqualified support. However, even these two countries were home to fierce interadministrative controversies on whether a more precise economic definition was needed. In the academic literature of the time, several such models were presented—theoretically therefore, this kind of knowledge would have been available. Particularly with its Orientation Laws of 1960 and 1962, France even introduced measures pointing in this direction on the national level.[47] On the European level, however, it acted quite differently. In Germany, resistance against more precise criteria was even stronger. In 1962, an Undersecretary of State in the Ministry for Agriculture who drafted a memorandum demanding tight economic criteria was so afraid of possible reactions that he only circulated it secretly among like-minded people.[48]

By and large, politicians in the six member-states as well as in Brussels found it very difficult to abandon their support for the family farm, even if they disliked the vague criteria defining CAP support for farmers. Adenauer, for instance, was put under pressure by the ministry of agriculture as well as the German farmers' union and transnational platforms like COPA. They managed to keep him on the course of unconditional support, and his successors as chancellors found themselves in a similar situation. Hence, even Germany, as the largest net payer of the CAP, did not push consistently for more precise criteria of support.[49] All in all, the image of the European family farm therefore had a massive impact on the political level, even if this cannot be neatly explained by member-states uploading their national interests.

Economically, the consequences of these decisions were also substantial. Certainly, the CAP reached most of its central goals—such as securing supplies for European consumers and raising productivity. But it also entailed problematic side effects such as skyrocketing costs and surplus production, and it had negative consequences for producers in non-EEC countries. For the family farm in particular, the results were highly paradoxical. Due to its unspecified focus on raising farmers' incomes, the CAP allocated its resources inefficiently: it did not strengthen farmers possessing viable enterprises systematically, nor did it ease the conversion of all others working in this sector to new jobs in alternative fields by social policy measurements.[50]

---

46. See the EC directives 72/159, 72/160, and 72/161.
47. See, e.g., Muller, 'La politique agricole française'; more generally on the French context, see Warlouzet, 'Quelle Europe économique'; for Germany, see, e.g., Lüschow, 'Die Produktivität bäuerlicher Familienbetriebe'; Planck, *Der bäuerliche Familienbetrieb.*
48. PA/AA, B 2/74, Rudolf Hüttebräuker, 'Gedanken zu Problemen der Agrarstruktur', 27 August 1962.
49. Patel, *Europäisierung wider Willen.*
50. Federico, 'Was the CAP the Worst?'

Nor did it secure all, or even just the majority, of farms—as proven by the fact that the sector has shrunk from some twenty-five percent of the workforce in the six original member-states in the late 1950s to less than five percent in today's EU. Despite the political rhetoric of protecting and beefing up family farms, the inner mechanics of the CAP favored highly efficient, big producers—independent of their type of enterprise, and without spelling out these economic realities. Ironically, European agriculture thus became similar to the much abhorred U.S. model of industrialized large-scale agriculture. Moreover, it was not least due to the CAP's rural image that marginal and submarginal farms often stayed in operation far longer than economic rationales would have allowed. Herein lies the paradox: the fixation on the vague formula of the family farm on the political level is an important reason why, economically, most of these enterprises have perished over the course of the last fifty years. The family farm idea, then, in contrast to the bifurcated picture of image and reality described by Milward, was both agent and victim of European agricultural production, and EEC policy, throughout this period.

*Figure 19.1* EU coloring book for children.
*Source:* Directorate General for Agriculture and Rural Development, *On the Farm*, 1; figure reproduced at http://ec.europa.eu/agriculture/publi/children/colouringbook.pdf (accessed on 1 December 2011).

Since the 1990s, the rural image has appeared somewhat differently in the discussions on the CAP. To some extent the image has simply been updated, for example, with the idea that land stewardship and not sheer productivity should be a key target. In most documents, however, the family farm is no longer singled out as the European ideal, as it was during the cold war.[51] Having said that, the withering of this concept has not led to its complete demise. Article 23 of the 1997 Polish Constitution, for instance, established the family farm (*gospodarstwo rodzinne*) as the basis of the agricultural economy; the 2007 French presidential candidate François Bayrou was an example of a politician arguing for a strong role for the family farm both on the national and the European Union level.[52] And a recent coloring book for children produced by the European Commission depicts an image reflecting the family farm model—with a small main building, three cows peacefully grazing in the meadows, a horse, a couple of chickens as well as sheep—but not the highly industrialized, large-scale farms that characterize the trend in today's European Union. Rural images thus continue to resonate well into the early twenty-first century Europe.

*

* *

Any historical interpretation is incomplete and partial, forever redone and in need of redoing because of our own cultural background and context as historians.[53] As such, we always build on earlier research, yet try to extend the agenda in order to arrive at ever-more nuanced interpretations. In line with Milward's approach to European integration history, this chapter has stressed the dimensions of long-term (dis-)continuities, and it has moved beyond a sheer 'intrinsic' approach. Thus, it showed that, ironically, the Swiss propagator of the European family farm model soon found himself marginalized in the discourse because of his nationality and that also the contrast with the United States was somewhat doubtful. Moreover, this chapter put transnational actors and their platforms back into the picture—such as groups and institutions for which Milward's interpretation left little room. Most importantly, it showed how the analysis of ideas and of the cultural dimension enriches our understanding of European integration in a concrete and conceptually controlled way; in line with some parts of Milward's work, but also transcending its methodological confines.

---

51. See, e.g., Knudsen, *Romanticising Europe*, 53–6.
52. See http://www.sejm.gov.pl/prawo/konst/angielski/kon1.htm and http://programme.bayrou.fr/programme_fbayrou_election_presidentielle.pdf (both accessed on 1 December 2011).
53. Bynum, 'Perspectives, Connections & Objects'.

A final consideration might be added: exploring the role of culture and ideas in European integration remains incomplete without considering the investigator's own historiographical background. Ironically, the scholar who deconstructed the lives and teachings of the (political) European saints has, through the intellectual power of his work, himself gained an almost celestial status within the realm of scholarly research. Despite some criticism leveled against his work, there is a broad consensus of Alan Milward's vital contribution to turning European integration history into what it is today: a lively, relevant, and serious field of academic scholarship.

# 20 The Scandinavian Rescue of the Nation-State?

## Scandinavia and Early European Integration, 1945–1955

*Johnny Laursen*

There is a strange paradox in the relationship of the Scandinavian states to the European Union (EU) and to the European integration process. On the one hand these states seem to be model member-states. Sweden, Finland, and Denmark are some of the EU member-states where EU legislation is passed with greatest expediency and observed most strictly. Even Denmark with an opt-out from the euro but with the Danish krone pegged to it has for years been pursuing monetary and fiscal policies in order to keep the national currency firmly within the bounds of the Growth and Stability Pact agreed in 1997. On the other hand none of these states were among the founding states of the European Communities, and none have a record for strong pro-Europeanism. Quite the opposite: They all own a record for euroskepticism, reservations, and general foot-dragging.

While historians writing on the history of the founding years of the European Economic Community (EEC) have focused on explaining why the original Six chose to set up the supranational European Communities, their Scandinavian counterparts have focused on why the Scandinavian countries could not, did not, and (in most cases according to these historians) should not engage in supranational integration. As a matter of fact, the only Scandinavian state unable to join the integration process was Finland. The other Scandinavian states had the choice of whether or not to join the process.[1] Throughout the 1950s they chose not to participate. In the historiography of European integration they have been lumped together with the United Kingdom as a group of countries, the Anglo-Scandinavian club, taking a different position on European integration from that of the Six. In 1950, while the Six rallied behind the Schuman Plan, the Anglo-Scandinavians joined behind the leadership of the *Union Jack* in the consultative Uniscan-club. While the Schuman Plan necessitated that member-states

1. For this reason this study is limited to Denmark, Norway, and Sweden and does not include Finland. Iceland did not contemplate participation in any West European plan in the 1950s. As the term *Nordic* tends to involve also cultural aspects, for this chapter I have used the term *Scandinavia/n*, except for formal names such as the Nordic Council.

would cede sovereignty to the High Authority and other community institutions, Uniscan involved little more than biannual, consultative meetings between top civil servants of the foreign ministries and economic ministries from the United Kingdom, Norway, Denmark, and Sweden.[2] Scandinavia became the reverse mirror, so to speak, of the experience of the Six in real life as well as in the historiography of European integration.

The Scandinavian case in the late 1940s and 1950s therefore offers an interesting possibility of testing the interpretative framework of the integration process of the Six against an alternative type of cooperative process and alternative choices of association. The Scandinavian countries exemplify a strategy for economic development—with a greater emphasis on welfare and full employment—and a choice between supranational and intergovernmental cooperation which differs from that of the Six. Moreover, they provide a possibility to contrast the path of the supranational integration process of the European Communities / Union with their attempt to establish an alternative type of regional integration in Northern Europe. In the following pages we will first take a look at the main interpretations of the early Scandinavian experience of cooperation. We will then briefly investigate two instances of Scandinavian cooperation plans: the creation of the Nordic Council in 1953 and the abortive attempts at closer economic cooperation in 1947–1950 and 1953–1959. We will finally discuss the possibility of applying some of the interpretative frameworks on the dynamics of European integration to the Scandinavian case.

## SCANDINAVIAN INTEGRATION THEORIES

Since the creation of the Nordic Council in 1953 a number of historical, institutional, and political science contributions have tried to make sense of the Scandinavian experience and of the specific forms of cooperation in the Scandinavian region. Views of the Nordic Council have been influenced especially by the writings of the secretary general of the Danish delegation to the Nordic Council, Frantz Wendt. Wendt's 1959 synthesis of the Nordic Council set the tone with the implicit thesis of continuity in Scandinavian cooperation and characteristics such as pragmatism and common sense in the cooperative approach in Scandinavia as opposed to the more binding institutional structures preferred by the Six.[3] In Wendt's interpretation the actual shape of Scandinavian cooperation was an expression of the virtue of the possible and not of the failure of the could-have-beens. This view was

2. Aunesluoma, 'An Elusive Partnership'. Apart from discussions on the development of the integration plans of the Six, the meetings focused on economic trends, production prognoses, and Scandinavian holdings of the British pound sterling.
3. Wendt, *The Nordic Council.*

strengthened in his 1979 synthesis of Scandinavian cooperation.[4] Amitai Etzioni, in turn, saw Scandinavian cooperation as a 'stable union' and an 'associational web' that was not likely to expand into more committing forms of cooperation. Etzioni stressed the weakness of the utilitarian-administrative ties and of the consultative design of Scandinavian cooperation. In the North there was no regional center of power, and the Nordic Council was more a 'symbol of the relative unimportance of regional institutions and their weakness than a focus of identification.'[5]

One of the most influential attempts to explain the form of cooperation in Scandinavia came from the political scientist Nils Andrén. He saw the ethos of Scandinavian cooperation as shaped by the existing emotional *Nordism* and by the prevalence of pragmatic-utilitarian approaches to cooperation in the region.[6] Accordingly, practical cooperation was propelled by the political idealism represented in the Nordic Council and concentrated on what were then considered to be practical low-policy areas such as economic and social policy cooperation. In the Nordic Council the Scandinavian 'community method' of cooperation was—according to Andrén—markedly different from the form of cooperation in the supranational EEC. This Scandinavian form of cooperation was termed 'cob-web' integration since it appeared as weaving a web of small relationships of cooperation and interdependence, but without central, authoritative institutions.

Many subsequent studies of Scandinavian cooperation have taken this view of Scandinavian cooperation as their point of departure and seen this special path or *Sonderweg* to integration as an expression of a Scandinavian exceptionalism based on structures of society or political cultures different from those of the rest of Europe. It could even be said that this historiography—like that of the European Community—has its own 'saints'—especially, as we shall see, the Danish Prime Minister Hans Hedtoft—in the form of pioneers of Scandinavian unity.[7]

The authors of the two main monographs on the Nordic Council, Stanley V. Anderson and Eric Solem, both dedicate a great deal of attention to the workings and powers of the Council. Anderson has largely seen the Council as a pressure group, even though it is unclear how it exerts its pressure and how successful it has been. An example of the clout of Scandinavian lobbying is what Anderson called 'the Phoenix effect' on Scandinavian

4. Wendt, *Nordisk Råd.*
5. Etzioni, *Political Unification*, 224 f., 227 f., and 305.
6. Andrén, 'Nordisk integration', 377–378 and 384. *Nordism* is the Scandinavian equivalent to *Europeanism*. Norden associations were created in the Scandinavian states after World War I. The concept denotes not only support for Scandinavian unity, but also implies a strong sentiment of Scandinavian cultural and political exceptionalism.
7. The term 'saint' is borrowed from Milward, 'The Lives and Teachings of the European Saints', Chapter 6 of his *The European Rescue of the Nation-State*, 318–344.

cooperation.[8] This phenomenon involves situations where Scandinavian cooperation efforts failed, or where other policy options, such as for example Danish relations with West Germany or with the EEC, prevailed over closer Scandinavian ties. In these cases the considerations of the domestic political backlash of Scandinavian failure prompted decision-makers to launch new compensatory initiatives. In this sense each failure of a grand scheme was followed by a small step forward in pragmatic cooperation.

Instead of becoming a coordinating center itself, the Presidium and secretariats of the Council, according to Anderson, have chosen to work directly on the governments through infiltration and lobbying. Anderson locates two forms of lobbying, directly on the governments and indirectly through public opinion, both with seemingly little leverage:

> As a force external to government, then, the Nordic Council has been able to rally little effective support. Consequently, the leadership has turned its efforts toward integrating the Council into the administrative apparatus, toward making the Council an inter-governmental organ as well as an inter-parliamentarian one.[9]

For his part Solem equivocates between stressing the importance of the Council and its weakness. He first underscores the wide-ranging political representation in the Council and, second, the importance of mixing cabinet ministers with parliamentarians at the Council sessions. Noting the failure to make progress in economic cooperation as well as the occasional lack of consistency between Scandinavian ideals and practice, by giving priority to national interests, Solem, however, tends to stress the vulnerability of the network of cooperation.[10]

The historians Bo Stråth and Bernt Schiller have switched attention to the role of external pressures on Scandinavia. Stråth strongly refuted the tradition of seeing Scandinavian alignment as an alternative to Europe. The ups and downs of Scandinavian cooperation were, he argued, immersed in the ebb and flow of European developments. Thus, Stråth sees the dynamics and limits of Scandinavian cooperation in the interaction with external forces, and only to a lesser degree in intrinsic Scandinavian forces. He interprets the Nordic customs union negotiations in the 1950s as a politically motivated strategy to strengthen the Scandinavian position vis-à-vis the European free trade negotiations. The economic motives, on the other hand, are seen as lukewarm 'lubricants'.[11] A related position has been presented by Bernt Schiller who also underscored the role of governments in the making, and particularly in the failures, of Scandinavian cooperation,

---

8. S. Anderson, *The Nordic Council*, 119.
9. Ibid., 117–118, quotation on 120.
10. Solem, *The Nordic Council*, 162–165.
11. Stråth, 'The Illusory Nordic Alternative', 112.

together with the commanding role of external pressures in facilitating the dynamics of cooperation.[12] Barbara Haskel's conclusion in her case study of Scandinavian economic cooperation is that so few intra-Scandinavian institutions were developed, not because of conflicting interests, but because there was no convergence of policies. She interprets the plan, known as the Harpsund initiative in 1954, which I discuss later, as being based on internal Norwegian motives to facilitate economic modernization and appease the Left wing of the Norwegian Labor Party. The weakness of the plan was, according to Haskel, that there were no political spin-off benefits to support it when it came under pressure.[13] The political scientist Toivo Miljan's 1977 study of the attitudes of the Scandinavian countries toward European integration reached the conclusion that each time a decision to integrate had been made it was on the basis of practical necessity, rather than as a matter of community building. He concluded that although the three post-1945 decades had seen a considerable increase in intra-Nordic interactions conducive to community building '[t]he desire to conserve the nation in the form of a sovereign independent nation-state has produced not only reluctant Europeans, but reluctant Nordics of the Nordic countries.'[14]

Many studies of the positions of individual Scandinavian countries in the integration process have tended to emphasize the dimension of *Realpolitik*—especially the national economic interest—in the European policy-making of these countries.[15] Already in 1952 William Diebold noted that Denmark and Norway represented economies caught in structural problems by the European trade and payments system in the late 1940s and early 1950s. This is indeed one of the very reasons why Denmark and Norway feature more in Alan Milward's *The Reconstruction of Western Europe, 1945–51,* than Sweden. Since the interwar period the Danish and Norwegian economies had been satellites of the British economy and specialized in the export of food products, fish, timber, and metals. After the 1930s the currency reserves and domestic industries of both countries had been protected by extensive quota restrictions. As the quota restrictions were being dismantled by the trade liberalization process that was taking place under the aegis of the Organization for European Economic Cooperation (OEEC) both countries were being stripped of their main means of industrial protection, while some of their main exports—food products and fish—were more or less exempted from intra-European trade liberalization.[16] While Denmark and Norway suffered from acute structural weaknesses in relation to European economic cooperation, the Swedish economy

12. Schiller, 'At Gun Point'.
13. Haskel, *The Scandinavian Option*, 106, 108–109, and 129–130.
14. Miljan, *The Reluctant Europeans*, 284.
15. For an early contribution see Pharo, 'Bridgebuilding and Reconstruction'.
16. Diebold, *Trade and Payments*, 193 f. and 247–266.

was considerably more robust in terms of both its actual payments position as well as its industrial competitiveness.

During the 1980s and early 1990s Scandinavian historians working on the history of European integration were influenced by the work of Alan Milward. The latter's *The Reconstruction of Western Europe* included not only the six founding members of the European Coal and Steel Community but also those countries which remained aloof from the integration process of the Six. In addition, Milward offered an overall interpretation:

> There is no intention in this book to deny a certain welcome leaven of idealism to these men [the European pioneers] [ . . . ] But the policies from which a limited measure of economic integration did emerge were, so the evidence clearly indicates, created by national bureaucracies out of the internal expression of national political interest, not by the great statesmen who implemented them. The Schuman Plan, for example, was based on two and a half years of the evolution of policy in the French Ministry of Foreign Affairs.[17]

Milward's work and ideas exerted much influence over Scandinavian research throughout the 1990s. The focus on economic factors and motives fitted well with historiographies dominated by both the role played by social democratic labor movements and the emergence of modern welfare states. In 1987 the historian Vibeke Sørensen defended a doctoral thesis advancing the interpretation that the early choices of the Danish Social Democratic government, 1947–1950, on the Marshall Plan and European economic integration should be seen in the context of its strategy toward national economic modernization.[18] Sørensen pointed out that this was the case with regard to the Scandinavian economic integration plans in the 1950s as well.[19] Milward's synthesis on the emergence of the European integration process and the national choices connected to it, *The European Rescue of the Nation-State,* was also influential for historians of Scandinavia, even though the Scandinavian countries did not initially, in the 1950s, choose supranational integration.[20] Milward's underlying argument that national choices of how to approach the integration process were strongly motivated by national policy choices on welfare, full employment, economic growth, and prosperity found strong resonance among historians of Scandinavia.

> The development of the European Community, the process of European integration, was, so runs the argument of this book, a part of

17. Milward, *The Reconstruction of Western Europe*, 492.
18. V. Sørensen, 'Social Democratic Government'.
19. V. Sørensen, 'Nordic Cooperation'.
20. See Olesen, 'Nationalstaten og den europæiske integration', and Tor Egil Førland, 'EFs betydning for nasjonalstaten'.

> that post-war rescue of the European nation-state, because the new political consensus on which this rescue was built required the process of integration, the surrender of limited areas of national sovereignty to the supranation.[21]

The emphasis on the role of the state and on class coalitions fitted well with the perception of Scandinavian political and socioeconomic history since the 1930s, where red-green coalitions with extensive state intervention had secured political and social stability.

> The post-war state was reconstructed on a much wider political consensus than that which had shaped policy in the inter-war period. Into this consensus were brought three large, overlapping categories of voters whose demands on central government had been hitherto imperfectly met or even refused: labour, agricultural producers, and a diffuse alliance of lower and middle income beneficiaries of the welfare state.[22]

It was also amplified by the poor track record of Europeanist idealism among the Scandinavian political parties and in intellectual life as well as by the programmatic refusal to combine European integration with security issues. Milward's criticism of the classical idealist interpretation of European integration as initiated by visionary European statesmen—'the European saints'—also fell on fertile ground among Scandinavian historians unable to dust up any such visionaries of Scandinavian provenance: 'The historiography of European integration is dominated by legends of great men. Most histories emphasize the role of a small band of leading statesmen with a shared vision.'[23]

This framework of interpretation was developed in *The Frontier of National Sovereignty*.[24] In Milward's words:

> Integration, the surrender of some limited measure of national sovereignty, is, we suggested, a new form of agreed international framework created by the nation-states to advance particular sets of national domestic policies which could not be pursued, or not be pursued so successfully, through the already existing international framework of co-operation between interdependent states, nor by renouncing international interdependence.[25]

---

21. Milward, *The European Rescue*, 4.
22. Ibid., 27.
23. Ibid., 318.
24. Milward et al., *The Frontier of National Sovereignty*.
25. Milward, 'Conclusions: The Value of History', ibid., 182–201 (quotation on 182).

The reasoning of how nations and their governments made choices on the basis of national interests or national strategies was not without influence on the relevant volumes of the official Norwegian foreign policy history published in 1997 and of its Danish counterpart in 2005. Both official histories dedicated substantial attention to the emergence and failure of the Scandinavian plans for closer economic cooperation.[26] By contrast Milward's use of the concept 'allegiance' had much less—if any—resonance among historians of Scandinavia.[27]

Milward's interpretation of how and why nation-states would choose to cede limited areas of national sovereignty to international organizations was primarily modeled on the Schuman Plan and on the European Economic Community. Accordingly, Scandinavian historians have mostly utilized the same framework of interpretation to explain the policy of individual Scandinavian states toward the supranational integration process in Europe. However, if the approach could be applied to British European policies in the period up to the first British application for EEC membership in 1961, why should it not be an equally useful approach to explain how the Scandinavian states positioned themselves in relation to closer cooperation in Scandinavia and to the creation of Scandinavian cooperative institutions? [28]

## THE NORDIC COUNCIL AND THE SCANDINAVIAN SONDERWEG

Since the 1920s 'Norden' associations had functioned as pressure groups for closer Scandinavian cooperation. Together with a post-1945 surge in 'Scandinavism' (or 'Nordism'), this caused numerous attempts to increase the cooperation among Scandinavian states in the late 1940s and early 1950s. These initiatives took place at the interministerial level as well as at intra-Scandinavian parliamentary meetings. In 1951 an interparliamentary committee to facilitate travel, traffic, and communications across the Scandinavian countries was established. As a result, the Scandinavian Passport Union was set up in July 1952. In 1954 a Scandinavian labor market was effectively put into operation.[29] The most ambitious initiative was the failed attempt in 1948–1949 to establish a Scandinavian defense alliance.

---

26. Eriksen and Pharo, *Kald krig og internasjonalisering*; Olesen and Villaume, *I blokopdelingens tegn 1945–72*, 257–268. There is no Swedish equivalent. The best account of Sweden's European policy is Af Malmborg, *Den ståndaktiga nationalstaten*.
27. Milward, 'Allegiance: The Past and the Future'.
28. See Milward, *The Rise and Fall of a National Strategy*.
29. Wendt, *The Nordic Council*, 66–68 and 86–87; S. Anderson, *The Nordic Council*, 19–22; Gunnar P. Nielsson, 'The Parallel National Action Process'.

The idea for a Scandinavian parliamentary assembly had been raised in 1948 by the Danish government. In their view such a body would be preferable to the existing Nordic Inter-Parliamentarian Union which was seen as too weak to infuse dynamism into Scandinavian cooperation.[30] On 8–9 September 1948 the Danish foreign minister put forward for the consideration of his Scandinavian colleagues a proposal for the creation of an inter-Scandinavian parliamentary assembly, though without success.[31] In August 1951 the leader of the Danish Social Democrats, Hans Hedtoft, raised the issue again at the meeting of the Nordic Inter-Parliamentarian Union. Despite the Norwegians' concern, the proposal was accepted and a small committee appointed to elaborate a proposal.[32] Hedtoft had in mind an institutional innovation to infuse momentum into Scandinavian cooperation.[33] In Norway on the other hand, outright antagonism to the plan existed in the bourgeois opposition and much hesitation in the governing Social Democratic Party. The main concern was the preservation of national sovereignty.[34]

The statute drafted by the 'constitutional fathers' was therefore carefully designed in order to be nonoffensive to national sovereignty. There was a manifest Norwegian wish to organize the Council according to national delegations, instead of along party lines. The Danes, on the contrary, wanted the Council to reflect the lines of division in the national parliaments in order to strengthen the political character of the assembly. The Danish participants in the work on the Council, among others Hedtoft—then leader of the opposition—and the liberal leader and Prime Minister Erik Eriksen, had also wanted a common inter-Scandinavian Council secretariat. This, however, turned out to be impossible.[35]

Thus, at the Scandinavian foreign ministers' meeting of 15–16 March 1952 the Danes had to accept a more limited inter-Scandinavian parliament. The Norwegian foreign minister, Halvard Lange, flatly refused to allow the participation of prime ministers and foreign ministers in the Council and did not want to cede voting rights to cabinet ministers. The Swedish foreign minister, Östen Undén, supported this position, while favoring the participation of cabinet ministers in Council proceedings. Faced with such staunch opposition the Danish foreign minister, Ole Bjørn Kraft, although highly

30. Archive of the Danish Ministry of Foreign Affairs, National Archive Copenhagen (henceforth UM), 5.F.114.a/I: Extract from the minutes of Foreign Ministers meeting held in Stockholm on 8 and 9 September 1948.
31. UM 5.F.114.a/I: Note dated 14 September 1948.
32. Herlitz, 'Nordiska rådets tillkomst', S5–11 and S39–47; Wendt, 'Hans Hedtoft', 466 ff.
33. For Hedtoft's views see Thorsen, 'Norden', 209 ff.; Wendt, 'Hans Hedtoft', 466 ff.
34. Eriksen and Pharo, *Kald krig og internasjonalisering*, 153–154.
35. Wendt, 'Hans Hedtoft'; Herlitz, 'Nordiska rådets tillkomst', 10 ff. and 32; S. Anderson, 'Negotiations for the Nordic Council', 24 f.

dissatisfied, agreed to compromise on the voting rights of cabinet ministers. His disappointment was shared in the Danish parliament's Foreign Policy Committee and especially in the Social Democratic Party. The eventual compromise was that cabinet ministers could participate in Council proceedings but could not vote. After this, a long debate followed on the role of the secretariats. Lange wanted the role of the secretariats limited to that of a mere parliamentary bureau and to keep the leadership firmly in the hands of the Council Presidium. Once again the Danish foreign minister yielded while protesting: 'It was desirable that the secretariat was set up as an institution able to contribute to making the Council a decisive body in inter-Scandinavian cooperation'.[36] The Presidium and national delegations were consequently served by small national secretariats attached to the national delegations. The national secretary generals nevertheless became important actors in inter-Scandinavian policy-making thanks to their omnipresence, mediating position, and concentrated occupation with Scandinavian affairs. In 1953 the Danish prime minister, Hedtoft, made a point of appointing the executive director of the Danish Norden association, Frantz Wendt, to be secretary general of the Danish delegation to the Nordic Council and attaching inter-Scandinavian affairs to the Prime Minister's Office instead of to the Foreign Ministry. It was not least around the axis between Wendt and the likewise strong Swedish secretariat that the executive functions of the Council came to revolve in the 1950s and 1960s.[37] Finally, the Danes had originally wanted to establish the institution by means of a treaty, but here also they had to face Norwegian and Swedish resistance. Eventually, Denmark enacted the decision to set up the Council by a law that was promulgated as a treaty, while in Norway and Sweden their parliaments approved the statute of the Council by form of parliamentary resolutions.[38]

The Council that assembled for the first time in 1953 in Copenhagen was, after this display of Scandinavian pragmatism, a consultative body deprived of every vestige of transnational institutionalism.[39] It was scheduled to meet for a few days annually in sessions rotating between the national parliaments. Cabinet members were members of the Council outside the national delegations and had the right to take part in the plenary assembly without

---

36. UM 5.F.114.a/II: Extract from the minutes of the Nordic Foreign Ministers meeting held in Copenhagen on 15 and 16 March 1952 (author's translation).
37. Wendt, *The Nordic Council*, 110–111; Wendt, 'Hans Hedtoft', 468 and 470; Herlitz, 'Nordiska rådets tillkomst', 10 and 32; S. Anderson, 'Negotiations for the Nordic Council', 24; S. Anderson, *The Nordic Council*, 40 ff. and 54–55; Sørensen, 'Nordic Cooperation'.
38. S. Anderson, 'Negotiations for the Nordic Council', 24.
39. On the Council procedures and rules described below see Wendt, *The Nordic Council*, 106 ff.; S. Anderson, *The Nordic Council*, 56–100; and Petrén, 'The Nordic Council', 346–362.

the right to vote. It happened that they were also invited to take part in the deliberations of the committees. The Council had no decision-making power of its own, and could only pass recommendations.[40]

## ECONOMIC COOPERATION IN SCANDINAVIA

Throughout 1947 to 1950, 1950 to 1954, and 1954 to 1959 the Scandinavian governments attempted to address the possibilities for closer economic cooperation through three rounds of investigations. The Norwegian initiative, in 1947, for a study group on a Scandinavian customs union was largely—if not exclusively—motivated by external requirements; primarily the United States' pressure for regional integration initiatives in the framework of the Committee of European Economic Cooperation and the Marshall Plan. In the words of Alan Milward:

> At this point [of disagreement between Denmark and Norway on a European customs union] Halvard Lange, the Norwegian Foreign Minister, played the card of Scandinavian co-operation and suggested they discuss how far they could nevertheless co-operate economically and put forward a common policy. In these hopeless circumstances the idea of a Scandinavian association, perhaps even a customs union, was put forward. It was no more than a way of saving face and refusing to admit to the world the reality of profound Scandinavian disunity.[41]

At a conference in February 1948 the Scandinavian countries established an intergovernmental committee (known as the 'Bramsnæs Committee') to study closer economic cooperation.[42] The work of the committee was cumbersome due to diverging national economic interests and views on institutional matters. In Norway the opportunity to instrumentalize Scandinavian cooperation in order to modernize and further regulate the economy was weighed against the fears of the adverse effects of Swedish and Danish industrial competition on the Norwegian domestic industry. The Swedish government was positive but opposed to any increase in the public

---

40. S. Anderson, *The Nordic Council*, 179 ff.
41. Milward, *The Reconstruction of Western Europe*, 251.
42. Sogner, 'Norges holdning'; Amstrup, 'Nordisk samarbejde', 174; Stråth, 'The Illusory Nordic Alternative', 106–107 and 109; Haskel, *The Scandinavian Option*, 94 ff.; Eriksen and Pharo, *Kald krig og internasjonalisering*, 155. The formal name of the committee was The Nordic Intergovernmental Committee for Nordic Economic Cooperation. The chairman, Carl Valdemar Bramsnæs, was a former director of the Danish central bank (1933–1949). Bramsnæs was also chairman for the Danish Norden Association and a strong supporter of closer Scandinavian cooperation.

control over the economy.[43] In Denmark a broad majority favored closer Scandinavian cooperation as an answer to Denmark's strong dependence on international markets and weak bargaining position. The Danes were, in the 1950s, acutely aware of the rising economic and political importance of West Germany and vacillated between closer cooperation with the Six on the one hand or with Scandinavia on the other. But also a quite 'un-Scandinavian' outlook played a role: Danish politicians had watched the creation of the Benelux, the economic union that was established in 1946 among the neighboring countries of Belgium, the Netherlands, and Luxemburg, and were inclined to follow this example. The Danes had simply many fewer qualms about strong cooperative institutions than their Scandinavian partners.[44] In 1950 forceful tensions erupted in the Bramsnæs Committee between the delegations of Denmark and Sweden, on the one side, and of Norway, on the other. The Norwegians doubted that a customs union would be favorable to their economy.[45] In the preliminary report of the Bramsnæs Committee, drafted early in 1950, the Norwegian members submitted a minority statement warning against the adverse consequences to the Norwegian economy of liberalizing intra-Scandinavian trade.[46] After this failure the Committee received a new mandate to investigate a range of industries in order to prepare for a more limited tariff cooperation. In March 1954, after four years of work, the Committee submitted its final report which carried, once again, a negative Norwegian minority conclusion against a favorable Danish-Swedish one which pointed out the long-term advantages of a Scandinavian economic division of labor.[47]

Most research on Scandinavian cooperation tends to bundle all the plans for Scandinavian economic cooperation, from 1947 until 1970, into one package. The Bramsnæs Committee investigations have therefore been seen as symptomatic of the failed attempts to create a Scandinavian common market after 1945. There is, however, much evidence suggesting that there was a marked difference between the studies initiated in 1947 and the new attempt set in motion in 1954.

---

43. Amstrup, 'Nordisk samarbejde', 157–158, 162–166, and 168–169.
44. Nielsson, 'Denmark and European Integration', 242–244.
45. Archive of the Norwegian Foreign Office (henceforth UD), 44–3/4: Memorandum entitled 'Nordic economic cooperation—conversation with the Danish ambassador Mathias Wassard', 19 January 1950; UD 44–3/4: O.S.: Meeting in Copenhagen 3 January 1950 and Joint Committee for Economic Cooperation, 5 January 1950.
46. Fælles Nordiske Udvalg for økonomisk Samarbejde, *Nordisk økonomisk samarbejde*, 22–24 and 43; Eriksen and Pharo, *Kald krig og internasjonalisering*, 156.
47. Anon., *Nordisk økonomisk samarbeid*, 75 and 82–88; UD 44.3/4: 'The Joint Nordic Economic Committee' by K. Christiansen, 20 February 1954; Eriksen and Pharo, 157.

Several factors contributed to a beginning or 'relance' of Scandinavian economic cooperation in 1952–1953. First, on the political level prominent politicians had participated in the creation of the Nordic Council, and the potential political embarrassment of a subsequent breakdown of the customs union investigations tended to mollify positions. Second, by 1953 the Norwegian economy had become more robust, and liberalization pressures from the OEEC were becoming more evident. Hence, some kind of opening of the Norwegian market to Scandinavian competition had become less of a taboo. Third, by 1953 the Scandinavian countries were beginning to realize that solutions to their dependence on the British and West German economies were unlikely to emerge within the framework of the OEEC.

Early in 1952 the Norwegian foreign ministry brought forward a new approach to the Scandinavian question. It considered that some kind of partial customs union, combined with a common commercial policy in the OEEC and the General Agreement on Tariff and Trade (GATT) might become a useful tool in the foreign economic relations of the Scandinavian countries.[48] This idea was cautiously condoned by foreign minister Halvard Lange, and in April the idea was brought to the fore by the Danish permanent under secretary of state Erling Sveinbjørnsson. The latter was mildly skeptical about the Norwegian government's newfound dedication to Scandinavism. Nevertheless, the forthcoming enforcement of the Treaty establishing the European Coal and Steel Community (ECSC), which had been signed in April 1951, the shift in British commercial policies from OEEC cooperation toward a greater emphasis on tariffs and trade with the Commonwealth, and the stalemate in the GATT attempts to reduce international tariff duties made a Scandinavian approach 'with real content' promising in Danish eyes.[49]

Such views were now increasingly shared in Oslo among a small group of politicians and top civil servants who saw the need for a Scandinavian approach to respond to the nascent ECSC and the British disengagement with the work of the OEEC.[50] When in April 1952 the Danish ambassador in Oslo, Mathias Wassard, met the Norwegian state secretary, Johan Melander, their respective views began to converge, even though the Danish view still implied the most radical departure from Uniscan and British leadership in Europe. The Danish preference was to establish a full customs

48. UD 44.3/4: 'The resumption of discussions on a Nordic Customs Union' by Norwegian Foreign Ministry secretary Otto Christian Malterud, 1 February 1952.
49. UD 44.3/4: State secretary in the Norwegian Foreign Ministry Johan Melander to Otto Christian Malterud, 11 March 1952; UM 73.B.51.a/III: Memorandum by Erling Sveinbjørnsson, 7 April 1952. Sveinbjørnsson was a member of the inter-Scandinavian committee on closer economic cooperation.
50. UD 44.3/4: State secretary Johan Melander to the Norwegian foreign minister Halvard Lange, 24 April 1952.

union 'ad modem Benelux' with the commitment to united action vis-à-vis the large Western European powers and international organizations. But also the Norwegians were beginning to fear that the British economy could not continue to constitute the point of reference for the Scandinavians:

> Melander admitted that Norway had been more oriented towards the West in its economy than what could be justified based on later experiences, and that Norway's views of the strength in and the value of economic co-operation among the Continental countries was in need of a revision. In short: Melander was largely arriving at what we in Denmark have seen as the natural and correct points of view for all three Scandinavian countries.[51]

In December 1953 *The New York Times* reported an imminent move in Scandinavia toward a regional grouping which was to remove quantitative trade restrictions between each other. The approach should also be a new one, as the anonymous source noted:

> In the past ministers have told their officials to see what the difficulties would be if a decision were made to go ahead with such a scheme. This time they have told us that they are going ahead with the scheme, and that we should tell them what difficulties to expect. There is a world of difference.[52]

This was indeed a far cry from Nils Andrén's cob-web method. The change had especially been nurtured in the circle around the influential Norwegian minister of commerce, Erik Brofoss (from May 1954 director of the Norwegian central bank). The latter and a circle of politicians and civil servants had come to consider Scandinavian cooperation a potential road to economic modernization and a counterweight to what they considered to be the growing economic influence on the part of West Germany.[53]

In May 1954 Brofoss gave a talk on Scandinavian economic cooperation at the annual inter-Scandinavian Social Democrat meeting. He argued that changes in the external environment had actualized closer Scandinavian cooperation. The weakening of the OEEC, the economic dependency

---

51. UM 73.B.51.a/III: Ambassador Mathias Wassard to the permanent under secretary of the Danish Foreign Office Nils Svenningsen, 23 April 1952. Author's translation of Danish original.
52. UD 44.3/4: 'Scandinavia Plans for a Free Trade Area', *The New York Times*, 19 December 1953, 4.
53. Erik Brofoss' private archive, The Norwegian Labor Archive, Oslo (henceforth EB PA), box 51: The Norwegian ambassador to the OEEC in Paris, Arne Skaug, to the Norwegian minister of commerce Erik Brofoss, 12 January 1954; Eriksen and Pharo, *Kald krig og internasjonalisering*, 157–158 and 288–290.

on Germany, and the Scandinavian payments problems in the European Payments Union made Scandinavian economic cooperation more necessary than ever. Presenting a blueprint for the cooperative scheme, he proposed a Scandinavian division of labor in industrial production and trade, as well as a concerted economic policy. This would create larger economic units, abate the dependency on imports, and alleviate in particular dependency on West Germany.[54]

In August 1954 the intention to proceed with a Scandinavian common market with a new more determined approach was condoned by the Nordic Council.[55] In Denmark the Council recommendation was greeted with enthusiasm. At a meeting of Norden associations in Copenhagen, in early July, prime minister Hans Hedtoft branded Scandinavian economic cooperation as a vital necessity:

> Now, and as far as we can see into the future, there is no more urgent task for the Nordic Council and for the individual governments and parliaments than to promote the economic cooperation in Scandinavia. We must adapt the economies of our countries to the demands of modern technology in order to be able to preserve our place under the sun.[56]

On 30–31 October 1954 representatives of the Scandinavian governments involved gathered at the Swedish prime minister's summer retreat at Harpsund outside Stockholm in order to discuss the proposal. The Norwegian participants stressed that the concept was an integrated package with the common market linked to concrete production planning and investment. The Swedish position was positive but not very committed, especially with regard to institutional matters. The Danes on their side charged ahead into the new opening. Danish cabinet ministers, backed with the positive views expressed by their industry (farmers remaining critical), trade unions, and a large parliamentary majority, urged for the plan to be as extensive as possible. They stressed the need to establish a strong steering group and a Scandinavian secretariat along the lines of the OEEC secretariat. This was a step too far for their Norwegian and Swedish counterparts.[57]

The conference eventually agreed to map out inter-Scandinavian commerce in order to locate areas with low tariff or quota restrictions, where a Scandinavian common market with an external common tariff could be

---

54. EB PA, Box 158: Protocol for the meeting of the Nordic Council of Cooperation of 24 May 1954.
55. UD 44.3/4: Untitled and undated note; and Memorandum on the 2nd session of the Nordic Council, August 1954, 152–53 and 158.
56. 'Nordic Common Market an Urgent Necessity', *Social-Demokraten*, 7 July 1954. Author's translation of the original in Danish.
57. EB PA, Box 152: Unofficial minutes of the meeting held in Harpsund on 30 and 31 October 1954, drafted by the Norwegian ambassador in Stockholm, Jens Schive and dated 1 November 1954.

established quickly. Apart from this commodity group, four sectors were selected for further cooperation: chemical and pharmaceutical products, iron and steel products, metals and semifabricated goods, and finally, electrotechnical and metallurgical products. Apart from the Scandinavian common market the investigations embraced the coordination of production activities, a concerted commercial policy, and the study of the relative terms of competition. The negotiations were organized around a strong inter-Scandinavian committee of ministers, an executive group of high civil servants, and a number of working groups of specialists.[58]

Like the future Messina mandate, the Harpsund mandate was not purely a result of immaterial Scandinavian or pro-European-unity idealism, but a carefully balanced compromise among all the economic interests at stake. Thus, it was from the outset clear that several sectors and provisions had been included in order to satisfy the Norwegians' claims. It was not least the ambition to build a tariff-protected Scandinavian steel market in which to plan investments in the Swedish and Norwegian steel industries. This ran counter to Denmark's long battle against price discrimination on its steel imports from ECSC countries and for better security for coal and steel provisions, which constituted a crucial issue for the attempts to build a viable Danish export industry in machinery, shipbuilding, and consumer goods. In 1954–1955 brief feelers had been tested between the High Authority and the Danish government on the possibility for partial Danish membership or association with the ECSC. The Danish Foreign Ministry, recognizing the explosiveness of these contacts in relation to the Scandinavian negotiations, was quick to classify the relevant documents as strictly confidential, which in fact meant a higher classification than normal.[59] The main reason why these contacts were terminated was that the Harpsund plans in 1955–56 were expanded to include machinery and broader parts of inter-Scandinavian trade.[60]

Agriculture was conspicuously absent from the scheme, which in fact represented a substantial concession from Denmark, which had a large, competitive, and export-oriented agricultural sector. For the Danes,

58. The Cabinet Economic Committee (CEC), Kurt Hansen's archive, Ministry of Economic Affairs, National Archive Copenhagen, box 6, file 5: Minutes from the Harpsund meeting of 30–31 October 1954.
59. Commission des Communautés européennes, Archives Bruxelles, EU Historial Archives, Florence, CEAB 5/63: P.U. (Pierre Uri): 'Note sur le Danemark', 4 July 1955; UM 74.C.13.f./I: J.C.: 'Notat vedrørende dansk og skandinavisk samarbejde med CECA' (Note concerning Danish and Scandinavian cooperation with the ECSC), 15 October 1955. For the early Danish contacts with the ECSC, see Laursen, 'The Supranational Seven', especially 211–216.
60. CEC 7/11: CEC 7/11: 'Danmarks forhold til Det Europæiske Kul- og Stålfællesskab' (Denmark's relationship with the ECSC), 15 May 1956; UM, B.32.c: Danish Committee on Scandinavian Economic Cooperation, 27th meeting, 20 December 1955.

choosing Scandinavia instead of closer ties with the rest of Western Europe implied giving priority to the development of an industrial export sector over traditional agricultural exports to Britain and West Germany. On the other hand the inclusion of electrotechnical and pharmaceutical products, both sectors with great dynamism in Denmark, also reflected Danish interests. It was, however, still a very vague compromise, with many difficulties remaining to be solved, not least the divergence in the meaning of a common market among the Scandinavians. If the Messina meeting of the Six was a 'relance' after the failure of the European Defense Community, as the traditional accounts of European integration maintain, then the Harpsund meeting was no less of a 'relance' after the failure of the Bramsnæs Committee's investigations. However, in 1955, after the Messina meeting, the Scandinavian star began to wane. The British proposal in early 1957 for an OEEC-wide free trade area and the signing of the Treaties of Rome in March 1957 sent the Scandinavian cohesion into wreckage, and in early 1959 all post-Harpsund planning was eventually scrapped in favor of the European Free Trade Association.[61]

## SCANDINAVIA AND THE INTERPRETATION OF EUROPEAN INTEGRATION

Our brief study of the two cases of Scandinavian cooperation—the founding of the Nordic Council and the attempts at closer economic cooperation in 1947–1955—suggests that the early interpretations of the nature of Scandinavian cooperation have a number of inherent weaknesses. Just as the early European integration theories had been influenced by the idealistic rhetoric of the pioneers of European integration, the early theories or interpretations of Scandinavian cooperation were ideologically imbued with a strong dose of pro-Scandinavian partisanship. It is, on the one hand, apparent that the assumptions about the Scandinavian cooperation process as characterized by pragmatism, incremental progress, and cob-web cooperation do not hold up against the weight of the empirical evidence. On the other hand it does seem that at least some of the contemporary decision-makers were moved by strong political convictions and motivations with regard to both the value of closer cooperation in Scandinavia as well as of the domestic and diplomatic political benefits from Scandinavian cooperation. It is also apparent especially from the track record of the economic cooperation discussions from 1947 until the mid-1950s that the implicit assumption about continuity in the nature of the Scandinavian cooperation efforts is unsustainable. In many ways, the Harpsund initiative of 1954 constituted

61. Jens Otto Krag on the Common Nordic Market: *Politiken*, 16 December 1954, 6. The EFTA Convention was agreed in Stockholm in November 1959. It entered into force on 3 May 1960.

a new departure that had more in common with the process initiated by the Six at Messina—or even more: with the Spaak Committee—than it had with the early feeble attempts at Scandinavian economic cooperation from 1947 onward. In other words, it seems that the hypothesis about a Scandinavian special path or '*Sonderweg*' in regional cooperation does not hold up against the test of the two cases.

If then the Scandinavian case/cases are applied as case studies of a general interpretation of the forces behind European integration a number of puzzling questions remain. Can, for example, the available interpretative frameworks—not to speak of theories—of European integration accommodate the Schuman Plan as well as the Scandinavian cooperation experience in the late 1940s and during the 1950s? Implicit in this is of course that the Scandinavian economic integration plans are seen as a category of integration choice on a par with that of the Six. In other words, did the Scandinavian integration process in the 1950s represent enough critical mass of commitment for us to say that it was a kind of choice at the same systematic level as that taken by the Six founding members of the ECSC? Could the choice of Scandinavia be qualified as representing a common strategy for integration?

Of the cases that we have studied here, only the Harpsund 'relance' of a Scandinavian common market in 1954 can be qualified as properly containing the sum of different national strategies aiming at securing crucial national aims such as welfare, full employment, and economic modernization. Indeed, it was so primarily for Norway and Denmark, while the economic motives for Sweden were less compelling. But there can be little doubt that the Harpsund initiative in its bloom in 1955–1956 offered a solution to problems that would be insoluble for the individual Scandinavian states on their own. Hans Hedtoft's speech in August 1954 (quoted above) is an expression of the awareness of at least some contemporary Scandinavians that the small Scandinavian states faced a challenge which had consequences not only on welfare but also on the viability of their political independence. While the customs union discussions in the period 1947–1954 resounded with Scandinavian disunity, conflicting end goals, and diverging views about the relationship to the major economic and political forces in Western Europe, the Harpsund negotiations did for a brief while unite the Scandinavian governments in a common purpose. This purpose was, in Alan Milward's words, to 'advance particular sets of national domestic policies'.[62] For a brief period of time there was, in the framework of Scandinavian cooperation, a convergence of possible national strategies—in the sense used by Milward—offering a lever for national policy aims for all three countries as well as a counterweight to the dependency on the major

62. Milward, 'Conclusions', in *The Frontier of National Sovereignty*, quotation on 182.

European economies. None of these strategies were domestically without contention. Giving priority to economic modernization in the framework of a Scandinavian market involved painful domestic decisions for Norwegian industry as well as for Danish farmers.

The major difference with the integration process taking place in the rest of the continent had to do with size and with the degree of economic dependency. All three states also saw cooperation as a remedy to their dependency on the dominating economic and political forces, such as Great Britain and West Germany. In this sense Scandinavian cooperation had a strong dimension of small-state strategy. Scandinavian cooperation was not only a 'rescue of the nation-state' in the sense that it promised solutions to domestic national policy aims, but also in the sense that it offered stronger European bargaining clout compared to the weak bargaining positions of the individual Scandinavian states. However, it also meant that the three Scandinavian states would need to sacrifice, if not sovereignty in full, at least some degree of decision-making authority to mutual decision-making procedures. This was exactly what at least two of the Scandinavian states, Norway and Sweden, found so difficult. They continued throughout the negotiations to insist on institutional solutions which did not infringe national sovereignty.

For all three countries the choice for Scandinavia cannot be isolated from the challenges which other European initiatives at integration, such as the Schuman Plan, or at cooperation, such as the OEEC or Uniscan, represented. A Scandinavian common market would under all circumstances need to find its place within a broader European economic order. This was most obvious between 1947 and 1950 with the initiative in favor of closer economic cooperation in Scandinavia, which in the overall view was little more than a gesture to satisfy the Marshall Plan administrators in the United States. This is not to say that political leaders in individual Scandinavian countries—such as Denmark—did not see it differently. Moreover, the Scandinavian steel market, which was part of the 1954 Harpsund plans, cannot be seen in isolation from the ECSC. This raises the question whether the Scandinavian economic cooperation plans—and the national positions on them—can be analyzed and understood by themselves. That is, can Sweden's position on a Scandinavian steel market be understood in terms of the nature of this market, or in terms of the nature of its effects on Sweden's commercial relationship to the ECSC member-states? Thus, the Scandinavian option was not an exclusive choice in relation to other European initiatives, but it certainly was a way to approach them, in particular the broader question of European Community integration.

Even though individual Scandinavian countries rallied behind this or that integration initiative, they might have done so for quite different motives and causes. Moreover, even if they did choose, say, Scandinavian economic cooperation instead of closer ties with the Six, there is little evidence that they all did so based on the institutional type of integration, namely, with reference to the intergovernmental or supranational nature of the choice. At least for the representatives of Danish and Norwegian industry the choice of a Scandinavian common market was preferable to a Western European common market, where they would face tough industrial competition from especially the West German industry. It was a matter of industrial jobs rather more than of institutional choices. At the same time, while the Norwegian and Swedish choices of Scandinavian cooperation reflected a preference for intergovernmental, less committing institutions, this was much less the case for Denmark. Danish representatives even pressed for stronger institutional, though admittedly not supranational, commitments in both the Scandinavian common market plans and the Nordic Council. As we have seen, there is evidence that Danish decision-makers and diplomats had close contacts with the High Authority of the ECSC in the mid-1950s. So, in the Scandinavian case, the strength of the argument in favor of the 'rescue' thesis, is—at least in one of the three cases—not necessarily evidence of an institutional choice for or against intergovernmental or supranational institutions.

The brief evidence reviewed here also suggests that the ideological—or what some might refer to as the idealistic—and political dimensions weighed heavily in the Scandinavian cases in the period under discussion. But they are also of a different nature. There is no doubt that Scandinavian idealism was a powerful political force in Denmark and Sweden, and to some—although a lesser—degree in Norway, in the immediate postwar years. This seems to indicate that the political dimension of closer Scandinavian cooperation, in particular in the case of the Nordic Council, weighed heavily on the minds of the Scandinavian decision-makers when determining the nature of this intra-Scandinavian parliamentarian institution. Held up against the 'rescue' thesis this suggests that the exposed position of the small Scandinavian states in geopolitical and security terms—and the perception of this in the voting population—was a relatively stronger concern in Scandinavia than in the larger West European powers. It should also be kept in mind that governments and central bureaucracies had powerful interests invested in avoiding an alienation of their Scandinavian partners. The foreign policy consultations and the often successful attempts to coordinate positions in the United Nations, the OEEC, and in—in the cases of Denmark and Norway—the North Atlantic Treaty Organization, remained an important asset that was not to be gambled with.

There were, however, also less idealistic domestic political dynamics giving weight to Scandinavian cooperation. Due to the strength of pro-Scandinavian-cooperation sympathies in the populations it was never without cost to choose a European solution rather than a Scandinavian one. There would therefore often be a strong tendency for a Phoenix effect, that is, to throw up some new Scandinavian initiatives from the ashes of failed projects as a consolation prize. Several times throughout 1945 to 1972 such compensatory initiatives came from Norway, at least partly in order to avoid carrying the responsibility for the breakdown in prior Scandinavian cooperation talks. The emergence of the Nordic Council in 1953 added extra weight to such dynamics through the public accountability of the governments in the Council.

Finally, it might well be that the continuity thesis in Scandinavian cooperation has blinded us to the qualitative changes in the nature of Scandinavian cooperation as well as in the conditions under which the choices were made. It seems evident that the choice in favor of Scandinavian investigations in 1947 were taken against the background of a much weaker competitive and monetary position in Norway than the decisions taken in 1954, not to speak of the decisions on the creation of EFTA in 1959 and on applying for EEC membership in 1961. The industrial and economic repercussions of a common market would simply be less severe after the mid-1950s than in the late 1940s. This had consequences for the nature of the welfare and employment considerations inherent in those choices. Instead of focusing on a presumed continuity in Scandinavian cooperation until at least 1973, historians will have to pay closer attention to the epochal shifts in the domestic and external conditions under which decisions for and against Scandinavian cooperation were taken. Timing is—this should be no surprise for historians—of the essence for the interpretation of Scandinavian cooperation. The Harpsund initiative in 1954 came at precisely the right time between the waning of the OEEC as a framework for economic cooperation in Western Europe and the ascendancy of the European Community as a new force in European integration. There is much to be said in favor of seeing the developments in European integration in 1957–1958 as a critical watershed in the external conditions for Scandinavian cooperation. The coming into force of the Treaties of Rome and the rise of the European Commission as an international actor qualitatively changed the environment in which any Scandinavian economic cooperation would have to exist.

*

* *

The time might have come to review the place of the Scandinavian states in the beginnings of the European integration process and their place in the historiography of European integration. What were the factors that shaped the choices made by the Scandinavian states when faced with the Schuman Plan and the Messina conference? A closer look at the role of the Scandinavian states in the Marshall Plan and the OEEC reveals that these states were faced with much the same choices, challenges, and dilemmas as the Six. The Scandinavian states were all confronted with the need to modernize and liberalize their economies and prepare them for international competition. Instead of searching for structural differences and generic factors historians will have to turn to the similarities between the

Scandinavian states and the Six, as well as the dissimilarities and internal dynamics among the Scandinavian states, in order to build a more complex understanding of the Scandinavian cases in European integration. Adopting a revised understanding of the role of the Scandinavian states as less unique and exotic implies in turn an understanding of the Six as less unique too. Such an approach to Scandinavian-European history will necessitate an interpretation of the dynamics and causes behind the choices of nation-states to engage in the European integration process as more dependent on small margins of causation and on temporal sequence.

# 21 The European Rescue of Britain

*James Ellison*

In the first edition of *The European Rescue of the Nation-State*, Alan S. Milward wrote a final chapter entitled 'Britain and Western Europe' which did not fit readily with the rest of the book.[1] As Britain's course was not that of the six countries which created the European Communities in the 1950s ('the Six'), the British nation-state was not 'rescued' by Europe in the 1950s. In the chapter, Milward included a brief section on 'Britain and the Treaties of Rome' which was not free of censure.[2] The barrage of his criticism of Britain's response to the Six's efforts had various targets but one of particular note was 'the civil service and particularly [ . . . ] the Foreign Office,' whose recruitment, Milward wrote, 'was designed to perpetuate the rule of a monied upper class with an elitist structure based on access to expensive private education and privileged entry into two universities notable for the irrelevance of the knowledge they imparted to the task at hand'.[3] Even a casual reader would not see in this sentiment much to have endeared Milward to those who appointed historians to Britain's official history series, yet it was he who was chosen in the early 1990s to write two volumes on the history of the United Kingdom and the European Community (EC). This came as a surprise to many in the field. Why would Milward, whose horizons and hypotheses were always wider than just one country, not least Britain, accept this role? Why, moreover, would those who had it to offer appoint a brilliant economic historian who was in print little interested in diplomacy in all senses? In any case, it was Milward who was chosen, and his book was much awaited. Unsurprisingly, *The Rise and Fall of a National Strategy, 1945–1963,* was yet another monumental monograph which, like *The European Rescue*, was both fascinating and frustrating.[4] It is nevertheless the benchmark study on the subject, and it was a great pity that Milward was unable to complete the second volume

---

1. Milward, *The European Rescue of the Nation-State.*
2. Ibid., 424–433.
3. Ibid., 431.
4. Milward, *The United Kingdom and the European Community, vol. 1, The Rise and Fall of a National Strategy, 1945–1963.*

(which planned to cover the period up to the 1980s). While *The Rise and Fall* marked Milward's first extended analysis of 'Britain and Europe' (as the field has become known), it actually represented the culmination of ideas which began with his study of the effects of the wars on Britain and in his seminal book on postwar economic history.[5] The evolution of Milward's research and the significance of his arguments for our understanding of Britain's fraught relationship with the process of postwar Western European integration are the subject matter of this chapter.

## FROM RECONSTRUCTION TO RESCUE

Milward first wrote about Britain's response to the early development of postwar Western European integration in *The Reconstruction of Western Europe, 1945–51*. In that book's description of 'institutionalized, international economic interdependence' among Western European powers in the Marshall Plan era, Milward made a contribution to the new and growing literature on the European policies of Clement Attlee's government.[6] The mid-1980s saw the first examples of what might be described as a revisionist school in the study of 'Britain and Europe' which attempted to depict Attlee's foreign secretary, Ernest Bevin, and the Foreign Office officials who advised him, as proponents of closer Anglo-European unity, not of immediate postwar special Atlantic ties.[7] Bevin was portrayed as 'remarkably integrationist,' embracing 'the idea of Britain, through close collaboration with her European neighbours, holding an intermediate and cooperative position between the two new Superpowers—a "third force".'[8] In these diplomatic histories of the Attlee government's foreign policy, Britain was seen searching for postwar resurgence not through immediate association with the United States and opposition toward the Soviet Union but as a power with European and imperial ambitions which were curtailed by cold war realities.

In his analysis of the formation of Western European economic interdependence in the implementation of the Marshall Plan, Milward offered a different perspective on Britain's involvement with the early postwar efforts toward unity. While his contemporaries focused mainly on diplomatic relations between Britain and France and on security issues in the emerging

5. Milward, *The Economic Effects of the Two World Wars on Britain* and *The Reconstruction of Western Europe, 1945–51*.
6. Ibid., xvi.
7. A prominent example of these works is J. W. Young, *Britain, France and the Unity of Europe*. Also see Greenwood, *The Alternative Alliance*. For a description of the historiographical evolution of the field of Britain and Europe see James Ellison, 'Britain and Europe', and also Daddow, *Britain and Europe since 1945*.
8. Greenwood, *Britain and European Cooperation since 1945*, 8.

cold war, Milward's interest was in political economy and patterns of trade and payments. In particular, he sought to understand why the British did not embrace the French proposal for a customs union made three weeks after the inauguration of the Committee of European Economic Cooperation in 1947. His explanation of Britain's rejection established themes of enquiry and a style of analysis and argument which would be sustained in his later work.

Milward made the observation that 'the almost unanimous opinion of civil servants, as well as of the few academic economists who were consulted' was that membership in a customs union would lead 'to much closer forms of political union as well as to the harmonization of economic policy.' Consequently, 'the attraction to the existing economic state of affairs was naturally strong', and thus Britain's extra-European priorities and assets—the Commonwealth, the Empire, and the sterling area—represented 'greater apparent possibilities for increasing trade and exports' in the pursuit of restored great power status.[9] While Milward had some sympathy for this stance—'[ . . . ] the long-run continuation of existing expensive domestic economic policies and even perhaps of eventual independence of political and economic action from the United States—did not then seem to the British as fragile as they now seem in retrospect'—he argued forcefully that the British civil service failed its country.[10] The Board of Trade received harsh comment—their attitude had 'no real merit or intelligence'—and while Treasury officials were right to prioritize extra-European assets (i.e., sterling reserves), they too were described as hamstrung by lack of imagination.[11] It was the conservative and defensive outlook of British decision-makers which Milward found so objectionable, as he would once again when first analyzing British reactions to European plans in the mid-1950s. Only Bevin emerges from Milward's account as singly farsighted. In describing the foreign secretary's recognition of the benefits to Britain of increased trade with Western European developed economies via a customs union Milward thus aligned himself with others who emphasized Bevin's European aspirations. Beyond that, he asked why British policy should 'have been formulated on such short-term considerations? The longest period of future time the Treasury envisaged [ . . . ] was four years and its image of what it expected to find on that horizon was extraordinarily wishful, a mirage made of optimism and complacency.'[12] Other historians had found the economic ministries wanting on the question of a European customs union, but Milward's criticism was caustic:

9. Milward, *Reconstruction*, 236.
10. Ibid., 236–237 for the quotation.
11. Ibid., 237.
12. Ibid., 248.

> At the highest levels of the three ministries mainly concerned with the decision advice was often formulated in self-indulgent memoranda in an outmoded literary vein in which the subtleties of opinion and the elegance of expression do not hide the almost complete absence of knowledge of the things that needed to be known or the extraordinary prejudices about national character which influenced the generalizations.[13]

Such British myopia was a theme of *The Reconstruction* to which Milward returned at the close of the book. Throughout, he accepted that Britain's global trade and payments network separated it from Western Europe and aligned it with the United States in terms of international political economy. Later in his career, he would see this as a defensible position for the British, but in the mid-1980s, he produced a pointed critique. Essentially, he criticized Britain's lack of awareness of the popular support for, and political will behind, a European customs union as the kernel of something much greater in future Western European economic integration. Hence, he concluded his book (in part) with a comparison between British and French decisions at the dawn of postwar European unity. The British came off worse: 'One question has had to be repeatedly posed. How did France, starting from so weak a position in 1945 and pursuing an unrealizable set of foreign policy objectives, arrive at such a satisfactory long-term political and economic solution?' The answer was not that 'the French policy-making machine was in any way superior to that in Britain,' but that 'the German threat to French national security simply would not go away and, because it was always there, forced French policy-formulation to consider a more distant horizon.'[14] As such, Milward's argument rested on an external security threat as a motive for remarkable prudence which yielded long-term dividends. In this analysis, we perhaps see a flaw in Milward's judgment about Britain's choices. No doubt he was right to find short-term shortcomings in British decision-making in the late 1940s, but was he also right to underplay the cultural influence of Britain's long-held great power status upon ministers and officials in London? Was he also right to neglect the global roles that the British were carrying out by choice, invitation, or necessity, the extent of which did not trouble the French in the late 1940s?

Criticism of Milward's reading of Britain's decision to follow a global rather than a new European course at the close of the 1940s was not taken up in response to the publication of *The Reconstruction*. There are two main reasons for that. First, the book's impact was greatest in its challenging argument about the Marshall Plan; it caused less of a stir in the study of

13. Ibid., 249.
14. Ibid., 501.

British foreign policy.[15] Second, Milward's analysis was methodologically challenging; he fought his battles on different ground from that of his British academic contemporaries who were predominantly diplomatic historians. What he achieved in *The Reconstruction* was nevertheless highly important, and perhaps all the more so in retrospect, given the later evolution of his ideas. He had drawn unparalleled attention to the economic aspects of Britain's policy decisions, and in Britain's unique trade and payments profile found a powerful explanation for its rejection of certain forms of economic cooperation with Western Europe. That said, he felt it necessary to go beyond pure explanation to criticize British policy-makers for a failure to see the future, implying that a long-term national price was paid as a result. This was his mark on the field, and in his next major book he would make it with yet greater impact and significance.

The 'magisterial' *The European Rescue of the Nation-State* elevated Milward to historiographical deity in the field of European integration history.[16] While controversial, the book's central argument was brilliantly ironic. Whatever flaws reviewers found in *The European Rescue*, there was a consensus that it was a work which greatly advanced the field of historical enquiry in absorbing and stimulating new ways.[17] Oddly, the book's final chapter on Britain's response to the formation of the European Economic Community in the 1950s was only partly pioneering and not entirely of the quality of its overall thesis. In fact, the section covering 'Britain and the Treaties of Rome' was rather disappointing (and, as we shall see, it enjoyed the greatest revisions in a second edition). Milward began the chapter in the way he began the book: by asking a critical historical question ('why did the United Kingdom play so small and distant a role in the historical processes analysed here?') and by describing existing explanations as inadequate.[18] Those explanations, written mainly by diplomatic and political historians, placed explanatory weight on Britain's Anglo-American and Commonwealth foreign and defense policy priorities, as well as on a fundamental aversion to European supranationality.[19] Furthermore, they did not express the frustration that Milward did with the contemporary political debate in Britain about its relations with the European Community as a motive for understanding the past. 'In its essentials', Milward wrote, 'it is a debate about history as much as about the future, but both the past and

15. On Milward's historiographical impact, see Dinan, 'The Historiography of European Integration'.
16. Andrew Moravcsik described the book as a 'magisterial history' while also criticizing it. See Moravcsik's review of *The European Rescue of the Nation-State,* 128.
17. Dinan, 'Historiography', cit., 310–323.
18. Milward, *Rescue* (1st ed., 1992), 345–347 (quotation on 345).
19. For example, Bullen, 'Britain and "Europe", 1950–1957'. Also see Greenwood, *Britain and European Cooperation*, 7–78, and J. W. Young, *Britain and European Unity*, 1–81.

the present are represented by images of childlike simplicity.'[20] A reading of the opening and close to the chapter on Britain shows Milward's exasperation to be patent, and somewhat mismatched with the detached authority he conveys in the chapter's main sections, namely sterling–dollar relations, sterling and Western Europe, British and German manufacturing in the postwar period, and competition in cars. In each of these areas, Milward is persuasive. His concentration on Britain's external economic policies, particularly its pursuit of sterling-dollar convertibility to restore the pound's status as an international reserve currency, produced a compelling counterbalance to the different (though ultimately similar) arguments of diplomatic historians. However, when Milward introduced arguments beyond the economic into his analysis, his interpretation had both conventional and unconventional elements.

The chapter on Britain not only works toward an answer to Milward's main question—why Britain remained outside of the formation of the European Community—but also to another: 'Does the general explanation of European integration which has been developed in this book explain also why the United Kingdom did not participate?'[21] When *The European Rescue* was published in 1992, Milward's final judgments on these questions were eagerly awaited by a new wave of historians writing Ph.D. theses and books on Britain and Europe in the key phase from 1955 to 1963. On one level, the conclusions that he reached in the section on Britain and the Treaties of Rome were surprisingly analogous to existing accounts. The Eden government's response to the Messina conference and Spaak Committee was roundly judged as a grand failure by Milward's contemporaries and himself.[22] His version simply served to underline, with idiosyncratic verve, similar factors: the reaffirmation in 1955–56 of policies created in 1950; the 'casualness' of Britain's consideration of the common market proposals; the expectation of the Six's failure; the misreading of the Six's objectives; and the move toward an alternative policy in 'Plan G', the proposal for a European Free Trade Area to encapsulate the Six's Common Market.[23] It was in his broader arguments that Milward presented an explanation which was historiographically fertile but methodologically fragile.

In a very brief section based upon sparse evidence, he extended the criticisms of the British civil service that he had raised in *The Reconstruction* (denouncing Foreign Office advice as 'frequently amateurish and socially prejudiced') and suggested that anti-European chauvinism among the British establishment partly explained Britain's dismissive response to the Six's

20. *Rescue* (1st ed., 1992), 347.
21. Ibidem.
22. See Ellison, *Threatening Europe*, 32–36.
23. Milward, *Rescue* (1st ed., 1992), 424–433 (quotation on 426). Two classic accounts had already made similar points, Burgess and Edwards, 'The Six plus One', 393–413, and J. W. Young, 'The Parting of the Ways'.

plans.[24] The examples of 'ignorance and prejudice clothed as patriotism' outside the civil service were Sir George Bolton, as chairman of the Bank of London and South America, Lord Salisbury, as secretary of state for commonwealth relations, as well as Winston Churchill and Harold Macmillan, both as prime ministers. To illuminate his point, Milward quoted Churchill's comment at a State Department dinner in 1954—'only the English-speaking peoples count; [ . . . ] together they can rule the world'—and Macmillan's statement to colleagues at Chequers in 1959—'there were three elements who wanted supra-nationalism [ . . . ] the Jews, the Planners and the old cosmopolitan element'. To accentuate the supposed longevity of such attitudes, Milward went on: 'Cultural prejudice is usually a wish to misrepresent the world to oneself; it is as coded clues to those aspects of reality which could not be faced that such absurd comments should be taken. They have been matched by many similar atavistic outbursts since 1979.'[25]

The idea that an overwhelming cultural prejudice influenced the British view of European integration in the mid-1950s and beyond was, and is, historically fascinating, yet it was but a token in Milward's overall analysis and had meager evidential support. It is nevertheless clear that he saw it as an essential element of the difference that separated Britain from the Six. Milward's final argument rested on measurable facts of political economy ('the commitment to welfare was more cautious' in Britain; its industrial and commercial policies were 'dominated by the free-trade rhetoric of the "one-world system",' and the 'political economy of agricultural protection in Britain was also different') and upon immeasurable facts of history, memory, and identity: 'There were therefore substantial differences in the balance of perceived political and economic interest between Britain and the Six. They were widened by Britain's distinctive history which fed a national myth which readily turned towards nationalism and even more readily turned against Europe.'[26] It was the emphasis that Milward placed upon the economic in British decision-making which distinguished him from others working on this subject in the mid-1990s, for they too referred to Britain's historic uniqueness in explaining its initial rejection of the European Communities.[27] Even Milward's ultimate disapproval of the path taken by the Conservative governments of the mid-1950s ('the failure to sign the Treaties of Rome was a serious mistake [ . . . ] and the benefits from not having joined the Communities were reduced to no more than the preservation of that same illusion of independence which led to the mistake in the first place') was shared in other works published

24. Milward, *Rescue* (1st ed., 1992), 431 for the quotation.
25. Ibid., 432 for all the quotations.
26. Ibid., 433.
27. See, for example, the conclusions to J. W. Young, *Britain and European Unity*, 184–202. Also, in general, George, *An Awkward Partner.*

simultaneously.[28] Consequently, while *The European Rescue* was revolutionary in its nation-state thesis, it was much less so in its findings on Britain's policies and motives toward Western European integration initiatives.[29] What one reviewer described as Milward's 'frustrat[ions] with his country's current antifederalist opposition' may indeed have influenced some of his judgments and undermined the impact of his work.[30] It nevertheless remains true that the economic aspects of his arguments inspired a group of young scholars of Britain and Europe to integrate economics with diplomacy and politics in their essentially diplomatic histories of the period from 1955 to 1963.[31]

That the first edition of *The European Rescue of the Nation-State* was imperfect in its treatment of Britain was made clear by Milward himself. The second edition of the book, which came eight years later, completely revised the chapter on Britain and Western Europe in structure and argument. It is to Milward's great credit that he modified his views in print as significantly as he did. Gone was the censorious tone of the first edition; gone was its cultural prejudice argument; and gone was its condemnation of Britain's rejection of the Treaties of Rome. Now, British leaders were described as being 'only too aware that what they had inherited from the war was an almost empty simulacrum of world power.'[32] Moreover, their attempt to bargain what economic assets Britain still enjoyed on a world, rather than a European, stage was the right course: 'To construe this as mistakenly acting like a world power is to postulate an alternative policy of giving away advantages, for nothing.'[33] In this much more balanced account of Britain's pursuit of its one-world strategy, Milward placed far less emphasis on Britain's political difference from its continental neighbors and instead presented a new argument which rested on his area of expertise. Preempting the thesis that he would present in his official history, Milward explained that Britain attempted to maximize its two long-term assets: sterling's role as an international reserve currency and 'the huge value and volume of the United Kingdom's international trade'.[34] He described how British governments 'put together three successive strategies for prosperity and safety' after 1945, all of which were 'based on the pursuit of a multilateral framework of trade and settlements as worldwide as possible' and 'relied ultimately, albeit in different ways, on alliance with

28. For example, Bartlett, *British Foreign Policy in the Twentieth Century*, 117 and J. W. Young, *Britain and European Unity*, 52–56. Milward, *Rescue* (1st ed., 1992), 433 for the quotation.
29. Milward did not advance his findings on Britain and Europe in *The Frontier of National Sovereignty*, 17.
30. The review was Moravcsik's, 127.
31. For example, Ellison, *Threatening Europe*; Kaiser, *Using Europe, Abusing the Europeans*; Lee, *An Uneasy Partnership*; N. P. Ludlow, *Dealing with Britain*; and Schaad, *Bullying Bonn*.
32. Milward, *Rescue* (2nd ed., 2000), 347.
33. Ibidem.
34. Ibid., 348.

the USA'.[35] In basing his analysis on these three strategies—Bretton Woods; a multilateral Atlantic–Western European free-trading regime; and the European Free Trade Area—Milward accentuated the financial and commercial motives of British policy in a much clearer and more convincing manner than he had done previously. He also adapted his view of the importance which British decision-makers placed on Europe: 'Three failed strategies in thirteen and a half years is likely to be attributable to more than bad luck, but it hardly seems the case that these strategies, whatever their defects, were founded on any underestimation of the major importance of western Europe to Britain's post-war prosperity.'[36] Thus the rejection of the Treaties of Rome, in Milward's new view, was no longer 'a serious mistake' resulting from flawed policy-making and diplomacy tinged with chauvinism. Now, Britain's response—in its third strategy, the Free Trade Area—was depicted as rational and appropriate though essentially unattractive politically and economically to the Six. And, moreover, Milward now gave a much more compelling judgment on the applicability of his book's grand thesis to Britain's postwar path: 'There was no European rescue of the British nation-state except in very different circumstances from those prevailing in the 1950s.'[37] These circumstances came when Britain's fourth strategy—membership in the European Community—was realized in the early 1970s and when Britain reaped economic and political benefits in a global framework from within the EC. 'Only in that sense', Milward concluded, 'was there a European rescue of the British member-state.'[38] His nation-state thesis had matured, and so had his verdict on Britain's policies: 'Looking at the evidence for the 1950s it is difficult to see how it could have been otherwise.'[39]

The second edition of *The European Rescue* thus presented a much more authoritative account of Britain's response to the creation of the European Communities in the 1950s. It still had the flaws of omission that the first edition displayed—for example, Milward placed very little weight on foreign policy factors unrelated to finance and commerce and did not mention the cold war—but it was a significant advance. Why Milward changed his views so dramatically is a question worthy of a moment's consideration. He had been affected by the work of other historians and by his own now increasingly British-centered research. In the period between the publication of the first edition of *The European Rescue* and the second, the historical study of Britain and Europe entered what now seems to be a golden age when established and young scholars produced a large body of impressive work. John Young's distinguished 1993 survey, a kind of antidote to Milward's work,

35. Ibidem.
36. Ibid., 350.
37. Ibid., 423.
38. Ibid., 424.
39. Ibidem.

was the foundation upon which much research was based.[40] As the decade progressed, a succession of conferences produced excellent edited volumes, and important doctoral theses became books.[41] All of these works added complexity and depth to a field which gained interest beyond its specialist borders, not least because it was still a controversial issue of contemporary political debate.[42] A contender for Milward's 'magisterial' title also entered the ring with an argument which challenged his nation-state thesis and his interpretation of Britain's policies. Writ large, Andrew Moravcsik's state-centric liberal intergovernmentalist theory on European integration was a refinement of Milward's in that its focus rested specifically upon commercial interests.[43] On the question of Britain's reaction to European unity in the 1950s Moravcsik also sought to improve upon what Milward had written in the first edition of *The European Rescue*. '[I]f we begin from the assumption that British policy-makers were primarily pursuing commercial objectives,' Moravcsik wrote, 'there is no need for recourse to attributions of ignorance or irrationality. The information available to British policy-makers—little different from that available to their Continental counterparts—fully justified the skeptical attitude they took toward Messina'. Furthermore, while Milward had always been reluctant to accept that geopolitical factors influenced British decisions, Moravcsik noted their importance but simply described them as 'secondary' to the economic. Above all, reflecting the kind of balanced judgments found in some other recent historiography, Moravcsik distinguished himself from Milward's early conclusions by arguing that 'British policy constituted a rational, remarkably flexible, even far-sighted defense of enduring British economic interests'.[44] Such an argument was close to what Milward himself would write in brief in the second edition of *The European Rescue* and in full in his official history. His peers had clearly influenced his thoughts, but he too had been part of this scholarly milieu on Britain and Europe in the 1990s.

---

40. Young, *Britain and European Unity*.
41. Notable conferences produced Brivati and Jones, *From Reconstruction to Integration*; Broad and Preston, *Moored to the Continent?*; Griffiths and Ward, *Courting the Common Market*; and Wilkes (ed.), *Britain's Failure to Enter the European Community*. Doctoral theses that became books: Bange, *The EEC Crisis of 1963*; Ellison, *Threatening Europe*; Kaiser, *Using Europe*; Lee, *Uneasy Partnership*; Ludlow, *Dealing with Britain*; and Schaad, *Bullying Bonn*.
42. It thus attracted a distinguished journalist who wrote a book for the popular press which though polemical has many attributes: Young, *This Blessed Plot*.
43. Moravcsik, *The Choice for Europe*; on the significance of Moravcsik's work, see Dinan, 'Historiography', 317–318.
44. Moravcsik, *The Choice for Europe*, 122–135 (quotation on 123). For similar views, see Ellison, *Threatening Europe*, and Schaad, *Bullying Bonn*.

In 1996 Milward and George Brennan published a detailed study of the British use of quantitative import controls from 1945 to 1960.[45] This specialist and little-referenced work represents in part the evolution of Milward's ideas about Britain and Europe and somewhat explains the difference between the two editions of *The European Rescue*. Milward and Brennan argued that British governments did not fully comprehend how far Britain's postwar recovery in trade was dependent upon import controls which were expected to be a temporary measure. The result was an overestimation of the strength of British commerce which in turn perpetuated attachment to the one-world policy and significantly influenced Britain's response to the Six's plans for economic integration. In response to a thoughtful and sympathetic review of the book, Milward subsequently elaborated upon his and Brennan's notions in relation to Britain's European policies. In essence, he argued that Britain's postwar foreign economic policies were appropriate given its financial and commercial interests. Moreover, he acknowledged the power of politics in Britain's decision to pursue a global rather than a European course, stating that 'the whole of public and political opinion' wished to preserve the nation and empire that had been 'fought [for] so valiantly'. Milward explained that 'successive governments in the 1950s [thus] had to struggle forwards towards the unrealizable one-world system with obviously diminishing chances of success'; by the second half of the 1950s, Britain had nowhere to go but into the European Communities.[46] This was the story that Milward was to elaborate upon in his official history, the summit of his work on Britain and Europe.

## THE RISE AND FALL

As a result of Milward's writings on Britain and Europe prior to his official history of the subject, all serious historians had to accept that political and diplomatic factors alone could only offer partial historical explanations of Britain's involvement with European integration after 1945. Whether Milward would accept that the opposite was also true and, given the historiographical dominance of political and diplomatic accounts, incorporate the noneconomic into his analysis, was a question that many specialists pondered over before the publication in 2002 of *The Rise and Fall of a National Strategy, 1945–1963*. As Milward had always specialized in revisionism of the epochal, much was expected of this book. It being an official

45. Milward and Brennan, *Britain's Place in the World*.
46. Gamble's review of *Britain's Place in the World* and Milward's response can be found on the Institute of Historical Research's online reviews in history; see http://www.history.ac.uk/reviews/review/38 and http://www.history.ac.uk/reviews/review/38/response respectively (last accessed on 30 December 2011).

history, it had to produce a detailed narrative of policy and events based predominantly on unrestricted access to British governmental sources with reference to the secondary literature at key points of debate. That it did with great authority in 483 pages written mainly for an informed audience. It also went beyond this strict definition of an official account to set its narrative within an overall explanatory concept: the national strategy thesis. This compelling and controversial idea represented the culmination of Milward's views from the first edition of *The European Rescue* ten years earlier. He depicted postwar British policy as a rational choice for a country which had few advantages in Western Europe in 1945 and whose assets were largely extra-European, principally tariff preferences on Commonwealth markets, London's centrality as a financial hub, the ability to build and deploy nuclear weapons, and Britain's strategic utility to the United States of America, especially due to its large colonial empire and its armed forces. Hence, successive British governments implemented a national strategy which aimed to make the best of what Britain had to barter with in full knowledge of the limited endurance of its global reach and power, and in the hope of securing a long-term settlement to provide economic and physical security for the British people. The central element of achieving that new settlement was to bargain Commonwealth preferences in a grand tariff agreement which would see a reduction in U.S. tariffs and the creation of a one-world system which had unique benefits for Britain.[47]

This thesis, which formalized and elaborated upon the three-strategies argument of the second edition of *The European Rescue*, was historiographically innovative. Since the 1960s, as somewhat of an adjunct to the literature on British decline, prominent writers have argued that the European Communities constituted Britain's missed opportunity for postwar national renewal. Through a fated attachment to former glory and a lack of foresight, British ministers and officials forfeited ready opportunities to mold and lead postwar European unity and benefit from the economic growth enjoyed by the Six in the 1950s and 1960s.[48] That Milward rejected this perspective did not set him apart; it had been avoided by all objective historical research for some time. It was the connection between his dismissal of it and his overriding thesis that was so effective. He rendered invalid 'the simplistic question of whether the United Kingdom should have joined the European Communities' by adopting the premise that this was not Britain's aim as long as the national strategy existed.[49] Few other studies before Milward's official history described so convincingly Britain's European policies as a component of Britain's wider foreign and economic policies. The links had of course been made, not least by Moravcsik on

47. Milward, *The Rise and Fall*, 1–9.
48. Two prominent examples of this view are Dell, *The Schuman Plan and the British Abdication*, and H. Young, *This Blessed Plot*.
49. Milward, *The Rise and Fall*, 6.

commercial policy, but not with the force or profundity of *The Rise and Fall*.[50] The national strategy, which was established by 1950, explained the limited British cooperation with nascent Western European economic integration in the decade that followed. However, while Europe was only one aspect of the strategy at its inception, it was the cause of its demise: 'In 1962 in the negotiations for entry into the European Community, a major element of [the strategy], the importance attached to trade preferences in the Commonwealth, had to be abandoned, and the search for a new strategy had to begin.'[51] It was Britain's inability to sustain its postwar aims, above all its commercial policies, in the face of the European Economic Community (EEC), which rendered the national strategy defunct. Combined with wider issues, not least the changing trajectory of British and Commonwealth trade, and the United States' concentration on tariff negotiations with the Six and not Britain, the failure of the Brussels negotiations on Britain's first EEC application forced British governments to adopt a new national strategy: to revise the one-world policy which had dominated British decision-making since 1950 and to concentrate singly on achieving Community membership.

Milward's account of official policy formulation and implementation dealt with all moments of narrative significance and responded to key historiographical debates. In his judgment, Britain's decision not to join the European Coal and Steel Community was fitting given the United Kingdom's economic imperatives. Moreover, there was no historic parting of the ways in 1950; that came in 1955 over Messina, and Britain's fundamental decision at that stage was essentially understandable due to the attachment to its national strategy.[52] The impartiality of these judgments did not make Milward an apologist for British decisions. While he saw Britain's Free Trade Area proposal of 1957 and its first EEC application of 1961 as positive advances in policy (defeated not by the political strength of the Six but because 'Britain's international economic and financial position became too weak to take advantage of France's uncertainty, while Germany's increasing economic strength held the Community together'), he found fundamental flaws in particular aspects of such a policy and, more generally, in the reluctance of British ministers and political parties to adjust relations with the Commonwealth and thus Britain's overall strategy.[53] In their attempt to protect ties with the Commonwealth, British leaders paid too much attention to the global rather than the European and thus undermined the reception of their policies among the Six. Moreover, they failed to recognize the commercial bargains at the heart of the Community and

50. On the broader literature, see Ellison, 'Britain and Europe', 520–522.
51. Milward, *The Rise and Fall*, 7.
52. Ibid., 77 and 229.
53. Ibid. (419 for the quotation).

France's particular attachment to them. For Milward, then, the story of Britain and Europe was, in effect, an Anglo–French struggle:

> Britain's weakness in the [first EEC enlargement] negotiations did not spring from its tactics but from direct conflict between its own worldwide strategy, which in the Conservative Party still had powerful adherents, and that of France. It was not a part of the United Kingdom's strategy to base its economic or political future on European preferences. France, however, would accept nothing less and the outcome was de Gaulle's veto.[54]

At base, therefore, Milward's arguments were still essentially about financial and commercial policies but that is not to say that he failed to engage with political or diplomatic factors or historiographical arguments based upon them. He did, but as an inveterate economic historian, he found them to have less explanatory force. For example, on the much-debated motives for de Gaulle's 1963 veto he wrote this:

> It seems perverse to ignore a total of three years of deadlock between Britain and France in economic negotiations and to suppose that something else—the organisation of NATO, the lack of help for the development of French nuclear weapons, or France's determination to challenge the USA's dominance over western Europe—was the cause of [the] final breakdown [of the Brussels negotiations for EEC British membership].[55]

In making such a case, Milward's analysis shared similarities with that of Moravcsik; indeed, the rationality argument that runs through *The Rise and Fall* is reminiscent of Moravcsik's line in *The Choice for Europe* although it is more far-reaching.[56] There was also much that was familiar about Milward's narrative, yet it was far from derivative, and his conclusions added to the debates on controversial events rather than providing the final word.

What then was historiographically original about *The Rise and Fall*? Milward was aware that his national strategy thesis would not appeal to all readers but he nevertheless hoped that doubters might still find it 'a valuable, though abstract, tool for comprehending and judging British policy towards the European Communities in their first decade.'[57] Its critics might argue that it was overly abstract, but it is difficult to judge exactly what the historical community thought of the book as it did not cause the impact

54. Ibid., 483.
55. Ibid., 472.
56. Moravcsik, *The Choice for Europe*, 122–123 and 164–176.
57. Milward, *The Rise and Fall*, 7.

that might have been expected. At the time of its publication, the popularity of historical research on Britain and Europe had peaked and, since then, historians have moved on to deal with the national and international politics of Britain's relations with the European Communities in the 1960s and 1970s. Additionally, a combination of the loss of senior supervisors in the field, the decline of doctoral funding for diplomatic history, and the waning of economic history at any level (in the United Kingdom especially), has meant that scholars have yet to interrogate the national strategy thesis or extrapolate from it. This is a pity as it remains a stimulating analytical framework. The national strategy thesis describes Britain's choices in terms of political economy—the one-world system and the sought-after commercial bargain to reduce tariffs—but is fundamentally political in that it is intrinsically about Britain's position as a global power rather than a European one. As such, it raises many questions about Britain's democratic governmental system, its attitude toward power, its national identity, and the manner in which each of these factors was affected by the increasing globalization of the postwar era. In the same way that critics of *The European Rescue* argued that the nation-state thesis did not amount to a total theory and was too restrictive in rejecting alternative explanatory factors, it might be said that the national strategy thesis is similarly imperfect. For instance, was Britain's attachment to the one-world system so complete that it, more than, say, an antipathy toward federalism, governed policy toward the emergent Community? And was Harold Macmillan, to take one prominent actor as an example, a politician and prime minister who thought first of trade and second of Britain's place in the cold war in deciding upon his country's policies? Answers to such questions would not necessarily render the national strategy thesis null and void, but instead refine it profitably. Indeed, its most valuable application might come in the era when Britain sought to achieve its objectives from within the European Community. After all, as a member-state, Britain has continued to hanker, both commercially and geopolitically, after global ties and a world role. It is a great loss that Alan Milward was unable to explore such possibilities himself and build on the foundations of *The Rise and Fall* to write yet another seminal work.

# 22 The Establishment of the EEC as an International Actor

## The Development of the Common Commercial Policy in the GATT Negotiations of the Kennedy Round, 1962–1967

*Lucia Coppolaro*

One of Alan S. Milward's most significant historiographical contributions to the history of contemporary Europe has been his explanation of the creation of the European Economic Community (EEC) in which he focused on the trade interests and the commercial policies of the Western European states. By facing the economic questions, Milward has reoriented a historiography dominated by diplomatic historians, has shown the relevance of commercial interests, and has placed the analysis of the EEC Treaty of Rome in the context of the policies pursued by the Western European states after 1945 to favor economic growth and social and political stability. Milward has shown that one of the motivations leading to the establishment of the EEC, with a customs union at its foundations, was to favor freer trade at the regional level through a new form of intra-European cooperation labeled as 'integration' in order to sustain economic growth. Milward qualified this as a 'rescue' operation of those nation-states and illustrated how the ultimate aim of the pooling of sovereignty through integration was not to get rid of the nation-state itself, but rather to strengthen it. Integration allowed governments to pursue those policies that were considered as indispensable for the political and social stability of the state, but that governments could not sustain by themselves. As such, integration gave the nation-state the tools to regain legitimacy. Milward concluded that there was no antithesis between the nation-state and the supranational character of the EEC. Far from undermining nation-states, as neofunctionalism and federalism had held, Milward viewed European integration as an essential instrument used to enhance the authority of the national governments involved. The drive toward further integration was propelled by the Communities' member-states and their national interests. The supranational institutions were not the motor of integration but rather instruments used by member-states to forward their own national interests.[1]

---

1. Milward, *The European Rescue of the Nation-State*, 1–46.

Milward's analysis, in addition, provided the first incursion into the origins of the EEC's common commercial policy. This second contribution is no less relevant than the first if we consider the fundamental role that trade had been playing in European integration. The customs union was the most important single undertaking of the Treaty of Rome, and foreign trade immediately became a field in which the original members of the Communities pooled sovereignty by voluntarily delegating their authority to the EEC. Today the European Union—the ultimate institutional development emerging from the previous three European Communities—is a leading player in the World Trade Organization. International trade remains one of the few fields in which the European Union of today is able to speak with a single and powerful voice.

Grounded in Milward's theoretical approach to European integration, his emphasis on the role of the nation-state, and his analysis of the impact of foreign trade, this chapter analyzes the participation of the EEC in the international negotiations for trade liberalization that were convened under the aegis of the General Agreement on Tariffs and Trade (GATT) and took place from 1962 to 1967, in Geneva, known as the Kennedy Round.[2]

The specific aim of the chapter is to show how these GATT negotiations enhanced the definition of the common commercial policy by the original member-states of the EEC, at the time known as 'the Six', and vividly marked the subsequent experience of the EEC as a single actor in world affairs. In order to attend the negotiations in Geneva the Six had first to define their common commercial policy and agree on how open to world trade the EEC should become. The Round fostered this definition, and in 1967 the EEC established itself as a liberal actor for industrial trade, but as a major protectionist actor in the field of agricultural trade. Furthermore, by demonstrating its ability to participate in a major international negotiation with a unified voice, the EEC proved to be able to act as a single and powerful trading unit on the world stage. Rightly so: it was in the arena of international trade and through the implementation of a common commercial policy that the EEC became an international power. Its participation in the Kennedy Round provided the EEC with an incipient international political identity and represented the first manifestation of a common foreign policy. Moreover, the analysis of the EEC's participation in this Round shows how the EEC and its supranational institution, the European Commission, were instrumental to the interests of the member-states. It was only to better defend their trading interests that member-states allowed the EEC and the Commission to strengthen their role in GATT.

2. This chapter is based on the author's Ph.D. thesis 'Trade and Politics across the Atlantic'.

## ACCEPTING THE ROUND, WITH SOME QUALIFICATIONS

The year 1962 was a busy one for the six member-states of the EEC in terms of favoring integration at their regional level. Following the specifications of the EEC Treaty of Rome of 25 March 1957, the Six established the customs union by progressively dismantling internal trade barriers and implementing the Common External Tariff (CET). They were also busy elaborating the Common Agricultural Policy (CAP) and discussing the form of association of former colonies. Moreover, they were engaged in negotiations with the British government, which in 1961 had asked to join the Communities.

With this already busy agenda, a new issue turned up: U.S. President John F. Kennedy proposed the launching of a new GATT round leading to a sweeping reduction in trade barriers worldwide. From the U.S. perspective, the EEC was both a challenge and an opportunity. It represented a challenge because it could develop into an inward-looking and discriminatory trading bloc. This had already been a concern of former President Dwight D. Eisenhower when the EEC was established in 1957. By the time Kennedy entered the White House in 1961, concern increased because of the challenging policy of the French president, Charles de Gaulle, and the growing deficit in the U.S. balance of payments. From 1959 to 1961, the deficit averaged \$3.2 billion per year, as compared to an average \$1.1 billion per year between 1952 and 1958.[3] But, at the same time, the EEC provided an opportunity for tariff reduction worldwide. For the first time since the establishment of GATT in 1947, a trade partner was able to offer valuable negotiated counter-concessions due to the size of its market. For this reason the Kennedy administration was able to obtain from the U.S. Congress the authority to launch a new offer for far-reaching international trade liberalization. The 1962 'Trade Expansion Act', by which congressional authorization was granted to the executive, allowed the reduction of tariffs in the industrial sector in a linear way—that is to say by a uniform percentage—up to 50% and, in some cases, up to the complete removal of existing duties. This implied the possibility of abandoning the item-by-item negotiation procedure that had characterized all previous rounds in GATT. For the first time since the establishment of the GATT in 1947, the U.S. government intended to include agriculture in the negotiations, as a way of responding to the establishment of the

3. USDC, *Survey on Current Business*, Washington, 1968. On the United States' policy toward European integration see Lundestad, *Empire by Integration*. On Kennedy's policy toward Western Europe see Brinkley and Griffiths, *John F. Kennedy and Europe*. For an analysis of how the deficits in the balance of payments affected U.S.-Western Europe relations see Gavin, *Gold, Dollars, and Power*.

regional CAP and in order to moderate the discriminatory aspects of that emerging common policy.[4]

The American initiative affected every aspect of the EEC, from the customs union to the CAP and the association agreements with former colonies. But it affected more generally the trade policy of the Six as it implied that intra-Community trade liberalization would be accompanied by trade liberalization at the multilateral level. At this point the EEC had to state whether it supported the drastic liberalization apparently sought by the United States or favored more limited reductions in trade barriers. The EEC had to choose the position it wanted to assume in the future world trading system and decide how regional trade integration was to be complemented by increasing trade integration worldwide. By taking a position on Kennedy's initiative and then attending the new GATT round, the Six were forced to speed up the definition of the common features of the Community's commercial policy. This represented a fundamental step in defining the Community's trade integration patterns both at the regional and multilateral levels.

The Six agreed to attend the new GATT round in order to expand their exports to the United States and the rest of Western Europe. As Table 22.1 shows, they all had relevant trade interests outside the EEC. After at least one decade of export-led growth non-EEC international trade liberalization appeared attractive even to the governments of those countries, such as France and Italy, that had traditionally held a more protectionist record. However, a too drastic reduction in duties was rejected by all in Brussels as it would undermine the intra-Community trade system which was then taken as essential for the overall economic performance of the six economies. Table 22.1 shows how important exports at the regional level of the EEC were for each of the Six and how dramatically intra-EEC exports increased in the period running from 1958, the year before the implementation of the customs union began, to 1963. Thus the dismantling of internal barriers strengthened the process of regionalization of trade that had already begun in 1954.[5]

The EEC might well find its economic position in the industrialized world eroded if the full potential of its internal market were not achieved because of a sudden and drastic external tariff reduction. The CET was a fundamental part of the Community, the latter not yet developed sufficiently to afford the loss of such an important protectionist feature. Moreover, tariff protection did not have the same meaning on the two sides of the Atlantic: for the Six the CET constituted an important element of cohesion and an

---

4. On the U.S. initiative for the new round see Zeiler, *American Trade and Power in the 1960s*.
5. For the trade patterns among the Six before 1957 and how they led to the creation of the EEC see Milward, *The European Rescue of the Nation-State*, 119–223.

**Table 22.1 EEC Member States' Exports 1954-1963 by Destination (in million of US$ at current prices)**

| The Federal Republic of Germany | | | | The Netherlands | | | | BLEU* | | | | France | | | | Italy | | | |
|---|---|---|---|---|---|---|---|---|---|---|---|---|---|---|---|---|---|---|---|
| Dest. | 1954 | 1958 | 1963 | Dest. | 1954 | 1958 | 1963 | Dest. | 1954 | 1958 | 1963 | Dest. | 1954 | 1958 | 1963 | Dest. | 1954 | 1958 | 1963 |
| EFTA | 1524 | 2649 | 3967 | EFTA | 584 | 847 | 1036 | EFTA | 423 | 524 | 674 | EFTA | 616 | 760 | 1313 | EFTA | 398 | 642 | 959 |
| % total | 29.2 | 27.1 | 27.2 | % total | 24.8 | 23.7 | 21 | % total | 18.6 | 16 | 14 | % total | 17 | 14.2 | 16.3 | % total | 24.6 | 22.3 | 19 |
| Index growth | 100 | 174 | 260 | Index growth | 100 | 145 | 177 | Index growth | 100 | 154 | 297 | Index growth | 134 | 123 | 213 | Index growth | 100 | 161 | 241 |
| EEC | 1534 | 2731 | 5455 | EEC | 862 | 1597 | 2646 | EEC | 991 | 1522 | 2941 | EEC | 907 | 1527 | 3093 | EEC | 356 | 792 | 1799 |
| % total | 29.3 | 27.9 | 37.4 | % total | 37 | 44.6 | 53.6 | % total | 43.5 | 46.4 | 61 | % total | 25 | 28.5 | 38.3 | % total | 22 | 27.5 | 35.7 |
| Index growth | 100 | 178 | 356 | Index growth | 100 | 185 | 306 | Index growth | 100 | 154 | 297 | Index growth | 100 | 168 | 341 | Index growth | 100 | 222 | 505 |
| USA | 295 | 913 | 1051 | USA | 158 | 209 | 203 | USA | 191 | 444 | 411 | USA | 156 | 470 | 421 | USA | 129 | 345 | 480 |
| % total | 5.6 | 9.3 | 7.2 | % total | 6.7 | 5.8 | 4.1 | % total | 8.3 | 13.5 | 8.5 | % total | 4.3 | 8.7 | 5.2 | % total | 8 | 12 | 9.5 |
| Index growth | 100 | 309 | 356 | Index growth | 100 | 132 | 128 | Index growth | 100 | 232 | 215 | Index growth | 100 | 301 | 270 | Index growth | 100 | 267 | 372 |
| Rest of the world | 1873 | 3463 | 4112 | Rest of the world | 747 | 926 | 1049 | Rest of the world | 673 | 789 | 798 | Rest of the world | 1952 | 2593 | 3238 | Rest of the world | 732 | 1097 | 1801 |
| % total | 35.9 | 37.7 | 28.2 | % total | 31.5 | 25.9 | 21.3 | % total | 29.6 | 24.1 | 16.5 | % total | 53.7 | 48.6 | 40.2 | % total | 45.4 | 38.3 | 35.8 |
| Index growth | 100 | 185 | 220 | Index growth | 100 | 124 | 140 | Index growth | 100 | 117 | 119 | Index growth | 100 | 133 | 166 | Index growth | 100 | 150 | 246 |

*Source* : Direction of trade statistics historical, 1948-1980 (Washington, D.C.: International Monetary Fund, 2002). Note: (*) Belgium and Luxembourg

element of the EEC's identity in world trade and affairs. As Milward notes, the CET was like a Constitution that usually identifies nation-states.[6] As a result, a too far-reaching liberalization of trade was rejected by the representatives in Brussels of both the traditionally more protectionist countries of Italy and France and the traditionally more liberally oriented countries of the Benelux and the Federal Republic of Germany.[7]

Notwithstanding this basic agreement, differences existed between the industrial and agricultural sectors. For the industrial sector, the Six had to decide if the CET was to be reduced by 50%, as suggested by Washington. To understand the attitude of the member-states, it should be recalled that, as Table 22.2 shows, in 1958 the CET was formed by averaging the high tariffs of France and Italy with the much lower tariffs of the Federal Republic and Benelux. As a result, low Benelux and German duties were raised, whereas high French and Italian duties were lowered.[8] The representatives of the Federal Republic and Benelux governments approved the 50% reduction if some sectors were to be exempted. In joining the CET, the frontier duties in the four countries had been raised, and the reduction of 50% at the multilateral level simply meant regaining the 1958 level. On the other hand, duties in France and Italy were progressively being reduced to match the common CET levels. In both countries many feared the effects of cumulative tariff reduction forced by the CET and the forthcoming GATT negotiations.

But this was not the only element that caused differences. The Federal government aimed at further expanding exports to both the rest of Western Europe and the United States and at using the reduction in CET duties as a bargaining tool. To many in the Federal Republic it seemed that the EEC ought to adopt a liberal stance so that international trade could be liberalized and German exports further expanded. After the French veto of the British application to join the EEC in 1963, which reconfirmed the trade division of Western Europe, a lowering of tariffs at multilateral level appeared more urgent than ever in order to attenuate the discriminatory effects of such division. On the other hand, the opening of the French and Italian economies was taking place cautiously, at the EEC regional level, taking advantage of the preferential access to the large and dynamic market of the Federal Republic. Thus, while sharing a clear interest in expanding exports to the rest of Western Europe and the United States, the ruling governments adopted a cautious position.[9]

---

6. Milward, 'Tariffs as Constitutions', in *The International Politics of Surplus Capacity*, edited by Strange and Tooze, 57–66.
7. Archives Council of Ministers of the European Union, Brussels (hereafter CM2) 1963/946 Note S/628/62, 'Eléments qui pourraient faire l'objet d'études ultérieures au sein de la Communauté', 30 November 1962.
8. For a more in-depth discussion of the establishment of the CET see Nême and Nême, *Economie Européenne*, 58–61.
9. CM2 1963/947 Procès verbaux (PV) de la 101ème session du Conseil de la CEE, Brussels, 8–10 May 1963.

*Table 22.2* Average *Ad Valorem* Percentage Incidence of Import Duties of the Six in 1958 and of the CET

| SITC | Products | Benelux | France | Germany | Italy | CET |
|---|---|---|---|---|---|---|
| 5 | All Chemicals | 7 | 16 | 8 | 17 | 14 |
| 61 | Leather manufactures | 11 | 11 | 13 | 18 | 12 |
| 62 | Rubber manufactures | 17 | 17 | 10 | 19 | 18 |
| 63 | Wood and cork manufactures, except furniture | 11 | 19 | 7 | 22 | 16 |
| 64 | Paper and board manufactures | 14 | 16 | 8 | 18 | 15 |
| 65 | Textiles, except clothing | 14 | 19 | 11 | 20 | 16 |
| 66 | Nonmetallic mineral manufactures | 12 | 16 | 6 | 21 | 13 |
| 67 | Silver, platinum, gems, jewellery | 5 | 13 | 3 | 7 | 6 |
| 681 | Iron and steel | 5 | 13 | 7 | 17 | 10 |
| 6841 | Primary aluminum | 0 | 20 | 0 | 25 | 9 |
| 691 | Ordnance | 9 | 14 | 7 | 17 | 11 |
| 699 | Manufactures of metal | 11 | 20 | 10 | 23 | 16 |
| 71 | Machinery other than electric | 8 | 18 | 5 | 20 | 13 |
| 72 | Electrical machinery | 11 | 19 | 6 | 21 | 15 |
| 73 | Transport equipment | 17 | 29 | 12 | 34 | 22 |
| 81 | Building parts and fittings | 15 | 19 | 8 | 25 | 17 |
| 821 | Furniture | 13 | 23 | 8 | 21 | 17 |
| 84 | Clothing | 20 | 16 | 13 | 25 | 21 |
| 851 | Footwear | 20 | 21 | 10 | 21 | 19 |
| 86 | Instruments | 13 | 25 | 8 | 20 | 16 |

*Source*: GATT, Spec(61)37, Working Party on Examination of Common Tariff of EEC-Secret-General Incidence of the Common Tariff of the European Economic Community, 2 February 1961.

Differences also existed concerning the agricultural sector. In defining the CAP, a process that had started in 1958 and was still ongoing when the Kennedy Round negotiations opened, the EEC members had to work out a common position, despite their conflicting interests, over the desired impact of the CAP on imports from third countries as well as the pace at which the CAP was to be implemented.[10] On the one hand, France, a larger and more efficient producer of most agricultural products than the rest of the EEC member-states, sought to limit preferential export access within the EEC to the Six. If France accepted the inclusion of agriculture in the Geneva talks it was only to push EEC members, notably the Federal Republic, to move ahead in fully establishing this policy. Since the beginning of the elaboration

10. The reasons leading to the inclusion of a common policy for agriculture in the EEC Treaty of Rome have been extensively analyzed by Milward, *The European Rescue of the Nation-State*, 224–317.

of the CAP, the Federal Republic had shown reluctance to move ahead with the approval of this common policy. In 1962, in particular, it opposed the setting of the unified grain price, a basic element of the CAP. Within the EEC, the Federal Republic had the highest prices, and it refused to set common prices to the level proposed by the Commission, halfway between the German and the much lower French price, as it maintained that this would only cause a reduction in German farmers' remuneration.[11] With the completion of the CAP due at the end of the transitional period, in 1970, if the Six were to attend the agricultural side of the Kennedy Round as a trading unit, they would have to anticipate the definition of this policy. As such, the Kennedy Round gave France the possibility of further increasing pressure on the Federal Republic to move ahead with the CAP. On the other hand, Germany, Italy, and the Netherlands imported cheap food from outside the EEC and looked at the GATT negotiations as an opportunity to maintain that flow.[12]

It was with these different trading interests that the Six had to formulate a common position for the Kennedy Round. By obliging them to determine the level of tariff cuts, the level of CET duties, and the treatment of agricultural trade under the GATT rules, the American move put the Six in the position of having to delineate their trade policy. But the U.S. move had another implication: it forced the Six to demonstrate their ability to negotiate as a single unit. The establishment of the common commercial policy meant that the authority to enter into negotiations with non-EEC countries passed from the member-states to the EEC. It now required the development of unified instruments for negotiation and the capacity of the Six to act as a Community. In short, the EEC had now to prove its ability to act as an international actor.

## AGREEMENTS DESPITE THE QUARRELS

The Six had to elaborate their common position to attend the GATT talks during the crisis atmosphere caused by both de Gaulle's veto of the British membership application in January 1963 and by the way the veto had been announced. Yet, whereas tensions remained high in Brussels, fueled also by disagreement over the CAP, the economic and political reasons that had led to the signing of the EEC Treaty of Rome were too relevant to be dismissed.[13] The participation in the new GATT round helped the Six to find a

11. For the German resistance to setting common prices for grain and the negotiations on the elaboration of the CAP from 1962 to 1964, see Knudsen, *Farmers on Welfare*, 207–265.
12. On the stances of the member-states on agriculture in the Kennedy Round, see CM2 1963/947 PV de la 101ème session du Conseil de la CEE, 8–10 May 1963.
13. On the tension between the Six caused by the French veto and the elaboration of the CAP, see N. P. Ludlow, *The European Community and the Crises of the 1960s*, 15–32.

degree of unity during the transitional phase established by the EEC Treaty and in the face of the United States.

The Kennedy Round was launched at the GATT ministerial meeting of May 1963. Trade negotiations in GATT consisted of a preliminary phase during which the objectives and the rules of the bargain would be established. Then attention would move to the reduction of trade barriers. In the Kennedy Round, the United States, the EEC, the United Kingdom, and Japan agreed that the negotiations would be devoted to the reduction of tariffs in the industrial sector, to trade in the agricultural sector, to the harmonization of nontariff barriers, and to the barriers which prevented the expansion of exports of the developing countries. In the course of the bargain attention mostly concentrated on the first two objectives, which corresponded to the main interest of the major actors involved and, in particular, of the United States and the European Community. In effect, from the outset the Round was dominated by these two actors with the result that when an agreement was reached between Brussels and Washington it was almost impossible for the other trading partners—including the United Kingdom—to challenge the deal.

In the first year of the Round, attention was devoted to the rules to reduce duties and to deal with agriculture. After much quibbling on whether duties had to be reduced by 50% across the board, as Washington asked, or harmonized, as the EEC required, it was decided to accept the 50% across-the-board reduction, even if tempered by the possibility to table lists of exceptions, notably for products that would be partially or totally exempted from the general rule. This basic agreement was enough to put the industrial negotiations on track and showed that, despite the quarrels, the EEC and the United States had a strong common interest in reducing duties.[14] By contrast, no rules were elaborated for agriculture, due to the persistent disagreement across the Atlantic on how to treat this sector and the parallel EEC clash on the elaboration of the CAP. Until the end of 1964, the Six bitterly quarreled over the CAP, with the Germans dragging their feet over the approval of unified grain prices and the French threatening to leave the EEC.[15]

What is relevant here is that despite internal tension, the Six were able to set their list of exceptions to be tabled in Geneva on 14 November 1964 when attending the industrial negotiations. None of the Six intended to allow the internal wrangles to endanger their participation in the Kennedy

14. CM2 1964/389, PV de la 60ème réunion du Comité 111, 6 May 1964; Telegram 2007 from President Kennedy's Special Representative for Trade Negotiations Christian A. Herter to State Department 6 May 1964, NSF (National Security File)—Subject files, Trade: Kennedy Round, Box 48, Lyndon B. Johnson Library (hereafter LBJL).
15. Telegram 2004 for White House National Security Advisor McGeorge Bundy from Herter, 7 May 1964, Bator Papers, box 12, LBJL; CM2 1964/134 PV de la 146ème session du Conseil de la CEE, 19–21 October 1964.

Round for the industrial sector. This fact is revealing as drawing up the list of exceptions was a complicated process for all governments because of the lobbying pressure exercised by the different sectors' interest groups. For the EEC it was even more difficult as six governments, subjected to lobbying pressures, had to compromise their positions in one stance. Moreover, for the Six the drawing up of the list had a special significance. First, it implied reaffirming their capability to move from six national commercial policies to a common commercial policy. Second, deciding which products would be subjected to the 50% linear reduction and which exempted meant in fact defining the degree of liberalism / protectionism of the EEC toward the rest of the world in commercial terms.

The EEC list was formulated by the Council of Ministers in a four-day marathon meeting in November 1964 based on proposals tabled by the European Commission. The latter institution formulated a liberal list covering 6.1% of total EEC industrial imports and 14.4% of EEC industrial dutiable imports, so that 85.6% of industrial imports paying duties when entering the markets of the Six were to be subjected to the 50% reduction. Confronted with the Commission's proposals, the representatives of Italy, France, and, to a lesser extent, Belgium, called for more exceptions, the Federal Republic and the Netherlands for fewer, while Luxembourg approved the list as it stood. As it is not possible to describe the negotiations for all the products, in order to understand how the list was set, four sectors are considered: machinery and transport equipment, chemicals, aluminum, and textiles. These sectors are chosen either for their importance in world trade or because they exemplify the mechanics incurred in reaching compromises.[16]

The machinery and transport equipment sector was of major importance in the Kennedy Round talks. In 1964, it represented 36% of OECD members' imports of manufactured items and was the largest trading sector.[17]

16. The description of the negotiations between the Six over the exception list is based on the following archival sources: Archives European Commission Brussels (hereafter AECB) BAC 122/1991–24 Rapport du Comité 111 en ce qui concerne la proposition de la Commission relative à la liste d'exceptions de la Communauté, 4 November 1964; Ministère des Affaires Etrangères (Quai d'Orsay), Paris (hereafter MAEF), DE/CE, 1961–1966 GATT 932, Note de la Direction des Relations Economiques Extérieurs (DREE)—Ministre des Finances, 4 November 1964; CM2 1964/143 PV de la 149ème session du Conseil de la CEE, 10–15 November 1964; Historical Archives European Union Florence—MAEF Olivier Wormser (hereafter OW) 36 R.132, Note reporting the Commission's attitude toward the list of exceptions as described by Robert Marjolin, vice president of the Commission of the EEC, 13 November 1964; AECB BAC 122/1991–24, Mise en œuvre des décisions prises par le Conseil, 16 November 1964.
17. Author's calculation based on the OECD data base on foreign trade (Standard International Trade Classification Revision 2), Historical Series 1961–1990, OECD, 2000.

*Table 22.3* Composition of Total Exports of the Six in 1964 in Percentage

| SITC | France | Italy | Germany | BLEU | Netherlan. |
|---|---|---|---|---|---|
| 0 Food and live animals | 12.7 | 22.7 | 1.8 | 5.2 | 22.7 |
| 1 Beverages and tobacco | 3.3 | 1.2 | 0.3 | 0.6 | 1.2 |
| 2 Crude materials, inedible, except fuels | 7.1 | 7.9 | 2.7 | 6.2 | 7.9 |
| 3 Mineral fuels, lubricants and related materials | 3.5 | 9.2 | 4.9 | 4.0 | 9.2 |
| 4 Animal and vegetable oils, fats and waxes | 0.3 | 0.8 | 0.3 | 0.2 | 0.8 |
| 5 Chemicals and related products, n.e.s. | 9.7 | 9.2 | 4.9 | 4.0 | 9.2 |
| 6 Manufactured goods classified chiefly by material | 28.4 | 19.4 | 22.0 | 50.0 | 19.4 |
| 7 Machinery and transport equipment | 25.4 | 23.6 | 46.2 | 19.0 | 23.6 |
| 8 Miscellaneous manufactured articles | 9.1 | 5.2 | 9.0 | 7.2 | 5.2 |
| 9 Commodities and transactions, n.e.c. | 0.6 | 0.9 | 1.3 | 2.2 | 0.9 |
| Total | 100 | 100 | 100 | 100 | 100 |

*Source*: *OECD SITC Rev.2—Historical Series 1961–1990* (Paris: OECD, 2000). Note: n.e.c. and n.e.s. stand for 'not elsewhere classified' and 'not elsewhere specified' respectively.

Table 22.3 illustrates the major importance which this sector had for the EEC members.

Moreover, the German manufacturers were worldwide leaders. Their exports represented one-third of their country's total exports, and the sector registered an important trade surplus with the United States. Hence, the Federal government had a main interest in reducing CET duties by 50% so as to bargain for equivalent reductions in European Free Trade Association (EFTA) and U.S. tariffs. By contrast, in France and Italy, an across-the-board 50% reduction was rejected so as to avoid the reduction in intra-EEC preference, the weakening of their preferential access to the German market, and any increased competition from the United States and the EFTA countries. A common position therefore implied finding a middle course between the French and Italian stances, which privileged regionalism, and the German and the Dutch positions, which favored multilateralism. This sector saw the toughest confrontation, but all the Six knew that they had to make concessions if they wanted to attend the GATT negotiations as a unit. The final compromise was built around the proposals drawn up by the Commission which represented a balanced and complicated set of concessions between member-states. Cars would be subjected to the 50% reduction, as German representatives requested, despite the opposition of the Italians; trucks heavier than four tons, buses, and their detached pieces and accessories would be totally exempted, to the satisfaction of French producers. As for the key mechanical, electrical and electronic sector, while the representatives of France and Italy withdrew 30% of their requests for exceptions, the representatives of West Germany eased their position. In the end, exceptions were limited to sewing-machines, certain machine tools, computers and electronic calculating machines, nuclear reactors, radios, public work machines, airplanes, bicycles, diesel motors, tractors and their parts, and optical equipment.

The same pattern of interests was replicated in the chemical sector. West Germany had a worldwide competitive industry, enjoyed a trade surplus with the United States, and, supported by the Benelux countries, was willing to reduce tariffs. On the other hand, France and Italy had a less competitive industry and were prepared to make only moderate cuts. The task of setting a common position was facilitated by the existence of the American Selling Price (ASP), a customs valuation system, which hit this sector heavily. Due to the tough insistence of the French and to the bewilderment of the Germans, the Council of Ministers put the entire chemical sector on the exceptions list and declared itself to be ready to reconsider its stance only if Washington abolished the ASP. The Six adopted an apparently intransigent position, hoping to persuade the U.S. government to remove the ASP, but tactically this position was a response to the American pressure in favor of far-reaching liberalization in other sectors.

The case of aluminum was completely different. Here the largest EEC industrial producer was France, which was trying to establish a regional market in which to export at prices which were not competitive by any international comparison. Thus the French government had no intention in Geneva of offering any reduction in protection. By contrast the governments of the Federal Republic and the Benelux countries wished to reduce the CET on aluminum in order to continue importing from their traditional low-price sources outside the EEC and offer reductions to the Nordic countries in exchange for compensation in other sectors. Clashes between the French position, on the one hand, and that of the Benelux, the Federal Republic, and Commission representatives, on the other, which lasted throughout the Kennedy Round, had failed to produce any change in the French position by May 1967. The very fact that a member-state had no exporting interests, but rather an interest in retaining the common market as its own protected preferential market, impeded reaching a consensus. The same pattern was followed in the paper sector, where the governments of France and Italy, wanting to protect their industries from Nordic competition, allowed only token reductions.

While the aforementioned sectors were characterized by a strong German attitude toward duty reduction and a more cautious attitude expressed by French and Italian representatives, the situation was different in cotton textiles where all the Six asked for protection. Here the industrialized countries together faced competition from the less-developed countries and were united in calling for protection.[18] Within the EEC, Italy was the largest

18. For an excellent account of the textile sector in this context, see Kohlhase and Schwamm, *La Négociation CEE-Suisse dans le Kennedy Round*, 139–157.

textile producer and its government aimed at preserving the preferential area of the EEC, whereas the industries of the other five Community members were already coping with the competition from the Italian industry and were not willing to be exposed to increased worldwide competition. Trade in cotton textiles was regulated by the Long Term Arrangement on Cotton Textiles (LTA), approved in 1962 and due to expire in 1967. The LTA was a worldwide market-control scheme by which the importing countries—mostly the advanced industrial ones—imposed on the exporting countries—mostly less-developed ones, plus Japan and Hong Kong—quotas to limit their exports. Against this situation, the Six easily agreed in Geneva to ask for the renewal of this arrangement and the maintenance of their protectionist policy.

After the exception lists were tabled in November 1964, the negotiations in the industrial sector got underway in Geneva. In the end, out of 1,588 tariff items, about 1,148 were submitted to a general linear reduction of 50%, 409 excepted (117 totally and 292 partially), and 31 reduced conditionally. Mostly because of Italian and French requests, the Council of Ministers added exceptions for a further 4.6% to EEC dutiable imports compared to what the Commission had suggested. The final list of exemptions covered 19–20% of Community dutiable industrial imports and 9% of all EEC industrial imports.[19] In this sense, it can be affirmed that the Six defined the EEC common commercial policy along liberal lines, even if important sectors remained well protected.

It is notable that at a time when the EEC was struggling through the intense quarrels over the definition of the CAP, the Six were able to approve their list of industrial exceptions to the 50% across-the-board tariff reduction. Despite all their other existing disputes, their collective willingness to reach a final compromise was never put in doubt, and all of them showed the necessary flexibility to make concessions. The capacity of the Six to set up a common list, an exercise that could easily have led them to paralysis, showed the paramount interest they had in attending the Kennedy Round with a view to lowering tariffs, and in doing so as a single, unified trading unit. These two interests combined forged a convergence of commercial policies which resulted in a *common commercial policy*. It should be noted, nevertheless, that the Community's commercial policy was not yet completely common since some sectors were not included within the EEC administration. In addition to textiles, a case in point was trade with Japan and the Eastern European countries, with which imports and exports were negotiated bilaterally by each of the member-states on the basis of quantitative restrictions.

The adoption of the exceptions list also sheds light on the EEC trade policy-making and, in particular, on the role the Commission played in

---

19. AECB Commissioner Marjolin's cabinet papers, Box 791, Liste d'exceptions de la Communauté économique européenne pour les produits industriels, 4 December 1964.

it. The latter was able to provide the essential technical expertise necessary for mediating between the member-states' interests and for reaching a final compromise. As such, this institution played a central role and was able to strengthen its stance in Brussels.[20] As for the agricultural sector, in December 1964 the West German government eventually acquiesced in approving unified grain prices, thereby enabling the negotiations over agriculture in Geneva to begin. As a result, in May 1965, the Kennedy Round had gained a certain amount of momentum: negotiations over the lists of exceptions continued, discussions over an international grain agreement were initiated, and a date, September 1965, was approved to make offers in agriculture.[21]

Yet beneath this serene surface, the situation was far more complicated. First, the Six still had to agree on the financing of the CAP for the period of 1966 to 1969, and second, frustration existed in Bonn, Rome, and the Hague over the way in which the French dominated the EEC. At the end of June 1965, all these tensions erupted with the representative of the French government leaving the Council of Ministers and not attending any of its meetings until the following January.[22] Still, the 'empty chair' crisis did not impede the EEC's participation in the GATT talks. Despite French absence from the Council, the main decision-making institution in Brussels, the other five members agreed that under the existing Council mandates, the Commission continued to negotiate in Geneva over the industrial sector and grain, even if it could not present offers for other agricultural staples. As for the French malcontents, despite de Gaulle's attack on the EEC, the French government never obstructed the work of the EEC in Geneva nor questioned the negotiating rights of the Commission. As a result, during the crisis, the Six kept on negotiating and maintained their unity in Geneva. They had paramount economic and political interests in avoiding the dismantling of the EEC, as well as in limiting the impact of any internal crisis on the action of the Community at the GATT talks. Once the crisis was over, in January 1966, and the last phase of the Kennedy Round had started, the GATT talks had a positive effect on the cohesion of the Six. Although it had been badly shaken by the 'empty chair' crisis, the need to confront the United States with a united position in order to defend the regional dimension of the EEC allowed the Six to recover their unity and cohesion, at least in trade relations with third countries.[23]

---

20. For a detailed description of the EEC trade policymaking see Johnson, *European Community Trade Policy and the Article 113 Committee.*
21. Preeg, *Traders and Diplomats*, 150–155.
22. On the crisis see N. P. Ludlow, *The European Community and the Crises of the 1960s*, 115–123.
23. The capacity and willingness of the Six to keep negotiating in Geneva during the crisis is described in Coppolaro, 'The Empty Chair Crisis and the Kennedy Round of GATT Negotiations'.

## THE FINAL BARGAIN: SETTING THE CORE OF EUROPEAN REGIONALISM IN GLOBAL TRADE

In October 1966 the Kennedy Round entered its last phase. Until then, member-states had played an active role in Geneva. They attended the bargaining between the Commission, which negotiated on behalf of the EEC, and the other GATT partners and enjoyed speaking rights. In the last phase, they became aware that to effectively enhance their trade interests, the EEC had to be represented by a sole negotiator that could speak with a single voice to third countries. A unified voice reinforced their bargaining strength. Thus they allowed the Commission to be the sole negotiator and, consequently, to strengthen its role because this was in line with their interests. Yet the fact remained that member-states intervened at every stage of the negotiations, checking the treatment of every single item—from needles for sewing-machines to wooden packing-cases—with the Commission having to constantly shuttle between Geneva and Brussels to get instructions from the Council of Ministers.

In the industrial sector, the reciprocal interest in reducing protectionism that existed on both sides of the Atlantic led the EEC, the United States, and the EFTA countries to agree on a reduction in their respective trade barriers so that valuable results were within reach.[24] The United States had tabled a list of products to be exempted from the 50% tariff cut, which was of the same length as that of the EEC, whereas the United Kingdom had opted for a shorter list. The rest of the EFTA countries stuck to a general 50% tariff reduction and threatened to retract their offer unless the EEC countries agreed to limit their exceptions. They counted above all on the German interest in reducing protection. In effect, the German authorities had already started to put pressure on their French and Italian counterparts. Because of the overall importance of the machinery and transport equipment sector for the Kennedy Round, the French and Italian representatives were well aware of the need to improve offers. Thus they agreed both to reduce the exceptions and to transfer public work machines and, above all, electrical machines to regular tariff-reduction treatment. The EEC, however, because of French and Italian opposition, exempted business machines and electronics, two new industries that they wanted to protect from U.S. and Japanese competition. With an average reduction of 45% in actual tariff levels, machinery was the industrial sector in which the greatest cuts were offered. This was surely a major concession by the EEC, given the already low CET duties (between 6% and 12% *ad valorem*), which served as a point of departure for new

24. The following description of the result of industrial negotiations is based on Curtis and Vastine, *The Kennedy Round and the Future of American Trade*, and Coppolaro, 'Trade and Politics across the Atlantic', 360–392.

reductions, and given the fact that U.S. and British producers were more competitive than those of the Six.[25]

The negotiations on chemicals became a tough confrontation between Washington and Brussels. With the EEC making the removal of the ASP a precondition for any tariff negotiations on the entire sector, unless the United States was ready to seriously discuss the issue, disappointing results in this crucial sector of world trade were to be expected.[26] After lengthy negotiations in Geneva, an agreement was reached on the basis of the U.S. proposal for a two-package deal. The EEC and the United Kingdom would reduce tariffs by 20% unconditionally, whereas the United States would make a 50% cut. Then on condition that the United States transformed the ASP into a tariff protection and reduced the resulting duties to an average level of 20%, the EEC and the United Kingdom would make a further 30% reduction.[27] The agreement reached in Geneva could have had a major impact on the liberalization of this sector, but, due to the growing protectionist impulses that existed in the United States, in 1970 the U.S. Congress refused to ratify the agreement. As a result U.S. tariffs were reduced by 50%, but the ASP was kept, while the EEC and the United Kingdom reduced their tariffs by 20%.

Whereas in the two sectors previously discussed an important degree of trade liberalization was achieved, the situation for aluminum and textiles was rather different. In the aluminum sector, the French remained intransigent, and in response the Nordic countries, which were already disappointed by the small cuts in the paper sector, withdrew part of their offers in the mechanical sector. Norway, in particular, decided to offer a limited 20% duty reduction on cars, to the great disappointment of the Federal Republic. Even worse was the outcome in the textile sector. In renewing the LTA for three years, the United States, the EEC, and the United Kingdom only agreed to slightly enlarge the respective import quotas and offer a limited 20% tariff reduction. As a result, the divorce between free trade and textiles was complete. The EEC members, moreover, maintained their bilateral quota restrictions, which further delayed the implementation of a common commercial policy for this sector.[28]

25. CM2 1967/17 PV de la 212ème session du Conseil de la CEE, 10–12 April 1967.
26. Memorandum for Francis M. Bator (Deputy Special Assistant to President Lyndon B. Johnson for National Security Affairs) and Harry McPherson (Special Counsel to the President) from William M. Roth (Special Representative for Trade Negotiations), 25 April 1966, Roth Papers, box 2, LBJL.
27. CM2 1966/34 PV de la 188ème réunion du Conseil de la CEE, 13–14 June 1966 ; telegram 3668 from Roth to Bator, 15 May 1967, Roth papers, box 3, LBJL.
28. CM2 1967/28 PV de la 216ème réunion du Conseil de la CEE, 10–11 May 1967 and Department of State—Administrative History, Vol. 1, Part 8, box 2, LBJL.

Despite this notable exception, in the industrial sector the Kennedy Round produced valuable results. It cut duties by 35% on average, with about two-thirds of the cuts reaching a 50% level. The average 1964 level of the CET (12%) was to be reduced by 33.4%, which meant placing it at a new average level of 8% *ad valorem*, whereas Japan had an average tariff level of 11.5%, the United Kingdom of 10.4%, and the United States of 9.4%. Achievements varied across sectors as illustrated by Table 22.4, which reports the tariff cuts made by the United States and the EEC according to main categories of products.

It is worth noting that the exceptions rule allowed the United States, EFTA, and the EEC to remove the most sensitive sectors from the linear cuts, allowing them to pursue the neomercantilism which had previously characterized their commercial policies. In effect, as noted by Milward, it would be misguided to think that the Western governments—and in particular the Western Europeans—moved from the extreme protectionism of the 1930s to free trade in the 1960s. They were constrained by the fact that a decision to move toward trade liberalization could provoke a negative reaction in those sectors that aimed for protection. Moreover, while

*Table 22.4* EEC and U.S. Tariffs before and after the Kennedy Round (KR)

| | US duties before the KR | EEC duties before the KR | US duties after the KR | EEC duties after KR |
|---|---|---|---|---|
| All chemicals | 17.8 | 14.3 | 9.3 | 7.6 |
| Leather manufactures | 16.2 | 9.2 | 10.4 | 5.7 |
| Rubber manufactures | 11.3 | 15 | 6 | 7.8 |
| Wood and cork manufactures, except furniture | 7.1 | 10.9 | 6.8 | 8.8 |
| Paper and board manufactures | 10.9 | 10.7 | 5.5 | 7.5 |
| Textiles | 21.4 | 16 | 20.1 | 15.6 |
| Mineral manufactures | 9.9 | 9.4 | 7.5 | 5.5 |
| Iron and steel | 6.5 | 9.4 | 5.7 | 6.7 |
| Manufactures of metal | 14.7 | 12.8 | 7.7 | 7.2 |
| Machinery other than electrical | 11.9 | 11.1 | 6 | 6.4 |
| Electrical machinery | 13.6 | 14.2 | 7.1 | 9.1 |
| Transport equipment | 7.1 | 15.4 | 3.5 | 9.9 |
| Footwear | 21.1 | 17.8 | 12.1 | 12.4 |
| Instruments | 21.1 | 13.3 | 13.1 | 8.4 |

*Source*: E. Preeg, *Traders and Diplomats: An Analysis of the Kennedy Round of Negotiations under the GATT* (Washington DC, 1970), 208–209.

governments held that liberalization of foreign trade encouraged the growth of productivity and incomes while satisfying consumer demands, they also held protectionism as necessary to foster technological modernization and more sophisticated manufacturing sectors. The tariff policy was made by governments which were reorganizing industries and, although with different intensity, intervening to actively promote long-term economic and social welfare. This circumstance influenced their tariff policy. The link between industrial and commercial policies and between investment and trade led to the assumption that trade liberalization was not only a question of tariff reductions. Frontier controls on commerce became part of a wider political economy employed for ever-broader policy objectives. The situation gave the trade policies of the period their peculiar mixture of liberalism and protectionism.[29]

In any case, the interest in lowering the tariff levels of other participants led to a substantial reduction in protectionism both across the Atlantic and in Western Europe, even if some sectors remained outside the liberalization process. The EEC, while maintaining its regionalism, was not in fact a stumbling block. On the contrary, it ended the GATT talks with a liberal common commercial policy in the making, and, with its regionalism, it contributed to multilateral liberalization. The outcome of the agricultural part of the GATT talks was, however, totally different. Because of the protectionist policies of the Western European countries during the 1950s, GATT rules were not applied to agriculture. With the creation of the CAP, the United States and other major exporters, such as Australia and Canada, started to ask for the extension of GATT rules to the trade of agricultural commodities as a way of reducing the likely impact of EEC discrimination.[30]

In order to reinforce their stance U.S. negotiators took a strong line in the Kennedy Round, claiming that they would not conclude the negotiations unless meaningful results were achieved for agriculture. Despite this stance, the White House and the State Department were aware that it was not feasible to miss the opportunity of getting a 50% reduction of tariffs in the industrial sector—which in terms of volume of trade and export potential was much more important than the agricultural sector—in order to get reductions in agriculture. From the outset, U.S. negotiators were aware that their chances of success in the agricultural field were limited. Whereas in the industrial sector a reciprocal interest in reducing discrimination existed, this was not the case in agriculture. Since the EEC was more interested in protecting its agricultural production than in exporting its agricultural surpluses it had no incentive to reduce the level

---

29. Milward, *The European Rescue of the Nation-State*, 121–132.
30. The best account of the treatment of agriculture in GATT remains Josling et al., *Agriculture in the GATT*. For an account of protectionism of agriculture in Europe see Tracy, *Government and Agriculture in Western Europe*.

of protection. In effect, while agricultural exports to the EEC had great importance for the United States, the EEC did not have any urgency to enhance its exports. For the time being, therefore, pressure to liberalize could not come from GATT.[31]

Negotiations in Geneva centered above all on grain, a basic commodity which had implications for the treatment of meat and dairy products as well. Moreover, this was the commodity which constituted the bulk of U.S. exports to the EEC, representing 37.6% of total U.S. agricultural exports to the Community in 1964.[32] Most importantly, the Six in defining the CAP had started with grain so that its inclusion in GATT negotiations represented the test of how this common policy would be lodged in the world trade system. Washington wanted to negotiate an international grain agreement based on assured quantities and a food aid program. This agreement was to provide importing countries with the guarantee of a given volume of supply and exporting countries with the possibility of having their fair share in growing world consumption. The food aid program no doubt responded to the goal of sharing the responsibility of helping poor and developing countries, but it also served for the management of surpluses. To the extent that other industrialized countries diverted excess production to food aid, the food aid program would make room for commercial imports and reduce the pressure on export markets.[33]

Achieving a compromise to negotiate over grain in Geneva meant that the EEC would have to hold some sort of international trade negotiation on a smaller scale in Brussels. Its members were divided between exporters and importers. More exactly, France was a significant exporter, while the other countries were all net importers. The different stances of France, on the one hand, and the other five members, on the other, are illustrated by Tables 22.5 and 22.6. Table 22.5 illustrates the self-sufficiency rate (the ratio of total production to total domestic consumption) for grain of the EEC members. France was the only country to be self-sufficient for all grain and having a potential as exporter, whereas the other five members were not self-sufficient, with the exception of the Federal Republic on rye. Table 22.6

---

31. Letter from MacGeorge Bundy to Dean Acheson (former U.S. Secretary of State under the Truman Administration), 29 October 1964, Bator Papers, box 12, LBJL.
32. Author's calculation based on OECD (2010), 'SITC Revision 2', International Trade by Commodity Statistics. Available at: http://www.oecd-ilibrary.org/trade/data/international-trade-by-commodity-statistics/sitc-revision-2_data-00055-en;jsessionid=1sqgcu2m5m29o.delta?isPartOf=/content/datacollection/itcs-data-en (accessed on 17 December 2010).
33. United States National Archives, College Park, MA (hereafter NARA), 364 Recs. of the USTR on the Kennedy Round, box 5, telegrams 2343 and 2349 from State Department reporting conversation between U.S. Under Secretary of State Ball, USTR Herter, U.S. Secretary of Agriculture Freeman, Commissioner Rey, and Commission's official Rabot in Washington, 27 May 1966.

*Table 22.5* Rate of EEC Self-sufficiency in Grain in 1964

| | EEC | Germany | France | Italy | Netherlands | BLEU |
|---|---|---|---|---|---|---|
| Wheat | 90 | 70 | 109 | 95 | 32 | 68 |
| Rye | 98 | 107 | 103 | 46 | 75 | 69 |
| Barley | 84 | 65 | 123 | 48 | 39 | 47 |
| Oat | 92 | 91 | 101 | 85 | 68 | 86 |
| Maize | 64 | 2 | 105 | 79 | - | 1 |
| Average | 85 | 77 | 110 | 87 | 35 | 51 |

*Source*: Istituto Statistico delle Comunità europee, *Annuario di statistica agraria*, 1970.

*Table 22.6* Imports of Cereals of EEC Members—Excluding France—in 1964, by Country of Origin (in tons)

| SITC | Country of origin | Argentina | Australia | United States | Canada | France | Rest of the world |
|---|---|---|---|---|---|---|---|
| Italy | | | | | | | |
| 041 | Wheat | 150 | 0 | 112,000 | 66,111 | 202,000 | 11,000 |
| 043 | Barley | 280,037 | 28,155 | 212,678 | 40,678 | 28,096 | 272,998 |
| 044 | Maize | 2,212,609 | 0 | 2,162,184 | 2,649 | 61,000 | 714,173 |
| 045 | Other cereals | 149,426 | 11,858 | 274 | 6,974 | 1,853 | 13,599 |
| Fed. Rep. of Germany | | | | | | | |
| 041 | Wheat | 137,000 | 105,000 | 394,000 | 676,000 | 170,000 | 161,000 |
| 043 | Barley | 88,561 | 63,302 | 285,169 | 687 | 383,905 | 382,247 |
| 044 | Maize | 139,000 | 0 | 1,079,000 | 2,000 | 364,000 | 410,000 |
| 045 | Other cereals | 177,181 | 125,319 | 166,392 | 56,773 | 16,828 | 136,462 |
| The Netherlands | | | | | | | |
| 041 | Wheat | 119,000 | 4,000 | 377,000 | 58,000 | 45,000 | 2,000 |
| 043 | Barley | 7,140 | 17,643 | 103,576 | 3,869 | 62,706 | 28,274 |
| 044 | Maize | 165,000 | 0 | 1,578,000 | 63,000 | 5,000 | 19,000 |
| 045 | Other cereals | 157,222 | 10,035 | 671,173 | 93,016 | 1,844 | 62,521 |
| BLEU | | | | | | | |
| 041 | Wheat | 37,000 | 1,000 | 58,000 | 267,000 | 134,000 | 1,000 |
| 043 | Barley | 102 | 1,781 | 12,368 | - | 153,778 | 56,333 |
| 044 | Maize | 163,000 | 0 | 464,000 | 1,000 | 6,000 | 72,000 |
| 045 | Other cereals | 86,235 | 995 | 43,275 | 17,822 | 27,952 | 25,175 |

*Source*: OECD *SITC Rev.2—Historical Series 1961–1990* (Paris: OECD 2000).

shows the origin of grain supply of the EEC members, excluding France. All of them imported more cheaply from outside the EEC.

The working out of a common position required a compromise between the opposing interests of the exporter, France, and importers, the other five. The latter aimed at maintaining their imports of cheap cereals from outside the EEC while France saw the EEC as a preferential area for its own agricultural exports and aimed at excluding competition from abroad. To reach their goal, the EEC importers were disposed to give a guarantee to third countries of minimum purchases. This, however, was rejected by France ostensibly on the grounds that quantitative guarantees were incompatible with the CAP system based on prices, but actually because they ran counter to French trading interests. Instead, the French suggested lowering the level of the unified grain price: a suggestion that was refused by the Germans.[34]

Clearly the adoption of the variable-levy system and the approval of a high common price for grain had already indicated that the EEC as a whole was moving toward increased protectionism. Then, the French veto of quantitative guarantees and the parallel German veto of the price reduction showed that there was not much left to negotiate in GATT. In effect, the deadlock in Geneva over grain ended when the U.S. negotiators eventually decided to drop their demand for quantitative assurances and proposed to negotiate an international wheat arrangement limited to the setting of an international reference price for wheat and a food aid program.[35] In this sense, the EEC ended the round as a major stumbling block in agricultural trade liberalization. Italy, the Federal Republic, and the Netherlands concerned themselves with maintaining imports from outside the EEC, but this concern was not strong enough to push them to modify in Geneva the agreement that had been previously reached on the CAP in Brussels. All of the Six gave priority to the EEC regional market and the protection of their farmers. This applied also to Bonn: if in the industrial sector the German authorities pushed their Community counterparts toward freer trade, in agriculture they were as protectionist as the rest.

## CONCLUSIONS

This chapter shows that the early definition of the EEC commercial policy was the result of a compromise among the different and diverging trading interests of the Six and that this definition was prompted by the GATT

34. MAEF DE/CE GATT 931 Note 'Session du groupe céréales du GATT', 20 March 1964; CM2 1964/11 PV de la 141ème session du Conseil de la CEE, 28–30 July 1964; CM2 1967/17 PV de la 212ème session du Conseil de la CEE, 10–12 April 1967.
35. Memo 'The Kennedy Round Crisis April–June 1967', NSF National Security Council History, Book 1-TABSI-6, LBJL.

negotiations of the Kennedy Round. In effect it was by responding to the U.S. initiative for a new GATT round that the Six were forced to define a common position concerning the multilateral trading system, which implied defining their commercial policy in common and, consequently, the patterns of their regional and multilateral integration. In the industrial sector the EEC outlined a liberal commercial policy. Having a major interest in exporting to third countries it agreed to reduce tariffs in a reciprocal way in order to enhance exports. The traditionally more liberal countries, the Benelux and the Federal Republic, and the traditionally more protectionist countries, France and Italy, reached compromises that should be defined as constituting a liberal commercial policy for the industrial sector. The Six accepted that liberalization at the regional level would move hand in hand with liberalization at the multilateral level. The position in the agricultural field was completely different. The EEC was implementing a protectionist common policy, and even if countries such as Italy, the Federal Republic, and the Netherlands were interested in importing cheap foodstuffs worldwide, they had no intention of calling into question the principles along which the CAP was being defined. Thus the EEC gathered in Geneva with a protectionist policy and found no stimulus to change it. The GATT, which worked like a bazaar, could not then give the push toward the liberalization of agricultural trade. This analysis of the participation of the EEC in the Kennedy Round allows conclusions about the relationship between the member-states and the European Commission to be drawn. In Brussels, thanks to the technical skills of the European Commission, this institution was an important source of compromises, whereas in Geneva member-states allowed it to be the sole negotiator on their behalf. The Kennedy Round marked the EEC's existence as a single powerful trading actor on the world stage. Despite frequent and intense internal quarrels, the EEC was able to participate in important international negotiations with a single voice and ended the talks showing that it had become one of the leading commercial actors in the then multilateral system. It was through the implementation of a common commercial policy that the EEC became an international actor.

# 23 Allegiance and the European Union

*Michael Newman*

Alan Milward sought to promote the idea of allegiance in an article in 1995 in the first issue of the *Journal of European Integration History*.[1] He suggested that the concept could be used to link together allegedly separate historical continuities into a single hypothesis from which an eventual model of integration might be constructed. He also outlined possible research questions on the topic and subsequently initiated a program at the European University Institute (EUI) designed to answer some of them. He thus directed a new interdisciplinary project and seminar series on allegiance at the EUI in 1996, continuing periodic discussions of this kind until 2002. However, his hope that such work might provide a fruitful link between researchers across conventional disciplinary divisions, thereby promoting a new understanding of the history and development of allegiance, was never fully realized, and few analysts of the EU have explicitly made the concept a central part of their work.

This chapter begins by outlining and exploring Milward's approach to the issue, arguing that it was an integral part of his understanding of European integration that needs to be appreciated in relation to his general historical ideas. Noting the paradox that he promoted the concept just at the time of a marked *decline* in popular support for the EU, it then turns to two contributions of particular relevance to the issues of allegiance in an era of euroskepticism—those of Kees van Kersbergen and Stefano Bartolini. Finally, the chapter asks how helpful Milward's ideas remain in an analysis of the contemporary European Union.

## HISTORY AND ALLEGIANCE

Milward's approach to the question was rooted in his interpretation of the origins of European integration and his belief in the primacy of *history*

1. Milward, 'Allegiance: The Past and the Future', *Journal of European Integration History* 1: 1 (1995): 7–19. This was republished as 'The Springs of Integration', in *The Question of Europe*, by Anderson and Gowan, 5–20. Subsequent references are to the latter version, under the title 'Allegiance'.

in any valid theorization in the social sciences. His ideas on the concept were already discernible in an embryonic form in *The Reconstruction of Western Europe, 1945–51*.[2] Behind his detailed analysis of trade statistics, machine tool production, and comparative growth rates, he identified the political imperatives of the postwar European order and argued that the potential conflict between Western Europe and the United States, first evident in 1947, lay in the danger that American priorities would prevent the continuation of West European economic expansion. Such expansion was built on full employment and welfare, and Milward maintained that European governments pursued these policies even at the risk of an impossible external payments position because they sought a fundamental reversal of their experience in the 1930s. Nor was this simply because of the particular ideological inclinations of those in power:

> High and increasing output, increasing foreign trade, full employment, industrialization and modernization had become in different countries, as a result of their experience of the 1930s and the war, inescapable policy choices, *because governments could find no other basis for political consensus* [my emphasis].[3]

Milward had not yet used the word 'allegiance', but he was already implying something similar in his suggestion that full employment and welfare were prerequisites for domestic support. In 1947 there was no clear blueprint for a trading and payments system that would secure such goals, but a common recognition that the U.S.-led Bretton Woods system was not fit for this purpose. It was, he argued, also clear that the creation of a successful framework for domestic reconstruction would be impossible without a very rapid growth of foreign trade. Between 1948 and 1951 this took place through the European Payments Union, the revival of West Germany, and the establishment of the European Coal and Steel Community. In his view, by 'rejecting the ultimate implications of American policy in Western Europe after 1947, Western Europe made its own peace settlement [ . . . ] a restricted but workable institutional framework for economic interdependence which has proved more effective than any previous peace settlement'.[4]

Governments had negotiated to reconcile their national interests, but the result, he believed, was the creation of something with significance beyond the bargaining process, both because it created a new Franco–German relationship and incorporated aspirations that elevated this above a traditional alliance:

---

2. Milward, *The Reconstruction of Western Europe, 1945–51* (London: Methuen, 1984).
3. Milward, *Reconstruction*, 466.
4. Ibid., 476–7.

> And this in turn gave the alliance a deeper meaning and a nobler purpose for many in the population of both countries, no matter how frequently these beliefs were traduced at government level. By extension, the same difference was created between the EEC and an alliance. In a period when the extent of political participation was increasing, the process of integration could stimulate participation in its own support and thus attach that support to the complex technicalities of formalized economic interdependence on which the European peace settlement was founded.[5]

This implied a two-level process. Political and economic elites were involved in a process of bargaining in which long-term calculations about gains and losses led to a new kind of structure. The mass of the population would not be deeply informed about 'complex technicalities' but nevertheless appreciated and supported this new entity. These ideas were developed more fully in *The European Rescue of the Nation-State* (henceforth, *Rescue*).[6]

The primary theme of *Rescue* was to develop and defend Milward's revisionist account of the process of integration against both nonhistorical theoretical approaches and versions that he regarded as propagandist. Much of the controversy about the book therefore focused on his contention that integration strengthened state power, particularly as he sometimes expressed his views rather provocatively. But Milward's argument was far richer than this, and his conception of allegiance was integral to it. The kernel of the claim was that each of the original six member-states had sought to build full employment welfare states in a situation of interdependence where none could guarantee the attainment of such goals autonomously. Interdependence was a fact of life, but governments needed to *manage* this, and there was nothing predetermined about their success. As Milward and his collaborators argued in *The Frontier of National Sovereignty*, integration was a specific means of achieving this, and the limited form of supranationalism that this involved guaranteed significant progress that would not otherwise have been possible.[7] Furthermore, it was highly unlikely that this degree of integration would subsequently be abandoned, particularly because the construction of

> a wholly new framework for foreign commercial policy would have been too risky an undertaking without a commitment from the Federal Republic, which was as near as it was possible to come in international

5. Ibid., 500.
6. Milward, *The European Rescue of the Nation-State* (2nd ed., 2000). Except where specifically stated subsequent references are to the second edition.
7. Milward and Sørensen, 'Interdependence or Integration? A National Choice', in Milward, Lynch, Ranieri, Romero, and Sørensen, *The Frontier of National Sovereignty*.

> relations to a permanent commitment, that it would continue to function as the key piece in that framework.[8]

In 1992 he also believed that a new form of allegiance provided an additional barrier against the unraveling of integration.[9]

Milward first introduced the relationship between integration and allegiance in *Rescue* as follows:

> the historical evidence points to the further conclusion that without the process of integration the west European nation-state might well not have retained the allegiance and support of its citizens in the way that it has. The European Community has been its buttress, an indispensable part of the nation-state's post-war construction. Without it, the nation-state could not have offered to its citizens the same measure of security and prosperity which it has provided and which has justified its survival. After 1945 the European nation-state rescued itself from collapse, created a new political consensus as the basis of its legitimacy, and through changes in its response to its citizens which meant a sweeping extension of its functions and ambitions reasserted itself as the fundamental unit of political organization. The European Community only evolved as an aspect of that national reassertion and without it the reassertion might well have proved impossible.[10]

This passage might appear to imply that Milward regarded European integration as a necessary, but wholly subordinate, element in this revival. But he surely meant more than this—that the construction of the European Community had played an integral role in the transformation of the nature of both the West European state and allegiance.

The modern state, he argued, had been created on such buttresses as nationalism, ethnicity, and revolution, and allegiance had been 'obtained through a mixture of power, myth and the protection of property'. However, from the late-nineteenth century onward 'a different conception of the nation-state as a more complex network of mutual political obligations of rulers and ruled' had emerged, and this tendency had been accelerated by both World Wars, which had simultaneously demanded feats of organization and a degree of allegiance beyond anything in previous experience.[11] Yet in the interwar period most states could not even fulfil their oldest and primary duty—the defense of national territory and the protection of their

8. Milward, *Rescue*, 429.
9. Milward, *Rescue*, 1992 edition, 445. The relevant sentence was removed from the second edition of *Rescue*, indicating Milward's declining confidence about the growth of European allegiance.
10. Milward, *Rescue*, 3.
11. Ibid., 4.

citizens—while Nazi Germany 'offered as little hope to mankind as any political organization which had existed'.[12] The rescue of the nation-state from this collapse was the most salient aspect of Europe's postwar history, but European integration was a part of this rescue because the new political consensus on which it was built required 'the surrender of limited areas of national sovereignty to the supranation': 'The history of that surrender is but a small part of the post-war history of the nation-state, though it may eventually seem to have been the most significant.'[13]

He was a little uncertain whether a formal definition of allegiance should include the role of state repressive powers or whether repression and allegiance should be regarded as mutually exclusive, but his interest was in support based on consent.[14] Nation-states had always made unremitting efforts to create this kind of allegiance, but normally without success:

> Flags, national anthems, the nationalistic rhetoric of politicians and state-servants, the hours devoted in schools to instruction in a carefully constructed myth of national history, the publicity which is built up around national sporting successes, leave a large part of the population sceptical or only spasmodically enthusiastic. All such propagandistic attempts to win allegiance by the creation and dissemination of national myth are filtered down through a thick and complex mesh of social class, regional, group and family affinities and at every stage encounter a natural human resistance to demands for conformity and subservience.[15]

Apart from Sweden and Norway, no European state had secured a reliable form of allegiance in the interwar period based on a political consensus. However, the postwar state had done so by bringing in three large and overlapping categories of voters: labor, agricultural producers, and a diffuse alliance of lower- and middle- income beneficiaries of the welfare state. Political parties undertook the necessary brokerage at the center to keep the new consensus together. And it was the reassertion of the nation-state that initiated the high growth rates that then led by 1960 to 'a degree of power and a legitimacy founded on an allegiance stronger than any in its previous

12. Ibid.
13. Ibid.
14. He initially stated: 'Force was to remain as it always had been the core of the state. The cruel penalties imposed by its judges, the weapons of its police and armed forces were what, finally, commanded allegiance' (*Rescue*, 24). However, in his subsequent article he wrote: 'By allegiance is meant the range of all those elements which induce citizens to give their loyalty to institutions of governance [ . . . ] It excludes repression' (Milward, 'Allegiance', 11).
15. Milward, *Rescue*, 25.

history', with the general motive of rescuing the capitalist economy by eliminating a waste of human resources and an economic injustice.[16]

Since the Community was designed to uphold and stabilize the postwar consensus, based on full employment and the welfare state, there was, he argued, no contradiction between national and European allegiance. Citing work by Miles Hewston on attitudes toward the Community,[17] he suggested:

> National allegiance remains undiminished, but national citizens have developed a strong secondary allegiance during the Community's existence. In almost every member-state a majority of them believes that the extent to which national policy now has to coexist with other policies arising from membership of the Community, and the degree to which national law and power are moderated also by European Community membership, are desirable. The majority would not wish to see a withdrawal from the Community and the nation left standing on its own. In general, the interests of citizens appear to be conjointly satisfied by both forms of governance. A theoretical explanation of integration would also need to show how this double allegiance has become so strong without weakening the primary allegiance.[18]

In the hope that he had established the importance of his concept of double allegiance, in his 1995 article Milward also outlined possible research questions on the topic. On the assumption that the notion of security had broadened, the first set of fundamental questions concerned the explanation for the growth of allegiance to the EC, and whether or not this would be permanently subsidiary to, and dependent on, that tendered to national or regional government. He proposed that a pragmatic analysis should begin with voting evidence to investigate the extent to which individual material calculations were determinants of allegiance. As a second strand of research, he suggested an examination of the economic and social issues determining national allegiance, which would involve an exploration of the connection between personal income, taxation, security in the widest possible sense of the word, and accepted common policies of the Communities. A third key area of research would be into the symbolic role of 'Europe' in political rhetoric, which changed the way it entered into national political discourse. Was this 'European' allegiance cultural, economic, idealistically political, realistically political, or simply born from fear or prejudice? And how had it changed since 1945?[19]

---

16. Ibid., 28–29.
17. Hewston, *Understanding Attitudes to the European Community.*
18. Milward, *Rescue*, 19.
19. Milward, 'Allegiance', 13–15.

Milward was raising questions of crucial importance to which he also provided some interesting preliminary answers. However, as already noted, he did not shift the agenda in the way that he had hoped, primarily because contemporary historical changes were undermining the very development in allegiance that he had regarded as so significant.

## UNDERMINING ALLEGIANCE

The defeat of the Danish government in the 1992 referendum on Maastricht, followed by the narrowness of the French victory three months later, heralded the new era of waning popular support for elite-driven bargains at EU level. Attempts to enhance popular enthusiasm, whether through symbols, a new currency, a Charter of Fundamental Rights, or a Constitution, were largely ineffective, and the prevailing tendency since the early 1990s has been a rising 'euroskepticism', with xenophobic forces on the populist Right making gains across Europe. In these circumstances, few governments remained confident that their electorates would accept major new developments in the EU, and this culminated in the painful process through which the Lisbon Treaty was eventually ratified. Nor, of course, were such problems evident solely in relation to the EU. There were also increasing signs of disaffection from domestic politics in most member-states, with a trend of decline in electoral turnout, party membership, traditional forms of political participation, and trust in politicians and governments, again reflected in the rise in the populist Right. Meanwhile, the continuing transformation from a full employment/welfare economy to a broadly neoliberal one eroded the socioeconomic conditions that Milward had highlighted in relation to enhanced national and European allegiance in the postwar era.

In these circumstances, a research agenda based on a claim about a new form of double allegiance had little resonance. Instead academic attention shifted to a quite different set of questions. There have thus been endless debates as to whether support for the EU might increase if it were more democratic, whether democracy is possible at this level, how legitimacy might be enhanced, whether a *polis* requires a form of identity, and, if so, whether this can exist at a European level. At the same time, much attention has been paid to the changes in the economy, and their impact upon social inequalities and popular attitudes, including the rise of euroskepticism. In one sense, the increasing sophistication of such research is in line with some of Milward's hopes, but the underlying assumptions have generally been far more pessimistic than those that had led him to suggest that there were new forms of allegiance.

Of course, he was quite aware of the changing context and disliked much of what he saw. In the Preface to the 1992 edition of *Rescue*, he thus contrasted the ideas of those who had reconstructed the postwar era with 'the managerial claptrap and narrow authoritarian deductions from abstract economic principles which dominated policy discussions in the 1980s'.[20] Nor had the research questions that he posed in 1995 necessarily implied that allegiance was bound to grow. In particular, he asked the very pertinent question of whether the ending of capital controls, the development of overseas bank accounts, and perhaps the movement of peoples might have *weakened* some people's national allegiance. If so, he further speculated that national allegiance might have reached its height during the 1960s because of the increased state benefits, with a subsequent decline suggesting a return to the nineteenth-century situation when national allegiance was much weaker.[21] However, he was unable to provide a new interpretive framework that rivaled that of *Rescue*, apparently believing that the notion of double allegiance remained valid even if both governments and the EU were currently experiencing difficulties in maintaining popular support. Nevertheless, his own confidence in this proposition was probably waning, as indicated, for example, by a reversal of his attitude toward strengthening the European Parliament, on the grounds that allegiance to the EU was so weak that there was no basis for any substantial new powers.[22]

It therefore seems that both recent historical trends, and Milward's own inability to demonstrate the continuing validity of his ideas in response to those trends, might imply that his concept of double allegiance had limited durability. This impression appears to be reinforced by the contributions of two theorists, whose writings have particular relevance.

## WELFARE REFORM AND ALLEGIANCE: THE CRITIQUE OF KEES VAN KERSBERGEN

Kees van Kersbergen presented a paper in Milward's allegiance seminar series at the European University Institute in 1996.[23] This was the first of several contributions on the issue in which his continued emphasis was on an exchange relationship as the central element in a definition of allegiance:

> [a]llegiance is defined—somewhat idiosyncratically perhaps—as the willingness of a national public to approve of and to support the decisions made by a government, in return for a more or less immediate and straightforward reward or benefit to which the public feels entitled on the basis of it having rendered approval and support.[24]

20. Milward, *Rescue*, 'Preface', xi.
21. Milward, 'Allegiance', 17–18.
22. Milward, *Politics and Economics in the History of the European Union*, 3.
23. Van Kersbergen, 'Double Allegiance in European Integration'.
24. Van Kersbergen, 'Political Allegiance and European Integration', 4.

By concentrating on this exchange aspect, originally derived from the feudal relationship between a liege and overlord, he not only sought to differentiate between allegiance and allied concepts, but also to demonstrate the irrelevance of many questions that are frequently raised about the explanation for particular attitudes toward European integration:

> The *general hypothesis* is that European allegiance does not depend on how people look at European integration. How a public understands the European Community or Union [ . . . ] in a general way is most likely largely inconsequential. Moreover, it is unlikely that people evaluate the legitimacy of the EC or EU's political institutions and decision-making processes in any meaningful sense. Finally, the extent to which people are attached to locality, region or country is arguably not directly related to their 'European' attachment [emphasis in original].[25]

Having whittled the notion of allegiance down to an exchange relationship, he then retained the idea—suggested by Milward—that allegiance to the EU rested on the *primary* allegiance that citizens held toward the nation-state. If states were delivering the immediate economic and social rewards that citizens expected, and if political elites suggested that European integration was necessary in order to deliver such benefits, people were prepared to offer a secondary allegiance to the EU. However, if governments failed to deliver, the central element in the exchange relationship would be removed. Furthermore, if welfare state construction had been an essential element in building support for nation-states in the early postwar era, the threat posed to existing social welfare systems in the neoliberal age posed a particularly sharp threat to national allegiance. This in itself would undermine secondary allegiance to the European Union; but if, as was also the case from the 1990s onward, the combination of neoliberalism and the austerity measures associated with EMU meant that European integration itself was perceived to be a major cause of economic and social insecurity and threats to the welfare state system, the undermining of European allegiance would become still more intense. In such circumstances, Europe no longer helped rescue the nation-state, but could lead to a situation in which 'allegiance is in double trouble, for both secondary and primary allegiance are threatened'.[26]

In 2003 van Kersbergen explored the relationship between domestic political allegiance and developments in welfare policy further. Endorsing classifications elaborated by Paul Pierson,[27] he suggested that 're-commodification', cost containment, and 'recalibration' had led to a radical

25. Van Kersbergen, 'Double Allegiance in European Integration', 1.
26. Van Kersbergen, 'Political Allegiance and European Integration', 14.
27. Pierson, 'The New Politics of the Welfare State'.

reconfiguration of the welfare state.[28] This could affect the existing patterns of allegiance and power, both between social groups and the state, and also between those groups and both Social Democratic and Christian Democratic parties, which had depended upon particular versions of the welfare state in order to build their own support.[29] If the state and major party formations could not guarantee security and equity, social and political cohesion would be endangered. In particular, political support for the welfare state would be weakened, 'giving rise to electoral instability, ungovernability, and anti-politics sentiments and populist politics.'[30] Van Kersbergen also made two further predictions. First, parties and governments would attempt to formulate their reform strategies in such a way as to protect their core political constituencies by shifting costs to weaker electoral groups and to migrant workers. Second, while this strategy might have short-term electoral advantages, it would 'produce a *systemic* logic that is "ineffective" for political integration, legitimacy, stability and political allegiance in the long run.'[31] It followed from his general view that this would further undermine European allegiance, and he turned to this issue in a subsequent article, coauthored with Catherine de Vries.[32]

This argued that there had been two dominant perspectives on the declining support for European integration and the rise in euroskepticism: one approach was based on utilitarian self-interest and the other on national identity. Both could take more than one form. A macroeconomic utilitarian perspective argued that support for the EU was dependent upon the success of national economic performance, while a second version focused on microeconomic considerations, noting that more mobile citizens with higher levels of income, education, and occupational skills tended to be far more favorable toward the EU than manual workers exposed to the pressures of the single market. In contrast, those taking a national identity approach argued that negative attitudes toward the EU were not dependent upon cost/benefit calculations, but on fear of, or hostility toward, other cultures. Following other authors, van Kersbergen and de Vries distinguished between *exclusive* and *inclusive* forms of national identity and also noted that euroskeptic Right wing parties could play a key role in political mobilization around the notion of *exclusive* national identity.[33] They argued that both the utilitarian and national identity approaches were valid, but that neither could explain the causal mechanisms involved. Instead they claimed that the political allegiance perspective could do so, but their definition of the concept now underwent a notable modification, the significance of

28. Van Kersbergen, 'Welfare State Reform and Political Allegiance', 565.
29. Ibid., 568.
30. Ibid., 569.
31. Ibid.
32. De Vries and van Kersbergen, 'Interests, Identity and Political Allegiance'.
33. Ibid., 308–311.

which will be discussed later. When explaining that people offered support to governments in return for their ability to guarantee security and well-being, van Kersbergen and de Vries now added *psychological* factors to the more familiar list of territorial, physical, social, and economic ones.

Using the 2003 Eurobarometer data, they then sought to examine the applicability of this concept of political allegiance by testing two main hypotheses. First, that the interaction between feelings of economic anxiety and exclusive identity was negatively related to EU support; second, that high levels of trust in national political institutions and satisfaction with national democracy would coincide with high levels of support for the EU. The empirical results appeared to uphold their expectations. Support for the EU was lowest among respondents with strong feelings of exclusive national identity and high levels of economic anxiety, and euroskeptic Right wing extremist parties were able to mobilize such feelings of identity against the EU. Furthermore, support for European integration among respondents with a feeling of exclusive national identity decreased rapidly with an enhanced feeling of economic anxiety, whereas similar economic worries led to significantly less decline in support for the EU among those who had an inclusive national identity. In the view of van Kersbergen and de Vries, these results vindicated their theoretical concept of double allegiance.

Milward had developed the idea of 'double allegiance' with the firm conviction that primary allegiance was to the state. He had also highlighted the central importance of the full employment/welfare state system in the construction of both forms of allegiance, and had argued that political parties played a key role in linking states to citizens. Behind all this he had emphasized European integration as the fundamental guarantor of the framework in which the new forms of state and allegiance had been built. Van Kersbergen's work is therefore important for its insights into the problems faced by both contemporary states and the European Union in securing support from key social and political groups, thereby calling into question the significance of some of the claims that Milward had made. Yet, in my view, van Kersbergen's work fails to dislodge the kernel of Milward's argument about double allegiance because it is based on a theoretical oversimplification.

In his first contribution, van Kersbergen sought to make Milward's concept of allegiance more rigorous, maintaining that in both conceptual and substantive terms there was some ambivalence in the argument because the exact meaning of allegiance had not been clearly defined. In particular, he questioned the fact that Milward had suggested that allegiance could be a basis for legitimacy,[34] regarding it as crucial to distinguish between the two. These were valid criticisms, for there was certainly a degree of imprecision in Milward's definitions. However, van Kersbergen himself obviously found

34. Milward, *Rescue*, 27.

some difficulty in distinguishing between allegiance and legitimacy. Thus in 1997 he regarded one difference as that 'allegiance has a more "active" connotation as it presupposes the subject's broad and active support for the ruler and not merely passive acquiescence or express consent.'[35] However, in 2000, the relevant part of the distinction had been reformulated as follows: '[A]llegiance presupposes the subject's broad, *although not necessarily active*, support for the actual ruler rather than a mere acquiescence with the system, an express consent with the institution or a diffuse democratic consensus' [my emphasis].[36] This reformulation suited van Kersbergen's general inclination to treat allegiance as a population's essentially submissive support for a ruler (on condition that the latter provided benefits). However, this gave the concept an unnecessarily restricted meaning, which was not the case with Milward. The other very significant inconsistency was between all his previous versions and that in the joint article in 2007. Until then the stress had been on an exchange relationship and, as noted, he had even suggested that feelings and attitudes were irrelevant to issues of allegiance to the EU. But the 2007 article stated that 'The more citizens perceive integration to threaten both *their feelings of economic and social-psychological security and well-being*, the less likely they will support the EU' [my emphasis].[37]And van Kersbergen and his coauthor claimed that their results upheld their theoretical concept of double allegiance, with the results indicating that

> support for national institutions depends on the extent to which supranational institutions allow national political elites to provide political, *social-psychological* and socio-economic security and well-being. Our conclusion is that we have reason to underline the notion that EU support is nested in citizens' primary allegiance to the national system. Double allegiance exists in a trade-off with the extent to which security (and prosperity for that matter), both in economic and *cultural terms*, are safeguarded [my emphasis].[38]

But once the discussion enters the realm of *feelings* and subjective perceptions of cultural identity, it must surely jettison the simplistic notion that (even secondary) allegiances necessarily depend upon receiving a 'more or less immediate and straightforward reward'.

The main problem with van Kersbergen's approach lay in his attempt to narrow the concept of allegiance by confining it to an exchange relationship between rulers and ruled in which the role of the latter was essentially

---

35. Van Kersbergen, 'Double Allegiance in European Integration', 6.
36. Van Kersbergen, 'Political Allegiance and European Integration', 7–8.
37. De Vries and van Kersbergen, 'Interests, Identity and Political Allegiance', 323.
38. Ibid., 324.

passive. Given its feudal origins, it might be thought that Milward had deliberately introduced the term because of such connotations, and Perry Anderson thought that this was the case.[39] Yet this seems unlikely. In common usage the term 'allegiance' is applied in numerous ways without such associations—for example, with reference to supporters of a football team or adherents of a political party or trade union. Similarly, some political theorists have talked of allegiance in a quite different way to suggest active commitment and participation rather than passivity and hierarchy.[40] It therefore seems more likely that Milward revived the term because of its historical significance and his belief that the contemporary era constituted a momentous change. Certainly, he stressed the importance of the welfare system in providing a wider form of security. But there was nothing in his work that suggested that this had entirely been constructed from above rather than as a new consensus arising partly out of pressures from below, and he specifically stated that he was only telling one part of the story.[41] Nor, unlike van Kersbergen (until 2007), did he believe that the disposition of allegiance rested entirely on materialistic factors to the exclusion of the symbolic, cultural, and discursive spheres.[42] It is true that his ideas remained underdeveloped, but they were not unduly restrictive. By contrast van Kersbergen's work is significant in tracing the relationship between changes in political economy and welfare to problems in relation to allegiance, but his interpretation of the concept itself appears reductionist and too passive.

## FRAGMENTING THE NETWORKS OF ALLEGIANCE: THE CHALLENGE OF STEFANO BARTOLINI

Stefano Bartolini's immensely ambitious work, *Reconstructing Europe*, seeks to explain European construction in relation to the long-term development of the nation-state over five centuries.[43] Although he does not use the term 'allegiance' to define his key arguments, he draws particularly on Stein Rokkan and Albert O. Hirschman for his theoretical concepts, and the work of both these authors has great bearing on the idea. Rokkan's emphasis was upon nation and state formation consciousness, focusing on structural relationships, while Hirschman's enormously influential text *Exit, Voice and Loyalty* effectively analyzes the notion of individual allegiances

39. Anderson, 'Under the Sign of the Interim', in *The Question of Europe*, by Anderson and Gowan, 65.
40. Laski, *Studies in the Problem of Sovereignty*, 11–23.
41. Milward, *Reconstruction*, xvi–xvii; 463.
42. Milward, 'Allegiance', 14.
43. Bartolini, *Restructuring Europe*.

by exploring the relationships between his three central concepts.[44] In fact, his emphasis on the complex interactions between attitudes and behavior on the one hand and the impact on organizations and institutions on the other adds dimensions to the concept of allegiance that are virtually ignored by Milward. By considering developments in the European state system through a creative reworking of such theoretical ideas, Bartolini presents a major challenge to Milward's ideas.

The difference does not lie in the interpretation of the origins of the European Community, for Bartolini endorses the argument in *Rescue* about the main drivers of European integration and the interrelationship between ideas and material forces. However, he argues that there was a fundamental transformation of the integration process from the 1970s onward, as the drift toward market-opening and neoliberalism became ever-more dominant, and this had a major impact on the system as a whole and the behavior and attitudes of the actors within it. In Bartolini's view, the rise of the European nation-state system depended on boundary formation and differentiation in which there was a general, but never total, congruence between political, military, and economic frontiers. The postwar welfare state had constituted the zenith of this system, for it enabled states to bring about forms of distribution that enhanced social cohesion. Applying Hirschman's notions to collective, rather than individual, actors, Bartolini argued that the appropriate mix of exit, voice, and loyalty also depended on a degree of boundary closure. Complete closure, permitting no exit through emigration, was not conducive to voice, for people were effectively trapped within a state. But a situation in which exit was effectively available only to those with capital and exceptional skills was also disadvantageous because it could lead to a severe weakening of the voice of those who remained. Voice, and therefore also loyalty, were more likely to be effective when there was a reasonable congruence of the different forms of boundary with some possibility of movement across frontiers. Taking this as his framework of interpretation, he argued that the first phase of European integration had maintained the existing structures and internal relationships and networks, but the subsequent complexity of differential boundaries, in an overall context of deregulation and open capital movements, led to a new situation with differential opportunities for exit (movement) for the different socioeconomic groups. Furthermore, he argued that

> this specific construction of differential boundary transcendence was carried out in order to free European political elites from the growing

44. Rokkan, 'Dimensions of State Formation and Nation-building'; Hirschman, *Exit, Voice, and Loyalty*. Van Kersbergen also cites Rokkan as an inspiration for his own approach, noting that Rokkan provided a synthesis of the approaches of Talcott Parsons and Hirschman (van Kersbergen, 'Political Allegiance and European Integration', 1–4).

> constraints of their internal national, democratic and welfare states. These political elites find it easier and preferable to agree on external constraints that 'objectify' the need for internal discipline. More precisely the setting of a core economic constitution as an external constraint was a way to externalize the pressure for domestic change and reform and, at the same time, to externalize the political costs of economic rationalization.[45]

The combination of political, bureaucratic, and socioeconomic developments resulting from such decisions simultaneously fractured internal networks of solidarity and weakened effective state power in relation to redistribution and welfare activity. States became more dependent upon the voice of those with the ability to 'exit' than of those who had little choice but to stay, further reinforcing the downward pressures on public services. Such tendencies also weakened social and political movements within states without creating countervailing forces at European level. At the same time there was a further differentiation between the tendency of ordinary people to adopt euroskeptic attitudes, while those more able to benefit were more likely to support the EU. Finally, Bartolini argued persuasively that such developments were inherent in the later phase of the integration process.

Milward viewed European integration as a buttress for the state, so that double allegiance was effectively a structural feature of the relationship between states and the EU. However, Bartolini rejected the premise by suggesting that, rather than enhancing the power of the state, the later development of the EC/EU was actively dismantling key aspects of the nexus of economic, social, and legal relationships on which the postwar state had been constructed. The networks on which allegiance had depended were therefore fragmented without being reconstructed in any effective form at the European level. Furthermore, Bartolini provided a rather pessimistic perspective on the difficulties of rebuilding those ties at supranational and transnational levels, both because elites had deliberately chosen a European strategy to sever them and because the structural basis for their reestablishment at European level was so weak.

Bartolini's critical account of the later phases of European integration implies a major challenge to Milward's arguments because he suggests a quite different interpretation of the structure of the system and the roles, actions, and attitudes of the actors within it. It follows that such phenomena as political disaffection and euroskepticism are not simply historical contingencies, but are structurally embedded in a system of fragmentation that has been a deliberate elite choice, and that the problems are liable to intensify. If so, it would surely seem inappropriate to talk of a double

45. Bartolini, *Restructuring Europe*, 246–247.

allegiance. However, the differences between Bartolini and Milward may be rather less than they appear.

## CONCLUSION: REBUILDING ALLEGIANCE?

Milward formed his views about European integration primarily through his immensely detailed historical research on its origins and early development. His emphasis on a double allegiance thus reflects the postwar era of welfare state construction and the belief that this constituted a major advance over the interwar era of mass unemployment and dictatorship. This did not mean that he failed to appreciate the significance of later developments. As he put it in *Rescue*:

> The European Community was the European rescue of the nation-state. Since all history is change, that rescue would only be temporary and the process of economic development itself has eroded the political consensus which sustained both nation and supranation after the war.[46]

He also noted the possible relevance of the free movement of capital and the decline of progressive taxation in relation to allegiance and in the second edition of *Rescue* even suggested that political parties were no longer playing a democratic role in formulating domestic policy choices.[47] Yet these factors were not stressed in Milward's work, and more critical analyses of the later period of European appear more obviously in tune with current tendencies. However, it is important to recall some of his fundamental beliefs about European integration if his work on allegiance is to be appreciated.

His starting point was his skepticism about the 'official' versions of the origins of the EC and his desire to produce a more valid history. But this did not make him skeptical about the importance of integration itself. On the contrary, he believed that it was imperative to understand what had been constructed in postwar Europe rather than to create a myth that could not withstand genuine historical research. And this was tied to his beliefs both about academic integrity and the nature of allegiance. If those who wrote about the history of European integration propounded idealized myths about its creation, they were guilty of propaganda rather than scholarship. Nor could any form of allegiance endure if based solely on myths. But he certainly rejected a wholly negative approach that might undermine integration itself. Completing *The Reconstruction of Western Europe* in the era of Margaret Thatcher, he thus ended his book with a warning note:

---

46. Milward, *Rescue*, 428.
47. Ibid., 436.

> Let all those who wish to reconstruct the roof on fundamentally new principles think first that never except beneath that roof has western Europe known so long a peace nor a life so prosperous and humane.[48]

Similarly, in the Preface to the first edition of *Rescue* he argued that the ideas called upon by the state and Community in the postwar era had been genuinely creative and that it was now necessary to match their scope. He clearly wanted the continuation of the full-employment/welfare state, underpinned by the EC/EU and double allegiance. However, he was much less adept in evaluating the significance of the neoliberal age. In fact, he may even have persisted with his allegiance project at a time when support for European integration seemed to be in decline partly because he sought to uphold the system of beliefs embedded in the underlying political and economic realities of the earlier period. This meant that he could sometimes sound unduly optimistic about popular attitudes to the EU or to citizens of other member-states.[49] Yet despite the depth of Bartolini's critique of the current trend in European integration as the source of fundamental problems, he also argued that the EU was the 'only possible solution to them'.[50] Thus he shared Milward's conviction that the establishment of European integration was of momentous historical importance and, in effect, endorsed the view that allegiance could never again be focused exclusively on the nation-state. In fact, he took the argument still further in some respects, for his insistence on the necessary congruence between boundaries and effective political power implied the ultimate need for a still greater shift in allegiances beyond the nation-state than Milward had envisaged. Yet if this appears to confirm the structural basis for double allegiance, there were also two important respects in which Milward's ideas were underdeveloped.

The first weakness was in his conception of democracy in relationship to allegiance. Certainly, he suggested that the postwar system had been built from below as well as above, but he never explored the contribution made by ordinary people, trade unions, or parties. Similarly, while he was a firm believer in democracy his interpretation of it remained rather shallow, implying that elections were a sufficient test of public opinion and preferences. But neoliberalism was surely launched primarily by governments and economic elites rather than by electorates, and it was this new model that undermined the framework that played so crucial a role in the construction of double allegiance. Of course, it would be unreasonable to suggest that any historian could analyze all dimensions of the construction of the postwar state, and Milward's contribution was immense. Yet his failure to explore the structures, processes, and political philosophies in which

48. Milward, *Reconstruction*, 502.
49. Milward, *Rescue*, 434
50. Bartolini, *Restructuring Europe*, 412.

democratic forms of allegiance were lodged left him a little bemused when the foundations of the full-employment/welfare state were dismantled. His antipathy towards the new orthodoxy was quite evident, but he seemed to effect a personal 'exit' from contemporary developments rather than providing a critique or alternative proposals.

The second weakness lay in Milward's tendency to treat allegiance as something that was either absent or present, rather than as a quality of variable intensities and types.[51] In reality, he knew that allegiance had many shades and tones. Thus when he argued that the postwar state had succeeded in overcoming the failures of the interwar period he did not mean that there had previously been a complete absence of allegiance. Nor could he have suggested that the nation-state remained the primary focus for allegiance unless he also believed that European allegiance was less intense. His interest was in identifying a new structural duality of the national and the European, rather than in exploring a more elusive phenomenon through a qualitative approach. Yet the extent to which a stronger European allegiance might ultimately develop will surely be dependent upon its ability to nurture the rather feeble roots that currently exist.

This leads to a final point. In his work, Milward demonstrated the possibility of retaining a *critical* perspective while maintaining a form of allegiance. He was a great debunker of historical myths, but he certainly believed that the construction of a new Europe had been of immense importance and should develop further. This is instructive, for it is too easy to overlook the positive achievements while concentrating on necessary critiques.

51. Newman, 'Allegiance, Legitimation, Democracy and the European Union'.

# Conclusions and Perspectives for Future Research

*Sigfrido M. Ramírez Pérez*

Alan Steele Milward was not just a scholar but also an intellectual, an intellectual of his time. As academics have been experiencing a period of acute transformation of their social conditions, as a result of the place attributed to universities in the knowledge-based economy, the temptation of looking at his work as merely related to the internal dynamics of 'excellent' research seems to be clearly insufficient for an author who actively collaborated in creating academic institutions and wrote about relevant issues for the broader political debate. Despite having more than 100 pages of introductory exegesis to the maestro's work and academic life, this volume cannot exhaustively reply to the fundamental question of which kind of historian and intellectual Alan Milward was. I will not attempt here such a perilous exercise, something I hope to do elsewhere. Yet it must be underlined, as mentioned in various texts in this book, that he was intellectually embedded in a larger constellation of Left-wing British intellectuals, such as Eric Hobsbawm, Perry Anderson, and Tony Judt, as well as European scholars—in particular the Italian scholars around the Gramsci Institute.[1] This is to say, that like any other historian formed during the cold war era, his work and interventions *also* have to be understood in the context of how he positioned himself within the various constellations of contemporary historians. Reducing Alan Milward to a heroic, 'bourgeois' scholar obsessed with excellence in the ivory towers of elite universities will not serve us for the purpose of this conclusion. Instead, we must coherently take stock of what the contributors to this volume believe is the actual relevance of Milward's work for current and future research, not only in history and social sciences, but also for the discussion about the future of European societies. The following chapter is structured in four thematic sections. The first section deals with what is left of Milward's contribution to the current trends in economic history (Vera Zamagni, Pedro Lains, Guðmundur Jónsson, and Eamonn Noonan). It will then look at his contribution to the history of the state

1. See the continuous references to Milward's work in Romero and Segreto, 'Italia, Europa, America: l'integrazione internazionale dell'economia italiana (1945–1963)'.

during the interwar period (Charles S. Maier, John Gillingham, Larry Neal, and Hans Otto Frøland) and European postwar reconstruction (David W. Ellwood, Federico Romero, and Anjo G. Harryvan). The third section deals with the debate about European integration (Jan van der Harst, Ben Rosamond, Michael Newman, and Wilfried Loth) before concluding with a discussion of his contribution to the current trends in the history of the policies of the ECSC (Ruggero Ranieri, Tobias Witschke, and Charles Barthel) and the EEC (Lucia Coppolaro, Kiran Klaus Patel, Maud Anne Bracke, James Ellison, and Johnny Laursen).[2]

## THE HISTORIAN OF POLITICAL ECONOMY AND SOCIETY

What was Alan Milward's contribution to economic history? The chapter by Vera Zamagni in this volume uses Milward as the paradigm of what the economic historian of the twenty-first century should be, paraphrasing the Nobel Prize laureate John Hicks, one of the fathers of the neo-Keynesian/neoclassical synthesis: more than just an economist. Regarding the ongoing institutional and intellectual debates about the role that economic history has to play within broader historiography and the social sciences, she calls for a renewal of the discipline by complementing the 'cliometric revolution' of the New Economic History and building on the 'Political Economy' paradigm that in her view characterized Milward's scholarship. Such a paradigm may be defined as the historical study of the impact of state institutions on the economy, and the other way around. To be sure, she is fully aware that such a change requires the institutional and intellectual autonomy of economic history in relation to economics in order to gain much more contact with other social sciences. Reducing economic history to retrospective economics will not be a positive sum game for both disciplines. This text should be read and interpreted within the larger debate about the past and present of economic and social history that is taking place in forums like the Economic History Society and the International Economic History Association, both of which Milward attended at different moments of his career.[3]

Eamonn Noonan goes even further by considering Alan Milward as a model in the necessary return to John Maynard Keynes' concept of economics as a moral and not a natural science. This seems to him a necessary return to political economic analysis after the failure of mathematically and

---

2. These conclusions are directly derived from the chapters of the present volume, and references already quoted in each of the chapters will not be repeated in further footnotes here.
3. For an overview of the discipline by worldwide practitioners, see Hudson, *Living Economic and Social History*. On page 467 there is an entry including Alan Milward within the Bio-Bibliography among the 700 worldwide scholars.

model-driven economics to forecast and understand the current Great Recession of 2008 onwards. In his chapter, Noonan reconstructs, with the help of Milward's book reviews and punctual references in his major books, the views of the British historian about the period in which Keynes gained a reputation: the interwar period and in particular the crisis of 1929. He added the most particular contribution of Milward to the debate on how Nazi Germany surmounted the crisis against the failure of other European countries to do so at a similar pace. The central Milwardian hypothesis concerns the existence of a durable political coalition whose economic policies at home, in particular fiscal policy, and abroad—*Grossraumwirtschaft* in the German case—were the reflection of the aggregate interests of contending groups. It is to Noonan's merit to remind us that Milward also had an admiration for the German tradition of *Finanzsoziologie*, which ultimately reveals that the maestro was indeed a sociopolitical historian interested in the relationship between different social groups and the nation-state. It is in this direct relationship between the modern nation-state and socioeconomic groups that the former's economic and industrial policies have to be documented, qualified, quantified, and evaluated without the prior dogmatic assumptions typical of economic modeling. The aim of historical enquiry into these public policies was to identify in each case the hidden structures and long-run trends which the historian must interpret after a detailed analysis, correlation, and contextualization of facts and statistical evidence.

Noonan's chapter also clarifies the centrality which the study of the role of the state in economic development had for Milward—rejecting any a priori generalization about it. This is precisely one of the fundamental elements of Pedro Lains' contribution studying the long-term trends of industrialization in the European periphery, subsequently making a direct link between the analysis of Milward and that developed by Alexander Gerschenkron. Departing from the contemporary economic history of Germany, both economic historians strongly opposed the different attempts by other historians, in particular the cold warrior Walt W. Rostow, who argued that there is just one single path for economic development. For this Portuguese historian, the emergence from backwardness of the Southern European countries only took place during the interwar period as a result of the catching-up process explained by national economic policies emanating mostly from dictatorial regimes. The chapter by Guðmundur Jónsson confirms that for historical political economists, there are distinct national paths of development instead of 'one best way' of reaching growth, such as the British model of capitalism during the nineteenth century or the American model during the twentieth. Like previous authors, this historian from Iceland introduces economic perspectives which are analytically useful for economic history. He does so through the use of the hypothesis, derived from institutional economics, that the study of economic growth should distinguish between production and social technologies. This author focuses, following Milward's writings on the European strategies for development in the agricultural sector, on the reasons for the failed transfer of the export-oriented Danish agricultural model into Iceland from 1870 to 1929, which he attributed to the mismatching of both kinds of institutional technologies.

In conclusion, most of the contributions to this book suggest that the 'historical political economy' approach practiced by Milward is of full relevance and centrality for the future renewal of economic history in a historical period which is marked by the failure of neoclassical economics to come to terms with the most important economic crisis since that of 1929. The path for a future research agenda in this field should encourage the collaboration of 'Milwardian' historians with political economists and economic sociologists who share with them a departure from the classical authors mentioned by the contributors to this volume, such as Keynes (post-Keynesians), Schumpeter (neo-Schumpeterians), and Gerschenkron (institutional economists of development). It is maybe of particular relevance to involve the French Regulation School in the dialogue, which provides a great deal of original synthesis of these approaches and Marxian economics for the interpretation of economic history. Given the fundamental role that Milward attributed to the national institutional models of development, a fruitful collaboration with their scientific discussion about the varieties of capitalism could be of great relevance for having the work of economic historians fully integrated in the contemporary scholarly debate with those social sciences which reject the fallacy of methodological individualism marking neoclassical economics.[4]

## THE HISTORY OF THE EUROPEAN NATION-STATE: WAR AND RECONSTRUCTION BETWEEN GERMAN DOMINATION AND AMERICAN HEGEMONY

Understanding the question of the role of the state in European economic development made Milward's worldwide reputation as a contemporary European historian in his pioneering studies about the period from 1929 to 1949. One of his most acclaimed partners in this adventure, and contemporary historian from the other side of the Atlantic, Charles Maier, has attempted in his contribution to this volume to extract from Milward's research a retrospective reflection on the underlying questions across fields of inquiry that both shared as historians of Germany and of Western European reconstruction. The first conclusion is that apart from

4. See their journal *Revue de la Régulation, Capitalisme, institutions, pouvoirs* (http://regulation.revues.org/) (accessed on 1 July 2011). About varieties of capitalism see Society for the Advance of Socio-Economics and its journal Socio-Economic Review (http://www.sase.org/) (accessed on 1 July 2011).

being an economic historian, Alan Milward was also a historian of the state and its administration. The German case inaugurated his enduring interest in the history of the European nation-state through looking at political motivations. Like Maier, Milward was convinced that political and economic issues could not really be disentangled, as economic policies were the result of domestic politics and not of market forces or international hegemons such as Nazi Germany or cold war America. This conclusion is fully shared by Larry Neal in his own chapter when stating that the real fascination and motivation of Milward's scholarship was to study the 'hysteresis of planning' brought about by the Second World War. Planning remained in place during the reconstruction period, embodying the continuity and structural direction of national economies, despite occasional transformations instigated by the limited choices of politicians.

According to Maier, he and Milward shared the same notion that Nazism was a form of European Fascism instead of resulting from a German *Sonderweg*. This European dimension of Fascism was a common project on the continental level. The New Order, which aimed to defend the Fascist revolution against Communism and Liberalism on the basis of a common political program, shared an antimaterialist utopia of a stable society unshaken by capitalist growth and antagonistic to the liberal principle of the individual. According to one of the contributors to this volume, who has excelled in the history of the European New Order, John Gillingham, Milward's analysis introduced the original interpretation of Nazi Blitzkrieg as not only a warfare technique, but also the central 'strategic synthesis' designed to organize this project in Hitler's international diplomacy and economic governance. That this was not systematically applied until very late during the war was exclusively due to the existence in Nazi Germany of a plurality of interests. According to Gillingham and Maier, the most recent research has challenged Milward on this point by showing that Hitler had already prepared Germany from the very beginning for total war and not just for Blitzkrieg. Nevertheless, his most fundamental characterization of the totalitarian state as a fragmented polity traversed by rivalries, with diverse interests and rationalities, is now a unanimously accepted conclusion. According to his fellow historian Larry Neal, Milward opened for future historians the black box of Nazi Germany as he considered it a political system capable of strategic planning and obtaining economic success through war. This scholarly obligation to understand his object of study without the prejudices of the present was not, as Neal points out, an easy task as it broke several myths and prejudices. The impact was so strong that it even raised criticisms that Milward somehow sympathized with his object of study since he tried to define under which conditions the Nazi strategy would have worked. Indeed, this was a giant step for future scholarship about the history of World War II, even when it was unpleasant for tenants of the liberal dogma to learn that wars could be fully functional for the industrial and economic development of the combatants.

Milward's subsequent contribution to the history of the European state during the Second World War aimed to test whether the New Order was coherent and functional for all the European states sharing the same ideological basis of Fascism. His monographic studies about Vichy France and Fascist Norway under Nazi Occupation still pass the test of time too. They confirmed that this European New Order implied the creation of an organized German empire whose viability would have terminated the European nation-state. Therefore, it comes as no surprise that national bureaucracies within both occupied France and Norway opposed abandoning their own plans for development within the New Order, as this would have implied their subordination to those of the Nazi technocracy. In his contribution, Hans Otto Frøland makes an erudite and detailed analysis *à la Milward* on the reaction of the aluminum industry to the Nazi *Grossraumwirtschaft* during the war. Given its strategic nature for the aeronautical sector, this industrial sector is an important test case for the practical application of the New Order, and precisely for this reason Milward dedicated individual chapters to the German exploitation of the aluminum industry in his books about France and Norway. For the Norwegian historian, Milward's pioneering contribution for the first time articulated an analysis about the behavior of industrial circles in Germany and the occupied countries toward the Nazi administration of the European economy. New evidence now available from Norwegian companies partially invalidates Milward's conclusions by showing that indigenous businesses willingly acted to influence German administrations in order to preserve their own interests in the new economic situation without being completely subordinated to a national arrangement between German firms and administrations. But on the whole, they confirm Milward's views that Nazi planning in this sector failed to be coordinated despite the active collaboration of business circles in Germany and Norway, precisely due to the mutual neutralization between different administrative and business alliances in both countries.

Last, but not least, with his synthetic volume about the economic and social impact of the war in all belligerents, Milward can also be considered a pioneer in the global interpretation of the Second World War, providing the basis for the current attempts to write a genuine international history of this conflict which changed the course of history. That Milward's pioneering approach about the nature of the economy in Fascist states have better survived the passing of time than his partial conclusions about them would not be a surprise for those who share with him the principle that all history is provisional. When new evidence and unknown facts arise, they demand a revision of previously held views. What is relevant for the future historical agenda is that the rediscovery of his work, and its contextualization as in this volume, keeps inspiring pathbreaking research about the topics that he devoted his energy to studying. An example of this spirit is the agenda-setting proposal made by Frøland in his contribution. He suggests carrying out a transborder study of private business collaboration under the New Order, which is perhaps the only genuine path toward answering Milward's still pertinent question of whether the Nazi New Order was doomed to fail or had any opportunity to be legitimized by the different organized interests and sociopolitical groups of Fascist Europe.

When looking at the post-1945 period, both Maier and Neal make clear that Milward maintained the same question regarding the resistance of the European nation-state to becoming obsolete when confronted with the rise of the new Empires born from the ashes of defeat of the New Order: the Soviet Union and the United States. Indeed, the cold war was also fought in the historians' classrooms, where the Marshall Plan and its motives and impact on the European postwar recovery became one of the central topics that shaped Milward's reputation as a scholar. It was in these debates that he gained a reputation for shattering the myths of official histories and revisionist approaches based on a massive variety of governmental sources elaborated by entrenched national administrations that had risen during the war. Maier concludes that he and Milward shared the view that the attempts by the United States to set up its hegemony over Western European nation-states were dictated by domestic political considerations of the United States more than by the European necessity to kick start the economic recovery that was happening in any case. This partial agreement between these two outstanding historians of twentieth-century Europe is also stressed by the contribution of Federico Romero, who currently holds Milward's chair at the European University Institute in Florence and collaborated with Milward in the writing of *The European Rescue*. For him, Maier and Milward coincided in their rejection of the shortcomings of the historiographical controversy between orthodox diplomatic historians and revisionist Marxist scholars about the nature of the United States as an empire. Despite their partial postrevisionist consensus about the exceptionality and peculiar nature of American hegemony, American scholars were equally guilty of their ignorance and lack of interest in understanding the reception of the Marshall Plan in Europe and its actual impact on the European countries that it was supposed to help. However, both Milward and Maier disagreed about the fundamental point on the agency of the political changes that permitted the reconstruction. For Milward, these were previous to the public adoption of the rhetoric and symbolism of the politics of productivity typical of the American model that the Marshall Plan aimed to transfer into European lands.

It is precisely on this point that the contribution of David Ellwood departs, introducing a new element in the study of the Marshall Plan that Milward did not really explore: the domestic roots of the American postwar projects to solve the European problems not only of war, but also of political radicalization toward the Right and the Left, which American statesmen associated with the stagnation of the economy. Ellwood argues that the Marshall Plan embodied not just a solution to an emergency, but part of the American modernizing challenge to Europe that had been planned by various American elites to control the internal instabilities of the European nation-state. From the external and internal challenges to the nation-state, the reconciliation of the Europeans with the American style of economic growth and the development of social welfare policies was born. That Ellwood decided to dedicate his own research to study the intellectual and cultural roots of American projects to shape the European continent and its reception in Europe clearly demonstrates that Milward's work had moved the cursor about the impact of the Marshall Plan from economics to the symbolic. In this volume, this is confirmed by Anjo Harryvan as well in his chapter about Milward's contribution to understanding the impact of the Marshall Plan in the Netherlands. In his view, Milward turned upside down the prevalent view that without the Marshall Plan the Netherlands would not have been able to recover the path to prosperity. By inspiring studies, he confirmed that if American aid was qualitatively important it was by no means fundamental for the rebound of the Dutch economy—it only accelerated its growth at most by eight months. Bringing the Marshall Plan from the celestial heights of the myth to the tough reality of history did not make many friends for this British historian, who had to endure many gratuitous disqualifications by those actors in the Netherlands, and elsewhere, who were involved at the time in that difficult starting moment of the cold war.

Indeed, it would have been natural for Milward to explore the roots and structure of American hegemony after having theorized the 'strategic synthesis' of an imperial project like that of Nazi Germany. But as Romero recalls, Milward never touched upon the strategic and ideological framework of the cold war, nor participated in the debates which took place around this, in particular about those security considerations which had been at the center of his own analysis of the Second World War. This seems to be Milward's main vulnerability as a historian of the postwar period in the framework of the new cold war history—to which Romero has devoted a great deal of his own intellectual attention. In Milward's defense, Maier pointed out that his last research about the 'national strategy' of Great Britain represented the heyday of his reflection about the fate of the European nation-state in this postwar international context. This new concept of 'national strategy' summarized all the dilemmas that Britain had to confront in order to limit the rise of the new hegemon and the counter-hegemonic European project led by France, in the attempt to stop its own imperial decline. Indeed, this concept became one of the most decisive legacies of Milward and is directly descended from his concept of strategic synthesis applied to Nazi Germany but elaborated further in his Graz lectures, as quoted by Maier. The American historian did not fail to notice that Milward had not fully formulated the dynamics of that complex relationship between the policy choices and outcomes of nation-states in international relations, where choosing between power and plenty, between cannons and butter, has no straightforward answer and is in need of constant rethinking as the other actors act. Even so, it is my impression that for Milward, as an attentive student of contemporary debates in German history, the *Primat der Innenpolitik* was always dominant as a causal element of last resort in the modification of a national strategy.

This seems to be confirmed by Professor Romero's suggestion that the fundamental part of Milward's legacy in the study of the European nation-state was the notion of allegiance. This keyword summarized his explicit agenda for the future study of postwar European integration and implied exploring the different ways that nation-states managed to ensure the economic security and well-being of their citizens in order to maintain their material cohesion, with particular attention to the new role that party politics played in democratic regimes after World War II. This emphasis of the new social and democratic pact in studying the nature of the postwar European nation-state was obviously central in Milward's inquiry about the origins of European integration. However, it is important to remember that this focus on citizenship needs to be contextualized within the sociological approaches that are theoretically behind this principle of social citizenship as the political basis of the welfare state, as reflected upon by the British sociologist Thomas H. Marshall.

To my mind, the major conclusions that we can deduce from Alan Milward's contribution as historian of the European nation-state is that the future Milwardian agenda needs to develop along two trajectories. The first is indeed to depart from the agenda he pointed out about allegiance and, in particular, about the changing role that political parties have played in the trend toward the progressive subordination of parliaments toward the national executives and the concomitant rise of the administrative state with the multiplication of agencies and other technocratic bodies. The evolution of the welfare state and coalition politics is of fundamental importance for reconstructing the diverse models of welfare state development in Europe. Correspondingly, this focus should account for the kind of international institutions that they have required in order to ensure their sustainability. Again, the literature on the institutional change of various trajectories and models of capitalism seems an obvious point of departure for such a research agenda.[5]

This brings us to the second element of a Milwardian research on the nation-state, which will consist of linking national strategies with research on international political economy. This linkage should not only consider the rise of the hegemons, but the counterhegemonic projects of each of the declining European empires or rising new international powers. This obviously will require a more complex framework than the one pushed forward

5. Streeck and Thelen, *Beyond Continuity: Institutional Change in Advanced Political Economies*.

by the Realist school of international relations, and considering Milward's unspoken attraction for the question of how to build hegemony, it may be adequate to engage in direct dialogue with those Gramscian scholars who have explicitly addressed the question of Trans-Atlantic hegemony that Alan Milward never fully articulated, according to Romero.[6] Such a step will imply introducing into the picture other cultural, social, and economic actors of international relations in line with those economic sociologists departing from Karl Polanyi on how international markets have been institutionally embedded and disembedded during the twentieth century.[7]

## EUROPEAN INTEGRATION: BETWEEN THEORY AND HISTORY

Romero's chapter clarifies that the Milwardian agenda on allegiance derived from a particularly inductive epistemological and methodological approach to history: document-based, evidence-driven, knowledge-enhancing. But whether this approach has given way to a historiographical school is an open question put forward by Harryvan. In his view, a distinctive approach to historical change can be identified, and therefore this precondition for creating a lineage of studies within the disciples of the maestro was satisfied. He confirms that in the early 1990s there was a Milwardian school which flourished under the British historian and his successor at the European University Institute chair, Richard T. Griffiths '*plus milwardien que Milward*'. This school focused on the topic of the history of European integration, something partially reflected in the chapters written for this volume by different authors. But which was precisely Milward's contribution to the history of European integration?

The long-serving president of the EU Liaison Committee of Historians, Wilfried Loth, elaborates in his chapter on how Milward's approach to the history of European integration was distinct from that of his predecessor at the EUI chair, Walter Lipgens, who was Loth's professor. Lipgens argued that the founding act of European integration, the Schuman Plan of May 1950, was the result of a long-term struggle by European antiwar elites, who since the end of the First World War aimed to limit the expansion of nationalism, symbolized by the European nation-state of the Second World War. European federalist circles, which had participated in the resistance to Fascism, counted on U.S. support within the Marshall Plan to force a passing of sovereignty to supranational institutions as theorized by Jean Monnet and put into practice by the Catholics Robert Schuman from France, Alcide de Gasperi from Italy, and Konrad Adenauer from Germany. This

6. Van Apeldoorn, 'Transnational Historical Materialism'.
7. Block and Evans, 'The State and the Economy'.

conclusion, based on the archives of European movements, strongly contrasted with that drawn by Milward from his reading of national archives. Milward concluded that in reality the European nation-state, in ceding part of its economic sovereignty through integration, was able to reassert itself and gain legitimacy in the eyes of its population. Loth concurs that these conclusions were not necessarily antithetical, as they both were critical of the realist interpretation offered by historians of diplomacy for whom the determinant of European integration was foreign policy and security matters, instead of decisions made by transnational elites for social and economic reasons. In his view, both men shared a critical appraisal of the basic static concept of this traditional school: that national interest is an aim in itself, seeking superiority based on power and hegemony. Both authors also departed from a common diagnosis that the European nation-state had reached an impasse, whereby the postwar problems which it confronted were irresolvable in its current form due to a lack of legitimacy.

After stating the shortcomings of both authors, Loth presents his own work as a synthesis to overcome the limits of both Lipgens and Milward. He develops a model of four driving forces of European integration: preserving peace between nations, the German question, economic competitiveness, and self-assertion toward hegemons, arguing that each force was dominant during particular stages of European integration. In his chapter, he then briefly presents the way this model serves to understand the history of European integration up to the Lisbon Treaty, following Milward's two fundamental questions on European integration: the reasons for its continuation and the exact nature of current integration. It is Loth's merit to remind us that, whatever the discussion, the overall result has always been more and not less Europe, making clear that the discipline still has a bright future in explaining how we have gotten to the point we are in the twenty-first century. In my view, Loth's chapter also opens up the fundamental question of the direct relationship between, first, the kind of explanation reached and, second, the ongoing process of European integration. More directly, are historical explanatory models contingent on the time in which they are elaborated? Does their validity expire at a certain date, making them obsolete as we move forward in time and new questions become more salient? One does not need to adhere entirely to Walter Benjamin's thesis on history—the famous *Angelus Novus* thesis in particular—to concur that all history is contemporary history, and this might be the case to a certain extent, which depends on the cumulative knowledge of history, itself limited by the available historical sources.

The logical question is whether this new synthesis effectively surpasses, or at least encompasses, Milward's scholarship, along with some of the members of the Milwardian school at the EUI, and whether it has developed a complementary or alternative historical approach to the history of European integration. At this point, the chapter by Jan van der Harst is quite illustrative. A former student of Milward, this Dutch member of the EU Liaison Committee actually explains why in his opinion

Milward's scholarship is somehow *passé* as a historical approach, even if some of his conclusions are still valid in explaining the process of European integration. He defines Milward's conceptual thinking as derived from a materialist conception of interest in which ideas, visions, and ideals played a minor role. Milwards's heroes were not 'Saints' but rather pragmatic politicians who saw in European integration a way of strengthening national governing elites and preserving their executive capacity, "rescuing" in this way the European nation-state. This empowerment of the postwar nation through transferring sovereignty was not a general formula, but applied to commercial affairs and particular economic sectors which allowed European states a new path toward full employment and welfare provisions, which subsequently have been integral elements of their historical evolution.

Van der Harst's chapter considerably enlarges the framework by placing Milward's contribution to European integration within the larger debate between historians and political scientists writing about European integration. He credits Milward for having pioneered the debate with other social sciences, despite the fact that this was often in a polemical tone. At first, he attacked the early neofunctionalist political scientists who theorized that political integration was an automatic and inexorable evolution of the European nation-state and managed to rally some liberal intergovernmentalist scholars to take historical research seriously in their theorization. However, Milward's intellectual leadership did not stay for long as a new generation of historians and political scientists increasingly challenged it, bolstered by the historical transformations following the European dynamics of deepening and enlarging at the end of the cold war and the Treaty of Maastricht. Milward's work was increasingly seen as inadequate for three reasons: first, due to its state-centrism focused on a history from above populated by coherent governments and bureaucracies without dealing with the history from below of nonstate transnational actors as postulated by the 'governance' paradigm in political sciences; second, his approach was too close to the sources and national archives, thus producing a sum of national studies but not a truly European perspective. This prevented him from taking seriously the impact of European institutions on state and nonstate actors as elaborated by institutionalist perspectives in social sciences. Last but not least, his materialist and rationalist approach directly conflicted with the new trend toward constructivism, in particular emphasizing the role that incentives, ideals, and ideas have in the construction of a community of values overcoming economic considerations. The conclusion is without much appeal: the potentiality for a Milwardian school of his own and subsequent generation of students of Milward waned. Many of his students have effectively taken their own way in three directions consistent with these critiques: network multilevel governance analysis of transnational European actors such as political parties; sociological institutionalist analysis of the European Communities as a political system with a capacity to institutionalize the European project thanks to the Council of Ministers or the European Commission; and last but not least, departing from social constructivism to develop a hermeneutic analysis of European discourses by political elites and supranational European entrepreneurs in order to identify how ideas have contributed to the legitimation and/or delegitimation of European integration for citizens. We could conclude that the proto-Milwardian school disintegrated before it matured due to the intellectual ascendancy of a renewed political science and the turn in historiography toward it. If we follow the Dutch scholar, nothing seems to have survived from the supremacy of history over theory and the relations between both disciplines.

So what is left of Milward? After the symbolic sacrifice of the father, like in any ritual ceremony accomplished by those European intellectuals socialized after 1968, Van der Harst concedes the substantial relevance of two topics for the current political and intellectual debate on the state of the European Union. On the one hand, we can salvage Milward's hypothesis that the European rescue of the nation-state was a temporary phenomenon in which the legitimation of the European project depended on a simultaneous strengthening of the nation-state. This hypothesis appears to be working but in an opposite direction already perceived by Milward: that the current weakening of the European welfare state due to globalization is also weakening and delegitimizing the European project. On the other hand, Milward's position on the democratization of European integration has revealed all its validity in the current political context. He favored enhancing the position of national parliaments, instead of the European Parliament, unless there is a clear transfer of taxation competencies to the European level. He considered this the crucial moment when there would be a qualitatively new transfer of sovereignty. About the central element of Milward's thesis Van der Harst concludes that the nation-state still dominates all policy choices and that the ongoing Great Recession has proven Milward right. The future of the European Monetary Union will depend on national policy choices.

Indeed, these conclusions seem at odds with those of an attentive reader of Milward's research agenda, in particular a reader building from the concept of allegiance that Van der Harst does not really take into account in his chapter. Michael Newman's chapter is a good counterpoint to this chapter as it is entirely devoted to this question and how it had evolved in discussion with political scientists. He rightly pointed out that Milward's attempts to renew research on European integration started in the mid-1990s from his seminal article in the first issue of the *Journal of European Integration History*, edited by the EU Liaison Committee, and later developed in his seminars at the European University Institute in Florence during his second period as professor from 1996 until his retirement. Despite the fact that its aim was very clearly to provide the framework for a robust interdisciplinary dialogue, he acknowledged that this hope to materialize this project was never fully completed, but it eventually bore some fruits, which are not irrelevant for a future agenda.

As we saw in the previous section, the concept of allegiance was already *in nuce* in Milward's previous works dealing with Nazi Germany and the Second World War, even if it took a more precise form, however, in his research about European integration. The story runs as follows: in order to gain the loyalty of its citizens from the late-nineteenth century, the European nation-state had progressively developed a welfare state based on full employment that had to be reconciled with a situation of increasing economic interdependence. European integration, which is a political and not an economic concept, was born to manage these two opposing demands: protection of citizens by economic and social security versus a hegemonic pressure for the liberalization of markets. In this way, European integration became not just a secondary element of the relegitimation of the state, but an integral part of this search for allegiance. For this reason, it had to be analyzed within the larger history of the transformation of the nation-state. At the same time, allegiance as a concept did not contain an element of repression characteristic of the traditional means of the state to govern its subjects. It was, on the contrary, based on the consent that elites had created through national symbols and nationalism of which, for Milward, national history and the creation of national myths had been a central component. The postwar specificity of this trajectory of consensus-building resided in the capacity of political parties to broker a political agreement between organized labor, farmers, and the middle classes. The economic prosperity of the postwar mixed economy depended on this stability. For this reason, European integration was created to support this consensus, and allegiance to it was not in opposition to national allegiance because both reinforced each other. According to Newman, the allegiance agenda at first intended to check whether this allegiance to the European Communities would be, in different ways, permanently subsidiary: at first Milward suggested conducting a voting analysis to check whether material calculations determined allegiance. Then he argued for exploring the connection between the policies of the EEC and the evolution of personal income, taxation, social security, and economic stability in order to test the variables which determined allegiance. Last, but not least for our purpose here, he argued for researching the symbolic role of Europe in political rhetoric, an agenda complementary with what Van der Harst has been recently developing in his own scholarship. Milward's agenda on European and national allegiance surprises by its coherence and search for a political, economic, or cultural basis of allegiance, thus rejecting any suggestion that it rested a priori only on materialistic factors, but also giving space to the symbolic, cultural, and discursive spheres.

Newman concludes that despite this precise agenda, which at the same time departed from his previous research but went much further, Milward did not manage to shift the agenda of EU studies as decisively as he had changed the historiography on European integration. He rather points to the impact of the changes in the process of European integration since the Maastricht Treaty of 1992, and in particular to the crisis of legitimacy of European integration and the European welfare state, thus moving the research agenda to questions of how to solve this disaffection in the context of a neoliberal turn in economic policies. Milward was aware of this change but did not demonstrate the continuous validity of these ideas in the new context. It is most likely that he concluded, as Van der Harst rightly pointed out, that the most contemporaneous events did not invalidate his conclusions, but just implied a typical backwards swing of the pendulum of the history of the nation-state. Newman, on the contrary, concludes that social scientists who have used Milward's concept have argued the temporary validity of his concept of double allegiance, and contrary to appearance, did not pose a fundamental challenge to it. In particular, some of these scholars go as far as arguing that the elites of the EEC-EU have dismantled this nexus of national allegiance, substituting European integration without reconstructing allegiance at a supranational level. Even so, most researchers will agree that it is impossible to reconstruct allegiance in Europe exclusively on the basis of the nation-state, making plain that the double allegiance agenda is still pertinent.

For these reasons, the Milwardian agenda is not yet passé. However, it requires an expansion of those points on which it appeared the weakest but which can be explored using Milward's hypotheses. In particular, Newman suggests doing so through an exploration of social actors (trade unions, parties, and ordinary people), structures, processes, and political philosophies in which democratic forms of allegiances manifested themselves outside of the traditional electoral channels of parliamentary democracy. The second element that he is suggesting needs to be qualified and explored further is the treatment of allegiance as a quality of variable intensity and type in history.

It is interesting to note that these conclusions by Newman are partially shared, in particular about its epistemology, in the contribution of one of the brightest political scientists who has specialized in EU studies: Ben Rosamond. Like Newman, he reached slightly different conclusions from those of Van der Harst about the reasons for Milward's wariness to make a clear distinction between the territory of the historian and the political scientist, yet without endorsing an interdisciplinary approach. In one of Milward's last articles, precisely about the relationship between both disciplines in the field of European integration, he makes clear that each discipline has its own agenda: history studies why European integration happened at the historical moment where it took place, whereas political theory is focused on understanding European integration as an instance of a larger principle. This distinction serves to frame Milward's critiques of neofunctionalism during the early 1990s. He was reacting against a revival of that school of interpretation, which he considered as a false basis for constructing a genuine interdisciplinarity, as it cannot be genuine research to limit oneself to those theories accepting only those 'scientific' proofs which fit their theoretical interpretation, and demonstrating an unwillingness to follow the historical record and its conclusions.

Like Newman, Rosamond also suggests a structural transformation of the agenda between 'historians à la Milward' and those political scientists interested in maintaining the multidisciplinarity of European Union studies. From this situation, it appears as if Milward would have been more successful in his dialogue with political scientists than with historians. Toward that purpose, Rosamond briefly introduces the three important trends of political science focusing on EU studies, which have to be considered in any future agenda: first, there is a tendency to move the focus from explaining integration as such to explaining the European Communities as a fully-fledged political system from the very beginning. The second trend, which contradicts the previous one, is to conceptualize the European level as nothing more than an illustration of a larger move toward a regulatory state like other Western countries. And last but not least is the rising role of ideas in EU political research and, more concretely, the endeavor to synthesize the artificial separation of rationalist and constructivist approaches, by considering that the full acceptance of ideational dynamics is part of the construction of interests. On this basis, it is possible to forge a genuine partnership that may serve to develop clear projects and answer puzzles for historians following Milward's example of taking constructivism seriously. The request from this political scientist is that EU historians should be prepared to look for outcomes based both on the logic of appropriateness (behavior from norms, identities, and values) and not just of the logic of consequences (from rational calculus).

My conclusion is that Newman and Rosamond made a clear proposal for such a convergence, even when one cannot fail to notice that it is a fact of contemporary academic power that social scientists, in this case political scientists, have managed to dominate EU studies while historians keep failing to organize themselves enough to transform this field of studies decisively. Indeed, a new historical society is needed where the professional historians working on European integration, broadly speaking, can participate and define the future of the profession. There is currently a fragmentation of the forums where the history of European integration is discussed. It is obvious that what is needed for any serious interdisciplinary research is an active professional association similar to the European Consortium for Political Research, which the EU Liaison Committee, for all its virtues and achievements, has not yet managed to create. Without it, the trend of historians is to continue subordinating themselves and their agendas to discussions in the field of political science, even if their suggestions are of great interest to illuminate future research convergences and common agendas.

## IS THERE A MILWARDIAN SCHOOL OF HISTORY OF EUROPEAN INTEGRATION? FROM THE ECSC TO THE EEC

The remaining chapters included in this volume can be subsumed under the heading of history of European integration. To a large extent, they cover various core economic policies of the European Communities from the creation of the European Coal and Steel Community up to the current situation. Some of those who have contributed to these chapters are Milward's former doctoral students and can be considered as representatives of the Milwardian school of European integration. Unfortunately, the editors of this book did not manage, for various reasons related to space or availability, to include papers from all those former students who wrote a doctoral thesis about European integration under Milward's direction. It can be said, however, by reading Appendix 3 of this volume—the list of the topics of the doctoral candidates that he directed at the European University Institute during his second period (1996–2003)—that he was actually advancing the research agenda and coming to terms with some of the shortcomings of his own previous scholarship. This is confirmed further when we add to those works the titles of the theses of those candidates whom he did not manage to supervise to completion due to his illness, like myself, and those for whom he was a member of the jury as second supervisor. Anybody who knew Alan Milward was aware that he was his own fiercest critic. He undertook a constant process of self-revision, and rectification if necessary, as can be demonstrated by the substantial changes made to several second editions of some of his most widely acclaimed books.

This is also verified in the chapter by one of the staunchest practitioners of the Milward method, Professor Ruggero Ranieri. This representative of the first generation of Milward's doctoral students in Florence takes stock of his systematic research into the origins of the Schuman Plan to verify whether Milward's scholarship in this transcendental founding moment of European integration stands the test of time. He systematically reviews how this central episode was repeatedly explained, and revised, by Milward from his early work to his most recent scholarship in the context of the evolving historiographical debate. He clarifies that this chapter is fundamental to his overall interpretation of the process of European integration: in particular, his finding that, contrary to what was believed, the Schuman Plan was not an exclusive invention of Jean Monnet and his circle at the Planning Commissariat of France in Spring 1950. It was already in place in the Allied London conference of 1948–1949 on Germany by the action of French diplomats crucially challenging France's foreign policy toward German reconstruction. In this sense, it is fundamental for the understanding of Milward's scholarship that he considered that the Schuman Plan was simultaneously motivated by political and economic objectives and not just economic aims as it is generally interpreted by a superficial reading of Milward's work. The analysis by Milward of French motives and actions in the path from the Schuman Plan to the ECSC Treaty demonstrates that the final shape of the first institution of European integration corresponded more to the influence of French policy-makers like Robert Schuman than to the action of technocrats like Jean Monnet and his circle. Against a misrepresentation that Milward refused on principle to take into account the position of nonstate actors, Ranieri elucidates that Milward clarified that what was at stake in this plan, particularly in relationship to the companies operating in the steel and coal sector, was none other than establishing political control over economic policy in a period marked by the fresh wounds of nationalization and economic planning. This initial approach from above to the foundation of the ECSC was later complemented in successive research by a perspective from below through looking at the case of Belgian coal. The Belgian case is important because it illustrates how the ECSC was instrumental in a managed reconversion of a strategic sector of the Belgian economy through regional policies which amounted to sustaining employment and welfare provisions in this sector, vividly illustrating why it is possible to consider this industry as the object of a European rescue. It goes without saying that Ranieri himself has documented in detail how this interpretation applied to European steel sectors in Italy but also to other countries, in particular Britain, which refused to adhere to the negotiated compromises of the Schuman Plan. This British rejection to join is also analyzed in Ranieri's chapter, providing an answer to why some European countries decided to join and others not. The key concept in this case is that of national strategy, which is applied to explain that Britain, contrary to France, enjoyed political assets from its previous hegemonic position. This position at the end of the war pushed Britain toward rejecting adherence to an exclusive European involvement in order to advance its welfare state strategy without breaking its domestic consensus, which would have included going against nonstate actors. Ranieri concludes his vindication of Milward's historiographical validity by pointing out that Milward may in no way be considered a realist or an intergovernmentalist as he did not reduce the supranational dimension to a merely instrumental level, but as an integral part of the evolution of the nation-state, incorporating an important element of supranational symbolism. In my opinion, Ranieri's most interesting insights for the future agenda are his concluding remarks, which make a direct link between Milward's reflection and that of John Maynard Keynes and Andrew Shonfield. The three British intellectuals believed that the welfare state was not an exogenous factor of postwar economic growth, but an integral part which explained the success of the mixed economy of postwar Europe. It was this issue, the economic consequences of the postwar political consensus, which was the theme most dear to the British historian.

Another of Milward's students from Florence in this volume, Tobias Witschke, takes up where Ranieri leaves off by complementing his analysis of the origins of the ECSC and testing Milward's hypothesis during the first years of the functioning of this supranational institution. His chapter here deals innovatively with the actual working of the institution in the pioneering field of competition policy and also serves explicitly to refute the charge that Milward's interpretations were state-centric. This chapter also makes clear that Milward understood supranational institutions, in this case the ECSC, with the concept of a 'protoplasmic organization' capable of dynamically adapting itself to the pressures of various actors, particularly nation-states. Witschke demonstrates that in this way his scholarship can be become a basis for renewing the agenda of the history of European integration. The author suggests following an interdisciplinary agenda from the perspective of policy implementation based on the principal-agent approach in which historians will contribute with their research in investigating the origins of supranational law and institutions of the European Union. This chapter on the origins of the ECSC competition articles during the Treaty negotiations and their subsequent implementation from 1954 to 1962 on the central question of merger control is a fundamental illustration of such an agenda. This seminal chapter uses a myriad of archival sources and perspectives (governments, parliaments, companies, European institutions) to discuss the existing scholarship on the issue at stake for which this law and its corresponding regulation were issued: the European control, French in particular, of the future reconstitution of the mighty German steel industry. This chapter intensively follows the demystifying Milwardian style when showing that actually domestic choices determined the implementation of competition rules, but the authoritative role was symbolically, hence politically, to settle an open conflict at the core of Franco–German relations. The High Authority, the agent, received from the principal, the states, two simultaneous mandates: one explicit, antimerger control, and the other implicit, regulating the reconcentration of the German steel industry, which was ultimately settled by agreements among nation-states in the Council of Ministers with the cooperation of the High Authority.

Another chapter in this volume has the merit of complementing previous analyses about the origins and functioning of the ECSC after 1962. It explains how the other provision of competition policy, anticartel law, of the High Authority of the ECSC functioned until the end of its autonomous administrative existence in 1967 with the fusion of the executives of the European Communities. The contribution from Charles Barthel concludes along lines very similar to Ranieri's and Witschke's regarding the confirmation of Milward's hypothesis about the real functioning of the ECSC and its intrinsic dependence on the nation-states to confront the power of the steel industry, which, at least since 1961, reconstructed a cartelized agreement to manage the sector. The traumatic failure of the ECSC anticartel action motivated by the need to preserve the *raison d'être* of this supranational institution was symptomatic of the strong 'protoplasmic' nature of this institution. Confronted with a failure to challenge a transnational network of European steelmakers, it had little alternative but to rely on the support of nation-states to bring these industrialists to the negotiating table from which they had previously been unable to work together toward a genuine European industrial policy to manage the sector. As Milward had understood, at the end of the day, when the High Authority disappeared in 1967, the steel sector contemplated a forceful return to national steel policies which later would be coordinated at a supranational level. This was in spite of the legal capacity of the ECSC to have organized the sector at a supranational level. Indeed, with these elaborations on the history of the ECSC, this volume contributes to the debate about the actual validity of the most recent research in the history of the initial institutions of European integration.

As far as the history of the EEC is concerned, this volume also contains chapters which take on three different fields of research in which Milward had direct interest during his last period as a scholar. The first concerns the common policies of the EEC and in particular those which directly deal with two of the central supranational policies: agriculture and trade. The second, which was the object of the Schumpeter lectures book, is related to the impact of the EEC in third countries like Britain and the Nordic countries. Last but not least, a chapter by one of his last students from the European University Institute examines the evolution of the position of political parties in the process of European integration.

Lucia Coppolaro's chapter on the development of the European Economic Community as an actor in international trade derived from her doctoral dissertation, which was supervised by Milward. She seems to suggest that the Milwardian School was very much alive in the last period of the British historian at the EUI. The 'protoplasmic' nature of a supranational institution, in this case the European Commission, is confirmed by examining the commercial policy that the European Community developed during the Kennedy Round of the GATT negotiations between 1962 and 1967. Indeed, commercial policy was, for an economic historian like Milward, a test case for the validity of his hypothesis about when supranational integration is more adequate than classical interdependence as represented by free-trade agreements. The conclusions of the chapter cannot be clearer: if the EEC endeavored to be a liberal proponent for industrial trade—but without losing its neomercantilist strategy, which continued through exempting certain industries from tariff reductions—it became protectionist as soon as agricultural trade was concerned, despite considerable pressure from the United States to open up this issue in order to establish the international management of global surpluses. Indeed, simultaneously defending on the one hand a neomercantilist-based liberalization of target sectors, and on the other hand protectionism in agriculture, was not a question of ideals or ideology but of the direct material interests of nation-states and their organized lobbies. This capacity to act with a single voice served the EEC to counter the challenge of the U.S. hegemon, which continued offering, such as after the end of the Bretton Woods system, a multilateral system of economic interdependence which would serve to sustain the political struggle against Communism. The successful negotiation of the Kennedy Round, which was accepted by all major commercial partners, provided the EEC with its first important attempt to set up the common foreign policy and identity of the new economic community in an international society which accepted it as a legitimate partner. This can be considered another case in which the principal-agent relationship directly illustrates the results of negotiations in both fields throughout the period, with a particular emphasis on understanding how the 'empty chair' crisis did not fundamentally affect the capacity of the Community to maintain commercial policy in spite of the French boycott's limiting effect on the functioning of European institutions.

Indeed, this text opens up an entire avenue of research about the European Communities as an international actor which can be complementary to that presented in this volume by one of the successors of Alan Milward at the EUI, a professor of European Union history and transatlantic relations, Kiran Patel. To be sure, this German expert on the Common Agricultural Policy (CAP) acknowledges that Milward has made a lasting contribution to the dominant interpretation about this central policy of the EEC by refuting the superficial idea that the CAP was little more than an intergovernmental horse trade that Germany reluctantly accepted in exchange for its access to the French market of industrial goods. In particular, the British historian elucidated the fundamental role played by the Dutch government and politicians in defining the CAP, providing a detailed analysis of national positions which included both state and nonstate actors. Despite incorporating the role of ideas to some extent in the definition of agricultural policies, Alan Milward privileged material interests as the most important explanatory variable. Patel's chapter makes a genuine attempt to go further and discuss whether it is possible in this policy field to demonstrate that ideas and cultural factors have any impact on the definition of European public policies. In the case of the CAP, the author individualizes the polymorphous and resilient representation of the concept of the 'family farm'. He is very explicit in his aim to complement and develop Milward's suggestions for research by looking at the impact generated by transnational institutions and nonstate actors in a larger historical perspective which avoids focusing only on the inner dynamics of member-states. This chapter complements the conclusions about the CAP developed by Milward himself and his Ph.D. student at the EUI, Ann-Christina Knudsen, who confirmed, in full consistency with the double allegiance agenda, that the CAP was a means of welfare statism meant to improve the economic situation of farmers despite its negative impact on consumers or international actors.

In her contribution to this volume, another of Milward's former doctoral candidates, Maud Bracke, introduces a chapter partly derived from her dissertation written at the EUI in Florence, proving that Milward's intellectual agenda aimed to develop innovative research about topics consistent with his allegiance agenda that he had not developed himself. In this case, Bracke presents the way in which the Italian Communist Party (PCI) developed a genuine allegiance toward the European Economic Communities from 1962 onward in clear contrast with both the official Soviet discourse and the ideological prejudices of the French Communist Party (PCF), thus balancing a triple allegiance: to the nation, to the USSR, and last to the European project. Even if the author does not make any direct reference to it, the chapter is authentically Milwardian in its conclusions. The primacy of domestic political strategy, coupled with the ambitions of the party leadership in the early 1960s to bring the party as close as possible to power, gave way to the creation of a European identity. When international relations entered into the *détente* process, the PCI carried out a genuine investment into the European project which ultimately made the PCI the most favorable and autonomous Communist party to follow the road to Strasbourg's parliamentary assembly. It is of 'Milwardian' importance that the author noted that an important element in this turn came out of the reflection made by the Communist trade union leaders, in particular by the leader of the metal-mechanical section, Bruno Trentin, that European economic integration had led to an increase of the real wages of Italian workers, something later confirmed by the secretary general of the PCI, Palmiro Togliatti, in his political testament. The crisis of the EEC and NATO due the Gaullist challenge to both institutions in the mid-1960s managed to complete this historical turning point. The PCI found itself trying to conciliate its national and internationalist dimension with a new European identity based on antimonopolistic economic reforms put forward by Togliatti's successor Luigi Longo until the early 1970s. During the subsequent phase directed by Enrico Berlinguer, the PCI took a clear new direction with the concept of eurocommunism and the rejection of Italy's entrance into the European Monetary System in 1979. This episode did not break the trend toward increasing adhesion to the European project in a critical mode, as it cannot be interpreted as a sign of anti-Europeanism. It was, on the contrary, evidence of PCI's genuine engagement with European integration, given that the reasons for the rejection derived from a socio-economic interpretation of the impact of the EMS on Italy and not from ideological grounds or fidelity to Moscow.

Bracke's chapter opens up the question of the international impact of European integration for those actors who were not 'present at the creation'. This obviously brings us back to the other strand of research that Milward explored with former doctoral students of the EUI in Florence: the reasons for outsiders to adhere, or not, to the European project. Milward presented part of these reflections in his Schumpeter lectures with the idea that by looking at those who stayed outside like the United Kingdom, we could open another path of his collective research strategy toward understanding the nature of European integration. In his chapter for this volume,

James Ellison makes an impressive evaluation of this fundamental case, an unachieved endeavor given that Milward was unable for health reasons to complete the second volume of the official history of Britain and the European Communities, which included the period of adhesion from de Gaulle's veto in 1963 until at least British entrance into the EEC. The chapter discusses the ways in which Milward proceeded toward a serious revision of his initial conclusions about the reasons Britain had decided to opt out from European integration and instead pursue a distinctive national strategy of international interdependence. Ellison does so by putiing Milward's work into perspective with that of both British diplomatic historians and a new generation of young scholars who had written doctoral dissertations about this precise topic. The major historiographical innovation of Milward's initial interpretation, based on unrestricted access to all the relevant British government records, is that the British refusal to join was not based on foreign or defense priorities, aversion to European supranationality or, as he had originally argued himself, cultural ignorance and prejudices among the ruling elites of Britain, in particular of diplomats. Such a conclusion evolved progressively to come to terms with what Milward called Britain's one-world strategy. It was rather based on the development of the idea that Britain pursued a strategy which aimed to put Britain at the center of three international arrangements: the Bretton Woods system, the sterling area, and a free trade area in Europe. But such a strategy was no longer considered a serious mistake, as he had maintained in earlier investigations, but a conscious and well-informed choice which became obsolete in 1961–1962. This was precisely when the United Kingdom requested to join the European Communities and the Kennedy Round negotiations began. Ellison concludes that the 'national strategy' thesis may still be considered too abstract to be useful. Nevertheless, this was part of Milward's agenda to develop stimulating analytic frameworks for discussions about the British case or those of other countries, like France. He did so by reconstructing their global position and reconciling it with issues related to the difficulties which democratic governments faced in relation to retaining power and coping with the effects of globalization and regionalization. Part of this effort to document the national strategies is the chapter by Johnny Laursen, which presents us with one of the most interesting case studies of this approach to the national strategies: the Scandinavian countries. He explains how these countries rejected managing their place in the world on the basis of a regional project based on a sense of a common cultural background: Nordic integration. His conclusion, after analyzing the creation of the Nordic Council, is that the Scandanavian countries avoided issues of economic integration, focusing instead on political and symbolic questions. Economic cooperation in Scandinavia failed to go further than intergovernmentalism along the path toward integration, despite suffering many of the same dilemmas member-states of the EEC had to come to terms with. In conclusion, Laursen's chapter poses the fundamental question of whether the Milwardian method can be applied, as he does in the Scandinavian case, to other processes of regional integration and interdependence and the role of multilateral agreements in the national strategies of nation-states.

## CONCLUSION: AFTER-MILWARD? AN AGENDA FOR RESEARCH

On 30 September 2010, the European University Institute organized a whole day workshop between authors to discuss some of the papers which were to be included in this volume. As organizer of the event, during the previous day, I received a phone call from the head of the Department of History and Civilization of the EUI, Bartolomé Yun Casalilla, who had gently supported this activity, in which he informed me that Alan Milward had passed away on 28 September 2010. After having consulted the co-organizer, Kiran Patel and the successor in Milward's chair, Federico Romero, we decided to maintain the debate as the best homage to his memory. The meeting happened to be extremely useful to discuss what was left of Alan Milward's contribution and gave me the possibility to offer some personal reflections as the complement to the central question of this volume. These reflections are indeed fed by all the papers submitted by all those who generously offered to contribute to the project. They are also fed by a workshop held on 20 January 2003, organized at the EUI in order to honor the departure of Professor Milward from his chair. It also benefited from some other lectures that the British historian gave in different places after that time, in particular Paris and Brussels. They aim to be the research perspectives that Milward himself had put forward for a future agenda and that I have not seen presented systematically elsewhere, but which I understand can be updated, complemented, and defined within the perspectives of our present time.

A general point concerns the question of the basis on which the history of European integration should be written. As a matter of fact, we enjoy greater possibilities than ever possessed by previous generations of historians with an exponential multiplication of sources previously unknown or unavailable. This is derived partly from a greater transparency of public and also private sources concerning the history of the twentieth century in general, and European integration in particular. If the challenge of digital humanities has still to be tackled fully by a new generation of historians, these transformations enable the introduction of topics and methodological questions to the agenda, which it would have been very difficult seriously to contemplate even in the most recent past. The accessibility of sources coupled with new technologies allows historians to better document the facts which are at the basis of their craft. Therefore, we now can document events and interview actors which in the past were impossible to manage by an individual historian, or even by a research group. Milward always defended himself against those who criticized his obsession with facts and figures, pointing out that the establishment and categorization of facts are central elements of historiographical practice going back to the Enlightenment in the cosmopolitan variant represented by Gibbon and Voltaire. For this school of history, historical knowledge serves to empower citizens if based on the interpretation of facts, and not just on beliefs.[8]

No doubt Milwards's position was clear and he gave sure advice against the excesses of the postmodern turn in historiography without renouncing the insights that this historiographical trend might provide to the interpretation of history. In any case, this general point does not prevent the possibility of inducing a conceptual shift in order to study the process of European integration by inserting it within the larger context of the history of European construction. There should be a clear distinction between the former process, which started in 1951, and is based on the voluntary and legal cessation of sovereignty, and the latter, which included attempts to construct European unity by other means, for example through force, such as during the Nazi World Order; ideas or movements, for example the Europeanist movements from the First World War; or through building international institutions, such as the United States with the Marshall Plan, the OEEC and NATO. The connections and actual transfers between both historical processes is an issue which needs to be documented and established without any a priori assumption as demonstrated by the patient and massive work in both fields developed already by first-class scholars like Michel Dumoulin, Eric Bussière, Sylvain Schirmann, and Antonio Varsori in the editorial project Euroclio.[9]

From these premises and following Milward's suggestions, there may be four directions of research in European integration and the construction of Europe:

1) *Linguistic archeology of the central concepts which have structured European integration.* This will focus on the way decision-makers involved in European integration presented their ideas in public discourses and try to find in which way contending concepts of European integration traveled from different contexts or were derived from the work of intellectuals, academics, civil servants, or other experts into policy. Milward suggested this as a new field of research which has

8. For the first massive and systematic collection of oral archives in the history of European integration see Dumoulin *La Commission Européenne, 1958–1972: Histoire et mémoire d'une institution.*
9. For an overview of the work developed around this distinction see the editorial project and publications of the Euroclio collection. http://www.peterlang.de/index.cfm?cid=5&event=cmp.ccc.seitenstruktur.detailseiten&seitentyp=series&pk=287&concordeid=EUROED (accessed 15 June 2011).

already been explored by political scientists,[10] but also by those historians who are interested in the relationship between law and history within the paradigm of integration by law.[11]

2) *Analysis of sociopolitical and socioeconomic networks invested in European integration.* Such an endeavor requires a more systematic approach in order to understand who was influenced by whom and how key decision-makers were related to each other and with civil servants. Indeed this needs to be applied not only to study the influence of European movements, but also to the European actions of political parties, trade unions, and multinational corporations. This research line seems to be already producing some fruits in recent works, but it should be considered here as a complement to the *acquis Milwardien* rather than implying that the simple existence of European networks, transnational or national, automatically implied an impact on European policies.[12] It is in this direction where my own contribution has occurred, in trying to introduce the role of multinational corporations and business associations in the process of European integration.[13]
3) *European integration as a regulatory pillar to govern global capitalism.* It is obvious at this point that Milward did not focus on a question which others consider to have been of central importance: the impact of the cold war on the process of European integration. This impact is something that needs to be at the top of the agenda, and it is indeed so in the publications of the networks specializing in the history of the cold war with scholars such as Piers Ludlow.[14] However, what Milward actually suggested was to focus the attention on a more long-term economic dimension by researching whether the EEC/EU was one of the ways to regulate or organize the return to globalization that had originally manifested itself at end of the nineteenth century. More precisely, this research direction will imply dealing with the relationship between the history of the European project and other international institutions such as the United Nations and GATT, or the development of external relations of the European Communities since their foundation, for instance focusing on the relationship with Third World countries. This problematic question was partly attempted with the 'Breakthrough Project' in the beginnings of the

10. White, 'Theory Guiding Practice: The Neofunctionalists and the Hallstein EEC Commission'.
11. Rasmussen, 'From *Costa v. ENEL* to the Treaties of Rome'.
12. Kaiser, Leucht, and Rasmussen, *The History of the European Union*.
13. Ramírez Pérez, 'Public Policies, European Integration and Multinational Corporations in the Automobile Sector: the French and Italian cases in a comparative perspective 1945-1973'; 'Transnational Business Networks Propagating EC Industrial Policy'; and 'The European Committee for Economic and Social Progress'.
14. Ludlow, *European Integration and the Cold War*.

past decade, which was coordinated by Alan Milward and Fernando Guirao and aimed at putting into perspective the questions and implications of the first enlargement of the EEC in 1973. It is currently being explored in a larger perspective by the French scholar Eric Bussière in the project 'European and global governance since the 1970s', following his previous reflections upon the French case.[15]

4) *Transformation of the democratic welfare state and its relationship with European integration.* This is basically a continuation of the allegiance agenda, but taking as point of departure that European integration has to be considered as an idiosyncratic process of state-building, which has created a confederation of states with federalist elements. In this agenda, therefore, history of the transformation of the relationship of the welfare state with its citizens under the economic and political impact of European integration should be included. Milward considered it of particular importance to deal with the way in which the political systems of democratic states have changed with the progressive subordination of the legislative to the executive. This process has indeed been reinforced by the transformation of political parties from mass-parties to electoral machines financed by the state and oriented toward safeguarding particular interests and lobbies. Such an agenda brings us directly to the fundamental question of the history of the democratization and economic, social, and political identities of the European Union since its origins. This topic has been partially discussed in a recent volume by the historical editor of the *New Left Review*, Perry Anderson, who dedicated this book to Milward.[16]

If we add these four dimensions to those introduced in the first subsections of this chapter about political economy, plus those suggested by the different contributors in their chapters, a post-Milwardian approach, yet standing on his shoulders, will allow historians to maintain Milward's legacy in order to better understand the moving waters of European construction and integration without losing sight of the intense flow of historical research. As to how Milward's historical scholarship relates to the broader intellectual debate about European integration, as demonstrated in his interrupted dialogue with Perry Anderson, I hope to elucidate this issue elsewhere.[17]

15. Bussière, *Georges Pompidou face à la mutation économique de l'Occident.*
16. Anderson, *The New Old World.*
17. For a first attempt on the use of Milward's scholarship in the French debate on European integration see my 'Europe néo-libérale? Les limites d'une interprétation téléologique de l'intégration européenne'. For an alternative view see Rasmussen, 'European Rescue of the Nation-State? Tracing the Role of Economics and Business'.

# Appendix 1
## Career History of Alan S. Milward

**Education:**

- 1953–1956, University College, London. BA (First Class Honours) in Medieval and Modern History
- 1956–1959, London School of Economics and Political Science (LSE), University of London. Ph.D. in Economic History. Ph.D. thesis, 'The Armaments Industry in the German Economy in the Second World War' (1960)

**Career:**

- 1959–1960, Assistant Lecturer in Indian Archaeology, The School of Oriental and African Studies, University of London
- 1960–1965, Assistant Lecturer, then Lecturer, in Economic History, University of Edinburgh
- 1965–1968, Lecturer, then Senior Lecturer, The School of Social Studies, University of East Anglia
- 1969–1971, Tenured Associate Professor of Economics, Stanford University
- 1971–1983, Professor of European Studies, University of Manchester Institute of Science and Technology (UMIST)
- 1983–1986, Professor of the History of European Integration, European University Institute (EUI), Florence
- 1986–1996, Professor of Economic History, Department of Economic History, LSE
- 1996–2003, Professor of the History of European Integration, EUI, Florence
- 1993–2007, Official Historian at the Cabinet Office contracted to write the Official History of the Accession of the United Kingdom to

the European Community and its subsequent relations with the Community up to the mid-1980s

- 2002–2003, Senior Visiting Research Fellow, St John's College, Oxford

## Visiting Teaching Appointments:

- February 1966, Social Sciences Research Council Visiting Fellow, *Ecole des Hautes Etudes en Sciences Sociales*, Paris
- Academic Year 1966–67, Visiting Associate Professor of Economics, Stanford University
- September 1978–January 1979, Visiting Professor of Economics, University of Illinois at Urbana-Champaign
- March–July 1980, *Gastprofessor des Forschungsinstituts für Geistes- und Sozialwissenschaften, Universität-Gesamthochschule Siegen*
- March 1982, *Directeur d'Etudes*, *Ecole des Hautes Etudes en Sciences Sociales*, Paris
- 1986–1992, External Professor, EUI, Florence
- October 1990, *Directeur d'Etudes*, *Ecole des Hautes Etudes en Sciences Sociales*, Paris
- January–July 1991, Norwegian Social Science Research Council Visiting Professor, University of Oslo
- 1991–1996, Visiting Professor, *Collège d'Europe*, Bruges
- October 1992, Visiting Professor, University of Århus
- 1993–2000, Visiting Professor, University of Trondheim
- February 1999, Visiting Fellow, *Institut für die Wissenschaften vom Menschen*, Vienna
- 2000–2004, Associate of the London European Research Centre, University of North London

## Elected Distinctions:

- 1987, Fellow of the British Academy
- 1994, Fellow of the Royal Norwegian Society of Sciences and Letters

## Honorary Awards:

- 1976, MA, University of Manchester
- 1996, Professor Emeritus of Economic History, London School of Economics

# Appendix 2
## Published work of Professor Alan S. Milward, 1964–2007

### Books

*The German Economy at War*. London: Athlone Press of the University of London, 1965. Reprinted: 1967. Translations: *Die deutsche Kriegswirtschafts 1939–1945*. Translated by Elisabeth Maria Petzina. Stuttgart: Deutsche Verlags-Anstalt, 1966.

*L'economia di guerra della Germania*. Translated by Marcello De Cecco. Milan: Franco Angeli, 1971. Reprinted: 1978.

*The New Order and the French Economy*. Oxford: The Clarendon Press, 1970. Aldershot: Gregg Revivals, 1993.

*The Economic Effects of the Two World Wars on Britain*. London: Macmillan, 1970. (With the title *The Economic Effects of the World Wars on Britain*.) Reprinted: 1972, 1973, 1977, 1979. 2nd ed. London: Macmillan, 1984. Reprinted: 1987, 1991. Translations: *Ryoutaisen ni okeru iguirisuno keizaiteki kiketsu*. Translated by Kenzou Mizukami. Tokyo: Aya Hiroshi's cultural bookstore, 1990.

*The Fascist Economy in Norway*. Oxford: The Clarendon Press, 1972.

*Der Zweite Weltkrieg: Krieg, Wirtschaft und Gesellschaft, 1939–1945*. Munich: Deutsche Taschenbuch Verlag, 1977.

*War, Economy and Society, 1939–1945*. London: Allen Lane, 1977. Berkeley: University of California Press, 1977. Paperback edition: 1979. Harmondsworth: Penguin, 1984. Reprinted: 1987. Translations: *Guerra, economia e società, 1939–1945*. Translated by Guido Abbatista. Milan: ETAS libri, 1983. Reprinted: 1989.

*La Segunda Guerra Mundial, 1935–1945*. Translated by Antonio Menduiña and Juan Tugores. Barcelona: Crítica, 1986. Barcelona: Folio, 1997.

*The Reconstruction of Western Europe, 1945–51*. London: Methuen, 1984. Paperback edition with revisions in text and bibliography: 1987. Berkeley: University of California Press, 1984. London: Routledge, 1992. Reprinted: 1994, 2003, 2006, and 2011.

*The European Rescue of the Nation-State*. With the assistance of George Brennan and Federico Romero. London: Routledge, 1992. Paperback edition with revisions in last chapter: 1994. Berkeley: University of California Press, 1992. 2nd ed. London: Routledge, 2000. Hardcover and paperback editions. Also available as a talking book in the Norwegian Library of Talking Books and Braille, 2007.

*The United Kingdom and the European Community. Vol. I: The Rise and Fall of a National Strategy, 1945–1963*. London: Whitehall History Publishing in association with Frank Cass, 2002.

*Politics and Economics in the History of the European Union*. London: Routledge, 2005.

### *With Samuel Berrick Saul:*

*The Economic Development of Continental Europe, 1780–1870*. London: Allen and Unwin, 1973. Hardcover and paperback editions. Totowa: Rowman and Littlefield, 1973. Vol. 1 (With the title: *The Economic Development of Continental Europe*.) 2nd ed. London: Allen and Unwin, 1979. Reprinted by Routledge, London and New York, 2011 in hardback and to be reprinted in 2012 in paperback. Translations 1st ed.: *Storia economica dell'Europa continentale: 1780–1870*. Translated by Franco Bassani. Bologna: Il Mulino, 1973. Reprinted: 1977. *Desarrollo económico de la Europa Continental: los países adelantados, 1780–1870*. Translated by María José Triviño. Madrid: Tecnos, 1979.

*The Development of the Economies of Continental Europe, 1850–1914*. London: Allen and Unwin, 1977. Hardcover and paperback editions. Cambridge: Harvard University Press, 1977. Reprinted by Routledge, London and New York, 2011 in hardback and to be reprinted in 2012 in paperback. Translation 1st ed.: *Storia economica dell'Europa continentale: 1850–1914*. Translated by Emanuele Barié. Bologna: Il Mulino, 1979.

### *With Frances M. B. Lynch, Ruggero Ranieri, Federico Romero, and Vibeke Sørensen:*

*The Frontier of National Sovereignty: History and Theory, 1945–1992*. London: Routledge, 1993. Paperback edition: 1994. Reprinted: 1995.

### *With George Brennan:*

*Britain's Place in the World: A Historical Enquiry into Import Controls, 1945–60*. London: Routledge, 1996.

### *Edited with Bernd Martin:*

*Agriculture and Food Supply in the Second World War / Landwirtschaft und Ernährung im zweiten Weltkrieg*. Ostfildern: Scripta Mercaturae Verlag, 1985.

### *Edited with Erik Aerts:*

*Economic Planning in the Post-1945 Period*. Leuven: Leuven University Press, 1990.

### *Edited with Anne Deighton:*

*Widening, Deepening and Acceleration: The European Economic Community, 1957–1963*. Baden-Baden and Brussels: Nomos Verlag and Bruylant, 1999.

## ARTICLES

1. "The End of the Blitzkrieg." *The Economic History Review* 16: 3 (April 1964): 499–518.
2. "Fritz Todt als Minister für Bewaffnung und Munition." *Vierteljahrshefte für Zeitgeschichte* 14 (1966): 40–58.
3. "Could Sweden have Stopped the Second World War?" *Scandinavian Economic History Review* 15: 1–2 (1967): 127–138.
4. "French Labour and the German Economy, 1942–45: An Essay on the Nature of the Fascist New Order." *The Economic History Review* 23: 2 (August 1970): 336–351.
5. "The European Studies Movement: What's in a Name?" *Journal of Common Market Studies* 14: 1 (September 1975): 69–80.
6. "Probleme der Landwirtschaft im Zweiten Weltkrieg." *Studia Historiae Oeconomicae* 17 (1982): 59–69.
7. "Nationale Wirtschaftsinteressen im Vordergrund—Neue Erkenntnisse statt überholter Schulweisheiten." *Integration* 10: 3 (1987): 100–106. Republished in *Die Europäische Union als Prozeß: Verfassungsentwicklungen im Spiegel von 20 Jahren der Zeitschrift Integration: Zu Ehren von Heinrich Schneider,* edited by Rudolf Hrbek, Mathias Jopp, Barbara Lippert, and Wolfgang Wessels. Bonn: Europa Union Verlag, 1998, 255–262.
8. "Was the Marshall Plan Necessary?" *Diplomatic History* 13: 2 (April 1989): 231–253. See book review item 112. Reprinted in *The Reconstruction of the International Economy, 1945–1960,* edited by Barry Eichengreen. Cheltenham: Edward Elgar, 1996, 176–198.
9. "Etats-Nations et Communauté: Le Paradoxe de l'Europe?" *Revue de synthèse* 111: 3 (July–September 1990): 253–270.
10. "Le Plan Marshall: Interviews: Alan S. Milward." *Revue d'économie financière* 14 (1990): 125–127.
11. "Economic Warfare in the Cold War: The First Historical Research." *Historisk Tidsskrift* 4 (1992): 420–440. See book review item 147.
12. "Allegiance: The Past and the Future." *Journal of European Integration History* 1: 1 (1995): 7–19. Reprinted after some editing as "The Springs of Integration." In *The Question of Europe,* edited by Peter Gowan and Perry Anderson. London: Verso, 1997, 5–20.
13. "Approaching Reality: Euro-Money and the Left." *New Left Review* 216 (March–April 1996): 55–65. Reprinted as "The Social Bases of Monetary Union?" In *The Question of Europe,* edited by Peter Gowan and Perry Anderson. London: Verso, 1997, 149–161.
14. "Le changement dans la continuité." *Le Débat* 91 (September–October 1996): 134–142.
15. "La Unión Europea y el estado-nación." *Revista de Libros* 11 (November 1997): 20–24.
16. "Foreign Light on Italy's Foreign Policy." *Storia delle Relazioni Internazionali* 13: 2 (1998) 14: 1 (1999): 377–381.
17. "Keynes, Keynesianism, and the International Economy." *Proceedings of the British Academy* 105 (2000): 225–251.
18. "A comment on the Article by Andrew Moravcsik." *Journal of Cold War Studies* 2: 3 (2000): 77–80.
19. "Les Unions Monétaires Européennes." *Archives do Centre Cultural Calouste Gulbenkian* 40 (December 2000): 37–48.
20. "European Uses of Neutrality: An Essay on the Occasion of a New Conference Volume." *Wiener Beiträge zur Geschichte der Neuzeit* 1: 1 (2001): 103–116.

21. "Historical Teleologies." *EU Studies in Japan* 21 (2001): 107–125. Also published as: "The Challenge for the EU Historical Teleologies." In *European Integration in the 21st Century: Unity in Diversity?* edited by Mary Farrell, Stefano Fella, and Michael Newman. London: SAGE, 2002, 15–28.

## CONTRIBUTIONS

1. "Hitlers Konzept des Blitzkrieges." In *Probleme des Zweiten Weltkrieges*, edited by Andreas Hillgruber. Cologne: Kiepenheuer & Witsch, 1967, 19–40.
2. "German Economic Policy towards France, 1942–1944." In *Studies in International History: Essays Presented to W. Norton Medlicott,* edited by K. Bourne and D. C. Watt. London: Longmans, 1967, 423–443.
3. "Germany and World War II: Unit 21." In *Open University: War and Society; Block VII.* Milton Keynes: The Open University Press, 1973.
4. "Der deutsche Handel und der Welthandel 1925–1939." In *Industrielles System und politische Entwicklung in der Weimarer Republik*, edited by Hans Mommsen, Dietmar Petzina, and Bernd Weisbrod. Düsseldorf: Droste, 1974, 472–484.
5. "The Economic and Strategic Effectiveness of Resistance." In *Resistance in Europe, 1939–1945*, edited by Stephen Hawes and Ralph White. London: Penguin Allen Lane, 1975, 186–203.
6. "Der Einfluss ökonomischer und nicht-ökonomischer Faktoren auf die Strategie des Blitzkrieges." In *Wirtschaft und Rüstung am Vorabend des Zweiten Weltkrieges*, edited by Friedrich Forstmeier and Hans-Erich Volkmann. Düsseldorf: Droste, 1975, 189–201.
7. "Now as available as pornography. . . ." In *25 Jahre Institut für Zeitgeschichte*, edited by Institut für Zeitgeschichte. Stuttgart: Deutsche Verlags-Anstalt, 1975, 92–94.
8. "Fascism and the Economy." In *Fascism: A Reader's Guide; Analyses, Interpretations, Bibliography*, edited by Walter Laqueur. London: Wildwood House and Penguin Allen Lane; Berkeley: University of California Press, 1976, 409–453.
9. "Arbeitspolitik und Produktivität in der deutschen Kriegswirtschaft unter vergleichendem Aspekt." In *Kriegswirtschaft und Rüstung, 1939–1945*, edited by Friedrich Forstmeier and Hans-Erich Volkmann. Düsseldorf: Droste, 1977, 73–91.
10. "Les placements français à l'étranger et les deux guerres mondiales." In *La position internationale de la France: Aspects économiques et financiers XIXe–XXe siècles*, edited by Maurice Lévy-Leboyer. Paris: Editions de l'Ecole des Hautes Etudes en Sciences Sociales, 1977, 299–311.
11. "Strategies for Development in Agriculture: The Nineteenth-Century European Experience." In *The Search for Wealth and Stability: Essays in Economic and Social History Presented to M. W. Flinn*, edited by T. C. Smout. London: Macmillan, 1979, 21–42.
12. "Towards a Political Economy of Fascism." In *Who Were the Fascists?* edited by Stein Ugelvik Larsen, Bernt Hagtvet, and Jan Petter Myklebust. Bergen: Universitetsforlaget, 1980, 56–65.
13. "Cyclical Fluctuations and Economic Growth in Developed Europe, 1870–1913." In *Konjunktur, Krise, Gesellschaft*, edited by Dietmar Petzina and Ger van Roon. Stuttgart: Klett-Cotta, 1981, 42–53.
14. "The Reichsmark Bloc and the International Economy." In *Der Führerstaat: Mythos und Realität*, edited by Gerhard Hirschfeld and Lothar Kettenacker. Stuttgart: Klett-Cotta, 1981, 377–413. Reprinted in *Aspects of the Third*

*Reich*, edited by H. W. Koch. London: Macmillan, 1985, 331–359. Reprinted in *The Disintegration of the World Economy Between the World Wars*, edited by Mark Thomas. Cheltenham: Edward Elgar, 1996. Vol. 2, 371–411.

15. "Tariffs as Constitutions." In *The International Politics of Surplus Capacity: Competition for Market Shares in the World Recession*, edited by Susan Strange and Roger Tooze. London: George Allen and Unwin, 1981, 58–66. Reprinted in *The International Trading System, Globalization and History*, edited by Kevin H. O'Rourke. Cheltenham: Edward Elgar, 2005. Vol. 1, 39–48.
16. "The Committee of European Economic Co-operation (CEEC) and the Advent of the Customs Union." In *A History of European Integration, Part 1, 1945–1947*, edited by Walter Lipgens; with contributions by Wilfried Loth and Alan Milward. Oxford: Clarendon Press, 1982, 507–569.
17. "L'integrazione dell'Europa occidentale negli anni dell'ERP: l'esperienza del Gruppo di Studio Europeo per l'Unione Doganale." In *Il Piano Marshall e l'Europa*, edited by Elena Aga Rossi. Rome: Istituto della Enciclopedia Italiana, 1983, 109–118.
18. "Grossbritannien, Deutschland, und der Wiederaufbau Westeuropas." In *Wirtschaftspolitik im britischen Besatzungsgebiet 1945–1949*, edited by Dietmar Petzina and Walter Euchner. Düsseldorf: Schwann, 1984, 25–40.
19. "Comments on Some Theories of Historical Change." In *Economic Theory and History*, edited by Jürgen Kocka and György Ránki. Budapest: Akadémiai Kiadó, 1985, 157–164.
20. "The Second World War and Long-Term Change in World Agriculture." In *Agriculture and Food Supply in the Second World War / Landwirtschaft und Ernährung im zweiten Weltkrieg*, edited by Bernd Martin and Alan S. Milward. Ostfildern: Scripta Mercaturae Verlag, 1985, 5–15.
21. "Entscheidungsphasen der Westintegration." In *Westdeutschland, 1945–1955: Unterwerfung, Kontrolle, Integration*, edited by Ludolf Herbst. Munich: R. Oldenbourg, 1986, 231–246.
22. (with Richard T. Griffiths) "The Beyen Plan and the European Political Community." In *Noi si mura: Selected Working Papers of the European University Institute*, edited by Werner Maihofer. Florence: European University Institute, 1986, 595–621.
23. (with Richard T. Griffiths) *The European Agricultural Community, 1948–1954*. Florence: European University Institute, 1986. (EUI working paper 86/254.)
24. "Belgium and Western European Interdependence in the 1950s: Some Unexplained Problems." In *La Belgique et les débuts de la construction européenne: de la guerre aux traités de Rome*, edited by Michel Dumoulin. Louvain-la-Neuve: CIACO, 1987, 145–152.
25. "Der historische Revisionismus zur Einigungsgeschichte West-Europas: neue historische Erkenntnisse statt überholter Schulweisheiten." In *Die Europäische Union als Prozess: Verfassungsentwicklungen im Spiegel von 20 Jahren der Zeitschrift Integration: Zu Ehren von Heinrich Schneider*, edited by Rudolf Hrbek. Bonn: Europa Union Verlag, 1998. (Previously published as: "Nationale Wirtschaftsinteressen im Vordergrund: Neue Erkenntnisse statt überholter Schulweisheiten", *Integration* 10: 3 (1987): 100–106.
26. "The Belgian Coal and Steel Industries and the Schuman Plan." In *Die Anfänge des Schuman-Plans = The Beginnings of the Schuman Plan*, edited by Klaus Schwabe. Baden-Baden: Nomos, 1988, 437–454.
27. "The Origins of the Treaty of Rome." In *Development Options in Europe*, edited by Björn Hettne. United Nations University, European Perspectives Project, 1986–1987, Padrigu Papers, Göteborg, 1988, 1–13.

28. "Motives for Currency Convertibility: The Pound and the Deutschmark, 1950–5." In *Interactions in the World Economy: Perspectives from International Economic History*, edited by Carl-Ludwig Holtfrerich. Hemel Hempstead: Harvester Wheatsheaf, 1989, 260–284.
29. "Introduction." In *Economic Planning in the Post-1945 Period*, edited by Erik Aerts and Alan S. Milward. Leuven: Leuven University Press, 1990, 3–5.
30. "La planification française et la réconstruction européenne." In *Modernisation ou décadence: études, témoignages et documents sur la planification française*, edited by Bernard Cazes and Philippe Mioche. Aix-en-Provence: Université de Provence, 1990, 77–115.
31. "Lessons from the Marshall Plan." In *The Helsinki Process and the Future of Europe*, edited by Samuel F. Wells, Jr. Washington, D.C.: Wilson Center Press, 1990, 125–132.
32. "The War, the Netherlands and the Development of the European Economic Community." In *Holland at War Against Hitler: Anglo-Dutch Relations, 1940–1945*, edited by M. R. D. Foot. London: Frank Cass, 1990, 200–212.
33. "The Marshall Plan and German Foreign Trade." In *The Marshall Plan and Germany*, edited by Charles S. Maier. Leamington Spa: Berg, 1991, 452–487.
34. "Benelux und die europäische Gemeinschaft, 1945–1958." In *Nationale Identität und Europäische Einigung*, edited by Michael Salewski. Göttingen: Muster-Schmidt, 1992, 87–112.
35. "El sector exterior en la expansión de los años cincuenta: comparación de las exportaciones españolas, italianas y portuguesas." In *El desarrollo económico en la Europa del Sur: España e Italia en perspectiva histórica*, edited by Leandro Prados de la Escosura and Vera Zamagni. Madrid: Alianza Universidad, 1992, 444–461.
36. "L'Europa in formazione." In *Storia d'Europa. Vol. 1: L'Europa oggi*, edited by Perry Anderson et al. Turin: Einaudi, 1993, 161–219.
37. "La livre sterling, le franc et le Deutschemark, 1950–5." In Ministère de l'Economie et du Budget and Comité pour l'histoire économique et financière de la France, *Du franc Poincaré à l'écu*. Paris: Comité pour l'histoire économique et financière de la France, 1993, 405–418.
38. "The European Monetary Agreement, 1955." In *Die europäische Integration vom Schuman-Plan bis zu den Verträgen von Rom = The European Integration from the Schuman Plan to the Treaties of Rome*, edited by Gilbert Trausch. Baden-Baden: Nomos, 1993, 115–128.
39. "The Marshall Plan and Europe's Foreign Trade." In *Le Plan Marshall et le relèvement économique de l'Europe*, edited by René Girault and Maurice Lévy-Leboyer. Paris: Comité pour l'histoire économique et financière de la France, 1993, 641–650.
40. (with Vibeke Sørensen) "Interdependence or Integration? A National Choice." In Milward, Lynch, Ranieri, Romero, and Sørensen, *The Frontier of National Sovereignty*, 1–32.
41. "Conclusions: The Value of History." In Milward, Lynch, Ranieri, Romero, and Sørensen, *The Frontier of National Sovereignty*, 182–201.
42. "Como Tudo Começou." In *Convertibilidade Cambial*, edited by Jorge Braga de Macedo, Barry Eichengreen, and Jaime Reis. Lisbon: Banco de Portugal e Fundação Luso-Americana para o Desenvolvimento, 1995, 113–129. Republished as: "The Origins of the Gold Standard." In *Currency Convertibility: The Gold Standard and Beyond*, edited by Jorge Braga de Macedo, Barry Eichengreen, and Jaime Reis. London and New York: Routledge, 1996, 87–101.

43. "Economie de guerre" and "Reconstruction." In *1938–1948: les années de tourmente; de Munich à Prague: dictionnaire critique*, edited by Jean-Pierre Azéma and François Bédarida. Paris: Flammarion, 1995, 177–190 and 247–259 respectively.
44. "The Origins of the Fixed-Rate Dollar System." In *International Monetary Systems in Historical Perspective*, edited by Jaime Reis. Basingstoke: Macmillan, 1995, 135–152.
45. "The Frontier of National Sovereignty." In *The Future of the Nation-State: Essays on Cultural Pluralism and Political Integration*, edited by Sverker Gustavsson and Leif Lewin. London: Routledge; Stockholm: Nerenius & Santérus, 1996, 149–167.
46. "Was the Marshall Plan Necessary?" In *The Reconstruction of the International Economy, 1945–1960*, edited by Barry Eichengreen. Cheltenham: Edward Elgar, 1996, 176–198. Previously published in: *Diplomatic History* 13: 2 (April 1989): 231–252.
47. "The Springs of Integration" and "The Social Bases of Monetary Union?" In *The Question of Europe*, edited by Peter Gowan and Perry Anderson. London: Verso, 1997, 5–20 and 149–161. See items nos. 12 and 13 under 'Articles'.
48. "Voraussetzungen der Wirtschaftspolitik in den westlichen Besatzungszonen." In *Markt oder Plan. Wirtschaftsordnungen in Deutschland 1945–1961*, edited by Haus der Geschichte der Bundesrepublik Deutschland. Frankfurt am Main: Campus, 1997, 46–61.
49. "Die Auswirkungen des Marshall-Plans." In Haus der Geschichte der Bundesrepublik Deutschland and German Marshall Fund of the United States, *50 Jahre Marshall Plan*. Bonn: Haus der Geschichte der Bundesrepublik Deutschland; Berlin: Argon, 1997, 46–54.
50. "La construction de l'Europe." In *L'Europe dans son histoire: La vision d'Alphonse Dupront*, edited by François Crouzet and François Furet. Paris: Presses universitaires de France, 1998, 335–355.
51. "Interpreting the European Union." In *National Interest and the EEC/EC/EU*, edited by Svein Dahl. Trondheim: Tapir, 1999, 9–14
52. "The European Communities, The United Kingdom, and NATO, 1950–1963." In *Von Truman bis Harmel: Die Bundesrepublik Deutschland im Spannungsfeld von NATO und europäischer Integration*, edited by Hans-Joachim Harder. Munich: Oldenbourg, 2000, 109–120.
53. "Le Gouvernement Heath, le Trésor Britannique, et le Rapport Werner." In *Le Rôle des Ministères de Finances et de l'Economie dans la Construction Européenne (1957–1978)*, edited by Ministère pour l'Economie, des Finances et du Budget. Paris: Ministère pour l'Economie, des Finances et du Budget; Comité Pour l'Histoire Economique et Financière de la France, 2001. Vol. 1: 315–327.
54. "Childe Harold's Pilgrimage." In *Britain and Germany in Europe 1949–1990*, edited by Jeremy Noakes, Peter Wende, and Jonathan Wright. Oxford: Oxford University Press, 2002, 49–66.
55. "The Challenge for the EU Historical Teleologies." In *European Integration in the 21st Century: Unity in Diversity?* edited by Mary Farrell, Stefano Fella, and Michael Newman. London: SAGE, 2002, 15–28. Previously published as: "Historical Teleologies." In *EU Studies in Japan* 21, 2001, 107–125.
56. "Gaetano Martino and Russell Bretherton." In *Gaetano Martino. Scienziato Rettore Statista (1900–1967)*, edited by Marcello Saija. Messina: Trisform, 2002, 323–328.
57. "Politische Ökonomie, Unilateralismus und Sicherheit im „Dritten Reich"." In *Wirtschaftsordnung, Staat und Unternehmen: Neue Forschungen zur Wirtschaftsgeschichte des Nationalsozialismus*, edited by Werner Abelshauser, Jan-Otmar Hesse, and Werner Plumpe. Essen: Klartext, 2003, 221–229.

58. "Economic Warfare in Perspective." In *East-West Trade and the Cold War*, edited by Jari Eloranta and Jari Ojala. Jyväskylä: University of Jyväskylä, 2005, 201–207.
59. "Was the Middle East the Birthplace of a Common European Foreign Policy?" In *Controlling the Uncontrollable? The Great Powers in the Middle East*, edited by Tore T. Petersen. Trondheim: Tapir Academic Press, 2006, 23–36.
60. "History, Political Science and European Integration." In *Handbook of European Union Politics*, edited by Knud Erik Jørgensen, Mark A. Pollack, and Ben Rosamond. London: SAGE, 2007, 99–103.

## VIDEO RECORDINGS

(with Hugh Redwald Trevor-Roper) "Hitler's World Policy" and "Hitler's War?" London: Audio-Visual Learning, 1972.

"The Nazi New Order". [Milton Keynes]: Open University, 1973.

(with Ian Kershaw) "The Third Reich—A Social Revolution?" London: Audio-Visual Learning, 1978.

(with Ian Kershaw) "Comparative Fascism". London: Audio-Visual Learning, 1980.

## BOOK REVIEWS

The references of book reviews listed below have been obtained from the following databases (consulted in November and December 2010): *Business Source Elite*. Ipswich: EBSCO, 1997. http://www.ebscohost.com/academic/business-source-elite; *EconLit*. Ipswich: EBSCO, 2002. http://www.ebscohost.com/academic/econlit; *International Bibliography of the Social Sciences: IBSS*. Ann Arbor: ProQuest, 2010. http://www.proquest.co.uk/en-UK/catalogs/databases/detail/ibss-set-c.shtml; *ISI Web of Knowledge*. Philadelphia: Thomson Reuters, 2002. http://isiknowledge.com/; *JSTOR*. New York: JSTOR, 2000. http://www.jstor.org; *Oxford Journals*. Oxford: Oxford University Press, 2008. http://www.oxfordjournals.org/; *Periodicals Index Online*. Cambridge: Bell & Howell Information and Learning Company, 2001. http://pio.chadwyck.co.uk/marketing.do; *Project Muse Online: Scholarly Journals Online*. Baltimore: Johns Hopkins University, 1993. http://muse.jhu.edu; *ScienceDirect*. Amsterdam: Elsevier, 2003. http://www.sciencedirect.com/; *Wiley Online Library*. Hoboken: John Wiley & Sons, 1999. http://onlinelibrary.wiley.com/; *Wilson Humanities Index*. New York: OVID, [199–]. http://www.ovid.com/site/catalog/DataBase/184.jsp?top=2&mid=3&bottom=7&subsection=10.

1. Total Warfare and Compulsory Labour: A Study of the Military-Industrial Complex in Germany during World War I, by Robert B. Armeson. *The Economic History Review* 18: 3 (1965): 675–676.
2. *L'Europe de l'abondance*, by François Hetman, and *Wirtschaftsordnung und Wirtschaftspolitik: Studien und Konzepte zur Sozialen Markwirtschaft und zur Europaischen Integration*, by Alfred Müller-Armack. *International Affairs*

(henceforth always referring to the journal published by the Royal Institute of International Affairs since 1944) 44: 4 (October 1968): 784–785.

3. *Design for Total War: Arms and Economics in the Third Reich*, by Berenice A. Carroll. *The Journal of Economic History* 29: 2 (June 1969): 329–330.
4. *La crise de 1929*, by Jacques Néré. *The English Historical Review* 85: 334 (January 1970): 207.
5. *Economic History of Europe: Twentieth Century*, by Shepard B. Clough, Thomas Moodie, and Carol Moodie. *International Affairs* 46: 2 (April 1970): 353.
6. *Autarkiepolitik im Dritten Reich: Der Nationalsozialistische Vierjahresplan*, by Dieter Petzina. *The Economic History Review* 23: 2 (August 1970): 390–392.
7. *The Ordeal of Total War, 1939–1945*, by Gordon Wright. *The English Historical Review* 85: 337 (October 1970): 879.
8. *La France dans la compétition économique: Quatre débats à l'Académie des sciences morales et politiques*, by Raymond Aron; *Central Planning for the Market Economy: An Analysis of the French Theory and Experience*, by Vera Lutz; and *Modern Capitalistic Planning: The French Model*, by Stephen S. Cohen. *International Affairs* 47: 1 (January 1971): 153–154.
9. *95 Regions*, by Bernard Kayser and Jean-Louis Kayser. *International Affairs* 48: 2 (April 1972): 311.
10. *Quisling, Rosenberg und Terboven: zur Vorgeschichte und Geschichte der Nationalsozialistischen Revolution in Norwegen*, by Hans-Dietrich Loock. *International Affairs* 49: 1 (January 1973): 74–75.
11. *The French Economy, 1913–39: The History of a Decline*, by Tom Kemp. *International Affairs* 49: 2 (April 1973): 274–275.
12. *The Social Economy of France*, by Peter Coffey; and *The Social Economy of West Germany*, by Graham Hallett. *International Affairs* 50: 3 (July 1974): 477.
13. *Le IIIe Reich et la réorganisation économique de l'Europe, 1940–1942: Origines et projets*, by Jean Freymond. *International Affairs* 51: 3 (July 1975): 422–424.
14. *War and Economic Development: Essays in Memory of David Joslin*, edited by J. M. Winter. *The Times Literary Supplement* 3831 (15 August 1975): 923.
15. *German Steel and Swedish Iron Ore, 1939–1945*, by Martin Fritz; and *German Coal and Swedish Fuel, 1939–1945*, by Sven-Olof Olsson. *Scandinavian Economic History Review* 24: 1 (1976): 88.
16. *National Economic Planning in France*, by David Liggins. *International Affairs* 52: 1 (January 1976): 112–113.
17. *The Rise of German Industrial Power, 1834–1914*, by William Otto Henderson. *The Manchester School of Economic and Social Studies* 44: 2 (June 1976): 193–194.
18. *Les camps de concentration dans l'économie du Reich hitlérien*, by Joseph Billig. *The Journal of Modern History* 48: 3 (September 1976): 567–568.
19. *French Economic Growth*, by Jean-Jacques Carré, Paul Dubois, and Edmond Malinvaud. *International Affairs* 52: 4 (October 1976): 642–644.
20. *The Great Rumanian Peasant Revolt of 1907: Origins of a Modern Jacquerie*, by Philip Gabriel Eidelberg. *The English Historical Review* 92: 362 (January 1977): 161–163.
21. *Social Structure in Divided Germany*, by Jaroslav Krejci. *International Affairs* 53: 2 (April 1977): 303.
22. *The Emerging European Enterprise: Strategy and Structure in French and German Industry*, by Gareth P. Dyas and Heinz T. Thanheiser. *International Affairs* 53: 3 (July 1977): 485–486.

23. *The End of French Predominance in Europe: The Financial Crisis of 1924 and the Adoption of the Dawes Plan*, by Stephen A. Schuker. *Journal of Common Market Studies* 16: 4 (December 1977): 362–363.
24. *The Nationality Problem in Austria-Hungary: The Reports of Alexander Vaida to Archduke Franz Ferdinand's Chancellery*, edited by Keith Hitchins. *European Studies Review* 8: 3 (1978): 381–382.
25. *Supplying War: Logistics from Wallenstein to Patton*, by M. Van Creveld. *The Journal of Strategic Studies* 1: 2 (1978): 227–229.
26. *The Fontana Economic History of Europe. Vol. 5 (2 parts): The Twentieth Century*, and *Vol. 6 (2 parts): Contemporary Economies*, by Carlo M. Cipolla. *The English Historical Review* 93: 367 (April 1978): 421–424.
27. *Political Strategies for Industrial Order: State, Market and Industry in France*, by John Zysman. *International Affairs* 54: 2 (April 1978): 324–325.
28. *Population and Society in Twentieth-Century France*, by Colin Dyer. *International Affairs* 54: 4 (October 1978): 673–674.
29. *Iron and Steel in the German Inflation, 1916–23*, by Gerald D. Feldman. *The Economic History Review* 31: 4 (November 1978): 695–696.
30. *The Political Economy of Germany, 1815–1914*, by Martin Kitchen. *The Manchester School of Economic and Social Studies* 46: 4 (December 1978): 404.
31. *Handbuch der deutschen Wirtschafts- und Sozialgeschichte, Bd. I: Von der Frühzeit bis zum Ende des 18. Jahrhunderts. Bd. II: Das 19. und 20. Jahrhundert*, edited by Hermann Aubin and Wolfgang Zorn, in *Geschichte und Gesellschaft* 5: 2 (1979): 251.
32. *Contemporary Europe: Social Structures and Cultural Patterns*, by Salvador Giner and Margaret Scotford Archer. *Regional Studies* 13: 1 (February 1979): 116–117.
33. *The Decision to Divide Germany: American Foreign Policy in Transition*, by John H. Backer. *The Economic Journal* 89: 353 (March 1979): 202.
34. *Le IIIe Reich et le pétrole roumain, 1938–1940*, by Philippe Marguerat. *The English Historical Review* 94: 371 (April 1979): 472–473.
35. *War Economy, 1942–1945: Australia in the War of 1939–1945*, by Sydney James Butlin and Carl Boris Schedvin. *The Economic History Review* 32: 3 (August 1979): 445–446.
36. *The Cambridge Economic History of Europe VII: The Industrial Economies; Capital, Labour and Enterprise, Parts 1 and 2*, by Peter Mathias and M. M. Postan. *The English Historical Review* 94: 373 (October 1979): 885–889.
37. *The Secret Betrayal: 1944–1947*, by Nikolai Tolstoy. *Slavic Review* 38: 4 (December 1979): 679–680.
38. *The World Economy: History and Prospect*, by Walt Whitman Rostow. *The English Historical Review* 95: 374 (January 1980): 188–189.
39. *Communist Power in Europe, 1944–1949*, edited by Martin McCauley. *Slavic Review* 39: 2 (June 1980): 329–330.
40. *Schwedens Wirtschaftsbeziehungen zum Dritten Reich, 1933–1945*, by Klaus Wittmann. *The Journal of Modern History* 52: 2 (June 1980): 362–364.
41. *Lend-Lease, Loans, and the Coming of the Cold War: A Study of the Implementation of Foreign Policy*, by Leon Martel. *Slavic Review* 40: 1 (Spring 1981): 119–120.
42. *Histoire économique et sociale de la France*, by Fernand Braudel and Ernest Labrousse. *The Journal of Modern History* 53: 2 (June 1981): 341–344.
43. *Managerial Hierarchies: Comparative Perspectives on the Rise of the Modern Industrial Enterprise*, by Alfred D. Chandler, Jr. and Herman Daems. *The Economic History Review* 34: 3 (August 1981): 503.

44. *Collaborationism in France during the Second World War*, by Bertram M. Gordon. *The International History Review* 3: 4 (October 1981): 601–604.
45. *Businessmen and Politics in the Rhineland, 1789–1834*, by Jeffery M. Diefendorf. *Business History* 23: 3 (November 1981): 368.
46. *Women Workers in the First World War*, by Gail Braybon. *The Economic History Review* 34: 4 (November 1981): 665–666.
47. *Economic Diplomacy and the Origins of the Second World War: Germany, Britain, France, and Eastern Europe, 1930–1939*, by David E. Kaiser. *The American Historical Review* 86: 5 (December 1981): 1066–1067.
48. *The Political Economy of Germany in the Twentieth Century*, by Karl Hardach. *The Economic Journal* 91: 364 (December 1981): 1097–1098.
49. *West Germany: A European and Global Power*, by Wilfrid L. Kohl and Georgio Basevi. *International Affairs* 58: 1 (Winter 1981–1982): 149–150.
50. *Hitler's 'Mein Kampf' in Britain and America: A Publishing History, 1930–1939*, by James J. Barnes and Patience P. Barnes; *Faschismus Forschung: Positionen, Probleme, Polemik*, edited by Dietrich Eichholtz and Kurt Gossweiler; *Young Mussolini and the Intellectual Origins of Fascism*, by A. James Gregor; *Italian Fascism and Developmental Dictatorship*, by A. James Gregor; *Anmerkungen zu Hitler*, by Sebastian Haffner; *Art in the Third Reich*, by Berthold Hinz; *Der Hitler-Mythos: Volksmeinung und Propaganda im Dritten Reich*, by Ian Kershaw; *The Coming of Austrian Fascism*, by Martin Kitchen; *Who were the Fascists? Social Roots of European Fascism*, edited by Stein Ugelvik Larsen, Bernt Hagtvet, and Jan Petter Myklebust; *Ernst Krieck und die Nationalsozialistische Wissenschaftsreform: Motive und Tendenzen eine Wissenschaftslehre und Hochschul-Reform im Dritten Reich*, by Gerhard Müller; *Fascism: Comparison and Definition*, by Stanley G. Payne; *Kunst und Kultur im deutschen Faschismus*, edited by Rolf Schnell; *Sabers and Brown Shirts: The German Students' Path to National Socialism, 1918–1935*, by Michael Stephen Steinberg; *The Nazi Organization of Women*, by Jill Stephenson; *Hitler*, by Norman Stone; and *The Dynamics of Nazism: Leadership, Ideology and the Holocaust*, by Fred Weinstein. *History* 67: 219 (January 1982): 47–62.
51. *Polish Society Under German Occupation: The Generalgouvernement, 1939–1944*, by Jan Tomasz Gross. *The English Historical Review* 97: 382 (January 1982): 231.
52. *Reparation in World Politics: France and European Economic Diplomacy, 1916–1923*, by Marc Trachtenberg. *The Journal of Modern History* 54: 1 (March 1982): 131–133.
53. *Capitalism and the State in Modern France: Renovation and Economic Management in the Twentieth Century*, by Richard F. Kuisel. *International Affairs* 58: 2 (Spring 1982): 365.
54. *Historische Konjunkturforschung*, by Wilhelm H. Schröder and Reinhard Spree. *Business History* 24: 2 (July 1982): 230–231.
55. *The Beginnings of Communist Rule in Poland December 1943–June 1945*, edited by Antony Polonsky and Boleslaw Drukier. *The English Historical Review* 97: 385 (October 1982): 942–943.
56. *The Nazi Question: An Essay on the Interpretations of National Socialism (1922–1975)*, by Pierre Ayçoberry. *History* 67: 221 (October 1982): 518–519.
57. *The Industrialization of the Continental Powers, 1780–1914*, by Clive Trebilcock. *The Economic History Review* 35: 4 (November 1982): 646–648.
58. *From Embargo to Ostpolitik*, by Angela Stent. *The Economic Journal* 92: 368 (December 1982): 1004.

59. *The Adaptable Nation: Essays in Swedish Economy during the Second World War*, by Martin Fritz et al. *Scandinavian Economic History Review* 31: 3 (1983): 221–223.
60. *Technological Diffusion and Industrialisation before 1914*, by A. George Kenwood and Alan L. Lougheed. *The Economic History Review* 36: 1 (February 1983): 175–176.
61. *Mobilization for Total War: The Canadian, American and British Experience, 1914–1918, 1939–1945*, edited by Nándor F. Dreisziger. *The Journal of Strategic Studies* 6: 1 (March 1983): 97–98.
62. *Anglo-American Economic Collaboration in War and Peace, 1942–1949*, by Richard Clarke and Alec Cairncross. *International Affairs* 59: 2 (Spring 1983): 287–288.
63. *The Economic History of Britain since 1700*, by Roderick Floud and Donald McCloskey. *The English Historical Review* 98: 387 (April 1983): 378–379.
64. *British Economic and Strategic Planning, 1905–1915*, by David French. *The Journal of Economic History* 43: 2 (June 1983): 511–512.
65. *Internationale Beziehungen in der Weltwirtschaftskrise, 1929–1933*, by Josef Becker and Klaus Hildebrand. *The English Historical Review* 98: 389 (October 1983): 929.
66. *Die Deutsche Inflation: Eine Zwischenbilanz*, edited by Gerald Feldman et al. *Business History* 25: 3 (November 1983): 333–335.
67. *The Nazi Economic Recovery, 1932–1938*, by Richard J. Overy. *The Economic History Review* 36: 4 (November 1983): 652–654.
68. *The Depression and the Developing World, 1914–1939*, by A.J.H. Latham, in *The English Historical Review* 99: 390 (January 1984): 219.
69. *The Inner Nazi: A Critical Analysis of Mein Kampf*, by Hans Staudinger. *History* 69: 225 (January 1984): 176.
70. *Investing in Europe's Future*, edited by Arnold A. Heertje, and *State Investment Companies in Western Europe: Picking Winners or Backing Losers?* edited by Brian Hindley. *Journal of Common Market Studies* 22: 4 (June 1984): 408.
71. *Sterling in Decline: The Devaluations of 1931, 1949 and 1967*, by Alec Cairncross and Barry Eichengreen. *Journal of Common Market Studies* 23: 1 (September 1984): 88.
72. *România şi trusturile petroliere internaţionale până la 1929* [*Romania and International Oil Trusts by 1929*], by Gheorghe Buzatu. *The English Historical Review* 99: 393 (October 1984): 929–930.
73. *Goering: The Iron Man*, by Richard J. Overy. *The Times Literary Supplement* 4269 (25 January 1985): 82.
74. *Järn och Potatis: Jordbruk, Teknik och Social Omvandling i Skaraborgs Län, 1750–1860 [Iron and Potatoes: Agriculture, Technique, and Social Change in the County of Skaraborg, 1750–1860]*, by Carl-Johan Gadd. *The American Historical Review* 90: 1 (February 1985): 153.
75. *Evolution of the European Idea, 1914–1932*, by Carl H. Pegg. *The Journal of Modern History* 57: 1 (March 1985): 109–110.
76. *International Banking in the 19th and 20th Centuries*, by Karl-Erich Born, *The Journal of Modern History* 57: 1 (March 1985): 112–114.
77. *Political Life in Romania, 1918–1921*, by Mircea Muşat and Ion Ardeleanu. *The English Historical Review* 100: 395 (April 1985): 454–455.
78. *Hitler and the Final Solution*, by Gerald Fleming; *Hitler in History*, by Eberhard Jäckel; and *Albert Speer: The End of a Myth*, by Matthias Schmidt. *London Review of Books* 7: 8 (2 May 1985): 3–6.
79. *Capitalism since World War II: The Making and Breaking of the Great Boom*, by Philip Armstrong, Andrew Glyn, and John Harrison. *Journal of Common Market Studies* 23: 4 (June 1985): 385–386.

80. *The Marshall Plan Revisited: The European Recovery Program in Economic Perspective*, by Imanuel Wexler. *The Journal of Modern History* 57: 2 (June 1985): 341–343.
81. *German Big Business and the Rise of Hitler*, by Henry Ashby Turner. *The Times Literary Supplement* 4292 (5 July 1985): 744.
82. *The Economic Rise of the Habsburg Empire, 1750–1914*, by David F. Good. *The Economic History Review* 38: 3 (August 1985): 470–471.
83. *Depression and Protectionism: Britain between the Wars*, by Forrest Capie. *The Journal of Imperial and Commonwealth History* 14: 1 (October 1985): 124–125.
84. *The History of Anti-Semitism. Vol. 4: Suicidal Europe, 1870–1933*, by Léon Poliakov. *London Review of Books* 7: 18 (17 October 1985).
85. *German Yearbook on Business History. Business History* 28: 1 (January 1986): 147–148.
86. *Hitler: Memoirs of a Confidant*, edited by Henry Ashby Turner; *Blood and Soil: Walther Darré and Hitler's 'Green Party'*, by Anna Bramwell; *Industry and Politics in the Third Reich: Ruhr Coal, Hitler and Europe*, by John Gillingham; and *Geschichte der Deutschen Kriegswirtschaft, 1939–1945. Vol. 2: 1941–1943*, by Dietrich Eichholtz. *London Review of Books* 8: 1 (23 January 1986): 21–22.
87. *Hitler's Apocalypse: Jews and the Nazi Legacy*, by Robert Wistrich. *The Times Literary Supplement* 4322 (31 January 1986): 105.
88. *Autarkie und Grossraumwirtschaft in Deutschaland, 1930–1939: Aussenwirtschaftspolitische Konzeptionen zwischen Wirtschaftskrise und Zweitem Weltkrieg*, by Eckart Teichert. *The American Historical Review* 91: 1 (February 1986): 139–140.
89. *Britain, America and the Sinews of War, 1914–1918*, by Kathleen Burk. *The Economic History Review* 39: 1 (February 1986): 152.
90. *The European Experience: A Historical Critique of Development Theory*, by Dieter Senghaas and K. M. Kimmig. *International Affairs* 62: 2 (Spring 1986): 314–315.
91. *Il capitale tedesco in Italia. Dall'Unità alla Prima Guerra Mondiale. Banche miste e sviluppo economico italiano*, by Peter Hertner. *The Journal of Modern History* 58: 1 (March 1986): 348–349.
92. *Istoria Parlamentului şi a vieţii parlamentare din România până la 1918*, edited by Paraschiva Câncea, Mircea Iosa, and Apostol Stan. *The English Historical Review* 101: 399 (April 1986): 545–546.
93. *Selling Hitler: The Story of the Hitler Diaries*, by Robert Harris. *London Review of Books* 8: 6 (3 April 1986): 8–9.
94. *My Father Rudolf Hess*, by Wolf Rüdiger Hess; *Long Knives and Short Memories: The Spandau Prison Story*, by Jack Fishman; *Zwangssterilisation im Nationalsozialismus: Studien zur Rassenpolitik und Frauenpolitik*, by Gisela Bock; and *Prelude to Genocide: Nazi Ideology and the Struggle for Power*, by Simon Taylor. *London Review of Books* 8: 14 (7 August 1986): 16–17.
95. *Economy and Foreign Policy: The Struggle of the Great Powers for Hegemony in the Danube Valley, 1919–1939*, by György Ránki. *The English Historical Review* 101: 401 (October 1986): 1033–1034.
96. *Russia and the Formation of the Romanian National State, 1821–1878*, by Barbara Jelavich. *The English Historical Review* 102: 402 (January 1987): 245–246.
97. *The Great War and the British People*, by J. M. Winter. *The Economic History Review* 40: 2 (May 1987): 312–313.
98. *The Price of War: British Policy on German Reparations, 1941–1949*, by Alec Cairncross. *The Economic Journal* 97: 386 (June 1987): 527–528.

99. *Economic Security and the Origins of the Cold War, 1945–1950*, by Robert A. Pollard. *The Slavonic and East European Review* 65: 3 (July 1987): 493–494.
100. *Origins of the European Integration, March 1948–May 1950*, edited by Raymond Poidevin. *Journal of Common Market Studies* 26: 1 (September 1987): 87.
101. *Energy in History: The 11th Symposium of the International Cooperation in History of Technology Committee (ICOHTEC)*, by Jaroslav Purš. *The English Historical Review* 102: 405 (October 1987): 1080.
102. *Historia agraria de la España contemporánea, Volumen 3, El fin de la agricultura tradicional (1900–1960)*, by Ramon Garrabou, Carlos Barciela, and J. I. Jiménez Blanco. *The Agricultural History Review* 36: 2 (1988): 221–222.
103. *Robert Schuman: Homme d'Etat, 1886–1963*, by Raymond Poidevin. *Journal of Common Market Studies* 26: 3 (March 1988): 344–345.
104. *War, Prosperity and Depression: The US Economy, 1917–1945*, by Peter Fearon. *The Economic Journal* 98: 392 (September 1988): 912.
105. *An Historical Geography of Europe, 1800–1914*, by N.J.G. Pounds. *The English Historical Review* 103: 409 (October 1988): 1071–1073.
106. *Warschau unter dem Hakenkreuz: Leben und Alltag im besetzten Warschau, 1939 bis 1944*, by Tomasz Szarota. *The English Historical Review* 103: 409 (October 1988): 1094.
107. *An Economic and Social History of Europe, 1890–1939: An Economic and Social History of Europe from 1939 to the Present*, by Frank B. Tipton and Robert Aldrich. *The Economic History Review* 41: 4 (November 1988): 660–661.
108. *Economic Behavior in Adversity*, by Jack Hirshleifer. *The Manchester School of Economic and Social Studies* 56: 4 (December 1988): 399–400.
109. *Munich: The Eleventh Hour*, by Robert Kee; *Peace for our Time*, by Robert Rothschild; and *A Class Divided: Appeasement and the Road to Munich, 1938*, by Robert Shepherd. *London Review of Books* 11: 1 (5 January 1989): 17.
110. *External Economic Policy since the War. Vol. 1: The Post-War Financial Settlement*, by L. S. Pressnell. *International Affairs* 65: 2 (Spring 1989): 345–345.
111. *Growth to Limits: The Western European Welfare States since World War II. Vol. 1: Sweden, Norway, Finland, Denmark. Vol. 2: Germany, United Kingdom, Ireland, Italy. Vol. 4: Appendices*, edited by Peter Flora; and *Wealth and Taxation in Central Europe: The History and Sociology of Public Finance*, edited by Peter-Christian Witt. *European History Quarterly* 19: 4 (October 1989): 568–571.
112. *The Marshall Plan: America, Britain, and the Reconstruction of Western Europe, 1947–1952*, by Michael J. Hogan. *Diplomatic History* 13: 2 (Spring 1989): 231–253.
113. *The Rise and Fall of the Great Powers: Economic Change and Military Conflict from 1500 to 2000*, by Paul Kennedy. *Millennium: Journal of International Studies* 18: 1 (Spring 1989): 99–102.
114. *Industry and Ideology: IG Farben in the Nazi Era*, by Peter Hayes. *The American Historical Review* 94: 2 (April 1989): 474–475.
115. *The Bulgarian Economy in the Twentieth Century*, by John R. Lampe. *The English Historical Review* 104: 411 (April 1989): 549–550.
116. *The Marshall Plan: America, Britain and the Reconstruction of Western Europe, 1947–1952*, by Michael J. Hogan. *Journal of Common Market Studies* 27: 4 (June 1989): 373–373.

117. *America and the Reconstruction of Italy, 1945–1948*, by John Lamberton Harper. *The English Historical Review* 104: 413 (October 1989): 1084–1085.
118. *Multinational Enterprise in Historical Perspective*, edited by Alice Teichova, Maurice Lévy-Leboyer, and Helga Nussbaum. *European History Quarterly* 19: 4 (October 1989): 555–557.
119. *British Technology and European Industrialization: The Norwegian Textile Industry in the Mid-nineteenth Century*, by Kristine Bruland. *The Economic Journal* 99: 398 (December 1989): 1233.
120. *German Macroeconomic History, 1880–1979: A Study of the Effects of Economic Policy on Inflation, Currency Depreciation and Growth*, by Andrea Sommariva and Giuseppe Tullio. *German History* 8: 1 (January 1990): 104–106.
121. *In Search of Detente: The Politics of East-West Relations since 1945*, by S. R. Ashton; *Cold War, Third-World: An Essay on Soviet-American Relations*, by Fred Halliday; *United States-Soviet Relations*, by Karl W. Ryavec; and *The Global Rivals*, by Seweryn Bialer and Michael Mandelbaum. *The Times Literary Supplement* 4530 (26 January 1990): 81–82.
122. *In Search of Stability: Explorations in Historical Political Economy*, by Charles S. Maier. *The Journal of Modern History* 62: 1 (March 1990): 105–108.
123. *The German Economy, 1945–1947: Charles P. Kindleberger's Letters from the Field*, by Charles P. Kindleberger. *The Journal of Economic History* 50: 1 (March 1990): 203–204.
124. *Banque et investissement industriel: Paribas, le pétrole roumain et la politique française, 1919–1939*, by Philippe Marguerat. *The English Historical Review* 105: 415 (April 1990): 533–534.
125. *German Liberalism and the Dissolution of the Weimar Party System, 1918–1933*, by Larry Eugene Jones. *International Affairs* 66: 2 (April 1990): 386–387.
126. *The Nazi Party in Dissolution: Hitler and the Verbotzeit, 1923–25*, by David Jablonsky. *International Affairs* 66: 3 (July 1990): 596.
127. *Britain and the Marshall Plan*, by Henry Pelling. *The Economic History Review* 43: 3 (August 1990): 509.
128. *Trente ans d'expérience Euratom: La Naissance d'une Europe nucléaire*, by Olivier Pirotte, Pascal Girerd, Pierre Marsal, and Sylviane Morson. *Journal of Common Market Studies* 29: 1 (September 1990): 87–88.
129. *The European Payments Union: Financial Diplomacy in the 1950s*, by Jacob J. Kaplan and Gunther Schleiminger. *The Economic History Review* 43: 4 (November 1990): 767–768.
130. *Ruhrstahl und Europa: Die Wirtschaftsvereinigung Eisen- und Stahlindustrie und die Anfänge der europäischen Integration, 1945–1952*, by Werner Bührer. *The American Historical Review* 95: 5 (December 1990): 1570–1571.
131. *Die Okkupationspolitik Nazideutschlands in Polen, 1939–1945*, by Czesław Madajczyk. *The English Historical Review* 106: 418 (January 1991): 259–261.
132. *Reconstruction in Post-War Germany: British Occupation Policy and the Western Zones, 1945–1955*, edited by Ian Turner. *German History* 9: 1 (January 1991): 113–115.
133. *A Social and Economic History of Twentieth-Century Europe*, by Gerold Ambrosius and William H. Hubbard. *Business History* 33: 2 (April 1991): 327–328.

134. *The Cambridge Economic History of Europe. Vol. 8: The Industrial Economies: The Development of Economic and Social Policies*, by Peter Mathias and Sidney Pollard. *The English Historical Review* 106: 419 (April 1991): 408–412.
135. *Elusive Stability: Essays in the History of International Finance, 1919–1939*, by Barry Eichengreen. *The Economic Journal* 101: 406 (May 1991): 684.
136. *The French Economy in the Nineteenth Century: An Essay in Econometric Analysis*, by Maurice Lévy-Leboyer and François Bourguignon. *The Economic Journal* 101: 406 (May 1991): 684.
137. *Krieg zur Friedenssicherung: Die Deutschlandplanung der britischen Regierung während des Zweiten Weltkrieges*, by Lothar Kettenacker. *History* 76: 247 (June 1991): 367–368.
138. *Real Wages in Nineteenth- and Twentieth-Century Europe*, edited by Peter Scholliers. *Journal of Historical Geography* 17: 3 (July 1991): 330–331.
139. *World War II and the West: Reshaping the Economy*, by Gerald D. Nash. *The International History Review* 13: 3 (August 1991): 628–629.
140. *The Netherlands and the Economic Integration of Europe, 1945–1957*, edited by Richard T. Griffiths. *The Economic History Review* 44: 4 (November 1991): 746–747.
141. *Protectionism and Economic Revival: The British Interwar Economy*, by Michael Kitson and Solomos Solomou. *Vierteljahrschrift für Sozial- und Wirtschaftsgeschichte* 79: 2 (1992): 265.
142. *Bauern, Agrarkrise und Volksernährung in der Europäischen Zwischenkriegszeit: Studien zur Agrargesellschaft und -Wirtschaft der Republik Österreich, 1918 bis 1938*, by Ulrich Kluge. *The English Historical Review* 107: 422 (January 1992): 261–262.
143. *The Fruits of Fascism: Postwar Prosperity in Historical Perspective*, by Simon Reich. *German History* 10: 1 (January 1992): 126–127.
144. *The German Economy in the Twentieth Century: The German Reich and the Federal Republic*, by Hans-Joachim Braun. *International Affairs* 68: 1 (January 1992): 168–169.
145. *Coal, Steel, and the Rebirth of Europe, 1945–1955: The Germans and French from Ruhr Conflict to Economic Community*, by John Gillingham. *German History* 10: 2 (1992): 264–265.
146. *The West German Economy, 1945–1955*, by Alan Kramer. *German History* 10: 2 (1992): 262–264.
147. 'Cold Economic Warfare: The Creation and Prime of COCOM, 1948–1954.' Doctoral dissertation by Tor Egil Førland, University of Oslo, 1991. *Historisk Tidsskrift* 4 (1992): 420–440.
148. *The Bread of Affliction: The Food Supply in the USSR during World War II*, by William Moskoff. *The Slavonic and East European Review* 70: 2 (April 1992): 358–359.
149. *Reshaping Europe in the Twenty-First Century*, by Patrick Robertson. *International Affairs* 68: 3 (July 1992): 546.
150. *The Two Germanies since 1945*, by Henry Ashby Turner; *Zwei Staaten, eine Nation: Deutsche Geschichte, 1955–1970*, by Christoph Klessmann; *Politische Kultur und deutsche Frage: Materialien zum Staats- und Nationalbewusstsein in der Bundesrepublik Deutschland*, edited by Werner Weidenfeld; *Die Verletzte Nation: Über den Versuch der Deutschen, Ihren Charakter zu Ändern*, by Elisabeth Noelle-Neumann and Renate Köcher; *Von Stalingrad zur Währungsreform: Zur Sozialgeschichte des Umbruchs in Deutschland*, edited by Martin Broszat, Klaus-Dietmar Henke, and Hans Woller; *Die Wiedereingliederung Westdeutschlands in die Weltwirtschaft, 1945–1958*, by Christoph Buchheim; *Sozialpolitische Entscheidungen im*

*Nachkriegsdeutschland: Alliierte und deutsche Sozialversicherungspolitik 1945 bis 1957*, by Hans-Günter Hockerts. *Vierteljahrshefte für Zeitgeschichte* 40: 3 (July 1992): 449–465.

151. *The United States and the Making of Postwar France, 1945–1954*, by Irwin M. Wall. *The International History Review* 14: 4 (November 1992): 839–840.
152. *L'Etat, les finances et l'économie: Histoire d'une conversion, 1932–1952*, vols. 1 & 2, by Michel Margairaz. *Revue de Synthèse* 114: 1 (1993): 154–156.
153. *Betriebspolitik im 'Dritten Reich': Deutsche Arbeitsfront, Unternehmer und Staatsbürokratie in der westdeutschen Grossindustrie, 1933–1939*, by Matthias Frese. *German History* 11: 2 (April 1993): 257–258.
154. *The Internationalization of the German Political Economy: Evolution of a Hegemonic Project*, by William D. Graf. *International Affairs* 69: 2 (April 1993): 383.
155. *War Finance, Reconstruction, Hyperinflation, and Stabilization in Hungary, 1938–48*, by Pierre L. Siklos. *The International History Review* 15: 2 (May 1993): 389–390.
156. *German Industry and German Industrialization: Essays in German Economic and Business History in the Nineteenth and Twentieth Centuries*, edited by W. Robert Lee. *History* 78: 253 (June 1993): 334.
157. *Histoire, économie et société*, 1990, 9: 1. *The Journal of Transport History* 14: 2 (September 1993): 204.
158. *Economy and Society: European Industrialisation and its Social Consequences: Essays Presented to Sidney Pollard*, edited by Colin Holmes and Alan Booth. *The Economic History Review* 46: 4 (November 1993): 831–832.
159. *State Capitalism and Working-Class Radicalism in the French Aircraft Industry*, by Herrick Chapman. *The Journal of Modern History* 66: 1 (March 1994): 171–172.
160. *Governments, Industries and Markets: Aspects of Government-Industry Relations in the UK, Japan, West Germany and the USA since 1945*, edited by Martin Chick. *The English Historical Review* 109: 431 (April 1994): 544.
161. *Industrialisation and Everyday Life*, by Rudolf Braun. *The English Historical Review* 109: 431 (April 1994): 469.
162. *Jumpstart: The Economic Unification of Germany*, by Gerline Sinn and Hans-Werner Sinn. *International Affairs* 70: 2 (April 1994): 363–364.
163. *The Fading Miracle: Four Decades of Market Economy in Germany*, by Herbert Giersch, Karl-Heinz Paqué, and Holger Schmieding. *The Economic History Review* 47: 2 (May 1994): 433–434.
164. *The Economics of the Second World War*, by György Ránki. *The English Historical Review* 109: 432 (June 1994): 669–670.
165. *War and Economy in the Third Reich*, by Richard J. Overy. *The Times Literary Supplement* 4757 (3 June 1994): 28.
166. *The United States and the European Trade Union Movement, 1944–1951*, by Federico Romero. *The International History Review* 16: 3 (August 1994): 627–629.
167. *The Battle for Coal: Miners and the Politics of Nationalization in France, 1940–1950*, by Darryl Holter. *History* 79: 257 (October 1994): 542.
168. *The Economic History of Italy, 1860–1990: Recovery after Decline*, by Vera Zamagni. *Business History* 36: 4 (October 1994): 143–144.
169. *The Sinews of War: Essays on the Economic History of World War II*, by Geofrey T. Mills and Hugh Rockoff. *Journal of Economic Literature* 32: 4 (December 1994): 1922–1924.

170. *Reviving the European Union*, by C. Randall Henning, Eduard Hochreiter, and Gary Clyde Hufbauer. *International Affairs* 71: 1 (January 1995): 168–169.
171. *Finance and Financiers in European History, 1880–1960*, by Youssef Cassis. *The English Historical Review* 110: 435 (February 1995): 243–244.
172. *Der Stille Krieg: der Wirtschaftskrieg zwischen Grossbritannien und der Schweiz in Zweiten Weltkrieg*, by Oswald Inglin. *The English Historical Review* 110: 437 (June 1995): 809–810.
173. *Jacques Delors and European Integration*, by George Ross, and *Regional Integration: The West European Experience*, by William Wallace. *The Times Literary Supplement* 4825 (22 September 1995): 4–5.
174. *Capitalism in Crisis: International Responses to the Great Depression*, edited by William R. Garside. *The English Historical Review* 111: 440 (February 1996): 264–265.
175. *France, Germany, and the Western Alliance*, by Philip H. Gordon, and *The European Sisyphus: Essays on Europe, 1964–1994*, by Stanley Hoffmann. *The International History Review* 18: 2 (May 1996): 478–479.
176. *The Crisis of Representation in Europe*, edited by Jack Hayward; *British Politics and European Elections, 1994*, by David Butler and Martin Westlake; *National Parliaments and the European Union*, by Philip Norton; and *Parliaments and Parties: The European Parliament in the Political Life of Europe*, edited by Roger Morgan and Clare Tame. *The Times Literary Supplement* 4858 (10 May 1996): 6.
177. *The Stateless Market: The European Dilemma of Integration and Civilization*, by Paul Kapteyn; and *Democracy, Sovereignty and the European Union*, by Michael Newman. *The Times Literary Supplement* 4877 (20 September 1996): 13.
178. *British Protectionism and the International Economy: Overseas Commercial Policy in the 1930s*, by Tim Rooth. *Vierteljahrschrift für Sozial- und Wirtschaftsgeschichte* 84: 3 (1997): 423–424.
179. *The Schuman Plan and the British Abdication of Leadership in Europe*, by Edmund Dell. *The Journal of European Integration History* 3: 2 (1997): 99–100.
180. *A History of Money: From Ancient Times to the Present Day*, by Glyn Davies. *The English Historical Review* 112: 446 (April 1997): 553–554.
181. *Economic Change in Europe since 1918*, by Derek H. Aldcroft. *The English Historical Review* 112: 446 (April 1997): 540.
182. *The United States and the Integration of Europe: Legacies of the Postwar Era*, by Francis H. Heller and John R. Gillingham. *The International History Review* 19: 2 (May 1997): 439–440.
183. *A Grand Illusion? An Essay on Europe*, by Tony Judt, and *Our Currency, Our Country: The Dangers of European Monetary Union*, by John Redwood. *The Times Literary Supplement* 4920 (18 July 1997): 30.
184. *The German Predicament: Memory and Power in the New Europe*, by Andrei S. Markovits and Simon Reich. *The Times Literary Supplement* 4932 (10 October 1997): 8.
185. *From EC to EU: An Historical and Political Survey*, by R. McAllister. *Journal of Common Market Studies* 36: 2 (June 1998): 273–274.
186. *Using Europe, Abusing the Europeans: Britain and European Integration, 1945–1963*, by Wolfram Kaiser. *International History Review* 20: 3 (September 1998): 741–743.
187. *The Currency of Ideas: Monetary Politics in the European Union*, by Kathleen R. McNamara; *Europe's Economic Dilemma*, by John Mills; *A 'Coming Home' Or Poisoned Chalice?* edited by Helen Szamuely and Bill Jamieson;

and *Globalisation vs. Sovereignty? The European Response*, by Leon Brittan. *The Times Literary Supplement* 4982 (25 September 1998): 4–5.

188. *Nationalsozialistische Rüstungspolitik und Unternehmerischer Entscheidungsspielraum: Vergleichende Fallstudien zur württembergischern Maschinenbauindustrie*, by Astrid Gehrig. *The English Historical Review* 113: 454 (November 1998): 1377–1378.
189. *Tariffs, Trade and European Integration, 1947–1957*, by Wendy Asbeek Brusse. *The American Historical Review* 104: 1 (February 1999): 241.
190. *The United States and European Reconstruction, 1945–1960*, by John Killick. *The Journal of Economic History* 59: 2 (June 1999): 559–560.
191. *Twilight of the West*, by Christopher Coker. *The International History Review* 21: 3 (September 1999): 843–844.
192. *Economic Crises and Restructuring in History: Experiences of Small Countries*, by Timo Myllyntaus. *The Economic History Review* 53: 1 (February 2000): 210–211.
193. *War and Welfare: Europe and the United States, 1945 to the Present*, by Jytte Klausen. *The International History Review* 22: 1 (March 2000): 217–218.
194. *The Politics of Retribution in Europe: World War II and its Aftermath*, edited by Istvan Deak, Jan T. Gross, and Tony Judt; *The Legacy of Nazi Occupation: Patriotic Memory and National Recovery in Western Europe, 1945–1965*, by Pieter Lagrou; and *Vectors of Memory: Legacies of Trauma in Post-War Europe*, by Nancy Wood. *The Times Literary Supplement* 5063 (14 April 2000): 7–8.
195. *Free Trade, Free World: The Advent of GATT*, by Thomas W. Zeiler. *The American Historical Review* 105: 4 (October 2000): 1272–1273.
196. *Fremdarbeiter: Politik und Praxis des 'Ausländer-Einsatzes' in der Kriegswirtschaft des Dritten Reiches*, by Ulrich Herbert. *The English Historical Review* 115: 464 (November 2000): 1364–1365.
197. *European Industrial Policy: The Twentieth-Century Experience*, by James Foreman-Peck and Giovanni Federico. *The Journal of Economic History* 60: 4 (December 2000): 1133–1134.
198. *Die Neutralen und die Europäische Integration, 1945–1995*, edited by Michael Gehler and Rolf Steininger. *Wiener Beiträge zur Geschichte der Neuzeit* 1: 1 (2001): 103–116.
199. *The Cash Nexus: Money and Power in the Modern World, 1700–2000*, by Niall Ferguson. *The Times Literary Supplement* 5116 (20 April 2001): 14.
200. *The End of Globalization: Lessons from the Great Depression*, by Harold James. *The Times Literary Supplement* 5143 (26 October 2001): 4.
201. *Rethinking Europe's Future*, by David Calleo. *New Left Review* 12 (November–December 2001): 161–167.
202. *The Economic Cold War: America, Britain, and East-West Trade, 1948–1963*, by Ian Jackson. *The Journal of Economic History* 62: 2 (June 2002): 636–637.
203. *Threatening Europe: Britain and the Creation of the European Economic Community, 1955–58*, by James Ellison. *The Political Quarterly* 73: 3 (July–September 2002): 371–374.
204. *The Marshall Plan in Austria*, by Günter Bischof, Anton Pelinka, and Dieter Stiefel. *The English Historical Review* 117: 473 (September 2002): 1036–1037.
205. *A History of the European Economy, 1000–2000*, by François Crouzet. *History* 88: 289 (January 2003): 89–90.
206. *The Marshall Plan: Fifty Years After*, by Martin Schain, and *Denmark's Social Democratic Government and the Marshall Plan, 1947–1950*, by

Vibeke Sørensen and Mogens Rüdiger. *The International History Review* 25: 1 (March 2003): 207–210.

207. *Grand Designs and Visions of Unity: The Atlantic Powers and the Reorganization of Western Europe, 1955–1963*, by Jeffrey Glen Giauque. *Journal of Cold War Studies* 6: 2 (Spring 2004): 88–89.
208. *A Question of Self-Esteem: The United States and the Cold War Choices in France and Italy, 1944–1958*, by Alessandro Brogi. *Journal of Cold War Studies* 6: 3 (Summer 2004): 156–158.
209. *Mémoires*, by Jacques Delors. *New Left Review* 29 (September–October 2004): 145–151.
210. 'The European Union as a Superstate', a review article of: *We, the People of Europe? Reflections on Transnational Citizenship*, by Etienne Balibar and James Swenson; *The European Union: How does it Work?* by Elizabeth Bomberg and Alexander Stubb; *The Politics of Europeanization*, by Kevin Featherstone and Claudio M. Radaelli; *European Integration, 1950–2003: Superstate or New Market Economy?* by John Gillingham; *Framing Europe: Attitudes to European Integration in Germany, Spain, and the United Kingdom*, by Juan Díez Medrano; *A Certain Idea of Europe*, by Craig Parsons; *The Engines of European Integration: Delegation, Agency, and Agenda Setting in the EU*, by Mark A. Pollack; and *Europe's Foreign and Security Policy: The Institutionalization of Cooperation*, by Michael E. Smith. *The International History Review* 27: 1 (March 2005): 90–105.
211. *The American Century in Europe*, edited by R. Laurence Moore and Maurizio Vaudagna. *Journal of Cold War Studies* 8: 2 (Spring 2006): 170–172.
212. *Building Europe's Parliament: Democratic Representation Beyond the Nation-State*, by Berthold Rittberger. *The International History Review* 28: 4 (December 2006): 922–924.
213. *Die Bundesrepublik Deutschland und die europäische Einigung, 1949–2000*, by Mareike Konig and Matthias Schulz. *The English Historical Review* 122: 498 (September 2007): 1112–1113.

# Appendix 3
## List of completed Ph.D. theses for which Alan S. Milward was the main supervisor

| | | |
|---|---|---|
| 1981 | Frances M. B. Lynch | The Political and Economic Reconstruction of France, 1944–1947, in the International Context [The University of Manchester] |
| 1987 | Sabine S. Peters-Godts | La politique européenne du gouvernement belge, septembre 1944–mai 1950 [EUI]. |
| 1987 | Vibeke Sørensen | Social Democratic Government in Denmark under the Marshall Plan, 1947–1950 [EUI] published as *Denmark's Social Democratic Government and the Marshall Plan 1947–1950* (edited by Mogens Rüdiger), Copenhagen: Museum Tusculanum Press, 2001. |
| 1988 | Jan van der Harst | European Union and Atlantic Partnership: Political, Military and Economic Aspects of Dutch Defence, 1948–1954, and the Impact of the European Defence Community [EUI] published as *The Atlantic Priority: Dutch Defence Policy at the Time of the European Defence Community*, Florence: European Press Academic Publishing, 2003. |
| 1988 | Ruggero Ranieri | L'espansione alla prova del negoziato—l'industria italiana e la Comunità del Carbone e dell'Acciaio, 1945–1955 [EUI]. |
| 1989 | Peter Fischer | Die Anfänge der Atompolitik in der Bundesrepublik Deutschland im Spannungsfeld von Kontrolle, Kooperation und Konkurrenz (1949–1955) [EUI] published as *Atomenergie und staatliches Interesse: die Anfänge der Atompolitik in der Bundesrepublik Deutschland, 1949–1955*, Baden-Baden: Nomos, 1994. |
| 1990 | Valeria Camporesi | Mass Culture and the Defence of National Traditions: The BBC and American Broadcasting, 1922–1954 [EUI] published as *Mass Culture and National Traditions: The B.B.C. and American Broadcasting, 1922–1954*, Fucecchio, Italy: European Press Academic Publishing, 2000. |

| | | |
|---|---|---|
| 1991 | Jordi Catalán | Fábrica y franquismo, 1939–1958. El modelo español de desarrollo en el marco de las economías del sur de Europa [Universitat de Barcelona–EUI]* published as *La economía española y la Segunda Guerra Mundial*, Barcelona: Ariel, 1995. |
| 1991 | Catherine R. Schenk | British Management of the Sterling Area, 1950–8 [LSE] published as *Britain and the Sterling Area: From Devaluation to Convertibility in the 1950s*, London and New York: Routledge, 1994. |
| 1991 | Isabel Warner | The Deconcentration of the West German Steel Industry 1949–1953 [EUI] published as *Steel and Sovereignty: The Deconcentration of the West German Steel Industry, 1949–54*, Mainz: P. von Zabern, 1996. |
| 1992 | Christoph Dartmann | Re-distribution of Power, Joint Consultation or Productivity Coalitions? Labour and Post-war Reconstruction in Germany and Britain, 1945–1953 [EUI] published as *Re-distribution of Power, Joint Consultation or Productivity Coalitions? Labour and Postwar Reconstruction in Germany and Britain, 1945–1953*, Bochum: Brockmeyer, 1996. |
| 1992 | Guðmundur Jónsson | The State and the Icelandic Economy, 1870–1930 [LSE]. |
| 1992 | Pedro Lains e Silva | Foreign Trade and Economic Growth in the European Periphery: Portugal, 1851–1913 [EUI] published as *A economia portuguesa no século XIX: crescimento económico e comércio externo, 1851–1913*, Lisbon: Imprensa Nacional Casa da Moeda, 1995, and *L'économie portugaise au XIXe siècle. Croissance économique et commerce extérieur, 1851–1913*, Paris: L'Harmattan, 1999. |
| 1993 | Régine Perron | Le marché du charbon, 1945–1958, un enjeu dans les relations Europe/Etats-Unis de 1945 à 1958 [Ecole des Hautes Etudes, Paris–EUI]* published as *Le marché du charbon, un enjeu entre l'Europe et les Etats-Unis de 1945 à 1958*, Paris: Publications de la Sorbonne, 1996. |
| 1993 | Max-Stephan Schulze | The Economic Development of Austria–Hungary's Machine Building Industry, 1870–1913 [London School of Economics and Political Science (LSE)] published as *Engineering and Economic Growth: The Development of Austria-Hungary's Machine-building Industry in the Late Nineteenth Century*, Frankfurt am Main and New York: Peter Lang, 1996. |

* Alan Milward co-supervised theses at the EUI which were submitted for their defense in the candidate's home country.

| | | |
|---|---|---|
| 1994 | Carl Glatt | Reparations and the Transfer of Scientific and Industrial Technology from Germany: A Case Study of the Roots of British Industrial Policy and of Aspects of British Occupation Policy in Germany between Post-World War II Reconstruction and the Korean War, 1943–1951 [EUI]. |
| 1994 | Götz von Thadden | Inflation and Reconstruction in Poland, 1918–27 [LSE]. |
| 1995 | Eamonn M. Noonan | Choosing Confrontation: Commercial Policy in Britain and Germany, 1929–1936 [EUI]. |
| 1996 | Simon Niziol | British Technologies and Polish Economic Development 1815–1863 [LSE]. |
| 1996 | J. Adam Tooze | Official Statistics and Economic Governance in Inter-War Germany [LSE] published as *Statistics and the German state, 1900–1945: The Making of Modern Economic Knowledge*, Cambridge (UK) and New York: Cambridge University Press, 2001. |
| 1997 | Markus Schulte | Industry, Politics and Trade Discrimination in West Germany's European Policy, 1957–1963 [LSE]. |
| 1997 | Sylvia Schwaag | International Monetary Cooperation: Britain, Germany and France in the Return to Convertibility, December 1958 [LSE]. |
| 1998 | Kurt Wayne Schake | Strategic Frontier: American Bomber Bases Overseas, 1950–1960 [Norwegian University of Science and Technology] published as *Strategic Frontier: American Bomber Bases Overseas, 1950–1960*, Dragvoll: Historisk institutt, Norges teknisk-naturvitenskapelige universitet, 1998. |
| 2000 | Ute Ackermann | Geheimrezept oder chemische Reaktion? Die westdeutsche chemische Industrie (1950–1964): Firmen, Produkte und Märkte [EUI]. |
| 2000 | Marta Craveri | Ascesa, crisi e disgregazione del lavoro forzato in Unione Sovietica. La resistenza dei prigionieri nei campi staliniani 1945–1956 [EUI] published as *Resistenza nel Gulag: un capitolo inedito della destalinizzazione in Unione Sovietica,* Soveria Mannelli: Rubbettino, 2003. |
| 2000 | Ann-Christina Knudsen | Defining the Policies of the Common Agricultural Policy: A Historical Study [EUI] published as *Farmers on Welfare: The Making of Europe's Common Agricultural Policy*, Ithaca: Cornell University Press, 2009. |
| 2001 | George Kritikos | Greek Orthodox Refugees: Integration and the Making of a New Greek National Community (1923–1930) [EUI]. |
| 2003 | David Alexander Gilgen | Entstehung und Wirkung des deutschen Patentsystems im Kaiserreich. Eine neoinstitutionalistische Analyse [EUI]. |

| | | |
|---|---|---|
| 2003 | Thomas Michael Witschke | Gefahr für den Wettbewerb? Die Fusionskontrolle der Europäischen Gemeinschaft für Kohle und Stahl (EGKS) und die "Rekonzentration" der Ruhrstahlindustrie 1950–1963 [EUI] published as *Gefahr für den Wettbewerb?: die Fusionskontrolle der Europäischen Gemeinschaft für Kohle und Stahl und die "Rekonzentration" der Ruhrstahlindustrie 1950–1963*, Berlin: Akademie Verlag Berlin, 2009. |
| 2004 | Maude Bracke | Is it Possible to be Revolutionary without being Internationalist? West European Communism, Proletarian Internationalism and the Czechoslovak Crisis of 1968–69: A Comparative Study of the Italian and French Communist Parties [EUI] published as *Which Socialism, Whose Détente? West European Communism and the Czechoslovak Crisis of 1968*, Budapest: Central European University Press, 2007. |
| 2004 | Alexandre Nicolau Andresen Leitão | The Unexpected Guest: Portugal and European Integration (1956–1963) [EUI] published as *Estado novo, democracia e Europa: 1947–1986*, Lisboa: Imprensa de Ciências Sociais, 2007. |
| 2004 | Morten Rasmussen | Joining the European Communities—Denmark's Road to EC Membership, 1961–1973 [EUI]. |
| 2005 | Aoife Ni Lochlainn | 'A Question of Allegiance?' Ideology, Agency and Structure: British-based Unions in Ireland, 1922–1960 [EUI]. |
| 2005 | Steffen Prauser | Rom in deutscher Hand. Die deutsche Besatzungszeit in der ewigen Stadt 1943/44 [EUI]. |
| 2005 | Stephanie Seul | Appeasement und Propaganda, 1938–1940, Chamberlains Außenpolitik zwischen NS-Regierung und deutschem Volk [EUI]. |
| 2005 | Markus Wien | Markt und Modernisierung. Deutsch-Bulgarische Wirtschaftsbeziehungen 1918–1944 in ihren konzeptionellen Grundlagen [EUI] published as *Markt und Modernisierung: Deutsch-bulgarische Wirtschaftsbeziehungen 1918–1944 in ihren konzeptionellen Grundlagen*, Munich: R. Oldenbourg Verlag, 2007. |
| 2006 | Lucia Coppolaro | Trade and Politics across the Atlantic: The European Economic Community and the United States of America in the GATT Negotiations of the Kennedy Round (1962–1967) [EUI]. |

# Contributors

## EDITORS

**Fernando Guirao** is Jean Monnet Professor of European Integration History at Pompeu Fabra University (Barcelona, Spain), member of the Editorial Board of the *Journal of European Integration History*, the only international peer-reviewed journal in its field, and member of the European Union Liaison Committee of Historians, a Committee established in 1982 to disseminate research on the postwar history of Europe, to advise the European Community and facilitate access to research facilities, to encourage academic research, promote new areas of historical research, and to promote cooperation between European universities. His best-known publication is *Spain and the Reconstruction of Western Europe, 1945–57: Challenge and Response*, London and New York: Macmillan/ St. Martin's Press, 1998. At present he is completing two monographs: *Franco's Spain and the Integration of Europe, 1950–1975: Dealing with Dictatorships*; and *The Role of the European Community in the Spanish Transit towards Democracy, 1969–77*. His five most recent publications appear in: *Nota d'Economia* 88 (2007): 41–57; *Beyond the Customs Union: The European Community's Quest for Deepening, Widening and Completion, 1969–1975*, 2007; *Economía y economistas españoles en la Guerra Civil*, vol. 2, 2009; *Journal of European Integration History* 16: 2 (2010); (coauthor Del Pero, Gavín, and Varsori) *Democrazie: L'Europa meridionale e la fine delle dittature*, 2010.

**Frances M. B. Lynch** is reader in French studies at the University of Westminster where she has run a Master's degree program in European studies for several years. She gained her Ph.D. in economic history and taught in this field for fifteen years at the University of Manchester. She has conducted a number of research projects focusing on the transformation of the French economy and France's role in the international economy under the Fourth Republic, technological cooperation in Europe, and most recently on the subject of the history of personal taxation and of fiscal harmonization in Europe. Her most significant publications include: (with Alan S. Milward, Ruggero Ranieri, Federico Romero, and Vibeke Sørensen) *The Frontier of National Sovereignty: History and Theory, 1945–1992*, London: Routledge, 1993; reprinted in *The Economic Development of the EEC*, 1997; *France and the International Economy: From Vichy to the Treaty of Rome*, 1997; *Contemporary European History* 9:1 (2000).

As a result of an ESRC-funded research project she has produced an interactive computer program, known as EuroPTax, which calculates what individuals and households, at all levels of income, have paid in personal taxes and social security contributions in nine west European countries in the period of 1958 to 2007. This database forms part of the UK Data Archive (Study no. 6358; EuroPTax Who Pays for the State? The Evolution of Personal Taxation in Post-war Europe, 1958–2007), where it can be freely accessed by the international community.

**Sigfrido M. Ramírez Pérez** is currently a researcher and member of the international steering committee within the Permanent Group for the Study of the Automobile Industry and its Employees (GERPISA), Ecole Normale Supérieure Cachan (Paris), where he works for the project 'The European Government of Industries' financed by the French Agency for Research. He graduated in contemporary history, political sciences, and foreign languages from the Universities of Lyon III (France) and Granada (Spain) and read graduate courses in economics, political sciences, and sociology at the University of California, Berkeley and the *Ecole des Hautes Etudes en Sciences Sociales* before obtaining a Ph.D. in History and Civilization from the European University Institute, Florence, in 2007. Until 2010 he was postdoctoral research fellow of the Spanish Foundation of Science and Technology at the Department of Institutional Analysis and Public Management of the University Bocconi in Milan (Italy). Recent publications in English and French appear in: *Europe organisée, Europé du libre-échange*, 2007; *From Common Market to European Union Building: 50 Years of the Rome Treaties, 1957–2007*, 2008; *Histoire, Economie et Société*, March 2008; *The History of the European Union: Origins of a Trans- and Supranational Polity 1950–1972*, 2009; *Transnational Networks in Regional Integration: Governing Europe 1945–1983*, 2010; *Trends in Technological Innovation and the European Construction: the Emerging of Enduring Dynamics*, 2010.

## CHAPTER AUTHORS

**Charles Barthel**, head of the *Centre d'études et de recherches européennes Robert Schuman*, Luxembourg, secretary general of the editorial board of the *Journal of European Integration History.* Recent publications appear in: *Robert Schuman et les pères de l'Europe*, 2008; *The Bank of the European Union: The EIB, 1958–2008*, 2009; and (with Brandt, Kohl, and Schroeder) *Terres rouges: Histoire de la sidérurgie luxembourgeoise*, 2010.

**Maud Anne Bracke** is a lecturer in Modern European history at the University of Glasgow. She has published numerous articles in journals including *Contemporary European History*, *European History Quarterly*, *Journal of European Integration History*, *Women's History Review*, and *Modern Italy*, dealing with the Prague Spring, the French and Italian Left, and May 1968. A notable recent publication is: *Which Socialism, Whose Détente? West European Communism and the 1968 Czechoslovak Crisis*, 2007. She is currently preparing a monograph on Italian second-wave feminism in an international context.

**Lucia Coppolaro** is a postdoctoral reseacher at the Instituto de Ciências Sociais da Universidade de Lisboa, Portugal. She holds a Ph.D. from the European University Institute, Florence (2006). Publications appear in: *Visions, Votes and Vetoes*, 2006; *Beyond the Customs Union: The European Community's Quest for Deepening, Widening and Completion, 1969–1975*, 2007; *Orderly Change: International Monetary Relations Since Bretton Woods*, 2008.

**James Ellison** is reader in international history, Department of History, Queen Mary, University of London. His main publications include: *Threatening Europe: Britain and the Creation of the European Community, 1955–1958*, 2000; *The United States, Britain and the Transatlantic Crisis: Rising to the Gaullist Challenge, 1963–68*, 2007; and 'Stabilising the West and looking to the East', in *European Integration and the Cold War*, 2007.

**David W. Ellwood** is associate professor in international history, University of Bologna, and professorial lecturer in European-American relations, Johns Hopkins University, SAIS, Bologna Center. His most recent publications in English appear in: *Transatlantica*, 2009; *Defining the Atlantic Community: Culture, Intellectuals and Policies in the Mid-Twentieth Century*, 2010; *On the Idea of America: Perspectives from the Engelsberg seminar, 2009*, 2010.

**Hans Otto Frøland** is professor of European contemporary history, Department of History and Classical Studies, Norwegian University of Science and Technology, Trondheim, Norway. His most recent foreign-language publications appear in: *Scandinavian Economic History Review* 2–3 (2004); *Grenzen der Wiedergutmachung: Die Entschädigung für NS-Verfolgte in Ost- und West-Europa, 1945–2000*, 2006;

*Contemporary European History* 15: 4 (2006); *Pathbreakers: Small European Countries Responding to Globalisation and Deglobalisation*, 2008; *Between Nordic Ideology, Economic Interests and Political Reality. New Perspectives on Nordek*, 2010.

**John Gillingham** is University of Missouri Board of Curators Professor. Publications include: *Coal, Steel and the Rebirth of Europe, 1945–1955: The Germans and French from Ruhr Conflict to Economic Community*, 1991; reprinted, 2005; *European Integration, 1950–2003: Superstate or New Market Economy*, 2003; *Design for a New Europe*, 2006; *Progetto per una nuova Europa*, 2009.

**Anjo G. Harryvan** is a lecturer in international relations at Groningen University. His main publications in English include: (with J. van der Harst) *Documents on European Union*, 1997, and *Max Kohnstamm: A European's Life and Work*, 2011; *In Pursuit of Influence: The Netherlands' European Policy during the Formative Years of the European Union, 1952–1973*, 2009.

**Guðmundur Jónsson** is professor of history, University of Iceland in Reykjavík. He is the editor (with Magnússon) of *Icelandic Historical Statistics*, 1997, and his main publications in English appear in *Scandinavian Economic History Review* 41: 2 (1993); *Exploring Economic Growth: Essays in Measurement and Analysis*, 2004; *Pathbreakers. Small European Countries Responding to Globalisation and Deglobalisation*, 2008, and *EFTA 1960–2010: Elements of 50 Years of European History*, 2010.

**Pedro Lains** is research professor at the Instituto de Ciências Sociais, University of Lisbon, and visiting professor at Católica-Lisbon School of Business and Economics. His most recent publications in English include: *Classical Trade Protectionism, 1815–1914*, 2006; (with V. Pinilla) (eds.) *Agriculture and Economic Development in Europe since 1870*, 2009; (with J. L. Cardoso) (eds.) *Paying for the Liberal State: The Rise of Public Finances in Nineteenth Century Europe*, 2010. Other publications appear in *Research in Economic History* 24 (2007); *Open Economies Review*, 19: 5 (2008); *Historical Research* 81 (August 2008).

**Johnny Laursen** is associate professor of contemporary European history, Aarhus University, Denmark. His most recent publications include: 'The Enlargement of the European Community, 1950–95', in Loth, *Experiencing Europe* (2009); 'The Supranational Seven?', in Gehler, *From Common Market to European Union* (2009); *Politiets Efterretningstjeneste 1945–68* (The Danish Security and Intelligence Service, 1945–68) (2009).

**Wilfried Loth** is professor of modern and contemporary history at the University of Duisburg-Essen / Germany and Chairman of the European Union Liaison Committee of Historians. He has authored numerous publications on the history of political Catholicism, contemporary France, the cold war, and European integration. Most recently: *Die Sowjetunion und die deutsche Frage: Studien zur sowjetischen Deutschlandpolitik von Stalin bis Chruschtschow*, 2007; (with Georges-Henri Soutou) (eds.) *The Making of Détente: Eastern and Western Europe in the Cold War, 1965–75*, 2008; *Experiencing Europe: 50 Years of European Construction, 1957–2007*, 2009.

**Charles S. Maier** is the Leverett Saltonstall Professor of History at Harvard University, where he teaches courses on the era of the World Wars, international history (with Niall Ferguson), and modern global history. He has recently been a senior fellow at the Woodrow Wilson Center for Scholars in Washington, DC, where he has been working on a history of territoriality since 1500. His books include: *In Search of Stability: Explorations in Historical Political Economy*, 1988; *The Unmasterable Past: History, Holocaust, and German National Identity*, 1988; *Dissolution: The Crisis of Communism and the End of East Germany*, 1997; *Among Empires: American Ascendancy and its Predecessors*, 2006.

**Larry Neal** is professor emeritus of economics at the University of Illinois at Urbana-Champaign and founding director of the European Union Center at Illinois. Currently, he is visiting professor at the London School of Economics and previously at UCLA. He has authored numerous articles in American and European economic and financial history. His main publications include: *The Rise of Financial Capitalism: International Capital Markets in the Age of Reason*, 1990; (with Daniel Barbezat) *The Economics of the European Union and the Economies of Europe*, 1998; (with Rondo Cameron) *A Concise Economic History of the World*, 4th ed., 2002; *The Economics of Europe and the European Union*, 2007; (with Jeremy Atack) *The Origins and Development of Financial Markets and Institutions*, 2009.

**Michael Newman** is emeritus professor at London Metropolitan University and holds a Personal Jean Monnet Chair in European studies. He has written widely on European integration and jointly organized two seminars with Alan Milward on the issue of allegiance, leading to his earlier paper 'Allegiance, Legitimation, Democracy and the European Union' (European University Institute Working Paper, 2001). He has also published several books on the Left, and has recently worked on issues of peace and conflict. His latest book, *Humanitarian Intervention: Confronting the Contradictions*, was published by Hurst & Co.

and Columbia University Press in 2009, and he is now carrying out research on transitional justice.

**Eamonn Noonan** holds a doctorate from the EUI, where he was a student of Alan Milward. His dissertation dealt with British and German commercial policy in the 1930s. He previously studied at University College Cork and at the Institute for European History in Mainz. He has worked in the Irish foreign service and as an official of the European Parliament, and in 2005 became chief clerk of Norway's Contact Committee on Immigration (KIM). He is now CEO of the Campbell Collaboration, an academic network devoted to applied social science research. Publications: 'Wurttemberg's Exporters and German Protectionism, 1931–36' (EUI working paper), European University Institute, 1987; 'Choosing Confrontation: Commercial Policy in Britain and Germany, 1929–1936' (EUI working paper), European University Institute, 1995.

**Kiran Klaus Patel** is professor of European and global history at the University of Maastricht. His most recent publications include: (ed. with Mauch) *The United States and Germany during the 20th Century: Competition and Convergence*, 2010; (ed. with Conway) *Europeanization in the Twentieth Century: Historical Approaches*, 2009; *Europäisierung wider Willen: Die Rolle der Bundesrepublik in der Agrarintegration der EWG, 1955–1975*, 2009; (ed.) *Fertile Ground for Europe? The History of European Integration and the Common Agricultural Policy since 1945*, 2009.

**Ruggero Ranieri** is currently visiting professor at the Universities of Padova and Perugia. He is also president of the Uguccione Ranieri di Sorbello Foundation. He is currently working on three chapters on the post-1945 history of the IRI-Finsider for the official project 'Storia dell'IRI'. Selected publications: *The Frontier of National Sovereignty—History and Theory, 1945–1992*, 1993 (2nd ed. 1994); (with Aylen and Gibellieri) (eds.) *The Steel Industry in the New Millennium*, 2 vols., London, 1998; (with Tosi) (eds.) *La Comunità Europea del Carbone e dell'Acciaio (1952–2002): Gli esiti del Trattato in Europa e in Italia*, 2004; (with Aylen) (eds.) *Ribbon of Fire. The History of the Wide Strip Mill in Europe*, forthcoming.

**Federico Romero** is professor of history of postwar European cooperation and integration at the European University Institute. His publications include: *Emigrazione e Integrazione Europea, 1945–1973*, 1991; *The United States and the European Trade Union Movement, 1944–1951*, 1993; *Storia internazionale del Novecento*, 2001; (with Silvio Pons) (eds.) *Reinterpreting the End of the Cold War*, 2005; (with Mario Del Pero) (eds.) *Le crisi transatlantiche: Continuità e trasformazioni*, 2007; *Storia della guerra fredda*, 2009.

**Ben Rosamond** is professor of political science at the University of Copenhagen. His main publications include: *Theories of European Integration*, 2000; (with Barrie Axford, Gary K. Browning, and Richard Huggins) *Politics: An Introduction*, 2002 (2nd ed.); *Globalization and the European Union*, forthcoming.

**Jan van der Harst** is professor of history and theory of European integration at the University of Groningen. His main publications include: (with Anjo G. Harryvan) *Documents on European Union*, 1997, and *Max Kohnstamm: A European's Life and Work*, 2011; *The Atlantic Priority: Dutch Defence Policy at the Time of the European Defence Community*, 2003; (ed.) *Beyond the Customs Union: The European Community's Quest for Deepening, Widening and Completion, 1969–1975*, 2007.

**Tobias Witschke** works for the European Commission's Directorate General for Regional Policy. He completed his Ph.D. at the European University Institute, Florence, under the supervision of Alan S. Milward on the historical roots of European competition policy (ECSC) and the 'reconcentration' of the West German steel industry from 1950 to 1963. He has a Master's degree in European studies from the College of Europe in Natolin/Poland. His main publications are: 'Steel prices, trade and producers' strategies in the European Coal and Steel Community from 1952 to 1964', in *Transnational Companies. 19th and 20th centuries*, 2002; and *Gefahr für den Wettbewerb? Die Fusionskontrolle der Europäischen Gemeinschaft für Kohle und Stahl und die "Rekonzentration" der Ruhrstahlindustrie, 1950–1963*, 2009.

**Vera Zamagni** is professor of economic history at the University of Bologna, and visiting professor of European economic history at the Bologna Center of the Johns Hopkins University. Her most recent publications in English include: *Revue Economique* 51: 2 (2000); *Italy Since 1945*, 2000; *Business History Review*, spring 2006; *The Global Chemical Industry in the Age of the Petrochemical Revolution*, 2006.

# Bibliography

Aarts, Kees, and Henk van der Kolk, eds. *Nederlanders en Europa: Het referendum over de Europese grondwet*. Amsterdam: Bert Bakker, 2005.

Abelshauser, Werner. 'Germany: Guns, Butter, and Economic Miracles'. In Harrison, *The Economics of World War II*, 122–176.

Abrams, Philip. 'The Failure of Social Reform, 1918–1920'. *Past and Present* 24: 1 (1963): 43–64.

Acemoglu, Daron, Simon H. Johnson, and James A. Robinson. 'The Rise of Europe: Atlantic Trade, Institutional Change and Economic Growth'. *American Economic Review* 95: 3 (2005): 546–579.

Af Malmborg, Mikael. *Den ståndaktiga nationalstaten: Sverige och den västeuropeiska integrationen, 1945–59*. Lund: Lund University Press, 1994.

Aga-Rossi, Elena, and Gaetano Quagliariello. *L'altra faccia della luna: I rapporti tra PCI, PCF e Unione sovietica*. Bologna: Il Mulino, 1997.

Aldcroft, Derek H. *The European Economy, 1914–1970*. New York: St Martin's Press, 1977. Most recent update: *The European Economy, 1914–2000*. London: Routledge, 2001.

———. *Europe's Third World: The European Periphery in the Interwar Years*. London: Ashgate, 2006.

———. Review of *The Development of the Economies of Continental Europe*, by Milward and Saul. *History* 64: 210 (1979): 144–145.

Aldenhoff-Hübinger, Rita. *Agrarpolitik und Protektionismus: Deutschland und Frankreich im Vergleich, 1879–1914*. Göttingen: Vandenhoeck & Ruprecht, 2002.

Alter, Karen J., and David Steinberg. 'The Theory and Reality of the European Coal and Steel Community'. In *Making History: European Integration and Institutional Change at Fifty*, edited by Sophie Meunier and Kathleen R. McNamara, 89–104. Oxford: Oxford University Press, 2007.

*Alþingistíðindi*. Vol. 1928. Reykjavík: 1933.

Amendola, Giorgio. 'Movimento e organizzazione delle masse'. *Critica Marxista* 5–6 (September–December 1963).

———. 'Unità e autonomia della classe operaia'. *Critica Marxista* 1 (January–February 1963).

Amstrup, Niels. 'Nordisk samarbejde—myte eller realitet? Planerne om økonomisk samarbejde fra 1945 til 1950'. In *Nær og Fjern: Samspillet mellem indre og ydre politik*, edited by Tage Kaarsted, Knud Larsen, Ole Karup Petersen, and Jørgen Sevaldsen, 155–180. København: Forlaget Politiske Studier, 1980.

Amyot, Grant. *The Italian Communist Party: The Crisis of the Popular Front Strategy*. London: Croom Helm, 1981.

Andersen, Ketil Gjølme. *Flaggskip i fremmed eie: Hydro, 1905–1945*. Oslo: Pax Forlag, 2005.

———, and Gunnar Yttri. *Et forsøk verdt: forskning og utvikling i Norsk Hydro gjennom 90 år*. Oslo: Universitetsforlaget, 1997.

Anderson, Perry. *The New Old World*. London and New York: Verso, 2009.

———. 'Under the Sign of the Interim'. *London Review of Books* (4 January 1996): 13–17. Reprinted in Anderson and Gowan, *The Question of Europe*, 51–74.

———, and Peter Gowan, eds. *The Question of Europe*. London and New York: Verso, 1997.

Anderson, Stanley V. 'Negotiations for the Nordic Council'. *Nordisk Tidsskrift for International Ret* 33: 1 (1963): 22–33.

———. 'The Nordic Council and the 1962 Helsinki Agreement'. *Nordisk Tidsskrift for International Ret* 34: 2 (1964): 278–300.

———. *The Nordic Council: A Study in Scandinavian Regionalism*. Seattle and London: University of Washington Press; New York: The American-Scandinavian Foundation, 1967.

Andreev, E., L. Darskii, and T. Khar'kova. 'Otsenka liudskikh poter' v period Velikoi Otechestvennoi voiny'. *Vestnik statistiki* 10 (1990): 26–27.

Andrén, Nils. 'Nordic Integration and Cooperation—Illusion or Reality'. *Cooperation and Conflict* 19: 3 (1984): 251–262.

———. 'Nordisk integration—synspunkter och problemställningar'. *Internasjonal Politikk* 4: 4 (1966): 370–387.

———. 'A Note on a Note'. *Cooperation and Conflict* 2: 2 (1967): 235–237.

Andrzejewski, Stanislaw. *Military Organisation and Society*. London: Routledge & Kegan Paul, 1954.

Angell, Norman. *The Great Illusion*. New York and London: G. P. Putnam's Sons, 1913 (first published as *Europe's Optical Illusion*. London: Simpkin, Marshall & Co., 1909).

Anonymous. 'Guns and Butter'. Review of *The German Economy at War*, by Milward. *The Economist*, 15 May 1965: 772.

Anonymous. Review of *War, Economy and Society*, by Milward. *The Economist*, 11 June 1977: 139.

Ásgeirsson, Ólafur. *Iðnbylting hugarfarsins: Átök um atvinnuþróun á Íslandi, 1900–1940*. Vol. 9: *Sagnfræðirannsóknir*. Reykjavík: Bókaútgáfa Menningarsjóðs, 1989.

Ashworth, J. Review of *The Development of the Economies of Continental Europe*, by Milward and Saul. *The Economic Journal* 88: 349 (March 1978): 178–179.

Atack, Jeremy, and Larry Neal, eds. *The Origins and Development of Financial Markets and Institutions: From the Seventeenth Century to the Present*. Cambridge and New York: Cambridge University Press, 2009.

Augustinos, Gerasimos. 'Development through the Market in Greece: The State, Entrepreneurs, and Society'. In *Diverse Paths to Modernity in Southeastern Europe: Essays in National Development*, edited by G. Augustinos, 89–133. New York: Greenwood Press, 1991.

Aunesluoma, Juhana. 'An Elusive Partnership: Europe, Economic Co-operation and British Policy towards Scandinavia 1949–1951'. *JEIH* 8: 1 (2002): 103–119.

Axford, Barrie, Gary K. Browning, Richard Huggins, and Ben Rosamond. *Politics: An Introduction*. London and New York: Routledge, 2002 (2nd ed.).

Azéma, Jean-Pierre. 'Vichy'. In Azéma and Bédarida, *1938–1948: Les années de tourmente*, 1083–1092.

———, and François Bédarida, eds. *1938–1948: Les années de tourmente; de Munich à Prague: dictionnaire critique*. Paris: Flammarion, 1995.

Baines, Dudley. review of *War, Economy and Society*, by Milward. *The Economic History Review* 31: 4 (November 1978): 693–694.

Bairoch, Paul. *Commerce extérieur et développement économique de l'Europe au XIX siècle.* Paris: Mouton, 1976.

Bajon, Philip Robert. 'Die konstitutionelle Krise der Europäischen Gemeinschaften 1965–66: Ursachen, Verlauf und Folgen.' Ph.D. thesis, Paris IV–Duisburg-Essen, 2010.

Baker, Ray Stannard, and Wm. E. Dodd, eds. *The Public Papers of Woodrow Wilson*, Vols. 5-6. *War and Peace: Presidential Messages, Addresses and Public Papers (1917–1924).* New York: Harper & Brothers, 1925–1927.

Baldwin, Richard E. 'A Domino Theory of Regionalism.' In *Expanding Membership of the European Union*, edited by R. E. Baldwin, P. Haaparanta, and J. Kiander. Cambridge: Cambridge University Press, 1995, 25–48.

Bange, Oliver. *The EEC Crisis of 1963: Kennedy, Macmillan, de Gaulle and Adenauer in Conflict.* London: Macmillan, 2000.

Bardach, Eugene. *The Implementation Game: What Happens After a Bill Becomes Law.* Cambridge: MIT Press, 1977.

Barents, René. *Een grondwet voor Europa: achtergronden en commentaar.* Deventer: Kluwer, 2005.

Barjot, Dominique, ed. *Catching Up with America: Productivity Missions and the Diffusion of American Economic and Technological Influence after the Second World War.* Paris: Presses de l'Université de Paris-Sorbonne, 2002.

Barnet, Richard. *The Alliance: America, Europe, Japan: Makers of the Post-War World.* New York: Simon & Schuster, 1983.

Barthel, Charles. 'Un aspect particulier de la culture politique luxembourgeoise: Joseph Bech et l'art de concilier les affaires étrangères avec la diplomatie du grand capital sidérurgique'. In *Robert Schuman et les pères de l'Europe*, edited by Sylvain Schirmann, Brussels: Peter Lang, 2008: 235–256.

———. *Bras de fer: Les maîtres de forges luxembourgeois, entre les débuts difficiles de l'UEBL et le Locarno sidérurgique des cartels internationaux, 1918–1929.* Luxembourg: Saint-Paul, 2006.

———. 'Une "crise manifeste" jamais déclarée: La Haute Autorité, le Club des Sidérurgistes et les cartels censés assainir les marchés de l'acier (1961–1965)'. In *'Ces chers voisins': L'Allemagne, la Belgique et la France en Europe du XIXe au XXIe siècle*, edited by Michel Dumoulin, Jürgen Elvert, and Sylvain Schirmann. Stuttgart: Franz Steiner Verlag, 2010.

———. 'De l'entente belgo-luxembourgeoise à la Convention de Bruxelles, 1948–1954'. In Dumoulin et al., *L'Europe du Patronat*, 29–62.

———. 'The problematic transfer of the EIB to the Grand Duchy'. In *The Bank of the European Union: The EIB, 1958–2008*, edited by Michel Dumoulin and Eric Bussière. Luxembourg: European Investment Bank, 2009.

———, Josef Brandt, Michel Kohl, and Corinne Schroeder, *Terres rouges. Histoire de la sidérurgie luxembourgeoise*, vol. 2. Luxembourg: Centre d'études et de recherches européennes Robert Schuman and Archives nationales de Luxembourg, 2010.

Bartlett, C. J. *British Foreign Policy in the Twentieth Century.* Basingstoke: Macmillan, 1989.

Bartolini, Stefano. *Restructuring Europe: Centre Formation, System Building and Political Structuring between the Nation-state and the European Union.* Oxford and New York: Oxford University Press, 2005.

Beck, Ulrich, and Edgar Grande. *Cosmopolitan Europe.* Cambridge: Polity Press, 2007.

Beckett, Ian F. W. 'Total War'. In *Warfare in the Twentieth Century: Theory and Practice*, edited by Colin McInnes and G. D. Sheffield, 1–23. London: Unwin Hyman, 1988. Reprinted in Emsley, Marwick, and Simpson, *War, Peace and Social Change in Twentieth Century Europe*, 26–44.

Bédarida, François. 'L'histoire de la résistance : Lectures d'hier, chantiers de demain'. *Vingtième Siècle: Revue d'histoire* 11 (July–September 1986): 75–90.

Beevor, Anthony, and Artemis Cooper. *Paris after the Liberation, 1944–1949.* London: Penguin, 2007.

Behrman, Greg. *The Most Noble Adventure: The Marshall Plan and the Time When America Helped Save Europe.* New York: Free Press, 2007.

Berend, Ivan T. *History Derailed: Central and Eastern Europe in the Long Nineteenth Century.* Berkeley: University of California Press, 2003.

———, and György Ránki. *The European Periphery and Industrialization, 1780–1914.* Cambridge: Cambridge University Press, 1982.

Berghahn, Volker. *The Americanization of West German Industry.* Leamington: Berg Publishers, 1986.

Berlinguer, Enrico, and Antonio Tato. *La politica internazionale dei comunisti italiani.* Rome: Editori Riuniti, 1976.

Besselink, Leonard F. M., ed. *Grondwet voor Europa: wettekst en vergelijking met de geldende basisverdragen.* Den Haag: SDU, 2005.

Birkenfeld, Wolfgang. Review of *The German Economy at War*, by Milward. *Vierteljahrschrift für Sozial- und Wirtschaftsgeschichte* 53: 4 (December 1966): 570–573.

Bischof, Günter, and Dieter Stiefel, eds. *Images of the Marshall Plan in Europe: Films, Photographs, Exhibits, Posters.* Innsbruck: Studien Verlag, 2009.

Bishop, Simon, and Michael Walker. *The Economics of EC Competition Law: Concepts, Application and Measurement.* London: Sweet & Maxwell, 2010.

Bissell, Richard M., Jr. 'The Impact of Rearmament on the Free World Economy'. *Foreign Affairs* 29 (April 1951): 385–405.

Bjørn, Claus, ed. *Det danske landbrugs historie*, vol. 3, *1810–1914.* Odense: Landbohistorisk selskab, 1988.

Blackmer, Donald, and Annie Kriegel. *The International Role of the Communist Parties of Italy and France.* Cambridge, MA: Harvard University Center of International Affairs / Harvard University Press, 1975.

Block, Fred, and Peter Evans, 'The State and the Economy.' In *Handbook of Economic Sociology*, edited by Neil Smelser and Richard Swedberg, 505–527. 2nd ed. Princeton: Princeton University Press, 2005.

Blok, Dirk Peter et al. *Algemene Geschiedenis der Nederlanden*, vol. 15. Bussum: Fibula-Van Dishoeck, 1982.

Bluche, Lorraine, and Kiran Klaus Patel. 'Der Europäer als Bauer: Das Motiv des bäuerlichen Familienbetriebs in Westeuropa nach 1945'. In *Der Europäer—ein Konstrukt: Wissensbestände—Diskurse—Praktiken*, edited by Lorraine Bluche, Veronika Lipphardt, and Kiran Klaus Patel, 135–157. Göttingen: Wallstein, 2009.

Boel, Bent. *The European Productivity Agency and Transatlantic Relations, 1953–1961.* Copenhagen: Museum Tusculanum Press, 2003.

Bohn, Robert. *Reichskommissariat Norwegen: Nationalsozialistische Neuordnung und Kriegswirtschaft.* Munich: Oldenburg Verlag, 2000.

Bossuat, Gérard. *La France, l'aide américaine et la construction européenne, 1944–1954.* 2 vols. Paris: Imprimerie Nationale, 1992 (2nd ed., 1997).

Bouwman, Bernard. 'De Britse historicus Milward zet vraagtekens: "Die hele Marshallhulp was niet meer dan een druppel in de oceaan".' *NRC Handelsblad*, 24 (May 1997), 21.

Bowley, Arthur L. *Some Economic Consequences of the Great War.* London: Thornton Butterworth Ltd, 1930.

Bracke, Maud. *Which Socialism, Whose Détente? West European Communism and the 1968 Czechoslovak Crisis.* Budapest and New York: Central European University Press, 2007. Italian translation with Carocci Editore, 2008.

Brand, Urs. Review of *The New Order and the French Economy*, by Milward. *Schweizerische Zeitschrift für Geschichte* 21 (1971): 202–203.

Breit, Frederick J. Review of *The Reconstruction of Western Europe*, by Milward. *The Annals of the American Academy of Political and Social Science* 478 (March 1985): 187–188.

Brinkley, Douglas, and Richard T. Griffiths, eds. *John F. Kennedy and Europe.* Baton Rouge: Louisiana State University Press, 1999.

Brivati, Brian, and Harriet Jones, eds. *From Reconstruction to Integration: Britain and Europe since 1945.* Leicester: Leicester University Press, 1993.

Broad, Roger, and Virginia Preston, eds. *Moored to the Continent? Britain and European Integration.* London: Institute of Historical Research, 2001.

Broadberry, Stephen, and Mark Harrison, eds. *The Economics of World War I.* Cambridge: Cambridge University Press, 2005.

———, and Kevin O'Rourke, eds. *The Cambridge Economic History of Modern Europe.* 2 vols. Cambridge: Cambridge University Press, 2010.

Brustein, William. 'An Endogenous Explanation of French Internal Peripheries'. In *Internal Peripheries in European History*, edited by Hans-Heinrich Nolte, 91–117. Göttingen: Muster-Schmidt Verlag, 1991.

Buchheim, Christoph. 'Unternehmen in Deutschland und NS-Regime, 1933–1945. Versuch einer Synthese'. *Historische Zeitschrift* 282: 2 (2006): 351–390.

Budrass, Lutz. *Flugzeugindustrie und Luftrüstung in Deutschland, 1918–1945.* Düsseldorf: Droste Verlag, 1998.

———. 'Unternehmer im Nationalsozialismus: Der „Sonderbevollmächtigte des Generalfeldmarschalls Göring für die Herstellung der J. 88"'. In *Unternehmen zwischen Markt und Macht: Aspekte deutscher Unternehmens- und Industriegeschichte im 20 Jahrhundert*, edited by Werner Plumpe and Christian Kleinschmidt, 74–89. Essen: Klartext Verlag, 1992.

Bull, Hedley. *The Anarchical Society: A Study of Order in World Politics.* Basingstoke: Macmillan, 1977.

Bullen, Roger. 'Britain and "Europe" 1950–1957'. In Serra, *The Relaunching of Europe*, 315–338.

Burgess, Simon, and Geoffrey Edwards. 'The Six plus One: British Policy Making and the Question of European Economic Integration, 1955'. *International Affairs* 64: 3 (1988): 393–413.

Burk, Kathleen. 'The Marshall Plan: Filling in Some of the Blanks'. *Contemporary European History* 10: 2 (July 2001): 267–294.

Burn, Duncan L. *The Steel Industry, 1939–1959: A Study in Competition and Planning.* Cambridge: Cambridge University Press, 1961.

Bussière, Eric, ed. *Georges Pompidou face à la mutation économique de l'Occident, 1969–1974.* Paris: PUF, 2003.

Bynum, Caroline W. 'Perspectives, Connections & Objects: What's Happening in History Now?' *Daedalus* 138 (2009): 71–86.

Calleo, David P. *Rethinking Europe's Future.* Princeton, NJ: Princeton University Press, 2001.

Cameron, Rondo. *A Concise Economic History of the World: From Paleolithic Times to the Present.* New York and Oxford: Oxford University Press, 1989. With Larry Neal for its 4th ed., 2003.

———. Review of *The Development of the Economies of Continental Europe,* by Milward and Saul. *The American Historical Review*, 83: 3 (June 1978): 712–713.

Cappelletti, Mauro, Monica Seccombe, and Joseph Weiler. *Integration through Law: Europe and the American Federal Experience.* New York: Walter de Gruyter, 1985.

Cardoso, José Luís, and Pedro Lains. 'Public Finance in Portugal, 1796–1910'. In *Paying for the Liberal State: The Rise of Public Finance in Nineteenth Century Europe*, edited by Cardoso and Lains, 251–278. Cambridge: Cambridge University Press, 2010.

Cazes, Bernard, and Philippe Mioche, eds. *Modernisation ou décadence: Contribution à l'histoire du Plan Monnet et de la planification en France*. Aix-en-Provence: Publications de l'Université de Provence, 1990.

CEA (Confédération européenne de l'agriculture), ed. *Historique, organisation, activité: ouvrage publié à l'occasion du dixième anniversaire de la CEA, 1948–1958*. Brugg: Secrétariat général de la CEA, 1958.

Checkel, Jeffrey C. 'Constructivism and EU Politics'. In Jørgensen, Pollack, and Rosamond, *Handbook of European Union Politics*, 57–76.

Christiansen, Thomas, Knud Erik Jørgensen, and Antje Wiener, eds. *The Social Construction of Europe*. London, Thousand Oaks, New Delhi: Sage, 2001.

Cillekens, Caspar. 'Marshall-hulp: W-Europa uit klauwen Moskou houden'. *Brabants Dagblad*, 10 May 1997.

———. 'Minister vd Brink: Marshall-plan onontbeerlijk'. *De Stem*, 10 May 1997.

Cini, Michelle, and Lee McGowan. *Competition Policy in the European Union*. New York: Palgrave Macmillan, 1998.

Cipolla, Carlo. *Tra due culture: Introduzione alla storia economica*. Bologna: Il Mulino, 1988.

———, ed. *The Fontana Economic History of Europe*. Vol. 3: *The Industrial Revolution*. London and Glasgow: Collins/Fontana, 1973.

Clausen, C. A. Review of *The Fascist Economy in Norway*, by Milward. *Annals of the American Academy of Political and Social Science* 403 (September 1972): 191.

Clavel, Jean-Claude. 'La conférence de Milan'. *L'Information Agricole*, 1 April 1960.

Clavin, Patricia, and Kiran Klaus Patel. 'The Role of International Organizations in Europeanization: The Case of the League of Nations and the European Economic Community'. In *Europeanization in the Twentieth Century: Historical Approaches*, edited by Martin Conway and Kiran Klaus Patel, 110–131. New York: Palgrave, 2010.

Cleveland, Harold van Buren. *The Atlantic Idea and its European Rivals*. New York: MacGraw-Hill, 1966.

Comité intergouvernemental crée par la conférence de Messine, ed. *Rapport des chefs de délégation aux ministres des affaires étrangères*. Brussels: Secrétariat, 1956.

Commission sur la réforme de l'agriculture dans la C.E.E., ed. *Plan Mansholt / Rapport Vedel*. Paris: S.E.C.-L.A.F., 1969.

Communauté européenne, ed. *Recueil des documents de la Conférence agricole des Etats membres de la Communauté économique européenne à Stresa du 3 au 12 juillet 1958*. Luxembourg: Service des publications des Communautés européennes, 1958.

Conway, Martin, and Kiran Klaus Patel, eds. *Europeanization in the Twentieth Century: Historical Approaches*. New York: Palgrave - Macmillan, 2010.

Coppolaro, Lucia. 'The Empty Chair Crisis and the Kennedy Round of GATT Negotiations (1962–1967)'. In Palayret et al., *Visions, Votes and Vetoes*, 219–239.

———. 'Trade and Politics across the Atlantic: The European Economic Community and the United States of America in the GATT Negotiations of the Kennedy Round (1962–1967)'. Ph.D. thesis, European University Institute, Florence, 2006.

———. 'The United States and EEC enlargement (1969–1973): Reaffirming the Atlantic framework'. In J. van der Harst, *Beyond the Customs Union*, 135–162.

———. 'U.S. Payments Problems and the Kennedy Round of GATT Negotiations, 1961–1967'. In *Orderly Change: International Monetary Relations Since Bretton Woods*, edited by David M. Andrews. New York: Cornell University Press, 2008: 120–138.

Crafts, Nicholas F. R. 'The Golden Age of Economic Growth in Western Europe, 1950–1973'. *Economic History Review* 48: 3 (August 1995): 429–447.

———, and Gianni Toniolo, eds. *Economic Growth in Europe since 1945*. Cambridge: Cambridge University Press, 1996.

———. 'Post-war Growth: An Overview'. In Crafts and Toniolo, *Economic Growth in Europe*, 1–37.

Crouzet, François. Review of *The Economic Development of Continental Europe*, by Milward and Saul. *Revue d'histoire économique et social* 52 (1974): 460–461.

Cullis, Michael F. Review of *The Fascist Economy in Norway*, by Milward. *International Affairs* 48: 3 (July 1972): 505–507.

Curtis, Thomas B., and John R. Vastine. *The Kennedy Round and the Future of American Trade*. New York: Praeger, 1971.

Daalder, Hans. 'In Memory of Max Kohnstamm, First President of the EUI'. *EUI Review* (Winter 2010): 19–22.

Daddow, Oliver. *Britain and Europe since 1945: Historiographical Perspectives on Integration*. Manchester: Manchester University Press, 2004.

Dahl, Robert A. *Who Governs? Democracy and Power in an American City*. New Haven, CT: Yale University Press, 1961.

Daley, Anthony. *Steel, State, and Labor: Mobilization and Adjustment in France*. Pittsburgh: University of Pittsburgh Press, 1996.

David, Paul. 'Path Dependence: A Foundational Concept for Historical Social Science'. *Cliometrica* 1: 2 (2007): 91–114.

Dean, Vera Micheles. *Europe in Retreat*. New York: A. A. Knopf, 1939.

De Grazia, Victoria. *Irresistible Empire: America's Advance through 20th Century Europe*. Cambridge and London: Belknap Press, 2005.

Dell, Edmund. *The Schuman Plan and the British Abdication of Leadership in Europe*. Oxford: Oxford University Press, 1995.

DeLong, Bradford J., and Barry Eichengreen. 'The Marshall Plan: History's Most Successful Structural Adjustment Program'. Cambridge, MA: National Bureau of Economic Research working paper 3899, 1991. Reprinted in *Postwar Economic Reconstruction and Lessons for the East Today*, edited by Rudiger Dornbusch, Wilhelm Nölling, and Richard Layard, 189–230. Cambridge, MA: MIT Press, 1993.

Del Pero, Mario, Víctor Gavín, Fernando Guirao, and Antonio Varsori. *Democrazie: L'Europa meridionale e la fine delle dittature*. Milan: Mondatori Education—Quaderni di Storia—Le Monnier, 2010.

———, and Federico Romero, eds. *Le crisi transatlantiche. Continuità e trasformazioni*. Rome: Edizioni di Storia e Letteratura, 2007.

Demeulemeester, Jean-Luc, and Claude Diebolt. 'How Much Could Economics Gain from History: The Contribution of Econometrics'. *Cliometrica* 1: 1 (2007): 7–17.

Deutsch, Karl W. et al. *Political Community and the North Atlantic Area: International Organization in the Light of Historical Experience*. Princeton, NJ: Princeton University Press, 1957.

Deutsches Institut für Wirtschaftsforschung. *Die deutsche Industrie im Kriege, 1939–1945*. Berlin: Duncker & Humblot, 1954.

De Vries, Catherine E., and Kees Van Kersbergen. 'Interests, Identity and Political Allegiance in the European Union'. *Acta Politica* 42 (2007): 307–328.

Dewey, P. H. Review of *Agriculture and Food Supply in the Second World War*, edited by Martin and Milward. *The Economic History Review* (New Series) 40: 1 (February 1987): 151.

Diebold, William, Jr. *The Schuman Plan: A Study in Economic Cooperation, 1950–1959*. New York: Praeger, 1959.

———. *Trade and Payments in Western Europe: A Study in Economic Cooperation, 1947–51*. New York: Harper (for the Council on Foreign Relations), 1952.

Dierikx, Marc. *An Image of Freedom: The Netherlands and the United States, 1945 to the Present*. The Hague: SDU, 1997.

Dinan, Desmond, 'The Historiography of European Integration'. In Dinan, *Origins and Evolution*, 297–321.

———, ed. *Origins and Evolution of the European Union*. Oxford: Oxford University Press, 2006.

Directoraat-Generaal voor het Economische en Militaire Hulpprogramma, ed. *Herwonnen welvaart: De betekenis van het Marshallplan voor Nederland en de Europese samenwerking*. The Hague: DGEMH, 1954.

Directorate General for Agriculture and Rural Development. *On the Farm*. Brussels: European Union Publications Office, 2010.

Di Vaio, Gianfranco, and Jacob L. Weisdorf. 'Ranking Economic History Journals: A Citation-based Impact Adjusted Analysis'. *Cliometrica* 4: 1 (2010): 1–17.

Donohue, Kathleen M. *Freedom from Want: American Liberalism and the Idea of the Consumer*. Baltimore: Johns Hopkins University Press, 2003.

Dormois, Jean-Pierre, and Pedro Lains, eds. *Classic Trade Protectionism 1815–1914*. London: Routledge, 2006.

Dudley, G. F., and J. J. Richardson. *Politics and Steel in Britain, 1967–1988*. Aldershot & Brookfield: Dartmouth, 1990.

Dumoulin, Michel, ed. *La Commission Européenne, 1958–1972: Histoire et mémoire d'une institution*. Luxembourg: OPOCE, 2007.

———, René Girault, and Gilbert Trausch, eds. *L'Europe du Patronat: De la guerre froide aux années soixante*. Berne: Peter Lang, 1993.

Dyson, Kenneth. *The Road to Maastricht: Negotiating Economic and Monetary Union*. Oxford: Oxford University Press, 1999.

Easton, David. 'The Decline of Modern Political Theory'. *Journal of Politics* 13: 1 (1951): 36–58.

———. *The Political System: An Inquiry into the State of Political Science*. New York: Alfred A. Knopf, 1953.

Eckert, Sandra. 'Between Commitment and Control: Varieties of Delegation in the European Postal Sector'. *Journal of European Public Policy* 17: 8 (2010): 1231–1252.

Edgerton, David. *Britain's War Machine: Weapons, Resources and Experts in the Second World War*. London: Penguin, 2011.

Eggertsson, Þráinn. *Imperfect Institutions: Possibilities and Limits of Reform*. Ann Arbor: University of Michigan Press, 2004.

Eichengreen, Barry J. *The European Economy since 1945: Coordinated Capitalism and Beyond*. Princeton and Oxford: Princeton University Press, 2007.

———, ed. *Europe's Post-War Recovery*. Cambridge: Cambridge University Press, 1995.

———. 'Mainspring of Economic Recovery in Postwar Europe'. In Eichengreen, *Europe's Post-War Recovery*, 3–35.

———. *Reconstructing Europe's Trade and Payments: The European Payments Union*. Manchester: Manchester University Press, 1993.

Eichholtz, Dietrich. *Geschichte der deutschen Kriegswirtschaft, 1939–1945*. Vol. 1: *1939–1941*. Berlin: Akademie-Verlag, 1969.

———. *Geschichte der deutschen Kriegswirtschaft, 1939–1945*. Vol. 2: *1941–1943*. Berlin: Akademie-Verlag, 1985.

———. 'Die Norwegen-Denkschrift des IG-Farben-Konzerns von 1941'. *Bulletin des Arbeitskreises Zweiter Weltkrieg* 1–2 (1974): 4–66.

Eliassen, Finn-Einar, Jorgen Mikkelsen, and Bjorn Poulsen. 'Historical Regions and Regional History in the Nordic Countries'. In *Regional Integration in Early Modern Scandinavia*, edited by F.-E. Eliassen, J. Mikkelsen, and B. Poulsen, 7–13. Odense: Odense University Press, 2001.

Ellersieck, Heinz E. Review of *The Fascist Economy in Norway*, by Milward. *The American Historical Review* 78: 2 (April 1973): 457–458.

Ellison, James. 'Britain and Europe'. In *A Companion to Contemporary Britain, 1939–2000*, edited by Paul Addison and Harriet Jones, 517–538. Oxford: Blackwell, 2005.

———. 'Stabilising the West and looking to the East: Anglo-American relations, Europe and détente, 1965 to 1967'. In Ludlow, *European Integration and the Cold War*, 105–127.

———. *Threatening Europe: Britain and the Creation of the European Community, 1955–58*. Basingstoke: Macmillan, 2000.

———. *The United States, Britain and the Transatlantic Crisis: Rising to the Gaullist Challenge, 1963–68*. Basingstoke: Palgrave Macmillan, 2007.

Ellwood, David William. 'The American Challenge Revisited: soft power struggles in contemporary Europe'. In *On the Idea of America: Perspectives from the Engelsberg seminar 2009*, edited by Kurt Almqvist and Alexander Linklater. Stockholm: Ax:son Johnson Foundation, 2010: 95–104.

———. *Rebuilding Europe: Western Europe, America, and Postwar Reconstruction*. London: Longman, 1992.

———. *The Shock of America. Europe and the Challenge of the Century*. Oxford University Press, forthcoming.

———. 'Visualizing the Marshall Plan in Western Germany: films, exhibits, posters'. In Bischof and Stiefel, *Images of the Marshall Plan in Europe*.

———. 'What Winning Stories Teach: the Marshall Plan and Atlanticism as Enduring Narratives'. In *Defining the Atlantic Community: Culture, Intellectuals and Policies in the Mid-Twentieth Century*, edited by Mariano Marco. London and New York: Routledge, 2010: 111–131.

Emsley, Clive, Arthur Marwick, and Wendy Simpson. *War, Peace and Social Change in Twentieth Century Europe*. Milton Keynes: Open University Press, 1990.

Eriksen, Knut Einar, and Helge Pharo. *Kald krig og internasjonalisering: Norsk utenrikspolitisk historie, vol. 5*. Oslo: Universitetsforlaget, 1997.

Etter, Boris. 'The Assessment of Mergers in the EC under the Concept of Collective Dominance. An Analysis of the Recent Decisions and Judgments—by an Economic Approach'. *Journal of World Competition* 23: 3 (2000): 103–139.

Etzioni, Amitai. *Political Unification: A Comparative Study of Leaders and Forces*. New York: Holt Rinehart & Winston, 1965.

'Europas Brot-und-Butter-Plan' (Interview with Mansholt), *Der Spiegel*, 1 June 1960.

European Productivity Agency, ed. *The Small Family Farm: A European Problem; Methods for Creating Economically Viable Units*. Paris: European Productivity Agency of the OEEC, 1959.

Fabiani, Guido. 'L'agricoltura italiana nello sviluppo dell'Europa comunitaria'. In *Storia dell'Italia repubblicana: La trasformazione dell'Italia: sviluppo e squilibri*, edited by Fabiani Barbagallo et al., Vol. 2 (parte prima): 269–352. Turin: Einaudi, 1995.

Fælles Nordiske Udvalg for økonomisk Samarbejde. *Nordisk økonomisk samarbejde. Foreløbig rapport til regeringerne i Danmark, Island, Norge og Sverige, fra Det Fælles Nordiske Udvalg for Økonomisk Samarbejde*. Copenhagen: 1950.

Fasting, Kåre. *Norsk aluminium gjennom 50 år: forhistorie og historikk 1915–1965; Aktieselskapet Norsk Aluminium Company, A/S Nordisk aluminium industri*. Oslo: Høyang, 1965.

Federico, Giovanni. *Feeding the World: An Economic History of Agriculture, 1800–2000*. Princeton: Princeton University Press, 2005.

———. 'Was the CAP the Worst Agricultural Policy of the 20th Century?' In Patel, *Fertile Ground*, 257–271.

Feilberg, Peter. *Om Forholdene paa Island*. Copenhagen: J. Cohens Bogtrygkkeri, 1878.

———. 'Kulturarbejeder i Island'. *Ugeskrift for landmænd* 10 (1907): 143–145.

Ferguson, Niall. *High Financier: The Lives and Time of Siegmund Warburg*. London: Allen & Lane, 2010.

———. *The War of the World: Twentieth-Century Conflict and the Descent of the West*. Penguin: London, 2006.

Fischer, Wolfram. *Wirtschaft und Gesellschaft im Zeitalter der Industrialisierung*. Göttingen: Vandenhoeck & Ruprecht, 1972.

Foot, M. R. D. 'What Good Did Resistance Do?' In Hawes and White, *Resistance in Europe*: 204–220.

Førland, Tor Egil. 'EFs betydning for nasjonalstaten'. *Nytt Norsk Tidsskrift* 2 (1993): 180–190.

Forsyth, M. G. Review of *The German Economy at War*, by Milward. *International Affairs* 42: 1 (January 1966): 123–124.

Frank, Raymond. Review of *War, Economy and Society*, by Milward, and *War and Economy in the Third Reich*, by Overy. *Armed Forces & Society* 27: 3 (Spring 2001): 477–487.

Frank, Robert. 'La gauche et l'Europe'. In *Histoire des gauches en France*, edited by Jean Jacques Becker and Gilles Candar. Paris : La Découverte, 2004.

Fridenson, Patrick. 'French Enterprises under German Occupation, 1940–1944'. In *Enterprise in the Period of Fascism in Europe*, edited by Harold James and Jakob Tanner, 259–269. Aldershot: Ashgate, 2002.

Frøland, Hans Otto. 'Norway's Liberalisation of Trade and Payments in the 1950s'. *Scandinavian Economic History Review* 52: 2–3 (2004): 11–38.

———. 'Distrust, Dependency and Détente: Norway, the two Germanys and the German Question'. *Contemporary European History* 15: 4 (2006): 495–517.

———. '"Eine gewaltige, nicht beglichene Schuld". Die deutsche Entschädigung für NS-Verfolgte in Norwegen'. In *Grenzen der Wiedergutmachung. Die Entschädigung für NS-Verfolgte in Ost- und West-Europa 1945–2000*, edited by Günter Hockerts and Claudia Moisel. Göttingen: Wallstein Verlag, 2006: 285–356.

———. 'In Pursuit of Selective Protectionism: The Norwegian Experience 1920s-1950s'. In Müller and Myllyntaus, *Pathbreakers. Small European Countries Responding to Globalisation and Deglobalisation*, 349–374.

———. 'Norway's Policy towards the Nordek Negotiations'. In *Between Nordic Ideology, Economic Interests and Political Reality. New Perspectives on Nordek*, edited by Jan Hecker-Stampehl, 65–76. Helsinki: The Finnish Society of Science and Letters, 2009.

———, and Jan Thomas Kobberrød. 'The Norwegian Contribution to Göring's Megalomania: Norway's Aluminium Industry during World War II'. *Cahiers d'histoire de l'aluminium* 42/43 (2009): 131–147.

Fuentes Quintana, Enrique, and Francisco Comín Comín, eds. *Economía y economistas españoles en la Guerra Civil*. 2 vols. Barcelona: Galaxia Gutemberg / Círculo de Lectores, 2009.

Funck, Charles. *Une Europe . . . Un quart de siècle . . . Une sidérurgie . . . Un Club . . . (1951–1977)*. Luxembourg: Saint-Paul, 1977.

Funk, Arthur L. Review of *The New Order and the French Economy*, by Milward. *The Journal of Modern History* 44: 2 (June 1972): 313–314.

Gaddis, John L. 'The Emerging Post-Revisionist Synthesis on the Origins of the Cold War'. *Diplomatic History* 7: 3 (July 1983): 171–204.

———. *We Now Know*. Oxford and New York: Oxford University Press, 1997.

Gaddum, Eckart. *Die deutsche Europapolitik in den 80er Jahren: Interessen, Konflikte und Entscheidungen der Regierung Kohl*. Paderborn: Schöningh, 1994.

Galambos, Louis, Takashi Hikino, and Vera Zamagni, eds. *The Global Chemical Industry in the Age of the Petrochemical Revolution*. Cambridge: Cambridge University Press, 2006.

Galante, Severino. *Il partito comunista italiano e l'integrazione europea: Il decennio del rifiuto: 1947–57*. Padova: Liviana, 1988.

Galantière, Lewis, ed. *America and the Mind of Europe*. London: Hamish Hamilton, 1951.

Gamble, Andrew. Review of *Britain's Place in the World*, by Milward and Brennan. *Reviews in History* 38 (July 1997). http://www.history.ac.uk/reviews/review/38. (last accessed on 12 December 2011).

Garton Ash, Timothy. *In Europe's Name: Germany and the Divided Continent*. London and New York: Random House, 1993.

Gavin, Francis J. *Gold, Dollars, and Power: The Politics of International Monetary Relations 1958–1971*. Chapel Hill: University of North Carolina Press, 2004.

Gehler, Michael. *Deutschland: Von der Teilung zur Einigung 1945 bis heute*. Vienna, Cologne, Weimar: Böhlau, 2010.

———. *Vom gemeinsamen Markt zur Europäischen Unionsbildung: 50 Jahre Römische Verträge 1957–2007—From Common Market to European Union Building; 50 years of the Rome Treaties 1957–2007*. Vienna, Cologne, Weimar: Böhlau, 2008.

Genin, André. 'Vers l'ère nouvelle de l'agriculture européenne'. *L'Information Agricole*, 15 January 1962.

George, Stephen. *An Awkward Partner: Britain in the European Community*. Oxford: Clarendon Press, 1990.

———, ed. *Britain and the European Community: The Politics of Semi-Detachment*. Oxford: Oxford University Press, 1992.

Geppert, Dominik, ed. *The Postwar Challenge: Cultural, Social, and Political Change in Western Europe, 1945–58*. Oxford: Oxford University Press, 2003.

Gerber, David J. *Law and Competition in Twentieth Century Europe: Protecting Prometheus*. Oxford: Oxford University Press, 1998.

Gerbet, Pierre. 'La Genèse du Plan Schuman: Des origines à la déclaration du 9 mai 1950'. *Revue Française de Science Politique* (September 1956): 526–553.

Gerschenkron, Alexander. *Economic Backwardness in Historical Perspective*. Cambridge, MA: Harvard University Press, 1962.

Gilbert, Mark. 'Partners and Rivals: Assessing the American Role'. In Kaiser and Varsori, *European Union History*, 169–189.

Gillingham, John J. *Coal, Steel, and the Rebirth of Europe, 1945–1955: The Germans and French from Ruhr Conflict to Economic Community*. Cambridge: Cambridge University Press, 1991 (reprinted, 2005).

———. *Design for a New Europe*. Cambridge: Cambridge University Press, 2006. (Italian translation *Progetto per una nuova Europa*. Bologna: CLUEB, 2009.)

———. *European Integration, 1950–2003: Superstate or New Market Economy*. Cambridge: Cambridge University Press, 2003.

———. 'Solving the Ruhr Problem: German Heavy Industry and the Schuman Plan'. In Schwabe, *Die Anfänge des Schuman-Plans*, 1988: 399–436.

Giocoli, Nicola. 'Competition vs. Property Rights: American Antitrust Law, the Freiburg School and the Early Years of European Competition Policy'. *Journal of Competition Law and Economics* 5: 4 (2009): 747–786.

Gofas, Andreas, and Colin Hay, eds. *The Role of Ideas in Political Analysis*. London: Routledge, 2010.

Gollwitzer, Heinz. *Europäische Bauernparteien im 20: Jahrhundert*. Stuttgart and New York: Fischer, 1977.

Golson, Eric. 'Neutrality for Self-Benefit? Spanish Trade in the Second World War'. Paper delivered to London School of Economics Ph.D. thesis seminar, Lent 2010.

Good, David F. Review of *The Reconstruction of Western Europe*, by Milward. *The Journal of Modern History* 58: 2 (June 1986): 545–547.

———. 'The State and Economic Development in Central and Eastern Europe'. In *Nation, State, and the Economy in History*, edited by Alice Teichova and Herbert Matis, 133–158. Cambridge: Cambridge University Press, 2003.

Greenwood, Sean. *The Alternative Alliance: Anglo-French Relations before the Coming of NATO, 1944–48*. London: Minerva Press, 1996.

———. *Britain and European Cooperation since 1945*. Oxford: Blackwell, 1992.

Griffiths, Richard T. 'Economic Reconstruction Policy in the Netherlands and its International Consequences, May 1945–March 1951'. EUI working paper 76. Florence: 1983.

———. 'Het jaar 1947' in Griffiths et al., *Van strohalm tot strategie*. Assen: Van Gorcum, 1977, 5–15.

———, ed. *The Netherlands and the Integration of Europe, 1945–1957*. Amsterdam: NEHA, 1990.

———. 'The Schuman Plan Negotiations: The Economic Clauses'. In Schwabe, *Beginnings of the Schuman Plan*, 35–72.

———. 'The Stranglehold of Bilateralism'. In Griffiths, *The Netherlands and the Integration of Europe*, 1–26.

———, and Brian Girvin, eds. *The Green Pool and the Origins of the Common Agricultural Policy*. London: Lothian Press, 1995.

———, and Fernando Guirao. 'The First Proposals for a European Agricultural Community: The Pflimlin and Mansholt Plans'. In Griffiths and Girvin, *The Green Pool*, 1–19.

———, and Alan S. Milward. 'The European Agricultural Community, 1948–1954', EUI working paper 86/254. Florence: 1986.

———, Peter A. Schregardus, Gerard J. Telkamp, and Laurien W. M. Timmermans, eds. *Van strohalm tot strategie: Het Marshall-plan in perspectief*. Assen: Van Gorcum, 1997.

———, and Stuart Ward, eds. *Courting the Common Market: The First Attempt to Enlarge the European Community, 1961–1963*. London: Lothian Foundation Press, 1996.

Grigg, David B. *The Agricultural Systems of the World: An Evolutionary Approach*. Cambridge: Cambridge University Press, 1974.

Grofman, Bernard. 'Seven Durable Axes of Cleavage in Political Science'. In Monroe, *Contemporary Empirical Political Theory*, 73–86.

Grunert, Thomas. 'Decision-Making Processes in the Steel Crisis Policy of the EEC: Neocorporatist or Integrationist Tendencies'. In Mény and Wright, *The Politics of Steel*, 222–307.

Gualdesi, Marinella Neri. 'L'Italia e il processo di integrazione europea'. In *L'Italia e le organizzazioni internazionali*, edited by Luciano Tosi. Padova: CEDAM, 1999.

Gualtieri, Roberto. *L'Italia dal 1943 al 1992: DC e PCI nella storia della repubblica*. Rome: Carocci, 2006.

———. 'Il PCI, la DC e il vincolo esterno: una proposta di periodizzazzione'. In Gualtieri, *Il PCI nell'Italia repubblicana*, 47–99.

———, ed. *Il PCI nell'Italia repubblicana, 1943–1991*. Rome: Carocci, 2001.

Guasconi, Eleonora. *L'Europa tra continuità e cambiamento: Il vertice dell'Aja del 1969 e il rilancio della costruzione europea*. Florence: Edizioni Polistampa, 2004.

Guirao, Fernando. 'The European Community's Role in Promoting Democracy in Franco's Spain, 1970–1975'. In *Beyond the Customs Union*, edited by Van der Harst, 163–193.

———. 'L'evolució de la integració europea des de l'adhesió d'Espanya a la Comunitat fins a la Unió Europea d'avui (1986–2007): Una reflexió crítica'. *Nota d'Economia* 88 (2007): 41–57.

———. 'Introduction to the Special Issue on CAP Reform'. *JEIH* 16: 2 (2010): 13–24.

———. 'Naranjas y piritas: los embajadores de Franco en la inmediata segunda postguerra mundial'. In Fuentes Quintana (dir.) and Comín Comín (coord.), *Economía y economistas españoles en la Guerra Civil*, 555–603.

———. *Spain and the Reconstruction of Western Europe, 1945–57. Challenge and Response*. London: Macmillan Press, 1998.

———, and Víctor Gavín Munté. 'La dimensione internazionale della transizione politica spagnola, 1969–1982: Quale ruolo giocarono la Comunità europea e gli Stati Uniti'. In Del Pero, Gavín, Guirao, and Varsori, *Democrazie*, 173–264.

Guðmundsson, Gísli. *Samband íslenzkra samvinnufélaga, 1902–1942*. Reykjavík: SIS, 1943.

Gunst, Péter. 'Agrarian Developments in East Central Europe at the Turn of the Century'. In *Hungarian Agrarian Society from the Emancipation of Serfs (1848) to the Re-privatization of Land (1998)*, edited by P. Gunst, 23–49. Boulder, CO: Social Sciences Monographs, 1998.

Haan, Henk de. 'De invloed van het Marshall-plan op de Nederlandse economie'. In Griffiths et al., *Van strohalm tot strategie*, 114–122.

Haas, Ernst B. *Beyond the Nation-State: Functionalism and International Organization*. Stanford, CA: Stanford University Press, 1964.

———. 'Does Constructivism Subsume Neo-functionalism?' In Christiansen, Jørgensen, and Wiener, *The Social Construction of Europe*, 22–31.

———. 'Introduction: Institutionalism or Constructivism?' In Haas, *The Uniting of Europe: Political, Social and Economic Forces, 1950–1957*. (3rd ed.). Notre Dame, IN: University of Notre Dame Press, 2004, xii–lvi.

———. *The Uniting of Europe: Political, Social and Economic Forces, 1950–1957*. Stanford, CA: Stanford University Press, 1958.

Hahn, Frank. 'The Next Hundred Years'. *The Economic Journal* 101 (January 1991): 47–50.

Hansen, Alvin. *America's Role in the World Economy*. New York: W. W. Norton & Co., 1945.

Hansen, Roger D. 'European Integration: Reflections on a Decade of Theoretical Efforts'. *World Politics* 21: 2 (1969): 242–271.

Harper, John Lamberton. *American Visions of Europe: Franklin D. Roosevelt, George F. Kennan and Dean G. Acheson*. Cambridge: Cambridge University Press, 1994.

Harrison, Mark. 'The Economics of World War II: An Overview'. In Harrison, *The Economics of World War II*: 1–42.

———, ed. *The Economics of World War II: Six Great Powers in International Comparison*. Cambridge: Cambridge University Press, 1998.

———. 'Resource Mobilization for World War II: The U.S.A., U.K., U.S.S.R., and Germany, 1938–1945'. *The Economic History Review* 41: 2 (May 1988): 171–192.

———. *Soviet Planning in Peace and War 1939–1945*. Cambridge: Cambridge University Press, 1985.

———. 'The Soviet Union: The Defeated Victor'. In Harrison, *The Economics of World War II*, 268–301.

Harryvan, Anjo G. 'De historiografie van de Europese integratie, 1945–1985'. In *Europese eenwording in historisch perspectief: Factoren van integratie en desintegratie*, edited by W.A.F. Camphuis and C.G.J. Wildeboer Schut, 22–45. Zaltbommel: Europese Bibliotheek, 1991.

———. *In Pursuit of Influence: The Netherlands' European Policy during the Formative Years of the European Union, 1952–1973*. Brussels: Peter Lang, 2009.

———, and Jan van der Harst. *Documents on European Union*. London: Macmillan, 1997.

———. *Max Kohnstamm: Leven en werk van een Europeaan*. Utrecht: Het Spectrum, 2008. Translated into English as *Max Kohnstamm. A European's Life and Work*. Baden-Baden: Nomos, 2011.

Hartley, Anthony. 'How the European Community Really Came About'. Review of *The European Rescue of the Nation-State*, by Milward. *World Today* 50: 1 (January 1994): 19–20.

Haskel, Barbara. *The Scandinavian Option: Opportunities and Opportunity Costs in Postwar Scandinavian Foreign Policies*. Oslo: Universitetsforlaget, 1976.

Hawes, Stephen, and Ralph White, eds. *Resistance in Europe: 1939–1945*. London: Allen Lane, 1975.

Hayes, Paul. Review of *The Fascist Economy in Norway*, by Milward. *The Economic History Review* (New Series) 25: 4 (November 1972): 738.

Hayes, Peter. *Industry and Ideology: IG Farben in the Nazi Era*. Cambridge: Cambridge University Press, 1987.

Hearden, Patrick. *Architects of Globalism: Building a New World Order during World War II*. Fayetteville: University of Arkansas Press, 2002.

Heath, Jim F. Review of *War, Economy and Society*, by Milward. *Journal of Economic Literature* 16: 2 (June 1978): 598-599.

Hedbert, Peter, and Elias Håkansson. 'Did Germany Exploit its Small Trading Partners? The Nature of the German Interwar and Wartime trade Policies Revisited from the Swedish Experience'. *Scandinavian Economic History Review* 56: 3 (2008): 248–270.

Helgason, Ágúst. *Endurminningar*. Edited by Sigurður Einarsson. Akureyri: Norðri, 1951.

Henrich-Franke, Christian. 'Gescheiterte Integration: Die Europäische Wirtschaftsgemeinschaft und die Formulierung der gemeinsamen Verkehrspolitik (1958–1967)'. *JEIH* 15: 2 (2009): 125–148.

Henriksen, Ingrid. 'Avoiding Lock-In: Cooperative Creameries in Denmark, 1882–1903'. *European Review of Economic History* 3 (1999): 57–78.

———. 'The Contribution of Agriculture to Economic Growth in Denmark, 1870–1939'. In Lains and Pinilla, *Agriculture and Economic Development*, 143–144.

Hentschel, Volker. *Ludwig Erhard: Ein Politikerleben*. Munich: Olzog, 1996.

Herbst, Ludolf. *Der totale Krieg und die Ordnung der Wirtschaft: die Kriegswirtschaft im Spannungsfeld von Politik, Ideologie und Propaganda, 1939–1945, Studien zur Zeitgeschichte*. Stuttgart: DVA, 1982.

Herlitz, Nils. 'Nordiska rådets tillkomst: Minnen från 1951–1953'. *Nordisk Kontakt* (1962): 5–59.

Hettne, Björn, ed. *Development Options in Europe*. Gothenburg: United Nations University, 1988.

Hewston, Miles. *Understanding Attitudes to the European Community*. Cambridge: Cambridge University Press, 1986.

Hicks, John R. 'Education in Economics'. *Bulletin of the Manchester Statistical Society* (April 1941): 1–20.

Hiepel, Claudia. 'Willy Brandt—Georges Pompidou et la gouvernance européenne'. In Loth, *La gouvernance supranationale*, 163–183.

———. 'Willy Brandt und Georges Pompidou: Deutsch-französische Beziehungen und europäische Einigung'. 'Habilitationsschrift' for the University of Duisburg-Essen, 2010.

Hildebrand, Doris. *The Role of Economic Analysis in the EC Competition Rules*. Chicago: Kluwer, 2010.

Hillmann, H. C. Review of *The German Economy at War*, by Milward. *The Economic History Review* 18: 3 (1965): 676–677.

Hirschfeld, Gerhard, and Lothar Kettenacker, eds. *Der „Führerstaat": Mythos und Realität; Studien zur Struktur und Politik des Dritten Reiches*. Stuttgart: Klett-Cotta, 1981.

Hirschman, Albert O. *Exit, Voice, and Loyalty: Responses to Decline in Firms, Organizations, and States*. Cambridge, MA: Harvard University Press, 1970.

Hitchcock, William I. 'The Marshall Plan and the Creation of the West'. In Leffler and Westad, *The Cambridge History of the Cold War*. Vol. 1: *Origins*, 154–174.

Hix, Simon. 'The European Union as a Polity (I)'. In Jørgensen, Pollack, and Rosamond, *Handbook of European Union Politics*, 141–158.

———. 'The Study of the European Community: The Challenge to Comparative Politics'. *West European Politics* 17: 1 (1994): 1–30.

Hobsbawm, Eric. Review of *The Development of the Economies of Continental Europe*, by Milward and Saul. *The Economic History Review* (New Series) 31: 4 (November 1978): 692–693.

Hoffmann, Stanley. 'Obstinate or Obsolete? The Fate of the Nation-State and the Case of Western Europe'. *Daedalus* 95: 3 (1966): 862–915.

———, and Charles Maier, eds. *The Marshall Plan: A Retrospective*. Boulder, CO: Westview Press, 1984.

Hogan, Michael J., ed. *The Ambiguous Legacy: U.S. Foreign Relations in the 'American Century'*. Cambridge: Cambridge University Press, 1999.

———. 'European Integration and German Reintegration: Marshall Planners and the Search for Recovery and Security in Western Europe'. In Maier and Bischof, *The Marshall Plan and Germany*, 115–170.

———. *The Marshall Plan: America, Britain and the Reconstruction of Western Europe, 1947–1952*. Cambridge and New York: Cambridge University Press, 1987.

———. 'The Search for a "Creative Peace": The United States, European Unity, and the Origins of the Marshall Plan'. *Diplomatic History* 6: 3 (July 1982): 267–286.

Hohenberg, Paul M. Review of *War, Economy and Society*, by Milward. *The Journal of Economic History* 38: 2 (June 1978): 547–549.

Holland, Stuart. *Uncommon Market: Capital, Class and Power in the European Community*. London and Basingstoke: Macmillan, 1980.

Hooghe, Liesbet, and Gary Marks. *Multi-Level Governance and European Integration*. Lanham, MD: Rowman & Littlefield, 2001.

Hoover, Herbert. *The Memoirs of Herbert Hoover: Years of Adventure, 1874–1920*. New York: Macmillan, 1957.

———. *The Memoirs of Herbert Hoover: The Cabinet and the Presidency, 1920–1933*. New York: Macmillan, 1952.

———. *The Memoirs of Herbert Hoover: The Great Depression, 1929–1941*. New York: Macmillan, 1952.

Hudson, Pat, ed. *Living Economic and Social History. The Economic History Society: Essays to mark the 75h Anniversary of the Economic History Society*. Glasgow: Economic History Society, 2001.

Hull, Cordell. *The Memoirs of Cordell Hull*. Vols. 1 and 2. New York: Macmillan, 1948.

Hunt, Michael. 'The Long Crisis in U.S. Diplomatic History: Coming to Closure'. *Diplomatic History* 16: 1 (Winter 1992): 115–140.

Hurst, Michael. Review of *The German Economy at War*, by Milward. *The Oxford Magazine* (October 1965): 56–57.

Ibelings, Hans. *Americanism: Dutch Architecture and the Transatlantic Model*. Rotterdam: NAi, 1997.

Inklaar, Frank. *Van Amerika geleerd: Marshall-hulp en kennisimport in Nederland*. The Hague: SDU, 1997.

Iriye, Akira. *Global Community: The Role of International Organizations in the Making of the Contemporary World*. Berkeley and London: University of California Press, 2002.

Jachtenfuchs, Markus. 'The European Union as a Polity (II)'. In Jørgensen, Pollack, and Rosamond, *Handbook of European Union Politics*, 159–173.

Jackson, Julian. *France: The Dark Years, 1940–1944*. Oxford: Oxford University Press, 2001.

Jackson, Scott. 'Prologue to the Marshall Plan: The Origins of the American Commitment for a European Recovery Program'. *Journal of American History* 65: 4 (March 1979): 1043–1068.

Jager, Ronald. *The Fate of Family Farming: Variations on an American Idea*. Hanover, MA: University Press of New England, 2004.

James, Harold. Review of *War and Economy in the Third Reich*, by Overy. *The Journal of Modern History* 68: 2 (June 1996): 502–504.

Janos, Andrew C. *The Politics of Backwardness in Hungary, 1825–1945*. Princeton, NJ: Princeton University Press, 1982.

John, Richard R. 'Bringing Political Economy Back In'. *Enterprise and Society* 9: 3 (2008): 487–490.

John of Salisbury. *The Metalogicon: A Twelfth-Century Defense of the Verbal and Logical Arts of the Trivium*. Translated with an Introduction and Notes by Daniel D. McGarry. Berkeley and Los Angeles: University of California Press, 1962.

Johnson, Michael. *European Community Trade Policy and the Article 113 Committee*. London: Royal Institute of International Affairs, 1998.

Joly, Hervé. 'The Economy of Occupied and Vichy France: Constraints and Opportunities'. In *Working for the New Order: European Business under German Domination, 1939–1945*, edited by Joachim Lund, 93–104. Copenhagen: University Press of Southern Denmark, 2006.

Jones, Alison, and Brenda Sufrin. *EC Competition Law: Text, Cases, and Materials*. Oxford: Oxford University Press, 2010.

Jones, Joseph Marion. *The Fifteen Weeks (February 21–June 5, 1947)*. New York: Viking Press, 1955.

Jónsson, Agnar Kl. *Stjórnarráð Íslands, 1904–1964*. Vols 1 and 2. Reykjavík: Sögufélag, 1969.

Jónsson, Guðmundur. 'Á slóðum Bjarts í Sumarhúsum. Smábýlastefnan í íslenskum landbúnaði'. In *Vísindavefur: Ritgerðasafn til heiðurs Þorsteini Vilhjálmssyni sjötugum 27: september 2010*, edited by Gunnar Karlsson and Orri Vésteinsson, 55–72. Reykjavík: Hið íslenska bókmenntafélag, 2010.

———. 'Coming to Terms with Europe. Iceland's Entry into EFTA and its implications'. In *EFTA 1960–2010: Elements of 50 Years of European History*, edited by Kåre Bryn and Guðmundur Einarsson. Reykjavík: University of Iceland Press, 2010: 77–97.

———. *Hagvöxtur og iðnvæðing: Þjóðarframleiðsla á Íslandi, 1870–1945*. Reykjavík: Þjóðhagsstofnun, 1999.

———. 'Iceland's Response to European Economic Integration, 1945-1960'. In Müller and Myllyntaus, *Pathbreakers. Small European Countries Responding to Globalisation and Deglobalisation*, 2008.

———. 'Institutional Change in Icelandic Agriculture, 1780–1940'. *Scandinavian Economic History Review* 41: 2 (1993): 101–128.

———. 'The State and the Icelandic Economy, 1870–1930'. Ph.D. thesis, London School of Economics and Political Science, 1992.

———. 'The Transformation of the Icelandic Economy'. In *Exploring Economic Growth: Essays in Measurement and Analysis: A Festschrift for Riitta Hjerppe on her 60th Birthday*, edited by Sakari Heikkinen and Jan Luiten van Zanden, 131–166. Amsterdam: Aksant Academic Publishers, 2004.

———, and Magnús S. Magnússon, eds. *Hagskinna: Sögulegar hagtölur um Ísland. [Icelandic Historical Statistics]*. Reykjavík: Statistics Iceland, 1997.

Jónsson, Guðni. *Eimskipafélag Íslands tuttugu og fimm ára*. Reykjavík: H. F. Eimskipafélag Íslands, 1939.

Jónsson, Jónas. *Komandi ár* 1. Reykjavík: Ísafoldarprentsmiðja, 1923.

Jørgensen, Knud Erik, Mark Pollack, and Ben Rosamond, eds. *Handbook of European Union Politics*. London, California, New Delhi: Sage, 2007.

Josling, Timothy E., Stefan Tangermann, and Thorald K. Warley. *Agriculture in the GATT*. London, 1996.

Judt, Tony. 'Introduction'. In *The Marshall Plan: Fifty Years After*, edited by Martin Schain, 1–9. New York: Palgrave, 2001.

———. *Postwar: A History of Europe Since 1945*. New York: Penguin Press, 2005.

Kaiser, Wolfram. *Christian Democracy and the Origins of the European Union*. Cambridge: Cambridge University Press, 2007.

———. 'From State to Society? The Historiography of European Integration'. In *Palgrave Advances in European Union Studies*, edited by Michelle Cini and Angela K. Bourne, 190–208. Basingstoke: Palgrave Macmillan, 2006.

———. 'History Meets Politics: Overcoming Interdisciplinary *Volapük* in Research on the EU'. *Journal of European Public Policy* 15: 2 (2008): 300–313.

———. 'Transnational Networks in European Governance: The Informal Politics of Integration'. In Kaiser, Leucht, and Rasmussen, *The History of the European Union*, 12–34.

———. *Using Europe, Abusing the Europeans: Britain and European Integration, 1945–63*. Basingstoke: Macmillan, 1996 (hb), 1999 (pb).

———, and Brigitte Leucht. 'Informal Politics of Integration: Christian Democratic and Transatlantic Networks in the Creation of ECSC Core Europe'. *JEIH* 14: 1 (2008): 35–50.

———, Brigitte Leucht, and Michael Gehler, eds. *Transnational Networks in Regional Integration: Governing Europe, 1945–83*. Basingstoke: Palgrave Macmillan, 2010.

———, Brigitte Leucht, and Morten Rasmussen, eds. *The History of the European Union: Origins of a Trans- and Supranational Polity, 1950–72*. London and New York: Routledge, 2009.

———, and Antonio Varsori, eds. *European Union History: Themes and Debates*. Basingstoke and New York: Palgrave Macmillan, 2010.

Kaplan, Jacob J., and Gunther Schleiminger. *The European Payments Union: Financial Diplomacy in the 1950s*. Oxford: Clarendon Press, 1989.

Kaplan, Lawrence S. 'The Cold War and European Revisionism'. *Diplomatic History* 11: 2 (Spring 1987): 143–156.

Karlbom, Rolf. Review of *The Fascist Economy in Norway*, by Milward. *Scandinavian Economic History Review* 20: 2 (1972): 203–205.

Kassim, Hussein, and Anand Menon. 'The Principal-Agent Approach and the Study of the European Union: Promise Unfulfilled?' *Journal of European Public Policy* 10: 1 (2003): 121–139.

Katzenstein, Peter J., ed. *Between Power and Plenty: Foreign Economic Policies of Advanced Industrial States*. Madison: University of Wisconsin Press, 1978.

Kaufman-Osborn, Timothy V. 'Dividing the Domain of Political Science: On the Fetishism of Subfields'. *Polity* 38: 1 (2006): 41–71.

Kavanagh, Dennis. 'Why Political Science Needs History'. *Political Studies* 39: 3 (1991): 479–495.

Kemp, Tom. Review of *The Development of the Economies of Continental Europe*, by Milward and Saul. *The English Historical Review* 93: 369 (October 1978): 882–883.

Kershaw, Ian. *The Nazi Dictatorship: Problems and Perspectives of Interpretation.* (4th ed.). London: Edward Arnold, 2000.

Kersten, Albert E. 'Nederland en de buitenlandse politiek na 1945'. In Blok, *Algemene Geschiedenis der Nederlanden*, 382–400.

———. 'A Welcome Surprise? The Netherlands and the Schuman Plan Negotiations'. In Schwabe, *Beginnings of the Schuman Plan*, 285–303.

Keynes, John Maynard. *The Collected Writings of John Maynard Keynes.* Vol. 2: *The Economic Consequences of the Peace,* 1919. Reprint, Basingstoke: Macmillan, 1971.

———. *The Economic Consequences of the Peace.* London: Macmillan, 1919.

———. *How to Pay for the War: A Radical Plan for the Chancellor of the Exchequer.* London: Macmillan, 1940.

Killick, John. *The United States and European Reconstruction, 1945–60.* Keele: Keele University Press, 1997.

Kindleberger, Charles P. *Marshall Plan Days.* Boston: Allen & Unwin, 1987.

———. Review of *The New Order and the French Economy*, by Milward. *The Annals of the American Academy of Political and Social Science* 396 (July 1971): 160–161.

King, Gary, Robert O. Keohane, and Sidney Verba. *Designing Social Inquiry: Scientific Inference in Qualitative Research.* Princeton, NJ: Princeton University Press, 1994.

Kipping, Matthias. *Zwischen Kartellen und Konkurrenz: Der Schuman-Plan und die Ursprünge der europäischen Einigung, 1944–1952.* Berlin: Duncker & Humblot, 1996.

———, and Ove Bjarnar, eds. *The Americanisation of European Business: The Marshall Plan and the Transfer of US Management Models.* London: Routledge, 1998.

Kjaran, Birgir. 'Íslenzk utanríkisverzlun milli tveggja heimsstyrjalda'. *Frjáls verzlun* 2 (1940): 13–19, 31.

Kjartansson, Helgi Skúli. 'Áveiturnar miklu á Skeið og Flóa: Dæmi um umdeilanlega opinbera fjárfestingu'. *Skírnir* 162 (Fall 1988): 330–360.

Klein, Burton H. *Germany's Economic Preparations for War.* Cambridge, MA: Harvard University Press, 1959.

Knipping, Franz, and Matthias Schönwald, eds. *Aufbruch zum Europa der zweiten Generation: Die europäische Einigung, 1969–1984.* Trier: Wissenschaftlicher Verlag, 2004.

Knudsen, Ann-Christina Lauring. *Farmers on Welfare: The Making of Europe's Common Agricultural Policy.* Ithaca: Cornell University Press, 2009.

———. 'Ideas, Welfare, and Values: Framing the Common Agricultural Policy in the 1960s'. In Patel, *Fertile Ground for Europe?* 61–78.

———. 'Romanticising Europe? Rural Images in the European Union Policies'. *Kontur—Tidsskrift for Kulturstudier* 12 (2005): 49–58.

Kobberrød, Jan Thomas. 'Norwegian Alumina—A Key to Success in a Global Industry?' *Cahiers d'histoire de l'aluminium*, Special Issue 2 (2007): 53–66.

Kocka, Jürgen, and György Ránki, eds. *Economic Theory and History.* Budapest: Akadémiai Kiadó, 1985.

Kohlhase, Norbert, and Henri Schwamm, eds. *La Négociation CEE-Suisse dans le Kennedy Round.* Lausanne: Publications du Centre de recherches européennes, 1977.

Kolko, Joyce, and Gabriel Kolko. *The Limits of Power: The World and United States Foreign Policy, 1945–1954.* New York: Harper & Row, 1972.

Koper, Arnold. 'Een Amerikaans plan voor Europa'. *De Volkskrant*, 31 May 1997.

Kreisler, Harry. 'Science and Progress in International Relations: Conversation with Ernst B. Haas', 30 October 2000. Available at: http://globetrotter.berkeley.edu/people/Haas/haas-con3.html (last accessed on 15 December 2011).

Kuznets, Simon. *Modern Economic Growth: Rate, Structure, Spread*. New Haven: Yale University Press, 1965.

Lains, Pedro. 'Agriculture and Economic Development in Portugal, 1870–1973'. In Lains and Pinilla, *Agriculture and Economic Development in Europe*, 333–352.

———. 'Growth in a Protected Environment: Portugal, 1850–1950'. Research in Economic History 24 (2007): 121–163.

———. 'New Wine in Old Bottles. Output and Productivity Trends in Portuguese Agriculture, 1850–1950'. European Review of Economic History 7: 1 (2003): 43–72.

———. 'The Portuguese economy in the Irish mirror, 1960–2002'. Open Economies Review, 19: 5, 2008: 667–683.

———. 'Southern European Economic Backwardness Revisited: The Role of Open Economy Forces in Portugal and the Balkans'. *Scandinavian Economic History Review* 50: 1 (2002): 24–43.

———, and J. L. Cardoso, eds., *Paying for the Liberal State: The Rise of Public Finances in Nineteenth Century Europe*. Cambridge: Cambridge University Press, 2010.

———, and Vicente Pinilla, eds. *Agriculture and Economic Development in Europe since 1870*. London: Routledge, 2009.

Lama, Luciano. 'La relazione, il dibattito, e le decisioni del Comitato Direttivo della CGIL sulla partecipazione al VI Congresso FSM'. *Rassegna sindacale*, 17 October 1965.

Landes, David S. *The Unbound Prometheus: Technological Change and Industrial Development in Western Europe from 1750 to the Present*. Cambridge: Cambridge University Press, 1969.

———. *The Wealth and Poverty of Nations: Why Some Are So Rich and Some So Poor*. London: Little, Brown and Co., 1998.

Laqueur, Walter, ed. *Fascism: A Reader's Guide; Analyses, Interpretations, Bibliography*. London: Wildwood House, 1976; Berkeley: University of California Press, 1977.

Laschi, Giuliana. *L'agricoltura italiana e l'integrazione europea*. Bern: Peter Lang, 1999.

Laski, Harold J. *Studies in the Problem of Sovereignty*. New Haven: Yale University Press; London: Humphrey Milford, Oxford University Press, 1917.

Latham, Michael. 'Cooperation and Community in Europe'. In Schain, *The Marshall Plan: Fifty Years After*, 61–90.

Laursen, Johnny. 'The Enlargement of the European Community, 1950–95'. In Loth, *Experiencing Europe*, 269–305

———. 'A kingdom divided: Denmark'. In *European Union Enlargement: a comparative history*, edited by Wolfram Kaiser and Jürgen Elvert. Abingdon and New York: Routledge, 2004: 34–56.

———. *Politiets Efterretningstjeneste 1945–68*. Copenhagen: Schultz, 2009.

———. 'The Supranational Seven? Denmark, Scandinavia and the Schuman Plan, 1950–53'. In Gehler, *From Common Market to European Union*, 2008: 197–223.

———, and Thorsten B. Olesen. *Et Nordisk alternativ til Europa? : samspillet mellem Danmarks nordiske og europæiske politik, 1945–1999*. Aarhus: Systime, 1999.

———, and Tom Swienty. *Danmark i Europa, 1945–93*. Copenhagen: Munksgaard, 1994.

Lazar, Marc. *Maisons rouges: Les parties communistes français et italiens de la Libération à nos jours*. Paris: Aubier, 1992.

League of Nations, ed. 'European Conference on Rural Life'. National Monographs Series. Geneva: League of Nations, 1939/1940.

Le Boulay, Morgane. 'Investir l'arène européenne de la recherche: Le 'Groupe de Liaison' des historiens auprès de la Commission européenne'. *Politix: Revue des sciences sociales du politique* 23: 89 (2010): 103–124.

Lee, Sabine. *An Uneasy Partnership: British-German Relations between 1955 and 1961*. Bochum: Brockmeyer, 1996.

Lefèvre, Sylvie. 'Les sidérurgistes français propriétaires de charbonnages dans la Ruhr (1945–1954)'. In *Die deutsch-französischen Wirtschaftsbeziehungen, 1945–1960*, edited by Andreas Wilkens, 237–247. Sigmaringen: Jan Thorbecke Verlag, 1997.

Leffler, Melvyn P., and Odd Arne Westad, eds. *The Cambridge History of the Cold War*. Cambridge: Cambridge University Press, 2010.

Lemmes, Fabian. 'Collaboration in Wartime France, 1940–1944'. *European Review of History* 15: 2 (April 2008): 157–177.

Leontief, Wassily. 'Note on the Pluralistic Interpretation of History and the Problem of Interdisciplinary Cooperation'. *The Journal of Philosophy* 45: 23 (November 1948): 617–624.

Lepage, Solenne. 'La France et les institutions de Bretton Woods'. *Vingtième siècle: Revue d'histoire* 46 (April-June 1995): 182–184.

Leucht, Brigitte. 'Transatlantic Policy Networks in the Creation of the First European Anti-trust Law: Mediating between American Anti-trust and German Ordo-liberalism'. In Kaiser, Rasmussen, and Leucht, *History of the European Union*, 56–73.

———, and Katja Seidel. 'Du Traité de Paris au règlement 17/1962: Ruptures et continuités dans la politique européenne de concurrence, 1950–1962'. *Histoire, économie et société* 27:1 (2008): 35–46.

Lewis, Orion, and Sven Steinmo. 'Taking Evolution Seriously', ARENA working paper 19, Oslo, 2007.

Lieshout, Robert H., Matthieu L. L. Segers, and Anna van der Vleuten. 'De Gaulle, Moravcsik and *The Choice for Europe*'. *Journal of Cold War Studies* 6: 4 (2004): 89–139.

Lindberg, Leon N. *The Political Dynamics of European Economic Integration*. Stanford, CA: Stanford University Press, 1963.

Lipgens, Walter. *Die Anfänge der europäischen Einigungspolitik, 1945–1950, Erster Teil: 1945–1947*. Stuttgart: Klett-Cotta, 1977. (English edition, *A History of European Integration. Vol. 1: 1945–1947*. Oxford: Clarendon Press, 1982.)

———, ed. *Documents on the History of European Integration. Vol. 1: Continental Plans for European Union, 1939–1945*. Berlin and New York: de Gruyter, 1985. *Vol. 2: Plans for European Union in Great Britain and in Exile, 1939–1945*. Berlin and New York: de Gruyter, 1986.

———. *Europa-Föderationspläne der Widerstandsbewegungen, 1940–1945: eine Dokumentation*. Munich: Oldenbourg, 1968.

———. 'Die europäische Integration: Entwicklungsphasen und Stand'. *Ruperto Carola* 38 (December 1965): 23–43.

———. 'European Federation in the Political Thought of Resistance Movements during World War II'. In *European Integration*, edited by Frank Roy Willis, 1–18. New York: New Viewpoints, 1975.

———. *A History of European Integration, 1945–1947. Vol. 1: The Formation of the European Unity Movement*. Oxford: Clarendon Press, 1982.

———, ed. *45 Jahre Ringen um die Europäische Verfassung: Dokumente, 1939–1984*. Bonn: Europa-Union Verlag, 1986.

———. 'Der Zusammenschluss Westeuropas. Leitlinien für den historischen Unterricht'. *Geschichte in Wissenschaft und Unterricht* 34 (1983): 345–372.

———, and Wilfried Loth, eds. *Documents on the History of European Integration. Vol. 3: The Struggle for European Union by Political Parties and Pressure Groups in Western European Countries, 1945–1950*. Berlin and New York: de Gruyter, 1988. *Vol. 4: Transnational Organizations of Political Parties and Pressure Groups in the Struggle for European Union, 1945–1950*. Berlin and New York: de Gruyter, 1990.

Lippmann, Walter. *The Method of Freedom*. New York: Transaction Publishers, 1934.

Loock, Hans-Dietrich. *Quisling, Rosenberg und Terboven: Zur Geschichte der nationalsozialistischen Revolution in Norwegen*. Stuttgart: Deutsche Verlags-Anstalt, 1970.

———. Review of *The Fascist Economy in Norway*, by Milward. *Historische Zeitschrift* 217: 2 (1973): 473–475 (in German); and *The Journal of Modern History* 45: 3 (September 1973): 546–547 (in English).

Loth, Wilfried. 'Beiträge der Geschichtswissenschaft zur Deutung der europäischen Integration'. In *Theorien europäischer Integration*, edited by Loth and Wolfgang Wessels, 87–106. Opladen: Leske und Budrich, 2001.

———, ed. *Crises and Compromises: The European Project, 1963–1969*. Baden-Baden: Nomos, 2000.

———. 'De Gaulle und Europa: Eine Revision'. *Historische Zeitschrift* 253 (1991): 629–660.

———. 'Deutsche und französische Interessen auf dem Weg zu EWG und Euratom'. In *Die deutsch-französischen Wirtschaftsbeziehungen, 1945–1960*, edited by Andreas Wilkens, 178–187. Sigmaringen: Thorbecke, 1991.

———. 'Die Entstehung der Römischen Verträge'. In Gehler, *Vom gemeinsamen Markt*, 111–130.

———, ed. *Experiencing Europe: 50 Years of European Construction, 1957–2007*. Baden-Baden: Nomos, 2009.

———. 'Explaining European Integration: The Contribution from Historians'. *JEIH* 14: 1 (2008): 9–26.

———, ed. *La gouvernance supranationale dans la construction européenne*. Brussels: Bruylant, 2005.

———. 'Identity and Statehood in the Process of European Integration'. *JEIH* 6: 1 (2000): 19–31.

———. 'In memoriam Alan S. Milward (1935–2010)'. *JEIH* 16: 2 (December 2010): 5–7.

———. 'Mise en perspective historique de la constitution européenne'. In Loth, *La gouvernance supranationale*, 339–371.

———. 'Der Prozeß der europäischen Integration: Antriebskräfte, Entscheidungen, Perspektiven'. *Gewerkschaftliche Monatshefte* 46 (1995): 703–714.

———. *Die Sowjetunion und die deutsche Frage: Studien zur sowjetischen Deutschlandpolitik von Stalin bis Chruschtschow*. Göttingen: Vandenhoeck & Ruprecht, 2007.

———. *Sozialismus und Internationalismus: Die französischen Sozialisten und die Nachkriegsordnung Europas, 1940–1950*. Stuttgart: Deutsche Verlagsanstalt, 1977.

———. 'Die Verfassung für Europa in historischer Perspektive'. In *Europäische Gesellschaft: Grundlagen und Perspektiven*, edited by W. Loth, 244–264. Wiesbaden: VS Verlag für Sozialwissenschaften, 2005.

———. 'Walter Lipgens (1925–1984)'. In *Europa-Historiker: Ein biographisches Handbuch*, vol. 1, edited by Heinz Duchhardt, Malgorzata Morawiec, Wolfgang Schmale, and Winfried Schulze, 317–336. Göttingen: Vandenhoeck & Ruprecht, 2006.

———. *Der Weg nach Europa: Geschichte der europäischen Integration, 1939–1957*. Göttingen: Vandenhoeck & Ruprecht, 1990. (3rd ed. 1996).

———, and Georges-Henri Soutou. *The Making of Détente: Eastern and Western Europe in the Cold War, 1965–75*. London: Routledge, 2008.

———, William Wallace, and Wolfgang Wessels, eds. *Walter Hallstein: The Forgotten European?* London and New York: Macmillan, 1998.

Ludlow, N. Piers. *Dealing with Britain: The Six and the First UK Application to the EEC*. Cambridge: Cambridge University Press, 1997.

———. *The European Community and the Crises of the 1960s: Negotiating the Gaullist Challenge*. London and New York: Routledge, 2006.

———, ed. *European Integration and the Cold War: Ostpolitik-Westpolitik, 1965–1973*. London and New York: Routledge, 2007.

———. 'The Making of the CAP: Towards an Analysis of the EU's First Major Policy.' *Contemporary European History* 14 (2005): 347–371.

———. Review of *The Rise and Fall of a National Strategy*, by Milward. *Cold War History* 4: 3 (April 2004): 183–185.

Ludlow, Peter. *The Making of the New Europe: The European Councils in Brussels and Copenhagen, 2002*. Brussels: Eurocomment, 2005.

Lund, Joachim, ed. *Working for the New Order: European Business under German Domination, 1939–1945*. Copenhagen: University Press of Southern Denmark, 2006.

Lundestad, Geir. *Empire by Integration: The United States and European Integration, 1945–1997*. Oxford: Oxford University Press, 1998.

———. 'Empire by Invitation? The United States and Western Europe, 1945–1952'. *Journal of Peace Research* 23: 3 (1986): 263–277.

———. 'Moralism, Presentism, Exceptionalism, Provincialism, and Other Extravagancies in American Writings on the Early Cold War'. *Diplomatic History* 13: 4 (Fall 1989): 527–545.

Lüschow, Hans. 'Die Produktivität bäuerlicher Familienbetriebe', *Agrarwirtschaft* 7 (1958): 265–268.

Lynch, Frances M. B. *France and the International Economy: From Vichy to the Treaty of Rome*. London: Routledge, 1997.

———. 'De Gaulle's First Veto: France, the Rueff Plan and the Free Trade Area'. *Contemporary European History* 9: 1 (2000): 111–135.

———. 'Harmonization through Competition? The Evolution of Taxation in Postwar Europe'. In *Global Debates about Taxations*, edited by Holger Nehring and Florian Schui, 116–136. Basingstoke: Palgrave Macmillan, 2007.

———. 'Resolving the Paradox of the Monnet Plan: National and International Planning in French Reconstruction'. *The Economic History Review* 37: 2 (1984): 229–243.

Lyons, Bruce. 'An Economic Assessment of European Commission Merger Control: 1958–2007'. In *Competition Policy in the EU: Fifty Years on from the Treaty of Rome*, edited by Xavier Vives, 135–168. Oxford: Oxford University Press, 2009.

Lyons, John S., Louis P. Cain, and Samuel H. Williamson. *Reflections on the Cliometric Revolution*. London and New York: Routledge, 2008.

Mackenzie, Donald, Fabian Muniesa, and Lucia Siu, eds. *Do Economists Make Markets? On the Performativity of Economics*. Princeton, NJ: Princeton University Press, 2007.

Maddison, Angus. *The World Economy: A Millennial Perspective*. Paris: OECD, 2001.

Maggiorani, Mauro. *L'Europa degli altri. Comunisti italiani e integrazione europea 1957–1969*. Rome: Carocci, 1998.

———, and Paolo Ferrari, eds. *L'Europa da Togliatti a Berlinguer: testimonianze e documenti: 1945–1984*. Bologna: Il Mulino, 2005.

Maier, Charles S. *Among Empires: American Ascendancy and Its Predecessors*. Cambridge, MA, and London: Harvard University Press, 2006.

———. *Dissolution: The Crisis of Communism and the End of East Germany*. Princeton: Princeton University Press, 1997.

———. 'The Politics of Productivity: Foundations of American International Economic Policy after World War II'. Originally published in *International Organization* 31: 4 (1977): 607–634.

———. *In Search of Stability: Explorations in Historical Political Economy*. Cambridge: Cambridge University Press, 1988.

———. 'The Two Postwar Eras and the Conditions for Stability in Twentieth Century Europe.' *American Historical Review* 86: 2 (1981): 327–352.

———. *The Unmasterable Past: History, Holocaust, and German National Identity*. Cambridge MA: Harvard University Press, 1988.

———. 'The World Economy and the Cold War in the Middle of the Twentieth Century'. In Leffler and Westad, *The Cambridge History of the Cold War*, Vol. 1: *Origins*, 2010, 44–66.

———, ed., with the assistance of Günter Bischof. *The Marshall Plan and Germany: West German Development within the Framework of the European Recovery Program*. New York and Oxford: Berg, 1991.

Majone, Giandomenico. *Dilemmas of European Integration: The Ambiguities and Pitfalls of Integration by Stealth*. Oxford: Oxford University Press, 2005.

Makins, Christopher. Review of *The German Economy at War*, by Milward. *The Spectator*, 24 September 1965: 386.

Mansholt, Sicco. *Die Krise: Europa und die Grenzen des Wachstums*. Reinbek bei Hamburg: Rowohlt, 1974.

March, James G., and Johan P. Olsen. 'The Institutional Dynamics of International Political Orders'. *International Organization* 52: 4 (1998): 943–969.

Marks, G., L. Hooghe, and K. Blank. 'European Integration from the 1980s: State-centric versus Multi-level Governance'. *Journal of Common Market Studies* 34 (1996): 341–378.

Marks, Sally. Review of *The Reconstruction of Western Europe*, by Milward. *The American Historical Review* 90: 2 (April 1985): 408.

———. 'The World According to Washington'. *Diplomatic History* 11: 3 (Summer 1987): 265–282.

Martin, Stephen. 'Building on Coal and Steel: European Integration in the 1950s and 1960s'. In Dinan, *Origins and Evolution of the European Union*, 126–139.

Marwick, Arthur. *The Deluge: British Society and the First World War*. London: Bodley Head, 1965.

———. *Britain in the Century of Total War: War, Peace and Social Change, 1900–1967*. London: Bodley Head, 1968.

———, and Clive Emsley, 'Introduction'. In *War, Peace and Social Change in Twentieth Century Europe*, edited by Emsley, Marwick, and Simpson, 1–25. Milton Keynes: Open University Press, 1990.

Mason, Timothy W. 'Der Primat der Politik-Politik und Wirtschaft im Nationalsozialismus'. *Das Argument-Berliner Hefte für Probleme der Gesellschaft* 41 (1966): 473–494. (English version 'The Primacy of Politics—Politics and Economics in National Socialist Germany' In *Nazism and the Third Reich*, edited by Henry A. Turner, 175–200. New York: Quadrangle Books, 1972).

———. *Sozialpolitik im Dritten Reich: Arbeiterklasse und Volksgemeinschaft*. Opladen: Westdeutscher Verlag, 1977.

Mastenbroek, Ellen. 'EU Compliance: Still a "Black Hole"?' *Journal of European Public Policy* 12:6 (2005): 1103–1120.

Matteoli, Giovanni et al., eds. *Giorgio Amendola: comunista riformista*. Soveria Mannelli: Rubbettino, 2001.

Mauch, Christof, and Kiran Klaus Patel, eds. *The United States and Germany during the Twentieth Century: Competition and Convergence*. Cambridge: Cambridge University Press, 2010.

Mazower, Mark. *Dark Continent: Europe's Twentieth Century*. London: Penguin Press, 1998.

McGowan, Lee. *The Antitrust Revolution in Europe: Exploring the European Commission's Cartel Policy*. London: Edward Elgar, 2010.

———. 'Theorising European Integration: Revisiting Neofunctionalism and Testing its Suitability for Explaining the Development of EC Competition Policy?' European Integration online papers 11: 3 (2007). Available at: http://eiop.or.at/eiop/index.php/eiop/article/view/2007_003a (last accessed on 12 December 2011).

———, and Stephen Wilks. 'The First Supranational Policy in the European Union: Competition Policy'. *European Journal of Political Research* 28: 2 (1995) 141–169.

McGrew, William W. *Land and Revolution in Modern Greece, 1800–1881: The Transition in the Tenure and Exploitation of Land from Ottoman Rule to Independence*. Kent, OH: Kent State University Press, 1985.

McKenzie, Brian A. *Remaking France: Americanization, Public Diplomacy, and the Marshall Plan*. New York: Berghahn, 2005.

McLean, Iain. 'Political Science and History: Friends and Neighbours'. *Political Studies* 58: 2 (2010): 354–367.

McNeill, William Hardy. *The Greek Dilemma*. London: Victor Gollancz, 1947.

Medlicott, William Norton. *The Economic Blockade*. 2 vols. History of the Second World War, United Kingdom Civil Series, edited by Sir Keith Hancock. London: Her Majesty's Stationery Office and Longmans, Green & Co. Vol. 1, 1952 and vol. 2, 1959.

Mélandri, Pierre. 'La France et l'Alliance atlantique sous Georges Pompidou et Valerie Giscard d'Estaing'. In *La France et l'OTAN, 1949–1996*, edited by Maurice Vaïsse, Pierre Mélandri, and Frederic Bozo, 519–558. Brussels: Editions Complexe, 1996.

Mendès-France, Pierre. *Oeuvres complètes, II: Une politique de l'économie, 1943–1954*. Paris: Gallimard, 1985.

Menger, Manfred et al., eds. *Expansionsrichtung Nordeuropa: Dokumente zur Nordeuropapolitik des faschistischen deutschen Imperialismus 1939 bis 1945*. Berlin: Deutscher Verlag der Wissenschaften, 1987.

Mény, Yves, and Vincent Wright, eds. *The Politics of Steel: Western Europe and the Steel Industry in the Crisis Years (1974–1984)*. Berlin and New York: W. de Gruyter, 1987.

———. 'State and Steel in Western Europe'. In Mény and Wright, *The Politics of Steel*, 1–110.

Messing, F. 'Het economisch leven in Nederland, 1945–1980'. In Blok, *Algemene Geschiedenis der Nederlanden*, 159–201.

Mihic, Sophia, Stephen G. Engelmann, and Elizabeth Rose Wingrove. 'Making Sense In and Of Political Science: Facts, Values and "Real" Numbers'. In *The Politics of Method in the Human Sciences: Positivism and its Epistemological Others*, edited by George Steinmetz, 471–495. Durham, NC: Duke University Press, 2005.

Miljan, Toivo. *The Reluctant Europeans: The Attitude of the Nordic Countries towards European Integration*. London: C. Hurst & Co., 1977.

Millar, James R. *The Soviet economic experiment.* Edited and with an introduction by Susan J. Linz. Urbana: University of Illinois Press, 1990.

Miller, Perry. 'The Reimportation of Ideas'. In *The Impact of America on European Culture*, edited by Bertrand Russell et al. Boston: Beacon Press, 1951.

Mills, Geofrey T., and Hugh Rockoff, eds. *Sinews of War: Essays on the Economic History of World War II.* Ames, IA: Iowa State University Press, 1993.

Milward, Alan S. For all published works by this author, see Appendix 2 of this volume.

Mioche, Philippe. *Les cinquante années de l'Europe du charbon et de l'acier, 1952–2002.* Luxembourg: Office des publications officielles des Communautés européennes, 2004.

———. *Jacques Ferry et la sidérurgie française depuis la Seconde Guerre mondiale.* Aix-en-Provence: Publications de l'Université de Provence, 1993.

Mitchell, B. R. Review of *The Fascist Economy in Norway*, by Milward. *The Economic Journal* 82: 327 (September 1972): 1105–1107.

Modelski, George. 'The Long Cycle of Global Politics and the Nation-State'. *Comparative Studies in Society and History* 20: 2 (April 1978): 214–235.

Mokyr, Joel. 'Demand vs. Supply in the Industrial Revolution'. *Journal of Economic History* 37: 4 (1977): 981–1008.

———, ed. *The Economics of the Industrial Revolution.* London: George Allen & Unwin, 1985.

Mommsen, Hans, Dietmar Petzina, and Bernd Weisbrod, eds. *Industrielles System und politische Entwicklung in der Weimarer Republik: Verhandlungen des internationalen Symposiums in Bochum vom 12–17. Juni 1973.* Düsseldorf: Droste Verlag, 1974.

Monnet, Jean, and Robert Schuman. *Correspondance, 1947–1953.* Lausanne: Fondation Jean Monnet pour l'Europe, 1986.

Monroe, Kristen Renwick, ed. *Contemporary Empirical Political Theory.* Berkeley, CA: University of California Press, 1997.

———, ed. *Perestroika! The Raucous Rebellion in Political Science.* New Haven, CT: Yale University Press, 2005.

Moravcsik, Andrew. *The Choice for Europe: Social Purpose and State Power from Messina to Maastricht.* Ithaca and New York: Cornell University Press, 1998; London: UCL Press, 1999.

———. 'De Gaulle Between Grain and *Grandeur*: The Political Economy of French EC Policy, 1958–1970'. *Journal of Cold War Studies* 2: 2 (2000): 3–43 (Part 1) and 2: 3 (2000): 4–68 (Part 2).

———. 'In Defense of the "Democratic Deficit": Reassessing Legitimacy in the European Union'. *Journal of Common Market Studies* 40: 4 (2002): 603–624.

———. Review of *The European Rescue of the Nation-State*, by Milward. *The Journal of Modern History* 67: 1 (1995): 126–128.

Morgan, Roger. 'European Integration and National Interests'. Review. *Government and Opposition* 29: 1 (Winter 1994): 128–134.

Motta, Massimo. *Competition Policy. Theory and Practice.* Cambridge: Cambridge University Press, 2004.

Mougenot, Pierre. Review of *The Fascist Economy in Norway*, by Milward. *Revue Historique* 253: 514 (April–June 1975): 483–485.

Mozer, Alfred. *'Gastarbeider' in Europa.* Zutphen: De Walburg Pers, 1980.

Müller, Margrit, and Timo Myllyntaus, eds. *Pathbreakers. Small European Countries Responding to Globalisation and Deglobalisation.* Bern: Peter Lang, 2008.

Muller, Pierre. 'La politique agricole française: l'État et les organisations professionnelles'. *Économie rurale* 255 (2000): 33–39.

Müller, Rolf-Dieter. 'Albert Speer und die Rüstungspolitik im Totalen Krieg'. In *Das Deutsche Reich und der Zweite Weltkrieg*, Vol. 5: 2. *Organisation und*

*Mobilisierung des deutschen Machtbereichs: Kriegsverwaltung, Wirtschaft und personelle Ressourcen, 1942–1944/45*, edited by Militärgeschichtliches Forschungsamt, 275–776. Stuttgart: Deutsche Verlags-Anstalt, 1999.

Mutimer, David. '1992 and the Political Integration of Europe: Neofunctionalism Reconsidered'. *Journal of European Integration* 13: 4 (1989): 75–101.

Napolitano, Giorgio. *Dal PCI al socialismo europeo: un'autobiografia politica*. Rome-Bari: Laterza, 2006.

Nationale Conventie (Nederland), ed. *De Europese Unie als statenverbond. Gedachten over de finaliteit van de Europese integratie: Rapport van de werkgroep Europa*. The Hague: Nationale Conventie, 2006.

Neal, Larry. 'The Economics and Finance of Bilateral Clearing Agreements: Germany, 1934–1938'. *Economic History Review* 32 (August 1979): 391–404.

———. *The Economics of Europe and the European Union*. Cambridge and New York: Cambridge University Press, 2007.

———. Review of *War, Economy and Society*, by Milward. *Business History Review* 52: 3 (Autumn 1978): 441–443.

———. *The Rise of Financial Capitalism: International Capital Markets in the Age of Reason*. Cambridge: Cambridge University Press, 1993.

———, and Daniel Barbezat. *The Economics of the European Union and the Economies of Europe*. London and New York: Oxford University Press, 1998.

Neil, Robert F. Review of *The German Economy at War*, by Milward. *The Journal of Modern History* 38: 2 (June 1966): 216–217.

Nelson, Richard R., and Bhaven N. Sampat. 'Making Sense of Institutions as a Factor Shaping Economic Performance'. *Journal of Economic Behavior and Organization* 44: 1 (2001): 31–54.

Nême, J., and C. Nême. *Economie Européenne*. Paris: Presses Universitaires de France, 1970.

Néré, Jacques. *The Foreign Policy of France from 1914 to 1945*. London: Routledge, 1975.

Newman, Michael. 'Allegiance, Legitimation, Democracy and the European Union'. EUI working paper 2001/5 of the History and Civilization Department. Florence: December 2001. Available at: http://cadmus.eui.eu/dspace/bitstream/1814/57/1/hec01-05.pdf (last accessed on 12 December 2011).

———. *Humanitarian Intervention: Confronting the Contradictions*. London: C. Hurst & Co Publishers Ltd, 2009.

Nicholls A. J. Review of *The German Economy at War*, by Milward. *The English Historical Review* 81: 321 (October 1966): 873–875.

Nicolson, Harold. *The Future of the English-Speaking World*. Glasgow: Jackson, 1949.

Nielsson, Gunnar P. 'Denmark and European Integration: A Small Country at the Crossroads'. Ph.D. thesis, University of California, 1966.

———. 'The Parallel National Action Process: Scandinavian Experiences'. In *International Organisation: A Conceptual Approach*, edited by Paul Taylor and A.J.R. Groom, 270–316. London: Frances Pinter, 1978.

Niemann, Arne, and Philipp C. Schmitter. 'Neofunctionalism'. In Wiener and Diez, *European Integration Theory*, 45–66.

Njolstad, Olav. 'The Carter Administration and Italy: Keeping the Communists out of Power Without Interfering'. *Journal of Cold War Studies* 3 (Summer 2002): 56–94.

Nocken, Ulrich. 'International Cartels and Foreign Policy: The Formation of the International Steel Cartel, 1924–1926'. In *Internationale Kartelle und Außenpolitik*, edited by Clemens Wurm, 33–82. Stuttgart: Franz Steiner Verlag, 1989.

Noël, Gilbert. *Du Pool Vert à la Politique Agricole Commune: Les tentantives de Communauté agricole européenne entre 1945 et 1955*. Paris: Economica, 1988.

Noonan, Eamonn. 'Choosing Confrontation: Commercial Policy in Britain and Germany, 1929–1936'. Ph.D. thesis, European University Institute, Florence, 1995.

———. 'Wurttemberg's Exporters and German Protectionism, 1931–36'. EUI working paper 87/317. Florence: 1987.

*Nordisk økonomisk samarbejde: Foreløbig rapport fra Det Fælles Nordiske Udvalg for økonomisk Samarbejde*, Copenhagen: Joint Nordic Committee for Economic Cooperation, 1950.

North, Douglass C. 'Epilogue: Economic Performance through Time'. In *Empirical Studies in Institutional Change*, edited by Lee J. Alston, Thráinne Eggertsson, and North, 342–343. Cambridge: Cambridge University Press, 1996.

———. Review of *The Economic Development of Continental Europe*, by Milward and Saul. *The Journal of Economic Literature* 12: 3 (September 1974): 910–911.

———. *Structure and Change in Economic History*. New York: W. W. Norton, 1982.

———. *Understanding the Process of Economic Growth*. Princeton, NJ: Princeton University Press, 2005.

Nuti, Leopoldo. *Gli Stati uniti e l'apertura a sinistra: Importanza e limiti della presenza Americana in Italia*. Rome-Bari: Laterza, 1999.

O'Brien, Patrick K. 'Do We Have a Typology for the Study of European Industrialization in the Nineteenth Century?' *Journal of European Economic History* 15 (1986): 291–333.

———, and Çaglar Keyder. *Economic Growth in Britain and France, 1780–1914: Two Paths to the Twentieth Century*. London: G. Allen & Unwin, 1978.

Occhino, Filippo, Kim Oosterlinck, and Eugene N. White. 'How Much Can a Victor Force the Vanquished to Pay?' *Journal of Economic History* 68: 1 (March 2008): 1–45.

Olesen, Thorsten Borring. 'Nationalstaten og den europæiske integration i teori og praksis'. *Nyt fra historien* 1 (1994): 1–11.

———, and Poul Villaume. *I blokopdelingens tegn, 1945–72* (*Dansk Udenrigspolitiks historie 5*). Copenhagen: Gyldendals Leksikon, 2005.

Olsen, Johan P. 'Reforming Institutions of European Governance'. *Journal of Common Market Studies* 40: 4 (2002): 581–602.

Ophüls, Marcel, dir. *Le Chagrin et la Pitié: Chronique d'une ville sous l'occupation*. France: Télévision Rencontre, 1969. Documentary film.

Oren, Ido. *Our Enemies and US: America's Rivalries and the Making of Political Science*. Ithaca, NY: Cornell University Press, 2003.

Orwell, George. 'Toward European Unity'. *Partisan Review* 14: 4 (July–Aug 1947): 346–351.

Ory, Pascal. 'Introduction to an Era of Doubt: Cultural Reflections of "French Power" around the Year 1948'. In *Power in Europe? Great Britain, France, Italy and Germany in a Postwar World, 1945–1950*, edited by J. Becker and F. Knipping, 397–408. Berlin and New York: De Gruyter, 1986.

Overy, Richard J. 'Business in the *Grossraumwirtschaft*: Eastern Europe, 1938–1945'. In *Enterprise in the Period of Fascism in Europe*, edited by Harold James and Jakob Tanner, 151–177. Aldershot: Ashgate, 2002.

———. 'Germany, "Domestic Crisis" and War in 1939'. *Past and Present* 116 (16 August 1987): 138–168.

———. *Goering: The Iron Man*. London: Routledge & Kegan Paul, 1984.

———. 'Hitler's War and the German Economy: A Reinterpretation'. *The Economic History Review* (2nd Series) 35: 2 (May 1982): 272–291.

———. Review of the 1987 paperback edition of *War, Economy and Society*, by Milward. *European History Quarterly* 21: 1 (January 1991): 158–160.

———. *War and Economy in the Third Reich*. New York: Oxford University Press, 1994.

Owen, Geoffrey. *From Empire to Europe: The Decline and Revival of British Industry since the Second World War.* London and New York: Harper Collins Publishers, 1999.

Palairet, Michael P. *The Balkan Economies c.1800–1914: Evolution without Development.* Cambridge: Cambridge University Press, 2003.

Palayret, Jean-Marie. 'Jean Monnet, la Haute Autorité de la CECA face au problème de la reconcentration de la sidérurgie dans la Ruhr (1950–1958)'. *Revue d'Histoire diplomatique* 105 (1991), 307–348.

———, Helen Wallace, and Pascaline Winand, eds. *Visions, Votes and Vetoes: The Empty Chair Crisis and the Luxembourg Compromise Forty Years on.* Brussels: Peter Lang, 2006.

Pálsson, Lýður. 'Rjómabú. „Áfram með smjörið góðir hálsar"'. *Sagnir* 9 (1988): 72–81.

Parker, William N. 'Europe in an American Mirror: Reflections on Industrialization and Ideology'. In *Patterns of European Industrialization: The Nineteenth Century,* edited by Richard Sylla and Gianni Toniolo, 80–91. London and New York: Routledge, 1991. Reprinted as 'European Industrialization in an American Mirror' in *Europe, America, and the Wider World: Essays on the Economic History of Western Capitalism. Vol. 2: America and the Wider World,* edited by William N. Parker, 298–310. Cambridge and New York: Cambridge University Press, 1991.

———, ed. *Europe, America, and the Wider World: Essays on the Economic History of Western Capitalism. Vol. 1: Europe and the World Economy.* Cambridge and New York: Cambridge University Press, 1984.

———. Review of *The Development of the Economies of Continental Europe,* by Milward and Saul. *The Journal of Economic History* 38: 3 (September 1978): 799–801.

Parlato, V. 'La classe operaia e le tendenze del capitalismo europeo'. *Rinascita* 27, 3 July 1965.

Parsons, Craig. *A Certain Idea of Europe.* Ithaca, NY: Cornell University Press, 2003.

Patel, Kiran Klaus. 'Europäische Integrationsgeschichte auf dem Weg zur doppelten Neuorientierung: Ein Forschungsbericht'. *Archiv für Sozialgeschichte* 50 (2010): 595–642.

———. *Europäisierung wider Willen: Die Bundesrepublik Deutschland in der Agrarintegration der EWG, 1955–1973; Studien zur internationalen Geschichte* 23. Munich: Oldenbourg, 2009.

———, ed. *Fertile Ground for Europe? The History of European Integration and the Common Agricultural Policy since 1945.* Baden-Baden: Nomos, 2009.

———. 'Paradefall der Integration? Die Gemeinsame Agrarpolitik der EWG und die Agrarintegration nach dem Zweiten Weltkrieg'. In *Internationalismus und Europäische Integration im Vergleich: Fallstudien zu Währungen, Fallstudien zu Währungen, Landwirtschaft, Verkehrs- und Nachrichtenwesen,* edited by Christian Henrich-Franke, Cornelius Neutsch, and Guido Thiemeyer, 203–219. Baden-Baden: Nomos, 2007.

———. *Soldiers of Labor: Labor Service in Nazi Germany and New Deal America, 1933–1945.* Cambridge and New York: Cambridge University Press, 2005.

Paxton, Robert O., and Nicolas Wahl, eds. *De Gaulle and the United States: A Centennial Reappraisal.* Oxford: Berg, 1994.

Peggio, Eugenio. 'Intervento'. In *Tendenze del capitalismo europeo: Atti del convegno organizzato dall'Istituto Gramsci, Roma 25–27 giugno 1965,* edited by A. A. Arzumanian et al. Rome: Editori Riuniti-Istituto Gramsci, 1966.

Peltonen, Matti. 'Agrarian World Market and Finnish Farm Economy: The Agrarian Transition in Finland in Late Nineteenth and Early Twentieth Centuries'. *Scandinavian Economic History Review* 36: 1 (1988): 26–45.

Pen, Jan. 'Het onderschatte Marshall-wonder'. *Het Parool*, 24 May 1997.

———. 'Nieuw Marshall-plan?' *Het Parool*, 5 April 1997.

Pescatore, Pierre. 'Some Critical Remarks on the Single European Act'. *Common Market Law Review* 24 (1987): 9–18.

Petersen, Tore T., ed. *Controlling the Uncontrollable? The Great Powers in the Middle East*. Trondheim: Tapir Academic Press, 2006.

Petmezas, Socrates. 'Agriculture and Economic Development in Greece, 1870–1973'. In Lains and Pinilla, *Agriculture and Economic Development*, 353–374.

Petrén, Gustav. 'The Nordic Council: A Unique Factor in International Law'. *Nordisk Tidsskrift for International Ret* 29: 4 (1959): 346–362.

Petrick, Fritz. *Der ‚Leichtmetallausbau Norwegen', 1940–1945: Eine Studie zur deutschen Expansions- und Okkupationspolitik in Nordeuropa*. Frankfurt am Main: Peter Lang, 1992.

———. Review of *The Fascist Economy in Norway*, by Milward. *Zeitschrift für Geschichtswissenschaft* 22: 12 (1974): 1388.

———. 'Zwei Schlüsseldokumente zur faschistischen „Aufteilung der europäischen Aluminiumindustrie"'. *Jahrbuch für Wirtschaftsgeschichte* 17: 1 (1977): 249–268.

Petzina, Dietmar. *Autarkiepolitik im Dritten Reich: Der nationalsozialistische Vierjahresplan*. Stuttgart: Deutsche Verlagsanstalt, 1968.

———. Review of *Der Zweite Weltkrieg: Krieg, Wirtschaft und Gesellschaft*, by Milward. *Historische Zeitschrift* 226: 3 (June 1978): 761–763.

Pharo, Helge. 'Bridgebuilding and Reconstruction: Norway Faces the Marshall Plan'. *Scandinavian Journal of History* 1: 1–4 (1976): 125–153.

———. Review of *The Fascist Economy in Norway*, by Milward. *Historisk Tidsskrift* (Oslo): 52 (1973): 97–100.

Philips, Louis. *Competition Policy: A Game-Theoretic Perspective*. Cambridge: Cambridge University Press, 1995.

Philipse, A. H. 'Het Marshallplan gezien vanuit de Nederlandse ambassade te Washington'. In *Herwonnen welvaart*, edited by the Directoraat-Generaal voor het Economische en Militaire Hulp-programma, 113–121.

Pierson, Paul. 'The New Politics of the Welfare State'. *World Politics* 48: 2 (1996): 143–179.

———. 'The Path to European Integration: A Historical and Institutionalist Analysis'. *Comparative Political Studies* 29 (1996): 123–163.

Pijpers, A. *De mythe van het democratisch tekort: Een discussiebijdrage over de Europese politiek*. The Hague: Instituut Clingendael, 1999.

Pine, Melissa. 'European Integration: A Meeting Ground for History and Political Science? A Historian Responds to Andrew Moravcsik'. *JEIH* 14: 1 (2008): 87–104.

Planck, Ulrich. *Der bäuerliche Familienbetrieb: Zwischen Patriarchat und Partnerschaft*. Stuttgart: Enke, 1964.

Plumpe, Gottfried. *Die I.G. Farbenindustrie AG: Wirtschaft, Technik und Politik, 1904–1945*. Berlin: Duncker & Humblot, 1990.

Pohl, Manfred. *VIAG Aktiengesellschaft, 1923–1998: Vom Staatsunternehmen zum internationalen Konzern*. München: Piper, 1998.

Poidevin, Raymond. *Robert Schuman—Homme d'état, 1886–1963*. Paris: Imprimerie nationale, 1986.

Polanyi, Karl. *The Great Transformation: The Political and Economic Origins of our Time*. New York: Farrar & Rinehart, 1944.

———. *Trade and Market in the Early Empires*. Glencoe, IL: The Free Press, 1957.

Pollack, Mark A. *The Engines of European Integration: Delegation, Agency and Agenda Setting in the EU*. Oxford: Oxford University Press, 2003.

———. 'Principal-Agent Analysis and International Delegation: Red Herrings, Theoretical Clarifications and Empirical Disputes'. *College of Europe*, Political Research Paper 2. Bruges: February 2007.

Pollard, Robert A. *Economic Security and the Origins of the Cold War, 1945–50.* New York: Columbia University Press, 1985.

Pollard, Sidney. *Peaceful Conquest: The Industrialization of Europe, 1760–1970.* Oxford: Oxford University Press, 1981.

Pons, Silvio. *Berlinguer e la fine del comunismo*. Turin: Einaudi, 2006.

———, and Federico Romero, eds. *Reinterpreting the End of the Cold War.* London: Frank Cass, 2005.

Pounds, Norman J. G. *An Historical Geography of Europe, 1800–1914.* Cambridge: Cambridge University Press, 1985.

Preeg, Ernest H. *Traders and Diplomats: An Analysis of the Kennedy Round of Negotiations under the GATT.* Washington, DC: Brookings Institution, 1970.

Price, Harry Bayard. *The Marshall Plan and Its Meaning.* Ithaca, NY: Cornell University Press, 1955.

Rambour, Muriel. 'Les réformes institutionnelles dans l'Union Européenne avant et après Nice'. In Loth, *La gouvernance supranationale*, 283–308.

Ramírez Pérez, Sigfrido M. 'Antitrust ou anti US? L'industrie automobile européenne et les origines de la politique de la concurrence de la CEE'. In *Europe organisée, Europe du libre-échange*, edited by Éric Bussière, Michel Dumoulin and Sylvain Schirmann. Bern: Peter Lang, 2007: 203–229.

———. 'Automobile Standardisation in Europe: Between Technological Choices and Neo-protectionism'. In *Trends in Technological Innovation and the European Construction: the Emerging of Enduring Dynamics?*, edited by Christophe Bouneau, David Burigana, and Antonio Varsori, 187–205. Brussels: P.I.E. Peter Lang, 2010.

———. 'Europe néo-libérale? Les limites d'une interprétation téléologique de l'intégration européenne'. *Raison Publique* 13 (2010): 261–280.

———. 'The European Committee for Economic and Social Progress: Business Networks between Atlantic and European Communities'. In *Transnational Networks in Regional Integration*, edited by Kaiser, Leucht, and Gehler, 2010: 61–85.

———. 'The European Search for a New Industrial Policy (1970-1992)'. In *Back to Maastricht: Obstacles to Constitutional Reform within the EU Treaty (1991–2007)*, edited by Stefania Baroncelli, Carlo Spagnolo, and Leila Simona Talani, 303–324. Newcastle: Cambridge Scholars Publishing, 2008.

———. 'The French automobile industry and the Treaty of Rome: Between Welfare State and Multinational Corporations (1955–1958)'. In Gehler, *From Common Market to European Union Building*, 169–194.

———. 'La politique de la concurrence de la Communauté Economique Européenne et l'industrie européenne: les accords sur la distribution automobile (1972–1985)'. *Histoire, Economie et Société* 27: 1 (2008): 63–79.

———. 'Public Policies, European Integration and Multinational Corporations in the Automobile Sector: the French and Italian cases in a comparative perspective 1945-1973', Ph.D. thesis, European University Institute, Florence, 2007.

———. 'Transnational Business Networks Propagating EC Industrial Policy: The Role of the Committee of Common Market Automobile Constructors'. In Kaiser, Leucht, and Rasmussen, *The History of the European Union*, 74–93.

Range, Willard. *Franklin D. Roosevelt's World Order.* Athens, GA: University of Georgia Press, 1959.

Ranieri, Ruggero. 'Assessing the Implications of Mass Production and European Integration: The Debate Inside the Italian Steel Industry (1945–1960)'. In Dumoulin et al., *L'Europe du Patronat*, 77–100.

———. 'L'espansione alla prova del negoziato—l'industria italiana e la Comunità del Carbone e dell'Acciaio, 1945–1955', Ph.D thesis, European University Institute, Florence, 1988.

———. 'L'espansione siderurgica italiana nel primo quindicennio del trattato CECA (1952–1967)'. In Ranieri and Tosi, *La Comunità Europea del Carbone e dell'Acciaio*, 153–228.

———. 'Inside or Outside the Magic Circle? The Italian and the British Steel Industries Face to Face with the Schuman Plan and the European Coal and Steel Community'. In Milward, Lynch, Ranieri, Romero, and Sørensen, *The Frontier of National Sovereignty*, 117–154.

———, and Luciano Tosi, eds. *La Comunità Europea del Carbone e dell'Acciaio (1952–2002). Gli esiti del Trattato in Europa e in Italia*. Padova: Casa Editrice Dott. Antonio Dilani, 2004.

Ránki, György. *The Economics of the Second World War.* Vienna, Cologne, Weimar: Böhlaus zeitgeschichtliche Bibliothek, 1993.

Rappaport, Armin. 'The United States and European Integration: The First Phase', *Diplomatic History* 5: 2 (April 1981): 121–150.

Rasmussen, Morten. 'From *Costa v. ENEL* to the Treaties of Rome: A Brief History of a Legal Revolution'. In *The Past and Future of EU Law: The Classics of EU Law Revisited on the 50th Anniversary of the Rome Treaty*, edited by Miguel Poiares Maduro and Loïc Azoulai, 69–86. Oxford: Hart Publishing, 2010.

———. 'European Rescue of the Nation-State? Tracing the Role of Economics and Business'. In Kaiser and Varsori, *European Union History—Themes and Debates*, 128–149.

———, and Ann Christina Lauring Knudsen. 'A European Political System in the Making, 1958–1970: The Relevance of Emerging Committee Structures'. *JEIH* 14: 1 (2008): 51–68.

Ratner, Sidney. Review of *The German Economy at War*, by Milward. *The American Historical Review* 71: 2 (January 1966): 615–616.

Rauh, Cornelia. *Schweizer Aluminium für Hitlers Krieg? Zur Geschichte der ‚Alusuisse', 1918–1950.* Munich: C. H. Beck, 2009.

Reichlin, Lucrezia. 'The Marshall Plan Reconsidered'. In Eichengreen, *Europe's Post-War Recovery*, 39–67.

Reis, Jaime. 'Bank Structures, Gerschenkron and Portugal (pre-1914)'. In *The Origins of National Financial Systems: Alexander Gerschenkron Reconsidered*, edited by Douglas J. Forsyth and Daviel Verdier, 182–204. London: Routledge, 2002.

*Report of the Committee appointed by the Prime Minister under the Chairmanship of Lord Robbins*, Cmnd. 2154 (London, HMSO, 1963). Available at: http://www.educationengland.org.uk/documents/robbins/ (last accessed on 12 December 2011).

Riker, William H. 'The Ferment of the 1950s'. In Monroe, *Contemporary Empirical Political Theory*, 191–201.

Risse, T. 'Social Constructivism and European Integration'. In Wiener and Diez, *European Integration Theory*, 159–176.

Risso, Linda. *Divided We Stand: The French and Italian Political Parties and the Rearmament of West Germany.* Cambridge: Cambridge Scholars Publishing, 2007.

Ritschl, Albrecht. 'Nazi Economic Imperialism and the Exploitation of the Small: Evidence from Germany's Secret Foreign Exchange Balance, 1938–1940'. *The Economic History Review* 54: 2 (May 2001): 324–345.

Rittberger, Berthold. 'Which Institutions for Post-war Europe? Explaining the Institutional Design of Europe's First Community'. *Journal of European Public Policy* 8: 5 (2001): 673–708.

Robinson, Austin. Review of *The German Economy at War,* by Milward. *The Economic Journal* 76: 302 (June 1966): 418–424.

Rokkan, Stein. 'Dimensions of State Formation and Nation-building: A Possible Paradigm for Research on Variations within Europe'. In *The Formation of National States in Western Europe*, edited by Charles Tilly, 575–591. Princeton, NJ: Princeton University Press, 1975.

Romer, Christina D. 'The End of Economic History?' *Journal of Economic Education* 25: 1 (1994): 49–66.

Romero, Federico. *Emigrazione e Integrazione Europea, 1945–1973*. Rome: Edizioni Lavoro, 1991.

———. *Storia della guerra fredda: L'ultimo conflitto per l'Europa*. Torino: Einaudi, 2009.

———. *Storia internazionale del Novecento*. Rome: Carocci, 2001.

———. *The United States and the European Trade Union Movement, 1944–1951*. Chapel Hill: University of North Carolina Press, 1993.

———, and Luciano Segreto, eds. 'Italia, Europa, America: l'integrazione internazionale dell'economia italiana (1945–1963)'. *Studi Storici: Rivista Trimestrale dell'Istituto Gramsci* 37: 1 (1996): 5–362.

Rometsch, Dietrich. *Die Rolle und Funktionsweise der Europäischen Kommission in der Ära Delors*. Frankfurt am Main: Peter Lang, 1999.

Röndings, Uwe. *Globalisierung und europäische Integration: Der Strukturwandel des Energiesektors und die Politik der Montanunion, 1952–1962*. Baden-Baden: Nomos, 2000.

Rosamond, Ben. 'European Integration and the Social Science of EU Studies: The Disciplinary Politics of a Subfield'. *International Affairs* 83: 2 (2007): 231–252.

———. *Globalization and the European Union*. Basingstoke: Palgrave Macmillan, forthcoming.

———. 'Open Political Science, Methodological Nationalism and European Union studies'. *Government and Opposition* 43: 4 (2008): 599–612.

———. 'The Political Sciences of European Integration: Disciplinary History and EU Studies'. In Jørgensen, Pollack, and Rosamond, *Handbook of European Union Politics*, 7–30.

———. *Theories of European Integration*. Basingstoke: Macmillan, 2000.

———. 'The Uniting of Europe and the Foundation of EU Studies: Revisiting the Neofunctionalism of Ernst B. Haas'. *Journal of European Public Policy* 12: 2 (2005): 237–254.

Roseman, Mark. 'World War II and Social Change in Germany'. In *Total War and Social Change,* edited by Arthur Marwick, 58–78. London and New York: Macmillan and St. Martin's Press, 1988.

Rosenberg, Emily. *Spreading the American Dream: American Economic and Cultural Expansion, 1890–1945*. New York: Hill & Wang, 1982.

Rostow, Walter Whitman. *How it All Began: Origins of the Modern Economy.* New York: McGraw-Hill, 1975.

———. Review of *The Development of the Economies of Continental Europe*, by Milward and Saul. *The Journal of Modern History* 50: 4 (December 1978): 727–728.

———. *The Stages of Economic Growth: A Non-Communist Manifesto*. Cambridge: Cambridge University Press, 1960.

Rousso, Henry. *The Vichy Syndrome: History and Memory in France since 1944.* Cambridge, MA: Harvard University Press, 1991.

Ruggie, John G., Peter J. Katzenstein, Robert O. Keohane, and Philippe C. Schmitter. 'Transformations in World Politics: The Intellectual Contributions of Ernst B. Haas'. *Annual Review of Political Science* 8 (2005): 271–296.

Rumford, Chris, and Philomena Murray. 'Globalization and the Limitations of European Integration Studies: Interdisciplinary Considerations'. *Journal of Contemporary European Studies* 11: 1 (2002): 85–93.

Santamaria, Yves, and Andrea Guiso. *La colomba e la spada: lotta per la pace e antiamericanismo nella politica del PCI, 1949–1954*. Saverio Manella: Rubbettino, 2006.

Santoro, Carlo Maria. *Diffidence and Ambition: The Intellectual Sources of U.S. Foreign Policy*. Boulder, CO: Westview Press, 1992.

Sarotte, Mary Elise. *Dealing with the Devil: East Germany, Détente and Ostpolitik, 1969–1973*. Chapel Hill: University of North Carolina Press, 2001.

Saul, S. Berrick. *The Myth of the Great Depression, 1873–1896*. London: Macmillan, 1968.

Saunier, Georges. 'Le tandem François Mitterrand—Helmut Kohl: Une gouvernance franco-allemande symbolique?' In Loth, *La gouvernance supranationale*, 239–254.

Schaad, Martin P. C. *Bullying Bonn: Anglo-German Diplomacy on European Integration, 1955–61*. Basingstoke: Macmillan, 2000.

Schain, Martin, ed. *The Marshall Plan: Fifty Years After*. New York: Palgrave, 2001.

Schelling, Thomas C. *The Strategy of Conflict*. Cambridge, MA: Harvard University Press, 1960.

Scherner, Jonas. 'Das Verhältnis zwischen NS Regime und Industrieunternehmen: Zwang oder Kooperation?'. *Zeitschrift für Unternehmensgeschichte / Journal of Business History* 51: 2 (2006): 166–190.

———. 'Nazi Germany's Preparation for War: Evidence from Revised Industrial Investment Series'. *European Review of Economic History* 14 (August 2010): 433–468.

Schiller, Bernt. 'At Gun Point: A Critical Perspective on the Attempts of the Nordic Governments to Achieve Unity after the Second World War'. *Scandinavian Journal of History* 9: 3 (1984): 221–238.

Schimmelfennig, Frank. 'The Community Trap: Liberal Norms, Rhetorical Action, and the Eastern Enlargement of the European Union'. *International Organization* 55: 1 (2001): 47–80.

Schlesinger, Arthur M., Jr. 'Origins of the Cold War'. *Foreign Affairs* 46 (1967): 22–52.

Schmidt, Louis Bernard. *The Family Farm in the Machine Age* (third *The Challenge to Democracy* bulletin). Ames: Iowa State College, 1941.

Schmidt, Vivien A. *Democracy in Europe: The EU and National Polities*. Oxford: Oxford University Press, 2006.

Schneider, Andrea, and G. D. Feldman, eds. 'Die Vereinigte Industrieunternehmungen AG (VIAG) und der Vierjahresplan'. Working paper 3/1998 of the research project 'Unternehmen im Nationalsozialismus'. Frankfurt am Main: Gesellschaft für Unternehmensgeschichte, 1998.

Schneider, Gerald, Matthew Gabel, and Simon Hix. '*European Union Politics* Editorial Statement'. *European Union Politics* 1: 1 (2000): 5–8.

Schumann, Wolfgang, and Gerhard Lozek. 'Die faschistische Okkupationspolitik im Spiegel der Historiographie der beiden deutschen Staaten'. *Zeitschrift für Geschichtswissenschaft* 12 (1964): 213–230.

Schumpeter, Joseph. *History of Economic Analysis*. New York: Oxford University Press, 1954.

Schwabe, Klaus, ed. *Die Anfänge des Schuman-Plans / The Beginnings of the Schuman Plan*. Brussels and Baden-Baden: Nomos, 1988.

Schwartz, Thomas. Review of *The Reconstruction of Western Europe*, by Milward. *Business History Review* 61: 4 (Winter 1987): 666–669.

Schwarz, Hans-Peter. *Adenauer: Der Aufstieg; 1876–1952*. Stuttgart: Deutsche Verlagsanstalt, 1986.

———. *Adenauer: Der Staatsmann; 1952–1967*. Stuttgart: Deutsche Verlagsanstalt, 1991.

———. 'Adenauer und Europa'. *Vierteljahrshefte für Zeitgeschichte* 27 (1979): 472–523.

Schweitzer, Arthur. Review of *The German Economy at War*, by Milward. *Annals of the American Academy of Political and Social Science* 362 (November 1965): 173.

———. Review of *The New Order and the French Economy*, by Milward. *Political Science Quarterly* 88: 1 (March 1973): 126.

Segers, Mathieu L. L. *Tussen verzoening en verval: De nationale standpuntbepaling van de Bondsrepubliek Duitsland gedurende de beraadslagingen en onderhandelingen over de verdragen van Rome*. Nijmegen: Radboud University, 2006.

Serra, Enrico, ed. *The Relaunching of Europe and the Treaties of Rome / Il Rilancio dell' Europa e i Trattati di Roma*. Brussels / Milan / Paris / Baden-Baden: Bruylant / Giuffrè / L.G.D.J. / Nomos Verlag, 1989.

Sharp, Tony. Review of *War, Economy and Society*, by Milward. *International Affairs* 55:2 (April 1979): 288–289.

Sheehan, James J. *Where Have All the Soldiers Gone? The Transformation of Modern Europe*. Boston: Houghton Mifflin, 2008.

Shively, W. Phillips. *The Craft of Political Research*. (7th ed.). Upper Saddle River, NJ: Pearson Prentice Hall, 2009.

Siegfried, André. 'Can Europe Use American Methods?' *Foreign Affairs* 30: 4 (July 1952): 660–668.

Sigurðsson, Sigurður. 'Búnaðarhagir'. *Búnaðarfélag Íslands: Aldarminning*. Reykjavík: Síðara bindi, 1936.

———. *Landbrug og landboforhold i Island: Danmarks indsats for det islandske landbrugs udvikling*. Copenhagen: Ejnar Munksgaard, 1940.

Sigurjónsson, Arnór. 'Útflutningsverzlun Íslendinga með landbúnaðarafurðir'. *Árbók landbúnaðarins*, 1954: 222–235.

Skidelsky, Robert. 'How to Rebuild a Shamed Subject'. *Financial Times*, 6 August 2009.

Skjöl Búnaðarfélags Íslands. *Lánastofnanir fyrir landbúnað*. Reykjavík: The National Archives of Iceland, 25 January 1925.

*Sláturfélag Suðurlands 1907–28. Janúar–1932. Aldarfjórðungs minningarrit*. Reykjavík: Sláturfélag Suðurlands, 1932.

Smout, Thomas C., ed. *The Search for Wealth and Stability: Essays in Economic and Social History Presented to M. W. Flinn*. London: Macmillan, 1979.

Snyder, David J. 'United States Diplomacy in the New Netherlands, 1948–1958'. Ph.D. thesis, Southern Illinois University, 2006.

Sogner, Ingrid. *Norges holdning til nordisk økonomisk samarbeid, 1947–1957*. M.A. dissertation, Oslo University, 1992.

Solem, Eric. *The Nordic Council and Scandinavian Integration*. New York: Praeger, 1977.

Sørensen, Anders Thornvig. 'Denmark, the Netherlands and European Agricultural Integration, 1945–1960'. Ph.D. thesis, European University Institute, Florence, 2008.

Sørensen, Vibeke. *Denmark's Social Democratic Government and the Marshall Plan, 1947–1950*, edited by Mogens Rüdiger. Copenhagen: Museum Tusculanum Press and University of Copenhagen, 2001.

———. 'Nordic Cooperation—A Social Democratic Alternative to Europe?' In *Interdependence versus Integration: Denmark, Scandinavia and Western*

*Europe, 1945–1960*, edited by Thorsten Borring Olesen, 40–61. Odense: Odense University Press, 1995.

———. 'Social Democratic Government in Denmark under the Marshall Plan'. Ph.D. thesis, European University Institute, Florence, 1987.

Soutou, Georges. *L'Alliance incertaine: Les rapports politico-stratégiques Franco-allemands, 1954–1996*. Paris: Fayard, 1996.

Spagnolo, Carlo. 'Reinterpreting the Marshall Plan: The Impact of the European Recovery Programme in Britain, France, Western Germany, and Italy (1947–1952)'. In Geppert, *The Postwar Challenge*, 275–298.

———. *Sul memoriale di Yalta: Togliatti e la crisi del movimento comunista internazionale (1956–1964)*. Rome: Carocci, 2007.

Speer, Albert. *Erinnerungen*. Berlin: Propyläen Verlag, 1969. (English translation: *Inside the Third Reich: Memoirs*. London: Weidenfeld & Nicolson, 1970).

———. *Spandauer Tagebücher*. Frankfurt am Maine, Berlin, and Vienna: Propyläen Verlag, 1975. (English translation: *Spandau, the Secret Diaries*. London: Collins, 1976.)

Spencer, Frank. Review of *The German Economy at War*, by Milward. *History* 51: 173 (1966): 385–386.

Spierenburg, Dirk, and Raymond Poidevin. *Histoire de la Haute Autorité de la Communauté européenne du charbon et de l'acier: Une expérience supranationale*. Bruxelles: Bruylant, 1993; *The History of the High Authority of the European Coal and Steel Community: Supranationality in Operation*. London: Weidenfeld & Nicolson Ltd, 1994.

Stephenson, Paul J. 'The Role of Working Groups of Commissioners in Co-ordinating Policy Implementation: The Case of Trans-European Networks (TENs)'. *Journal of Common Market Studies* 48: 3 (2010): 309–335.

Stettinius, Edward A. *Roosevelt and the Russians: The Yalta Conference*. London: Jonathan Cape, 1950.

Stobart, Jon. *The First Industrial Region: North-West England, c.1700–1760*. Manchester: Manchester University Press, 2004.

Storli, Espen. 'Out of Norway Falls Aluminium: The Norwegian Aluminium Industry in the International Economy, 1908–1940'. Ph.D. thesis, Norwegian University of Science and Technology, Trondheim, 2010.

Strange, Susan, and Roger Tooze, eds. *The International Politics of Surplus Capacity: Competition for Market Shares in the World Recession*. New York: Routledge, 2009.

Stråth, Bo. 'The Illusory Nordic Alternative to Europe'. *Cooperation and Conflict* 15: 2 (1980): 103–114.

———. *Nordic Industry and Nordic Economic Cooperation: The Nordic Industrial Federations and the Nordic Customs Union Negotiations, 1947–1959*. Stockholm: Almqvist & Wiksell, 1978.

Streeck, Wolfgang, and Kathleen Thelen, eds. *Beyond Continuity: Institutional Change in Advanced Political Economies*. Oxford: Oxford University Press, 2005.

Sundhaussen, Holm. *Wirtschaftsgeschichte Kroatiens im nationalsozialistischen Grossraum, 1941–1945: Das Scheitern einer Ausbeutungsstrategie*. Stuttgart: Deutsche Verlagsanstalt, 1983.

Supple, Barry. Review of *The Rise and Fall of a National Strategy*, by Milward. *The English Historical Review* 121: 492 (June 2006): 892–894.

Suri, Jeremy. *Power and Protest: Global Revolution and the Rise of Détente*. Cambridge, MA: Harvard University Press, 2003.

*Svenskt aluminium under tio ar: Minnesskrift till Aktiebolaget Svenska Aluminiumkompaniets tioarsjubileum, 1934–1944, pa bolagets uppdrag utarbetad av Tekniska Museet*. Stockholm: Nordisk Rotogravyr, 1945.

Swann, Dennis, and Donald L. McLachlan. *Competition Policy in the European Community*. London and New York: Oxford University Press, 1967.

Sweet, Alec Stone, Wayne Sandholtz, and Neil Fligstein, eds. *The Institutionalization of Europe*. Oxford: Oxford University Press, 2001.

Sylla, Richard, and Gianni Toniolo, eds. *Patterns of European Industrialization: The Nineteenth Century*. London: Routledge, 1991.

Teich, Mikulas, and Roy Porter, eds. *The Industrial Revolution in National Context: Europe and the USA*. Cambridge: Cambridge University Press, 1996.

Therborn, Göran. *European Modernity and Beyond*. London: Sage Publications, 1995.

Thiemeyer, Guido. *Europäische Integration: Motive—Prozesse—Strukturen*. Cologne: Böhlau, 2010.

———. *Vom 'Pool Vert' zur Europäischen Wirtschaftsgemeinschaft: Europäische Integration, Kalter Krieg und die Anfänge der Gemeinsamen Europäischen Agrarpolitik, 1950–1957*. Munich: Oldenbourg, 1999.

Thorsen, Svend. 'Norden'. In *Hans Hedtoft: Liv og virke*, edited by Hans Christian Hansen and Julius Bomholt, 209ff. København: Fremad, 1956.

Thue, Lars. *Statens kraft, 1890–1947: Kraftutbygging og samfunnsutvikling*. Oslo: Universitetsforlaget, 2006.

Tilly, Richard. Review of *The New Order and the French Economy*, by Milward. *The Journal of Economic History* 34: 2 (June 1974): 512–514.

Tinbergen, Jan. 'De betekenis van het Marshallplan voor de Nederlandse volkshuishouding'. In Directoraat-Generaal voor het Economische en Militaire Hulpprogramma, *Herwonnen welvaart*, 24–29.

Titmuss, Richard M. *Essays on the 'Welfare State'*. London: Allen & Unwin, 1958.

———. *Problems of Social Policy*. London: HMSO, 1950.

Togliatti, P. 'Promemoria sulle questioni del movimento operaio internazionale e della sua unità'. In Spagnolo, *Sul memoriale*, 262–271.

Tooze, J. Adam. 'No Room for Miracles: German Industrial Output in World War II Reassessed'. *Geschichte und Gesellschaft* 31 (2005): 439–464.

———. *The Wages of Destruction: The Making and Breaking of the Nazi Economy*. New York: Viking, 2006.

Trachtenberg, Marc. *A Constructed Peace: The Making of the European Settlement, 1945–1963*. Princeton, NJ: Princeton University Press, 1999.

Tracy, Michael. *Government and Agriculture in Western Europe, 1880–1988*. (3rd ed.). London: Granada; New York: Harvester Wheatsheaf, 1989.

Tranholm-Mikkelsen, Jeppe. 'Neo-functionalism: Obstinate or Obsolete? A Reappraisal in the Light of the New Dynamism of the EC'. *Millennium: Journal of International Studies* 20: 1 (1991): 1–22.

Trebilcock, Clive. *The Industrialization of the Continental Powers, 1780–1914*. New York: Longman, 1981.

Trevor-Roper, Hugh R. Review of *The German Economy at War*, by Milward. *Business History* 8: 1 (January 1966): 60–63.

Truman, David B. *The Governmental Process: Political Interests and Public Opinion*. New York: Knopf, 1951.

Tsoukalis, Loukas, and Robert Strauss. 'Community Policies on Steel, 1974–1982: A Case of Collective Management'. In Mény and Wright, *The Politics of Steel*, 186–221.

Umbreit, Hans. Review of *The New Order and the French Economy*, by Milward. *Historische Zeitschrift* 217: 3 (December 1973): 740–741.

United States Department of Commerce. *Survey on Current Business, 1968*. Washington, DC: USDC Bureau of Economic Analysis, 1968.

United States Farmers Home Administration. *Strengthening the Family Farm: A Report on Activities of the Farmers Home Administration in the 1946–47 Fiscal Year.* Washington, DC: The Administration, 1947.

United States' Strategic Bombing Survey (Overall Economic Effects Division). *The Effects of Strategic Bombing on the German War Economy.* Washington: USSBS, 31 October 1945. New edition, New York: Garland, 1976.

Urban, Joan Barth. 'The Four Faces of Eurocommunism'. In *Marxism in the Contemporary West*, edited by Charles F. Elliot and Carl A. Linden, 36–59. Boulder, CO: Westview Press, 1980.

———. *Moscow and the Italian Communist Party: From Togliatti to Berlinguer.* London: I B Tauris, 1986.

Urwin, Derek. Review of *The European Rescue of the Nation-State*, by Milward. *Journal of Common Market Studies* 32: 1 (March 1994): 112–113.

Vaïsse, Maurice. *La grandeur: Politique étrangère du général de Gaulle, 1958–1969.* Paris: Fayard, 1998.

Valdimarsson, Valdimar Unnar, and Halldór Bjarnason. *Saltfiskur í sögu þjóðar: Saga íslenskrar saltfiskframleiðslu og -verslunar frá 18; öld til okkar daga.* Vols. 1 and 2. Reykjavík: Hið íslenska bókmenntafélag, 1997.

Van Apeldoorn, Bastiaan, ed. 'Transnational Historical Materialism: The Amsterdam International Political Economy Project'. *Journal of International Relations and Development* 7: 2 (2004).

Van der Beugel, Ernst H. *From Marshall Aid to Atlantic Partnership.* Amsterdam: Elsevier, 1966.

Van der Eng, Pierre. *De Marshall-hulp: Een perspectief voor Nederland, 1947–1953.* Houten: De Haan, 1987.

Van der Harst, Jan. *The Atlantic Priority: Dutch Defence Policy at the Time of the European Defence Community.* Florence: European Press Academic Publishing, 2003.

———, ed. *Beyond the Customs Union: The European Community's Quest for Deepening, Widening and Completion, 1969–1975.* Baden-Baden: Nomos; Brussels: Bruylant; Paris: L.G.D.J., 2007.

———. 'Geschiedenis en theorie van Europese integratie: de erfenis van Alan Milward', inaugural lecture, University of Groningen, 21 April 2009.

———. 'Introduction: History and Theory'. *JEIH* 14: 1 (2008): 5–8.

Van der Hoeven, Pien. *Hoed af voor Marshall: De Marshall-hulp aan Nederland, 1947–1952.* Amsterdam: Bakker, 1997.

Van Houtte, J. A. et al., eds. *Algemene geschiedenis der Nederlanden.* Utrecht: W. de Haan, 1949.

Van Kersbergen, Kees. 'Double Allegiance in European Integration: Publics, Nation-States, and Social Policy'. EUI RSC working paper 97/15, Florence, February1997. Available at: www.eui.eu/RSCAS/WP-Texts/97_15.html (last accessed on 12 December 2011).

———. 'Political Allegiance and European Integration'. *European Journal of Political Research* 37: 1 (January 2000): 1–17.

———. 'Welfare State Reform and Political Allegiance'. *The European Legacy* 8: 5 (2003): 559–571.

Van Merriënboer, Johan. *Mansholt: Een biografie.* Amsterdam: Boom, 2006.

Van Zanden, Jan Luiten. *Een klein land in de 20e eeuw: Economische geschiedenis van Nederland, 1914–1995.* Utrecht: Het Spectrum, 1997.

———, and Richard T. Griffiths. *Economische geschiedenis van Nederland in de 20e eeuw.* Utrecht: Aula, 1989.

Vanke, Jeffrey. *Europeanism and European Union: Interests, Emotions and Systemic Integration, in the Early European Economic Union, 1954–1966.* Palo Alto: Academica Press, 2010.

Vogeler, Ingolf. *The Myth of the Family Farm: Agribusiness Dominance of U.S. Agriculture*. Boulder, CO: Westview Press, 1981.

Vogt, Hannah. *The Burden of Guilt: A Short History of Germany, 1914–1945*. Translated by Herbert Strauss. Oxford and New York: Oxford University Press, 1964.

Von Graevenitz, Fritz Georg. 'From Kaleidoscope to Architecture: Interdependence and Integration in Wheat Policies, 1927–1957'. In Patel, *Fertile Ground*, 27–45.

Von Simson, Werner. 'Reflections on Jean Monnet's Skillful Handling of Member States and People during the First Years of the Community'. In *Jean Monnet et l'Europe d'aujourd'hui*, edited by Giandomenico Majone, Emile Noël, and Peter van den Bossche, 29–36. Baden-Baden: Nomos, 1989.

Wall, Irwin. 'The Marshall Plan and French Politics'. In Schain, *The Marshall Plan*, 167–184.

Ward, Ian. 'The European Constitution and the Nation State'. Review of *The European Rescue of the Nation-State*, by Milward. *Oxford Journal of Legal Studies* 16: 1 (1996): 161–174.

Warlouzet, Laurent. 'Quelle Europe économique pour la France? La France et le marché commun industriel, 1955–1969'. Ph.D. thesis, Université Paris IV-Sorbonne, 2007.

Warner, Isabel. *Steel and Sovereignty: The Deconcentration of the West German Steel Industry, 1949–1954*. Mainz: Philipp von Zabern, 1996.

Watt, Donald Cameron. Review of *Documents on the History of European Integration*, Vol. 1: *Continental Plans for European Union, 1939–1945* and Vol. 2: *Plans for European Union in Great Britain and in Exile, 1939–1945*, edited by Lipgens; and Vol. 3: *The Struggle for European Union by Political Parties and Pressure Groups in Western European Countries, 1945–1950*, edited by Lipgens and Loth. Berlin: De Gruyter for the European University Institute, 1985, 1986, and 1988 respectively. *International Affairs* 66: 2 (April 1990): 392–393.

Weber, Eugen. *Peasants into Frenchmen: The Modernization of Rural France, 1870–1914*. Stanford, CA: Stanford University Press, 1976.

Weiler, Joseph H. H. *The Constitution of Europe: Essays on the Ends and Means of European Integration*. Cambridge: Cambridge University Press, 1999.

Weinachter, Michèle. *Valéry Giscard d'Estaing et l'Allemagne: Le double rêve inachevé*. Paris: Harmattan, 2004.

Welles, Sumner. *Time for Decision*. New York: Harper & Brothers, 1944.

Wells, Wyatt. *Antitrust and the Formation of the Postwar World*. New York: Columbia University Press, 2002.

Wenden, D. J. Review of *The New Order and the French Economy*, by Milward. *History* 57: 190 (1972): 312–313.

Wendt, Frantz. 'Hans Hedtoft og det nordiske samarbejde'. *Nordisk tidskrift för vetenskap, konst och industri* 63 (1987): 451–475.

———. *The Nordic Council and Co-operation in Scandinavia*. Copenhagen: Munksgaard, 1959.

———. *Nordisk Råd, 1952–78: Struktur—arbejde—resultater*. Stockholm: Almqvist and Wiksell, 1979.

Wessels, Wolfgang. *Das politische System der Europäischen Union*. Wiesbaden: VS Verlag für Sozialwissenschaften, 2008.

Westad, Odd Arne. 'The Cold War and the International History of the Twentieth Century'. In Leffler and Westad, *The Cambridge History of the Cold War*. Vol. 1: *Origins*, 1–19.

Wexler, Imanuel. *The Marshall Plan Revisited: The European Recovery Program in Economic Perspective*. Westport, CT: Greenwood Press, 1983.

White, Dan S. Review of *War, Economy and Society*, by Milward. *Journal of Interdisciplinary History* 9: 2 (Autumn 1978): 364–365.

White, Jonathan P. J. 'Theory Guiding Practice: The Neofunctionalists and the Hallstein EEC Commission'. *JEIH* 9: 1 (2003): 111–131.

Wieland, Volker. Review of *The New Order and the French Economy*, by Milward. *Francia: Forschungen zur westeuropäischen Geschichte* 2 (1974): 864–865.

Weiler, Joseph H. H. *The Constitution of Europe*. Cambridge: Cambridge University Press, 1999.

Wiener, Antje, and Thomas Diez, eds. *European Integration Theory*. Oxford: Oxford University Press, 2009.

Wightman, David. Review of *The Reconstruction of Western Europe*, by Milward. *Journal of Economic Literature* 23: 3 (September 1985): 1229–1230.

Wilkes, George, ed. *Britain's Failure to Enter the European Community, 1961–1963: The Enlargement Negotiations and Crises in European, Atlantic and Commonwealth Relations*. London: Frank Cass, 1997.

Wimmer, Andreas, and Nina Glick Schiller. 'Methodological Nationalism and Beyond: Nation-State Building, Migration and the Social Sciences'. *Global Networks* 2 (2002): 301–344.

Winkler, Allan M. 'American Opposition to Imperialism During World War II'. In *Eagle against Empire: American Opposition to European Imperialism, 1914–1982*, edited by Rhodri Jeffreys-Jones. Aix-en-Provence: Université de Provence, 1983.

Witschke, Tobias. *Gefahr für den Wettbewerb? Die Fusionskontrolle der Europäischen Gemeinschaft für Kohle und Stahl und die "Rekonzentration" der Ruhrstahlindustrie, 1950–1963*. Berlin: Akademie Verlag, 2009.

———. 'Steel prices, trade and producers' strategies in the European Coal and Steel Community from 1952 to 1964'. In *Transnational Companies. 19th and 20th centuries*, edited by Hubert Bonin, 815–830. Paris: Plage, 2002.

Wolfe, Martin. Review of *War, Economy and Society*, by Milward. *The American Historical Review* 83: 2 (April 1978): 409–409.

Woyke, Wichard. *Deutsch-französische Beziehungen seit der Wiedervereinigung: Das Tandem faßt wieder Tritt*. Opladen: Leske und Budrich, 2000.

Wright, Gavin. 'William Nelson Parker: Biographical Memoirs'. *Proceedings of the American Philosophical Society* 151: 2 (June 2007): 268–270.

Wurm, Clemens, ed. *Western Europe and Germany: The Beginnings of European Integration, 1945–1960*. Oxford and Washington: Berg Publishers, 1995.

Young, Hugo. *One of Us: A Biography of Margaret Thatcher*. London: Macmillan 1989.

———. *This Blessed Plot: Britain and Europe from Churchill to Blair*. London: Macmillan, 1998.

Young, John W. *Britain and European Unity, 1945–1999*. Basingstoke: Macmillan, 2000.

———. *Britain, France and the Unity of Europe, 1945–51*. Leicester: Leicester University Press, 1984.

———. '"The Parting of the Ways"? Britain, the Messina Conference and the Spaak Committee, June–December 1955'. In *British Foreign Policy, 1945–56*, edited by Michael Dockrill and John W. Young, 197–224. Basingstoke: Macmillan, 1989.

Zamagni, Vera. *The Economic History of Italy, 1860–1990: Recovery after Decline*. Oxford: Clarendon Press, 1993.

———. 'Evolution of the economy'. In *Italy since 1945*, edited by Patrick McCarthy, 42–68. Oxford: Oxford University Press, 2000.

———. *Dalla periferia al centro: La seconda rinascita economica dell'Italia, 1861–1981*. Bologna: Il Mulino, 1990.

———. 'The Political and Economic Impact of CST since 1891: Christian Democracy and Christian Labour Unions in Europe'. In *The True Wealth of Nations:*

*Catholic Social Thought and Economic Life*, edited by Daniel K. Finn, 95 ff. Oxford: Oxford University Press, 2010.

———. Review of *Coase revisited: Business groups in the Modern Economy*, by Mark Granovetter. *Business History Review* (Spring 2006): 159–61.

———. Review of *The Reconstruction of Western Europe, 1945–1951*, by Milward. *Rivista di storia economica* 3: 1 (February 1986): 129–132.

———. 'Southern Europe: from the periphery to the center?'. *Revue Economique* 51: 2 (2000): 303–313.

———. 'What is the Message of "Understanding the Process of Economic Change" for Economic Historians?' *Structural Change and Economic Dynamics* 21 (2010): 157–163.

Zeiler, Thomas W. *American Trade and Power in the 1960s*. New York: Columbia University Press, 1992.

Zunz, Olivier. *Why the American Century?* Chicago: University of Chicago Press, 1998.

# Index

## D

## J

## Y

Printed in Great Britain
by Amazon

22290513R00368